Foundations of [illegible]egy

Second Edition

Robert M. Grant &
Judith Jordan

WILEY

Registered office
John Wiley & Sons Ltd, The Atrium, Southern Gate, Chichester, West Sussex, PO19 8SQ, United Kingdom

For details of our global editorial offices, for customer services and for information about how to apply for permission to reuse the copyright material in this book please see our website at www.wiley.com.

Library of Congress Cataloging-in-Publication Data
Grant, Robert M., 1948-
Foundations of strategy / Robert M. Grant & Judith Jordan.—Second Edition.
pages cm
Includes index.
ISBN 978-1-118-91470-0 (pbk.)
1. Strategic planning. 2. Industrial management—Technological innovations.
I. Jordan, Judith. II. Title.
HD30.28.G7214 2015
658.4'012—dc23 2014039505

ISBN: 978-1-118-91470-0 (pbk)
ISBN: 978-1-119-00131-7 (ebk)
ISBN: 978-1-119-00127-0 (ebk)

A catalogue record for this book is available from the British Library.

Set in 10/12.5 Sabon LT Std by Aptara Inc., New Delhi, India
Printed and bound in Italy by Printer Trento Srl.

FSC
www.fsc.org
MIX
Paper from responsible sources
FSC® C015829

Reprinting September 2016

Brief contents

Contents

Preface to 2nd edition

The second edition retains its aim of providing a concise introduction to the key concepts, frameworks and techniques of strategy for those who are coming to the subject for the first time. The emphasis remains on practicality and how theory can be used to gain strategic insight into the challenges facing business organizations. At the same time, the content of the book has been revised to reflect recent developments in the business environment and in strategy research and to take into account feedback from instructors.

The distinctive features of the second edition include:

- changes and updates to opening and closing cases to reflect the current issues facing decision makers in a broad array of business organizations (Chapters 1 to 9);
- a more integrated approach to value creation and strategic analysis in not-for-profit contexts (particularly Chapter 1 but throughout the text);
- a stronger emphasis on strategic change that is structured around the challenges and ways of managing change and highlights the development of new capabilities and ways in which organizations seek to become more responsive and flexible (Chapter 5);
- a more concise and integrated treatment of strategy implementation; while the book maintains its emphasis on integrating strategy formulation and integration, Chapters 5 and 9 offer a more accessible and systematic approach to strategy execution;
- updates to the discussion of current trends in strategic management to reflect changes in the business climate and new strands of research including practice-based approaches (Chapter 10).

Like the first edition, the second edition of *Foundations of Strategy* draws heavily on the ideas, theories and evidence presented in Robert Grant's text *Contemporary Strategy Analysis*. It has also benefited from the feedback and suggestions of academic staff and students in the many universities and colleges where *Foundations of Strategy* has been adopted. We look forward to broadening and deepening our engagement with users.

We are also grateful for the professionalism and enthusiasm of the editorial, production, and sales and marketing teams at John Wiley & Sons Ltd.

Preface to 1st edition

Robert Grant's *Contemporary Strategy Analysis* is one of the market-leading text books used on MBA and advanced undergraduate courses around the world. During the continuing development of that text, now in its 8th edition, it has become apparent that there is also considerable demand for a more accessible and concise version of the text. In response to this demand, we have developed *Foundations of Strategy* as a brand new textbook. While maintaining the accessible writing style, clear approach and sound theoretical depth, this new text is better suited to the needs of both undergraduate students and Masters' students requiring a more concise treatment of the subject.

As all those with an interest recognise, the way in which business and management education is delivered continues to evolve and change over time. Strategy modules remain a key part of business and management programmes but are now delivered in a wide variety of different formats, to a diverse range of students using a variety of different technologies. Strategy educators frequently find themselves with the challenge of having to deliver strategy modules in relatively short time frames to students with limited prior knowledge and experience of business and management practice. This text is designed to assist educators and students meet this challenge. Our aim has been to cover the key areas of strategy as concisely as possible without sacrificing intellectual rigour. To that end we have:

- Made clear the learning objectives and provided summary tables against these objectives at the start and end of each chapter.
- Organised the book on the basis of ten chapters.
- Provided a range of short cases that students can read and digest quickly and that can be used as an alternative to, or in conjunction with, longer cases available on the web.
- Included worked examples relating to the opening case of each chapter demonstrating how theory can be applied to practice in order to gain insight into strategic decision-making.
- Highlighted key concepts in the margin.
- Provided a glossary of key terms.

Online teaching and learning resources

Visit **www.foundationsofstrategy.com** to access all the teaching and learning materials that accompany this text.

Instructors will find extensive teaching materials such as an **Instructor's Manual,** including **Case Teaching Notes,** a **Test Bank** and **PowerPoint Slides**. The website also features extra, longer **Case Studies** written by Robert M. Grant, as well as **Case Video Clips.**

Resources for students include **Self-Test Quizzes** and **Glossary Flashcards.**

Case list

Chapter	Opening Case	Closing Case
1. The concept of strategy	Strategy and success: Lady Gaga and Jeff Bezos	Tough Mudder LLC: Turning mud runs into a global business
2. Industry analysis	Pot of gold? The Colorado marijuana-growing industry	Fitness First and the UK health and fitness club industry
3. Resources and capabilities	Harley-Davidson, Inc.	Wal-Mart Stores, Inc.
4. The nature and sources of competitive advantage	Singapore Airlines (SIA)	Starbucks Corporation
5. Industry evolution and strategic change	The evolution of personal computers	Cirque du Soleil
6. Technology-based industries and the management of innovation	eBook readers	Nespresso
7. Corporate strategy	Tesco plc.: From food to finance	Diversification at Disney
8. Global strategies and the multinational corporation	IKEA's international strategy	Sharp and the production of liquid crystal displays
9. Realizing strategy	BP's environmental disasters	Designing and redesigning Cisco
10. Current trends in strategic management		

1

The concept of strategy

www.foundationsofstrategy.com

Introduction and objectives

Strategy is about success. This chapter explains what strategy is and why it is important to individuals and organizations in achieving their goals. We will distinguish strategy from planning. Strategy is not a detailed plan or programme of instructions; it is a unifying theme that gives coherence and direction to the actions and decisions of an individual or an organization.

The principal task of this chapter is to introduce the notion of strategy, to make you aware of some of the key debates in strategy and to present the basic framework for strategy analysis that underlies this book.

By the time you have completed this chapter, you will:

- appreciate the contribution that strategy can make to successful performance, both for individuals and for organizations;
- be aware of the origins of strategy and how views on strategy have changed over time;
- be familiar with some of the key questions and terminology in strategy;
- understand the debates that surround corporate values and social responsibility;
- gain familiarity with the challenges of strategy making in **not-for-profit organizations**;
- comprehend the basic approach to strategy that underlies this book.

Since the purpose of strategy is to help us to understand success, we start by looking at the role that strategy has played in enabling individuals to achieve their goals. Our Opening Case provides a brief outline of two different success stories: Lady Gaga's attainment of celebrity status and Jeff Bezos's building of Amazon. These two individuals working in very different fields offer fascinating insights into the foundations of success and the nature of strategy.

Opening Case

Strategy and success: Lady Gaga and Jeff Bezos

Lady Gaga

Stefani Joanne Angelina Germanotta, better known as Lady Gaga, is the most successful popular entertainer to emerge in the 21st century. Her three albums, *The Fame*, released August 2008, *Born This Way*, released May 2011, and *Artpop*, released November 2013, sold a total of 26 million copies by the end of 2013. Her Monster Ball completed a 2009 concert world tour that grossed $227.4 million (the highest for any debut artist). She has earned five Grammy music awards and 13 MTV video music awards and places on *Forbes'* listings of The World's 100 Most Powerful Women (though some way behind German Chancellor Angela Merkel).

Since dropping out of NYU's Tisch School of the Arts in 2005, she has shown total commitment to advancing her career as an entertainer and developing her Lady Gaga persona. Gaga's music is an appealing pastiche of Seventies glam, Eighties disco and Nineties Europop. One music critic, Simon Reynolds, described it as, 'ruthlessly catchy, noughties pop glazed with Auto-Tune and undergirded with R&B-ish beats'.[1] Her songs embody themes of stardom, love, religion, money, identity, liberation, sexuality and individualism.

However, music is only one element in the Lady Gaga phenomenon – her achievement is based less upon her abilities as a singer or songwriter and more upon her establishing a persona which transcends pop music. Like David Bowie and Madonna before her, Lady Gaga is famous for being Lady Gaga. The Gaga persona comprises a multimedia, multifaceted offering built from an integrated array of components that include her music, her stunning visual appearance, newsworthy events, distinctive social attitudes, her personality and a set of clearly communicated values. Key among these is visual impact and theatricality. Lady Gaga's outfits have set new standards in eccentricity and innovation. Her dresses – including her plastic bubble dress, meat dress and 'decapitated-corpse dress' – together with weird hairdos, extravagant hats and extreme footwear (she met President Obama in 16-inch heels) – are as well-known as her hit songs, and her music is promoted through visually stunning videos that combine fantasy, sex, sadism and science fiction. The variety of visual images she projects is such that her every appearance creates a buzz of anticipation as to her latest incarnation.

Lady Gaga has established a business model that recognizes the realities of the post-digital world of entertainment. Like Web 2.0 pioneers such as Facebook and Twitter, Gaga has followed the dictum 'first build market presence then monetize that presence'. She builds market presence through a range of online channels: her website, YouTube, Facebook and Twitter. With 2.8 billion YouTube views, 64 million Facebook fans and 41 million Twitter followers, she is outranked in online presence only by Justin Bieber and Katy Perry. Her emphasis on visual imagery reflects the ways in which her fame is converted into revenue. Music royalties are dwarfed by her concert earnings. Her other revenue sources – merchandizing deals, endorsements and product placements – are also linked to her market presence.

A distinctive feature of Gaga's market development is the emphasis she places on building relations with her fans. The devotion of her fans – her 'Little Monsters' – is based less on their desire to emulate her look as upon empathy with her values and attitudes. They recognize Gaga's images more as social statements of non-conformity than as fashion statements. In communicating her experiences of alienation and bullying at school and her values of individuality, sexual freedom and acceptance of differences – reinforced through her involvement in charities and gay rights events – she has built a global fan base that is unusual in its loyalty and commitment. As 'Mother Monster', Gaga is spokesperson and guru for this community, which is reinforced by her 'Monster Claw' greeting and the 'Manifesto of Little Monsters'.[2] To support her own talents as a singer, musician and songwriter, designer and showman, she created the Haus of Gaga as a creative workshop. Modelled on Andy Warhol's 'Factory', it includes choreographers, fashion designers, hair stylists, photographers, makeup artists, publicists, marketing professionals and is led by a creative director.[3]

Jeff Bezos and Amazon

In 1994, at the age of 30, Jeff Bezos left the investment firm D. E. Shaw & Company and travelled from New York to Seattle in order to set up an e-commerce business that a year later became Amazon. Since he was a child, Bezos had been obsessed with science and technology and while researching investment opportunities at D. E. Shaw he had become convinced that the Internet would offer a once-in-a-lifetime business opportunity.

On 3rd April 1995, Amazon made its first book sale through a primitive website which linked to a catalogue drawn from Books in Print. Amazon then ordered the book from a local book distributor and dispatched the book from its office, a converted garage, using the US Postal Service. The customer received the book within two weeks.

However, Bezos's goal was not to create an online bookselling business. His vision was the potential to use the Internet as an intermediary between manufacturers and customers, thereby offering an unprecedented range of products supported by information that could allow these products to be tailored to each customer's needs – what Bezos referred to as the 'everything store'. Books would be Bezos's first product: their durability, transportability and huge variety made them suitable for the online venture that Bezos envisaged.

Amazon was not the first online bookstore: books.com and Abacis preceded it – nor was it alone in its market space: by 1998 a host of new start-ups and established booksellers had established online businesses, including Borders and Barnes & Noble. However, what distinguished Amazon was Bezos's uncompromising ambition, its obsessive frugality and its unshakable belief in the potential of technology to transform the customer experience through augmented services and unprecedented efficiency.

Amazon's strategy was dominated by a single objective: growth. According to Bezos: 'This is a scale business ... fixed costs are very high and the variable costs of doing this business are extremely low. As a result our major strategic objective has always been GBF – Get Big Fast.' Achieving growth meant offering customers the cheapest deal possible, irrespective of its impact on profitability. Amazon's price cutting and offers of free delivery meant that as business grew so did Amazon's losses: not until the final quarter of 2001 did Amazon finally turn a profit. Achieving growth also meant continually augmenting customers' buying experience: designing the website to make customers' shopping experience quick, easy and interesting; allowing customers to review and rate books; offering personalized book recommendations; and constantly seeking new opportunities to surprise and delight customers.

Bezos viewed Amazon as, first and foremost, a technology company. Its mission 'to be Earth's most customer-centric company, where customers can find and discover anything they might want to buy online and that endeavours to offer its customers the lowest possible prices,' was to be achieved primarily through information technology. However, this also required the company to build leading logistical and merchandising capabilities which involved hiring executives from leaders in marketing and physical distribution companies such as Walmart, Coca-Cola, Allied Signal and the US Army. Amazon's basis in technology, its mission and its array of marketing, logistical and customer service capabilities meant that books were merely a starting point in fulfilling its growth ambitions: its online business system could be transferred to other products and replicated in other countries.

In 1998, Amazon diversified into audio CDs and DVDs and expanded into the UK and Germany. By the end of 2001, Amazon was offering a vast range of products that included computers and electronic products, software and video games, tools, toys and housewares. In addition, it was also hosting products from third-party suppliers – a move that further reinforced its identity as a technology platform rather than an online retailer.

Amazon's second decade (2005–2014) saw further diversification that proclaimed its credentials as one of the world's leading technology companies. Initiatives included:

- 2005 Mechanical Turk – crowdsourcing Internet marketplace where 'requesters' post tasks and 'responders' bid to do the work.
- 2006 Amazon Web Services – online services for other websites and client-side applications; by 2010, Amazon Web Services had established itself as the world's leading provider of cloud computing services.
- 2007 Kindle – Amazon's e-book reader was launched a year after the Sony Reader but soon dominated the market for dedicated e-book readers.
- 2014 Amazon Instant Video – Amazon's entry into streaming movies and TV shows began with Amazon Unbox in 2006 and was built through the acquisition of UK-based LoveFilm in 2011.

Case Insight 1.1

The basis of success

Our opening case describes two very different examples of outstanding success in highly competitive fields. Can their success be attributed to any common factors? Both Lady Gaga and Jeff Bezos are highly capable individuals, yet few would claim that Lady Gaga possesses outstanding talents as a popular musician or that Bezos was able to marshal stronger resources and capabilities than online rivals such as Barnes & Noble and Walmart. Nor can their success be attributed primarily to luck. Both have benefitted from lucky breaks, but both have suffered the cruel hand of fate: a hip injury forced Lady Gaga to cancel her Born This Way tour, while most of Amazon's acquisitions and investments of 1998–1999 were rendered worthless by the dot.com bust of 2000. Our contention is that underpinning the success of both Lady Gaga and Jeff Bezos was a soundly formulated and effectively implemented strategy. While these strategies existed more in the heads of the two leaders than as explicit plans, for both we can observe a consistency of direction based on a clear vision of a desired future and a keen awareness of how to manoeuvre into a position of advantage:

- Lady Gaga's career strategy has used music as a foundation upon which she has built her celebrity status by combining the generic tools of star creation – shock value, fashion leadership and media presence – with a uniquely differentiated image that has captured the imagination and affection of teenagers and young adults throughout the world.
- Jeff Bezos has honed a strategy for Amazon based upon the relentless pursuit of growth based on price leadership, the continual enhancement of the consumer experience and a relentless quest for new opportunities.

The role of strategy in success

What do these examples tell us about the characteristics of a strategy that are conducive to success? In both stories, four common factors stand out (Figure 1.1):

1 Goals that are simple, consistent and long term.

   a Stefani Germanotta has demonstrated a single-minded devotion to the pursuit of stardom for her alter ego, Lady Gaga.

   b The founding of Amazon and its relentless growth are a tribute to the focused ambition of Jeff Bezos to create a business that would exploit the power of the World Wide Web to revolutionize the way in which people bought goods and services.

2 Profound understanding of the competitive environment.

   a Lady Gaga's business model and strategic positioning show a keen awareness of the changing economics of the music business, the marketing potential of social networking and the needs of Generation Y.

   b Jeff Bezos's growth strategy for Amazon combines acute awareness of the business potential of the Web with insight into the role of low prices and superior convenience in driving consumer demand.

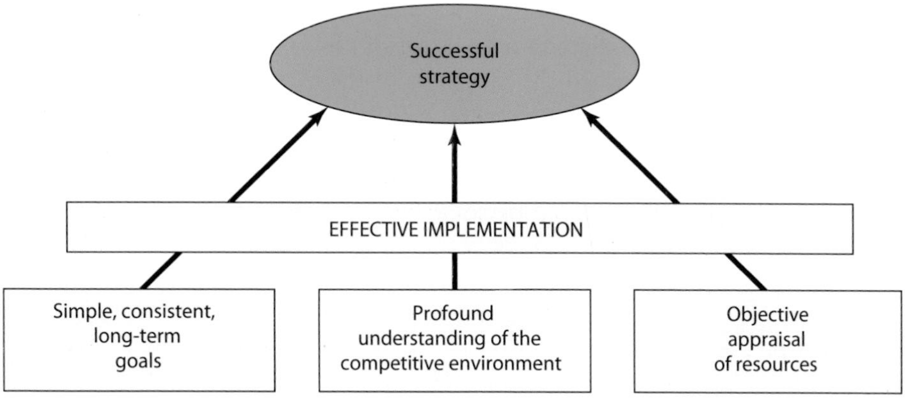

Figure 1.1 Common elements in successful strategies.

3 Objective appraisal of resources.

a In positioning herself as a celebrity performance artist, Lady Gaga has exploited her talents in relation to design, creativity, theatricality and self-promotion while astutely augmenting these skills with capabilities she has assembled within her Haus of Gaga.

b Jeff Bezos's leadership of Amazon has exploited his talent as a business and technological visionary and his attributes of persistence and ruthlessness while bringing in the technical, logistical and merchandising know-how that he lacked.

4 Effective implementation.

a Without effective implementation, even the best-laid strategies are likely to flounder. The ability of Lady Gaga and Amazon to beat the odds and establish outstanding success owes much to their leaders' determination and ability to encourage collaboration and commitment from others.

These observations about the role of strategy in success can be made in relation to most fields of human endeavour. Whether we look at warfare, chess, politics, sport or business, the success of individuals and organizations is seldom the outcome of a purely random process. Nor is superiority in initial endowments of skills and resources typically the determining factor. Strategies that build on the basic four elements almost always play an influential role.

Look at the 'high achievers' in any competitive area. Whether we review the world's political leaders, the CEOs of the Fortune 500 or our own circles of friends and acquaintances, those who have achieved outstanding success in their careers seldom possessed the greatest innate abilities. Success has gone to those who combine the four strategic factors mentioned above. They are goal focused; their career goals have taken primacy over the multitude of life's other goals – friendship, love, leisure, knowledge, spiritual fulfilment – which the majority of us spend most of our lives juggling and reconciling. They know the environments within which they play and tend to be fast learners in terms of understanding the keys to advancement. They know themselves in terms of both strengths and weaknesses. And they implement their career strategies with commitment, consistency and determination. As the late Peter Drucker observed: 'We must learn how to be the CEO of our own careers.'[4]

There is a downside, however. Focusing on a single goal may lead to outstanding success but may be matched by dismal failure in other areas of life.

Many people who have reached the pinnacles of their careers have led lives scarred by poor relationships with friends and families and stunted personal development. These include Howard Hughes and Steve Jobs in business, Richard Nixon and Joseph Stalin in politics, Marilyn Monroe and Elvis Presley in entertainment, Joe Louis and O. J. Simpson in sport and Bobby Fischer in chess. Fulfilment in our personal lives is likely to require broad-based lifetime strategies.[5]

A brief history of strategy

Origins

Enterprises need business strategies for much the same reasons that armies need military strategies: to give direction and purpose, to deploy resources in the most effective manner and to coordinate the decisions made by different individuals. Many of the concepts and theories of business strategy have their antecedents in military strategy. The term 'strategy' derives from the Greek word *strategia*, meaning 'generalship'. However, the concept of strategy did not originate with the Greeks. Sun Tzu's classic *The Art of War*, written in about 500 BC, is regarded as the first treatise on strategy.[6]

Military strategy and business strategy share a number of common concepts and principles, the most basic being the distinction between strategy and tactics. *Strategy* is the overall plan for deploying resources to establish a favourable position; a *tactic* is a scheme for a specific action. Whereas tactics are concerned with the manoeuvres necessary to win battles, strategy is concerned with winning the war. Strategic decisions, whether in military or business spheres, share three common characteristics:

- they are important;
- they involve a significant commitment of resources;
- they are not easily reversible.

Case Insight 1.2

Strategy versus tactics

A key lever for Amazon to drive sales growth was its shipping charges. During the 2000 and 2001 holiday seasons, Amazon began offering free shipping (initially to customers placing orders of a $100 or more). Such cuts in shipping costs were tactical measures – they could be introduced and withdrawn at relatively short notice, and while they were effective at boosting sales, they did not necessitate significant resource commitments. The introduction of Amazon Prime in 2005 was different. In charging a $79 fee to cover 12 months for free express delivery Amazon was, first, making a commitment for a year, second, it shifted consumers' behaviour: members of Prime had a huge incentive to maximize their purchases from Amazon, which then gave Amazon an incentive to broaden its range of merchandise. Prime was a strategic initiative.

The evolution of business strategy

The evolution of business strategy has been driven more by the practical needs of business than by the development of theory. During the 1950s and 1960s, senior executives were experiencing increasing difficulty in coordinating decisions and maintaining control in companies that were growing in size and complexity. Financial budgeting, in the form of annual financial planning and investment appraisal, provided short-term control and aided project selection but did little to guide the long-term development of the firm. Corporate planning (also known as *long-term planning*) was developed during the late 1950s to serve this purpose. Macroeconomic forecasts provided the foundation for the new corporate planning. The typical format was a five-year corporate planning document that set goals and objectives, forecast key economic trends (including market demand, market share, revenue, costs and margins), established priorities for different products and business areas of the firm and allocated capital expenditures. The diffusion of corporate planning was accelerated by a flood of articles and books addressing this new science.[7] The new techniques of corporate planning proved particularly useful for developing and guiding the diversification strategies that many large companies were pursuing during the 1960s. By the mid-1960s, most large US and European companies had set up corporate planning departments.

During the 1970s and early 1980s, confidence in corporate planning and infatuation with scientific approaches to management were severely shaken. Not only did diversification fail to deliver the anticipated synergies but also the oil shocks of 1974 and 1979 ushered in a new era of macroeconomic instability, combined with increased international competition from resurgent Japanese, European and Southeast Asian firms. Faced with a more turbulent business environment, firms could no longer plan their investments, new product introductions and personnel requirements three to five years ahead, simply because they couldn't forecast that far.

The result was a shift in emphasis from planning to strategy making, where the focus was less on the detailed management of companies' growth paths than on positioning the company in markets and in relation to competitors in order to maximize the potential for profit. This transition from corporate planning to what became termed strategic management was associated with increasing focus on competition as the central characteristic of the business environment and competitive advantage as the primary goal of strategy.

The emphasis on strategic management also directed attention to business performance. During the late 1970s and into the 1980s, attention focused on sources of profit within the industry environment. Michael Porter of Harvard Business School pioneered the application of industrial organization economics to analysing industry profitability.[8] Other studies focused on how profits were distributed between the different firms in an industry – in particular the impact of market share and experience upon costs and profits.[9]

During the 1990s, the focus of strategy analysis shifted from the sources of profit in the external environment to the sources of profit within the firm. Increasingly, the resources and capabilities of the firm became regarded as the main source of competitive advantage and the primary basis for formulating strategy.[10] This emphasis on what has been called the resource-based view of the firm (a theoretical perspective that highlights the role of resources and capabilities as the principal basis for a firm's strategy) represented a substantial shift in thinking. Rather than firms pursuing similar strategies, as in seeking attractive markets and favourable competitive positions, emphasis on internal resources and capabilities encouraged firms to identify how they were different from their competitors and to design strategies that exploited these differences. Michael Porter's answer to the question 'What is strategy?'

emphasized that: 'Competitive strategy is about being different. It means deliberately choosing a different set of activities to deliver a unique mix of value.'[11]

During the 21st century, new challenges have continued to shape the principles and practice of strategy. Digital technologies have had a massive impact on the competitive dynamics of many industries, creating winner-takes-all markets and standards wars.[12] Disruptive technologies[13] and accelerating rates of change have meant that strategy has become less and less about plans and more about creating options for the future[14], fostering strategic innovation[15] and seeking 'blue oceans'[16] of uncontested market space. The complexity of these challenges has meant being self-sufficient is no longer viable for most firms – they increasingly depend on other firms through outsourcing and strategic alliances.

The continuing challenges of the 21st century, including the recession of 2008/9, are encouraging new thinking about the purpose of business. Disillusion with 'shareholder value capitalism' has been accompanied by renewed interest in corporate social responsibility, ethics, sustainability of the natural environment and the role of **social legitimacy** in long-term corporate success.

Figure 1.2 summarizes the main developments in strategic management over the past 60 years.

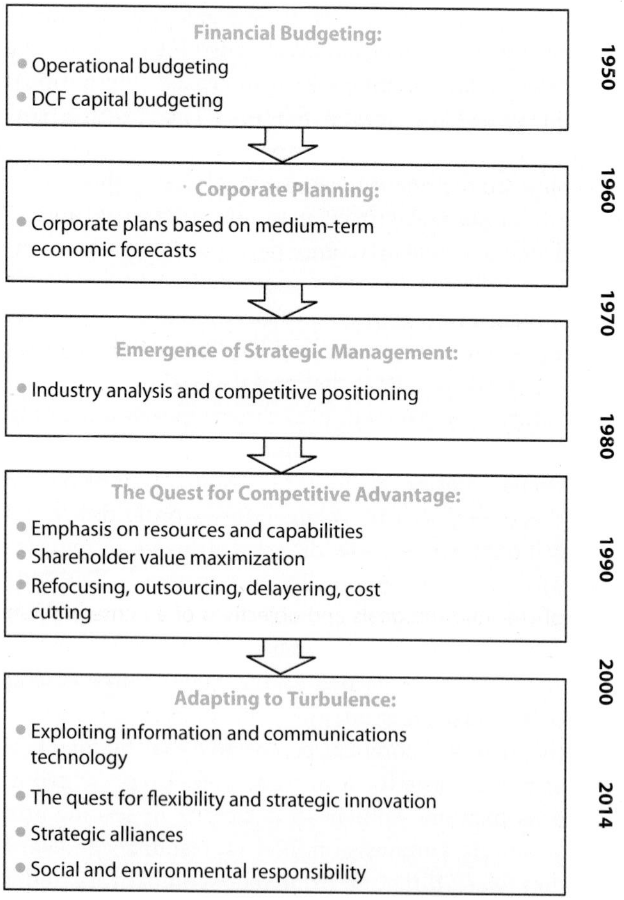

Figure 1.2 Evolution of strategic management: Dominant themes.

Strategy today

Having looked at the origins of strategy and how views on strategy have changed over time, we are ready to start our exploration of strategy today. We do this by posing a series of basic questions. What is strategy? How might we describe strategy? How do we go about identifying strategies in practice? How is strategy made? What purpose and whose interests does strategy serve? Can the concepts and tools of strategy be applied to not-for-profit organizations? In providing preliminary answers to these questions we introduce a number of key concepts and debates that we return to throughout this book. As you will see when you get further into the subject, strategy is a complex and contested field of study, so answers, which at first sight seem straightforward, can on deeper inspection raise further questions and force us to reflect on some things we may have previously taken for granted. For example, when we address the question of whose interests strategy serves, we find ourselves immediately propelled into considering whose interests strategy should serve. Before we get to that debate, we need to familiarize ourselves with some basic terminology and concepts and the obvious starting point is with the definition of the term 'strategy' itself.

What is strategy?

In its broadest sense, **strategy** is the means by which individuals or organizations achieve their objectives. Figure 1.3 presents a number of definitions of the term strategy. Common to definitions of business strategy is the notion that strategy is focused on achieving certain *goals*; that the critical actions which make up a strategy involve *allocation of resources*; and that strategy implies *consistency*, *integration* or *cohesiveness*.

Yet, as we have seen, the conception of firm strategy has changed greatly over the past half century. As the business environment has become more unstable and unpredictable, so strategy has become less concerned with detailed plans and more about the quest for success. This is consistent with our starting point to the chapter. If we think back to Jeff Bezos and Lady Gaga, neither wrote detailed strategic plans but both possessed clear ideas

- Strategy: a plan, method, or series of actions designed to achieve a specific goal or effect.

  – *Wordsmyth Dictionary*

- The determination of the long-run goals and objectives of an enterprise and the adoption of courses of action and the allocation of resources necessary for carrying out these goals.

  – Alfred Chandler, *Strategy and Structure* (Cambridge, MA: MIT Press, 1962)

- Strategy is the pattern of objectives, purposes, or goals and the major policies and plans for achieving these goals, stated in such a way as to define what business the company is in or is to be in and the kind of company it is or is to be.

  – Kenneth Andrews, *The Concept of Corporate Strategy* (Homewood, IL: Irwin, 1971)

Figure 1.3 Some definitions of strategy.

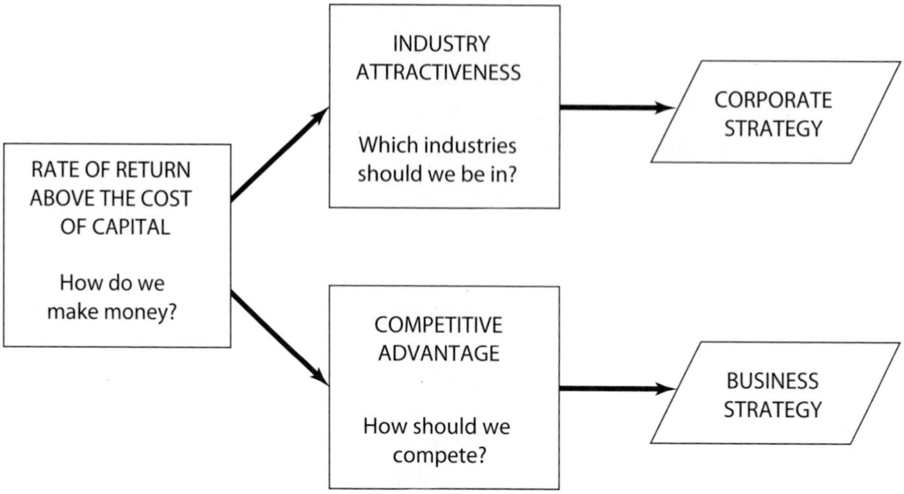

Figure 1.4 Corporate versus business strategy.

of what they wanted to achieve and how they would achieve it. This shift in emphasis from *strategy as plan* to *strategy as direction* does not imply any downgrading of the role of strategy. Certainly, in a turbulent environment, strategy must embrace flexibility and responsiveness. It is precisely in these conditions that strategy becomes more rather than less important. In an environment of uncertainty and change, a clear sense of direction is essential to the pursuit of objectives. When the firm is buffeted by unforeseen threats and when new opportunities are constantly appearing, strategy becomes a vital tool to navigate the firm through stormy seas.

When discussing strategy a distinction is commonly made between corporate strategy and business strategy (Figure 1.4).

- **Corporate strategy** defines the scope of the firm in terms of the industries and markets in which it competes. Corporate strategy decisions include investment in diversification, vertical integration, acquisitions and new ventures; the allocation of resources between the different businesses of the firm; and divestments.
- **Business strategy** is concerned with how the firm competes within a particular industry or market. If the firm is to prosper within an industry, it must establish a competitive advantage over its rivals. Hence, this area of strategy is also referred to as **competitive strategy**.

This distinction may be expressed in even simpler terms. The basic question facing the firm is: 'How do we make money?' The answer to this question corresponds to the two basic strategic choices we identified above: 'Where to compete?' and 'How to compete?' The distinction between corporate strategy and business strategy corresponds to the organizational structure of most large companies. Corporate strategy is typically the responsibility of the top management team and the corporate strategy staff. Business strategy is primarily the responsibility of divisional management.

Case Insight 1.3

Corporate versus business strategy

Lady Gaga's extension of her brand from recorded music to live concerts and interactive games illustrates the decisions she has taken at a corporate strategic level, because they are concerned with where she competes. In contrast her frequent changes in image, her emphasis on personal interaction with fans using digital media and her focus on theatricality are examples of how she chooses to compete and constitute decisions about business strategy.

As an integrated approach to firm strategy, this book deals with both business and corporate strategy. Our initial emphasis is on business strategy. This is because the critical requirement for a company's success is its ability to establish competitive advantage. Hence, issues of business strategy precede those of corporate strategy. At the same time, these two dimensions of strategy are intertwined: the scope of a firm's business has implications for the sources of competitive advantage; and the nature of a firm's competitive advantage determines the range of businesses in which it can be successful.

How do we describe a firm's strategy?

These same two questions 'Where is the firm competing?' and 'How is it competing?' also provide the basis upon which we can describe the strategy that a firm is pursuing. The *where* question has multiple dimensions. It relates to the industry or industries in which the firm is located, the products it supplies, the customer groups it targets, the countries and localities in which it operates and the vertical range of the activities it undertakes.

However, strategy is not simply about competing for today; it is also concerned with competing for tomorrow. This dynamic concept of strategy involves establishing objectives for the future and determining how they will be achieved. Future objectives relate to the overall purpose of the firm (*mission*), what it seeks to become (*vision*) and specific performance targets (Figure 1.5).

Strategy as Positioning	Strategy as Direction
• *Where are we competing?* -Product market scope -Geographical scope -Vertical scope • *How are we competing?* -What is the basis of our competitive advantage?	• *What do we want to become?* -Vision statement • *What do we want to achieve?* -Mission statement -Performance goals • *How will we get there?* -Guidelines for development -Priorities for capital expenditure, R & D -Growth modes: organic growth, M & A, alliances
COMPETING FOR THE PRESENT	*PREPARING FOR THE FUTURE*

Figure 1.5 Describing a firm's strategy: Competing in the present, preparing for the future.

How do we identify a firm's strategy?

Even if we know how to describe a firm's strategy, where do we look to find what strategy a firm is pursuing? Where does information of the type outlined in Figure 1.5 come from? Strategy is located in three places: in the heads of the chief executive, senior managers and other members of the organization; in the top management team's articulations of strategy in speeches and written documents; and in the decisions through which strategy is enacted. Only the last two are observable.

While the most explicit statements of strategy – in board minutes and strategic planning documents – are almost invariably confidential, most companies, and public companies in particular, see value in communicating their strategy to employees, customers, investors and business partners and, inevitably, to the public at large. Collis and Rukstad identify a hierarchy of strategy statements:[17]

- The mission statement is the basic statement of organizational purpose; it addresses 'Why we exist'.
- A statement of principles or values outlines 'What we believe in and how we will behave'.
- The vision statement projects 'What we want to be'.
- The strategy statement articulates 'What our competitive game plan will be'.

Collis and Rukstad argue that the game plan should comprise three definitive components of strategy: *objectives*, *scope* (where we will compete) and *advantage* (how we will compete).

A version of some or all of these statements is typically found on the corporate pages of companies' websites. Featured Example 1.1 illustrates this point. More detailed statements of strategy, including qualitative and quantitative medium-term targets, are often found in top management presentations to analysts which are typically included in the 'For investors' pages of company websites. More detailed information on scope (Where?) and advantage (How?) can be found in companies' annual reports but this kind of information can be difficult to find for privately owned companies.

The usefulness of public statements of strategy is, however, limited by their role as public relations vehicles. This is particularly evident in vision and mission statements, which are frequently grandiose and clichéd. Hence, explicit statements of strategy need to be checked against decisions and actions:

- Where is the company investing its money? Notes to financial statements often provide detailed breakdowns of capital expenditure by region and business segment.
- What technologies is the company developing? Identifying the patents that a company has filed (using the online databases of the US and EU patent offices) indicates the technological trajectory it is pursuing.
- What new products have been released, major investment projects initiated and/or top management hires made? A company's press releases usually announce these strategic decisions.

Identifying a firm's strategy requires drawing upon multiple sources of information in order to build an overall picture of what the company says it is doing and what it is actually doing.

Featured Example 1.1

Statements of company strategy: McDonald's and the Merck Group

McDonald's Plan to Win	The Merck Group's Mission and Strategy
McDonald's brand mission is to be our customers' favorite place and way to eat and drink. Our worldwide operations are aligned around a global strategy called the Plan to Win, which center on an exceptional customer experience – People, Products, Place, Price and Promotion. We are committed to continuously improving our operations and enhancing our customers' experience.	Our aspiration is to make great things happen. With our research-driven specialty businesses, we help patients, customers, partners and the communities in which we operate around the world to live a better life. We achieve entrepreneurial success through innovation.
Plan to Win provides a common framework that aligns our global business and allows for local adaptation. We continue to focus on our three global growth priorities of optimizing our menu, modernizing the customer experience, and broadening accessibility to Brand McDonald's within the framework of our Plan. We believe these priorities align with our customers' evolving needs, and – combined with our competitive advantages of convenience, menu variety, geographic diversification and system alignment – will drive long-term sustainable growth.	Merck focuses on innovative and top-quality high-tech products in the pharmaceutical and chemical sectors. The company's goal is sustainable and profitable growth. Merck intends to achieve this by growing primarily organically and by further developing its competencies, but also by making targeted acquisitions that complement and expand existing strengths in meaningful ways. Building on leading branded products in its four divisions, Merck aims to generate income that is largely independent of the prevailing economic cycles. Moreover, the aim is to further expand the strong market position in emerging markets in the medium to long term.
Source: www.aboutmcdonalds.com	*Source*: www.merckgroup.com

How is strategy made? Design versus emergence

How companies make strategy has been one of the most hotly debated issues in strategic management. Our emphasis on strategy analysis encourages the view that strategy is the result of managers engaging in deliberate, rational analysis. However, strategy may also emerge through adaptation to circumstances. In discussing Lady Gaga's career, we discerned a consistency and pattern to her career decisions that we described as a strategy, yet there is no evidence that she engaged in any systematic strategic planning. And this is the same with many successful companies: Walmart's winning strategy built on large store formats, hub-and-spoke distribution, small-town locations and employee motivation was not a product of grand design; it emerged from Sam Walton's hunches and a series of historical accidents.

Henry Mintzberg is a leading critic of rational approaches to strategy design. He distinguishes *intended*, *realized* and *emergent* strategies. **Intended strategy** is strategy as conceived of by the top management team. Even here, intended strategy is less a product of rational deliberation and more an outcome of negotiation, bargaining and compromise among the many individuals and groups involved in the process. However, **realized strategy**– the actual strategy that is implemented – is only partly related to that which was intended (Mintzberg suggests only 10–30% of intended strategy is realized). The primary determinant of realized strategy is what Mintzberg terms **emergent strategy**– the decisions that emerge from the complex processes in which individual managers interpret the intended strategy and adapt to changing external circumstances.[18] According to Mintzberg, not only is rational design an inaccurate account of how strategies are actually formulated, it is a poor way of making strategy.

'The notion that strategy is something that should happen way up there, far removed from the details of running an organization on a daily basis, is one of the great fallacies of conventional strategic management.'[19]

Featured Example 1.2

Honda's entry into the US motorcycle market

Honda's successful entry into the US motorcycle market has provided a central battleground between those who view strategy making as primarily a rational, analytical process of deliberate planning (*the design school*) and those who envisage strategy as emerging from a complex process of organizational decision making (the *emergence* or *learning school of strategy*).[20] The Boston Consulting Group lauded Honda for its single-minded pursuit of a global strategy based on exploiting economies of scale and learning to establish unassailable cost leadership.[21] However, subsequent interviews with the Honda managers in charge of US market entry revealed a different story: a haphazard entry with little analysis and no clear plan.[22] As Mintzberg observes: 'Brilliant as its strategy may have looked after the fact, Honda's managers made almost every conceivable mistake until the market finally hit them over the head with the right formula.'[23]

The emergent approaches to strategy making permit adaptation and learning though continuous interaction between strategy formulation and strategy implementation in which strategy is constantly being adjusted and revised in light of experience.

In practice, strategy making almost always involves a combination of centrally driven rational design and decentralized adaptation. The design aspect of strategy comprises a number of organizational processes through which strategy is deliberated, discussed and decided. In larger companies these include board meetings and a formalized process of strategic planning supplemented by more broadly participative events such as strategy workshops.

At the same time, strategy is being continually enacted through decisions that are made by every member of the organization, and by middle management especially. The decentralized, bottom-up strategy emergence may in fact lead to more formalized strategy formulation. Intel's historic decision to abandon memory chips and concentrate on microprocessors was initiated by incremental decisions taken by business unit and plant managers that were subsequently promulgated by top management into strategy.[24]

In all the companies we are familiar with, strategic planning combines design and emergence – a process that Grant refers to as **planned emergence**.[25] The balance between the two depends greatly upon the stability and predictability of a company's business environment. The Roman Catholic Church, for example, inhabits a relatively stable environment. For Google, Al Qaeda and Zimbabwe Banking Corporation, however, strategic planning will inevitably be restricted to a few principles and guidelines; the rest must emerge as circumstances unfold. As the business environment becomes more turbulent and less predictable, so strategy making becomes more concerned with guidelines and less with specific decisions. We return to these issues again throughout the book.

What roles does strategy perform?

The transition from corporate planning to strategic management has involved strategy moving from planning departments to the centre of corporate leadership. As such, strategy occupies multiple roles within organizations.

STRATEGY AS DECISION SUPPORT We have described strategy as a pattern or theme that gives coherence to the decisions of an individual or organization. But why can't individuals or organizations make optimal decisions in the absence of such a unifying theme? Consider the 1997 'man versus computer' chess epic in which Garry Kasparov was defeated by IBM's Deep Blue computer.

Deep Blue did not need strategy. Its phenomenal memory and computing power allowed it to identify its optimal moves based on a huge decision tree.[26] Kasparov, although the world's greatest chess player, was subject to bounded rationality: his decision analysis was subject to the cognitive limitations that constrain all human beings.[27] For chess players, a strategy offers guidelines and decision criteria that assist positioning and help create opportunities.

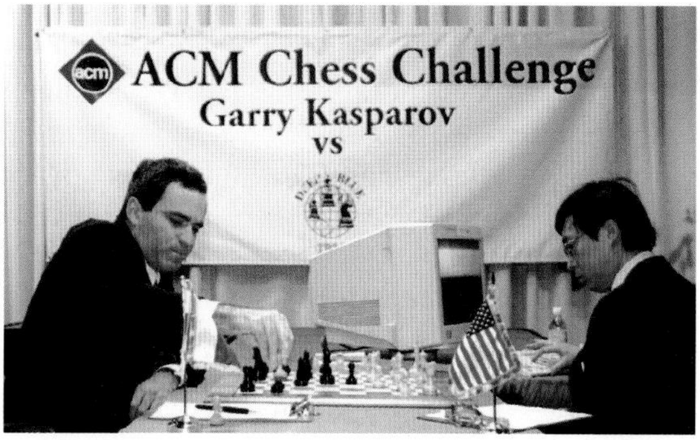

Credit: AFP/Getty Images

Strategy improves decision making in several ways. First, strategy simplifies decision making by *constraining* the range of decision alternatives considered and by acting as a *heuristic* (a rule of thumb) that reduces the search required to find an acceptable solution to a decision problem. Second, a strategy-making process permits the knowledge of different individuals to be pooled and integrated. Third, a strategy-making process facilitates the use of analytic tools: the frameworks and techniques that we will encounter in the ensuing chapters of this book.

STRATEGY AS A COORDINATING DEVICE The greatest challenge of managing an organization is coordinating the actions of different organizational members. Strategy can promote coordination in several ways. First, it is a communication device. Statements of strategy are a powerful means through which the CEO can communicate the identity, goals and positioning of the company to all organizational members. However, communication alone is not enough. For coordination to be effective, *buy-in* is essential from the different groups that make up the organization. The strategic planning process can provide a forum in which views are exchanged and consensus developed. Once formulated, the implementation of strategy through goals, commitments and performance targets that are monitored over the strategic planning period also provides a mechanism to ensure that the organization moves forward in a consistent direction.

STRATEGY AS TARGET Strategy is forward looking. It is concerned not only with how the firm will compete now but also with what the firm will become in the future. A key purpose of a forward-looking strategy is not only to establish a direction of the firm's development but also to set aspirations that can *motivate* and *inspire* the members of the organization. Gary Hamel and C. K. Prahalad use the term *strategic intent* to describe the articulation of a desired leadership position. They argue that: 'strategic intent creates an extreme misfit between resources and ambitions. Top management then challenges the organization to close the gap by building new competitive advantages.'[28] The implication they draw is that strategy should be less about fit and resource allocation and more about *stretch* and **resource leverage**.[29] The evidence from Toyota, Virgin and Southwest Airlines is that resource scarcity may engender ambition, innovation and a 'success against the odds' culture. Jim Collins and Jerry Porras make a similar point: US companies that have been sector leaders for 50 years or more – Merck, Walt Disney, 3M, IBM and Ford – have all generated commitment and drive through setting 'Big, Hairy, Ambitious Goals'.[30]

STRATEGY AS ANIMATION AND ORIENTATION Karl Weick popularized the story of a group of soldiers on reconnaissance in the Alps who, after a snowstorm, lose their way.[31] They are feeling cold and despondent until one of the party discovers a tattered map in a little-used pocket. Finding the map animates the group and gets group members walking until they are back on a familiar bearing. On reaching shelter they find that the map was of another mountain range, the Pyrenees. The moral of the story is that the map is like strategy. Often the most important role of strategy is to animate and orientate individuals within organizations so that they are mobilized, encouraged and work in concert to achieve focus and direction even if the plan isn't correct. It helps, of course, to work with a map or a plan that is as accurate as possible.

Strategy: In whose interest? Shareholders versus stakeholders

We have highlighted the multiple roles that strategy plays in organizations and its central role is assisting organizations to achieve their goals, but while it is easy to comprehend an individual having personal goals, the notion of organizations having goals is slightly more problematic. Organizations are composed of many different individuals and groups, many of which may have different agendas. As a consequence, firms are likely to have multiple goals some of which may, at times, conflict. Nonetheless, at the broadest level, all businesses seek to create value through the activities they undertake. This, of course, invites the questions about what we mean by value and who benefits from the value businesses create. Defining value is not straightforward, because it is rarely a matter of objective fact. Perceptions of value arise through the interplay of supply and demand and through processes of negotiation and argument but, in the business world, value is usually assessed in monetary terms through customers' willingness to pay for a good or service. Firms create value for their customers to the extent that the satisfaction customers gain exceeds the price they pay for the goods or services they purchase.

The 'value' created by firms is distributed among different parties: employees (wages and salaries), lenders (interest), landlords (rent), government (taxes) and owners (profit). Given that the value added by firms is distributed between these different parties, it is tempting to think of all businesses as operating for the benefit of multiple constituencies. This view of business organizations as coalitions of interest groups where top management's role to balance these different, often conflicting, interests is referred to as the **stakeholder approach** to the firm.[32]

Stakeholder analysis is a useful tool for identifying, understanding and prioritizing the needs of key stakeholders. The needs and goals of stakeholders often conflict, requiring organizations to engage in an ongoing process of balancing and managing multiple objectives and relationships. Bryson outlines a number of key steps in stakeholder analysis:[33]

- Identification of the list of potential stakeholders – this stage usually involves a brainstorming session between informed parties;
- Ranking stakeholders according to their importance and influence on the organization;
- For each stakeholder identifying the criteria that stakeholder would use to judge the organization's performance or the extent to which it is meeting stakeholders' expectations;
- Deciding how well the organization is doing from its stakeholders' perspective;
- Identifying what can be done to satisfy each stakeholder;
- Identifying and recording longer-term issues with individual stakeholders and stakeholders as a group.

To assist with this analysis Eden and Akerman suggest the use of *power interest grids* (Figure 1.6).[34] These grids array stakeholders in a matrix with stakeholder interest forming one dimension and stakeholder power the other.

Stakeholder interest refers to a particular stakeholder's political interest in an organization or issue rather than merely their degree of inquisitiveness. *Stakeholder power* refers to the stakeholder's ability to affect the organization's or the issue's future. Four categories of stakeholders result. Players are stakeholders who have both an interest and significant power; subjects are stakeholders with an interest but little power; context setters are stakeholders with power but little direct interest; and the crowd make up the final box comprising those with neither interest nor power. The grid is used to identify which stakeholder interests and power bases should be taken into account, but it also helps identify what coalitions amongst

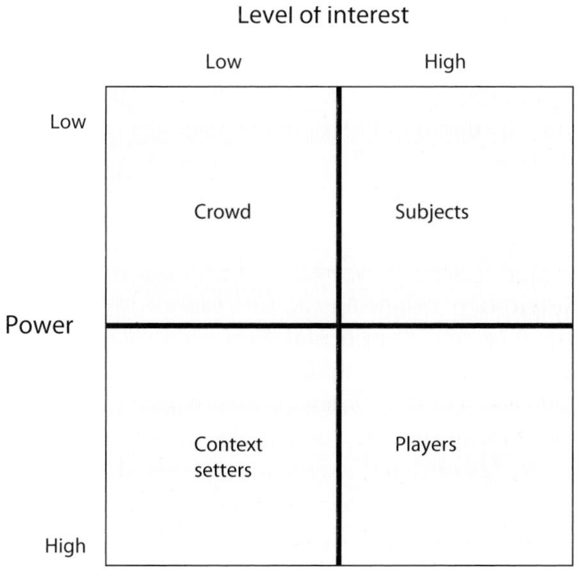

Figure 1.6 Stakeholder power/interest grid.
Source: C. Eden and F. Ackerman (1998) *Making Strategy: The Journey of Strategic Management* (London: Sage).

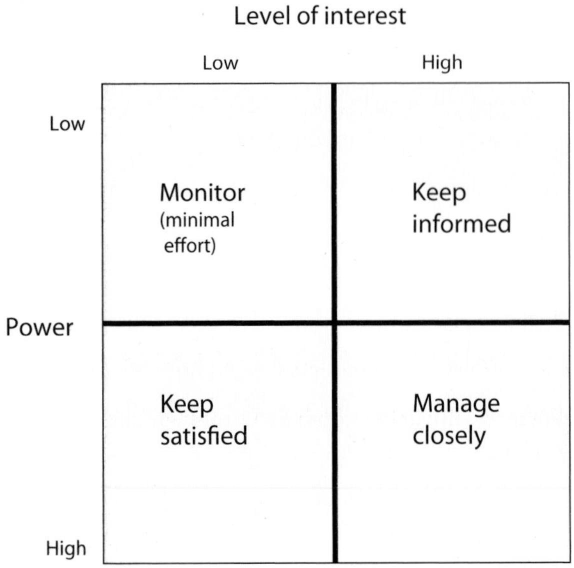

Figure 1.7 Responses to stakeholders' positions within the power/interest grid.

stakeholders managers may wish to encourage or discourage. Figure 1.7 redraws the matrix to show how managers may respond to different groups in order to gain their compliance. Obviously ensuring the acceptability of strategies to *players* is of key importance and relationships with these stakeholders need to be managed closely. In contrast stakeholders categorized as part of the *crowd* may be considered passive but they do have the potential to reposition by taking a more active interest so need to be monitored. Bryson suggests that stakeholder participation, if properly organized, can be of a positive assistance in strategy formulation, implementation and review.[35] This is particularly important in the public and not-for-profit sectors, where empowering stakeholders is often a key objective in its own right.

In contrast, however, in many countries the prime concern of firms is seen as producing profits for shareholders. The question of whose interests strategy *should* serve is the subject of much debate, particularly since the 2008 financial crisis revealed some of the shortcomings of shareholder capitalism so in the next section we review some of the main arguments.

Strategy: Whose interests **should** *be prioritized?*

The notion of the corporation balancing the interests of multiple stakeholders has a long tradition, especially in Asia and continental Europe. By contrast, most English-speaking countries have endorsed shareholder capitalism, where companies' overriding duty is to produce profits for owners. These differences are reflected in international differences in companies' legal obligations. In the US, Canada, the UK and Australia, company boards are required to act in the interests of shareholders. In continental European countries, companies are legally required to take account of the interests of employees, the state and the enterprise as a whole. Whether companies should operate exclusively in the interests of their owners or should also pursue the goals of other stakeholders is an ongoing debate.

During the 1990s, *Anglo-Saxon* shareholder capitalism was in the ascendancy – many continental European and Japanese companies changed their strategies and corporate governance to increase their responsiveness to shareholder interests. However, during the 21st century, shareholder value maximization has come to be associated with short-termism, financial manipulation (Enron, WorldCom), excessive CEO compensation and the failures of risk management that precipitated the 2008/9 financial crisis. The responsibilities of business to employees, customers, society and the natural environment are central ethical and social issues.

Featured Example 1.3

The Kraft takeover of Cadbury: Shareholders versus stakeholders

Cadbury plc was a globally recognized confectionery company, second only to the Mars-Wrigley group in size worldwide. Its brands included Crunchie, Flake, Creme Eggs, Roses and Milk Tray, to name but a few. In its long history Cadbury had acquired many other companies but in February 2010 the company itself became an acquisition target, was taken over by the US food giant Kraft and ceased to exist as an independent corporate entity.

The business was originally founded in the UK by John Cadbury in 1824 selling tea, coffee and drinking chocolate. The business flourished and John extended his activities into the production of cocoas and drinking chocolates and formed the partnership Cadbury Brothers of Birmingham with his brother Benjamin. The business gained particular momentum in the 1850s when a reduction in the high rate of import tax on cocoa and chocolate meant the Cadbury Brothers' products, which had hitherto been the preserve of the wealthy owing to their high cost, became more affordable to the general public. Around this time master confectioner Frederic Kinchelman joined the business, bringing with him his recipes and production secrets. This allowed Cadbury to move into the chocolate-covered confectionery products that eventually became the basis of the company's growth and development.

In due course, the business was taken over by John Cadbury's sons, who decided that they needed larger premises. They acquired land just outside Birmingham and their new Bournville factory opened in 1879. John's sons, like their father and uncle, were Quakers, that is to say members of a Protestant religious group that rejected ritual and formal creed and had a commitment to social reform. Acting in the Quaker philanthropic tradition, George Cadbury (one of John's sons) bought land adjacent to the new factory and built a model village for workers at his own expense in order to 'alleviate the evils of more cramped living conditions'. His aim was to operate a profitable company that cared for and nurtured its employees. The company retained its commitment to social philanthropy over time and was known for its caring attitude to its workers and for its charitable works. The company ethos proved so enduring that in 2010, when faced

Credit: AFP/Getty Images

with the hostile bid from Kraft, the then chief executive of Cadbury, Todd Stitzer, argued that his firm was the embodiment of a distinctive style of 'principled capitalism' that was 'woven into its fabric' by its founders. He saw the Cadbury culture as something distinctive that contributed to the company's competitive success and argued that this advantage would be lost if the company were acquired by Kraft.

Kraft eventually acquired control of Cadbury in February 2010 but the takeover was particularly controversial. Cadbury workers protested on the streets, the Royal Bank of Scotland was fiercely criticized for lending Kraft the money to close the deal and a few politicians tried to have the takeover blocked on competition grounds. At the heart of the debate over Cadbury's future was disagreement about whose interests were being served. Those who wished to block the bid argued that past history suggested that Kraft would prioritize shareholders' interests above those of other stakeholders and in the pursuit of profit would negate everything that Cadbury had previously stood for. Others saw no such conflict, arguing that doing good is good for business and, anyway, firms that do not pay attention to shareholders' interests do not survive.

In practice the extent to which firms take a narrow (shareholder) or broad (stakeholder) view of their purpose is probably more a matter of pragmatics than arbitrary choice. In a competitive labour market, firms that failed to take their employees into account would soon find themselves incurring costs of high labour turnover. Similarly, firms that failed to take the interests of customers or suppliers into account would be at a disadvantage relative to competitors with different policies. In practice what is important is the priority given to different groups and senior managements' judgement calls on the trade-offs required to satisfy important interest groups.

Profit and purpose

As the Cadbury example illustrates, there is more to business than making money. Profit maximization (enterprise value maximization, to be more precise) provides a convenient foundation for building our tools of strategy analysis, yet it is not the goal that inspired Henry Ford to build a business that precipitated a social revolution.

'I will build a motor car for the great multitude ... It will be so low in price that no man making good wages will be unable to own one and to enjoy with his family the blessing of hours of pleasure in God's great open spaces ... When I'm through, everyone will be able to afford one and everyone will have one.'[36]

We saw in our opening case that Lady Gaga and Jeff Bezos were not so much driven by the desire for riches as the desire to fulfil a broader vision. Likewise, the world's most consistently successful companies in terms of profits and shareholder value tend to be those that are motivated by factors other than profit. A succession of studies point to the role of strategic intent, vision and ambitious goals in driving sustained corporate success.[37] Indeed, the converse may also be true: companies that are most focused on profitability and the creation of shareholder value are often remarkably unsuccessful at achieving those goals.

Why does the pursuit of profit so often fail to realize its goal? First, profit will only be an effective guide to management action if managers know what determines profit. Obsession with profitability can blinker managers' perception of the real drivers of superior performance. Conversely, a strategic goal 'to build a motor car for the great multitude that everyone will be able to afford' (Ford) or to 'build great planes' (Boeing) or to 'become the company most known for changing the worldwide poor quality image associated with Japanese products' (Sony, 1950s) may lead a company to direct its efforts towards the sources of competitive advantage within its industry – ultimately leading to superior long-term profitability.

Some companies have kept alive a keen sense of purpose. It is embedded in organizational culture and implicit in strategy and in the behaviour of corporate leaders. However, sustaining a sense of purpose typically requires articulation in explicit statements of mission, vision and purpose. For example:

- Google's mission is: 'to organize the world's information and make it universally accessible and useful'.
- 'The IKEA vision is to create a better everyday life for the many people. They make this possible by offering a wide range of well-designed, functional home furnishing products at prices so low that as many people as possible will be able to afford them.'
- SAP strives to define and establish undisputed leadership in the emerging market for business process platform offerings and accelerate business innovation powered by IT for companies and industries worldwide.
- Oxfam aspires to create lasting solutions to poverty, hunger and social injustice.

The second factor concerns motivation. Success is the result of coordinated effort. The goal of maximizing the return to stockholders is unlikely to inspire employees and other company stakeholders and it's unlikely to be especially effective in inducing cooperation and unity between them. Dennis Bakke, founder of the international power company AES, offers the following analogy:

> Profits are to business as breathing is to life. Breathing is essential to life, but is not the purpose for living. Similarly, profits are essential for the existence of the corporation, but they are not the reason for its existence.[38]

A sense of purpose is common to most new, entrepreneurial enterprises and is also very evident in numerous non-private-sector organizations. But what about established companies? What happens to the sense of purpose that was presumably present at their founding?

Is organizational purpose instilled at birth or can companies choose or adapt their *raison d'être* during the course of their lives? Certainly many of the companies that are most closely identified with clarity of purpose – HP, Johnson & Johnson, Walt Disney – have a sense of mission that is little changed from that articulated by their founders. Yet, Cynthia Montgomery argues that 'forging a compelling organizational purpose' is the ongoing job of the CEO; indeed, it is the 'crowning responsibility of the CEO'.[39] The challenge is to link change with continuity. Some of the most successful corporate turnarounds have been engineered by corporate leaders – Gerstner at IBM, Eisner at Walt Disney – who have renewed and redirected organizational purpose while appealing to a continuity of tradition and values. We re-engage with this debate in Chapter 9, where we explore how strategy is realized in practice.

The debate over corporate social responsibility

This issue of 'whose interests should strategy serve' has re-emerged in recent years as part of the debate over corporate social responsibility (CSR). What are a company's obligations to society as a whole?

In a sharp rebuttal to calls for business to address the broader problems of society, free-market economist Milton Friedman declared CSR to be both unethical and undesirable. Unethical because it involved management spending owners' money on projects that owners had not approved of and undesirable because it involved corporate executives determining the interests of society. Once business enterprises accept responsibility for society, does this justify support for political groups, for religious movements, for elitist universities? According to Friedman:

> There is one and only one social responsibility of business – to use its resources and engage in activities designed to increase its profits so long as it stays within the rules of the game, which is to say, engages in open and free competition without deception or fraud.[40]

Some of the main arguments for prioritizing shareholder interests and seeking to maximize profits rather than returns to other stakeholders are:

- *Competition*. Competition erodes profitability. As competition increases, the interests of different stakeholders converge around the goal of survival. Survival requires that, over the long term, the firm earn a rate of profit that covers its cost of capital; otherwise, it will not be able to replace its assets. Across many sectors of industry, the heat of international competition is such that few companies have the luxury of pursuing goals that diverge from profit maximization.
- *The market for corporate control*. Management teams that fail to maximize the profits of their companies will be replaced by teams that do. In the *market for corporate control*, companies that underperform financially suffer a declining share price that acquirers – other public companies or private equity funds – will use as a basis for personnel replacement. Despite the admirable record of British chocolate maker Cadbury in relation to employees and local communities (Featured example 1.3), its poor return to shareholders between 2004 and 2009 meant that it was unable to resist acquisition by Kraft Foods. In addition, activist investors – both individuals and institutions – pressure boards of directors to dismiss CEOs who fail to create value for shareholders.[41]

- *Convergence of stakeholder interests*. Even beyond a common interest in the survival of the firm, there is likely to be more community of interests than conflict of interests among different stakeholders. Profitability over the long term requires loyalty from employees, trusting relationships with suppliers and customers and support from governments and communities.
- *Simplicity*. A key problem of the stakeholder approach is that considering multiple goals and specifying trade-offs between them vastly increase the complexity of decision making.[42] Virtually all the major tools of business decision making, from pricing rules to discounted cash flow analysis, are rooted in the assumption of profit maximization. Adopting stakeholder goals risks opening the door to political wrangling and management paralysis.

Despite these arguments, companies are increasingly accepting responsibilities that extend well beyond the immediate interests of their owners. The case for CSR is based on both ethics and efficacy. Ethical arguments about management responsibility depend, ultimately, upon what we conceive the firm to be. William Allen contrasts two different notions of the public corporation: *the property conception*, which views the firm as a set of assets owned by stockholders and the *social entity conception*, which views the firm as the community of individuals that is sustained and supported by its relationships with its social, political, economic and natural environment.[43] The **firm as property** view implies that management's responsibility is to operate in the interests of shareholders. The **firm as social entity** implies a responsibility to maintaining the firm within its overall network of relationships and dependencies. Charles Handy dismisses the 'firm as property' view as a hangover from the 19th century: in the 21st century shareholders invest in companies but are not 'owners' in any meaningful sense. To regard profit as the purpose for which companies exist, he argues, is a tragic confusion.[44]

Strategic management of not-for-profit organizations

When strategic management meant top-down, long-range planning, there was little distinction between business corporations and not-for-profit organizations: the techniques of forecast-based planning applied equally to both. As strategic management has become increasingly oriented towards the identification and exploitation of sources of profit, it has become more closely identified with for-profit organizations. So, can the concepts and tools of corporate and business strategy be applied to not-for-profit organizations? The short answer is yes. Strategy is as important in not-for-profit organizations as it is in business firms. The benefits we have attributed to strategic management in terms of improved decision making, achieving coordination and setting performance targets may be even more important in the non-profit sector. Moreover, many of the same concepts and tools of strategic analysis are readily applicable to not-for-profits, albeit with some adaptation. However, the not-for-profit sector encompasses a vast range of organizations. Both the nature of strategic planning and the appropriate tools for strategy analysis differ among these organizations.

The basic distinction here is between those not-for-profits that operate in competitive environments (most non-governmental, non-profit organizations) and those that do not (most government departments and government agencies). Among the not-for-profits that

Table 1.1 Applying the concepts and tools of strategic analysis to different types of not-for-profit organization.

	Organizations in competitive environments that charge users	Organizations in competitive environments that provide free services	Organizations sheltered from competition
Examples	Royal Opera House Guggenheim Museum Stanford University	Salvation Army Habitat for Humanity Greenpeace Linux	UK Ministry of Defence European Central Bank New York Police Dept World Health Organization
Analysis of goals and performance	Identification of mission, goals and performance indicators and establishing consistency between them is a critical area of strategy analysis for all non-profits		
Analysis of the competitive environment	Main tools of competitive analysis are the same as for for-profit firms	Main arena for competition and competitive strategy is the market for funding	Not important. However, there is inter-agency competition for public funding
Analysis of resources and capabilities	Identifying and exploiting distinctive resources and capabilities critical to designing strategies that confer competitive advantage		Analysis of resources and capabilities essential in determining priorities and designing strategies
Strategy implementation	The basic principles of organizational design, performance management and leadership are common to all organizational types		

inhabit competitive environments we may distinguish between those that charge for the services they provide (most private schools, non-profit-making private hospitals, social and sports clubs, etc.) and those that provide their services free – most charities and NGOs (non-governmental organizations). Table 1.1 summarizes some key differences between each of these organizations with regard to the applicability of the basic tools of strategy analysis. Among the tools of strategy analysis that are applicable to all types of not-for-profit organizations, those which relate to the role of strategy in specifying organizational goals and linking goals to resource-allocation decisions are especially important. For businesses, profit is always a key goal since it ensures survival and fuels development. But for not-for-profits, goals are typically complex. The mission of Harvard University is to 'create knowledge, to open the minds of students to that knowledge, and to enable students to take best advantage of their educational opportunities'. But how are these multiple objectives to be reconciled in practice? How should Harvard's budget be allocated between faculty research and financial aid for students? Is Harvard's mission better served by investing in graduate or undergraduate education? The strategic planning process of not-for-profits needs to be designed so that mission, goals, resource allocation and performance targets are closely aligned. Similarly, most of the principles and tools of strategy implementation – especially in relation to organizational structure, management systems, techniques of performance management and choice of leadership styles – are common to both for-profit and not-for-profit organizations.

In terms of the analysis of the external environment, there is little difference between the techniques of industry analysis applied to business enterprises and those relevant to not-for-profits that inhabit competitive environments and charge for their services. In many markets (theatres, sports clubs, vocational training) for-profits and not-for-profits may be in competition with one another. Indeed, for these types of not-for-profit organizations, the pressing need to break even in order to survive may mean that their strategies do not differ significantly from those of for-profit firms. In the case of not-for-profits that do not charge users for the services they offer (mostly charities), competition does not really exist at the final market level: different homeless shelters in San Francisco cannot really be said to be competing for the homeless. However, these organizations compete for funding: raising donations from individuals, winning grants from foundations or obtaining contracts from funding agencies. Competing in the market for funding is a key area of strategy for most not-for-profits. The analysis of resources and capabilities is important to all organizations that inhabit competitive environments and must deploy their internal resources and capabilities to establish a competitive advantage; however, even for those organizations that are monopolists – many government departments and other public agencies, for example – performance is enhanced by aligning strategy with internal strengths in resources and capabilities.

The approach taken in this book

Figure 1.8 shows the basic framework for strategy analysis that we use throughout the book. The four elements of a successful strategy that we outline at the start of this chapter and illustrate in Figure 1.1 are recast into two groups – the firm and the industry environment – with strategy forming a link between the two. The firm embodies three sets of these elements: goals and values ('simple, consistent, long-term goals'), resources and capabilities ('objective appraisal of resources') and structure and systems ('effective implementation').

The industry environment ('profound understanding of the competitive environment') represents the core of the firm's external environment and is defined by the firm's relationships with customers, competitors and suppliers. Hence, we view strategy as forming a link between the firm and its external environment.

Fundamental to this view of strategy as a link between the firm and its external environment is the notion of **strategic fit**. For a strategy to be successful, it must be consistent with the firm's external environment and with its internal environment – its goals and values, resources and capabilities and structure and systems. As we shall see, the failure of many companies is caused by a lack of consistency with either the internal or external environment. General Motors' long-term decline is a consequence of a strategy that has failed to break away from its long-established ideas about multibrand market segmentation and adapt to the changing market for cars. In other cases, many companies have failed to

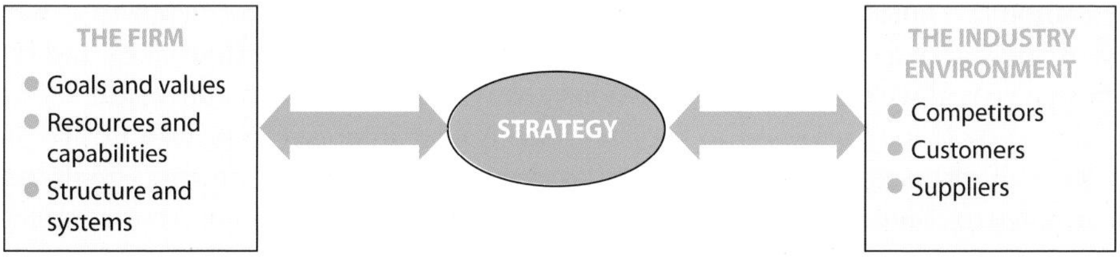

Figure 1.8 The basic framework: Strategy as a link between the firm and its environment.

align their strategies to their internal resources and capabilities. A critical issue for Nintendo in the coming years will be whether it possesses the financial and technological resources to continue to compete head-to-head with Sony and Microsoft in the market for video game consoles. We address the ways in which successful firms achieve *fit* in the first half of the book, exploring the key tools of strategic analysis. In Chapters 2, 3 and 4, we focus on business strategy and the quest for competitive advantage before exploring the ways in which business strategies need to adapt and change in response to different industry contexts in Chapters 5 and 6. In Chapters 7 and 8, we turn our attention to corporate strategy and the scope of a firm's activities and conclude in Chapters 9 and 10 by looking at the challenges of realizing strategy and recent thinking on ways organizations can adapt their strategies to deal with an ever-changing world.

Summary

This chapter covers a great deal of ground. If you are feeling a little overwhelmed, not to worry: we shall be returning to the themes and issues raised in this chapter in subsequent sections of the book. Through the examples provided in our opening case and our subsequent discussion, we have sought to show you the links between strategy and success and to outline the different ways of thinking about strategy. By posing a series of fundamental questions we have uncovered a number of central debates. Is strategy about planning or about recognizing patterns? Is strategy formulation the prerogative of the top management team or something that emerges? Whose interests *does* strategy serve and, equally importantly, whose interests *should* it serve? Can the concepts and tools of corporate and business strategy be applied to not-for-profit organizations or are they only of value to for-profit firms?

The strategic issues that individuals face in their careers and firms face in their business operations are too complex to lend themselves to simple solutions, and as we progress through this book and introduce an array of analytical tools and techniques, you will soon come to appreciate that the purpose of studying strategy is not to provide quick-fix answers (there aren't any!) but to understand the issues better. Most of the analytical concepts and techniques we introduce in this and subsequent chapters are designed to help us identify, classify and understand the principal factors relevant to strategic decisions. Often one of the most useful contributions strategic analysis makes is to enable us to make a start on unpicking problems. It helps us to find those initial threads that are the key to untangling complex knots.

We have seen that strategy is about providing common purpose, committing resources and creating value, so inevitably strategy is bound up with ethical questions. What values and principles should a business organization adopt? What are a business organization's broader obligations to society as a whole? As we progress through the illustrative cases and chapters of this book, we will see that strategic decisions always have an ethical dimension and that the pursuit of shareholder as opposed to broader stakeholder interests remains a hotly contested debate. We will also see that the pursuit of wider social and environmental goals does not necessarily have to conflict with shareholder interests. Strategy's main concern is about creating value for the future and this requires identifying and exploiting the fundamental drivers of value in a principled way.

Summary table

Learning objectives	Summary
Appreciate the contribution that strategy can make to successful performance, both for individuals and for organizations	Using the stories of Lady Gaga and Jeff Bezos to illustrate, we argue that success is associated with strategy. In particular success is linked to the adoption of goals that are simple, consistent and long term; having a profound understanding of the competitive environment; objective appraisal of resources; and effective implementation
Be aware of the origins of strategy and how views on strategy have changed over time	Strategy derives from the Greek word *strategia* but its roots can be traced to Sun Tzu's classic work *The Art of War*. Strategy has been driven by the practical needs of business and has moved from a focus on corporate planning to an emphasis on strategic management
Be familiar with some of the key questions and terminology in strategy	We have outlined six key questions: What is strategy? How can strategy be described? How can strategy be identified? How is strategy made? What roles does strategy perform? Whose interests does strategy serve? In our discussion of these issues we introduce a range of key terms and concepts
Understand the debates that surround corporate values and social responsibility	Our discussion of whose interests strategy serves leads to a further discussion of whose interests strategy *should* serve – shareholders or stakeholders? We review the arguments on both sides
Gain familiarity with the challenges of strategy making in not-for-profit organizations	Strategy is as important for not-for-profit organizations as it is for for-profit firms and many of the same concepts and tools are applicable to both types of organization. However, it is useful to distinguish between those not-for-profits that operate in competitive environments and those that do not. Appropriate tools for strategic analysis differ among these different types of organization
Comprehend the basic approach to strategy that underlies this book	Figure 1.8 outlines the basic framework for strategy analysis that we use throughout this book

Further reading

In his 1996 article, Michael Porter provides an excellent discussion on the difference between strategy and operational effectiveness and in a later article he provides some good insights into current debates about shareholder versus stakeholder values and corporate social responsibility. Campbell and Yeung's (1991) article on mission and vision is something of a classic, making clear the distinction between a firm's mission and attempts to create a 'sense of mission'. Henry Mintzberg's work is the obvious starting point for deeper insight into the ways in which strategy is made.

Campbell, A. and Yeung, S. (1991). Creating a sense of mission. *Long Range Planning*, 24(4), 10–20.

Mintzberg, H. (1985). Of strategies: Deliberate and emergent. *Strategic Management Journal*, 6, 257–72.

Porter, M. E. (1996). What is strategy? *Harvard Business Review*, 74(6), 61–78.

Porter, M. E. (2006). Strategy and society: The link between competitive advantage and corporate social responsibility. *Harvard Business Review*, 84(2), 78–92.

Self-study questions

1 Choose a company that has recently been celebrated in the media for its success and examine its performance in relation to the four characteristics of successful strategies (clear, consistent, long-term objectives; profound understanding of the environment; objective appraisal of resources; and effective implementation).

2 The discussion of the evolution of business strategy established that the characteristics of a firm's strategic plans and its strategic planning process are strongly influenced by the volatility and unpredictability of its external environment. On this basis, what differences would you expect in the strategic plans and strategic planning processes of the Coca-Cola Company and Google Inc?

3 Select a firm and use Internet resources to identify and describe its strategy. Use the template provided in Figure 1.5 to structure your answer.

4 What is your career strategy for the next five years? To what extent does your strategy fit with your long-term goals, the characteristics of the external environment and your own strengths and weaknesses?

5 'Firms abandon shareholder value maximization in favour of some woolly notion of stakeholder satisfaction at their peril.' Discuss, explaining the benefits and drawback of firms acting primarily in the interests of shareholders.

Closing Case
Tough Mudder LLC: Turning mud runs into a global business

> Really tough. But really fun. When I got back to the office on Monday morning, I looked at my colleagues and thought: 'And what did you do over the weekend?'
>
> *Tough Mudder participant*

Introduction

Tough Mudder LLC is a New York-based company that hosts endurance obstacle events – a rapidly growing sport also known as 'mud runs'. During 2014, over one million participants will each pay between $100 and $180 to tackle a 10- to 12-mile Tough Mudder course featuring 15 to 20 challenging obstacles at 60 different locations in nine different countries. The obstacles include wading through a dumpster filled with ice (the Arctic Enema), crawling through a series of pipes part-filled with mud (Boa Constrictor) and dashing through live wires carrying up to 10 000 volts (Electroshock Therapy). Tough Mudder's website describes the experience as follows:

> Tough Mudder events are hardcore obstacle courses designed to test your all around strength, stamina, mental grit and camaraderie. With the most innovative courses, over one million inspiring participants worldwide to date, and more than $5 million raised for the Wounded Warrior Project, Tough Mudder is the premier adventure challenge series in the world. But Tough Mudder is more than an event; it's a way of thinking. By running a Tough Mudder challenge, you'll unlock a true sense of accomplishment, have a great time and discover a camaraderie with your fellow participants that's experienced all too rarely these days.[45]

Tough Mudder was founded in 2010 by former British school pals Will Dean and Guy Livingston. While a Harvard MBA student, Dean entered Harvard Business School's annual business plan competition using Tough Guy, a UK obstacle race based on British Special Forces training, as the basis for his plan.[46] On graduating from Harvard, Dean and Livingstone launched their first Tough Mudder event on 21st May 2010 at Bear Creek Mountain, Pennsylvania attracting 4500 participants.

Growing the company, building the brand

Tough Mudder was targeting the market for endurance sports which comprised traditional endurance sports such as marathons, triathlons and orienteering and newer activities, including:

- Adventure races: off-road, triathlon-based events that typically include trekking/orienteering, mountain biking and paddling.
- Obstacle mud runs: cross-country running events with a variety of challenging obstacles.
- Novelty events: fun events such as 5 km races in which competitors are doused in paint (Color Run), running with real bulls (Great Bull Run) and food fights (Tomato Royale).

Obstacle mud runs were initiated in the UK in 1986 with the annual Tough Guy race and in the US with Warrior Dash launched in July 2009. Spartan Races began in May 2010 (the same time as Tough Mudder). A flood of new entries followed and by 2013 there were about 350 organizations offering obstacle mud runs. The surging popularity of mud runs pointed to the desire of the young (and not so young) to turn away from video screens and cossetted lifestyles and test their physical and emotional limits. One observer referred to the 'Walter Mitty weekend-warrior complex' noting that while the events draw endurance athletes and military veterans, 'the muddiest, most avid, most agro participants hail from Wall Street'.[47]

Tough Mudder's strategic priority was to establish leadership within an increasingly crowded market. How to position Tough Mudder in relation both to other endurance sports and to other obstacle runs was a key issue for Dean and Livingstone. They used several variables to analyse their market: degree of risk, competition vs. collaboration and the potential for brand building. While traditional endurance sports – such as marathons and triathlons – were low risk and highly competitive, they viewed the area of the market characterized by high risk and collaboration as 'white space'. Hence, Tough Mudder would be high risk (exhaustion, hypothermia, broken bones, electrocution and drowning) and collaborative – it would be untimed and team-based. Tough Mudder also needed to present itself as formidable ('Probably the Toughest Event on the Planet') while attracting a wide range of participants. Making it a collaborative event and giving participants the option to bypass individual obstacles helped reconcile these conflicting objectives. Team collaboration was a central theme: Tough Mudder would foster 'a true sense of camaraderie … We want everyone to compete, but being a Tough Mudder is also about making sure no man is left behind, not worrying about your finish time.'[48] This collaborative nature was a major inducement to corporations seeking to build trust, moral and motivation among employee groups.

The spirit of unity and collaboration provided a central element of Tough Mudder's marketing strategy. Tough Mudder has relied almost exclusively on Facebook for building its profile, encouraging participation and building community among its participants. Its Facebook ads target specific locations, demographics and 'likes' such as ice hockey and other physical sports. It also runs sponsored stories in Facebook's news and uses Facebook Exchange to show ads to people who visited the Tough Mudder website. Most important, Facebook is the ideal medium for Tough Mudder to exploit its greatest appeal to participants: the ability of participants to proclaim their courage, endurance and fighting spirit. As the *New York* magazine observes: 'the experience is perfect for bragging about on social media, and from the outset Tough Mudder has marketed to the boastful.'[49] By February 2014, Tough Mudder had 3.7 million Facebook 'likes'.

To reinforce its reputation for toughness, in 2011 Tough Mudder launched an annual competitive run to find 'The World's Toughest Mudder': individuals and teams competed to complete the greatest number of course laps during a 24-hour period. The *Financial Times* described the event: 'Le Mans on foot, through a Somme-like landscape with Marquis de Sade-inspired flourishes'.[50]

Partnering

Partnering with other organizations has been a central feature of Tough Mudder's growth. Its partnerships have been important for building market momentum, providing resources and capabilities that Tough Mudder lacked and generating additional sources of revenue.

Since its inaugural run in 2010, Tough Mudder has been an official sponsor of the Wounded Warriors Project, a charity that offers support to wounded veterans. The relationship reinforces Tough Mudder's military associations and helps legitimize Tough Mudder's image of toughness, resilience and bravery. Its military connections were further reinforced in September 2013 when the US Army Reserve agreed to sponsor eight Tough Mudder events for promotional and recruiting purposes.

Other sponsorships were primarily to generate revenue. Commercial sponsors include Under Armour, the official outfitter to Tough Mudder; Dos Equis, supplier of beer to refresh Tough Mudder finishers; General Mills, whose Wheaties are the official cereal of Tough Mudder; and several other consumer goods companies.

Management

As CEO of Tough Mudder LLC, Will Dean focuses upon key priorities. 'There are only two things a leader should worry about,' he told *Inc.* magazine, 'strategy and culture ... We aspire to become a household brand name, so mapping out a long-term strategy is crucial. I speak with Cristina DeVito, our chief strategy officer, every day, and I meet with the entire five-person strategy team once a week ... We go on retreats every quarter to a house in the Catskill Mountains ... There's no phone coverage, and the Internet connection is slow ... We started the retreats to get everyone thinking about the future.'[51]

At the core of Tough Mudder's strategy is its sense of identity, which is reinforced through the culture of the company: 'Since Day 1, we've had a clear brand and mission: to create life-changing experiences. That clear focus means that every employee is aligned on the same vision and knows what they're working toward ... We know who we are and what we stand for,' said Dean.[52] To sustain the culture, Tough Mudder has established a list of core values to guide the actions and behaviour of the management team.

The other key responsibility of Will Dean as CEO is hiring. Tough Mudder grew from eight employees in 2010 to over 200 by the end of 2013. 'A business is only as good as the people who build it,' observed Dean, who has been meticulous in seeking out the best available talent and ensuring that its new hires share his own passion and values. Hires included executives from ESPN, Diageo, Bain & Company and the London Olympic Committee – typically individuals who combined professional achievement with the quest for adventure.

Tough Mudder in 2014

By 2014, the industry appeared to be consolidating and the market leaders – Tough Mudder, Spartan Races and Warrior Dash – were vying for dominance (Figure 1.9). While Tough Mudder was generally regarded as the market leader, its margin of leadership over Spartan Races and Warrior Run was narrow. Spartan Races, which offered obstacle races of between three and 13 miles, was hosting 34 events in the US and Canada during 2014 as well as events in 11 other countries. In 2013, it signed Reebok as its lead partner. In 2014, Warrior Dash would offer its 5 km mud runs in 35 US locations plus seven in Mexico and two in Denmark.

Tough Mudder's success was a result of astute strategic positioning, effective brand building, careful product design, meticulous operational planning and obsessive focus on the quality of the customer experience. However, as leading rivals became increasingly sophisticated in design, marketing and operations, CEO Will Dean recognized that sustaining

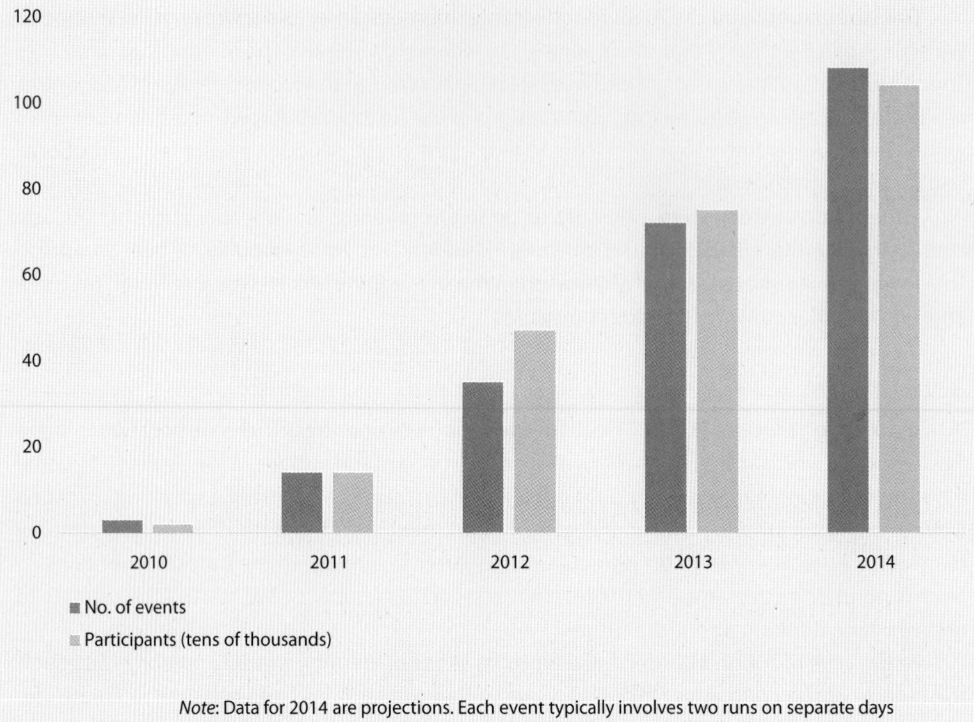

Figure 1.9 Tough Mudder: Growth 2010–2014.

Tough Mudder's growth and market leadership would be an ongoing challenge. This would require Tough Mudder enhancing its market presence and, most of all, delivering an experience that participants would want to come back for, time and time again. Staying ahead of the competition involved two major activities at Tough Mudder. First, meticulous attention to customer feedback: through customer surveys, on-site observations and following social media communities, Tough Mudder continually sought clues to how it could improve the experience of its participants. Second was the continual development of obstacles and course design. Achieving this continual enhancement while reinforcing the unconventional and edgy aspects of the Tough Mudder brand would require the company to maintain an innovative, dynamic and committed culture that matched the energy, determination and gung-ho spirit of the participants.

Case questions

- How would you describe Tough Mudder's strategy?
- Why has the strategy been successful?
- What do you think is the role of Tough Mudder's sense of identity ('We know who we are and what we stand for') in influencing the effectiveness with which it implements its strategy?

- Distinguish between the following concepts using examples drawn from the case:
  - corporate and competitive strategy;
  - strategy and tactics.
- What challenges and opportunities does Tough Mudder currently face and how should it adapt its strategy to meet these challenges and exploit the opportunities?
- Is Tough Mudder a socially responsible company? To what extent are Tough Mudder's corporate social responsibility activities a tool of competitive strategy?

Notes

1 S. Reynolds (2010) The 1980s revival that lasted and entire decade. *Guardian* 22nd January, www.theguardian.com/music/musicblog/2010/jan/22/eighties-revival-decade, accessed 29th September 2014.

2 S. Fry (2011) Lady Gaga takes tea with Mr Fry, *Financial Times*, 28th May.

3 We have drawn extensively on Mauro Sala's Bocconi University, BSc thesis, Milan, June 2011.

4 P. F. Drucker, 'Managing oneself', *Harvard Business Review* (March–April, 1999): 65–74.

5 S. Covey (*The Seven Habits of Highly Effective People*, Simon & Schuster, 1989) advises us to start at the end – to visualize our own funerals and imagine what we would like the funeral speakers to say about us and our lives. On this basis, he recommends that we develop lifetime mission statements based on the multiple roles that we occupy in life.

6 Sun Tzu, *The Art of Strategy: A New Translation of Sun Tzu's Classic 'The Art of War'*, trans. R. L. Wing (New York: Doubleday, 1988).

7 During the late 1950s, *Harvard Business Review* featured a number of articles on corporate planning, e.g. D. W. Ewing, 'Looking around: Long-range business planning', *Harvard Business Review* (July–August 1956): 135–46; B. Payne, 'Steps in long-range planning', *Harvard Business Review* (March–April 1957): 95–101.

8 M. E. Porter, *Competitive Strategy* (New York: Free Press, 1980).

9 Boston Consulting Group, *Perspectives on Experience* (Boston: Boston Consulting Group, 1978).

10 R. M. Grant, 'The resource-based theory of competitive advantage: Implications for strategy formulation', *California Management Review*, 33 (Spring 1991): 114–35; D. J. Collis and C. Montgomery, 'Competing on resources: Strategy in the 1990s', *Harvard Business Review* (July–August 1995): 119–28.

11 M. E. Porter, 'What is strategy?' *Harvard Business Review* (November–December 1996): 64.

12 C. Shapiro and H. R. Varian, *Information Rules* (Boston: Harvard Business School Press, 1998); R. H. Frank and P. J. Cook, *The Winner-Take-All Society* (New York: Penguin, 1997).

13 C. Christensen, *The Innovator's Dilemma* (Boston: Harvard Business School Press, 1997).

14 P. J. Williamson, 'Strategy as options on the future', *Sloan Management Review*, 40(3) (1999): 117–26.

15 C. Markides, 'Strategic innovation in established companies', *Sloan Management Review* (June 1998).

16 W. C. Kim and R. Mauborgne, 'Creating new market space', *Harvard Business Review* (January–February 1999): 83–93.

17 D. J. Collis and M. G. Rukstad, 'Can you say what your strategy is?' *Harvard Business Review* (April 2008): 63–73.

18 See H. Mintzberg, 'Patterns of strategy formulation', *Management Science*, 24 (1978): 934–48; 'Of strategies: Deliberate and emergent', *Strategic Management Journal*, 6 (1985): 257–72; *Mintzberg on Management: Inside our strange world of organizations* (New York: Free Press, 1988).

19 H. Mintzberg, 'The fall and rise of strategic planning', *Harvard Business Review* (January–February 1994): 107–14.

20 The two views of Honda are captured in two Harvard cases: *Honda [A]* (Boston: Harvard Business School, Case No. 384049, 1989) and *Honda [B]* (Boston: Harvard Business School, Case No. 384050, 1989).

21 Boston Consulting Group, *Strategy Alternatives for the British Motorcycle Industry* (London: Her Majesty's Stationery Office, 1975).

22 R. T. Pascale, 'Perspective on strategy: The real story behind Honda's success', *California Management Review*, 26 (Spring 1984): 47–72.

23 H. Mintzberg, 'Crafting strategy', *Harvard Business Review*, 65 (July–August 1987): 70.

24 R. A. Burgelman and A. Grove, 'Strategic dissonance', *California Management Review*, 38 (Winter 1996): 8–28.

25 R. M. Grant, 'Strategic planning in a turbulent environment: Evidence from the oil and gas majors', *Strategic Management Journal* 14 (June 2003): 491–517.

26 'Strategic intensity: A conversation with Garry Kasparov', *Harvard Business Review* (April 2005): 105–13.

27 The concept of bounded rationality was developed by Herbert Simon ('A behavioral model of rational choice', *Quarterly Journal of Economics*, 69 (1955): 99–118).

28 G. Hamel and C. K. Prahalad, 'Strategic intent', *Harvard Business Review* (May–June 1989): 63–77.

29 G. Hamel and C. K. Prahalad, 'Strategy as stretch and leverage', *Harvard Business Review* (March–April 1993): 75–84.

30 J. C. Collins and J. I. Porras, *Built to Last: Successful habits of visionary companies* (New York: HarperCollins, 1995).

31 K. E. Weick, *Sensemaking in Organizations* (Thousand Oaks, CA: Sage, 1995): 54.

32 T. Donaldson and L. E. Preston, The stakeholder theory of the corporation, *Academy of Management Review*, 20 (1995): 65–91.

33 J. M. Bryson, 'What to do when stakeholders matter: Stakeholder identification and analysis techniques', *Public Management Review*, 6 (2004): 21–53.

34 F. Akermann and C. Eden, 'Strategic Management of Stakeholders: Theory and practice', *Long Range Planning*, 44 (2011): 179–96.

35 J. M. Bryson, 'What to do when stakeholders matter: Stakeholder identification and analysis techniques', *Public Management Review*, 6 (2004): 21–53.

36 See www.abelard.org/ford, accessed 29th September 2014.

37 J. Collins and J. Porras, 'Building your company's vision', *Harvard Business Review* (September–October, 1996): 65–77.

38 Robert Grant's interview with Dennis Bakke.

39 C. A. Montgomery, 'Putting leadership back into strategy', *Harvard Business Review* (January, 2008): 54–60.

40 M. Friedman, *Capitalism and Freedom* (Chicago: University of Chicago Press, 1963). See also: M. Friedman, 'The social responsibility of business is to increase its profits', *New York Times Magazine* (13th September 1970).

41 J. Helwege, V. Intintoli and A. Zhang, 'Voting with their feet or activism? Institutional investors' impact on CEO turnover', *Journal of Corporate Finance*, 18 (2012): 22–37.

42 J. Figuero, S. Greco and M. Ehrgott, *Multiple Criteria Decision Analysis: State of the art surveys* (Berlin: Springer, 2005).

43 W. T. Allen, 'Our schizophrenic conception of the business corporation', *Cardozo Law Review*, 14 (1992): 261–81.

44 C. Handy, 'What's a business for?' *Harvard Business Review* (December, 2002): 133–43.

45 http://toughmudder.com/about/, accessed 29th September 2014.

46 http://toughmudder.com/history-of-tough-mudder/, accessed 29th September 2014.

47 J. D. Stein 'Forging a bond in mud and guts', *New York Times* (7th December 2012), http://www.nytimes.com/2012/12/09/fashion/extreme-obstacle-course-races-forge-a-bond-in-mud-and-guts.html?pagewanted=all&_r=0, accessed 29th September 2014.

48 http://toughmudder.com/about/, accessed 9th September 2014.

49 J. Grose 'Tough Mudder: There are riches in this mud pit', *New York Magazine* (29th September 2013), http://nymag.com/news/business/boom-brands/tough-mudder-2013-10, accessed 29th September 2014.

50 G. Stoddard 'Tough Mudder', *Financial Times* online edition (18th January 2013), http://www.ft.com/cms/s/2/7a80e610-603d-11e2-b657-00144feab49a.html#ixzz2nFzd1Xx4, accessed 29th September 2014.

51 Issie Lapowsky 'The Way I Work: Will Dean, Tough Mudder' *Inc Magazine* (13th February 2013), http://www.inc.com/magazine/201302/issie-lapowsky/the-way-i-work-will-dean-tough-mudder.html, accessed 29th September 2014.

52 W. Dean 'On the Streets of SoHo: Tough Mudder', http://issuu.com/accordion_partners/docs/q_a_will_dean_lite, accessed 29th September 2014.

2

Industry analysis

www.foundationsofstrategy.com

Introduction and objectives

In this chapter, we explore the external environment of the firm. In Chapter 1, we observed that profound understanding of the competitive environment is a critical ingredient of a successful strategy. We further noted that business strategy is essentially a quest for profit. The primary task for this chapter is to identify the sources of profit in the external environment. The firm's proximate environment is its industry environment, hence the primary focus of this chapter is on industry analysis.

By the time you have completed this chapter, you will:

- be familiar with a number of frameworks used to analyse an organization's external environment and understand how the structural features of an industry influence competition and profitability;
- be able to use evidence on structural trends within industries to forecast changes in competition and profitability and to develop appropriate strategies for the future;
- be able to define the boundaries of the industry within which a firm is located;
- be able to recognize the limits of the Porter five forces of competition framework (commonly known as the five forces framework) and extend the framework to include the role of complements as well as substitutes;
- be able to segment an industry into its constituent markets and appraise the relative attractiveness of different segments;
- be able to analyse competition and customer requirements in order to identify opportunities for competitive advantage within an industry (key success factors).

Opening Case

Pot of gold? The Colorado marijuana-growing industry

Legalization of the sale of marijuana by the states of Colorado and Washington in 2014 was a milestone in transition of America's marijuana business from a clandestine activity, where growers, dealers and consumers risked fines and jail sentences, to a legitimate economic activity on a par with tobacco and alcoholic beverages. By the end of 2014, only Colorado and Washington state allowed the sale of marijuana for recreational use, but 14 other states and the District of Colombia permitted its sale for medical use. Despite continuing concerns over the physical and psychological risks of marijuana consumption, several experts predicted that, by 2020, the majority of US states would legalize its recreational sale and use.

It was not only the 7.3% of Americans who were regular consumers of marijuana who welcomed the trend towards legality. With decriminalization, existing growers of marijuana could emerge from secrecy and newcomers were establishing cultivation. During 2013, it was estimated that 2000 to 4000 businesses were legally producing marijuana with sales of about $1.2 billion. New start-ups and the expansion of existing businesses required investment funds. Existing banks and venture capital funds were unwilling to finance marijuana-related businesses: the growing, sale and possession of marijuana was still a federal offence.

This created an opportunity for new sources of investment. Among the newly created venture capital funds investing in the marijuana industry, an early leader was Seattle-based Privateer Holdings. Founded by two investment analysts with Yale MBAs, Privateer hoped to raise $50 million in 2014 to acquire equity stakes in marijuana-based businesses. Another early leader was ArcView Group, which acted as an intermediary between businesses seeking investment funds and investors, mainly wealthy individuals. Investor interest was generated by a growing number of trade conventions and conferences. The annual CannaBusiness Conference in 2014 in Las Vegas attracted around 1500 industry professionals.

Despite being poised for rapid growth ('After 3D printing and cloud computing, marijuana is one of the fastest growing industries in the country'), the industry's profit prospects were less clear. The Motley Fool suggested that marijuana was a highly profitable crop: a 10 000-square-foot growing facility with five annual growing cycles could produce 1250 lb a year with a wholesale value of $2.75 million.[1] With production costs of $1.25 million, this implied a net margin of 55%. However, most Colorado marijuana suppliers reported much more modest margins: La Conte's Clone Bar & Dispensary earned a margin of just 6% on revenues of $4.2 million. Future profitability would depend heavily on marijuana prices. In March 2014, high-quality legal marijuana sold for between $280 and $340 an ounce in Colorado (including state taxes of about 28%); for medical marijuana, it was closer to $200 an ounce. However, with increasing production capacity, it seemed likely that prices would fall.

Setting up marijuana cultivation required obtaining a licence, an arduous process involving detailed background checks on applicants, and capital investment of at least $1 million. Marijuana-growing facilities are capital-intensive: plants are grown indoors under electric lights under tight security conditions and Colorado regulations require growing plants to be monitored with security cameras. Facilities tended to be 60 000 square feet or more with capital costs of at least $100 per square foot. The Colorado regulations favoured vertical integration: the licensed dispensaries that sold medical and recreational marijuana also grew most of their own supply.

The production process is complex and requires meticulous management. It comprises cloning, growing, flowering, processing and curing. It is labour-intensive, requires considerable know-how and the risk of crop loss is considerable. Labour and electricity are main variable costs.

Despite high capital costs and complex regulatory requirements, it looked as though Colorado and Washington would see a continuing stream of new entrants into the recreational marijuana industry. In each state the number of applications for supplying marijuana exceeded 2000 at the beginning of March 2014.

As competition in the industry hotted up, some producers hoped to achieve superior profit through differentiating their products on the basis of quality, service or by offering an array of cannabis-infused products such as cookies and candies. However, one barrier to branding by producers was that legal protection for trademarks did not extend to products that were illegal under federal law.

The legal marijuana industry was also threatened by competition from other sources. Most significant was competition from illegal supplies of marijuana. Illicit marijuana had a well-established supply chain with most supply coming from Mexico, where outdoor production and low-cost labour gave producers a huge cost advantage. Marijuana also competes with a host of other recreational drugs. These include cocaine, amphetamines, methamphetamine, ecstasy and a range of other 'designer drugs'.

In seeking to understand how the marijuana industry might evolve and to identify potential sources of its future profitability, several observers pointed to comparable industries such as tobacco and alcoholic beverages. In the case of tobacco it was noted that, despite falling consumption, tight regulation and heavy taxation, tobacco remained one of the most profitable industries in the US, with the major cigarette suppliers (Altria, Reynolds American, BAT and Lorillard) earning an average return on equity of 62% during 2012–2013. However, there were major differences between the structure of the tobacco and marijuana industries: while the former was highly concentrated with strongly entrenched brands, the latter was fragmented.

From environmental analysis to industry analysis

The **business environment** of a firm consists of all the external influences that affect its decisions and performance. Given the vast number and range of external influences, how can managers hope to monitor, let alone analyse, environmental conditions? The starting point is some kind of system or framework for organizing information. For example, environmental influences can be classified by source – e.g. political, economic, social and technological factors (PEST analysis) – or by proximity – the *micro-environment* or *task environment* can be distinguished from the wider influences that form the *macro-environment*.

PEST analysis has become popular as an environmental scanning framework because it provides a simple yet systematic approach to identifying factors that are likely to shape the competitive conditions within an industry.[2] Recognizing these *basic forces* is important in understanding and predicting how an industry may change and evolve over time and is a key initial step in thinking about future scenarios and the opportunities and threats that an industry may face. Case Insight 2.1 provides an example of PEST analysis based on the opening case.

Case Insight 2.1

An illustration of PEST analysis

Some illustrative examples of the PEST factors affecting firms in the marijuana industry include:

Political

- *Licensing:* the extent to which other states and other countries follow Colorado's lead in legalizing marijuana is of paramount importance to existing and potential marijuana producers, as are the regulations and processes surrounding the issue of licences. Strict regulatory regimes raise capital requirements, affect the cost structures and profitability of existing producers and influence the nature and extent of entry into this industry.
- *Taxation:* it seems likely that marijuana, like tobacco and alcohol, will be subject to heavy taxation and to relatively frequent changes in tax rates. The extent to which this will affect the industry depends, in large part, on how sensitive consumers are to changes in price.
- *Trademarks and intellectual property:* even though the use of marijuana for recreational use is now permitted in Colorado, it still remains a federal crime to sell 'pot'. As a consequence it is not currently possible for Colorado marijuana producers to get federal trademark protection for their brands outside the state. While this is a factor that marijuana producers need to take into consideration, the larger concern is the uncertainty created by the lack of alignment between state and federal policy. It is possible to imagine a scenario in which the federal government decides to enforce the federal prohibition on marijuana and shut down cannabis sellers in Colorado.

Economic

- *The costs of labour, capital and energy:* the production of marijuana is a labour-, capital- and energy-intensive process hence the profitability of individual producers, and the industry as a whole, is affected by movements in these cost categories. The overall impact of cost changes on the profitability of any given producer will, of course, depend on that firm's cost structure and the extent to which consumers are prepared to absorb cost increases through price rises.
- *The level of economic activity:* while it seems likely that the demand for marijuana will be affected by macro-factors such as levels of employment/unemployment or national income, the nature and extent of any effect is difficult to judge. On the one hand, it could be expected that as incomes rise consumption of marijuana would, all other things being equal, rise, but this is not necessarily the case. Marijuana may be viewed as a gateway drug and as incomes rise users may switch to other drugs (e.g. cocaine), to alcohol or other recreational activities. The hitherto illicit nature of much of this industry means that very little evidence is available, so it is difficult to judge the impact macro-economic factors have. In addition, there are likely to be important differences between those who consume marijuana for medical reasons and those who use it for recreational purposes.

Social

- *Shifting attitudes towards the consumption of marijuana:* the consumption of marijuana, particularly for recreational purposes, remains illegal in many states because of ongoing concerns over physical and psychological risks. Although in recent years support for legalization has grown markedly so has opposition and there are strong demographic and geographic differences in public opinion. Overall, the general public's attitudes towards marijuana consumption are ambivalent but will be shaped by the results of ongoing research into the impact of marijuana use on health and well-being and the evidence that emerges from the experience of states like Colorado that have lifted prohibitions.

Technological

Changes in technology are having a major impact on the way in which marijuana is grown and resulting in big cost savings. Industry sources suggest that the costs of producing a pound of premium cannabis in Colorado can range from around $385 to $1450 and that technological innovation accounts for much of the difference.[3] Key technologies include:

- *The use of advanced greenhouses:* modern cannabis greenhouses employ light diffusion and dehumidification technologies to modify the flowering cycle of the cannabis plants to generate higher yields. For example, by using recently developed LED lighting technology in a greenhouse environment as opposed to using high-pressure sodium lights in an indoor facility, growers can dramatically reduce their energy bills.
- *Automated fertilization and irrigation:* the nutrients and water requirements of plants are carefully controlled through the use of sensors, electronic injectors and sophisticated computer software.

Each of these factors is likely to have an important impact on the way in which the marijuana-growing industry evolves and changes over time.

Though systematic, continual scanning of the whole range of external influences may seem desirable, extensive environmental analysis incurs high costs and creates information overload. Merely listing large numbers of external factors that in some way influence firms' operations and performance is rarely helpful. Rather, the key to effective environmental analysis is to distinguish the vital from the merely important. For example, of the PEST factors listed in Case Insight 2.1 some are clearly more important than others. Changes in legislation will have a more direct and immediate impact than changes in the level of economic activity. For PEST analysis to be worthwhile, those undertaking the analysis need to exercise judgement and keep in mind the purpose of the exercise, which is to identify those factors that are likely to be the *most important* in shaping industry conditions. It is to industry conditions we turn next, but before we start it is worthwhile reminding ourselves of some basic principles.

First, for a firm to make a profit it must create value for customers. Hence, it must understand its customers. Second, in creating value, the firm acquires goods and services from suppliers. Hence, it must understand its suppliers and manage relationships with them. Third, the ability to generate profit depends on the intensity of competition among firms that compete for the same value-creating opportunities. Hence, the firm must understand competition. Thus, the core of the firm's business environment is formed by its relationships with three sets of players: customers, suppliers and competitors. This is its industry environment.

This is not to say that macro-level PEST factors such as general economic trends, changes in demographic structure or social and political trends are unimportant to strategy analysis. These factors are critical determinants of the threats and opportunities a company will face in the future, but the key issue is how these more general environmental factors affect the firm's industry environment (Figure 2.1).

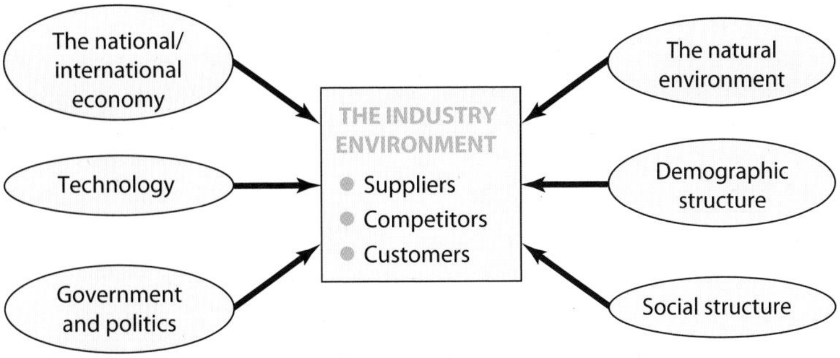

Figure 2.1 From PEST analysis to industry analysis.

Consider the threat of global warming. For most companies this is not an important strategic issue (at least, not for the next 100 years). However, for the producers of cars, global warming is a vital issue. But, to analyse the strategic implications of global warming, the car manufacturers need to trace its implications for their industry environment. For example, what will be the impact on consumers and their preferences? Will there be a switch from private to public transportation? With regard to competition, will there be new entry by manufacturers of electric vehicles into the car industry? Will increased R & D costs cause the industry to consolidate?

The determinants of industry profit: Demand and competition

The starting point for industry analysis is a simple question: 'What determines the level of profit in an industry?'

The prerequisite for profit is the creation of value for the customer. Value is created when the price the customer is willing to pay for a product exceeds the costs incurred by the firm. But value creation does not translate directly into profit. The surplus of value over cost is distributed between customers and producers by the forces of competition. The stronger the competition among producers, the more of the surplus is received by customers and the less of the surplus is received by producers. A single supplier of bottled water at an all-night rave can charge a price that fully exploits the dancers' thirst. If there are many suppliers of bottled water, then, in the absence of competitor complicity, competition causes the price of bottled water to fall towards the cost of supplying it.

Even when producers earn a surplus, this is not necessarily captured in profits. Where an industry has powerful suppliers – monopolistic suppliers of components or employees united by a strong labour union – a substantial part of the surplus may be appropriated by these suppliers (the profits of suppliers or premium wages of union members).

The profits earned by the firms in an industry are thus determined by three factors:

- the value of the product to customers;
- the intensity of competition;
- the bargaining power of the producers relative to their suppliers.

Industry analysis brings all three factors into a single analytic framework.

Table 2.1 The profitability of US industries: 2000–2010.

Industry	Median ROE 2000–2010 (%)	Leading companies
Tobacco	33.5	Philip Morris, Altria, Reynolds American
Household and personal products	27.8	Procter & Gamble, Kimberly-Clark, Colgate-Palmolive
Pharmaceuticals	20.5	Pfizer, Johnson & Johnson, Merck
Food consumer products	20.0	PepsiCo, Kraft Foods, General Mills
Food services	19.9	McDonald's, Yum Brands, Starbucks
Medical products and equipment	18.5	Medtronic, Baxter International, Boston Scientific
Petroleum refining	17.6	ExxonMobil, Chevron, ConocoPhillips
Mining, crude oil production	16.3	Occidental Petroleum, Devon Energy
Securities	15.9	KKR, BlackRock, Charles Schwab
Chemicals	15.7	Dow Chemical, Du Pont, PPG
Aerospace and defence	15.7	Boeing, United Technologies, Lockheed Martin
Construction and farm equipment	14.5	Caterpillar, Deere, Illinois Tool Works
IT services	14.1	IBM, Computer Sciences, SAIC
Specialty retailers (non-apparel)	13.9	Home Depot, Costco, Lowe's
Communications equipment	13.1	Cisco Systems, Motorola, Qualcomm
Healthcare insurance and managed care	13.1	UnitedHealth Group, WellPoint, Aetna
Commercial banks	12.4	Bank of America, JPMorgan Chase, Citigroup
Engineering, construction	12.3	Fluor, Jacobs Engineering, KBR
Computers, office equipment	12.1	Hewlett-Packard, Apple, Dell Computer
Diversified financials	12.0	General Electric, Fannie Mae
General merchandisers	11.6	Walmart, Target, Sears Holdings
Energy	11.4	AES, AEP, Constellation Energy,
Pipelines	11.1	Plains All American, Enterprise Products, ONEOK
Utilities: gas and electric	10.6	Execon, Southern, NextEra
Packaging and containers	10.2	Ball, Crown Holdings, Owens-Illinois
Automotive retailing and services	9.8	AutoNation, Penske, Hertz
Food and drug stores	9.6	CVS, Kroger, Walgreen
Insurance: property and casualty	9.5	Berkshire Hathaway, AIG, Allstate
Insurance: life and health	8.7	MetLife, Prudential, Aflac
Hotels, casinos, resorts	8.5	Marriott International, Caesars, Las Vegas Sands
Metals	8.2	Alcoa, US Steel, Nucor
Semiconductors and electronic components	7.7	Intel, Texas Instruments, Jamil Circuit
Forest and paper products	7.3	International Paper, Weyerhaeuser, Domtar
Food production	5.2	Archer Daniels Midland, Tyson Foods, Smithfield
Telecommunications	5.8	Verizon, AT&T, Sprint-Nextel
Motor vehicles and parts	4.4	GM, Ford, Johnson Controls
Entertainment	3.9	Time Warner, Walt Disney, News Corporation
Airlines	−11.3	AMR, UAL, Delta Airlines

Notes:

1 Median ROE for each industry averaged across the 11 years 2000–2010.

2 Industries with fewer than five firms were excluded (with the exception of tobacco). Also omitted were industries that were substantially redefined during the period.

Source: Data from Fortune 1000 by industry.

Analysing industry attractiveness

Table 2.1 shows the profitability of different US industries. Some industries (such as tobacco and pharmaceuticals) consistently earn high rates of profit; others (motor vehicles and parts, entertainment) earn much lower rates of profit or fail to cover their cost of capital (airlines). The basic premise that underlies industry analysis is that the level of industry profitability is neither random nor the result of entirely firm-specific influences; it is determined by the systematic influences of the industry's structure. The pharmaceutical industry and the personal-computer industry not only supply very different products but also have very different structures, which make one highly profitable and the other a nightmare of price competition and weak margins. The pharmaceutical industry produces highly differentiated products bought by price-insensitive consumers and new products receive monopoly privileges in the form of patents. The personal-computer industry comprises many firms, produces commoditized products and is squeezed by powerful suppliers (e.g. Intel and Microsoft).

Small markets can often support much higher profitability than large markets, for the simple reason that small markets can more easily be dominated by a single firm. Featured Example 2.1 offers examples of niche markets that are havens from the rigours of fierce competition.

Featured Example 2.1

Chewing tobacco, sausage skins and slot machines: The joys of niche markets

UST Inc was the most profitable company in the S&P500 over the period 2003–2008 (in 2008 it was acquired by Altria, the owner of Philip Morris) with an average annual ROCE (operating profit as a percentage of capital employed) of 63%. What's the secret of UST's profitability? In 2010 it accounted for 55% of the US market for 'smokeless tobacco' (chewing tobacco and snuff), with brands such as Skoal, Copenhagen and Red Seal. Despite its association with a bygone era of cowboys and farm workers, chewing tobacco has been a growth market in the US. UST's long-established brands, its distribution through tens of thousands of small retail outlets and restrictions on advertising tobacco products have created formidable barriers to entry into this market.

Devro plc, based in the Scottish village of Moodiesburn, is the world's leading supplier of collagen sausage skins ('casings'). 'From the British Banger to the Chinese Lap Cheong, from the French Merguez to the South American Chorizo, Devro makes the casing of choice for manufacturers across the globe.' Its overall world market share is around 60%, with about 80% of the UK and Australian markets. In recent years its ROCE has averaged 18%, significantly above average for the UK (FTSE 100) companies.

International Game Technology (IGT), based in Reno, Nevada, is the world's dominant manufacturer of slot machines for casinos. IGT maintains its 70% US market share through close relations with casino operators and a continual flow of new products. With heavy investment in R & D, new product saturation, tight control over distribution and servicing and a policy of leasing rather than selling machines, IGT offers little opportunity to rivals. During 2007–2011 IGT earned an average ROCE of 19% despite severe recession in the US casino industry.

Sources: www.ustinc.com, www.devro.com, www.igt.com.

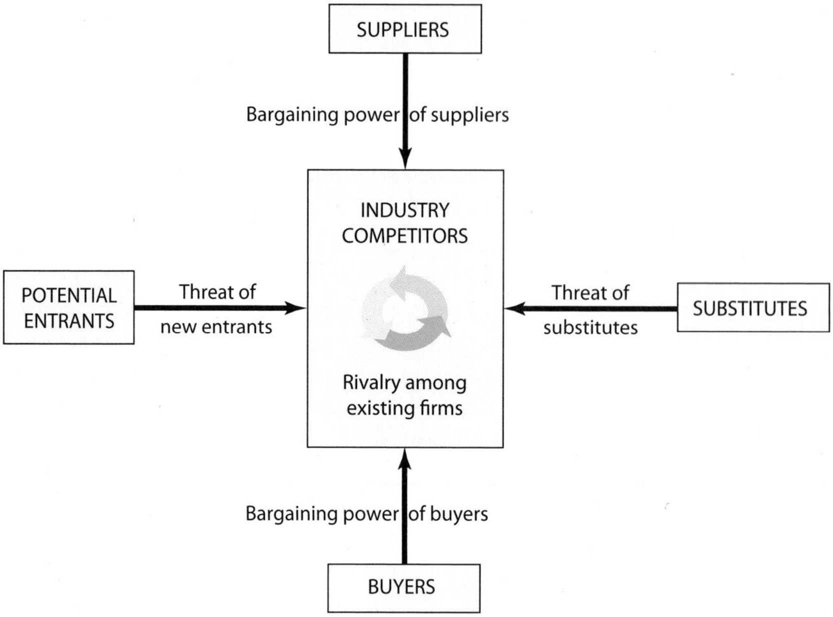

Figure 2.2 Porter's five forces of competition framework.
Source: Porter, M.E. (March–April 1979). 'How Competitive Forces Shape Strategy'. *Harvard Business Review*. Reproduced with permission.

Porter's five forces of competition framework

A helpful, widely used framework for classifying and analysing the factors that determine the intensity of competition and levels of competition in different industries was developed by Michael Porter of Harvard Business School.[4] Porter's five forces framework views the profitability of an industry (as indicated by its rate of return on capital relative to its cost of capital) as determined by five sources of competitive pressure. These five forces of competition include three sources of *horizontal* competition: competition from substitutes, competition from entrants and competition from established rivals; and two sources of *vertical* competition: the power of suppliers and power of buyers (Figure 2.2).

The strength of each of these competitive forces is determined by a number of key structural variables, as shown in Figure 2.3.

Competition from substitutes

The price customers are willing to pay for a product depends, in part, on the availability of substitute products. The absence of close substitutes for a product, as in the case of petrol or cigarettes, means that consumers are comparatively insensitive to price (i.e. demand is inelastic with respect to price). The existence of close substitutes means that customers will switch to substitutes in response to price increases for the product (i.e. demand is elastic with respect to price). The Internet has provided a new source of substitute competition that has proved devastating for a number of established industries. Travel agencies, newspapers and telecommunication providers have all suffered devastating competition from Internet-based substitutes.

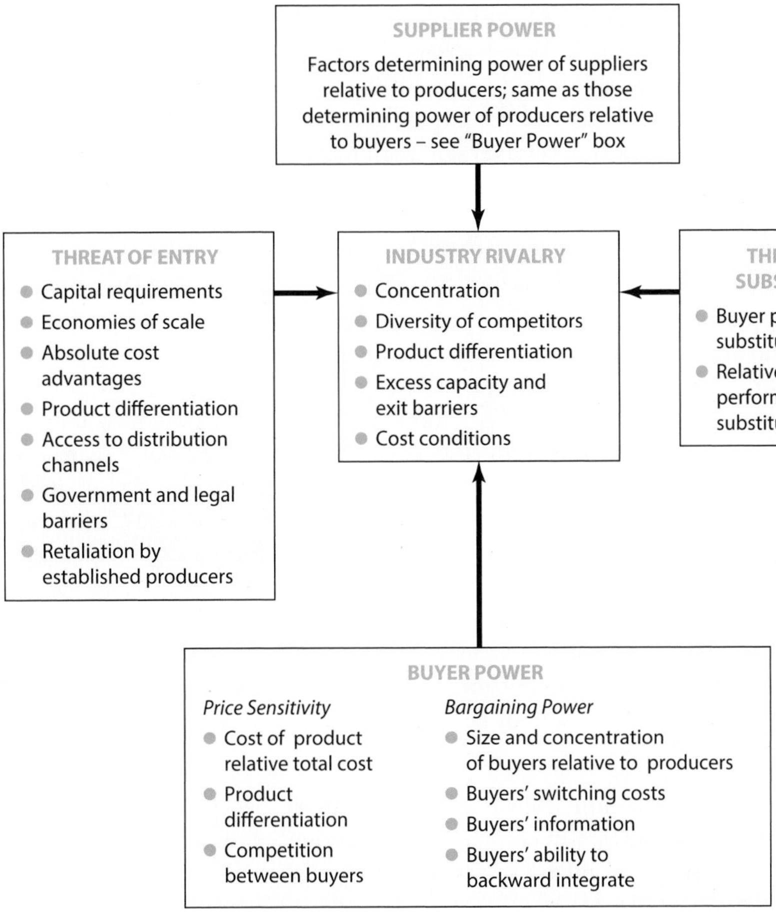

Figure 2.3 The structural determinants of the five forces of competition.

The extent to which substitutes depress prices and profits depends on the propensity of buyers to substitute between alternatives. Rare earths are elements that are critical to the production of everything from plasma TVs to mobile phones and guided missiles. In recent years China has controlled about 95% of the production of rare earths, and limited supply together with growing demand has led the prices of these minerals to rocket. Currently there are no replacements for rare earths in many high-tech products but the search is on for substitutes and ways of re-engineering products to reduce or eliminate their dependence on rare earths. For example, Toyota has reported that the company has developed a new motor for its hybrid cars that does not require lanthanum, neodymium and dysprosium; Honda has announced the opening of a rare earth recycling plant and scientists in laboratories around the world have shared details of progress in the search for synthetic alternatives. The fortunes of China's rare earth industry are likely to change significantly if these initiatives prove successful.

The threat of entry

If an industry earns a return on capital in excess of its cost of capital, it will act as a magnet to firms outside the industry. If the entry of new firms is unrestricted, the rate of profit will fall towards its competitive level. Increased health awareness in the US has encouraged increasing demand for fruit juice and smoothies. Low barriers to entry have resulted in about 4000 new juice and smoothie bars being established since 2000, resulting in market saturation and a high rate of business failures.[5] We also see the impact of entry restrictions in many professions. Why, for example, do orthodontists, on average, earn higher salaries than general dentists? The explanation lies, in part, with the need for qualified dentists to obtain a further licence to practise orthodontics. Restrictions on the number of licences create barriers to entry.

Threat of entry rather than actual entry may be sufficient to ensure that established firms constrain their prices to the competitive level. Eurostar is currently the only company offering a high-speed, passenger rail service through the Channel Tunnel that links Britain and France. Yet, Eurostar may be unwilling to exploit its monopoly power to the full given that European liberalization legislation means that other rail operators will soon be able to extend their operations to this route. An industry where no barriers to entry or exit exist is *contestable*: prices and profits tend towards the competitive level, regardless of the number of firms within the industry.[6] Contestability depends on the absence of **sunk costs** – investments whose value cannot be recovered on exit. An absence of sunk costs makes an industry vulnerable to hit-and-run entry whenever established firms raise their prices above the competitive level.

In most industries, however, new entrants cannot enter on equal terms with those of established firms. A **barrier to entry** is any advantage that established firms have over entrants. The height of a barrier to entry is usually measured as the unit cost disadvantage faced by would-be entrants. The principal sources of barriers to entry are discussed below.

CAPITAL REQUIREMENTS The capital costs of getting established in an industry can be so large as to discourage all but the largest companies. The duopoly of Boeing and Airbus in large passenger jets is protected by the huge capital costs of establishing R & D, production and service facilities for supplying these planes. Similarly with the business of launching commercial satellites: the costs of developing rockets and launch facilities make new entry highly unlikely. In other industries, entry costs can be modest. For example running a fitness boot camp in a local park requires very little capital, which is one reason why many such programmes have sprung up in recent years. Similarly, the costs of Internet ventures such as price comparison websites are typically small. Across the service sector more generally, start-up costs tend to be low. For example, start-up costs for a franchised pizza outlet begin at $150 000 for a Domino's and $638 000 for a Pizza Hut.[7]

ECONOMIES OF SCALE In industries that are capital or research or advertising intensive, efficiency requires large-scale operation. The problem for new entrants is that they are faced with the choice of either entering on a small scale and accepting high unit costs, or entering on a large scale and bearing the costs of under-utilized capacity. In the car industry, cost efficiency means producing at least three million vehicles a year. As a result, the only recent entrants into volume car production have been state-supported companies (e.g. Proton of Malaysia and Maruti of India). One of the main sources of **economies of scale** is new product development costs. Thus, developing and launching a new model of car typically costs over $1.5 billion. Airbus's A380 superjumbo cost about $18 billion to develop and must sell about 400 planes to break even. Once Airbus had committed to the project, Boeing was effectively excluded from the superjumbo segment of the market.

ABSOLUTE COST ADVANTAGES Established firms may have a unit cost advantage over entrants irrespective of scale. **Absolute cost advantages** often result from the acquisition of low-cost sources of raw materials. Saudi Aramco's access to the world's biggest and most accessible oil reserves give it an unassailable cost advantage over Shell, ExxonMobil and BP, whose costs per barrel are at least four times those of Saudi Aramco. Absolute cost advantages may also result from economies of learning. Sharp's cost advantage in LCD flat screen TVs results from its early entry into LCDs and from the wealth of experience it has accumulated.

PRODUCT DIFFERENTIATION In an industry where products are differentiated, established firms possess the advantages of brand recognition and customer loyalty. Consumers for whom brand is a key purchasing factor vary from 24% in Western Europe to 40% in China with brand loyalty highest for telecom services, consumer electronics and food and beverages.[8] New entrants to such markets must spend disproportionately heavily on advertising and promotion to gain levels of brand awareness and brand goodwill similar to that of established companies. One study found that, compared to early entrants, late entrants into consumer goods markets incurred additional advertising and promotional costs amounting to 2.12% of sales revenue.[9]

ACCESS TO CHANNELS OF DISTRIBUTION For many new suppliers of consumer goods, the principal barrier to entry is likely to be gaining distribution. Limited capacity within distribution channels (e.g. shelf space), risk aversion by retailers and the fixed costs associated with carrying an additional product result in retailers being reluctant to carry a new manufacturer's product. The battle for supermarket shelf space between the major food processors (typically involving 'slotting fees' to reserve shelf space) further disadvantages new entrants. One of the most important competitive impacts of the Internet has been allowing new businesses to circumvent barriers to distribution.

GOVERNMENTAL AND LEGAL BARRIERS Economists from the Chicago School claim that the only effective barriers to entry are those created by government. In taxicabs, banking, telecommunications and broadcasting, entry usually requires a licence from a public authority. From medieval times to the present day, companies and favoured individuals have benefited from governments granting them an exclusive right to ply a particular trade or offer a particular service. In knowledge-intensive industries, patents, copyrights and other legally protected forms of intellectual property are major barriers to entry. In the pharmaceutical industry, the major players seek to delay entry by generic drug makers by extending their original patents through changes in dosage and delivery methods. Regulatory requirements and environmental and safety standards often put new entrants at a disadvantage to established firms because compliance costs tend to weigh more heavily on newcomers.

RETALIATION Barriers to entry also depend on the entrants' expectations as to possible retaliation by established firms. Retaliation against a new entrant may take the form of aggressive price-cutting, increased advertising, sales promotion or litigation. The major airlines have a long history of retaliation against low-cost entrants. Southwest and other budget airlines have alleged that selective price cuts by American and other major airlines amounted to predatory pricing designed to prevent its entry into new routes.[10] To avoid retaliation by incumbents, new entrants may seek initial small-scale entry into less visible market segments. When Toyota, Nissan and Honda first entered the US car market, they targeted the small car segments, partly because this was a segment that had been written off by the Detroit Big Three as inherently unprofitable.[11]

THE EFFECTIVENESS OF BARRIERS TO ENTRY Industries protected by high entry barriers tend to earn above-average rates of profit.[12] Capital requirements and advertising appear to be particularly effective impediments to entry.[13]

The effectiveness of barriers to entry depends on the resources and capabilities that potential entrants possess. Barriers that are effective against new companies may be ineffective against established firms that are diversifying from other industries.[14] Google has used its massive Web presence as a platform for entering a number of other markets, including Microsoft's seemingly impregnable position in browsers and Apple's in the smartphone market.

Rivalry between established competitors

For most industries, the major determinant of the overall state of competition and the general level of profitability is competition among the firms within the industry. In some industries, firms compete aggressively – sometimes to the extent that prices are pushed below the level of costs and industry-wide losses are incurred. In other industries, price competition is muted and rivalry focuses on advertising, innovation and other non-price dimensions. The intensity of competition between established firms is the result of interactions between five factors. Let us look at each of them.

CONCENTRATION *Seller concentration* refers to the number and size distribution of firms competing within a market. It is most commonly measured by the concentration ratio (the combined market share of the leading firms. For example, the four-firm concentration ratio (CR4) is the market share of the four largest producers. In markets dominated by a single firm (e.g. P&G's Gillette in razor blades, Altria in the US smokeless tobacco market), the dominant firm can exercise considerable discretion over the prices it charges.

Where a market is dominated by a small group of leading companies (an oligopoly), price competition may also be restrained, either by outright collusion or more commonly through *parallelism* of pricing decisions.[15] Thus, in markets dominated by two companies, such as anti-virus software (Symantec and McAfee) and soft drinks (Coca-Cola and Pepsi), prices tend to be similar and competition focuses on advertising, promotion and product development. As the number of firms supplying a market increases, coordination of prices becomes more difficult and the likelihood that one firm will initiate price-cutting increases. However, despite the frequent observation that the exit of a competitor reduces price competition, while the entry of a new competitor stimulates it, there is little systematic evidence that seller concentration increases profitability. Richard Schmalensee concludes that: 'The relation, if any, between seller concentration and profitability is weak statistically and the estimated effect is usually small.'[16]

DIVERSITY OF COMPETITORS The extent to which a group of firms can avoid price competition in favour of collusive pricing practices depends on how similar they are in their origins, objectives, costs and strategies. The cosy atmosphere of the US car industry prior to the advent of import competition was greatly assisted by the similarities of the companies in terms of cost structures, strategies and top management mindsets. The intense competition that affects the car markets of Europe and North America today is partly due to the different national origins, costs, strategies and management styles of the competing firms. Similarly, the key challenge faced by OPEC is agreeing and enforcing output quotas among member countries that are sharply different in terms of objectives, production costs, politics and religion.

PRODUCT DIFFERENTIATION The more similar the offerings among rival firms, the more willing customers are to switch between them and the greater the inducement for firms to cut prices to boost sales. Where the products of rival firms are virtually indistinguishable, the product is a *commodity* and price is the sole basis for competition. Commodity industries such as agriculture, mining and petrochemicals tend to be plagued by price wars and low profits. By contrast, in industries where products are highly differentiated (perfumes, pharmaceuticals, restaurants, management consulting services), price competition tends to be weak, even though there may be many firms competing.

EXCESS CAPACITY AND EXIT BARRIERS Why does industry profitability tend to fall so drastically during periods of recession? The key is the balance between demand and capacity. Unused capacity encourages firms to offer price cuts to attract new business. Excess capacity may be cyclical (e.g. the boom–bust cycle in the semiconductor industry); it may also be part of a structural problem resulting from overinvestment and declining demand. In these latter situations, the key issue is whether excess capacity will leave the industry. Barriers to exit are costs associated with capacity leaving an industry. Where resources are durable and specialized and where employees are entitled to job protection, barriers to exit may be substantial.[17] In the European and North American car industry excess capacity together with high exit barriers have devastated industry profitability. Conversely, rapid demand growth creates capacity shortages that boost margins.

COST CONDITIONS: SCALE ECONOMIES AND THE RATIO OF FIXED TO VARIABLE COSTS When excess capacity causes price competition, how low will prices go? The key factor is cost structure. Where fixed costs are high relative to variable costs, firms will take on marginal business at any price that covers variable costs. The consequences for profitability can be disastrous. In the airline industry, the emergence of excess capacity almost invariably leads to price wars and industry-wide losses. The willingness of airlines to offer heavily discounted tickets on flights with low bookings reflects the very low variable costs of filling empty seats. During periods of recession the industries that have suffered the most drastic falls in profitability (cars, mining, hotels) have tended to be those where fixed costs were high and firms were willing to accept additional business at any price that covered variable costs.

The market for DRAM (dynamic random access memory) chips, used in electronic goods such as laptop computers and home games consoles, illustrates the link between demand, costs and industry profitability well. Demand for DRAM chips is closely correlated with global levels of economic activity, whereas the supply of DRAM chips is constrained by the size of fabrication plants and the rate at which production capacity can be ramped up. When demand is buoyant, it is difficult to add extra manufacturing capacity quickly. Similarly when demand falls away, because of the massive set-up costs and distinctive production processes of this industry, manufacturers cannot withdraw or cut back production easily or quickly. In 2013, for example, the price of DDR3-1600 chip fluctuated between approximately $127 and $36 with consequent effects on the profitability of producers of these chips.

Scale economies may also encourage companies to compete aggressively on price in order to gain the cost benefits of greater volume. If scale efficiency in the car industry means producing four million cars a year, a level that is currently achieved by only five companies, the outcome is a battle for market share as each firm tries to achieve critical mass.

Bargaining power of buyers

The firms in an industry compete in two types of markets: in the markets for inputs and in the markets for outputs. In input markets firms purchase raw materials, components and financial and labour services. In the markets for outputs firms sell their goods and services to customers (who may be distributors, consumers or other manufacturers). In both markets the transactions create value for both buyers and sellers. How this value is shared between them in terms of profitability depends on their relative economic power. Let us deal first with output markets. The strength of buying power that firms face from their customers depends on two sets of factors: buyers' price sensitivity and relative bargaining power.

BUYERS' PRICE SENSITIVITY The extent to which buyers are sensitive to the prices charged by the firms in an industry depends on four main factors:

- The greater the importance of an item as a proportion of total cost, the more sensitive buyers will be about the price they pay. Beverage manufacturers are highly sensitive to the costs of aluminium cans because this is one of their largest single cost items. Conversely, most companies are not sensitive to the fees charged by their auditors, since auditing costs are a tiny fraction of total company expenses.
- The less differentiated the products of the supplying industry, the more willing the buyer is to switch suppliers on the basis of price. The manufacturers of T-shirts and light bulbs have much more to fear from Tesco's buying power than have the suppliers of perfumes.
- The more intense the competition among buyers, the greater their eagerness for price reductions from their sellers. As competition in the world car industry has intensified, so component suppliers face greater pressures for lower prices.
- The more critical an industry's product to the quality of the buyer's product or service, the less sensitive are buyers to the prices they are charged. The buying power of personal computer manufacturers relative to the manufacturers of microprocessors

(Intel and AMD) is limited by the vital importance of these components to the functionality of PCs.

RELATIVE BARGAINING POWER Bargaining power rests, ultimately, on refusal to deal with the other party. The balance of power between the two parties to a transaction depends on the credibility and effectiveness with which each makes this threat. The key issue is the relative cost that each party sustains as a result of the transaction not being consummated. A second issue is each party's expertise in managing its position. Several factors influence the bargaining power of buyers relative to that of sellers:

- *Size and concentration of buyers relative to suppliers.* The smaller the number of buyers and the bigger their purchases, the greater the cost of losing one. Because of their size, health maintenance organizations (HMOs) can purchase healthcare from hospitals and doctors at much lower cost than can individual patients. Empirical studies show that buyer concentration lowers prices and profits in the supplying industry.[18]
- *Buyers' information.* The better-informed buyers are about suppliers and their prices and costs, the better they are able to bargain. Doctors and lawyers do not normally display the prices they charge, nor do traders in the bazaars of Tangier and Istanbul. Keeping customers ignorant of relative prices is an effective constraint on their buying power. But knowing prices is of little value if the quality of the product is unknown. In the markets for haircuts, interior design and management consulting, the ability of buyers to bargain over price is limited by uncertainty over the precise attributes of the product they are buying.
- *Ability to integrate vertically.* In refusing to deal with the other party, the alternative to finding another supplier or buyer is to do it yourself. Large food-processing companies such as Heinz and Campbell Soup have reduced their dependence on the manufacturers of metal cans by manufacturing their own. The leading retail chains have increasingly displaced their suppliers' brands with own-brand products. Backward integration need not necessarily occur – a credible threat may suffice.

Bargaining power of suppliers

Analysis of the determinants of relative power between the producers in an industry and their suppliers is comparable to analysis of the relationship between producers and their buyers. The only difference is that it is now the firms in the industry that are the buyers and the producers of inputs that are the suppliers. The key issues are the ease with which the firms in the industry can switch between different input suppliers and the relative bargaining power of each party.

Because raw materials, semi-finished products and components are often commodities supplied by small companies to large manufacturing companies, their suppliers usually lack bargaining power. Hence, commodity suppliers often seek to boost their bargaining power through cartelization (e.g. OPEC, the International Coffee Organization and farmers' marketing cooperatives). A similar logic explains labour unions. Conversely, the suppliers of complex, technically sophisticated components may be able to exert considerable bargaining power. The dismal profitability of the personal computer industry may be attributed to the power exercised by the suppliers of key components (processors, disk drives, LCD screens) and the dominant supplier of operating systems (Microsoft).

Case Insight 2.2

Porter's five forces of competition applied to the Colorado marijuana-growing industry

Competition from substitutes

There is a wide array of substitutes available for both recreational and medical-use marijuana; these include alcohol, other drugs (such as cocaine, amphetamines and ecstasy), painkillers and synthetic marijuana to name but a few. Each of these potential substitutes varies in price and performance relative to marijuana. For example, for recreational users, alcohol could be considered a good alternative to smoking marijuana, whereas amphetamines might not. For medical users, prescription drugs may offer similar benefits to marijuana but with very different price performance characteristics. The jury is out on the extent to which marijuana is addictive, but the more addictive the drug the lower the consumer's propensity to switch to substitutes.

Depending on the way in which we define the industry, we could also consider unlicensed, illegal suppliers to be providing a substitute for legally grown marijuana.

Taken as a whole, consumers have a relatively high propensity to substitute other products for marijuana, although the relative price and performance characteristics of different substitutes vary substantially.

Overall, the threat to industry profitability from substitution is likely to be moderate to high.

The threat of entry

The legalization of the sale of marijuana in Colorado may seem to pave the way for a flood of new entrants into the business, but there are some barriers to entry that disadvantage small start-ups. We noted in the opening case that obtaining a licence and fulfilling regulatory requirements is an arduous and expensive process and that the cultivation of marijuana is a complex and risky affair that requires considerable know-how. While the prohibition of the production and sale of marijuana encouraged the establishment of a large number of small-scale, illicit operations, decriminalization paves the way for industrial-scale production using up-to-date technology. The introduction of new technologies is likely to reduce labour but increase capital requirements, change cost structures (the ratio of fixed to variable costs) and generate economies of scale – all of which are likely to create barriers to small-scale entrants. Nonetheless, if the newly legalized industry is viewed as having the potential to offer superior returns, there is a real threat of entry by both entrepreneurs and larger players who are established in other industries or markets. Much will depend on the licensing policies adopted by the state legislature.

Overall, the threat from new entrants is likely to be moderate to high.

Rivalry between established competitors

The fact that the number of applications for licences for supplying marijuana in Colorado exceeded 2000 at the beginning of 2014 suggests that there are likely to be a large number of players in this industry, although it is not yet known how many licences will be granted or taken up once issued. Competitors are likely, in the first instance, to be rather diverse in character, and the existence of an illicit market adds another element of uncertainty and complexity that increases the likelihood of price competition. While suppliers will, undoubtedly, seek to protect themselves from price competition by differentiating their product offerings, it is difficult (though by no means impossible) to create unique products given the generic nature of cannabis plants, the limited trademark protection available given current federal law and the relative ease with which successful business models can be imitated. Nonetheless, marijuana users are likely to find it difficult to judge the quality of the product prior to purchase and face the risk of harm if they consume products of the wrong type or strength, so it is reasonable to assume that branding and reputation may become important as legalized markets develop. In the long term the appearance of strong brands may mute price competition.

Overall, rivalry is likely to be high.

Buyer and supplier power

Growing marijuana is akin to growing other specialist plants and forms part of the wider horticultural industry. There are a large number of established firms supplying the needs of specialist plant growers, and well-developed markets already exist for inputs such as fertilizers, lighting, irrigation equipment and security systems. At present retailers and dispensaries tend to grow, process and sell marijuana to end-users through online or retail stores. There are regulatory limits on the amounts that can be grown and purchased so sales are primarily to individuals who can only make small purchases at a given time.

The overall bargaining strength of both buyers and suppliers is likely to be low.

The overall attractiveness of the market

While the current price and cost structures and the absence of powerful buyers and sellers suggest that marijuana growing in Colorado offers attractive returns, rivalry and new entry look set to place pressure on margins. The presence of a significant number of substitutes is also likely to check firms' ability to earn above-average profits. Of course, our analysis of industry attractiveness depends, in part, on the way we have defined the industry in the first place. We discuss the issues raised by industry definition in more detail in Case Insight 2.4.

Applying industry analysis to forecasting industry profitability

Once we understand how industry structure drives competition we can apply this analysis to forecast industry profitability in the future.

Identifying industry structure

The first stage of any industry analysis is to identify the key elements of the industry's structure. In principle, this is a simple task. It requires identifying who are the main players – the producers, the customers, the input suppliers and the producers of substitute goods – and then examining some of the key structural characteristics of each of these groups that will determine competition and bargaining power.

In most manufacturing industries identifying the main groups of players is straightforward; in other industries, particularly in service industries, mapping the industry can be more difficult. Consider the US television broadcasting industry. Where do we draw the industry boundaries? Is there a single TV distribution industry or do we identify separate industries for TV airwaves broadcasting, cable TV and satellite TV? In terms of identifying buyers and sellers we see that the industry has quite a complex value chain which includes the producers of TV shows, the networks and cable channels that put together programme schedules and local TV stations and cable companies that undertake final distribution. The industry has two types of buyer: viewers and advertisers. Additional complexity is created by the fact that some companies are vertically integrated across several stages of the value chain – thus, network broadcasters such as Fox and NBC are backward integrated into TV production and forward integrated into final distribution through ownership of local TV stations. We shall return to issues of industry definition later in this chapter.

Forecasting industry profitability

We can use industry analysis to understand why profitability has been low in some industries and high in others but, ultimately, our interest is not to explain the past but to predict the future. Investment decisions made today will commit resources to an industry for years – often for a decade or more – hence, it is critical that we are able to predict what level of returns the industry is likely to offer in the future. Current profitability is a poor indicator of future profitability: industries such as newspapers, solar (photovoltaic) panels and mobile phone handsets have suffered catastrophic declines in profitability. Conversely, several industries where returns were low – steel, metals mining and several other commodity industries – have experienced remarkable revivals in profitability over the last 20 years. However, if an industry's profitability is determined by the structure of that industry then we can use observations of the structural trends in an industry to forecast the likely changes in competition and profitability. Changes in industry structure tend to be the result of fundamental shifts in customer buying behaviour, technology and firm strategies; these can often be anticipated well in advance of their impacts on competition and profitability.

To predict the future profitability of an industry, our analysis proceeds in three stages:

1. Examine how the industry's current and recent levels of competition and profitability are a consequence of its present structure.
2. Identify the trends that are changing the industry's structure. Is the industry consolidating? Are new players seeking to enter? Are the industry's products becoming more differentiated or more commoditized? Will additions to industry capacity outstrip growth of demand?
3. Identify how these structural changes will affect the five forces of competition and resulting profitability of the industry. Will the changes in industry structure cause competition to intensify or to weaken? Rarely do all the structural changes move competition in a consistent direction. Typically, some factors will cause competition to increase; others will cause competition to moderate. Hence, determining the overall impact on profitability tends to be a matter of judgement.

Featured Example 2.2

The future of horseracing

On 10th April 2010 around 60000 people crammed in to Oaklawn, a 106-year-old horseracing track in central Arkansas, USA to watch the Arkansas Derby, an event which has become a preview for the more famous Kentucky Derby that takes place three weeks later. Attendance was up by 38% on the previous year but the town of Oaklawn, which has a population of just under 40000, wasn't built for such crowds and so enterprising locals turned their lawns and shop fronts into car parking slots at $20–$25 a go.[19]

While events like the Arkansas and Kentucky Derbies in the US, the Grand National in the UK and the Melbourne Cup in Australia are as popular as ever, horseracing in general is going through more turbulent times. Although sometimes celebrated as the sport of kings, horseracing is a business like any other and is subject to fluctuations in its fortunes as the external environment changes.

One of the biggest factors triggering change in recent years has been the introduction of the Internet. The first online gambling site started in 1995 but such sites have grown rapidly in number and there are now estimated to be in excess of 2000. The advent of online gambling has not only increased the number of places a punter can place a bet; it has also changed the way in which horseracing takes place.

Horseracing as a sport is heavily dependent on money from betting. Practically every national racing association in the world takes a cut from bets placed on races. In Britain, for example, 10% of bookmakers' profits go to a statutory body that distributes these funds to British horseracing interests, for example the money goes to increase prize money, to support racetracks and horse breeders and to fund work in veterinary science. However, revenues from these kinds of levies are falling. Not only does the Internet provide an extended range of opportunities for those who wish to gamble to bet on sports other than horseracing but, more importantly, it means that betting on horseracing does not necessarily take place through bookmakers or at racetracks.

Britain and Australia have permitted the development of betting exchanges that allow people to bet with each other rather than going through licensed bookmakers. The companies that run betting exchanges charge the users a small commission in much the same way that eBay does. In Britain, one of the largest of these exchange providers is Betfair. Around 90% of bets placed through exchanges and more than half the bets made online in Britain are now through Betfair. Many traditional bookmakers are beginning to shut up shop, preferring to offer odds through Betfair to avoid taxes and levies. As a consequence the flow of funds into the horseracing industry is diminishing and, overall, the sport is in decline. While headline events still draw the crowds, everyday racing is much harder to sustain.

Some argue that this would have happened anyway. Bookmakers have always looked for ways of avoiding taxes and levies. For example, the bookmakers Ladbrokes and William Hill have already moved their betting operations from Britain to Gibraltar, where they are exempt from paying levies and the tax on betting is 2% rather than 15%. The answer, they argue, is in finding a new revenue model and paying closer attention to what the punters want. While the transformation that is taking place in the industry has taken some stakeholders by surprise, the impact of these environmental changes on competition has long been predicted.

Case Insight 2.3

Using industry analysis

Forecasting industry profitability in the Colorado marijuana-growing industry

Our prior analysis suggests that price competition is likely to intensify over time as existing producers improve the efficiency and increase the scale of their growing operations and new capacity enters the market. Ultimately, we can expect, as in the alcohol and tobacco industries, a shakeout to occur and a few large players with efficient growing operations and well-developed brands to dominate the industry. However, the role that branding and consolidation will play in this industry is by no means clear-cut and government regulation has a significant impact. The industry is currently very fragmented and while its legal status remains in the balance profit prospects will remain uncertain.

Using industry analysis to develop strategy

Once we understand how industry structure influences competition, which in turn determines industry profitability, we can use this knowledge to develop firm strategies. First, we can develop strategies that influence industry structure in order to moderate competition; second, we can position the firm to shelter it from the ravages of competition.

Strategies to alter industry structure

Understanding how the structural characteristics of an industry determine the intensity of competition and the level of profitability provides a basis for identifying opportunities for changing industry structure to alleviate competitive pressures. The first issue is to identify the key structural features of an industry that are responsible for depressing profitability. The second is to consider which of these structural features are amenable to change through appropriate strategic initiatives. For example:

- The remarkable profit revival in the world steel industry in this century was mainly the result of rising demand from China. However, it was also supported by the rapid consolidation of the industry, led by Mittal's merger with Arcelor, which was followed by the creation of Hebei Iron and Steel (China), Tata Steel taking over Corus (India) and the creation of the Nippon Steel & Sumitomo Metal Corporation (Japan).
- Excess capacity was a major problem in the European petrochemicals industry. Through a series of bilateral plant exchanges, each company built a leading position within a particular product area.
- In the US airline industry, the major airlines have struggled to change an unfavourable industry structure. In the absence of significant product differentiation, the airlines have used frequent-flyer schemes to build customer loyalty. Through hub-and-spoke route systems, the companies have achieved dominance of particular airports: American at Dallas/Fort Worth, US Airways at Charlotte, NC and Northwest at Detroit and Memphis. Mergers and alliances have reduced the numbers of competitors on many routes.[20]

- Building entry barriers is a vital strategy for preserving high profitability in the long run. A primary goal of the American Medical Association has been to maintain the incomes of its members by controlling the numbers of doctors trained in the United States and imposing barriers to the entry of doctors from overseas.

The idea of firms reshaping their industries to their own advantage has been developed by Michael Jacobides. He begins with the premise that industries are in a state of continual evolution and that all firms, even quite small ones, have the potential to influence the development of industry structure to suit their own interests – thereby achieving what he calls architectural advantage.[21] Jacobides encourages firms to look broadly at their industry – to see their entire value chain and links with firms producing complementary goods and services. The key is then to identify 'bottlenecks': activities where scarcity and the potential for control offer superior opportunities for profit. Architectural advantages results from three sources:

- *Creating one's own bottleneck:* Apple's dominance of the music download market through iTunes is achieved through a digital rights management (DRM) strategy that effectively locks in consumers through the incompatibility of its music files with other MP3 formats.[22]
- *Relieving bottlenecks in other parts of the value chain:* Google developed Android to prevent other firms from gaining a bottleneck in operating systems for mobile devices which could have threatened Google's ability to transfer its dominance of search services from fixed to mobile devices.
- *Redefining roles and responsibilities in the industries:* IKEA's ability to become the world's biggest and most successful supplier of furniture was based upon a strategy that required a transfer of furniture assembly from furniture manufacturers to consumers.

Positioning the company

Recognizing and understanding the competitive forces that a firm faces within its industry allows managers to position the firm where competitive forces are weakest. The record industry with its reliance on sales of CDs has been devastated by the substitute competition in the form of digital downloads, piracy and file sharing. Yet not all segments of the recorded music business have been equally affected. The old are less inclined to turn to digital downloading than younger listeners are, with the result that classical music, country and golden oldies have become comparatively more attractive than pop and hip-hop genres. Effective positioning requires the firm to anticipate changes in the competitive forces likely to affect its industry.

Case Insight 2.4

Using industry analysis to develop strategy

Strategies to alter industry structure

Ambitious growers and retailers may seek to alter industry structure to their own advantage in a number of ways. For example, expenditure of branding and marketing, if successful, could advantage incumbents and disadvantage de novo entrants; investment in capital equipment and sophisticated technology will favour firms that have sufficient scale to realize the efficiency gains associated with spreading indivisible, up-front costs; the unbundling of a hitherto highly vertically integrated supply chain will advantage firms with strong retailing or growing capabilities.

Positioning the firm

Prior to the change in legislation, the legal supplies of marijuana were available through a limited number of medical dispensaries to individuals who were recommended the drug by their doctors. A number of the dispensaries were established as cooperatives or collectives by 'patients' who grew and distributed their own supplies. The legalization of marijuana for recreational use has opened up new markets for these dispensers and has led many of them to apply for extended licences and to diversify into cannabis-related products, such as cakes and candies. For some firms, however, retaining a focus on the medical market offers the best prospects. Consumers using the product to alleviate medical conditions are likely to be less price-sensitive and more willing to pay a premium for quality-assured products and advice services (for example with regard to dosage, side effects or the latest research). Companies with well-established reputations and strong links with the medical profession may be best able to protect themselves from the intensification of price competition by adopting appropriate positioning strategies.

Defining an industry

One of the key challenges in industry analysis is defining 'an industry'. Economists define an industry as a group of firms that supplies a market. Hence, a close correspondence exists between markets and industries. So what's the difference between analysing industry structure and analysing market structure? The principal difference is that industry analysis looks at industry profitability being determined in two markets: product markets and input markets.

Everyday usage makes a bigger distinction between industries and markets. Typically, industries are identified with relatively broad sectors, whereas markets are related to specific products. Thus the firms within the packaging industry compete in many distinct product markets: glass containers, steel cans, aluminium cans, paper cartons, plastic containers and so on.

Similar issues arise in relation to geographical boundaries. From an economist's point of view, 'the US automobile industry' would denote all companies supplying the US auto market, irrespective of their location. In everyday usage, 'the US auto industry' typically refers to auto manufactures located in the US (about 14 companies) and is often restricted to US-owned automakers (Ford and General Motors).

To identify and define an industry, it makes sense to start with the idea of a market: which firms compete to supply a particular product or service? At the outset this approach may lead us to question conventional concepts of industry boundaries. For example, what is the industry commonly referred to as 'banking'? Institutions called banks supply a number of different products and services each comprising different sets of competitors. The most basic distinction is between retail banking, corporate banking and investment banking. Each of these can be disaggregated into several different product markets. Retail banking comprises deposit taking, transaction services, credit cards and mortgage lending. Investment banking includes corporate finance and underwriting, trading and advisory services.

The central issue in defining industries is to establish who is competing with whom. To do this we need to draw upon the principle of **substitutability**. There are two dimensions to this: substitutability on the demand side and substitutability on the supply side. Let us consider the market within which Jaguar Cars, a subsidiary of Tata Motors, operates. Starting with the demand side, are consumers willing to substitute only between Jaguars and other luxury cars or are they willing to substitute between Jaguars and mass-market brands on the basis of price difference? If the former, Jaguar's relevant industry is the luxury car industry; if the latter, Jaguar is part of the auto industry. If Jaguar customers are unwilling to substitute a Jaguar car for a truck or motorcycle on the basis of price then Jaguar should not be considered part of the motor vehicle industry.

But this fails to take account of substitutability on the supply side. If manufacturers were able to switch their production from family sedans to luxury cars and if Jaguar could enter other parts of the automobile market, then, on the basis of supply-side substitutability, we could regard Jaguar as part of the broader automobile industry. The same logic can be used to define the major domestic appliances as an industry. Although consumers are unwilling to substitute between refrigerators and dishwashers, manufacturers can use the same manufacturing plants and distribution channels for different appliances.

The same considerations apply to geographical boundaries. Should Jaguar view itself as competing in a single global market or in a series of separate national or regional markets? The criterion here again is substitutability. If customers are willing and able to substitute cars available on different national markets, or if manufacturers are willing and able to divert their output among different countries to take account of differences in margins, then a market is global. The key test of the geographical boundaries of a market is price: if price differences for the same product between different locations tend to be eroded by demand-side and supply-side substitution then these locations lie within a single market.

In practice, drawing the boundaries of markets and industries is a matter of judgement that depends on the purposes and context of the analysis. If Tata is considering the pricing and market positioning of its Jaguar cars, it must take a micro-level approach that defines markets in terms of individual models and individual countries. In considering decisions over investments in technology, component plants and new products, Tata will view Jaguar as competing in the global automobile industry. The longer term are the decisions being considered, the more broadly should we define the relevant industry – substitutability is higher in the long run than in the short term.

Second, the boundaries of a market or industry are seldom clear-cut. The market in which an offering competes is a continuum rather than a bounded space. Thus, we may view the competitive market of Disneyland, Anaheim as a set of concentric circles. The closest competitor is Universal Studios Tour. Slightly more distant are Sea World and Six Flags. Further still would be a trip to Las Vegas or a skiing weekend. Beyond these would be the broader leisure market that could include cinemas, beach vacations and video games.

For the purposes of applying the five forces framework, industry definition is seldom critical. We define an industry 'box' within which industry rivals compete, but because we include competitive forces outside the industry box, notably entrants and substitutes, the precise boundaries of the industry box are not greatly important. If we define Disneyland as competing within the broad entertainment industry then beach and ski resorts are rivals; if we define Disneyland as competing in the theme park industry then beach and ski resorts are substitutes.[23]

Case Insight 2.5
Defining the industry

On the demand side we have already noted that consumers may be willing to substitute other products for marijuana on the basis of price. For example if whisky is cheap relative to cannabis, a number of recreational users may substitute an evening in a bar for an evening smoking pot and we may consider both marijuana and alcohol to be part of the 'recreational intoxicants' industry.

On the supply side the resources and capabilities needed to grow marijuana are similar to those needed to grow other specialist plants that are sensitive to light and humidity, for example poinsettia (a plant that is a popular purchase at Christmastime in a number of countries) so we could consider marijuana a part of the horticultural industry.

The same arguments apply to geographical boundaries. Our case refers to the Colorado marijuana industry but we could consider the US marijuana industry or the global marijuana industry.

The way we define the industry has implications for the way we conduct our industry analysis. If, for example, we adopt a narrow definition and view the industry as comprising legal Colorado-based producers then growers and retailers operating in other states as well as illegal producers fall into the category of potential entrants and rivalry centres on Colorado-licensed producers. If, on the other hand, we adopt a broader definition of the market and explore the marijuana industry in the US, the way we label the competitive threat from different players changes. Fortunately, as long as we are clear about the purpose and focus of our analysis and are consistent in the way we delineate industry boundaries and appraise competitive forces, definitional issues are rarely critical.

Reviewing the five forces of competition framework

Porter's five forces framework has been subjected to two main attacks. Some have criticized its theoretical foundations, arguing that the 'structure–conduct–performance' approach to industrial organization that underlies it lacks rigour. Others have noted its empirical weaknesses. It appears that industry environment is a relatively minor determinant of a firm's profitability. Studies of the sources of inter-firm differences in profitability have produced very different results but all acknowledge that industry factors account for a minor part (less than 20%) of variation in return on assets among firms.

Do these findings imply that industry doesn't matter and we relegate the analysis of industry and competition to a minor role in our strategic analysis? We would argue not. Industry analysis is important because, without a deep understanding of their competitive environment, firms cannot make sound strategic decisions. Industry analysis is not relevant just to choosing which industries to locate within, as Michael Jacobides' concept of 'architectural advantage' reveals: industry analysis is also important for establishing competitive advantage within an industry. But if industry analysis is to fulfil this promise, it needs to go beyond the confines of the Porter five forces framework. We need to go further by extending Porter's framework, disaggregating broad industry sectors to

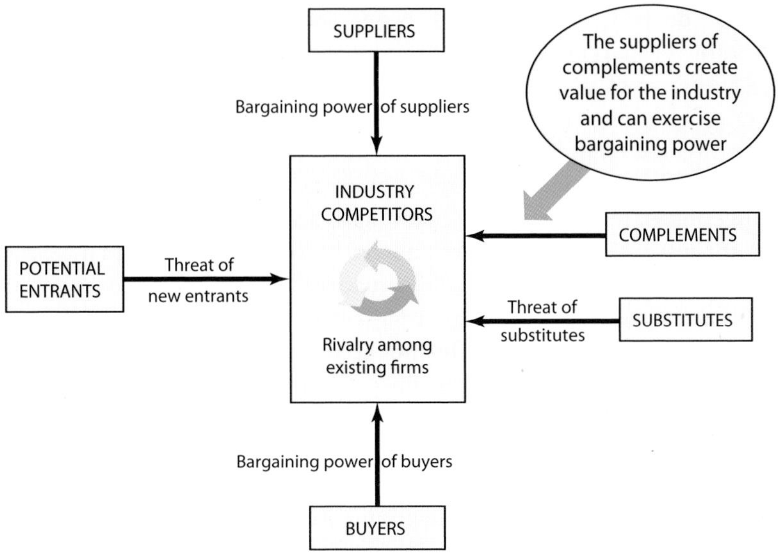

Figure 2.4 Five forces, or six?

examine competition within particular segments and giving thought to the dynamics of competition. This means we may also need to consider forces additional to those highlighted by Porter.

Complements: A missing force in the Porter model?

The Porter framework identifies the suppliers of substitute goods and services as one of the forces of competition that reduces the profit available to the firms within an industry. However, economic theory identifies two types of relationship between different products: substitutes and complements. Complements have the opposite effect to substitutes. While the presence of substitutes reduces the value of a product, complements increase it. For example, the availability of ink cartridges for my printer transforms its value to me.

Given the importance of complements to most products – the value of my car depends on the availability of petrol, insurance and repair services – our analysis of the competitive environment needs to take them into account. The simplest way is to add a sixth force to Porter's framework (Figure 2.4).[24]

Where products are close complements, they have little value to customers individually – customers value the whole system. But how is the value shared between the producers of the different complementary products? Bargaining power and its deployment is the key. During the early 1990s, Nintendo earned huge profits from its video game consoles. Although most of the revenue and consumer value was in the software – mostly supplied by independent developers – Nintendo was able to appropriate most of the profit potential of the entire system through establishing dominance over the games developers. Nintendo used its leadership in the console market and ownership of the console operating system to enforce restrictive developer licences to software producers of games and maintain tight control over the manufacture and distribution of games cartridges (from which Nintendo earned a large royalty).[25]

Where two products are complements to one another, profit will accrue to the supplier that builds the stronger market position and reduces the value contributed by the other. How is this done? The key is to achieve monopolization, differentiation and shortage of supply in one's own product while encouraging competition, commoditization and excess capacity in the production of the complementary product. IBM was attempting to shift the balance of power between hardware and software producers through its promotion of Linux and other open-source software programs. By pressing to differentiate its hardware products while commoditizing software, it could reduce the power of Microsoft and gain a bigger share of the profit returns from systems of hardware and software.[26]

It has also been suggested that the government be added to the model as an additional force. Indeed, Michael Porter considers this possibility when presenting his framework in his book *Competitive Strategy*, published in 1980.[27] Governments can have a strong impact on industry profitability. For example, the announcement in 2010 by the Australian government of proposals to raise taxes on the profits of mining companies like Rio Tinto and BHP Billiton resulted in an immediate fall in the valuation of these companies. While the government can directly affect industry attractiveness, as the mining example illustrates, it also has a powerful influence on each of the other five forces. The majority of analysts view the government as having such a pervasive influence on all aspects of industry competition that its influence is best captured through the existing five forces rather than added as a sixth.

Segmentation analysis

The difficulty of drawing industry boundaries and the need to define industries broadly or narrowly depending on the kinds of questions we are seeking to answer means that sometimes it is helpful to undertake more detailed, disaggregated analysis. One of the main approaches to 'within-' or 'intra-industry' analysis is market segmentation.

Segmentation is the processes of partitioning a market on the basis of characteristics that are likely to influence consumers' purchasing behaviour, and segmentation analysis is concerned with evaluating competitive conditions within segmented submarkets. Segmentation is particularly important if competition varies across these different submarkets such that some are more attractive than others. While Sony and Microsoft battled for dominance for leadership among so-called hard-core gamers with their technologically advanced PS3 and Xbox 360 consoles, Nintendo's Wii became a surprise market share leader by focusing on a large and underserved market segment: casual and older video game players. Essentially segmentation decisions are choices about which customers to serve and what to offer them.

The purpose of segmentation analysis is to identify attractive segments, to select strategies for different segments and to determine how many segments to serve. The analysis proceeds in five stages:

1 *Identify possible segmentation variables.* Essentially, segmentation decisions are choices about which customers to serve and what to offer them, hence segmentation variables relate to the characteristics of customers and the product. The most appropriate segmentation variables are those that partition the market most distinctly in terms of limits to substitution by customers (demand-side

substitutability) and producers (supply-side substitutability). Price differentials are a good guide to market segments. Thus, in the car industry, colour is probably not a good segmentation variable (white and red Honda Civics sell at much the same price); size is a better segmentation variable (full-size cars sell at a price premium over sub-compact cars).

2 *Construct a segmentation matrix*. Typically, segmentation analysis generates far too many segmentation variables so it is necessary to reduce the number of variables to make the analysis more manageable. This is usually done by selecting only those variables that are most important or closely correlated with each other. Reducing the number of variables allows individual segments to be identified in a two- or three-dimensional matrix.

3 *Analyse segment attractiveness*. Profitability within a segment is determined by the same structural forces that determine profitability within the industry as a whole so the five forces analysis can be applied to individual market segments.

4 *Identify key success factors in each segment*. By analysing buyers' purchase criteria and the basis of competition within individual segments, we can identify what a firm needs to do well in order to be successful in a particular segment.

5 *Select segment scope*. A firm needs to decide whether it wishes to be a segment specialist or compete across multiple segments. The advantage of a broad over a narrow focus depends on the similarity of key success factors and the presence of shared costs.

Case Insight 2.6

Segmentation analysis

In the opening case we chose to examine the Colorado marijuana industry as a whole but we could have looked in more detail at the competitive conditions influencing a particular subset of this industry. For example, we made frequent references to the difference between recreational users and those consuming marijuana for medical reasons. In other words, we segmented the industry on the basis of user motivation. But there are other ways in which we could have segmented this industry:

- *product attributes* – different strains of marijuana have different potency and flavour. We could distinguish between high-potency and low-potency products;
- *user characteristics* – age, lifestyle, socio-economic grouping;
- *geography*– e.g. UK, US, Russia.

A number of these variables may be correlated, for example those using marijuana for medical purposes may be older and more geographically dispersed than those consuming marijuana for recreational purposes. It seems likely that the key success factors in the medical segment of the market will be different from the recreational sector, so some firms may choose to be segment specialists.

Dealing with dynamic competition

Using five forces analysis to predict industry profitability supposes that industry structure is relatively stable and determines competitive behaviour in a predictable way, but this ignores the dynamic forces of innovation and entrepreneurship which transform industry structure. Joseph Schumpeter, one of the great economists of the early 20th century, viewed competition as a 'perennial gale of creative destruction' through which favourable industry structures – monopoly in particular – contain the seeds of their own destruction by attracting incursions from new and established firms deploying innovatory strategies and innovatory products to unseat incumbents.[28] The key consideration is the speed of structural change in the industry: if structural transformation is rapid, the five forces model has limited predictive value.

In practice, Schumpeter's process of 'creative destruction' tends to be more of a breeze than a gale. In established industries, entry occurs so slowly that profits are undermined only gradually,[29] while changes in industrial concentration tend to be slow.[30] One survey observes: 'the picture of the competitive process ... is, to say the least, sluggish in the extreme.'[31] As a result, both at the firm and at the industry level, profits tend to be highly persistent in the long run.[32]

What about recent decades? Has accelerating technological change and intensifying international competition reinforced the processes of 'creative destruction'? Rich D'Aveni argues that a general feature of industries today is **hypercompetition**: 'intense and rapid competitive moves, in which competitors must move quickly to build [new] advantages and erode the advantages of their rivals'.[33] If industries are hypercompetitive, their structures are likely to be less stable than in the past, superior profitability will tend to be transitory and the only route to sustained superior performance is through continually recreating and renewing competitive advantage.

Despite the plausibility of this thesis and everyday observations that markets are becoming more volatile and market leadership more tenuous, systematic evidence of this trend is elusive. One large-scale statistical study concluded: 'The heterogeneity and volatility of competitive advantage in US manufacturing industries has steadily and astonishingly increased since 1950. Industry structures are destabilizing. These results suggest that a shift towards hypercompetition has indeed occurred.'[34] This volatility is observed not just in technology-intensive and manufacturing industries.[35] However, another study found a 'lack of widespread evidence ... that markets are more unstable now than in the recent past'.[36]

From industry attractiveness to competitive advantage: Identifying key success factors

The five forces framework and the extensions to this framework allow us to determine an industry's potential for profit. But how is industry profit shared between the different firms competing in that industry? Let us look explicitly at the sources of competitive advantage within an industry. In subsequent chapters we develop a more comprehensive analysis of competitive advantage. Our goal here is to identify those factors within the firm's market environment that determine the firm's ability to survive and prosper: its **key success factors**.[37]

Our approach to identifying key success factors is straightforward and common sense. To survive and prosper in an industry, a firm must meet two criteria: first, it must supply what customers want to buy; second, it must survive competition. Hence, we may start by asking two questions:

- What do our customers want?
- What does the firm need to do to survive competition?

To answer the first question we need to look more closely at customers of the industry and to view them not as a threat to profitability because of their buying power but as the purpose of the industry and its underlying source of profit. This requires that we ask: Who are our customers? What are their needs? How do they choose between competing offerings? Once we recognize the basis of customers' preferences, we can identify the factors that confer success upon the individual firm. For example, if consumers choose supermarkets on the basis of price then cost efficiency is the primary basis for competitive advantage and the key success factors are the determinants of inter-firm cost differentials.

The second question requires us to examine the nature of competition in the industry. How intense is competition and what are its key dimensions? Thus, in airlines, it is not enough to offer low fares, convenience and safety. Survival requires sufficient financial strength to survive the intense price competition that accompanies cyclical downturns.

A basic framework for identifying key success factors is presented in Figure 2.5. Application of the framework to identify key success factors in three industries is outlined in Table 2.2.

The value of success factors in formulating strategy has been scorned by some strategy scholars. Pankaj Ghemawat observes that the 'whole idea of identifying a success factor and then chasing it seems to have something in common with the ill-considered medieval hunt for the philosopher's stone, a substance that would transmute everything it touched into gold'.[38] Our goal is not to identify 'generic strategies' that can guarantee success, simply to recognize commonalities in customer motivation and the nature of competition. In the fashion clothing business we identified key success factors (Table 2.2). However, unique resources and capabilities applied to common success factors results in the adoption of very different strategies.

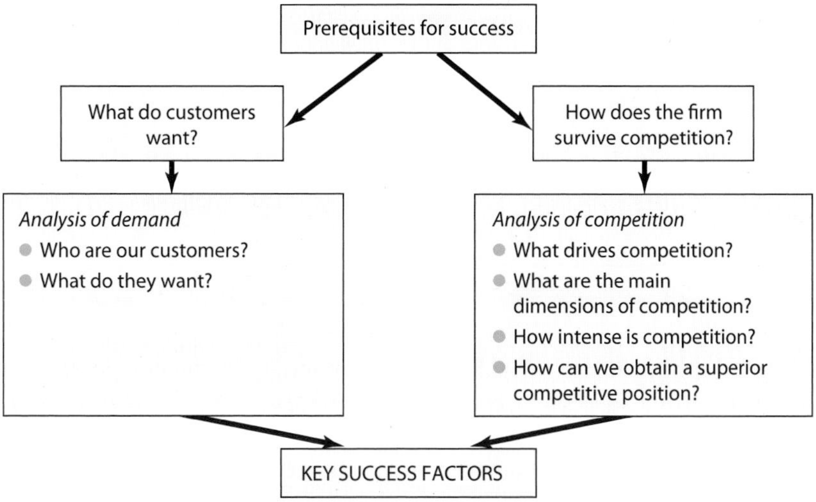

Figure 2.5 Identifying key success factors.

Table 2.2 Identifying key success factors: Steel, fashion clothing and supermarkets.

	What do customers want? (analysis of demand)	How do firms survive competition? (analysis of competition)	Key success factors
Steel	Low price Product consistency Reliability of supply Specific technical specifications for special steels	Commodity products, excess capacity, high fixed costs, exit barriers and substitute competition mean intense price competition and cyclical profitability Cost efficiency and financial strength essential	Cost efficiency requires: large-scale plants, low-cost location, rapid capacity adjustment Alternatively, high-technology, small-scale plants can achieve low costs through flexibility and high productivity Differentiation through technical specifications and service quality
Fashion clothing	Diversity of customer preferences in terms of garment type, style, quality, colour Customers willing to pay premium for brand, style, exclusivity and quality Mass market, highly price sensitive	Low barriers to entry and exit, low seller concentration and buying power of retail chains imply intense competition Differentiation can yield substantial price premium, but imitation is rapid	Combining differentiation with low costs Differentiation requires speed of response to changing fashions, style, reputation and quality
Supermarkets	Low prices Convenient location Wide range of products adapted to local preferences Fresh/quality produce, good service, ease of parking, pleasant ambience	Intensity of price competition depends on number and proximity of competitors Bargaining power a critical determinant of cost of bought-in goods	Cost efficiency requires manufacture in low-wage countries Low costs require operational efficiency, scale-efficient stores, large aggregate purchases, low wage costs Differentiation requires large stores (to allow wide product range), convenient location, familiarity with local customer preferences

Summary

In Chapter 1, we established that a profound understanding of the competitive environment is a critical ingredient of a successful strategy. In this chapter, we have developed a systematic approach to analysing a firm's industry environment in order to evaluate the industry's profit potential and to identify sources of competitive advantage. The centrepiece of this chapter has been Porter's five forces framework, which links the structure of an industry to the competitive intensity within it and to the profitability that it realizes. We have also introduced the notion of key success factors as a way of starting to get to grips with the question of how industry profits are shared between different firms competing in that industry.

By applying Porter's framework to some specific examples, we have revealed some of the challenges and limitations of the approach, recognizing, in particular, the need to exercise judgement when deciding how to define the scope of industry analysis and how finely grained such analysis needs to be. We have noted the potential for complementary products to add value and that we need to expand our strategy toolkit when it comes to looking at highly dynamic business environments. These are issues we return to in Chapters 5 and 6.

Summary table

Learning objectives	Summary
Be familiar with a number of frameworks used to analyse an organization's external environment and understand how the structural features of an industry influence competition and profitability	You have been introduced to systematic approaches to analysing a firm's industry environment using PEST and Porter's five forces framework. PEST analysis aims to identify those factors that are most likely to shape the competitive conditions within an industry. The five forces of competition framework classifies those features of an industry that drive competition and profitability. Although every industry is unique, industry attractiveness is the result of the systematic influences of the structure of that industry
Be able to use evidence on structural trends within industries to forecast changes in competition and profitability and to develop appropriate strategies for the future	The five forces framework can be used to explore future as well as current competitive conditions. It is useful for predicting industry profitability, identifying how the firm can improve industry attractiveness and positioning the firm in relation to these forces. Firm strategies can shape, as well as be shaped by, industry structure
Be able to define the boundaries of the industry within which a firm is located	The central issue in defining industries is to establish who is competing with whom, and to do this we drew on the notion of substitutability (both on the demand and the supply side). The boundaries of an industry are rarely clear-cut, but as long as we are clear about the purpose and focus of our analysis, industry definition is seldom critical
Be able to recognize the limits of the Porter five forces framework and extend the framework to include the role of complements as well as substitutes	Some critics have argued that Porter's five forces framework lacks rigour and supporting empirical evidence but we argue that industry analysis remains important. We also noted that while the Porter framework identifies the suppliers of substitute products as a force of competition it does not highlight the role of complements. Complements have the opposite effects to substitutes and are of growing importance in a number of industries so there is a case for adding them as a sixth force of competition
Be able to segment an industry into its constituent markets and appraise the relative attractiveness of different segments	For more detailed analysis of competition we often need to focus on markets that are drawn more narrowly in terms of products and geography. The process of disaggregating industries into specific markets we call segmentation
Be able to analyse competition and customer requirements in order to identify opportunities for competitive advantage within an industry (key success factors)	By combining the analysis of industry competition with a close examination of customer wants we were able to see how to identify key success factors, namely what firms need to do well to succeed in a particular industry

Further reading

In this particular area of study it is well worth returning to classic books and articles to gain a deeper understanding of the subject and to appreciate how debates have developed over time. That said, Ofek and Wathieu's short article in the *Harvard Business Review* gives some up-to-date examples of recent trends and the perils of ignoring them, and Michael Porter's 2008 article in the same journal provides an easy alternative to reading his original work, which was published in his 1980 book *Competitive Strategy*. In his more recent article he reaffirms and extends his five forces framework and comments on the practicalities of using this approach. It is often assumed that dominant firms or firms acting together can change their industry structure. Michael Jacobides introduces the notion of architectural advantage and suggests that all firms can potentially influence industry structure.The problems of defining markets and undertaking segmentation analysis are of key importance to marketeers so most standard marketing texts cover this area reasonably comprehensively. However, Gadiesh and Gilbert point out that markets are usually disaggregated horizontally by product, geography and customer group, but they can also be segmented vertically by identifying different value chain activities.

Gadiesh, O. and Gilbert, J. L. (1998). Profit pools: A fresh look at strategy. *Harvard Business Review*, May–June, 139–47.

Jacobides, M. G. (2008). Building architectural advantage: Don't just compete *in* your sector: Shape your sector and win! AIM White Paper, London Business School.

Ofek, E. and Wathieu, L. (2010). Are you ignoring trends that could shake up your business? *Harvard Business Review*, 88(7/8), 124–31.

Porter, M. E. (2008). The five competitive forces that shape strategy. *Harvard Business Review*, 57, 57–71.

Self-study questions

1. From Table 2.1 select a high-profit and a low-profit industry. From what you know about the structure of your selected industry, use the five forces framework to explain why profitability is high in one industry and low in the other.
2. 'The practical application of Porter's framework reveals its many limitations.' Discuss and suggest ways in which some of the limitations you identify could be overcome.
3. Aldi is a discount supermarket chain that has over 8000 retail stores worldwide, including in the UK, mainland Europe, Scandinavia, the US and Australia. Although Aldi operates internationally, most shoppers choose between retailers located within a few miles of each other. For the purposes of analysing profitability and competitive strategy, should Aldi consider the discount retailing industry global, national or local?
4. How would you segment the restaurant market in your home town? How would you advise someone thinking of starting a new restaurant what segments might be most attractive in terms of profit potential?
5. What do you think are the key success factors in the:
   a. pizza delivery industry?
   b. Formula One racing industry?

Closing Case

Fitness First and the UK health and fitness club industry

In July 2014, John Wartig, the chief financial officer of Fitness First Ltd, was preparing for a meeting with his CEO, Tony Cosslett, to review Fitness First's capital expenditure plans for the next five years. Both were relative newcomers to the company: following the acquisition of Fitness First by private equity firms Oaktree Capital and Marathon, Cosslett was installed as CEO in June 2012; Wartig was appointed CFO six months later. Fitness First claimed to be the world's largest privately owned health club group with 540 clubs and over one million members in 21 countries. In January 2014, Fitness First announced a £350 million five-year programme of capital investment which would include £50 million on upgrading and rebranding its UK clubs and £64 million on expanding its presence in Asia, including entry into China. John Wartig's concerns related to Fitness First's UK operations: given the intense competition within the UK health club sector, would Fitness First's investment in upgrading its facilities and repositioning within the market yield a satisfactory return to its owners?

Fitness First Ltd

In 1993, Mike Balfour established the first Fitness First health club in Bournemouth, England. The company's floatation on London's AIM in 1996 fuelled rapid expansion, initially in the UK, Germany and Belgium and then into Australia, Hong Kong, Spain, Malaysia, France, Holland and Italy. However, rapid expansion strained its finances and, following a steep fall in its share price, it was acquired by Cinven, a private equity firm in 2003. Following two years of restructuring and refocusing, Fitness First was bought by another private equity group, BC Partners, for £835 million. Yet, despite its market leadership in the UK, financial performance was poor. By 2011, Fitness First was teetering on the brink of bankruptcy and in 2012 was acquired by Oaktree Capital and Marathon Asset Management. The new management team closed some clubs and put others up for sale. By 2014, there were 80 Fitness First clubs in the UK, down from 161 in 2009. During 2014, CEO Tony Cosslett initiated an upmarket repositioning of the chain in an effort to enhance members' experiences and to avoid direct competition with budget chains. The new strategy comprised using IT to provide fuller information and a more customized experience, rebranding to establish Fitness First as a 'national authority' on fitness and exercise, a redesign of the clubs and retraining staff to enhance their knowledge and customer orientation.

The UK health club industry

Development

As in other countries, gymnasiums with facilities for weightlifting and general exercise and for sports such as gymnastics, boxing, wrestling and judo had long been a feature of the social infrastructure of urban Britain. Gymnasiums were operated both by local government authorities and by not-for-profit clubs. The emergence of health club chains owned and operated as business enterprises dates from the early 1980s and was associated with the rise of young urban professionals ('yuppies') as a social and cultural group.

The contrast between the new health clubs and the old gyms was stark. Gyms were typically scruffy, male-only facilities with limited equipment and very basic changing and showering facilities. The private health clubs featured sophisticated, technologically advanced exercise equipment; pools, saunas and steam rooms; individual and group instruction in a range of activities from yoga to weight training; individual consultation through personal trainers; and luxurious relaxation facilities including cafés and juice bars.

Early entrants into the industry were typically start-up companies which began with a single establishment then used venture capital funds to expand. These were often founded by individual enthusiasts and former sports personalities.

Early leaders such as Holmes Place (1980), David Lloyd Leisure (1982), Fitness First (1993) and Esporta (1994) initially drew upon venture capital finance and were later listed on the London Stock Exchange or AIM. Subsequently, many were bought out by private equity firms: their erratic profitability but good cash flow potential made them attractive, but more to private equity financiers than stock market investors. In addition to these start-ups, a number of established companies entered the industry. Richard Branson's Virgin Group entered the business in 1992 when it acquired South Africa's Health and Racquet Club. JJB Sports, a retail sportswear chain owned by Mike Ashby, opened JJB Sports Clubs (later to become DW Sports Fitness), and several hotel chains (including Marriott and Hilton) introduced health clubs within their hotels. Most of the leading chains owned and operated their individual health clubs, but some, such as the Swiss-based Kieser Training, adopted a franchising model.

Facilities, costs and pricing

Clubs differed in the sophistication and luxury and in the range of equipment and services they offered. Some clubs emphasized particular sports. For example, the David Lloyd club emphasized racquet sports (tennis, badminton and squash). Some clubs were women only.

While a small fitness club comprising an exercise room and changing facilities could be opened in leased premises for a start-up cost of around £400 000, a full-service health club of the type offered by the major chains involved an investment of around £2 million. The principal costs were converting the premises to install facilities such as a pool, Jacuzzi, showers and so forth and the cost of the equipment. Exercise machines have advanced substantially in sophistication and cost – individual items of equipment can cost over £25 000. Leading suppliers include Life Fitness (USA) and Technogym (Italy).

The typical pricing policy for health clubs was through annual membership contracts. These usually involved a one-time registration fee and a monthly fee of between £30 and £80. Because the costs of operating a health club were much the same irrespective of usage, health club operators were under considerable pressure to generate revenue through signing up new members. Competition took many forms. While health clubs were reluctant to compete on published membership fees, substantial discounts from list prices were offered. Initial sign-up fees were often waived, generous incentives were given to existing members for introducing new members, low-cost family deals and off-peak memberships were common and heavily discounted multiyear membership deals were offered.

An important source of profit for the industry was from consumers who signed up for membership but subsequently used their clubs rarely, if at all. However, this source of revenue was under attack. In a May 2011 court ruling, membership contracts of more than one year were declared unenforceable on the basis that such contacts were 'a trap into which the average consumer is likely to fall'.[39]

Widening competition

As the market grew, it was also becoming segmented among different groups of providers. A major challenge to Fitness First and the other market leaders was the emergence of a new group of budget fitness clubs. The Gym Group, Pure Gym, Fit4less and easyGym (owned by the EasyJet Group) offered monthly membership for £15 or less and even offered one-day memberships.

Growing competition also came from publicly owned gyms and sports centres. Many local government authorities had invested heavily in sports and fitness centres, including upgrading swimming pools by adding new gym facilities. Typically, these public sports and fitness facilities were much cheaper than private health clubs, even if they did offer less luxury and fewer services. However, the trend to outsource their management to not-for-profit social enterprises had brought greater efficiency, innovation and customer focus to these public facilities. Not-for-profit operators, such as Greenwich Leisure Ltd with 100 leisure centres, were equal in size to some of the biggest private chains. Table 2.3 compares private and public sectors within the industry.

Within the private sector of the health and fitness industry, Table 2.4 shows the UK's leading operators, while Table 2.5 gives financial information on selected companies.

Reflections

As John Wartig browsed through the most recent survey report of the UK health and fitness sector, he was struck by the basic contradiction that perplexed many of the entrepreneurs and investors who had flocked to the sector. In a society that was becoming increasingly health conscious with greater willingness to spend increasing amounts of disposable income on exercise and well-being, why was it that the private chains of health and fitness clubs found it so difficult to make money? Looking to the future, there were some positive signs – notably the increased growth in health club membership and the consolidation of the sector as the weaker players were bought out by financially stronger companies. At the same time, the prospects for the industry still looked precarious. The rise of the budget health clubs demonstrated the ease with which new companies were able to enter the industry. Even more worrying was the recognition that health and fitness clubs were not the only routes to health and fitness. Digital technology had enhanced the ability of individuals to conduct exercise programmes in their own homes, while traditional and new exercise forms such as running, cycling, yoga, Pilates and martial arts offered a vast array of possibilities that did not necessarily require membership of a health and fitness club.

Table 2.3 Private and public health and fitness clubs in the UK: 2011 and 2014.

	Private		Public	
	2011	2014	2011	2014
Number of clubs	3146	3269	2706	2750
Number of members (millions)	4.43	4.80	2.91	3.10
Average monthly fee	£38.39	£41.35	£29.57	£30.45

Sources: Leisure Database Company, Leisure Industry Academy and other sources.

Table 2.4 Leading UK private health and fitness club operators: 2014.

Company	No. of clubs[1]	No. of members[2]	Owner
Fitness First	150	336 000	Oaktree Capital, Marathon Asset Management
LA Fitness	80[3]	202 000	Owned by UK banks and other creditors
David Lloyd Leisure	76[4]	450 000	TDR Capital
Virgin Active	112[5]	435 000	Virgin Group
DW Sports Fitness	71	270 000	DW Fitness
Bannatyne's	59	185 000	Bannatyne Fitness
Pure Gym	33	198 000	CCMP Capital Advisors
Nuffield Health Fitness & Wellbeing	54	195 000	Nuffield Health
The Gym	44	195 000	Phoenix Equity Partners, Bridges Ventures
Marriott Leisure Club	42	Not known	Marriott International

Notes

1 Obtained from company websites and newspaper articles.

2 Mintel estimates for 2013.

3 33 of these clubs put up for sale in March 2014.

4 Includes racquet clubs.

5 Acquired 42 clubs from Esporta in 2011.

Table 2.5 Selected financial data for leading UK private health and fitness club operators (2010–2013).

Company	Year	Revenue £m	Operating profit (loss) £m	Net profit (loss) £m	Capital employed[1] (£m)
Fitness First Ltd	2012	40.6	(2.3)	(5.0)	378.7
	2011	43.1	(227.7)[2]	(214.4)	393.3
	2010	40.5	23.4	36.8	512.9
David Lloyd Leisure Ltd	2012	214.9	(40.8)	4.2	494.3
	2011	211.5	(60.1)	(16.4)	43.0
	2010	210.6	(3.5)	43.0	516.0
Virgin Active Ltd	2012	73.1	(1.6)	(0.3)	902.6[3]
	2011	71.2	7.4	0.3	556.3[3]
	2010	71.3	13.9	4.3	457.2[3]
Bannatyne Fitness Ltd	2013	88.8	13.6	9.4	160.2
	2012	89.5	8.6	3.6	161.8
	2011	89.1	(10.6)	(14.0)	152.2

Source: Company accounts filed with Companies House

Notes:

1 Shareholders' equity plus long-term liabilities.

2 Includes restructuring costs.

3 Includes current loans from other members of the Virgin Group.

Case questions

- How attractive is the UK health and fitness club industry in terms of its profit potential? Apply Porter's five forces framework to the industry to justify your answer.
- Should Fitness First cut back its investment in the UK and focus increasingly on expanding into Asia?
- How could this industry be segmented? Is Fitness First right to move upmarket and offer an enhanced range of services to its members? Are there alternative strategies that Fitness First could pursue?
- In what ways could Fitness First influence the course of the industry's evolution to its own advantage?
- What do you think are the key success factors in this industry?

Notes

1 J. Maxfield, 'Legalized drug dealing: An inside look at Colorado's massive marijuana industry', *Motley Fool* (5th January 2014), http://www.fool.com/investing/general/2014/01/05/legalized-drug-dealing-an-inside-look-at-colorados.aspx, accessed 29th September 2014.

2 PEST analysis is also referred to as 'STEP analysis' or 'PESTLE analysis' when legal and environmental categories are added.

3 http://mmjbusinessdaily.com/guest-column-top-technological-game-changers-for-cannabis-growers/, accessed 29th September 2014.

4 M. E. Porter, 'The five competitive forces that shape strategy', *Harvard Business Review*, 57 (January 2008): 57–71.

5 'Drink Up', Barron's (23rd July 2012); Juice & Smoothie Bars in the US: Market Research Report (IBIS World, February 2012).

6 W. J. Baumol, J. C. Panzar and R. D. Willig, *Contestable Markets and the Theory of Industry Structure* (New York: Harcourt Brace Jovanovich, 1982). See also M. Spence, 'Contestable markets and the theory of industry structure: A review article', *Journal of Economic Literature*, 21 (1983): 981–90.

7 'Annual Franchise 500', *Entrepreneur* (January 2009).

8 Ernst & Young, *This Time It's Personal: From consumer to co-creator,* EYGM Ltd (2012), http://www.ey.com/Publication/vwLUAssets/This_time_it_is_personal_-_from_consumer_to_co-creator_2012/$FILE/Consumer%20barometer_V9a.pdf, accessed 29th September 2014.

9 R. D. Buzzell and P. W. Farris, 'Marketing costs in consumer goods industries', in H. Thorelli (ed.), *Strategy – Structure – Performance* (Bloomington, IN: Indiana University Press, 1977): 128–9.

10 In October 1999, the Department of Justice alleged that American Airlines was using unfair means in attempting to monopolize air traffic out of Dallas/Fort Worth International Airport, http://www.aeroworldnet.com/1tw05179.htm, accessed 29th September 2014.

11 J. E. Kwoka, 'Market power and market change in the U.S. Automobile Industry', *Journal of Industrial Economics*, 32 (June 1984): 509–22.

12 See, for example, J. S. Bain, *Barriers to New Competition* (Cambridge, MA: Harvard University Press, 1956) and H. M. Mann, 'Seller concentration, entry barriers and rates of return in thirty industries', *Review of Economics and Statistics*, 48 (1966): 296–307.

13 W. S. Comanor and T. A. Wilson, *Advertising and Market Power* (Cambridge: Harvard University Press, 1974); J. L. Siegfried and L. B. Evans, 'Empirical studies of entry and exit: A survey of the evidence', *Review of Industrial Organization*, 9 (1994): 121–55.

14 G. S. Yip, 'Gateways to entry', *Harvard Business Review*, 60 (September–October 1982): 85–93.

15 F. M. Scherer and D. R. Ross, *Industrial Market Structure and Economic Performance*, 3rd edn (Boston: Houghton Mifflin, 1990); R. M. Grant, 'Pricing behaviour in the UK wholesale market for petrol: A "structure-conduct analysis"', *Journal of Industrial Economics*, 30 (March 1982): 271–92

16 R. Schmalensee, 'Inter-industry studies of structure and performance', in R. Schmalensee and R. D. Willig, *Handbook of Industrial Organisation*, 2nd edn (Amsterdam: North Holland, 1988): 976; M. A. Salinger, 'The concentration–margins relationship reconsidered', *Brookings Papers: Microeconomics* (1990): 287–335.

17 The problems caused by excess capacity and exit barriers are discussed in C. Baden-Fuller (ed.), *Strategic Management of Excess Capacity* (Oxford: Basil Blackwell, 1990).

18 S. H. Lustgarten, 'The impact of buyer concentration in manufacturing industries', *Review of Economics and Statistics*, 57 (1975): 125–32; T. Kelly and M. L. Gosman, 'Increased buyer concentration and its effects on profitability in the manufacturing sector', *Review of Industrial Organisation*, 17 (2000): 41–59.

19 'Lengthening odds: New betting options imperil horseracing's future', *The Economist* (8th July 2010).

20 M. Carnall, S. Berry and P. Spiller, 'Airline hubbing, costs and demand', in D. Lee (ed.), *Advances in Airline Economics: Vol. 1* (Amsterdam: Elsevier, 2006).

21 M. G. Jacobides, 'Creating and capturing value: From innovation to architectural advantage', *Business Insight* (London Business School, September 2008).

22 M. G. Jacobides, 'Strategy bottlenecks', *Capgemini Telecom and Media Insights*, 63 (2010), http://www.capgemini.com/resource-file-access/resource/pdf/Strategy_Bottlenecks__How_TME_Players_Can_Shape_and_Win_Control_of_their_Industry_Architecture.pdf, accessed 29th September 2014.

23 M. E. Porter, 'The five competitive forces that shape strategy', *Harvard Business Review*, 57 (January 2008): 57–71.

24 A. Brandenburger and B. Nalebuff (*Co-opetition*, New York: Doubleday, 1996) propose an alternative framework, the 'value net', for analysing the impact of complements.

25 A. Brandenburger, J. Kou and M. Burnett, *Power Play (A): Nintendo in 8-bit video games* (Harvard Business School Case No. 9-795-103, 1995).

26 C. Baldwin, S. O'Mahony and J. Quinn, *IBM and Linux (A)* (Harvard Business School Case No. 903-083, 2003).

27 M. E. Porter, *Competitive Strategy* (New York: Free Press, 1980): 129.

28 J. A. Schumpeter, *The Theory of Economic Development* (Cambridge, MA: Harvard University Press, 1934).

29 R. T. Masson and J. Shaanan, 'Stochastic Dynamic Limit Pricing: An empirical test', *Review of Economics and Statistics*, 64 (1982): 413–422; R. T. Masson and J. Shaanan, 'Optimal pricing and threat of entry: Canadian evidence', *International Journal of Industrial Organization*, 5 (1987): 520–35.

30 R. Caves and M. E. Porter, 'The dynamics of changing seller concentration', *Journal of Industrial Economics*, 19 (1980): 1–15; P. Hart and R. Clarke, *Concentration in British Industry* (Cambridge: Cambridge University Press, 1980).

31 P. A. Geroski and R. T. Masson, 'Dynamic market models in industrial organization', *International Journal of Industrial Organization*, 5 (1987): 1–13.

32 D. C. Mueller, *Profits in the Long Run* (Cambridge: Cambridge University Press, 1986).

33 R. D'Aveni, *Hypercompetition: Managing the dynamics of strategic maneuvering* (New York: Free Press, 1994): 217–18.

34 L. G. Thomas and R. D'Aveni, *The rise of hypercompetition in the US manufacturing sector: 1950–2002*, Tuck School of Business, Dartmouth College, Working Paper No. 2004-11 (2004).

35 R. R. Wiggins and T. W. Ruefli, 'Schumpeter's Ghost: Is hypercompetition making the best of times shorter?' *Strategic Management Journal*, 26 (2005): 887–911.

36 G. McNamara, P. M. Vaaler and C. Devers, 'Same as it ever was: The search for evidence of increasing hypercompetition', *Strategic Management Journal*, 24 (2003): 261–78.

37 The term was coined by Chuck Hofer and Dan Schendel (*Strategy Formulation: Analytical concepts*, St Paul, MN: West Publishing, 1977: 77). They define key success factors as 'those variables that management can influence through its decisions and that can affect significantly the overall competitive positions of the firms in an industry'.

38 P. Ghemawat, *Commitment: The dynamic of strategy* (New York: Free Press, 1991): 11.

39 http://www.theguardian.com/money/2013/jan/12/oft-to-acts-on-unfair-gym-contracts, accessed 29th September 2014.

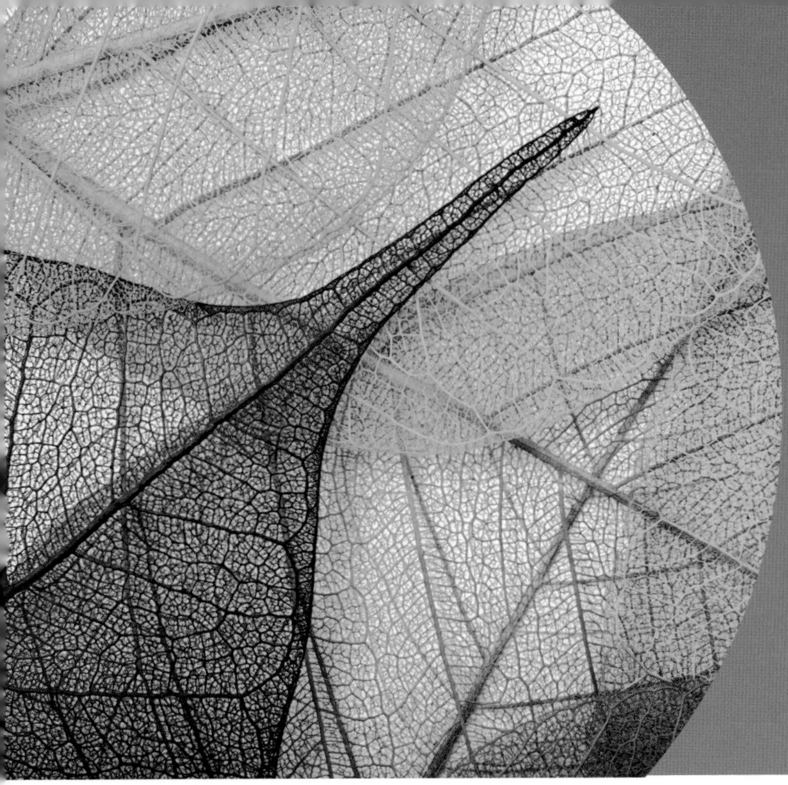

3

Resources and capabilities

www.foundationsofstrategy.com

Introduction and objectives

In this chapter, we shift our focus from the external environment to the internal environment. We look within the firm and concentrate our attention on the resources and capabilities that firms possess. In doing so, we build the foundations for our analysis of competitive advantage which began in Chapter 2 with the discussion of key success factors.

By the time you have completed this chapter, you will be able to:

- appreciate the role a firm's resources and capabilities play in formulating strategy;
- identify and appraise the resources and capabilities of a firm;
- evaluate the potential for a firm's resources and capabilities to confer sustainable competitive advantage;
- use the results of resource and capability analysis to formulate strategies that exploit internal strengths while defending against internal weaknesses.

Opening Case

Harley-Davidson, Inc.

In 2014, Harley-Davidson, Inc. was not only the world's oldest motorcycle company but also, after recovering from the trauma of the financial crisis of 2008/9, the world's most financially successful producer of motorcycles. Since its management buyout in 1981, it had grown its annual sales of motorcycles from 40 000 to 260 000 and its revenues from $0.5m to $5727m. Its sales margin and return on equity exceeded that of all its major rivals, and in heavyweight motorcycles it was the market leader in the US, Canada, Japan and Brazil. How was it possible that a company that had been on the brink of bankruptcy during the early 1980s could have outperformed the motorcycle divisions of automotive giants such as Honda and BMW? And, with its retro-styling and lack of leading-edge technology, could Harley-Davidson sustain its remarkable performance into the future (Table 3.1)?

Table 3.1 Indicators of Harley-Davidson performance: 1994–2013.

	2013	2012	2011	2010	2009	2008	2007	1994
Total shipments ('000s)	260	248	233	213	232	316	342	96
of which International ('000s)	95	87	81	79	78	97	89	22
Revenue ($m)	5900	5581	5311	4859	4781	5594	5727	1159
Operating income ($m)	1154	1000	829	559	197	1029	1426	154
of which Financial services ($m)	283	285	268	181	(117)	83	212	2
Net income ($m)	734	624	599	146	(55)	655	934	104
Operating margin (%)	25	18	4	12	16	18	20	13
Return on equity (%)	24	24	25	7	(3)	31	39	2

A brief history of Harley-Davidson: 1903–2013

Harley-Davidson, Inc. was founded in 1903 by William Harley and the Davidson brothers. In 1909, Harley introduced its throaty, V-twin engine, which has become the distinctive feature of Harley motorcycles to this day. With import competition, first from the British (BSA, Triumph and Norton) and then the Japanese (Honda, Suzuki, Yamaha and Kawasaki), Harley became sole survivor of the US motorcycle industry and was acquired by AMF, a US conglomerate.

In 1981, Harley's senior managers led a leveraged buyout and struggled for several years to keep the newly independent Harley-Davidson afloat in the midst of heavy debt and a declining market. After drastic cost cutting to stabilize Harley's finances, the management team embarked on a systematic rebuilding of the company. Production methods and working practices were revolutionized using lessons from the Japanese auto industry such as just-in-time scheduling and materials management, total quality management and worker–management cooperation.

Harley paid increasing attention to product development with a particular emphasis on reintroducing and updating traditional designs, improving paintwork and finish, making incremental engineering improvements and upgrading quality and reliability. It expanded its range of models around a standardized set of major components such as engines, frames, suspension systems and fuel tanks. It based its product strategy on the notion that every Harley rider should have the possibility of owning a unique personalized motorcycle. To that end, it created a wide range of customization opportunities and each year offered limited-edition, customized versions of some of its most popular models.

During this period, the demographic and socio-economic profile of its customers continued to shift. In the early years, its customers were primarily blue-collar youngsters, but by the 1990s, they were mainly middle-aged and upper income. To meet the preferences of these customers, the dealership network was overhauled. Harley dealerships were required to be exclusive and to offer a retail experience appropriate to the sale of high-priced leisure products to sophisticated customers.

Despite premium pricing (in 2014, US retail prices for Harley motorcycles ranged from $8250 to $32 500), Harley's share of the super-heavyweight market (over 850cc) grew from about 30% in 1986 to over 60% in 1990. The 1990s saw uninterrupted growth in the heavyweight motorcycle market and a continued increase in Harley's market share. The company's biggest challenge became that of systematically expanding production capacity to meet the surging demand for its products.

However, when Keith Wandell took over the reins as CEO in May 2009, Harley had suffered dramatic deterioration in its fortunes. The onset of the financial crisis of 2008/9 had radically shifted the balance of supply and demand: between 2007 and 2009, motorcycle shipments plunged from 342 100 to 232 400 and net income from $934m to a loss of $55m. After decades of customer waiting lists and capacity shortages, Harley-Davidson found itself in a very different position. In response Wandell laid off staff, instituted radical cost cutting, amalgamated plants to cut capacity and disposed of assets that were not central to Harley's core business.

Harley-Davidson in 2014

Some of the key features of Harley's business in 2014 included:

- *The product portfolio:* Compared to other motorcycle producers, Harley served a narrow market niche. Within the heavyweight segment (> 500cc), it was present only in super-heavyweight bikes (> 750cc) and here Harley produced only 'cruisers' (macho-styled, low-riding bikes for urban leisure use) and touring bikes (designed for long-distance travel). Performance motorcycles, the largest part of the heavyweight segment, Harley left to Japanese and European manufacturers. Harley's past efforts to expand into performance bikes and smaller models had been unsuccessful: in 2009, it closed its Buell motorcycle business and sold off the Italian motorcycle company, MV Agusta, that it had acquired a few years earlier. Within its model range, Harley remained committed to traditional designs and traditional technologies: its large capacity, V-twin, air-cooled engines made limited concessions to modern automotive technology. In addition, its focus on traditional bikes limited Harley's ability to grow its market share at the expense of rivals. Harley already accounted for more than 50% of the US heavyweight motorcycle market. Indeed, Harley's own market was vulnerable to competition. While no other company could replicate the emotional attachment of riders to the 'Harley Experience', younger motorcycle riders sought a different type of experience and became more attracted to the highly engineered sports models produced by European and Japanese manufacturers.

- *The brand:* Harley-Davidson's brand and the loyalty it engendered among its customers were its greatest assets. The famed spread eagle signified not just the brand of one of the world's oldest motorcycle companies but also an entire lifestyle and was an archetype of American style. Harley had a unique relationship with American culture. The values that Harley represented – individuality, freedom and adventure – could be traced back to the cowboy and frontiersman of yesteryear and before that to the quest for space and liberty that had brought people to America in the first place. As the sole survivor of the once-thriving American motorcycle industry, Harley-Davidson represented a tradition of US engineering and manufacturing.

  The appeal of the brand was central not just to Harley's marketing but also to its strategy as a whole. Harley-Davidson had long emphasized that it was not in the business of selling motorcycles: it was selling the 'Harley Experience'. A critical question for Harley was: 'How broad is the appeal of the brand and the Harley Experience?' Harley's core market was US white male baby-boomers: could the Harley image have the same appeal to younger generations and in overseas markets?

- *Operations:* Despite expanding capacity and upgrading its manufacturing operations, Harley's low production volumes and dispersed plants limited its access to scale economies. It also lacked the buying power of its bigger rivals. To offset its lack of purchasing power Harley fostered close relations with its key suppliers and placed purchasing managers at senior levels within its management structure.

- *Distribution:* In the past, Harley dealerships had been operated by enthusiasts, with erratic opening hours, poor stocks of bikes and spares and indifferent customer service. Recognizing that it was in the business of selling a lifestyle and an experience and that its dealers played a pivotal role in delivering that experience, Harley transformed its dealership network. Its dealer programme provided extensive support for dealers while requiring high standards of pre- and after-sales service. Dealers were obliged to carry a full line of Harley replacement parts and accessories and to perform services on Harley bikes. Training programmes helped dealers meet the higher service requirements and encouraged them to recognize and meet the needs of the professional, middle-class clientele that formed the bulk of Harley's customer base by offering test ride facilities, rider instruction classes, motorcycle rental and assistance in customizing bikes. About 85% of Harley's US dealerships were exclusive – far more than for any other motorcycle manufacturer.

- *Sales of related products:* Sales of parts, accessories and 'general merchandise' (clothing and collectibles) represented 20% of Harley's total revenue in 2008 – much higher than for any other motorcycle company. Clothing sales included not just traditional riding apparel but also a wide range of men's, women's and children's leisurewear. Almost all clothing, accessories, giftware, jewellery, toys and other products were produced by third-party manufacturers who paid licensing fees to Harley-Davidson. To expand sales of licensed products, Harley opened a number of secondary retail locations that sold clothing, accessories and giftware, but not motorcycles. In addition, Harley-Davidson Financial Services supplied credit, insurance and extended warranties to Harley customers and loans to Harley dealers. During the 2008/9 financial crisis, Harley's financial services subsidiary was hit by rising defaults and, unable to securitize its customer loans, was forced to retain many of these loans on its own balance sheet. However, by 2013 financial services were, once again, Harley's most profitable business.

Looking ahead: Threats and opportunities

Despite the confidence expressed by Keith Wandell in the strength of Harley-Davidson's recovery from the crisis of 2008/9 and its prospects for the future, while quality and effectiveness of its dealer network were key determinants of the strong demand for Harley's products, the market environment that Harley faced in 2014 presented several challenges.

With 54% of the US market for heavyweight motorcycles, a market share that had been fairly stable for 20 years, Harley had limited potential to grow within its core segment. As a result, Wandell's key strategic goal was 'to grow retail sales outside the U.S. faster than retail sales inside the U.S. and then to grow U.S. retail sales to outreach customer segments – women, young adults between 18 and 34, African Americans and Hispanics – faster than retail sales to our core customers'. To this end, the company introduced a new range of touring motorcycles, tagged with the 'project Rushmore' label that offered significantly improved functionality and announced the launch of a new range of 'Street' bikes aimed at younger, urban motorcyclists. Their emphasis remained on styling, customization, sound and reliability as sources of competitive advantage and the company viewed the availability of parts, accessories and ancillary services (such as finance, customer 'clubs' and social events delivered in partnership with dealers) to be vital in maintaining and enhancing a competitive advantage.

At the same time as extending the product range, the company endeavoured to open up new markets overseas by establishing more dealerships in Asia and Latin America and by running marketing campaigns with a stronger multigenerational and multicultural slant. On the operations side of the business, Harley reorganized its manufacturing to improve flexibility and reduce costs. However, international success remained elusive. Despite its strength in Japan and Australia and growing sales in Brazil, the Harley brand and image in overseas markets was weaker than in the US. In Europe, Harley's share of the heavyweight market was 12%: many European riders regarded Harley-Davidson motorcycles as unsophisticated, technologically backward and unwieldy compared to those supplied by its Japanese and European rivals.

Harley's pre-eminence within the US was also far from assured. Would Harley's macho image have the same appeal to upcoming generations of Americans as it had to baby-boomers? Indeed, would motorcycling maintain its appeal as a leisure activity? Even within its core segment, Harley faced increasing competition. All the major motorcycle producers offered V-twin cruiser bikes that imitated Harley's traditional style (but at significantly lower prices). In addition, several specialist suppliers had entered Harley's market space – most notably Polaris, which offered its Victory motorcycles and had acquired the resuscitated Indian brand.

The role of resources and capabilities in strategy formulation

We saw in Chapter 1 that strategy is concerned with matching a firm's resources and capabilities to the opportunities that arise in the external environment. In Chapter 2, our emphasis was on the identification of profit opportunities in the external environment of the firm. In this chapter, our emphasis shifts from the interface between strategy and the external environment towards the interface between strategy and the **internal environment** of the firm – more specifically, the relationship between strategy and the **resources** and **capabilities** of the firm (Figure 3.1). Moving from the external to the internal is a logical way of proceeding with our exploration of strategy that also resonates with a theme we noted in Chapter 1: the trend over time from seeing sources of profit as lying mainly in the external environment to seeing sources of profit being located within firms. Competitive advantage rather than industry attractiveness is the primary source of superior profitability.

Basing strategy on resources and capabilities

During the 1990s, ideas concerning the role of resources and capabilities as the principal basis for firm strategy and the primary source of profitability merged into what has become known as the resource-based view of the firm.[1]

To understand why the resource-based view has had a major impact on strategy thinking, let us go back to the starting point for strategy formulation, typically some statement of the firm's identity and purpose (often expressed in a mission statement). Conventionally, firms have answered the question 'What is our business?' in terms of the market they serve: 'Who are our customers?' and 'Which of their needs are we seeking to serve?' However, in a world where customer preferences are volatile and the identity of customers and the technologies for serving them are changing, a market-focused strategy may not provide the stability and constancy of direction needed to guide strategy over the long term.[2] When the external environment is in a state of flux, the firm itself, in terms of its bundle of resources and capabilities, may be a much more stable basis on which to define its identity.

The emphasis on resources and capabilities as the foundation of firm strategy was popularized by C.K. Prahalad and Gary Hamel in their landmark paper 'The Core Competence of the Corporation'.[3] The potential for capabilities to be the 'roots of competitiveness', the sources of new products and the foundation for strategy is exemplified be several companies, for example:

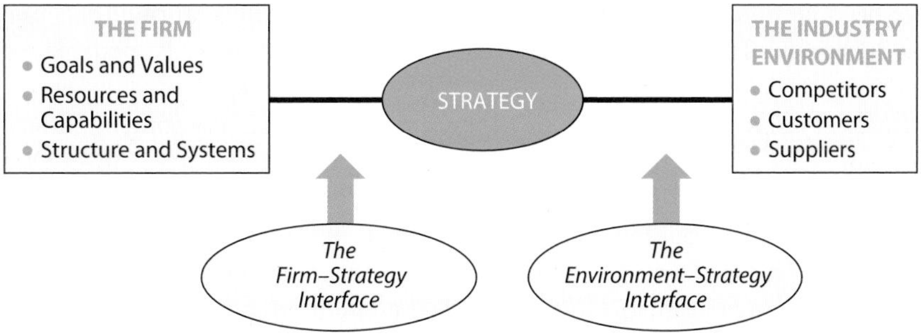

Figure 3.1 Analysing resources and capabilities: The interface between strategy and the firm.

Honda Motor Company is the world's biggest motorcycle producer and a lead supplier of cars, but it has never defined itself either as a motorcycle company or as a motor vehicle company. Since its foundation in 1948, its strategy has been built around its expertise in the development and manufacture of engines; this capability has successfully carried it from motorcycles to a wide range of gasoline-engine products.

Canon, Inc. had its first success producing 35mm cameras. Since then it has gone on to develop fax machines, calculators, copy machines, printers, video cameras, camcorders, semiconductor manufacturing equipment and many other products. Almost all Canon's products involve the application of three areas of technological capability: precision mechanics, microelectronics and fine optics.

3M Corporation expanded from sandpaper into adhesive tapes, audio and videotapes, road signs, medical products and floppy disks. Its product list now comprises over 30 000 products. Is it a conglomerate? Certainly not, claims 3M. Its vast product range rests on a foundation of key technologies relating to adhesives, thin-film coatings and materials sciences supported by outstanding capability in the development and launching of new products.

In general, the greater the rate of change in a firm's external environment, the more likely it is that internal resources and capabilities rather than external market focus will provide a secure foundation for long-term strategy. In fast-moving, technology-based industries, basing strategy upon capabilities can help firms outlive the lifecycles of their initial products. Microsoft's initial success was the result of its MS-DOS operating system for the IBM PC. However, by building outstanding capabilities in developing and launching complex software products and in managing an ecosystem of partner relationships, Microsoft extended its success to other operating systems (e.g. Windows), to applications software (e.g. Office) and to Internet services (e.g. Xbox Live). Similarly, Apple's remarkable ability to combine technology, aesthetics and ease of use has allowed it to expand beyond its initial focus on desktop and notebook computers into MP3 players (iPod), smartphones (iPhone) and tablet computers (iPad).

Conversely, those companies that when faced with radical technological change attempted to maintain their market focus have often experienced huge difficulties in building the new technological capabilities needed to serve their customers.

Eastman Kodak is a classic example. Its dominance of the world market for photographic products was threatened by digital imaging. From 1990 onwards, Kodak invested billions of dollars developing digital technologies and digital imaging products. Yet, in January 2012, continuing losses on digital products and services forced Kodak into bankruptcy. Might Kodak have been better off by sticking with its chemical know-how, allowing its photographic business to decline while developing its interests in specialty chemicals, pharmaceuticals and healthcare?[4]

Olivetti, the Italian manufacturer of typewriters and office equipment, offers a similar cautionary tale. Despite its early investments in electronic computing, Olivetti's attempt to recreate itself as a supplier of personal computers and printers was a failure. Might Olivetti have been better advised to deploy its existing expertise in electrical and precision engineering in other products?[5] This pattern of established firms failing to adjust to disruptive technological change within their own industries is well documented: in typesetting and in disk drive manufacturing, successive technological waves have caused market leaders to falter and have allowed new entrants to prosper.[6]

Identifying the organization's resources and capabilities

The first stage in the analysis of resources and capabilities is to identify the resources and capabilities of the firm – or, indeed, any organization since the analysis of resources and capabilities is as applicable to not-for-profit organizations as it is to business enterprises. It is important to distinguish between the *resources* and the *capabilities* of the firm: resources are the productive assets owned by the firm; capabilities are what the firm can do. Individual resources do not confer competitive advantage; they must work together to create organizational capability. Capability is the essence of superior performance. Figure 3.2 shows the relationships between resources, capabilities and competitive advantage.

Our discussion of key success factors (KSFs) – the sources of competitive advantage within an industry – in Chapter 2 offers a starting point for our identification of key resources and capabilities. Once we have identified the KSFs in an industry, it is a short step to identifying the resources and capabilities needed to deliver those success factors. For example:

- In budget airlines the KSF is low operating cost. This requires a standardized fleet of fuel-efficient planes; a young, motivated, non-unionized workforce; and a culture of frugality.
- In pharmaceuticals the KSF is the discovery and launch of new drugs. This requires high-quality researchers and drug-testing, marketing and distribution capability.

However, as we shall see, identifying KSFs is only a starting point. To develop a comprehensive picture of an organization's resources and capabilities we need systematic frameworks for identifying and classifying different resources and capabilities.

Identifying resources

Drawing up an inventory of a firm's resources can be surprisingly difficult. No such document exists within the accounting or management information systems of most corporations. The

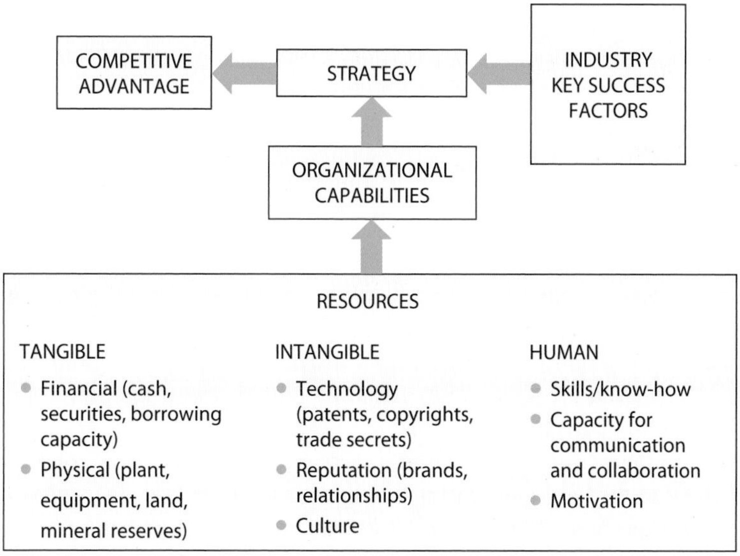

Figure 3.2 The links between resources, capabilities and competitive advantage.

corporate balance sheet provides a limited view of a firm's resources; it comprises mainly financial and physical resources. To take a wider view of a firm's resources it is helpful to identify three principal types of resource: tangible, intangible and human resources.

Featured Example 3.1

Focusing strategy around core capabilities: Lyor Cohen on Mariah Carey

2001 was a disastrous year for Mariah Carey. Her first movie, *Glitter*, was a flop, the soundtrack was Carey's most poorly received album in a decade, her $80 million recording contract was dropped by EMI and she suffered a nervous breakdown.

Lyor Cohen, the aggressive, workaholic chief executive of Island Def Jam records was quick to spot an opportunity: 'I cold-called her on the day of her release from EMI and I said, I think you are an unbelievable artist and you should hold your head up high', says Cohen. 'What I said stuck on her and she ended up signing with us.'

His strategic analysis of Carey's situation was concise: 'I said to her, what's your competitive advantage? A great voice, of course. And what else? You write every one of your songs – you're a great writer. So why did you stray from your competitive advantage? If you have this magnificent voice and you write such compelling songs, why are you dressing like that, why are you using all these collaborations [with other artists and other songwriters]? Why? It's like driving a Ferrari in first – you won't see what that Ferrari will do until you get into sixth gear.'

Cohen signed Carey in May 2002. Under Universal Music's Island Def Jam Records, Carey returned to her core strengths: her versatile voice, song-writing talents and ballad style. Her next album, *The Emancipation of Mimi*, was the biggest-selling album of 2005 and in 2006 she won a Grammy award.

Source: 'Rap's Unlikely Mogul' *Financial Times* (August 7, 2002). From the *Financial Times* © The Financial Times Ltd. 2002. All rights reserved.

TANGIBLE RESOURCES Tangible resources are the easiest to identify and evaluate: financial resources and physical assets are identified and valued in the firm's financial statements. Yet, balance sheets are renowned for their propensity to obscure strategically relevant information and to under- or overvalue assets. Historical cost valuation can provide little indication of an asset's market value. For example, Disney's movie library had a balance sheet value of $5.4 billion in 2008, based on production costs. Its land assets (including its 28 000 acres in Florida) were valued at a paltry $1.2 billion.

However, the primary goal of resource analysis is not to value a company's assets but to understand their potential for creating competitive advantage. Information that British Airways possessed fixed assets valued at £8 billion in 2013 is of little use in assessing the airline's strategic value. To assess British Airways' ability to compete effectively in the world airline industry we need to know about the composition of these assets: the location of land and buildings, the types of plane, the landing slots and gate facilities at airports and so on.

Once we have fuller information on a company's tangible resources we explore how we can create additional value from them. This requires that we address two key questions:

- *What opportunities exist for economizing on their use?* It may be possible to use fewer resources to support the same level of business, or to use the existing resources to support a larger volume of business. In the case of British Airways, there may be opportunities for consolidating administrative offices and engineering and service facilities. Improved inventory control may allow economies in inventories of parts and fuel. Better control of cash and receivables permits a business to operate with lower levels of cash and liquid financial resources.
- *What are the possibilities for employing existing assets more profitably?* Could British Airways generate better returns on some of its planes by redeploying them into cargo carrying? Should British Airways seek to redeploy its assets from Europe and the North Atlantic to Asia-Pacific? Might it reduce costs in its European network by reassigning routes to small franchised airlines?

INTANGIBLE RESOURCES For most companies, **intangible resources** are more valuable than tangible resources. Yet, in company financial statements, intangible resources remain largely invisible. The exclusion or undervaluation of intangible resources is a major reason for the large and growing divergence between companies' balance sheet valuations ('book values') and their stock market valuations (Table 3.2). Among the most important of these undervalued or unvalued intangible resources are brand names. Table 3.3 shows companies owning brands valued at $15 billion or more.

Brand names and other trademarks are a form of reputational asset: their value is in the confidence they instil in customers. The brand valuations in Table 3.3 are based upon the operating profits for each company (after taxation and a capital charge), estimating the proportion attributable to the brand and then capitalizing these returns.

Table 3.2 Large companies with the highest valuation ratios, April 2014.

Company	Valuation ratio	Country	Company	Valuation ratio	Country
Hindustan Unilever	46.6	India	Alexion Pharma.	11.9	US
Tesla Motors	37.7	US	Starbucks	11.8	US
Colgate-Palmolive	26.3	US	ITC Ltd.	11.7	India
Altria	18.3	US	MasterCard	11.4	USA
AbbVie	16.7	US	Roche Holding	11.3	Swz.
Yum! Brands	15.4	US	GlaxoSmithKline	11.0	UK
Regeneron Pharma.	15.0	US	Salesforce.com	11.0	US
Amazon	14.9	US	Hermes Intl.	11.0	France
British Sky Broadcasting	14.0	UK	ARM Holdings	10.7	UK
United Parcel Service	13.8	US	CSL	10.6	Australia

Note: the table shows companies from the FT Global 500 with the highest ratios of market capitalization to balance sheet net asset value ('market-to-book' ratios).
Source: Google Finance, Financial Times.

Table 3.3 The world's most valuable brands, 2013.

Rank	Brand	Value in 2013 ($ billion)	Change from 2012	Country of origin
1	Apple	98.3	+28%	US
2	Google	93.3	+34%	US
3	Coca-Cola	79.2	+2%	US
4	IBM	78.8	+4%	US
5	Microsoft	59.5	+3%	US
6	GE	46.9	+7%	US
7	McDonald's	42.0	+5%	US
8	Samsung	39.6	+20%	South Korea
9	Intel	37.2	−5%	US
10	Toyota	35.3	+17%	Japan
11	Mercedes-Benz	31.9	+6%	Germany
12	BMW	31.8	+10%	Germany
13	Cisco	29.0	+7%	US
14	Disney	28.1	+3%	US
15	Hewlett-Packard	25.8	−1%	US
16	Gillette	25.1	+1%	US
17	Louis Vuitton	24.9	+6%	France
18	Oracle	24.1	+9%	US
19	Amazon	23.6	+27%	US
20	Honda	18.5	+7%	Japan

Note: Brand values are calculated as the net present value of future earnings generated by the brand.
Source: Interbrand.

The value of a company's brands can be increased by extending the range of products over which a company markets its brands. Johnson & Johnson, Samsung and General Electric derive considerable economies from applying a single brand to a wide range of products. As a result, companies that succeed in building strong consumer brands have a powerful incentive to diversify, for example Nike's diversification from athletic shoes into apparel and sports equipment.

Like reputation, technology is an intangible asset whose value is not evident from most companies' balance sheets. Intellectual property – patents, copyrights, trade secrets and trademarks – comprises technological and artistic resources where ownership is defined in law. Over the past 20 years, companies have become more attentive to the value of their intellectual property. For IBM (with the world's biggest patent portfolio) and Qualcomm (with its patents relating to CDMA digital wireless telephony), intellectual property is the most valuable resource they own.

HUMAN RESOURCES Human resources of the firm comprise the expertise and effort offered by employees. Like intangible resources, human resources do not appear on the firm's balance sheet – for the simple reason that the firm does not own its employees; it purchases their services under employment contacts. The reason for including human resources as part of the resources of the firm is their stability. Although employees are free to move from one firm to another – most employment contracts require no more than a month's notice on the part of the employee – in practice most employment contracts are long term. In the US the average length of time an employee stays with an employer is four years; in Europe it is longer: 8.4 years in Britain to 13 and 11.7 in France and Italy respectively.[7]

Most firms devote considerable effort to appraising their human resources. This appraisal occurs at the hiring stage when potential employees are evaluated in relation to the requirements of their job and as part of an ongoing appraisal process of which annual employee reviews form the centrepiece. The purposes of appraisal are to assess past performance for the purposes of compensation and promotion, set future performance goals and establish employee development plans. Trends in appraisal include greater emphasis on assessing results in relation to performance targets (e.g. management-by-objectives) and broadening the basis of evaluation (e.g. 360-degree appraisal).

Over the past decade, human resource evaluation has become far more systematic and sophisticated. Many organizations have established assessment centres specifically for the purpose of providing comprehensive, quantitative assessments of the skills and attributes of individual employees, and increasingly appraisal criteria are based upon empirical research into the components and correlates of superior job performance. Competencies modelling involves identifying the set of skills, content knowledge, attitudes and values associated with superior performers within a particular job category and then assessing each employee against that profile.[8] An important finding of research into HR competencies is the critical role of psychological and social aptitudes in determining superior performance; typically these factors outweigh technical skills and educational and professional qualifications. Interest in emotional intelligence reflects the recognition of the importance of interpersonal skills and emotional awareness.[9] Overall, these findings explain the trend among companies to 'hire for attitude; train for skills'.

The ability of employees to harmonize their efforts and integrate their separate skills depends not only on their interpersonal skills but also on the organizational context. This organizational context as it affects internal collaboration is determined by a key intangible resource: the culture of the organization. The term organizational culture is notoriously ill defined. Sebastian Green defines organizational (or corporate) culture as 'an amalgam of shared beliefs, values, assumptions, significant meanings, myths, rituals, and symbols that are held to be distinctive'.[10] The observation that companies with sustained superior financial performance are frequently characterized by strong organizational cultures has led Jay Barney to view organizational culture as a firm resource of great strategic importance that is potentially very valuable.[11]

Identifying organizational capabilities

Resources are not productive on their own. A brain surgeon is close to useless without a radiologist, anaesthetist, nurses, surgical instruments, imaging equipment and a host of other resources. To perform a task, a team of resources must work together.

Case Insight 3.1

Illustrative examples of resources classified by type for Harley-Davidson, Inc.

Resource(s)	Illustrative example	Strategic relevance
Tangible	Headquarters and product development is in Milwaukee (WI); production plants are in York (PA), Kansas City (MI), Milwaukee County (WI), Manaus (Brazil) and Bawal (India)	Harley's production of 260 000 units is dispersed across six plants in three states; plants in Brazil and India assemble knocked-down motorcycles from the US; Harley's plants emphasize quality and flexibility; Harley lacks the scale economies of its rivals (Honda produced 17.2m bikes in 2013)
	Harley has 765 North American, full-service dealerships and 693 in the rest of the world. In addition 154 retail outlets sell other Harley-branded products	Harley's dealership network is central to the Harley Experience, reinforcing the brand image and supplying a wide range of services. Outside North America Harley's reach is limited by its sparse dealer network – just 14 in China
Intangible	Brand: the Harley brand, and the loyalty it engenders, is Harley's most valuable asset	The Harley brand forms the cornerstone of its strategy. At the core of the 'Harley Experience' is Harley's statement of purpose to 'fulfil dreams of personal freedom'
	Technology: annual R & D expenditure of $152m in 2013	Harley is unable to compete on technology (Honda spent almost $6 billion on R & D in 2013) but has made a virtue out of necessity by emphasizing the authenticity of its traditional motorcycles
Human	In 2013, Harley had 5800 employees in its motorcycle segment and 600 in financial services. Harley emphasizes training and employee loyalty, commitment, initiative and flexibility	Harley's employees, including managers, play a key role in reinforcing Harley's traditions and image, e.g. through participating in HOG events. Despite emphasis on open communication, team working and self-management Harley has experienced labour relations tensions (including a 2007 strike)

An **organizational capability** is a 'firm's capacity to deploy resources for a desired end result'.[12] Just as an individual may be capable of playing the violin, ice skating and speaking Mandarin, so an organization may possess the capabilities needed to manufacture widgets, distribute them globally and hedge the resulting foreign exchange exposure. We use the terms 'capability' and 'competence' interchangeably.[13]

Our primary interest is in those capabilities that can provide a basis for competitive advantage. Selznick uses **distinctive competence** to describe those things that an organization does particularly well relative to its competitors.[14] Prahalad and Hamel coined the term 'core competencies' to distinguish those capabilities fundamental to a firm's strategy and performance.[15] **Core competencies**, according to Hamel and Prahalad, are those that:

- make a disproportionate contribution to ultimate customer value, or to the efficiency with which that value is delivered; and
- provide a basis for entering new markets.[16]

Prahalad and Hamel criticize US companies for emphasizing products over capabilities. Global leaders are those companies that develop core competencies over the long term. Individual products may succeed or fail; the key is to learn from both success and failure in order to build capability.

CLASSIFYING CAPABILITIES Before deciding which organizational capabilities are 'distinctive' or 'core', a firm needs to take a comprehensive view of its full range of organizational capabilities. To identify a firm's capabilities, we need to have some basis for classifying and disaggregating its activities. Two approaches are commonly used:

1 A **functional analysis** identifies organizational capabilities in relation to each of the principal functional areas of the firm. Table 3.4 classifies the principal functions of the firm and identifies organizational capabilities located within each function, giving examples of firms that are widely recognized for their capabilities in particular functions.

Table 3.4 A functional classification of organizational capabilities.

Functional area	Capability	Exemplars
Corporate	Financial control	Exxon Mobil, PepsiCo
	Management development	General Electric, Shell
	Strategic innovation	Google, Haier
	Multidivisional coordination	Unilever, Shell
	Acquisition management	Cisco, Systems, Luxottica
	International management	Shell, Banco Santander
Management information	Comprehensive, integrated management information systems linked to managerial decision making	Walmart, Capital One, Dell Computer
Research and development	Research	IBM, Merck
	Innovative new product development	3M, Apple
	Fast-cycle new product development	Canon, Inditex (Zara)
Operations	Efficiency in volume manufacturing	Briggs & Stratton, YKK
	Continuous improvements in operations	Toyota, Harley-Davidson
	Flexibility and speed of response	Four Seasons Hotels
Product design	Design capability	Nokia, Apple
Marketing	Brand management	Procter & Gamble, Altria
	Building reputation for quality	Johnson & Johnson
	Responsiveness to market trends	MTV, L'Oréal
Sales and distribution	Effective sales promotion and execution	PepsiCo, Pfizer
	Efficiency and speed of order processing	L. L. Bean, Dell Computer
	Speed of distribution	Amazon
	Customer service	Singapore Airlines, Caterpillar

In Case Insight 3.2, we illustrate how this functional approach could be used to audit Harley-Davidson's capabilities. In some areas, Harley's capabilities are equivalent to those of other motorcycle manufacturers; in others, Harley has developed capabilities that are distinctive. We refer to capabilities that are common to all motorcycle manufacturers as 'threshold capabilities' because they comprise the essential set of capabilities that any firm needs to compete and survive in its chosen industry.

Case Insight 3.2

Some illustrative examples of Harley-Davidson's capabilities by function

Function	Illustrative capability
Product design	*Consumer-led design:* until recently, the company has stuck with classic styling and traditional technologies but has developed a strong capability in customizing designs to customers' requirements. Product upgrades are based on extensive market research and feedback from customers and dealers
Engineering	*A threshold capability:* Harley has made a virtue out of necessity by sticking to traditional technology and traditional design. Its smaller corporate size and inability to share R & D across cars and bikes (unlike Honda and BMW) has limited its ability to invest in new technology and implement the latest developments in engineering. In recent years it has started to access more up-to-date technologies through alliances with other companies
Operations	*Flexible production:* Harley has sought to enhance the flexibility of its manufacturing operations by introducing 'surge production' practices, moving away from model-dedicated production lines to lines that can produce multiple models and by strengthening its 'build to order' capability
Marketing and Distribution	*Enhanced retail service:* Harley has recognized the central role that dealers play in the relationship between the company and its customers so it places considerable emphasis on its relationship with dealers. Dealers are the vehicle through which Harley delivers add-on services such as test ride facilities, rider instruction classes, customization option, finance etc. Dealers receive support and training through the Harley-Davidson University, which was established to 'enhance dealer competencies in every area'
Customer Service	*Customer relationship management:* the appeal of the Harley motorcycle is tightly bound up with the image it conveys and the lifestyle it represents. Harley has tried to ensure that the reality lives up to the image by enhancing its customers' riding experience by establishing an owners' group, by organizing social and charity rallies and rides and creating a sense of community

2 **Value chain analysis** separates the activities of the firm into a sequential chain and explores the linkages between activities in order to gain insight into a firm's competitive position. Michael Porter's representation of the value chain distinguishes between primary activities (those involved with the transformation of inputs and interface with the customer) and support activities (Figure 3.3). Porter's generic value chain identifies

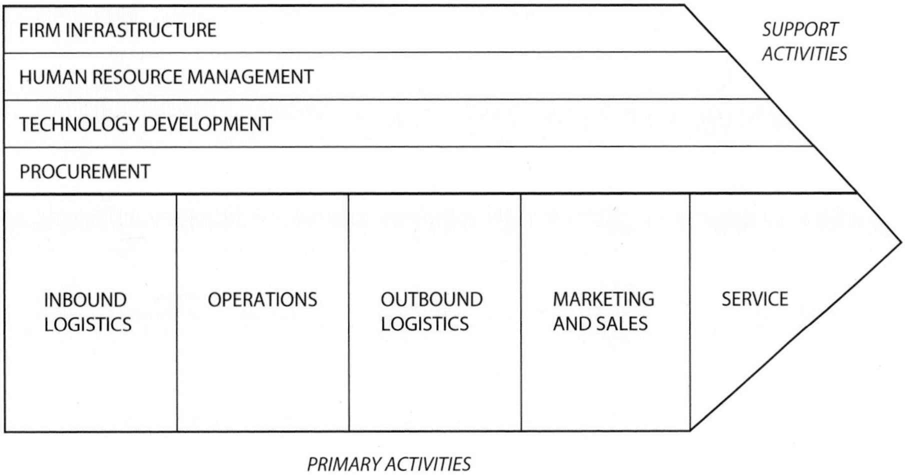

Figure 3.3 Porter's value chain.

Source: Adapted with the permission of Simon & Schuster Publishing Group from the Free Press edition of *Competitive Advantage: Creating and Sustaining Superior Performance* by Michael E. Porter.

a few broadly defined activities that can be separated to provide a more detailed identification of the firm's activities (and the capabilities that correspond to each activity). Case Insight 3.3 shows how this could look for firms like Harley-Davidson operating in the motorcycle industry. Thus, marketing can include market research, test marketing, advertising, promotion, pricing and dealer relations. By exploring different activities and, most crucially, the linkages between them, it is possible to gain a sense of an organization's main capabilities.

THE NATURE OF CAPABILITY Drawing up an inventory of a firm's resources is fairly straightforward. Organizational capabilities are more elusive, partly because they are idiosyncratic – every organization has features of its capabilities that are unique and difficult to capture using simple functional and value chain classifications. Consider Apple's product design and product development capabilities. Apple has a remarkable ability to combine hardware technology, software engineering, aesthetics, ergonomics and cognitive awareness to create products with a superior user interface and unrivalled market appeal. But identifying the components of this product design/development capability and establishing where and with whom within Apple this capability is located is no simple task. Let us explore more closely the nature and the determinants of organizational capability.

FROM RESOURCES TO CAPABILITIES: ROUTINES AND INTEGRATION Capabilities are based upon routinized behaviour. **Routinization** is an essential step in creating organizational capability – only when the activities of organizational members become routine can tasks be completed efficiently and reliably. In every McDonald's hamburger restaurant, operating manuals provide precise directions for a comprehensive range of tasks, from the placing

Case Insight 3.3

Using Porter's value chain to explore the capabilities of firms in the motorcycle industry

Type of activity	Generic value chain activity	Illustrative examples of activities and associated capabilities required in the motorcycle industry
Primary activities	Inbound logistics	Purchasing
		Supply chain management
		Component manufacture
	Operations	Design and product development
		Assembly
		Flexible manufacturing
		Quality control
	Outbound logistics	Distribution coordination and support
		Dealer relationships and management
	Marketing and sales	Market research
		Test marketing
		Advertising
		Promotion
		Pricing
	Service	Warranty and servicing arrangements
		Parts
		Recycling
Support activities	Infrastructure	Strategic management
		Managing external relations
		Financial and risk management
		Legal affairs
	Human resource management	Training and skills development
		Staff recruitment and retention
		Staff appraisal and performance management
	Technology development	Technology-managed design and manufacturing
		Integrated management information systems
		Technology linked manufacture and sales
	Procurement	Database management and IT controlled purchasing of parts and sub-assemblies
		Inventory management
		Supply chain integration and coordination

of the pickle on the burger to the maintenance of the milkshake machine. In practice, personnel are routinized through continual repetition, meaning operating manuals are seldom consulted.

These organizational routines – 'regular and predictable behavioral patterns [comprising] repetitive patterns of activity'[17] – are viewed by evolutionary economists as the fundamental building blocks of what firms do and who they are. It is through the adaptation and replication of routines that firms develop. Like individual skills, organizational routines develop through learning by doing. Just as individual skills become rusty when not used, so it is difficult for organizations to retain coordinated responses to contingencies that arise only rarely. Hence, there tends to be a trade-off between efficiency and flexibility. A limited repertoire of routines can be performed highly efficiently with near-perfect coordination. The same organization may find it extremely difficult to respond to novel situations.[18]

Creating organizational capability is not simply a matter of allowing routines to emerge. Combining resources to create capability requires conscious and systematic actions by management. These actions include: bringing the relevant resources together within an organizational unit, designing processes, creating motivation and aligning the activity with the overall strategy of the organization.

THE HIERARCHY OF CAPABILITIES Whether we start from a functional or value chain approach, the capabilities that we identify are likely to be broadly defined: operational capability, marketing capability, supply chain management capability. However, having recognized that capabilities are the outcome of processes and routines, it is evident that these broadly defined capabilities can be broken down into more specialist capabilities. For example, marketing capabilities can be separated into market research capability, product launch capability, advertising capability, pricing capability, dealer relations capability – and others too. We can also recognize that even broadly defined functional capabilities integrate to form wider cross-functional capabilities: new product development, business development, the provision of customer solutions. What we observe is a hierarchy of capabilities where more general, broadly defined capabilities are formed from the integration of more specialized capabilities. For example:

- A hospital's capability in treating heart disease depends on its integration of capabilities relating to patient diagnosis, physical medicine, cardiovascular surgery, pre- and post-operative care, as well as capabilities relating to training, information technology and various administrative and support functions.
- Toyota's manufacturing capability – its system of 'lean production' – integrates capabilities relating to the manufacture of components and sub-assemblies, supply chain management, production scheduling, assembly, quality control procedures, systems for managing innovation and continuous improvement and inventory control.

Figure 3.4 offers a partial view of the hierarchy of capabilities of a telecom equipment maker. As we ascend the hierarchy, capabilities become progressively more difficult to develop: higher-level capabilities require the broadest integration of know-how, typically across different functional departments.

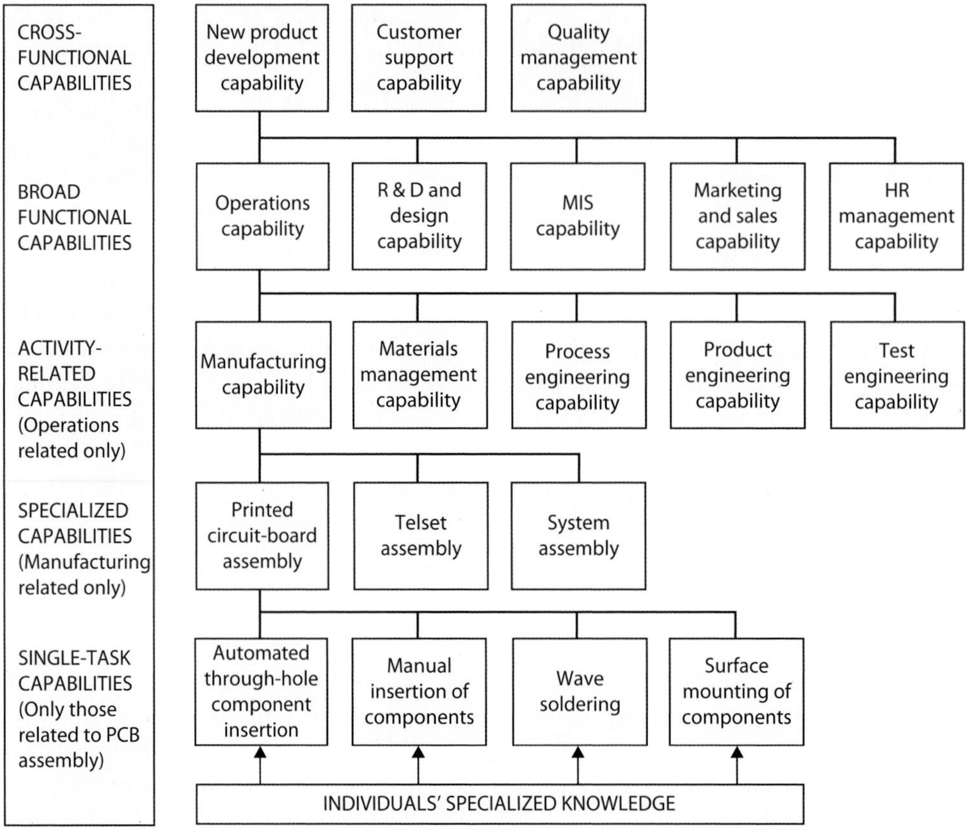

Figure 3.4 The hierarchy of organizational capabilities at a telecom equipment manufacturer.

Appraising resources and capabilities

Having identified the principal resources and capabilities of an organization, how do we appraise their potential for value creation? There are two fundamental issues: first, what is the strategic importance of different resources and capabilities and, second, what are the strengths of the focal firm in these resources and capabilities relative to competitors?

Appraising the strategic importance of resources and capabilities

Strategically important resources and capabilities are those with the potential to generate substantial streams of profit for the firm that owns them. This depends on three factors: establishing a competitive advantage, sustaining that competitive advantage and appropriating the returns from the competitive advantage. Each of these is determined by a number of resource characteristics. Figure 3.5 shows the key relationships.

ESTABLISHING COMPETITIVE ADVANTAGE For a resource or capability to establish a competitive advantage, two conditions must be present:

- *Scarcity:* If a resource or capability is widely available within the industry, it may be necessary in order to compete but it will not be a sufficient basis for competitive

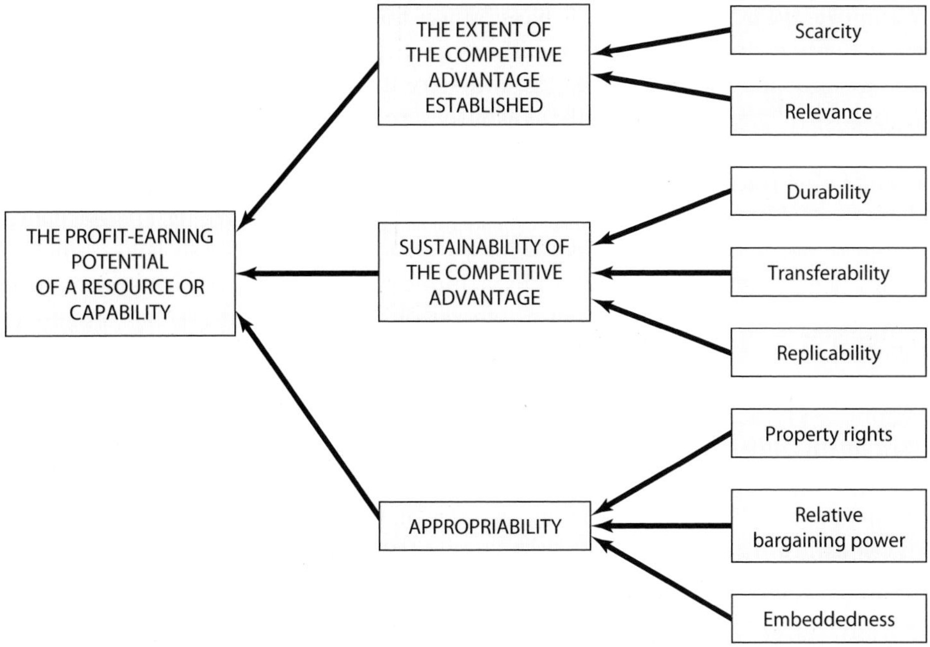

Figure 3.5 Appraising the strategic importance of resources and capabilities.

advantage. In oil and gas exploration, technologies such as directional drilling and 3D seismic analysis are widely available – hence they are 'needed to play' but they are not 'sufficient to win'.

- *Relevance:* A resource or capability must be relevant to the KSFs in the market. British coal mines produced some wonderful brass bands, but these musical capabilities did little to assist the mines in meeting competition from cheap imported coal and North Sea gas. As retail banking shifts towards automated teller machines and online transactions, so the retail branch networks of the banks have become less relevant for customer service.

SUSTAINING COMPETITIVE ADVANTAGE Once established, competitive advantage tends to diminish over time; three characteristics of resources and capabilities determine the sustainability of the competitive advantage they offer:

- *Durability:* The more durable a resource, the greater its ability to support a competitive advantage over the long term. For most resources, including capital equipment and proprietary technology, the quickening pace of technological innovation is shortening their lifespans. Brands, on the other hand, can show remarkable resilience to time. Heinz sauces, Kellogg's cereals, Guinness stout, Burberry raincoats and Coca-Cola have been market leaders for over a century.
- *Transferability:* Competitive advantage is undermined by competitive imitation. If resources and capabilities are transferable – they can be bought and sold – then

any competitive advantage that is based upon them will be eroded. Some resources, such as finance, raw materials, components, machines produced by equipment suppliers and employees with generic skills are transferable and can be bought and sold with little difficulty. Other resources and most capabilities are not easily transferred – either they are entirely firm-specific or their value depreciates on transfer. Some resources are immobile because they are specific to certain locations and cannot be relocated. A competitive advantage of the Laphroaig distillery and its 10-year-old, single malt whisky is its water spring on the Isle of Islay, which supplies water flavoured by peat and sea spray. Capabilities, because they combine multiple resources embedded in an organization's management systems, are also difficult to move from one firm to another. Another barrier to transferability is limited information regarding resource quality. In the case of human resources, hiring decisions are typically based on very little knowledge of how the new employee will perform. Sellers of resources have better information about the performance characteristics of resources than buyers do. This creates a problem of adverse selection for buyers.[19] Jay Barney has shown that different valuations of resources by firms can result in their being either underpriced or overpriced, giving rise to differences in profitability between firms.[20] Finally, resources are complementary: they are less productive when detached from their original home. Typically, brands lose value when transferred between companies: the purchase of European brands by Chinese companies – Aquascutum by YGM, Cerruti by Trinity Ltd., Volvo by Geely – risks the diminution of brand equity.

- *Replicability:* If a firm cannot buy a resource or capability, it must build it. In financial services, most new product innovations can be imitated easily by competitors. In retailing, too, competitive advantages that derive from store layout, point-of-sale technology and marketing methods are easy to observe and easy to replicate. Capabilities based on complex organizational routines are less easy to copy. Federal Express's national, next-day-delivery service and Singapore Airlines' superior in-flight services are complex capabilities based on carefully honed processes, well-developed HR practices and unique corporate cultures. Even when resources and capabilities can be copied, imitators are typically at a disadvantage to initiators.[21]

APPROPRIATING THE RETURNS TO COMPETITIVE ADVANTAGE Who gains the returns generated by superior resources and capabilities? Typically, the owner of that resource or capability. But ownership may not be clear-cut. Are organizational capabilities owned by the employees who provide skills and effort or by the firm which provides the processes and culture? In human-capital-intensive firms, there is an ongoing struggle between employees and shareholders as to the division of the rents arising from superior capabilities. This struggle is reminiscent of the conflict between labour and capital to capture surplus value described by Karl Marx. The prevalence of partnerships (rather than shareholder-owned companies) in law, accounting and consulting firms is one solution to this conflict over rent appropriation. The less clear are property rights in resources and capabilities, the greater the importance of relative bargaining power in determining the division of returns between the firm and its members. The more deeply embedded are individual skills and knowledge within organizational routines, and the more they depend on corporate systems and reputation, the weaker the employee is relative to the firm.

Case Insight 3.4

Building and sustaining competitive advantage at Harley-Davidson

Harley-Davidson's strategy is built around its brand and its ability to maintain and enhance its American pioneering image. The company's stated vision[22] is that of 'fulfilling its customers' dreams of personal freedom' and it endeavours to do this through its 'commitment to exceptional customer service' in everything it does. To that end the company makes it easy for customers to personalize their bikes, invests in its dealer network, offers financing and ancillary merchandise and organizes social events for owners.

But how sustainable is Harley's advantage? While the design, engineering, manufacturing and sales capabilities that Harley has are widely available throughout the industry, its marque is unique and has proved very enduring. The Harley-Davidson brand is rooted in the company's history and protected by a portfolio of trademarks, copyrights and patents. The gradual development and enhancement of the brand over time makes it difficult for others to achieve similar levels of brand awareness quickly or easily. The uniqueness of the company's image is reinforced by the complementarity and fit that Harley has achieved between different parts of its organization. It has built up complex organizational routines and relationships over time and integrated these into a unique company culture. Harley's competitive advantage, therefore, appears durable and difficult to acquire or imitate. The challenge, however, is whether the brand will transfer easily to new markets and market segments.

Appraising the relative strength of a firm's resources and capabilities

Having established which resources and capabilities are strategically most important, we need to assess how a firm measures up relative to its competitors. Making an objective appraisal of a company's resources and capabilities relative to its competitors' is difficult. Organizations frequently fall victim to past glories, hopes for the future and their own wishful thinking. The tendency toward hubris among companies, and their senior managers, means that business success often sows the seeds of its own destruction.[23] Royal Bank of Scotland's acquisition-fuelled growth during 2000–2007 was based upon its perceived excellence in targeting and integrating acquisitions. This perception, rooted in the success of its first major acquisition, NatWest Bank, culminated in the disastrous takeovers of Citizens Bank of Ohio in 2004 and ABN Amro in 2007.[24]

Benchmarking is 'the process of identifying, understanding, and adapting outstanding practices from organizations anywhere in the world to help your organization improve its performance'.[25] Benchmarking offers a systematic framework and methodology for identifying particular functions and processes and then for comparing their performance with other companies'. By establishing performance metrics for different capabilities, an organization can rate its relative position. The results can be salutary: Xerox Corporation, a pioneer of benchmarking during the 1980s, observed the massive superiority of its Japanese competitors in cost efficiency, quality and new-product development. Subsequent evidence showed wide gaps in most industries between average practices and best practices.[26]

Featured Example 3.2

Appropriating returns from superior capabilities: Employees vs. owners

Investment banks offer an illuminating arena to view the conflict between employees and owners to appropriate the returns to organizational capability. Historically, Goldman Sachs was widely regarded as possessing outstanding capability in relation to merger and acquisition services, underwriting new issues and proprietary trading. These capabilities combine several resources: a high level of employee skill, IT infrastructure, corporate reputation and the company's processes and culture. All but the first of these are owned by the company. However, the division of returns between employees and owners suggests that the former has had the upper hand in appropriating rents (Table 3.5).

Table 3.5 Profits, dividends and employee compensation at Goldman Sachs.

	2008	2009	2010	2011
Net profits	$4440m	$13 390m	$8354m	$4442m
Dividends to ordinary shareholders	$638m	$579m	$819m	$780m
Total employee compensation	$20 237m	$16 190m	$15 380m	$12 200m
Compensation per employee	$344 900	$498 000	$430 000	$366 360

In professional sport, it would appear that star players are well positioned to exploit the full value of their contribution to their team's performance. The $27.8 million salary paid to Kobe Bryant for the 2012/13 NBA season seems likely to fully exploit his value to the Los Angeles Lakers.

Similarly with CEOs. Disney's CEO, Robert Iger, was paid $31.4 million in 2011. But determining how much Iger contributed to Disney's 2011 net income of $5260 million as compared with that of Disney's other 156 000 employees is unknown.

The more an organization's performance can be identified with the expertise of an individual employee, the more mobile is that employee, and the more likely that the employee's skills can be deployed with another firm, the stronger is the bargaining position of that employee.

Hence, the emphasis that many investment banks, advertising agencies and other professional service firms give to team-based rather than individual skills. 'We believe our strength lies in … our unique team-based approach,' declares audit firm Grant Thornton. However, employees can reassert their bargaining power through emphasizing team mobility: in September 2010, most of UBS's energy team moved to Citi.

However, benchmarking carries risks. Dan Levinthal points to the danger of looking at specific practices without taking account of interdependencies with other processes and the organizational context more broadly: 'Companies should be cautious about benchmarking or imitating certain policies and practices of other firms … the implicit assumption in this thinking is that the policy that is benchmarked and adopted is independent of what my firm is already doing. The best human resource management practice for Nordstrom may not be the best for McDonald's. It may actually be dysfunctional.'[27]

The authors' own experiences with companies point to the need for benchmarking to be supplemented by more reflective approaches to recognizing strengths and weaknesses. It is useful to get groups of managers together to ask them to identify things that the company has done well in recent years and things that it has done badly, and then to ask whether any patterns emerge.

Case Insight 3.5

Appropriating the returns from competitive advantage

As Figure 3.6 illustrates, the results posted by Harley-Davidson from the mid-1990s onwards suggest that the company has been successful in appropriating the superior returns it earns from its unique resources and capabilities. The company's motorcycles sell at a premium price and its share price, revenue and net income have (the recent economic downturn apart) shown an upward trajectory. The strike at the York manufacturing plant in 2007 illustrates the struggle that is present in many companies between employees and shareholders as to the division of 'rents' between different stakeholders but, across the piece, Harley has a track record of harmonious relationships with its employees, suppliers and dealers.

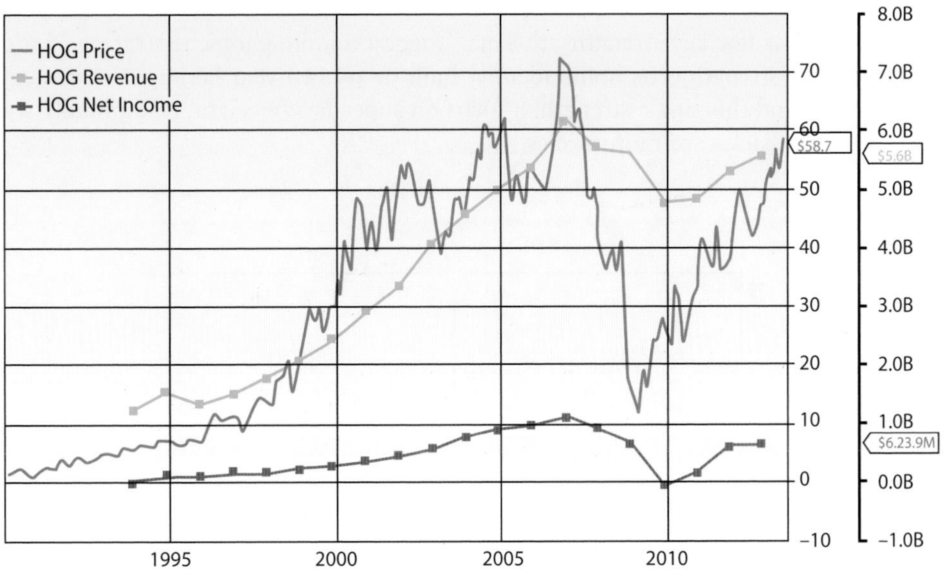

Figure 3.6 Harley-Davidson's share price, revenue and net income: 1995–2013.
Source: www.gurufocus.com.

Developing strategy implications

Our analysis so far – identifying resources and capabilities and appraising them in terms of strategic importance and relative strength – can be summarized in the form of a simple display (Figure 3.7).

Our key focus is on the two right-hand quadrants of Figure 3.7. How do we exploit our key strengths most effectively? How can we address our key weaknesses in terms of both reducing our vulnerability to them and correcting them? Finally, what about our 'inconsequential' strengths: are these really superfluous or are there ways in which we can deploy them to greater effect? Let us offer a few suggestions.

Exploiting key strengths

The foremost task is to ensure that the firm's critical strengths are deployed to the greatest effect:

- If some of Walt Disney's key strengths are the Disney brand, the worldwide affection that children and their parents have for Disney characters and the company's capabilities in the design and operation of theme parks, the implication is that Disney should not limit its theme park activities to six locations (Anaheim, Orlando, Paris, Tokyo, Hong Kong and Shanghai); it should open theme parks in other locations that have adequate market potential for year-round attendance.
- If a core competence of quality newspapers such as the *New York Times*, the *Guardian* (UK) and *Le Monde* (France) is their ability to interpret events (especially in their home countries), can this capability be used as a basis for establishing new businesses such as customized business intelligence and other types of consulting in order to supplement their declining revenues from newspaper sales?
- If a company has few key strengths, this may suggest adopting a niche strategy. Harley-Davidson's key strength is its brand identity built on its 110-year heritage. Its strategy has been built around this single strength: a focus on super-heavyweight, traditionally styled, technologically backward motorcycles.

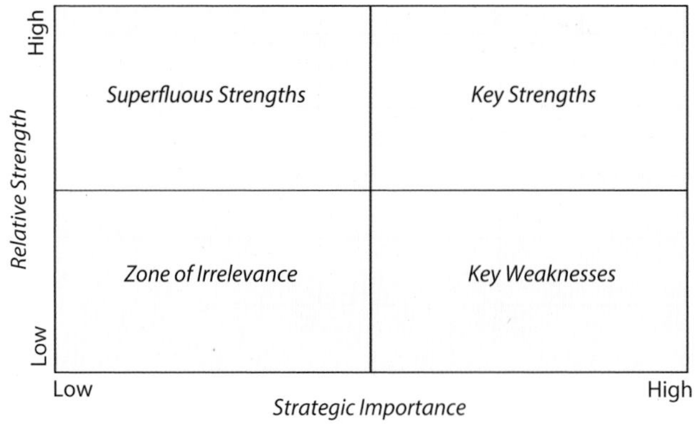

Figure 3.7 The framework for appraising resources and capabilities.

Managing key weaknesses

What does a company do about its key weaknesses? It is tempting to think of how companies can upgrade existing resources and capabilities to correct such weaknesses. However, converting weakness into strength is likely to be a long-term task for most companies. In the short to medium term, a company is likely to be stuck with the resources and capabilities that it has inherited.

The most decisive, and often most successful, solution to weaknesses in key functions is to *outsource*. Thus, in the automobile industry, companies have become increasingly selective in the activities they perform internally. During the 1930s, Ford was almost completely vertically integrated. At its massive River Rouge plant, which once employed over 100 000 people, coal and iron ore entered at one end, completed cars exited at the other. In 2004, Ford opened its Dearborn Truck Plant on the old River Rouge site. The new plant employed 3200 Ford workers and an equal number of suppliers' employees. Almost all component production was outsourced along with a major part of design, engineering, assembly, IT and security. In athletic shoes and clothing, Nike undertakes product design, marketing and overall 'systems integration', but manufacturing, logistics and many other functions are contracted out. We consider the extent to which firms are vertically integrated in greater depth in Chapter 8.

Clever strategy formulation can allow a firm to negate its vulnerability to key weaknesses. Returning to our opening case, Harley-Davidson cannot compete with Honda, Yamaha and BMW on technology. The solution? It has made a virtue of its outmoded technology and traditional designs. Harley-Davidson's old-fashioned, push-rod engines and recycled designs have become central to its retro-look authenticity.

What about superfluous strengths?

What about those resources and capabilities where a company has particular strengths that don't appear to be important sources of sustainable competitive advantage? One response may be to lower the level of investment into these resources and capabilities. If a retail bank has a strong but increasingly underutilized branch network, it may be time to prune its real-estate assets and invest in Web-based customer services.

However, in the same way that companies can turn apparent weaknesses into competitive strengths, it is possible to develop innovative strategies that turn apparently inconsequential strengths into key strategy differentiators. Edward Jones' network of brokerage offices and 8000-strong sales force looked increasingly irrelevant in an era when brokerage transactions were going online. However, by emphasizing personal service, trustworthiness and its traditional, conservative investment virtues, Edward Jones has built a successful contrarian strategy based on its network of local offices.[28]

In the fiercely competitive MBA market, business schools should also seek to differentiate on the basis of idiosyncratic resources and capabilities. Georgetown's Jesuit heritage is not an obvious source of competitive advantage for its MBA programmes. Yet, the Jesuit approach to education is about developing the whole person; this fits well with an emphasis on developing the values, integrity and emotional intelligence necessary to be a successful business leader. Similarly, Dartmouth College's location in the woods of New Hampshire far from any major business centre is not an obvious benefit to its business programmes. However, Dartmouth's Tuck Business School has used the isolation and natural beauty of its locale to create an MBA programme that features unparalleled community and social involvement which fosters personal development and close network ties.

Choosing the industry context

In appraising resources and capabilities on the basis of strategic importance and relative strength we need to acknowledge that both these variables are context-specific: both depend upon how we define the competitive environment of the focal firm. In the case of Harley-Davidson, if we view the relevant context as the world motorcycle industry then technology is a critically important resource. If we view Harley as competing in the heavyweight-cruiser segment, technology is less important. Similarly with the relative strength dimension: this depends critically upon which firms form our comparison set.

The choice of industry context is a matter of judgement. In general, it is best to define industry context relatively broadly; otherwise, there is a risk that our resource/capability analysis becomes limited by the focal firm's existing strategy and we tend to exclude both threats from distant competitors and opportunities for radically new strategic departures.

More generally, however, we need to be alert to the limitations and weaknesses of our strategy frameworks. In the case of the Porter five forces of competition framework, the theoretical foundations of the model are largely obsolete and empirical support for the model is weak. Nevertheless, the five forces framework is a useful and revealing analytical tool. The key is to recognize that our analytical frameworks are not scientific theories: they are tools. In the case of the approach to analysing resources and capabilities outlined here, our purpose is to make a start on identifying and understanding the resources and capabilities of organizations: the approach's value is in providing an overall picture of a firm's resource/capability profile within which more detailed analysis can then be pursued as illustrated in Case Insight 3.6.

Case Insight 3.6

Completing the picture

We are now in a position to bring the different strands in our analysis together. We can start with key success factors in the world motorcycle industry: low-cost production, attractively designed new models embodying the latest technologies, the financial strength to weather the cyclicality and heavy investment requirements of the industry and high levels of pre- and post-sales service. What capabilities and resources do these key success factors imply? They would include manufacturing capabilities, new product development capability, effective supply chain management and distribution, brand strength, scale-efficient plants with up-to-date capital equipment, a strong balance sheet and so on. To organize and categorize these various resources and capabilities, it is helpful to switch to the inside of Harley-Davidson using either a functional approach (as we did in Case Insight 3.2) or the value chain approach (illustrated in Case Insight 3.3). Table 3.6 shows how we may work through this step for Harley. The first column of the table lists Harley's principal resources and capabilities, which are derived from prior analyses of the types illustrated in Case Insights 3.1–3.3.

Table 3.6 Appraising Harley-Davidson's resources and capabilities.

	Strategic Importance (1 to 10)	Harley-Davidson's relative strength (1 to 10)
RESOURCES		
R1. Proprietary technology	3 Automotive technology is well-diffused throughout the industry	3 Harley has been a laggard rather than a leader in this area
R2. Location	4 Proximity to major markets, industry knowledge and low-cost inputs offer some advantages	6 Harley is well placed in terms of its established customer base but is poorly positioned in relation to the engineering centres of excellence or low-cost labour
R3. Brand	8 Brand image is important to customers; scarce and costly to replicate	10 Harley is an iconic brand that encompasses a lifestyle image
R4. Finance	7 Important for upgrading resources and capabilities	4 The company is small relative to many rivals and has limited financial resources
CAPABILITIES		
C1. Manufacturing	10 Capabilities with regard to efficiency, quality and flexibility are critical to cost and user satisfaction	5 Harley has reorganized production to improve efficiency, quality and flexibility but remains a small producer operating on multiple sites
C2. Design	7 Good design essential but designs relatively easy to replicate	8 Harley emphasizes traditional design and has a number of patents that cover some of its key design features
C3. Engineering	8 Key input into successful new product development	5 Has attempted to make a virtue of outdated engineering; recent innovations rely on partnerships with others
C4. New product development	10 Regular launch of new models critical to market presence	3 In the past Harley has relied on customization and incremental changes in product features rather than new product launches. Recent developments of 'Rushmore' and 'Street' bikes mark a change in strategy
C5. Marketing	6 Media advertising, promotion and community building important but marketing capability not rare	9 Very effective community building and enhancement of brand image
C6. Customer Service	7 Essential for brand reputation and sales of bikes and ancillary products	10 Strong reputation for customer service

Both scales range from 1 to 10 (1 = very low, 10 = very high).
Harley-Davidson's resources and capabilities are compared against those of BMW, Ducati, Honda, Suzuki, Yamaha and many more; 5 represents parity. The ratings are based on the authors' subjective judgements.

Many of Harley-Davidson's resources and capabilities are essential to compete in the business, but several of them are not scarce (e.g. engineering and marketing capabilities are widely diffused within the industry), while others (such as IT capabilities and provision of ancillary financial services) are often outsourced to external providers – in other words some resources and capabilities are 'needed to play' but not 'needed to win'. On the other hand, resources such as brand strength, effective distribution networks and fast-cycle new-product developments cannot be easily acquired or developed quickly yet they are critical to establishing and sustaining advantage. In the right-hand column of Table 3.6 we provide our subjective ranking of the relative strength of Harley-Davidson with respect to different resources and capabilities.

Having identified resources and capabilities that are important and where our company is strong relative to competitors, the key task is to formulate our strategy to ensure that these resources are deployed to the greatest effect. Given that the brand is a key strength of Harley, it makes sense for the company to differentiate itself from competitors by customizing its products to meet the demands of its target market. By trying to improve the efficiency and flexibility of its plants at the same time and offering locally customized products, Harley has been successful in providing its customers with perceived 'value for money'. To the extent that different companies within an industry have different capability profiles, this implies differentiation of strategies within the industry. Thus, Toyota's outstanding manufacturing capabilities and fast-cycle new-product development, VW's engineering excellence and Peugeot's design flair suggest that each company should be pursuing a distinctively different strategy.

In the case of Harley-Davidson, its capability in organizing social and charity events for its owners appears to exceed that which is required to operate effectively within the industry. However, when this capability is considered in conjunction with Harley's overall strategy of engendering customer loyalty it is easy to see why this particular capability is valued more highly by the company than the industry as a whole.

As we have seen in Chapter 2, the circumstances in which firms find themselves change over time. Technology and consumer tastes change, the economic climate alters, key personnel retire or leave the organization and, as a consequence, firms need to develop new resources and capabilities. This represents a serious challenge for both managers and academics, not least because our knowledge of the linkages between resources and capabilities are underdeveloped. This is a theme we return to in Chapter 5, where we explore the firm's ability to integrate, build and reconfigure its capabilities in response to external and internal change.

Summary

We have shifted the focus of our attention from the external to the internal environment of the firm. This internal environment comprises many features of the firm, but for the purposes of strategy analysis, the key issue is what the firm can *do*. This means looking at the resources of the firm and the way resources combine to create organizational capabilities. Our interest is the potential for resources and capabilities to establish sustainable competitive advantage. Systematic appraisal of a company's resources and capabilities provides the basis for formulating (or reformulating) strategy. How can the firm deploy its strengths to maximum advantage? How can it minimize its vulnerability to its weaknesses? Figure 3.8 provides a simplified view of the approach to resource analysis developed in this chapter.

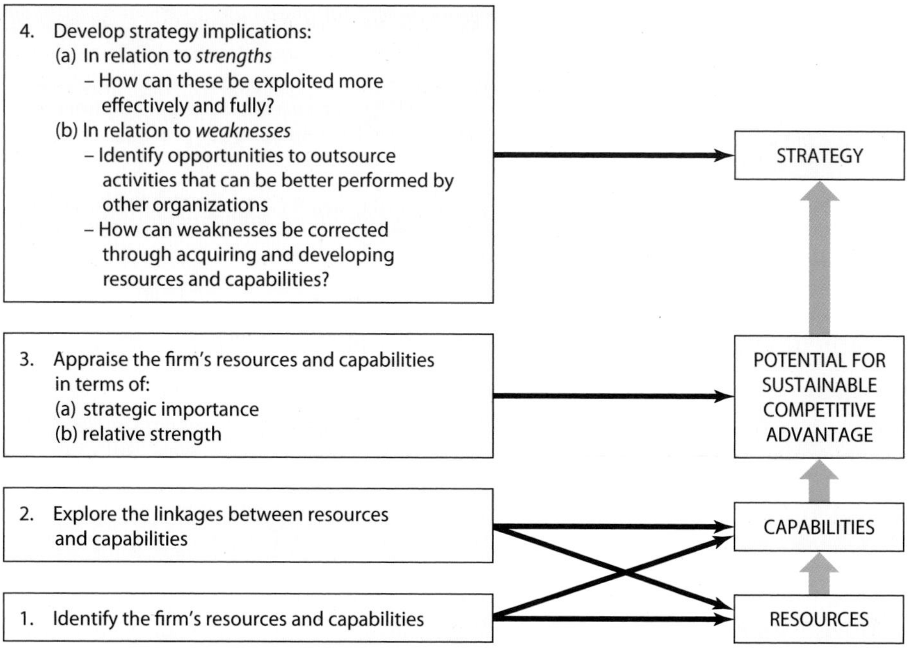

Figure 3.8 Summary: A framework for analysing resources and capabilities.

Although much of the discussion has been heavy on concepts and theory, the issues are practical. The management systems of most firms devote meticulous attention to the physical and financial assets that are valued on their balance sheets; much less attention has been paid to the critical intangible and human resources of the firm and even less to the identification, appraisal and development of organizational capability. In this chapter our emphasis has been on identifying, assessing and deploying a firm's existing resources and capabilities.

Summary table

Learning objectives	Summary
Appreciate the role firm's resources and capabilities play in formulating strategy	While the emphasis in Chapter 2 was on the external environment, this chapter highlights the importance of internal resources and capabilities. The interface between strategy and the internal environment of the firm has come increasingly to be seen as important because the external environment is perceived to have become more unstable and because research has indicated that competitive advantage rather than industry attractiveness is the primary source of superior profitability
Identify and appraise the resources and capabilities of a firm	Resources are what the firm 'has' or 'owns'; capabilities are what the firm can 'do'. Different ways of identifying and appraising resources and capabilities include functional and hierarchical classification schema and value chain analysis

Learning objectives	Summary
Evaluate the potential for a firm's resources and capabilities to confer sustainable competitive advantage	The profit-earning potential of a resource or capability depends on the extent to which it can be used to establish a competitive advantage. The key factors determining this potential are summarized in Figure 3.7
Use the results of resource and capability analysis to formulate strategies that exploit internal strengths while defending against internal weaknesses	A step-by-step approach to appraising resources and capabilities is outlined in the chapter together with an illustrative example based on Harley-Davidson, Inc.

Further reading

Classic articles which outline the central tenets of the resource-based view include:

Barney, J. B. (1991). Firms' resources and sustained competitive advantage. *Journal of Management*, 17, 99–120.

Grant, R. (1991). The resource-based theory of competitive advantage. *California Management Review*, 33, 114– 35.

Peteraf, M. A. (1993). The cornerstones of competitive advantage: A resource-based view. *Strategic Management Journal*, 14, 179–92.

An excellent critique and defence of the resource-based view is provided in the exchange between Richard Priem and John Butler on the one hand and Jay Barney on the other in the 2001 Issue 1 of the *Academy of Management Review*:

Priem, R. and Butler, J. (2001). Is the resource-based 'view' a useful perspective for strategic management research? *Academy of Management Review*, 26(1), 22–40.

Barney, J. (2001). Is the resource-based 'view' a useful perspective for strategic management research: Yes? *Academy of Management Review*, 26(1), 41–56.

Self-study questions

1 In recent years Google has expanded from an Internet search engine to a company that operates across a broad range of Internet services, including email, photo management, satellite maps, digital book libraries, blogger services and telephony. To what extent has Google's strategy focused on its resources and capabilities rather than specific customer needs? What are Google's principal resources and capabilities?

2 Through our opening case 'Harley-Davidson, Inc.' and the associated Case Insights (see particularly Case Insight 3.5) we have explored the ways in which Harley has sustained its competitive position over time. Do you think Harley's existing resources and capabilities fit well with its move into new overseas markets? What new capabilities may it need to develop?

3 Apply the approach outlined in the section 'Developing strategy implications' to your own place of study. Begin by identifying the resources and capabilities relevant to success

in the market for business education, appraise the resources and capabilities of your institution (e.g. your business school or university department) and then make strategy recommendations regarding such matters as the programmes to be offered and the overall positioning and differentiation of the school or department and its offerings.

4 Identify two sports teams: one that is rich in resources (e.g. talented players) but whose capabilities (as indicated by performance) have been poor and one that is resource-poor but has displayed strong team capabilities. What clues can you offer as to the determinants of capabilities among sports teams?

5 Many companies announce in their corporate communications: 'Our people are our greatest resource.' In terms of the criteria listed in Figure 3.5, can employees be considered of the utmost strategic importance?

Closing Case

Wal-Mart Stores, Inc.

Walmart is a discount retailer that sells a broad range of general merchandise covering everything from groceries to the latest electronic gadgets. The parent company, Wal-Mart Stores, Inc., operates retail stores in various formats under 69 different banners around the world. In 2013, it generated a total revenue of $469.2 billion,[29] made a profit of around $17 billion,[30] employed around 2.2 million people and topped the Fortune 500. The company operates retail stores through wholly owned subsidiaries in Argentina, Brazil, Canada, China, Japan and the UK, majority-owned subsidiaries in Africa, Central America, Chile, China and Mexico and joint ventures in India and China, but the US remains its central base, accounting for just under 60% of its net sales revenue.

A brief history of Walmart

Sam Walton opened his first discount retail store in Rogers, Arkansas in 1962 with the aim of bringing the kind of discounts and low prices found in big city stores to his part of America. He sold brand-name products to rural consumers at rock-bottom prices with the declared aim of 'saving people money so that they can live better'. The quest for low prices was something of an obsession for Walton, who, despite becoming one of the richest men in American, was legendary for his thriftiness.

Walton recognized from the start that to offer low prices he needed to take costs out of his business equation wherever possible and maximize the volume of sales. When on business trips he insisted that he and his business executives travel in the most economical way and share hotel rooms. He sought to hire as few people as possible, kept wages low and fiercely resisted any attempts at unionization. Even a cup of coffee in the office required a contribution in a tin.[31]

Even though Walton was at pains to minimize the Walmart wage bill, he encouraged all employees to view themselves as having a stake in the company and recruited them to his crusade to give customers the best possible deal. He referred to employees as 'associates' and encouraged them to share their ideas on ways of improving store performance. He introduced a profit-sharing scheme that allowed employees to use a certain percentage of their wages to buy Walmart shares at a subsidized price and emphasized the opportunities for employees to develop and succeed within the company. To reinforce his message Walton made frequent impromptu visits to stores, arriving in a personal aircraft that he piloted himself.

When Walton died in 1992, he left behind a set of business principles that endured. The values that Walton sought to instil in his workforce formed the basis of Walmart's corporate culture and contributed to the company's continuing success.

Key features of Walmart's operations

Walmart's ability to outperform its rivals rests on more than just the legacy it inherited from its founder. The company's strategy is based on an ecosystem of complex links between different parts of its operations embedded in relationships, practices and organizational routines. Key elements include:

Technology

One of the key aspects of Walmart's operations is its use of technology. Walmart has long been a pioneer in the use of information and communication technology to improve its efficiency. In the 1980s, the company introduced bar coding and electronic data interchange (EDI) tools to interact with suppliers and to manage the flow of merchandise to its stores. It invested large sums in sophisticated communications platforms like RetailLink, which gave its managers access to point-of-sale and inventory data on a store-by-store basis and has required all its suppliers to adopt this system. More recently, Walmart has introduced Radio Frequency Identification (RFID) to track pallets of merchandise moving along its supply chain.[32] All of these technologies have helped Walmart to minimize inventory, reduce shrinkage and out-of-stock occurrences and cut merchandise-handling costs significantly. The sophistication of Walmart's information and communication technology systems, in combination with its state-of-the art distribution networks, was highlighted when Hurricane Katrina hit New Orleans in 2005. Walmart was able to deliver much-needed food and supplies to those affected before the Federal Emergency Management Agency.

Stores formats

In the early years Walmart focused on serving customers in rural America and its stores were relatively small in terms of their square footage. As the cost advantages of larger-scale operations became apparent, Walmart introduced much larger supercentres to meet the growing demand for one-stop shopping. The number of supercentres now exceeds the number of discount stores by a considerable margin. Many of these superstores contain hair salons, opticians, cafés and restaurants and other speciality stores within their premises. Supercentres have extended opening hours, offer a wider range of products and generate higher sales volumes than the smaller outlets. This allows fixed costs to be spread over larger sales volume. In addition, Walmart also operates around 286 members-only warehouse stores under the label of 'Sam's Club' and a chain of around 600 or so smaller neighbourhood stores located in urban areas.

Supply and distribution

The scale of Walmart's operations means that it deals with tens of thousands of suppliers and has developed sophisticated systems for managing its supply chain relationships. The company likes to view its suppliers as partners; it provides them with advice and support including access to online training and a 46-page manual that outlines key policies and procedures and is known for paying promptly. In return, Walmart requires suppliers to align their systems and processes with those of Walmart and to make the investment necessary to fulfil their Walmart orders. The company rarely enters into long-term contracts with suppliers and tries to avoid becoming the supplier's main source of business. Walmart's immense bargaining power and emphasis on 'everyday low prices' means that suppliers are under considerable pressure not only to reduce their prices on a year-by-year basis but also to improve quality, delivery schedules, packaging and other aspects of their product offerings. Generally, suppliers deliver their products to Walmart distribution centres, from where merchandise is transported to stores. Walmart's distribution centres are large, highly automated warehouses that are strategically located. The company owns a large fleet of trucks and uses sophisticated logistical systems to optimize traffic flows.

People and public relations

In 2014, Walmart appeared 28th in the *Fortune* list of most admired companies and it still espouses the values and beliefs of its founder: service to customers, respect for the individual, acting with integrity and striving for excellence. Unfortunately, the company's image has been tarnished over time by a number of negative reports that have questioned the ethics of its low-cost approach. Critics accuse the company of paying excessively low wages, setting its frontline managers unrealistic performance targets, paying insufficient attention to the working conditions of those employed by its overseas suppliers and forcing small, local retailers out of business. In response, Walmart has mounted vigorous public relations and advertising campaigns that have included public pronouncements about its promotion of 250 000 US store employees and its move to change a significant number of store workers from temporary to part-time status. Walmart has also implemented policies to widen its supply base to include more local suppliers and suppliers from more diverse backgrounds.

International expansion

Walmart started to expand outside the US in 1991, when it moved across the border to Mexico. Since then it has increased its global presence and operates more than 5000 retail units outside the US. International expansion is a priority for Walmart because its dominant position in the US limits its domestic growth prospects. Overseas expansion has taken place through a combination of acquisitions (e.g. Asda in the UK and Bompreço in Brazil), partnerships (e.g. Bharti in India and Trust-Mart in Taiwan) and stand-alone ventures (e.g. Walmart Argentina and Walmart Canada) but it has not been without hiccups. The company has been dogged by a bribery scandal in Mexico and accused of holding down costs by using factories that ignore workers' rights and safety. Nonetheless, in 2013 Walmart International operated more than 6000 retail outlets in 26 countries.[33]

Future challenges

On 1st February 2014, Doug McMillon, formerly the head of Walmart's international business, succeeded Mike Duke as chief executive. He took over the company at a time when big changes looked increasingly necessary. Walmart faces a number of key challenges, in particular with regard to public relations, international expansion and competition. While Walmart's obsessive focus on keeping costs down has been central to its success, this has also eroded trust in the company. In 2014, for example, the US National Labor Relations Board accused Walmart of sacking and disciplining workers who went on strike in 2012. Walmart claims it acted lawfully but incidents of this type continue to dent the company's image.

Walmart's international expansion has come at a cost. In 2014, international business was expected to account for 28% of Walmart's sales but only 19% of its operating income and many commentators argue that Walmart has expanded overseas too rapidly. This is reflected in the company's decision to cut back on its planned store openings in a number of countries.

Perhaps the most worrying issue for Walmart is the rise in competition. Rivals such as CostCo, Target and Dollar General have seen their sales rise whereas Walmart same-store sales have dropped.[34] Online companies like Amazon have also been successful in drawing sales of bulky items like white goods, nappies and detergents away from Walmart. In response, Walmart has strengthened its online channel, Walmart.com, which not only retails Walmart's own products but also acts as a marketplace for products supplied by independent retailers. Nonetheless, if Walmart is able to flex its 'ecosystem' of shops, warehouses, delivery fleets and technology to match changes in the marketplace, it will remain very difficult for others to match.

Case questions

- Using the tools and techniques introduced in the chapter, identify Walmart's principal resources and capabilities at the case date.
- What is meant by 'a sustainable competitive advantage'? In your opinion, does Walmart have a sustainable competitive advantage? Justify your answer using the concepts outlined in Figure 3.5.
- What strategy recommendations would you offer Walmart's senior management team on the basis of your answer to the previous question?

Notes

1 The 'resource-based view' is described in J. B. Barney, 'Firm resources and sustained competitive advantage', *Journal of Management*, 17 (1991): 99–120; J. Mahoney and J. R. Pandian, 'The resource-based view within the conversation of strategic management', *Strategic Management Journal*, 13 (1992): 363–80; M. A. Peterlaf, 'The cornerstones of competitive advantage: A resource-based view', *Strategic Management Journal*, 14 (1993): 179–92; R. M. Grant, 'The resource-based theory of competitive advantage', *California Management Review*, 33 (1991): 114–35.

2 Ted Levitt ('Marketing myopia', *Harvard Business Review*, July–August 1960: 24–47) proposed that firms should define their strategies on the basis of customer needs rather than products, e.g. railroad companies should view themselves as in the transportation business. However, this fails to address the resource implication of serving these broad customer needs.

3 C. K. Prahalad and G. Hamel, 'The core competence of the corporation', *Harvard Business Review* (May–June 1990): 79–91.

4 'Eastman Kodak: Failing to meet the digital challenge', in R. M. Grant, *Cases to Accompany Contemporary Strategy Analysis*, 8th edn (Oxford: Blackwell, 2013).

5 E. Danneels, B. Provera and G. Verona, *Legitimizing Exploration: Olivetti's transition from mechanical to electronic technology*, Management Department, Bocconi University, Milan (2008).

6 M. Tripsas, 'Unraveling the process of creative destruction: Complementary assets and incumbent survival in the typesetter industry', *Strategic Management Journal* 18 (Summer 1997): 119–42; J. Bower and C. M. Christensen, 'Disruptive technologies: Catching the wave', *Harvard Business Review* (January/February 1995): 43–53.

7 *Economic Survey of the European Union*, 2007 (Paris: OECD, 2007).

8 E. Lawler, 'From job-based to competency-based organizations', *Journal of Organizational Behavior*, 15 (1994): 3–15; L. Spencer, D. McClelland and S. Spencer, *Competency Assessment Methods: History and state of the art* (Hay/McBer Research Group, 1994); L. Spencer and S. Spencer, *Competence At Work: Models for superior performance* (New York: John Wiley & Sons Ltd, 1993).

9 D. Goleman, *Emotional Intelligence* (New York: Bantam, 1995).

10 S. Green, 'Understanding corporate culture and its relation to strategy', *International Studies of Management and Organization*, 18 (1988): 6–28.

11 J. Barney, 'Organisational culture: Can it be a source of sustained competitive advantage?' *Academy of Management Review*, 11 (1986): 656–65.

12 C. E. Helfat and M. Lieberman, 'The birth of capabilities: Market entry and the importance of prehistory', *Industrial and Corporate Change*, 12 (2002): 725–60.

13 G. Hamel and C. K. Prahalad argue (*Harvard Business Review*, May–June (1992): 164–5) that 'the distinction between competences and capabilities is purely semantic'.

14 P. Selznick, *Leadership in Administration: A sociological interpretation* (New York: Harper & Row, 1957).

15 Prahalad and Hamel (1990), op. cit.

16 G. Hamel and C. K. Prahalad, 'Letter', *Harvard Business Review* (May–June 1992): 164–5.

17 R. R. Nelson and S. G. Winter, *An Evolutionary Theory of Economic Change* (Cambridge, MA: Belknap, 1982).

18 As a result, specialists perform well in stable environments, while generalists do well in variable conditions: see J. Freeman and M. Hannan, 'Niche width and the dynamics of organizational populations', *American Journal of Sociology*, 88 (1984): 1116–45.

19 See G. Akerlof, 'The market for lemons: Qualitative uncertainty and the market mechanism', *Quarterly Journal of Economics*, 84 (1970): 488–500.

20 J. B. Barney, 'Strategic factor markets: Expectations, luck and business strategy', *Management Science*, 32 (October 1986): 1231–41.

21 I. Dierickx and K. Cool ('Asset stock accumulation and sustainability of competitive advantage', *Management Science*, 35 (1989): 1504–13) point to two major disadvantages of imitation. They are subject to 'asset mass efficiencies' (the incumbent's strong initial resource position facilitates the subsequent accumulation of these resources) and 'time compression diseconomies' (additional costs incurred by an imitator when seeking to rapidly accumulate a resource or capability, e.g. 'crash programmes' of R & D and 'blitz advertising campaigns' tend to be costly and unproductive).

22 www.harley-davidson.com/en_US/Content/Pages/Company/company.html, accessed 29th September 2014.

23 D. Miller, *The Icarus Paradox: How exceptional companies bring about their own downfall* (New York: Harper-Business, 1990).

24 'Royal Bank of Scotland investigation: The full story of how the 'world's biggest bank' went bust', *The Telegraph* (5th March 2011), http://www.telegraph.co.uk/finance/newsbysector/banksandfinance/8363417/Royal-Bank-of-Scotland-investigation-the-full-story-of-how-the-worlds-biggest-bank-went-bust.html, accessed 29th September 2014.

25 'What is benchmarking?' *Benchnet: The Benchmarking Exchange*, http://www.benchnet.com/wib.htm, accessed 29th September 2014.

26 'The link between management and productivity', *McKinsey Quarterly* (February, 2006).

27 'A new tool for resurrecting an old theory of the firm', *Knowledge@Wharton*, (17th May 2006), http://knowledge.wharton.upenn.edu/article/1480.cfm, accessed 29th September 2014).

28 C. Markides, *All the Right Moves* (Boston: Harvard Business School Press, 1999).

29 Wal-Mart SEC Form 10 k (2013).

30 Wal-Mart Stores, Inc. Annual Report 2013.

31 http://www.corpwatch.org/article.php?id=13796, accessed 29th September 2014.

32 RFID transfers data stored on tags on a product or other object to operators, facilitating identification and tracking.

33 Wal-Mart Stores, Inc. Annual Report 2014.

34 'Walmart: Less amazing than Amazon', *The Economist* (1st February 2014).

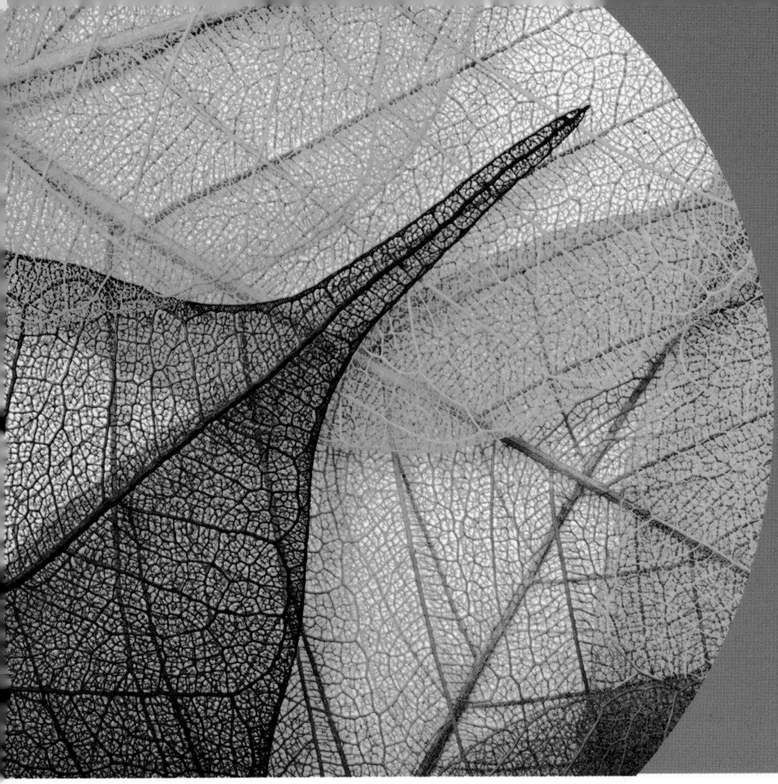

4

The nature and sources of competitive advantage

Introduction and objectives

In this chapter, we integrate and develop the elements of competitive advantage that we have analysed in prior chapters. We noted in earlier chapters that a firm could earn superior profits either by locating in an attractive industry or by establishing a competitive advantage over its rivals. Of these two, competitive advantage is the more important. As competition has intensified across almost all industries, very few industry environments can guarantee secure returns; hence, the primary goal of a strategy is to establish a position of competitive advantage for the firm.

Chapters 2 and 3 have provided the two primary building blocks for our analysis of competitive advantage. In Chapter 2, we analysed the *external* sources of competitive advantage: the key success factors within a market. In Chapter 3, we analysed the *internal* sources of competitive advantage: the potential for the firm to establish and sustain a competitive advantage on the basis of its resources and capabilities.

This chapter looks more deeply at competitive advantage. We focus on the dynamic relationship between competitive advantage and the competitive process. Competition provides the incentive for establishing advantage but is also the means by which advantage is worn away. By understanding the characteristics of competition in a market, we can identify the opportunities for, and the challenges to, competitive advantage.

By the time you have completed this chapter, you will be able to:

- understand the meaning of the term ‘competitive advantage’ and identify the circumstances in which a firm can create and sustain a competitive advantage over a rival;
- predict the potential for competition to wear away competitive advantage through imitation;
- recognize how resource conditions create imperfections in the competitive process that offer opportunities for competitive advantage;
- distinguish the two primary types of competitive advantage: cost advantage and differentiation advantage;
- identify potential sources of cost and differentiation advantage and recommend strategies to enhance competitiveness;
- appreciate the pitfalls of being ‘stuck in the middle’ and the challenge of achieving both effective differentiation and low cost.

Opening Case

Singapore Airlines (SIA)

Over the past four decades, Singapore Airlines (SIA) has developed an enviable reputation for providing its passengers with a high-quality air travel experience. The company prides itself on being the 'most awarded airline', a title it has gained through winning many prizes for its customer service standards. It was also ranked 18th in *Fortune* magazine's 'World's Most Admired Companies' in 2013. What is perhaps less well known is that SIA is also one of the most cost-effective operators in the airline business. The data listed in Table 4.1 illustrates this fact.

Table 4.1 Costs of available seat kilometres (ASK) between 2001 and 2009 in US cents.

Airline	Costs per ASK (US cents)
Singapore Airlines	4.58
Full service European airlines	8–16
US airlines	7–8
Asian airlines	5–7

Source: Heracleous, L. and Wirtz, J. (2010). 'Singapore Airlines' balancing act', *Harvard Business Review*, July–August, 145–9. Reproduced by permission of Harvard Business Publishing.

A brief history of SIA

The company can trace its roots back to 1947 but really took off as an independent entity in the early 1970s when it severed its ties with what would eventually become Malaysia Airlines. During the 1970s, the company grew rapidly, extending its scheduled routes from its Singapore hub to many destinations in India and Asia. In the 1980s, it added routes to the US, Canada and Europe and has continued to expand its network over time. Since its incorporation in 1972, SIA has been partly owned by the Singapore government, which has a 'golden share', but operationally it is free from government intervention.

SIA's strategy

SIA has based its strategy on two main pillars: its planes and its people. In terms of its aircraft, the company tries to keep its fleet 'young'. In April 2014, it was estimated that the average age of the SIA fleet was 81 months as opposed to the industry average of around 128 months.[1] SIA was the first airline to launch the Airbus A380 high-capacity jet and has continued to invest significant sums both in new aircraft and in new cabin products such as in-flight entertainment systems and ergonomically designed seats. The policy of operating a young fleet also means that SIA's aircraft are more fuel efficient and require less repair and maintenance than those of its rivals. Heracleous and Wirtz report that 'in 2008 repairs accounted for 4% of SIA's total costs compared with 5.9% for United Airlines and 4.8% for American Airlines'.[2] SIA's aircraft also spend less time in hangars and more time in the air – 13 hours on average per day versus the industry average of 11.3 hours.

In terms of its people, the Singapore International Airlines group as a whole (including cargo, repair and maintenance service, etc.) employed just under 23 000 people in 2013, of which 14 000 were employed by the airline business. While the company pays only average Singapore wages, it manages to attract first-class university graduates because it has a reputation for offering excellent training and experience. The company spends around $70 million a year putting each of its employees through 110 hours of retraining annually. Much of this training is focused on embedding the culture of customer service into everything employees do. Staff are, for example, trained to appreciate subtle cultural differences and to look for clever ways of personalizing passengers' flying experience – for example noticing that a laptop is out of power or a mother needs assistance with her child. As a consequence, crew members who leave the company usually find it easy to find employment with other operators.

While emphasis is given to customer service, any opportunity to cut costs, however small, is taken. The headquarters of the airline is housed in modest premises near Changi airport in Singapore and the central head count is kept to a minimum. Training takes place within the airline's offices and is delivered by senior members of the airline's own crew rather than by outside trainers. Staff are encouraged to find ways of reducing waste and bonus schemes are in place that incentivize cost-cutting behaviour. For example, even though two brands of high-quality champagne are available to business class travellers, cabin crew are encouraged to pour drinks from whichever bottle is open unless the passenger requests a specific brand. Similarly, pots of jam, which cabin crew noticed were frequently wasted, are now provided only on request. To make sure that cabin crew can give passengers personal attention SIA flights usually carry more flight attendants than other airlines, but this is reported to add only about 5% to labour costs and, as an expense that contributes strongly to the airline's reputation for excellent customer service, allows SIA to compete on factors other than price.

SIA tries to achieve both differentiation and cost saving through its approach to innovation. The company is willing to experiment and is fast to adopt any incremental innovations that improve customer service. It was one of the first airlines to introduce fully reclining seats (slumberettes), in-flight mobile telephones, fax services and biometric technology to simplify and speed up check-in times following global health scares. However, unlike some of its rivals, it has not developed highly customized and sophisticated yield management and other back-office software, preferring instead to buy tried-and-tested applications. It has also outsourced responsibility for maintaining non-strategic hardware and software to low-cost service providers in India.

Recent challenges

While the company seems to have very successfully reconciled the apparently contradictory strategies of cost minimization and differentiation, it does face problems. The company dominates the business class market segment on many of its routes and it is this segment that is particularly sensitive to the level of economic activity. The company was badly hit by the 2008 financial crisis and in 2009 posted its first full-year loss.[3] The company responded by cutting staff, reducing working hours and reviewing its routes and schedules. By 2013, it had returned to profit and continued to exceed industry average performance.

Competition, however, remains intense, particularly in the premium air travel segment, which has been aggressively targeted by Middle Eastern airlines such as Emirates, Etihad Airways and Qatar Airways.

To avoid excessive dependence on mature markets, SIA has also entered the low-cost segment of the airline business, first by acquiring shares in Tigerair (a budget carrier serving the Asia-Pacific region) and then by launching its own budget airline, Scoot, in 2012. Scoot operates medium- and long-haul flights from Singapore to Australia and China. At present little is known about Scoot's performance but there is a danger that this low-cost subsidiary could cannibalize its parent's traditional market and dilute its yield. It remains to be seen whether the distinctive culture of the company can remain intact as SIA seeks to simultaneously operate a budget and full-service airline.

How competitive advantage emerges and is sustained

To understand how **competitive advantage** emerges, we must first understand what competitive advantage is. Most of us can recognize competitive advantage when we see it: Walmart has a competitive advantage in discount retailing within the US; Toyota has a competitive advantage in making mass-produced cars; SAP has a competitive advantage in enterprise resource planning (ERP) software; but defining competitive advantage is troublesome. At a basic level, we can define it as follows:

> When two or more firms compete within the same market, one firm possesses a competitive advantage over its rivals when it earns (or has the potential to earn) a persistently higher rate of profit.

The problem here is that if we identify competitive advantage with superior profitability, why do we need the concept of competitive advantage at all? The key difference is that competitive advantage may not be revealed in higher profitability – a firm may forgo current profit in favour of investment in market share, technology, customer loyalty or executive perks.[4] In the long run, competition eliminates differences in profitability between competing firms, but external and internal changes can create short-term opportunities for creating an advantage.

The emergence of competitive advantage

The changes that generate competitive advantage can be either external or internal. Figure 4.1 outlines the basic relationships.

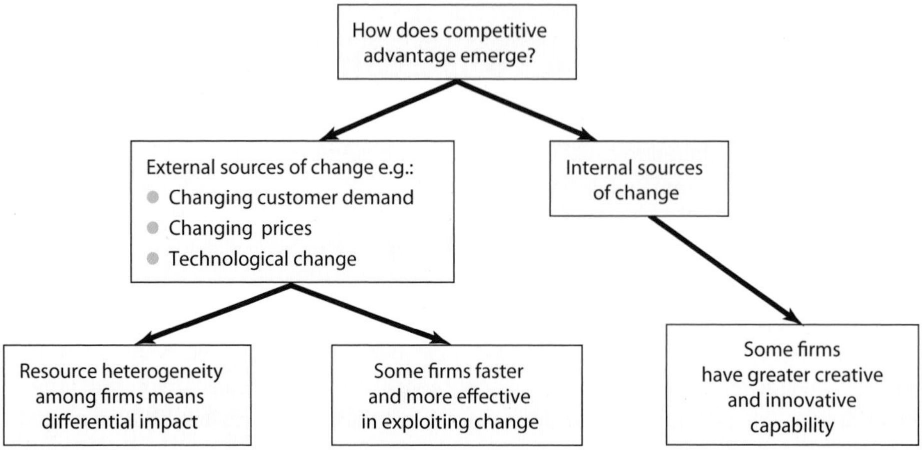

Figure 4.1 The emergence of competitive advantage.

EXTERNAL SOURCES OF CHANGE For an external change to create competitive advantage, the change must have differential effects on companies because of their different resources and capabilities or strategic positioning.

The global financial downturn of 2008/9 affected all car manufacturers but the US big three – General Motors, Ford and Chrysler – were hit harder than many of their European and Asian rivals because their market position had already been weakened by a decline in demand for their vehicles. The sales of US car producers were skewed towards sales of sports utility vehicles (SUVs) and pickup trucks that had, until the 2000s, been very popular with American consumers and offered high profit margins. In the period 2003–2008, the price of oil tripled and consumers turned away from these 'gas guzzlers' to smaller more fuel-efficient cars.[5] With fewer small cars in their product portfolios, US car manufacturers lost out to European and Asian rivals. The world financial crisis of 2008/9 hit the big three when they were already struggling with falling sales and mounting debts and pushed these firms to the edge of bankruptcy.

The extent to which external change creates competitive advantage and disadvantage depends on the magnitude of the change and the extent of firms' strategic differences. The more turbulent an industry's environment, the greater the number of sources of change, and the greater the differences in firms' resources and capabilities, the greater the dispersion of profitability within the industry. In the world tobacco industry, the external environment is fairly stable and the leading firms pursue similar strategies with similar resources and capabilities. Hence, competitive advantages, as reflected in inter-firm profit differentials, tend to be small. The toy industry, on the other hand, comprises a diverse group of firms that experience unpredictable shifts in consumer preferences and technology. As a result, profitability differences are wide and variable.

The competitive advantage that arises from external change also depends on firms' ability to respond to change. Any external change creates opportunities for profit, including opportunities for new business initiatives (what is known as entrepreneurship).

Responsiveness involves one of two key capabilities. The first is the ability to anticipate changes in the external environment. The second is speed. An unexpected rain shower creates an upsurge in the demand for umbrellas. Those street vendors who are quickest to position themselves outside a busy train station will benefit most.

As markets become more turbulent and unpredictable, so speed of response through greater flexibility has become increasingly important as a source of competitive advantage. The first requirement for quick response capability is information. As conventional economic and market forecasting has become less effective, so companies rely increasingly on 'early-warning systems' through direct relationships with customers, suppliers and even competitors. The second requirement is short cycle times that allow information on emerging market developments to be acted upon speedily.

In fashion retailing, a fast response to emerging fashion trends is critical to success. Zara, the chain of retail clothing stores owned by the Spanish company Inditex, has pioneered leading-edge fashion clothes for budget-minded young adults through a tightly integrated vertical structure that cuts the time between a garment's design and retail delivery to under three weeks (against an industry norm of three to six months).

The notion of speed as a source of competitive advantage was pioneered by the Boston Consulting Group with its concept of **time-based competition**. However, it was the advent of the Internet, real-time electronic data exchange and wireless communication that facilitated radical improvements in response capability across the business sector as a whole.

Case Insight 4.1

Singapore Airlines: Gaining or losing competitive advantage as a consequence of external change

Singapore Airlines' policy of investing in new aircraft sets it apart from many of its rivals but also means that external change affects it in different ways. By being the first company to introduce the Airbus 380 aircraft on long-haul flights, it altered its cost structure and load factors. The A380 is able to seat significantly more passengers than rival aircraft, but being a larger aircraft it consumes more fuel. The key to a profitable operation rests with the number of seats that are occupied. If the plane is full then, on a per seat kilometre basis, the aircraft is very fuel efficient; if the plane has few passengers then fuel costs per seat kilometre are high. SIA has deployed its A380s on routes where load factors are substantially higher than its network average, for example Singapore to London, and as long as passenger traffic holds up this is a cost-effective strategy. The introduction of these new aircraft therefore gives SIA an advantage over rivals with older fleets when fuel prices increase, but only if SIA can keep load factors high, meaning it is more vulnerable to falling passenger numbers on key routes.

INTERNAL SOURCES OF CHANGE: COMPETITIVE ADVANTAGE FROM INNOVATION

Competitive advantage may also be generated internally through innovation. Innovation creates competitive advantage for the innovator while undermining the competitive advantage of other firms. Although innovation is typically thought of as new products or processes that embody new technology, a key source of competitive advantage is strategic innovation: new approaches to doing business including new business models.

Strategic innovation typically involves creating value for customers from novel products, experiences or modes of product delivery. Thus, in the retail sector, competition is driven by a constant quest for new retail concepts and formats. This may take the form of: big-box stores with greater variety (Toys-R-Us, Staples, PetSmart); augmented customer service (John Lewis, Nordstrom); seamless, multichannel shopping (John Lewis, Marks and Spencer); and novel approaches to display and store layout (Sephora in cosmetics).

In other sectors too, competitive advantage typically goes to firms that have developed innovative strategies which have challenged conventional wisdom and reconceptualized the way of doing business:

- Southwest Airlines' point-to-point, no-frills airline service using a single type of plane and flexible working methods has made it not only the only consistently profitable airline in North America but also a model for budget airlines throughout the world.
- Nike built its large and successful business on a business system that totally redesigned the shoe industry's traditional value chain – notably by outsourcing manufacturing and concentrating upon design and marketing and orchestrating a vast global network of producers, logistics providers and retailers.
- Metro International is a Swedish company that publishes *Metro* newspapers – free, daily newspapers distributed to commuters in major cities. By October 2009, there were 56 daily editions in 19 countries in 15 languages across Europe, North and South America and Asia with 17 million daily readers.
- SixDegrees.com, launched in 1997, pioneered Web-based social networking, paving the way first for Myspace then Facebook.

Strategic innovations tend to involve pioneering along one or more dimensions of strategy:

- *New industries:* Some companies launch products that create a whole new market. Xerox created the plain-paper copier industry, Freddie Laker pioneered budget air travel and Craig McCaw and McCaw Communications launched the mass market for wireless telephony. For Kim and Mauborgne, creating new markets is the purest form of blue-ocean strategy – the creation of 'uncontested market space'.[6]
- *New customer segments:* Creating new customer segments for existing product concepts can also open up vast new market spaces. Apple did not invent the personal computer, but it launched the home market for computers. So too with the videocassette recorder (VCR): it was developed by Ampex for use in television studios but introduced into the home by Sony and Matsushita. The success of the Nintendo Wii video games console was based upon extending video gaming into new customer segments.
- *New sources of competitive advantage:* Most successful blue-ocean strategies do not launch whole new industries; they introduce novel approaches to creating customer value. Dell created an integrated system for ordering, assembling and distributing PCs, which permitted unprecedented customer choice and speed of fulfilment. Cirque du Soleil reinvented the circus as a multimedia entertainment spectacle.

McKinsey & Company identifies a key element of strategic innovation that it calls 'new game strategy' as it involves reconfiguring the industry value chain in order to change the 'rules of the game'.[7] (Southwest Airlines and Nike, mentioned above, are examples.) In their study of rejuvenation among mature firms, Charles Baden-Fuller and John Stopford observe that strategic innovation often involves combining performance dimensions that were previously viewed as conflicting. For example, Richardson, a UK kitchen knife producer, used an innovative design, process innovation and a lean, entrepreneurial management to supply kitchen knives that combined price competitiveness, durability, sharpness and responsive customer service.[8] However, Gary Hamel argues that firms need to go beyond strategic innovation: management innovations such as Procter & Gamble's brand management system and Toyota's lean production are likely to offer a more sustainable basis for competitive advantage.[9]

Sustaining competitive advantage

Once established, competitive advantage is eroded by competition. The speed with which competitive advantage is undermined depends on the ability of competitors to challenge either by imitation or by innovation. Imitation is the most direct form of competition; thus, for competitive advantage to be sustained over time, barriers to imitation must exist. Rumelt uses the term isolating mechanisms to describe the barriers that protect a firm's profits from being driven down by the competitive process.[10] The more effective these isolating mechanisms are, the longer competitive advantage can be sustained against the onslaught of rivals. In most industries the erosion of the competitive advantage of industry leaders is a slow process: inter-firm profit differentials often persist for a decade or more.[11] However, some commentators argue that, over time, competition in many industries has intensified and this has accelerated the erosion of profit.[12]

To identify the sources of isolating mechanisms, we need to examine the process of competitive imitation. For one firm successfully to imitate the strategy of another, it must meet four conditions:

- *Identification.* The firm must be able to identify that a rival possesses a competitive advantage.
- *Incentive.* Having identified that a rival possesses a competitive advantage (as shown by above-average profitability), the firm must believe that by investing in imitation it too can earn superior returns.
- *Diagnosis.* The firm must be able to diagnose the features of its rival's strategy that give rise to the competitive advantage.
- *Resource acquisition.* The firm must be able to acquire through transfer or replication the resources and capabilities necessary for imitating the strategy of the advantaged firm.

Figure 4.2 illustrates these stages and the types of isolating mechanism that exist at each stage.

IDENTIFICATION: OBSCURING SUPERIOR PERFORMANCE A simple barrier to imitation is to obscure the firm's superior profitability. According to George Stalk of the Boston Consulting Group, 'one way to throw competitors off balance is to mask high performance so rivals fail

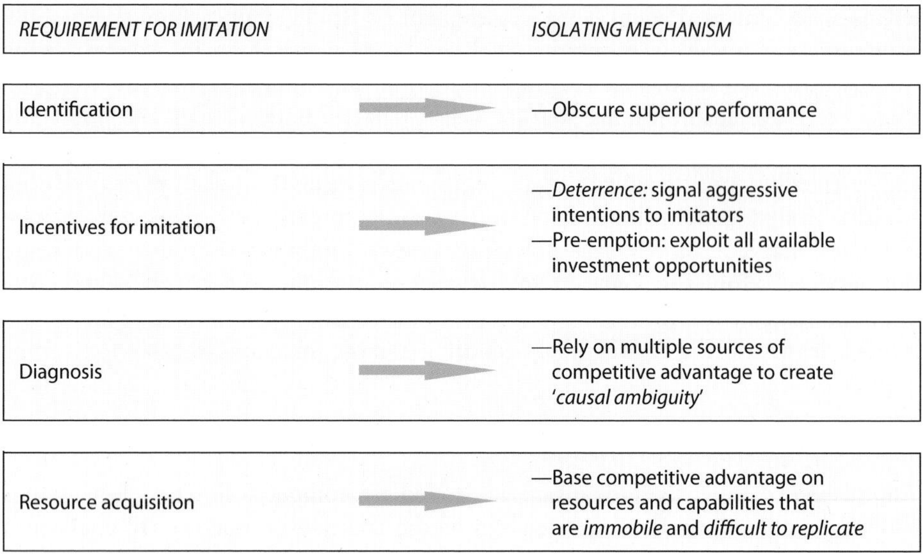

Figure 4.2 Sustaining competitive advantage: Types of isolating mechanism.

to see your success until it's too late'.[13] For example, in the 1948 movie classic *The Treasure of the Sierra Madre*, Humphrey Bogart and his partners went to great lengths to obscure their find from other gold prospectors.[14]

For firms that dominate a niche market, one of the attractions of remaining a private company is to avoid disclosing financial performance. Few food processors realized just how profitable cat and dog food could be until the UK Monopolies Commission revealed that the leading firm, Pedigree Petfoods (a subsidiary of Mars Inc.), earned a return on capital employed of 47%.[15]

The desire to avoid competition may be so strong as to cause companies to forgo short-run profits. The theory of limit pricing, in its simplest form, postulates that a firm in a strong market position sets prices at a level that just fails to attract entrants.[16]

DETERRENCE AND PRE-EMPTION A firm may avoid competition by undermining the incentives for imitation. If a firm can persuade rivals that imitation will be unprofitable, it may be able to avoid competitive challenges.

Reputation is critically important in making threats credible. Brandenburger and Nalebuff argue that in the aspartame market, NutraSweet's aggressive price war against the Holland Sweetener Company deterred other would-be entrants.[17]

A firm can also deter imitation by pre-emption: occupying existing and potential strategic niches to reduce the range of investment opportunities open to the challenger. Pre-emption can take many forms:

- Proliferation of product varieties by a market leader can leave new entrants and smaller rivals with few opportunities for establishing a market niche. Between 1950 and 1972, for example, the six leading suppliers of breakfast cereals introduced 80 new brands into the US market.[18]

- Large investments in production capacity ahead of the growth of market demand also pre-empt market opportunities for rivals. Monsanto's heavy investment in plants for producing NutraSweet ahead of its patent expiration was a clear threat to would-be producers of generic aspartame.
- Patent proliferation can protect technology-based advantage by limiting competitors' technical opportunities. In 1974, Xerox's dominant market position was protected by a wall of over 2000 patents, most of which were not used. When IBM introduced its first copier in 1970, Xerox sued it for infringing 22 of these patents.[19]

The ability to sustain competitive advantage through pre-emption depends on the presence of two flaws in the competitive process. First, the market must be small relative to the minimum efficient scale of production, such that only a very small number of competitors is viable. Second, there must be first-mover advantage that gives an incumbent preferential access to information and other resources, putting rivals at a disadvantage.

DIAGNOSING COMPETITIVE ADVANTAGE: 'CAUSAL AMBIGUITY' AND 'UNCERTAIN IMITABILITY' If a firm is to imitate the competitive advantage of another, it must understand the basis of its rival's success. In most industries, there is a serious identification problem in linking superior performance to the strategic decisions that generate that performance. Consider the remarkable success of Walmart in discount retailing which we explored in Chapter 3. For Walmart's struggling competitor, Sears Holdings (owner of the Kmart chain of discount stores), it is easy to point to the differences between Walmart and itself. As one Walmart executive commented: 'Retailing is an open book. There are no secrets. Our competitors can walk into our stores and see what we sell, how we sell it, and for how much.' The difficult task is to identify which differences are the critical determinants of superior profitability. Is it Walmart's store locations? Its tightly integrated supply chain? Its unique management system? The information and communication systems that supports Walmart's logistics and decision-making practices? Or is it a culture built on traditional rural American values of thrift and hard work?

Lippman and Rumelt identify this problem as **causal ambiguity**.[20] The more multidimensional a firm's competitive advantage and the more it is based on complex bundles of organizational capabilities, the more difficult it is for a competitor to diagnose the determinants of success. The outcome of causal ambiguity is **uncertain imitability**: where there is ambiguity associated with the causes of a competitor's success, any attempt to imitate that strategy is subject to uncertain success.

Research suggests that the problems of strategy imitation may run even deeper. Capabilities are the outcome of complex combinations of resources and different capabilities that interact together to confer competitive advantage. Work on complementarities among firms' activities suggests that these interactions extend across the whole range of management activities.[21] Porter and Siggelkow quote Urban Outfitters as an example of a unique 'activity system' (see Featured Example 4.1).[22] If company success is the outcome of a complex configuration of strategy, structure, management systems, personal leadership and a host of business processes, the implication is that imitation may well be impossible.

Featured Example 4.1

Urban Outfitters

During the three years to January 2009, Urban Outfitters, Inc., which comprises 130 Urban Outfitters stores (together with the Anthropologie and Free People chains) has grown at an average of 20% annually and earned a return on equity of 21%. The company describes itself as: 'targeting well-educated, urban-minded, young adults aged 18 to 30 through its unique merchandise mix and compelling store environment ... We create a unified environment in our stores that establishes an emotional bond with the customer. Every element of the environment is tailored to the aesthetic preferences of our target customers. Through creative design, much of the existing retail space is modified to incorporate a mosaic of fixtures, finishes and revealed architectural details. In our stores, merchandise is integrated into a variety of creative vignettes and displays designed to offer our customers an entire look at a distinct lifestyle.'

According to Porter and Siggelkow, Urban Outfitters offers a set of management practices that are both distinctive and highly interdependent. The urban-bohemian-styled product mix, which includes clothing, furnishings and gift items, is displayed within bazaar-like stores each of which has a unique design. To encourage frequent customer visits, the layout of each store is changed every two weeks, creating a new shopping experience whenever customers return. Emphasizing community with its customers, it forgoes traditional forms of advertising in favour of blogs and word-of-mouth transmission. Each practice makes little sense on its own, but together they represent a distinctive, integrated strategy. Attempts to imitate Urban Outfitters' competitive advantage would most likely fail because of the difficulty of replicating every aspect of the strategy then integrating them in the right manner.

Sources: Urban Outfitters Inc. 10-K Report to January 31, 2009 (Washington: SEC, 2008); M. E. Porter and N. Siggelkow, 'Contextuality within activity systems and sustainable competitive advantage', *Academy of Management Perspectives* **22** (May 2008): 34–56.

One of the challenges for the would-be imitator is deciding which management practices are generic best practices and which are 'contextual' (i.e. complementary with other management practices). For example, if we consider Sears Holdings' deliberation of which of Walmart's management practices to imitate in its Kmart stores, some practices (e.g. employees required to smile at customers, point-of-sale data transferred direct into the corporate database) are likely to be generically beneficial. Others – such as Walmart's 'everyday low prices' pricing policy, low advertising sales ratio and hub-and-spoke distribution – are likely to be beneficial only when combined with other practices.[23]

ACQUIRING RESOURCES AND CAPABILITIES Having diagnosed the sources of an incumbent's competitive advantage, the imitator can mount a competitive challenge only by assembling the resources and capabilities necessary for imitation. As we saw in Chapter 3, a firm can acquire resources and capabilities in two ways: it can buy them or it can build them. The period over which a competitive advantage can be sustained depends critically on the time it takes to acquire and mobilize the resources and capabilities needed to mount a competitive challenge. The imitation barriers here are limits to transferability and replicability of resources and capabilities that we discussed earlier (Chapter 3).

Case Insight 4.2

Is Singapore Airlines' competitive advantage sustainable?

In the opening case to this chapter, we argued that SIA has outperformed its rivals by referring to the number of awards it has achieved and the fact that it has consistently achieved returns that are in excess of the industry average. Its success has been based on its systematic design and development of a cost-effective approach to service excellence, supported by investments in its fleet, customer-focused innovation and staff training and development. But how sustainable is SIA's advantage? Can its approach be identified and replicated easily by competitors?

It would appear relatively straightforward for other airlines to unpick SIA's strategy – indeed, we have attempted to do that in our analysis – and they too can invest in new aircraft, staff training, new ticketing and check-in technologies and so on. What is much more difficult to identify and copy is the culture of cost-effective service excellence ingrained in the company and its people and the complex sets of linkages between SIA's different activities that create a virtuous circle of improvement. SIA's 'profit conscious' approach is made explicit in its vision statement (to be the most profitable rather than the largest airline), is evident in the way staff are rewarded and trained and is reinforced by its emphasis on feedback and benchmarking. Cabin crew members work together for significant periods of time and form closely knit teams, experienced staff deliver in-house staff training and the giving and receiving of feedback is encouraged – all of which creates a climate where there is peer pressure to perform. When these linked activities are combined with investment in a modern fleet and the infrastructure of its hub airport, Changi in Singapore, and put together with a successful track record of implementing customer-focused innovation, the whole becomes greater than the sum of the parts and much more difficult for competitors to imitate.

A key issue for would-be imitators is the extent to which **first-mover advantage** exists within the market. The idea of first-mover advantage is that the initial occupant of a strategic position or niche gains access to resources and capabilities that a follower cannot match. This is because the first mover is able to pre-empt the best resources or can use early entry to build superior resources and capabilities.[24] We shall return to the issue of first-mover advantage when we consider competitive advantage in technology-based industries in Chapter 6.

Types of competitive advantage: Cost and differentiation

A firm can achieve a higher rate of profit (or potential profit) over a rival in one of two ways: either it can supply an identical product or service at a lower cost or it can supply a product or service that is differentiated in such a way that the customer is willing to pay a price premium that exceeds the additional cost of the differentiation. In the former case, the firm possesses a **cost advantage**; in the latter, a **differentiation advantage**. In pursuing cost advantage, the goal

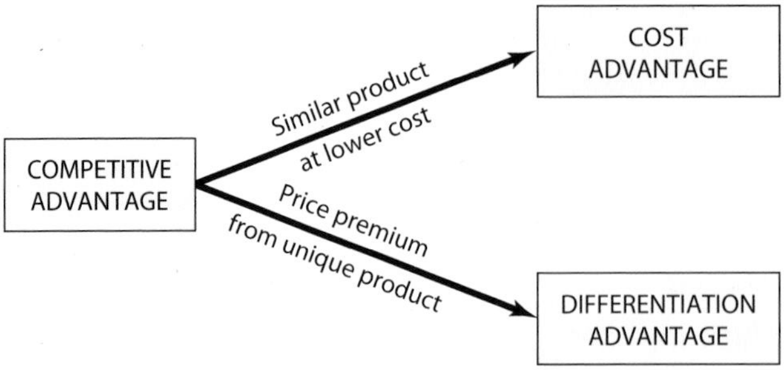

Figure 4.3 Sources of competitive advantage.

of the firm is to become the cost leader in its industry or industry segment. Cost leadership requires that the firm 'must find and exploit all sources of cost advantage [and] sell a standard, no-frills product'.[25] Differentiation by a firm from its competitors is achieved 'when it provides something unique that is valuable to buyers beyond simply offering a low price'.[26] Figure 4.3 illustrates these two types of advantage.

The two sources of competitive advantage define two fundamentally different approaches to business strategy. A firm that is competing on low cost is distinguishable from a firm that competes through differentiation in terms of market positioning, resources and capabilities, and organizational characteristics. Table 4.2 outlines some of the principal features of cost and differentiation strategies.

Strategy and cost advantage

There are seven principal determinants of a firm's unit costs (cost per unit of output) relative to its competitors; we refer to these as **cost drivers** (Figure 4.4).

The relative importance of these different cost drivers varies across industries, across firms within an industry and across the different activities within a firm. By examining each of these different cost drivers, in relation to a particular firm, we can analyse a firm's cost position

Table 4.2 Features of cost leadership and differentiation strategies.

Generic strategy	Key strategy elements	Resource and organizational requirements
Cost leadership	Scale-efficient plants Design for manufacture Control of overheads and R & D Process innovation Outsourcing (especially overseas) Avoidance of marginal customer accounts	Access to capital Process engineering skills Frequent reports Tight cost control Specialization of jobs and functions Incentives linked to quantitative targets
Differentiation	Emphasis on branding, advertising, design, service, quality and new product development	Marketing abilities Product engineering skills Cross-functional coordination Creativity Research capability Incentives linked to qualitative performance targets

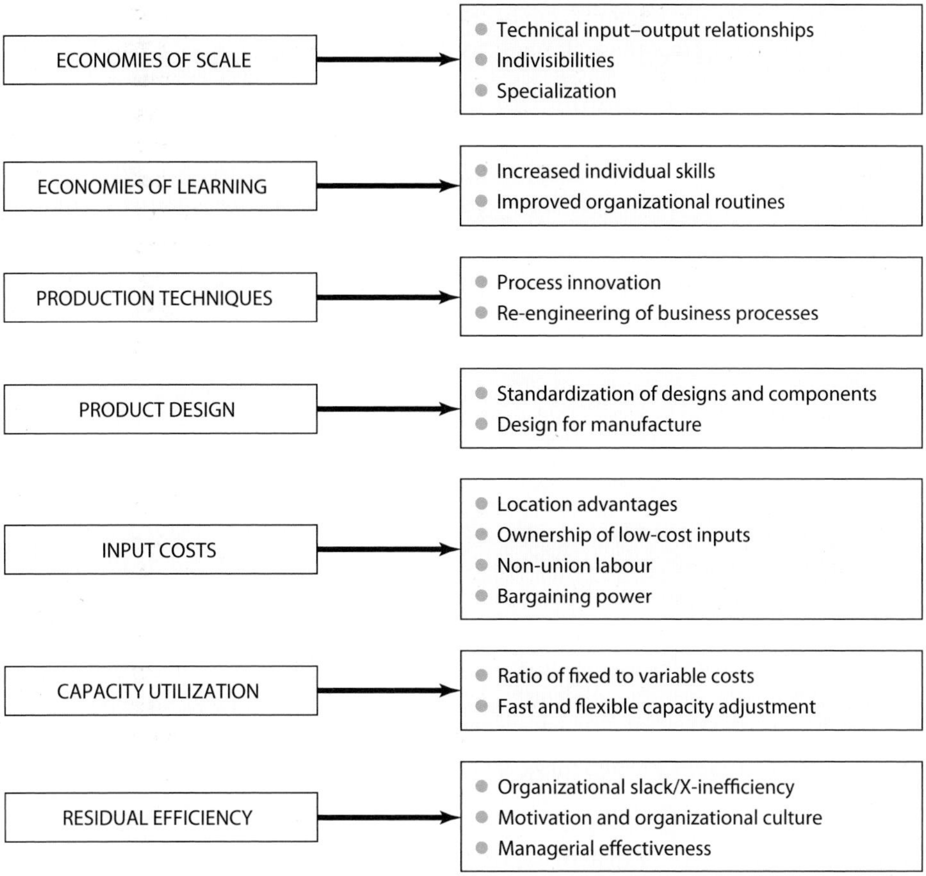

Figure 4.4 The drivers of cost advantage.

relative to its competitors and diagnose the sources of inefficiency and make recommendations as to how a firm can improve its cost efficiency.

The value chain is a useful framework with which to undertake this analysis. As we saw in Chapter 3, every business may be viewed as a chain of activities. Analysing costs requires breaking down the firm's value chain to identify:

- the relative importance of each activity with respect to total cost;
- the cost drivers for each activity and the comparative efficiency with which the firm performs each activity;
- how costs in one activity influence costs in another;
- which activities should be undertaken within the firm and which activities should be outsourced.

PRINCIPAL STAGES OF VALUE CHAIN ANALYSIS FOR COST ADVANTAGE To analyse a firm's cost position, we need to look at individual activities. Each activity tends to be subject to a different set of cost drivers, which give it a distinct cost structure. A value chain analysis of a firm's cost position comprises the following six stages:

1 *Break down the firm into separate activities.* Determining the appropriate value chain activities is a matter of judgement. It requires understanding the chain of processes involved in the transformation of inputs into output and its delivery to the customer. Very often, the firm's own divisional and departmental structure is a useful guide. Key considerations are:

   a the separateness of one activity from another;

   b the importance of an activity;

   c the dissimilarity of activities in terms of cost drivers;

   d the extent to which there are differences in the way competitors perform the particular activity.

2 *Establish the relative importance of different activities in the total cost of the product.* Our analysis needs to focus on the activities that are the major sources of cost. In separating costs, Michael Porter suggests the detailed assignment of operating costs and assets to each value activity. Though the adoption of activity-based costing has made such cost data more available, detailed cost allocation can be a major exercise.[27] Even without such detailed cost data, it is usually possible to identify the critical activities, establish which activities are performed relatively efficiently or inefficiently, identify cost drivers and offer recommendations.

3 *Compare costs by activity.* To establish which activities the firm performs relatively efficiently and which it does not, benchmark unit costs for each activity against those of competitors.

4 *Identify cost drivers.* For each activity, what factors determine the level of cost relative to other firms? For some activities, cost drivers are evident simply from the nature of the activity and the composition of costs. For capital-intensive activities, such as the operation of a body press in a car plant, the principal factors are likely to be capital equipment costs, weekly production volume and downtime between changes of dyes. For labour-intensive assembly activities, critical issues are wage rates, speed of work and defect rates.

5 *Identify linkages.* The costs of one activity may be determined, in part, by the way in which other activities are performed. Xerox discovered that its high service costs relative to competitors' reflected the complexity of design of its copiers, which required 30 different interrelated adjustments.

6 *Identify opportunities for reducing costs.* By identifying areas of comparative inefficiency and the cost drivers for each, opportunities for cost reduction become evident. For example:

   a If scale economies are a key cost driver, can volume be increased? One feature of Caterpillar's cost-reduction strategy was to broaden its model range and begin selling diesel engines to other vehicle manufacturers in order to expand its sales base.

   b Where wage costs are the issue, can wages be reduced either directly or by relocating production?

   c If a certain activity cannot be performed efficiently within the firm, can it be outsourced?

Case Insight 4.3

Using the value chain to explore Singapore Airlines' cost-saving initiatives and opportunities

Porter's category	Illustrative examples of airline activity fitting Porter's categories	Illustrative cost-saving opportunities and initiatives
Inbound logistics	Aircraft, fuel, food and drink	Young fleet – the lower average age of SIA's aircraft offers greater fuel efficiency and reduces maintenance costs. Staff are trained to reduce food and drink wastage
Operations	Airport and gate operations, ticketing, flight scheduling, baggage handling, repair and maintenance	SIA endeavours to reduce costs through improving efficiency and adopting best practices[28]
Outbound logistics	Flight connections Partnerships and alliances with other operators	Routes are constantly being added and subtracted from the company's route map to optimize load factors
Marketing and sales	Promotion, advertising	The company's success in achieving awards provides free publicity and promotes the company and its brand
Service	Pre- and post-flight service	Online booking of meals and seats allows better forward planning Social media is a low-cost means to build ties with customers
Firm infrastructure	Management systems – yield management, IT services, budgeting, etc.	Small headquarters in low-cost location
Human resources management	Recruitment and reward Training	Training is in-house by senior cabin crew rather than third parties Training emphasizes both attentive service and 'waste control' – no cost saving considered too small Employees incentivized by profit sharing, which attracts high-calibre employees despite non-premium compensation
Technology development	IT systems	Non-strategic IT services outsourced Tried-and-tested software systems bought 'off the shelf' in preference to customized applications
Procurement	Acquisition of aircraft and other inputs	A culture of hard bargaining for anything from aircraft to the negotiation of hotel rates for crew member stays when overseas

Strategy and differentiation advantage

A firm differentiates itself from its competitors when it provides something unique that is valuable to buyers beyond simply offering a low price. Differentiation advantage occurs when a firm is able to obtain from its differentiation a price premium in the market that exceeds the cost of providing the differentiation.

Every firm has opportunities for differentiating its offering to customers, although the range of differentiation opportunities depends on the characteristics of the product. A car or a restaurant offers greater potential for differentiation than cement, wheat or memory chips. These latter products are called 'commodities' precisely because they lack physical differentiation. Yet, even commodity products can be differentiated in ways that create customer value: 'Anything can be turned into a value-added product or service for a well-defined or newly created market,' claims Tom Peters.[29] Consider the following:

- Cement is the ultimate commodity product, yet Cemex, the Mexican-based supplier of cement and ready-mix concrete, has established itself as the world's biggest supplier using a strategy that emphasizes 'building solutions'. One component of this strategy is ensuring that 98% of its deliveries are on time (compared to 34% for the industry as a whole).[30]
- Online bookselling is inherently a commodity business – any online bookseller has access to the same titles and the same modes of distribution. Yet, Amazon has exploited the information generated by the business to offer a range of value-adding services: best-seller lists, reviews and customized recommendations.

The lesson is this: differentiation is not simply about offering different product features; it is about identifying and understanding every possible interaction between the firm and its customers, and asking how these interactions can be enhanced or changed in order to deliver additional value to the customer.

Analysing differentiation requires looking at both the firm (the supply side) and its customers (the demand side). While supply-side analysis identifies the firm's potential to create uniqueness, the critical issue is whether such differentiation creates value for customers and whether the value created exceeds the cost of the differentiation.

PRINCIPAL STAGES OF VALUE CHAIN ANALYSIS FOR DIFFERENTIATION ADVANTAGE In much the same way as we used the value chain to analyse the potential for a firm to gain a cost advantage relative to its rivals so we can use this framework to analyse opportunities for differentiation advantage. This involves four principal stages:

1. *Construct a value chain for the firm and the customer.* It may be useful to consider not just the immediate customer but also firms further downstream in the value chain. If the firm supplies different types of customers – for example, a steel company may supply steel strip to car manufacturers and white goods producers – draw separate value chains for each of the main categories of customer.
2. *Identify the drivers of uniqueness in each activity.* Assess the firm's potential for differentiating its product by examining each activity in the firm's value chain and identifying the variables and actions through which the firm can achieve uniqueness in

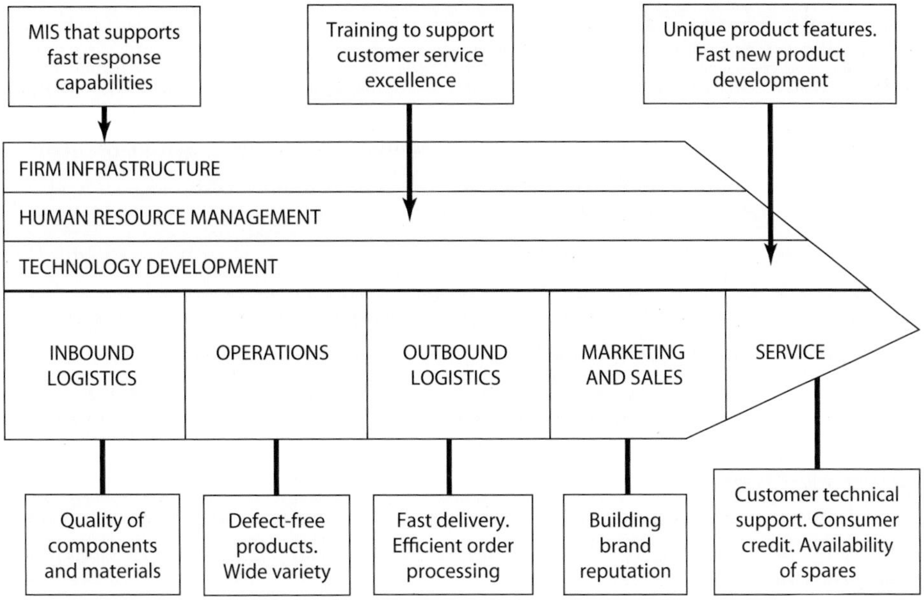

Figure 4.5 Using the value chain to identify differentiation potential on the supply side.

relation to competitors' offerings. Figure 4.5 identifies some illustrative sources of differentiation within Porter's generic value chain.

3 *Select the most promising differentiation variables for the firm.* Among the numerous drivers of uniqueness that we can identify within the firm, which one should be selected as the primary basis for the firm's differentiation strategy? On the supply side, there are three important considerations:

   a First, we must establish where the firm has greater potential for differentiating from, or can differentiate at lower cost than, rivals. This requires some analysis of the firm's internal strengths in terms of resources and capabilities.

   b Second, to identify the most promising aspects of differentiation, we also need to identify linkages among activities, since some differentiation variables may involve interaction among several activities. Thus, product reliability is likely to be the outcome of several linked activities: monitoring purchases of inputs from suppliers, the skill and motivation of production workers, and quality control and product testing.

   c Third, the ease with which different types of uniqueness can be sustained must be considered. The more differentiation is based on resources specific to the firm or skills that involve the complex coordination of a large number of individuals, the more difficult it will be for a competitor to imitate the particular source of differentiation. Thus, offering business class passengers wider seats and more legroom is an easily imitated source of differentiation. Achieving high levels of punctuality represents a more sustainable source of differentiation.

4 *Locate linkages between the value chain of the firm and that of the buyer.* The objective of differentiation is to yield a price premium for the firm. This requires the firm's differentiation to create value for the customer. Creating value for customers requires either that the firm lowers customers' costs or that customers' own product differentiation is facilitated. Thus, by reorganizing its product distribution around quick response technologies, Procter & Gamble has radically reduced distribution time and increased delivery reliability. This permits retailers to reduce costs of inventory while simultaneously increasing their reliability to shoppers through lowering the risk of stockouts. To identify the means by which a firm can create value for its customers, it must locate the linkages between differentiation of its own activities and cost reduction and differentiation within the customer's activities. Analysis of these linkages can also evaluate the potential profitability of differentiation. The value differentiation created for the customer represents the maximum price premium the customer will pay. If the provision of just-in-time delivery by a component supplier costs an additional €1000 a month but saves a car company €6000 a month in reduced inventory, warehousing and handling costs then it should be possible for the component manufacturer to obtain a price premium that easily exceeds the costs of the differentiation.

Featured Example 4.2

Adidas

Adidas, the German sportswear firm (named after its founder Adi Dassler), faces stiff competition from Nike, Puma, Reebok, Fila, New Balance and many others. Whereas Nike, the market leader, has promoted its brand through celebrity endorsements and big marketing campaigns, Adidas has chosen an altogether softer approach. For over a decade it has worked closely with ReD, a small Danish consultancy company founded by Mikkel Rasmussen. ReD takes a slightly unconventional approach. It hires ex-academics, largely anthropologists and ethnologists, to undertake detailed studies of customer motivation and feeds this information back to its clients. In the case of Adidas, for example, ReD put a group of the company's design staff through training in basic research techniques and then sent each of them to spend 24 hours with a customer to find out what motivated them to exercise. Adidas, like most other sportswear firms, had assumed that the majority of their customers were training to be good at specific sports, but the research revealed that fitness itself was the goal. This insight changed the way the designers approached their task. Similarly, ReD researchers spent several weeks with footballers at Bayern Munich football club to try to understand the players' perceptions of the key factors determining a footballer's success on the pitch. They discovered that while top European football clubs were excellent in teaching football skills the one critical thing they couldn't teach was speed. Adidas used this information to adapt one of its running shoes into a very light football boot that was an immediate hit. In an industry characterized by tight margins and intense competition, Adidas has managed to stay in profit and grow steadily by taking a different approach.

Case Insight 4.4

Using the value chain to explore Singapore Airlines' differentiation opportunities and initiatives

Porter's generic categories	Illustrative examples of airline activity fitting Porter's categories	Illustrative examples of differentiation opportunities and initiatives
Inbound logistics	Aircraft fuel Food and drink	Young fleet means a greater % of arrivals and departures are on time Food and drink customized to individuals' preferences through use of online booking system
Operations	Airport and gate operations Ticketing flight scheduling Baggage handling	SIA employs more cabin crew than other airlines so that more personal attention can be given to customers in-flight
Outbound logistics	Flight connections Partnerships and alliances with other operators	Changi airport regularly wins awards as the world's best airport and is an important hub for the Asia-Pacific region SIA is part of the Star Alliance
Marketing and Sales	Sales promotions Advertising	Use of customer relationship management (CRM) system in conjunction with training of cabin crew to personalize passengers' in-flight experience Publicity from winning awards
Service	Pre- and post-flight service	Loyalty marketing
Firm infrastructure	Management systems – yield management, IT services, budgeting, etc.	The constant reinforcement of a culture of customer service
Human resource management	Recruitment and reward Training	The company attracts first-class university students who like the idea of working for a leading local company The company invests heavily in training and enhancement of staff skills
Technology development	IT systems	SIA has invested in those technologies that improve the customer experience, for example after the scares over the SARS epidemic, SIA invested in biometric technology to speed up check-in
Procurement	Acquisition of aircraft	Has pioneered the introduction of brand-new aircraft, like the Airbus A380, to its fleet and has used this to generate publicity and to enhance its reputation as a leading airline Continues to invest heavily in cabin products such as in-flight entertainment and Internet connectivity

The aim of the analysis is not merely to identify and classify different elements of SIA's overall differentiation strategy but to spot where opportunities exist for further differentiation and to reinforce linkages between different parts of the value chain. For example, allowing passengers to state their preferences through online booking of meals when combined with judicious use of the CRM system and careful training of staff allows the airline to both 'personalize' and 'standardize' customer service.

Porter's generic strategies and being 'stuck in the middle'

By combining the two types of competitive advantage with the firm's choice of scope – broad market versus narrow segment – Michael Porter has defined three generic strategies: cost leadership, differentiation and focus (Figure 4.6). Porter views cost leadership and differentiation as mutually exclusive strategies. A firm that attempts to pursue both is 'stuck in the middle':

> The firm stuck in the middle is almost guaranteed low profitability. It either loses the high-volume customers who demand low prices or must bid away its profits to get this business from the low-cost firms. Yet it also loses high-margin business – the cream – to the firms who are focused on high-margin targets or have achieved differentiation overall. The firm that is stuck in the middle also probably suffers from a blurred corporate culture and a conflicting set of organisational arrangements and motivation system.[31]

In practice, few firms are faced with such stark alternatives. Differentiation is not simply an issue of 'to differentiate or not to differentiate'. All firms must make decisions as to which customer requirements to focus on, and where to position their product or service in the market. A cost leadership strategy typically implies a narrow-line, limited-feature, standardized offering. However, such a positioning does not necessarily imply that the product or service is an undifferentiated commodity. In the case of IKEA furniture and Southwest Airlines, a low-price, no-frills offering is also associated with clear market positioning and a unique brand image. The VW Beetle shows that a low-cost, utilitarian, mass-market product can achieve cult status. At the same time, firms that pursue differentiation strategies cannot be oblivious to cost.

In most industries, market leadership is held by firms that maximize customer appeal by reconciling effective differentiation with low cost – Toyota in cars, McDonald's in fast food, Nike in athletic shoes. Cost leaders are frequently not market leaders but smaller competitors with minimal overheads, non-union labour and cheaply acquired assets. In oil refining, the cost leaders tend to be independent refining companies rather than integrated giants such as ExxonMobil or Shell. In car rental, the cost leader is more likely to be Rent-A-Wreck (a division of Bundy American Corporation) rather than Hertz or Avis. Simultaneously pursuing differentiation, cost efficiency and innovation was a key element in the global success of Japanese companies in cars, motorcycles, consumer electronics and musical instruments. Reconciling different performance dimensions has been facilitated by new management techniques. For example, total quality management has refuted the perceived trade-off between quality and cost.

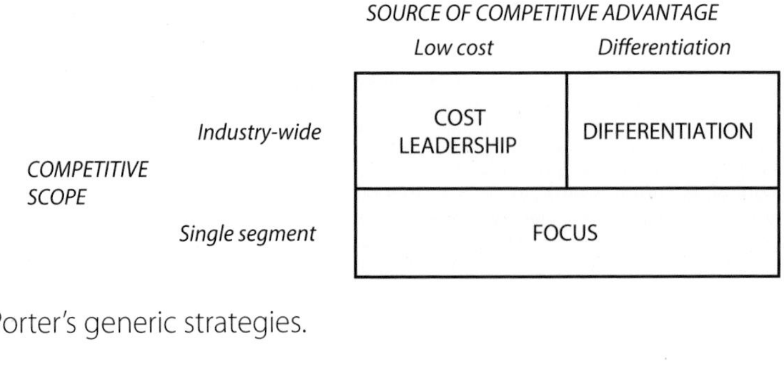

Figure 4.6 Porter's generic strategies.

Case Insight 4.5

Singapore Airlines: Reconciling differentiation with low costs

Porter argues that it is impossible for a firm to sustain cost leadership and differentiation over a sustained period of time without becoming 'stuck in the middle'.[32]

He bases this claim on the fact that such strategies usually entail contradictory investments, different organizational processes and different organizational mindsets. The SIA case illustrates that many companies do not face such stark alternatives and that, by developing appropriate cultures, thinking creatively and strategically about investment decisions and paying attention to the details, the best-performing companies often manage to reconcile what at first sight appear to be contradictory strategies. For example, by allowing customers to state their food preferences in advance the airline offers a personalized service while at the same time eliminating waste. By speeding up the check-in process, the airline enhances the travel experience of its passengers but also improves punctuality and reduces the costs incurred by delays.

Summary

Making money in business requires establishing and sustaining competitive advantage. Both these conditions for profitability demand profound insight into the nature and process of competition within a market. Competitive advantage depends critically on the presence of some faults in the competitive process – under perfect competition, profits are transitory. Our analysis of the imperfections of the competitive process has drawn us back to the resources and capabilities that are required to compete in different markets and to pursue different strategies. Sustaining competitive advantage depends on the existence of isolating mechanisms: barriers to rivals' imitation of successful strategies. The greater the difficulty that rivals face in accessing the resources and capabilities needed to imitate or substitute the competitive advantage of the incumbent firm, the greater the sustainability of that firm's competitive advantage. Hence, one outcome of our analysis is to reinforce the argument made in Chapter 3: the characteristics of a firm's resources and capability are fundamental to its strategy and its performance in decision making and long-term success.

Summary table

Learning Objectives	Summary
Understand the meaning of the term 'competitive advantage' and identify the circumstances in which a firm can create a competitive advantage over a rival	When two or more firms compete within the same market, one firm possesses a competitive advantage over its rivals when it earns (or has the potential to earn) a persistently higher rate of profit. Firms can create a competitive advantage when some kind of imperfection exists in the competitive process
Predict the potential for competition to wear away competitive advantage through imitation	In the long run competition wears away differences in profitability between firms but external and internal change can both create opportunities for advantage and destroy them
Recognize how resource conditions create imperfections in the competitive process that offer opportunities for competitive advantage	Owning resources or having capabilities that are in some way unique offers the firm some protection against imitation by rivals
Distinguish the two primary types of competitive advantage: cost advantage and differentiation advantage	A firm can achieve competitive advantage either by supplying an identical product or service at a lower cost or by supplying a product or service that is differentiated in such a way that the customer is willing to pay a premium price. Differentiation has some attraction over low cost as a basis for competitive advantage because it is less vulnerable to being overturned by changes in the external environment and is often more difficult to replicate
Identify potential sources of cost and differentiation advantage and recommend strategies to enhance competitiveness	The value chain views the firm as a series of linked activities and is an insightful tool for understanding sources of competitive advantage in an industry and for assessing the competitive position of a particular firm
Appreciate the pitfalls of being 'stuck in the middle' and the challenge of achieving effective differentiation and low cost	According to Porter, cost leadership and differentiation are mutually exclusive strategies and firms that are 'stuck in the middle' are almost guaranteed low profitability. Most firms do not face such stark alternatives. The most successful firms are often those who have managed to differentiate themselves in a highly cost-effective manner

Further reading

Jay Barney has developed a popular framework (VRIO) for analysing internal capabilities and the sustainability of competitive advantage, which is outlined in his article:

Barney, J. B. (1991). Firm resources and sustained competitive advantage. *Journal of Management*, 17(1), 99–120.

Michael Porter's original work is well worth reading as he provides a clear exposition of his basic arguments, particularly in Chapter 2, where he outlines his notion of generic strategies and the concept of being 'stuck in the middle'.

Porter, M. (1980). *Competitive Strategy: Techniques for Analysing Industries and Competitors*. New York: Free Press.

The article by Cronshaw *et al.*, while now rather dated in terms of its examples, nonetheless provides a nice critique of the concept of 'being stuck in the middle' and the problems of interpreting some of Porter's terminology.

Cronshaw, M., Evans, D. and Kay, J. (1994). On being stuck in the middle: Or good food costs less at Sainsbury's. *British Journal of Management*, 5(1), 19–32.

Heracleous and Jochen Wirtz have produced two articles that provide excellent detailed accounts of Singapore Airlines' strategy and organization. They are:

Heracleous, L. and Wirtz, J. (2009). Strategy and organization at Singapore Airlines: Achieving sustainable advantage through dual strategy. *Journal of Air Transport Management*, 15, 274–9.

Heracleous, L. and Wirtz, J. (2010). Singapore Airlines' balancing act. *Harvard Business Review*, July–August, 145–9.

Self-study questions

1. Explain the challenges Singapore Airlines faces in operating both a budget and a full-service airline?
2. Consider the implications for a business school of adopting a cost leadership strategy. How would a business school implementing a cost-leadership strategy differ from a business school pursuing a differentiation strategy in terms of its market position, resources and capabilities and organizational characteristics?
3. Apple has been highly successful in dominating the market for touch-screen tablet computers with its iPad product. Can Apple sustain its leadership in this market? If so, how?
4. Illy, the Italian-based supplier of quality coffee and coffee-making equipment, is launching an international chain of gourmet coffee shops. What advice would you offer Illy for how it can best build competitive advantage in the face of Starbucks' market leadership?
5. Target (the US discount retailer), H&M (the Swedish fashion clothing chain) and Primark (the UK discount clothing chain) have pioneered 'cheap chic' – combining discount store prices with fashion appeal. What are the principal challenges of designing and implementing a 'cheap chic' strategy? Design a 'cheap chic' strategy for a company entering another market (e.g. restaurants, sports shoes, cosmetics or office furniture).

Closing Case

Starbucks Corporation

Coffee drinking became popular in the Middle East and North Africa during the 16th century and spread to Europe in the 17th century with the opening of coffee houses in Venice, London, Paris and Amsterdam. By the early 20th century, coffee had become the most popular everyday beverage in continental Europe and throughout the Americas. The introduction of instant coffee in the 1950s further expanded the mass market for coffee. The fact that coffee drinking had been an established feature of Western culture for almost 500 years made it all the more remarkable that an appliance salesman from Brooklyn, New York could create a global chain of 21 000 coffee houses with a stock market value of $52 billion.

The rise of Starbucks: Wake up and smell the coffee

When Howard Schultz visited the Starbucks coffee store in Pike Place Market, Seattle, the coffee he sampled was a revelation. He joined the company in 1982 and, after a vacation in Italy, became convinced of the potential of Starbucks to sell brewed coffee as well as coffee beans in an effort to recreate the Italian coffee-drinking experience: 'I saw something. Not only the romance of coffee, but … a sense of community. And the connection that people had to coffee – the place and one another.'[33] The owners of Starbucks were not convinced, so Schultz left to set up his own coffee house. Later, when the opportunity arose, Schultz acquired the original Starbucks business and began its transformation and expansion.

Schultz's vision for Starbucks was based not just on serving superior coffee but also on creating an entire experience in which Starbucks coffee houses represented a 'third place' – somewhere other than home and work where people could engage socially while enjoying the shared experience of drinking good coffee. The strategy comprised several elements:

- Acquiring coffee beans of a high, consistent quality and carefully managing the chain of activities that resulted in their transformation into the best possible espresso coffee. 'We're passionate about ethically sourcing the finest coffee beans, roasting them with great care, and improving the lives of the people who grow them.'[34] Starbucks partnered with growers in order to promote best practice in coffee cultivation.

- Employee involvement. The counter staff at Starbucks stores – the baristas – were central in creating and sustaining the Starbucks Experience. Their role was not only to brew and serve coffee but also to engage customers in the unique ambiance of the Starbucks coffee shop. Starbucks' human resource practices were based upon a distinctive view of the company's relationship with its employees. If Starbucks was to engage customers in an experience which extended beyond the provision of good coffee, it was going to have to employ the right store employees who would be the critical providers of this experience. This required employees who were committed and enthusiastic communicators of the principles and values of Starbucks. This in turn required the company to regard its employees as business partners. Human resource practices aimed to attract and recruit people whose attitudes and personalities were consistent with the culture of the company and to foster trust, loyalty and a sense of belonging that would allow them to project that culture. Starbucks' employees were selected for their adaptability, dependability, capacity for teamwork and willingness to further Starbucks' principles and mission. Training extended beyond basic operational and customer-service skills and placed particular emphasis on educating employees about coffee. Unique among catering chains, Starbucks provided health insurance for almost all regular employees, including part-timers.

- Community relations and social purpose. Schultz viewed Starbucks as part of a broader vision of common humanity: 'I wanted to build the kind of company my father never had the chance to work for, where you would be valued and respected wherever you came from, whatever the color of your skin, whatever your level of education. Offering healthcare was a transforming event in the equity of the Starbucks brand that created unbelievable trust among our people. We wanted to build a company that linked shareholder value to the cultural values that we want to create with our people.'[35] Starbucks' social role extended from the local level where 'every store is part of a community, and we take our responsibility to be good neighbors seriously', to its global presence: 'we have the opportunity to be a different type of global company. One that makes a profit but at the same time demonstrates a social conscience.'
- The layout and design of Starbucks stores were integral to the overall ambiance. Starbucks' store design group was responsible for the furniture, fittings and layout of retail outlets and, following Schultz's dictum that 'retail is detail', subjected store design to meticulous analysis. Each Starbucks store was adapted to reflect its unique neighbourhood, while at the same time communicating a unifying theme: 'the clean, unadulterated crispness of the Pacific Northwest combined with the urban suavity of an espresso bar in Milan.'
- Starbucks' location strategy – its clustering of 20 or more stores in each urban hub – created a local 'Starbucks buzz' and facilitated loyalty by Starbucks' customers. Starbucks' analysis of sales by individual store found little evidence that closely located Starbucks stores cannibalized one another's sales. To expand sales of coffee-to-go, Starbucks added drive-through windows to some of its stores and built some new stores adjacent to major highways.

The results were stupendous: between 1993 and 2007 Starbucks expanded across the US and into 51 other countries growing revenues from $160 million to $9,412 million. During 2005–2007, it earned an operating margin of 29% and a return on equity of 26.5%.[36]

Crisis and renaissance

Schultz relinquished his position as Starbucks' CEO in 2000, while retaining his role as chairman. By 2007, even before the financial crisis had struck, problems were becoming apparent. In 2007, growth of same-store sales slowed dramatically and, during 2007–2008, profits slumped. After reaching a peak of $40 in October 2006, the share price declined by more than 75% over the next two years. Amidst increasing concern that the quest for rapid growth had compromised Starbucks' core values, Schultz returned as CEO at the beginning of 2008.

Schultz's turnaround strategy comprised retrenchment and rebuilding. Planned new US store openings were cut back; 600 stores in the US were closed along with most stores in Australia. Company-wide cost cutting measures were implemented and almost 6000 employees lost their jobs. Rebuilding comprised reaffirming Starbucks' values and business principles and reconnecting with its customers. Schultz reviewed operating practices to examine their consistency with the Starbucks' Experience and its reformulated mission statement: 'to inspire and nurture the human spirit – one person, one cup and one neighbourhood at a time'. Key changes included a return to 'hand-made' coffee – replacing automated espresso machines with machines requiring individual cups from freshly ground beans – and revision of Starbucks' food menu, including withdrawing toasted breakfast sandwiches, whose aromas masked that of the coffee. Starbucks increased its commitment to corporate social responsibility.

Reconnecting with customers involved Schulz in worldwide travel to meet with Starbucks' employees ('partners') in concert halls and theatres to remind them of Starbucks' values, to reignite their drive and enthusiasm and to recount inspiring tales of the 'humanity of Starbucks'.[37] It also involved extensive use of social media and mobile technology. Facebook offered a key platform for building loyalty and community among customers. Starbucks pioneered mobile payments – using its partnership with Square to introduce credit and debit payments by cell phone.

Rekindling growth

Once Starbucks had stabilized, Schultz returned to the quest for growth – however, in contrast to 2000–2007, growth would be 'disciplined'. Revenue growth was sought in two main areas: the grocery trade and international markets.

In the grocery trade, Starbucks head of Channel Development and Emerging Brands anticipated that sales of Starbucks' products through thousands of supermarkets and other food retailers would 'eventually rival Starbucks retail store portfolio in terms of size and profitability'. A range of new products would augment established products, such as Starbucks and Seattle Best ground and whole bean coffees and Tazo Teas. A major new product was the Via, a new type of instant coffee, launched in February 2009 at $2.95 for a pack of three individual servings. Via used a patented process to 'absolutely replicate the taste of Starbucks coffee'. It achieved sales of over $100m in its first year.

A key feature of Starbucks' strategy for the grocery trade was to use its own coffee houses to introduce new products and then to roll them out to other retailers. In relation to Via, Schultz explained: 'If we took Via and we put it into grocery stores and it sat on a shelf, it would have died. But we can integrate Via into the emotional connection we have with our customers in our stores. We did that for six to eight months and succeeded well beyond expectations in our stores. And as a result of that, we had a very easy time convincing the trade, because they wanted it so badly.'[38]

In relation to international markets, Schultz viewed emerging markets as a huge opportunity for Starbucks. While Starbucks had struggled in some well-developed coffee markets – in Australia and the UK strong competition made profits elusive – in emerging markets it pioneered a novel café experience that appealed to the Westernized tastes of the emerging middle classes. China and India were Starbucks' primary targets. China would have 1500 stores in 70 cities by 2015 and would be Starbucks' biggest market after the US. In India, a 50/50 joint venture with Tata Group was building a national chain of Starbucks coffee houses beginning in Mumbai, Delhi, Pune and Bangalore.

In addition, Starbucks diversified its range of retail outlets.[39] During 2011–2012, it acquired premium juice maker Evolution Fresh, teashop chain Teavana and the California bakery chain La Boulange.

Credit: AFP/Getty Images

The future

During fiscal years 2014 and 2015, Starbucks looked set to continue its impressive growth. Analysts expected average annual revenue growth of 11% and earnings growth of 14%. Yet, despite acclaim for Schultz's remarkable success in restoring Starbucks' profitability and growth, doubts remained as to the long-term sustainability of its performance. Starbucks faced competition from multiple sources. Starbucks' success had spawned many imitators – both independent coffee houses and chains. In addition to speciality coffee houses, most catering establishments in the US, whether restaurants or fast-food chains, served coffee as part of a broader menu of food and beverages. Increasingly, these chains – notably McDonald's with its McCafés – were competing directly with Starbucks by adding premium coffee drinks to their menus. Starbucks also faced competition from premium coffee roasters such as the Italian firms Illycaffè, Lavazza and Segafredo Zanetti, all of which were expanding their retail coffee houses. The gourmet coffee market was also seeing a revolution in home-brewed coffee: sales of espresso coffee makers (which used highly pressurized hot water) had grown rapidly – especially single-serve coffee pod systems pioneered by Nestlé's Nespresso subsidiary.

Some commentators wondered whether Schultz's multiple initiatives risked repeating the errors of the past by losing focus on Starbuck's core identity and foundations of its competitive advantage. Did diversification into tea, juices, instant coffee and sales through the grocery trade fit with Starbucks' mission and capabilities?

Case questions

- Summarize Starbucks' strategy in 2014.
- Why has Starbucks' strategy succeeded so well?
- Is Starbucks' competitive advantage sustainable? Give your reasons.
- Advise Mr Schultz on whether and how Starbucks should amend its strategy in order to remain successful.

Notes

1 SIA Annual Report 2012/13.

2 L. Heracleous and J. Wirtz, 'Singapore Airlines' balancing act', *Harvard Business Review* (July–August 2010): 145–9.

3 J. Burton, 'Singapore Airlines sees first full-year loss', *Financial Times* (30th July 2009).

4 Richard Rumelt argues that competitive advantage lacks a clear and consistent definition ('What in the world is competitive advantage?' *Policy Working Paper* 2003–105, Anderson School, UCLA, August 2003).

5 The term 'gas guzzler' was coined in the US and refers to a car that uses fuel inefficiently.

6 C. Kim and R. Mauborgne, 'Blue Ocean Strategy', *Harvard Business Review* (October 2004).

7 R. Buaron, 'New Game Strategies', *McKinsey Quarterly Anthology* (2000): 34–6.

8 C. Baden-Fuller and J. M. Stopford, *Rejuvenating the Mature Business* (London and New York: Routledge, 1992).

9 G. Hamel, 'The Why, What, and How of Management Innovation', *Harvard Business Review* (February 2006).

10 R. P. Rumelt, 'Toward a strategic theory of the firm', in R. Lamb (ed.), *Competitive Strategic Management* (Englewood Cliffs, NJ: Prentice Hall, 1984): 556–70.

11 See J. Cubbin and P. Geroski, 'The convergence of profits in the long run: Interfirm and interindustry comparisons', *Journal of Industrial Economics* 35 (1987): 427–42; R. Jacobsen, 'The persistence of abnormal returns', *Strategic Management Journal*, 9 (1988): 415–30; and R. R. Wiggins and T. W. Ruefli, 'Schumpeter's ghost: Is hypercompetition making the best of times shorter?' *Strategic Management Journal*, 26 (2005): 887–911.

12 See, for example, the work of Richard D'Aveni on hypercompetition: R. D'Aveni, *Hypercompetition: Managing the dynamics of strategic maneuvering* (New York: Free Press, 1994).

13 G. Stalk, 'Curveball: Strategies to fool the competition', *Harvard Business Review* (September 2006): 114–22.

14 The film was based on the book by B. Traven, *The Treasure of the Sierra Madre* (New York: Knopf, 1947).

15 Monopolies and Mergers Commission, *Cat and Dog Foods* (London: Her Majesty's Stationery Office, 1977).

16 S. Martin, *Advanced Industrial Economics*, 2nd edn (Oxford: Blackwell Publishing, 2001): Chapter 8.

17 A. Brandenburger and B. Nalebuff, *Co-opetition* (New York: Doubleday, 1996): 72–80.

18 R. Schmalensee, 'Entry deterrence in the ready-to-eat breakfast cereal industry', *Bell Journal of Economics* 9 (1978): 305–27.

19 Monopolies and Mergers Commission, *Indirect Electrostatic Reprographic Equipment* (London: Her Majesty's Stationery Office, 1976): 37, 56.

20 S. A. Lippman and R. P. Rumelt, 'Uncertain imitability: An analysis of interfirm differences in efficiency under competition', *Bell Journal of Economics*, 13 (1982): 418–38. See also R. Reed and R. DeFillippi, 'Causal ambiguity, barriers to imitation, and sustainable competitive advantage', *Academy of Management Review*, 15 (1990): 88–102.

21 P. R. Milgrom and J. Roberts, 'Complementarities and fit: Strategy, structure and organisational change in manufacturing', *Journal of Accounting and Economics*, 19 (1995): 179–208.

22 M. E. Porter and N. Siggelkow, 'Contextuality within activity systems and sustainable competitive advantage', *Academy of Management Perspectives*, 22 (May 2008): 34–56.

23 D. Ross, 'Learning to dominate', *Journal of Industrial Economics*, 34 (1986): 337–53.

24 For an analysis of first-mover advantage, see M. Lieberman and D. Montgomery, 'First-mover advantages', *Strategic Management Journal*, 9 (1988): 41–58; and M. Lieberman and D. Montgomery, 'First-mover (dis)advantages: Retrospective and link with the resource-based view', *Strategic Management Journal*, 19 (1998): 1111–25.

25 M. E. Porter, *Competitive Advantage* (New York: Free Press, 1985): 13.

26 Ibid.: 120.

27 On activity-based costing, see R. S. Kaplan and S. R. Anderson, 'Time-driven activity-based costing', *Harvard Business Review* (November 2004): 131–8; and J. Billington, 'The ABCs of ABC: Activity-based costing and management', *Harvard Management Update* (Boston: Harvard Business School Publishing, May 1999).

28 See, for example, the Centre for Aviation 2013 report, http://centreforaviation.com/analysis/asian-airline-cost-rankings-airasia-x-sia--thai-are-most-efficient-while-ana-is-highest-cost-118729, accessed 29th September 2014.

29 T. Peters, *Thriving on Chaos* (New York: Knopf, 1987): 56.

30 *Cemex: Cementing a global strategy*, Insead Case No. 307–233–1 (2007).

31 Porter (1985), op. cit.: 42.

32 Porter (1985), op. cit.

33 H. D. Schultz. (2014) The Biography.com website, http://www.biography.com/people/howard-schultz-21166227, accessed 29th September 2014.

34 http://www.starbucks.co.uk/about-us/company-information/mission-statement, accessed 29th September 2014.

35 Ibid.

36 Mintel Report on Coffee Shops, released March 2010.

37 H. Schultz, *Onward: How Starbucks fought for its life without losing its soul* (Chichester, John Wiley & Sons Ltd, 2011).

38 'The HBR interview: We had to own our own mistakes: An interview with Howard Schultz', *Harvard Business Review* (July–August 2010).

39 S. Johnson, 'Stealth Starbucks: Seattle-based coffee giant opening neighborhood shops in disguise', *Chicago Tribune* (17th July 2009).

5

Industry evolution and strategic change

www.foundationsofstrategy.com

Introduction and objectives

One of management's greatest challenges is to ensure that the enterprise adapts to its environment and to the changes occurring within that environment. Change in the industry environment is driven by the forces of technology, consumer need, politics, economic growth and a host of other influences. In some industries these forces for change combine to create massive, unpredictable changes. For example, in telecommunications new digital and wireless technologies combined with regulatory changes have resulted in the telecom industry of 2014 being almost unrecognizable from that which existed 20 years previously. In other industries – for example, food processing, house building and funeral services – change is more gradual and predictable. Change is the result both of external forces and of the competitive strategies of the firms within the industry. As we have seen, competition is a dynamic process in which firms vie for competitive advantage, only to see it eroded through imitation and innovation by rivals. The outcome is an industry environment that is being continually recreated by competition.

The purpose of this chapter is to help us understand how managers adapt their strategies to fit their environments, how they go about predicting change and adapting their strategies to cope with change. To do this we start by exploring different industry contexts and patterns of change that can help us to predict how industries are likely to evolve over time. While recognizing that every industry follows a unique development path, we will look for common drivers of change that produce similar patterns. Recognizing such patterns can help us to identify and exploit opportunities for competitive advantage.

Predicting changes in the industry environment is difficult. But even more difficult is ensuring the adaptation of the firm to these changes. For individuals, change is disruptive, costly and uncomfortable. For organizations, the forces of inertia are even stronger. So, we go on to explore the sources of inertia in organization and see how resistance to change can be overcome. Going beyond adaptation, some firms become initiators of change, but what determines the ability of some firms to become game-changers in their industries?

Whether a firm is adapting to or initiating change, competing in a changing world requires the development of new capabilities that can help renew competitive advantage. How difficult can this be? The short answer is, 'Very.' We conclude this chapter by considering the difficulties of building new capabilities and the approaches that organizations can take to overcome these difficulties.

By the time you have completed this chapter, you will:

- recognize the different stages of industry development and understand the factors that drive the process of industry evolution;
- identify the key success factors associated with industries at different stages of their development and the strategies appropriate to different stages in the industry lifecycle;

- appreciate the sources of organizational inertia that act as barriers to change;
- be familiar with different approaches to strategic change, including the quest for ambidexterity and the use of tools of strategic change management;
- be familiar with the concept of 'dynamic capabilities' and how firms can anticipate change and shape their futures;
- be aware of different approaches that firms have taken in developing organizational capabilities.

Opening Case

The evolution of personal computers

The origins of the personal computer (PC) can be traced back to the early 1970s following Intel's development of the microprocessor in 1968. Early machines were assembled from kits and programmed by their owners so were only of interest to knowledgeable hobbyists who enjoyed soldering and sorting out tangles of wires. Pre-assembled machines that included an operating system and applications software were launched in 1977 by Tandy, Commodore and Apple. By making microcomputers available to a much wider customer base, these machines signalled the birth of the PC industry. Like many of today's producers, the early manufacturers did little more than assemble bought-in components, but several of the early pioneers created their own operating systems.

The potential of this newly formed market was soon recognized and new firms started to pile in (Figure 5.1). By 1981, the worldwide market was estimated to be worth about $3 billion with around 150 companies producing microcomputers.[1] The first movers in the market succeeded in capturing an early lead with Apple having about 20% of the market, Tandy 15% and Commodore 7%. It is interesting to note that the initial leaders adopted significantly different strategies. While Tandy chose to restrict independent firms' access to its technology, Apple chose to adopt an open architecture by releasing all the technical information necessary for independent firms to produce products that were complementary to the Apple machine.

IBM's launch of its PC in 1981 marked the industry's second phase of development. After previously neglecting this market and continuing to focus on its mainframe computers, IBM

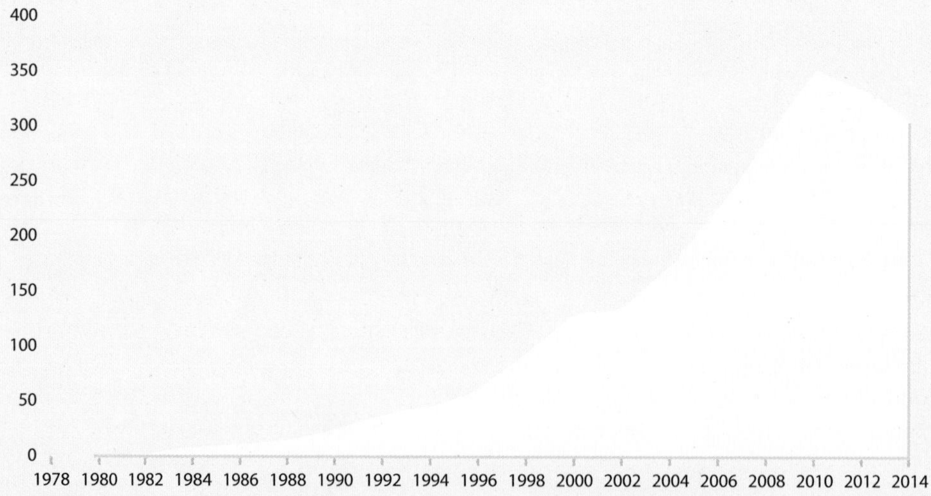

Figure 5.1 Worldwide shipments of personal computers 1978–2014 (millions of units).

Source: www.gartner.com.

now sought to enter the market quickly, so it set up a 'skunk works' operation in Florida.[2] This unit functioned entirely outside of the main IBM operation. This independence from IBM's strategy and traditions had an important impact on the design, production and marketing of PCs. Operating in isolation from the rest of the business, IBM's PC developers purchased key elements of the product – the operating system, the microprocessor, the screen, the disk drive – from third-party suppliers and adopted an open strategy which allowed third parties access to the technical details of its product so that complementary products could be developed. With a 4.77 MHz microprocessor, 16 kB of memory and a launch price of $1565 ($4025 in today's money), the IBM PC was an immediate hit. IBM's credibility meant that both users and software developers anticipated that the IBM PC would survive and prosper and were willing to invest in the platform. The open architecture strategy encouraged the development of a wide range of applications software creating a virtuous circle of growth.

In a short space of time IBM built a commanding share of the PC market, so much so that the IBM machine with its MS/DOS operating system became the de facto standard. However, the strategy that led to its success also contained within it the seeds of IBM's subsequent failure in personal computers. IBM's open strategy allowed the rapid development of its product but also meant that very little of its PC was proprietary: the intellectual property was owned primarily by Microsoft and Intel, who were the main beneficiaries. Moreover, the IBM PC was easily copied: clone products proliferated. Unwittingly, IBM's open strategy had reduced the barriers to entry into the PC market and new entrants flooded in. Competition was increasingly based on price rather than differentiation and the result was that although microcomputers became increasingly powerful their prices declined continually. By 2000, the world's leading PC suppliers were Compaq, Dell and Hewlett-Packard. However, the lion's share of the sector's profit pool was earned by its suppliers, notably Microsoft, which supplied the operating system (initially MS-DOS, then Windows), and Intel, which supplied microprocessors. Hence, though IBM had established the dominant design of the personal computer, the resulting technical standard – known as 'Wintel' – was owned by Microsoft and Intel. The implications for the personal computer manufacturers were dire. With the exception of Dell and Apple, all the PC makers earned wafer-thin margins and dismal rates of return on capital. The unattractiveness of the industry was confirmed by the exit of most of the early leaders, including IBM, Xerox, Olivetti, Radio Shack, Siemens-Nixdorf, Sharp and AST.

During 1998–2003, Wintel personal computers accounted for 96% of the world market, with the Apple Macintosh comprising most of the remainder. At Apple, Steve Jobs had pursued the opposite strategy to that of IBM. Rather than IBM's open standards strategy with extensive outsourcing of components and software, Jobs sought maximum control over his product by producing as much of his PCs as possible in-house, including peripherals and, critically, the operating system. Jobs' obsession with 'insanely great' products had resulted in a computer with outstanding design and unparalleled user friendliness, but the bandwagon effect created by the many producers of Wintel PCs and vast array of software applications from independent developers meant that the Apple Mac was engaged in a losing battle against the Wintel standard.[3] Apple's survival depended critically upon its dominance of a few niches of the market, notably desktop publishing and other segments of the media business. Only when Apple established compatibility with the Windows operating system was it able to grow its market share.

Yet, it was Jobs' relentless quest for 'insanely great' products that would eventually undermine the dominance of the Wintel standard and lead the personal computer industry into decline. Twenty-first-century technical advances in miniaturization, energy efficient microprocessors, third- and fourth-generation wireless communication, cloud computing and social networking ushered in a new era of mobile, Web-based communication and computing. With its iPod/iTunes, iPhone and iPad, Apple pioneered this new era. Innovation from other companies also chipped away at the dominance of the Wintel standard. Open source operating systems such as Linux and Google's Chrome displaced Windows at the lower end of the PC market. Specialist-use products such as e-readers (e.g. Amazon's Kindle) and game consoles (e.g. Sony's PS4) also displaced personal computers for certain applications. Most impactful was the transition from personal computers to tablet computers as more and more computer manufacturers sought to cash in on Apple's success with its iPad.

The impact on personal computer sales was brutal: during 2012–2013, worldwide shipments of personal computers declined by 16%. Revenues declined even more rapidly. The downward trend was expected to continue, though at a slower pace. In the face of such adversity, the PC makers were forced to rethink their strategies: at the time of writing some, such as Sony, are exiting the industry, some are seeking the elusive goal of differentiation advantage (which so far only Apple has done successfully), some are seeking a cost advantage through scale and efficiency (e.g. Acer and Asus) while others are diversifying into higher margin products (Dell into cloud computing; HP into software and services; Lenovo into servers and smartphones).

The industry lifecycle

One of the best-known and most enduring marketing concepts is the **product lifecycle**.[4] Products are born, their sales grow, they reach maturity, they go into decline and they ultimately die. If products have lifecycles, so too do the industries that produce them. The **industry lifecycle** is the supply-side equivalent of the product lifecycle. To the extent that an industry produces multiple generations of a product, the industry lifecycle is likely to be of longer duration than that of a single product.

The lifecycle comprises four phases: *introduction* (or *emergence*), *growth*, *maturity* and *decline* (Figure 5.2). Before we examine the features of each of these stages, let us examine the forces that drive industry evolution. Two factors are fundamental: demand growth and the production and diffusion of knowledge.

Demand growth

The lifecycle and the stages within it are defined primarily by changes in an industry's growth rate over time. The characteristic profile is an S-shaped growth curve.

- In the *introduction stage*, sales are small and the rate of market penetration is low because the industry's products are little known and customers are few. The novelty of the technology, small scale of production and lack of experience means high costs and low quality. Customers for new products tend to be affluent, innovation-oriented and risk-tolerant.
- The *growth stage* is characterized by accelerating market penetration as technical improvements and increased efficiency open up the mass market.
- Increasing market saturation causes the onset of the *maturity stage*. Once saturation is reached, demand is wholly for replacement.
- Finally, as the industry becomes challenged by new industries that produce technologically superior substitute products, the industry enters its *decline stage*.

The production and diffusion of knowledge

The second driver of the industry lifecycle is knowledge. New knowledge in the form of product innovation is responsible for an industry's birth, and the dual processes of knowledge creation and knowledge diffusion exert a major influence on industry evolution.

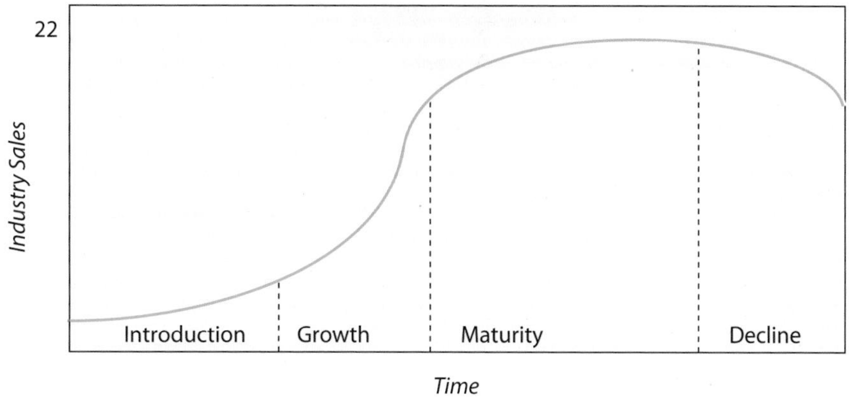

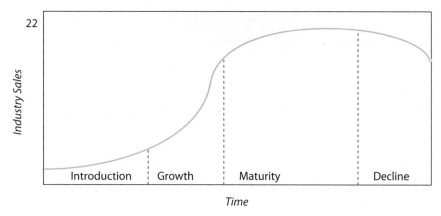

Figure 5.2 The industry lifecycle.

In the introduction stage, product technology advances rapidly. There is no dominant product technology and rival technologies compete for attention. Competition is primarily between alternative technologies and design configurations. Potential consumers often know little about the product and sales are primarily focused on enthusiasts and pioneers. Over the course of the lifecycle, customers become increasingly informed about the product and the market expands, but as customers become more knowledgeable about the performance attributes of manufacturers' products, so they are better able to judge value for money and become more price sensitive. The transition of an industry from its introduction to growth phase is reflected typically in the emergence of dominant designs and technical standards and in a change of focus away from product innovation towards process innovation.

Dominant designs and technical standards

A **dominant design** is a product architecture that defines the look, functionality and production method for the product and becomes accepted by the industry as a whole.

Dominant designs have included the following examples:

The Underwood Model 5 introduced in 1899 established the basic architecture and main features of typewriters for the 20th century: a moving carriage, the ability to see the characters being typed, a shift function or upper case and a replaceable, inked ribbon.[5]

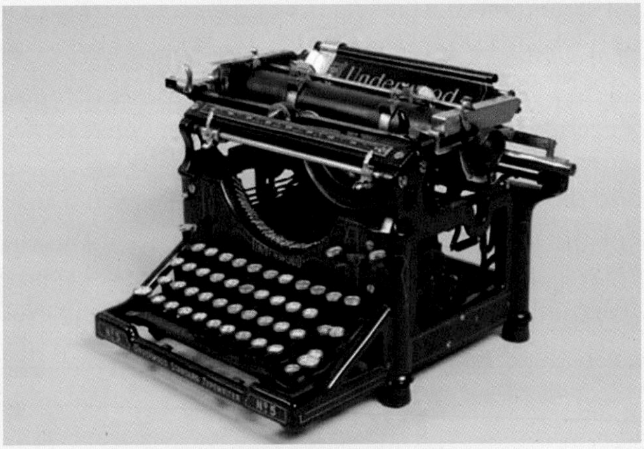

Courtesy of the Children's Museum of Indianapolis

Leica's Ur-Leica camera developed by Oskar Barnack and launched in Germany in 1924 established key features of the 35 mm camera, though it was not until Canon began mass-producing cameras based on the Leica original that this design of 35 mm camera came to dominate still photography.

When Ray Kroc opened his first McDonald's hamburger restaurant in Illinois in 1955, he established what would soon become a dominant design for the fast-food restaurant industry: a limited menu, no waiter service, eat-in and take-out options, roadside locations and a franchise system of ownership and control.

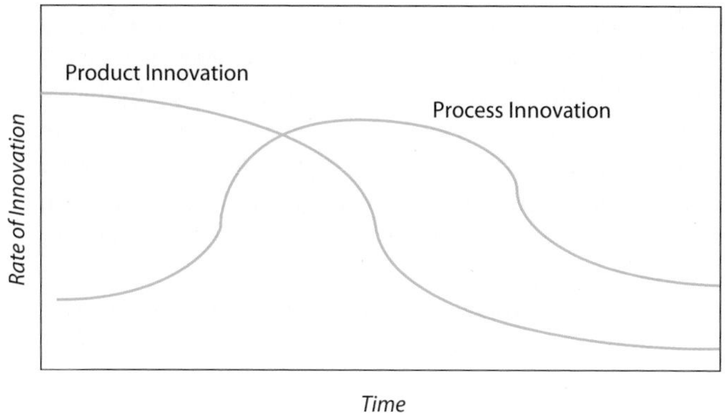

Figure 5.3 Product and process innovation over time.

Technical standards emerge where there are **network effects** – the need for users to connect in some way with one another. Network effects cause each customer to choose the same technology as everyone else to avoid being stranded. Unlike a proprietary technical standard, which is typically embodied in patents or copyrights, a firm that sets a dominant design does not normally own intellectual property in that design. So, except for some early-mover advantage, there is not necessarily any profit advantage from setting a dominant design. Dominant designs also exist in processes. In the flat glass industry there has been a succession of dominant process designs from glass cylinder blowing to continuous ribbon drawing to float glass.[6] Dominant designs are present too in business models. In many new markets, competition is between rival business models. In the UK, Internet start-up fashion retailers like Boo.com soon succumbed to competition from 'bricks 'n' clicks' retailers such as Marks & Spencer and Zara.

From product to process innovation

The emergence of a dominant design marks a critical juncture in an industry's evolution. Once the industry coalesces around a leading design, there is a shift from radical to incremental product innovation. This transition typically ushers in the industry's growth phase because greater standardization reduces risks to customers that they will be left with the 'wrong technology' and encourages firms to invest in manufacturing. The shift in emphasis from design to manufacture also tends to involve increased attention being paid to process innovation as firms seek to reduce costs and increase product reliability through large-scale production methods (Figure 5.3). The combination of process improvements, design modifications and scale economies results in falling costs and greater availability, which drive rapidly increasing market penetration.

Case Insight 5.1

The lifecycle pattern in the PC industry

In the opening case, we saw that, within a few decades, the PC industry has gone through a number of developmental phases. In the 1970s, the industry was in its introduction stage: the term 'personal computer' had yet to be coined and the earliest microcomputers needed to be built from kits, and were of interest only to knowledgeable enthusiasts. Early entrants offered diverse technologies and designs with differences in data storage systems (audio tapes vs.

floppy disks), visual displays (TV receivers vs. dedicated monitors), operating systems (CPM vs. DOS vs. Apple II) and microprocessors. Competition was primarily technology based as the early entrants into the market sought to improve the functionality and performance of their products.

The beginning of the 1980s marked the start of the industry's growth phase and sales soared. Successive waves of technical improvements increased the performance of computers in terms of their power and speed but also made them easier to operate and more user-friendly. The Apple II opened up the home and education markets to the personal computer, while IBM PC with its MS/DOS operating system and Intel x86 series of microprocessors made personal computers an essential tool for business and established the dominant design for the industry. This created the incentive for users to buy computers that were compatible with those of the IBM/Wintel architecture and established IBM/Wintel as the de facto standard for personal computing.

By the early 1990s, the market showed signs of maturity in the advanced industrialized economies: much of the demand became replacement demand, the rate of sales growth slowed. Innovation became incremental and predictable, based upon new generations of Intel microprocessors and new versions of Windows. However, in emerging markets, demand continued to grow strongly. Brand loyalty was weak and competition focused on price, resulting in a continuous decline in retail prices. The production of components and subsystems and the assembly of PCs have moved offshore to specialist contractors operating in low-cost countries, particularly China, with companies producing leading brands of PCs choosing to focus on their core competencies of product innovation, design and marketing.

How general is the lifecycle pattern?

To what extent do industries conform to this lifecycle pattern? To begin with, the duration of the lifecycle varies greatly from industry to industry:

- The introduction phase of the US railroad industry extended from the building of the first railroad, the Baltimore and Ohio in 1827, to the growth phase of the 1870s. By the late 1950s, the industry was entering its decline phase.
- The introduction stage of the US car industry lasted about 25 years, from the 1890s until growth took off in 1913–1915. Maturity set in during the mid-1950s, followed by decline during the past decade.
- Digital audio players (MP3 players) were first introduced by Saehan Information Systems and Diamond Multimedia during 1997–1998. With the launch of Apple's iPod in 2001, the industry entered its growth phase. By 2008/9, slackening growth indicated entry into the mature phase.

Over time, industry lifecycles have become increasingly compressed. This is especially evident in e-commerce. Businesses such as online gambling, business-to-business online auctions and online travel services went from initial introduction to maturity within a few years. Social networking was launched in 1997 by www.sixdegrees.com. By 2005, a number of sites were rapidly building their networks, including Myspace, Orkut (Google), Badoo and LinkedIn. However, it was Facebook that broke away from the pack achieving 12 million users by the end of 2006, 100 million by August 2008 and 600 million by the beginning of 2011. Since then, monthly growth has slowed to a modest 3.5%. Cusumano and Yoffie argue that 'competing on internet time' requires a radical rethink of strategies and management processes.[7]

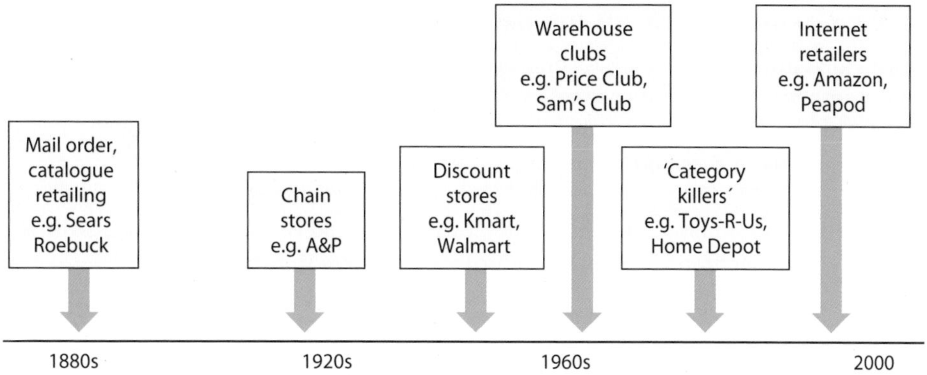

Figure 5.4 Innovation and renewal in the industry lifecycle: US retailing.

Patterns of evolution also differ. Industries supplying basic necessities such as residential construction, food processing and clothing may never enter a decline phase because it is unlikely that they become outdated and other industries may experience a rejuvenation of their lifecycle. In the 1960s, the world motorcycle industry, in decline in the US and Europe, re-entered its growth phase as Japanese manufacturers pioneered the recreational use of motorcycles. The market for TV receivers has experienced multiple revivals: colour TVs, computer monitors, flat-screen TVs and, most recently, HDTVs. Similar waves of innovation have revitalized retailing (Figure 5.4). These rejuvenations of the product lifecycle are not natural phenomena: they are typically the result of companies resisting the forces of maturity through breakthrough product innovations or developing new markets.

It is also important to note that an industry is likely to be at different stages of its lifecycle in different countries. Although the European, Japanese and US car markets have entered their decline phase, markets in China, India and Russia are in their growth phases. Multinational companies can exploit such differences: developing new products and introducing them into the advanced industrial countries, then shifting attention to other growth markets once maturity sets in.

Case Insight 5.2

Does the PC industry follow the lifecycle pattern?

The PC industry has gone through the stages of introduction, growth and maturity and has now entered its decline phase. Moreover, the characteristics of each phase correspond closely to the generic features of structure and competition outlined in Table 5.1. However, dating the transition between stages is difficult – not least because the cycle is at different stages in different countries. Another complication is that technological change has made it increasingly difficult to delineate the boundaries of the industry. For instance, should we view tablet computers as part of the industry or as a separate product? Forrester, an information technology research company, predicts that tablet sales will grow at a compound rate of 25.6% annually through to 2017 to reach 381 million – far exceeding the number of personal computers.[8] If we group PCs and tablets together, the industry is still growing.

Implications of the lifecycle for competition and strategy

Changes in demand growth and technology over the cycle have implications for industry structure, competition and the sources of competitive advantage. Table 5.1 summarizes the principal features of each stage of the industry lifecycle and outlines some of the key success factors associated with these different stages.

Categorizing industries according to their stages of development alerts us to the types of competition likely to emerge and the strategies that are likely to be effective, so it is worth examining the strategic implications of each of these phases in more detail.

Table 5.1 The evolution of industry structure and competition over the lifecycle.

	Introduction	Growth	Maturity	Decline
Demand	Limited to early adopters: high income, avant-garde	Rapidly increasing market penetration	Mass market, replacement/repeat buying Customers knowledgeable and price sensitive	Obsolescence
Technology	Competing technologies Rapid product innovation	Standardization around dominant technology Rapid process innovation	Well-diffused technical knowhow: quest for technological improvements	Little product or process innovation
Products	Poor quality Wide variety of features and technologies Frequent design changes	Design and quality improve Emergence of dominant design	Trend to commoditization Attempts to differentiate by branding, quality, bundling	Commodities the norm: differentiation difficult and unprofitable
Manufacturing and distribution	Short production runs High-skilled labour content Specialized distribution channels	Capacity shortages Mass production Competition for distribution	Emergence of overcapacity Deskilling of production Long production runs Distributors carry fewer lines	Chronic overcapacity Re-emergence of speciality channels
Trade	Producers and consumers in advanced countries	Exports from advanced countries to rest of world	Production shifts to newly industrializing then developing countries	Exports from countries with lowest labour costs
Competition	Few companies	Entry, mergers and exits	Shakeout Price competition increases	Price wars Exits
Key success factors	Product innovation Establishing credible image of firm and product	Design for manufacture Access to distribution Brand building Fast product development Process innovation	Cost efficiency through capital intensity, scale efficiency and low input costs	Low overheads Buyer selection Signalling commitment Rationalizing capacity

THE INTRODUCTION PHASE The number of firms in an industry increases rapidly during the early stages of an industry's lifecycle. Initially, an industry may be pioneered by a few firms but, as the industry gains legitimacy, failure rates will decline and the rate of new-firm formation increase. New entrants often have very different origins. Some are start-up companies (de novo entrants); others are established firms diversifying from related industries (**de alio entrants**).

The introduction stage typically features a wide variety of product types that reflect the diversity of technologies and designs and the lack of consensus over customer requirements. The basis of entry is product innovation so the introduction stage typically features a wide variety of product types that reflect the diversity of technologies and designs and the lack of consensus over customer requirements. Subsequent success comes from winning the battle for technological leadership. During this phase, gross margins can be high, but heavy investments in innovation and market development tend to depress return on capital.

New industries often begin in advanced industrial countries because of the presence of affluent consumers and the availability of technical and scientific resources. Traditionally, firms have built stable demand positions in their home markets before starting to internationalize. The advent of the Internet has, however, heralded the arrival of some start-ups that are 'born global'.[9] **Born global companies** are companies that operate internationally from their inception. These companies derive significant competitive advantage from the use of resources and the sale of output in multiple countries, for example, reaping the benefits of scale even though markets in individual locations are thin. Icebreaker, a New Zealand-based company producing thermal outdoor clothing from merino wool, has been able to market its product across the globe from the outset, because its products appeal to a specific group of individuals engaged in specialist outdoor pursuits that have very similar needs and preferences. In the Internet age, firms operating in the virtual domain can develop international operations relatively quickly and cheaply. For example, Eyeview is a company providing specialist advice to corporate clients on how to create effective websites. It uses video and audio materials developed in different languages to provide training sessions via the Internet.

Case Insight 5.3
De alio versus de novo entrants

In the PC industry, most of the pioneers were entrants from other industries (de alio entrants). Commodore, for example, was founded in 1954 as a typewriter manufacturing company but moved into the manufacture of electronic calculators when Japanese typewriters flooded the US market. From calculators, Commodore moved into home computers. Similarly, MITS, the maker of the popular Altair 8800 home computers, started out selling electronic calculator kits that hobbyists could assemble. Apple was, however, a de novo entrant. Over the past three decades, the leading firms have comprised both de novo entrants (e.g. Dell, Lenovo, Acer) and de alio entrants (e.g. IBM, HP, Samsung).

THE GROWTH PHASE As demand grows both in the domestic market and in other countries, a dominant design usually emerges. The key challenge then becomes scaling up. As the market expands, the firm needs to adapt its product design and manufacturing capability to large-scale production and so, in order to fully utilize manufacturing capacity, access to distribution becomes critical. Financial resources also become important as investment requirements grow. In addition, organizational growth creates the need for internal administrative and strategic skills.

During this phase, overseas demand may be serviced initially by exports, but the drive to reduce cost and associated changes in production processes reduces the need for sophisticated labour skills and makes production attractive in newly industrialized countries. Eventually, production and assembly may shift away from the advanced countries and these countries may start to import.

THE MATURITY PHASE With the maturity stage, competitive advantage is increasingly a quest for efficiency, particularly in industries that tend towards commoditization. Cost efficiency through scale economies, low wages and low overheads become the key success factors. With the onset of maturity, the number of firms begins to fall as product standardization and excess capacity stimulate price competition. Very often, industries go through one or more 'shakeout' phases during which the rate of firm failure increases sharply. The intensity of the shakeout depends a great deal on the capacity/demand balance and the extent of international competition.

In food retailing, airlines, motor vehicles, metals and insurance, maturity was associated with strong price competition and slender profitability. In household detergents, breakfast cereals, cosmetics and cigarettes, high seller concentration and successful maintenance of product differentiation has allowed subdued price rivalry and high profits.

Case Insight 5.4

The maturity phase in the PC industry

In the PC industry there was a significant shakeout from the mid- to late 1990s to the early 2000s. By 1999, only 20% of the firms that began producing PCs in the previous 22 years had survived. Hewlett-Packard merged with Compaq in 2001 and in 2004 IBM exited the PC market, selling its PC business to Lenovo, a large Chinese electronics firm. Whereas in 1987 there were 286 firms in the market, by 2010 six leading firms dominated – Acer, Apple, Dell, Hewlett-Packard, Lenovo and Toshiba – who between them accounted for around 60% of global sales.[10]

With maturity comes the commoditization and de-skilling of production processes, and production eventually shifts to developing countries where labour costs are lowest. At the beginning of the 1990s, the production of wireless handsets was concentrated in the US, Japan, Finland and Germany. By the end of the 1990s, South Korea had joined this leading group. During 2009, production in North America, Western Europe and Japan was in rapid decline as manufacturers shifted output to China, India, Brazil, Vietnam, Hungary and Romania. In the PC market, the vast majority of production now takes places in China.

THE DECLINE PHASE The transition from maturity to decline can be a result of technological substitution (typewriters, photographic film), changes in consumer preferences (canned food, men's suits), demographic shifts (children's toys in Europe) or foreign competition (textiles in the advanced industrialized countries). Shrinking market demand gives rise to acute strategic issues. Among the key features of declining industries are:

- excess capacity;
- lack of technical change (reflected in a lack of new product introduction and stability of process technology);
- a declining number of competitors, but some entry as new firms acquire the assets of exiting firms cheaply;
- high average age of both physical and human resources;
- aggressive price competition.

Despite the inhospitable environment offered by declining industries, research by Kathryn Harrigan has uncovered declining industries where at least some participants earned surprisingly high profits. These included electronic vacuum tubes, cigars and leather tanning. However, elsewhere – notably in prepared baby foods, rayon and meat processing – decline was accompanied by aggressive price competition, company failures and instability.[11]

What determines whether a declining industry becomes a competitive bloodbath? Two factors are critical: the balance between capacity and output and the nature of the demand for the product.

Achieving a balance between capacity and output is easier when decline can be predicted and firms can plan for it rather than being taken by surprise. For example, the decline in traditional photography and the rise in digital imaging was anticipated and planned for, whereas the decline in cinema attendance has been much more unpredictable, with blockbuster films and investments in multiplex cinemas making the extent and character of a long-term decline more difficult to judge. Similarly, in industries where capacity exits in an orderly fashion, decline can occur without trauma. Where substantial excess capacity persists, as has occurred in the steel industries of Europe, in the bakery industry, in gold mining and in long-haul bus transportation, the potential exists for destructive competition.

Although demand for an industry's output may be falling, there are often niches within markets where demand is more stable. Established firms have often been successful in cultivating high-price, high-quality segments within declining industries, for example Richemont has created a very profitable business based on mechanical watches (Lange & Söhne, Cartier, Piaget) and, similarly, has carved out a lucrative niche in fountain pens (Montblanc).

Key success factors and strategy

Our discussion of each of the phases of the industry lifecycle has highlighted the ways in which demand, technology and industry structure change as an industry evolves, with important implications for a firm's sources of competitive advantage and strategy. In particular:

- During the introductory stage, product innovation is the basis for initial entry and for subsequent success. Soon, however, other requirements for success emerge. In moving from the first generation of products to subsequent generations, investment requirements grow and financial resources become increasingly important. Capabilities in product development also need to be supported by capabilities in manufacturing, marketing and distribution.

- Once the growth stage is reached, the key challenge is scaling up. As the market expands, the firm needs to adapt its product design and its manufacturing capability to large-scale production. To utilize increased manufacturing capability, access to distribution becomes critical.
- With the maturity stage, competitive advantage is increasingly a quest for efficiency, particularly in industries that tend towards commoditization. Cost efficiency through scale economies, low wages and low overheads become the key success factors.
- The transition to decline intensifies pressures for cost cutting. It also requires maintaining stability by encouraging the orderly exit of industry capacity and capturing residual market demand. If, as seems the case in a number of sectors, product lifecycles are becoming shorter, systematic disengagement from product markets that are entering their decline phase is likely to become of increasing strategic importance. McGrath argues that businesses tend to focus on the introduction and growth phases of product lifecycles and that disengagement processes are often neglected.[12] To exit an industry gracefully the organization needs people who are good at detecting early signs of decline and who are willing and able to make the often difficult decision to stop doing something.

Case Insight 5.5

The future shape of the PC industry

The structure and boundaries of the PC industry are shifting rapidly as firms reshape their supply chains, their product portfolios and their relationships with related industries. The outsourcing model pioneered by IBM was extended by other US firms, and all major players became engaged in some form of outsourcing and contract manufacturing. As a consequence, firms like Foxconn in China and Quanta Computer in Taiwan were able to develop strong market positions as original design manufacturers of personal computers and other electronic devices. That is to say, they designed and manufactured electronic products as specified and eventually rebranded by US and other leading firms. However, the trend may be changing. Whereas, in the past, the PC industry has been characterized by vertical de-integration, some argue that the trend is now towards re-integration.[13] Even though Apple outsources production and assembly of its Mac computers, it designs its hardware and software in-house and has opened a chain of retail stores. Its development of the iPod, iPhone and iPad has taken place alongside the expansion of its digital content store, iTunes. The iTunes platform has allowed Apple to take a cut of each sale it makes through its digital storefront, and by integrating its various activities, it has enhanced its profitability.

Recent developments in the PC industry suggest that links between industry lifecycles, industry structure and firm strategy can be complex, leading some authors to suggest that managers should focus on industry architectures rather than industry lifecycles.[14] That is to say, rather than thinking primarily about the way in which the final market for a particular product or service is evolving (the industry lifecycle approach) and the implications this has for acquiring and maintaining competitive advantage, managers should be alert to the shifting vertical structures of clusters of related industries (the industry architecture approach) and consider the way they could adapt firm strategy accordingly.

Managing organizational adaptation and strategic change

We have established that industries change. But what about the companies within them? Let us turn our attention to business enterprises and consider both the impediments to change and the means by which change takes place.

Why is change so difficult? The sources of organizational inertia

At the heart of all approaches to change management is the recognition that organizations find change difficult. Why is this so? Different theories of organizational and industrial change emphasize different barriers to change:

- *Organizational routines:* Evolutionary economists emphasize the fact that capabilities are based on organizational routines – patterns of coordinated interactions among organizational members that develop through continual repetition. The more highly developed are an organization's routines, the more difficult it is to develop new routines. Hence, organizations get caught in **competency traps**[15] where 'core capabilities become core rigidities'.[16]
- *Social and political structures:* Organizations are both social systems and political systems. As social systems, organizations develop patterns of interaction that make organizational change stressful and disruptive.[17] As political systems, organizations develop stable distributions of power; change represents a threat to the power of those in positions of authority. Hence, as a result of rigidities in both social systems and political systems, organizations tend to resist change.
- *Conformity:* Institutional sociologists emphasize the propensity of firms to imitate one another in order to gain legitimacy. The process of **institutional isomorphism** locks organizations into common structures and strategies that make it difficult for them to adapt to change.[18] The pressures for conformity can be external: governments, investment analysts, banks and other resource providers encourage the adoption of similar strategies and structures. Isomorphism also results from voluntary imitation: risk aversion encourages companies to adopt similar strategies and structures to their peers.[19]
- *Limited search:* The Carnegie School of Organizational Theory (associated with Herbert Simon, Jim March and Richard Cyert) views search as the primary driver of organizational change. Organizations tend to limit search to areas close to their existing activities – they prefer *exploitation* of existing knowledge over *exploration* for new opportunities.[20] Limited search is reinforced, first, by bounded rationality – human beings have limited information processing capacity, which constrains the set of choices they can consider – and, second, **satisficing** – the propensity for individuals (and organizations) to terminate the search for better solutions when they reach a satisfactory level of performance rather than to pursue optimal performance. The implication is that organizational change is triggered by a decline in performance.
- *Complementarities between strategy, structure and systems:* Organizational economics,[21] socio-technical systems[22] and complexity theory[23] have all emphasized the importance of fit between an organization's strategy, structure, management systems, culture, employee skills – indeed, all the characteristics of an organization. Organizations struggle to establish complex, idiosyncratic combinations of multiple characteristics

during their early phases of development that match the conditions of their business environment. However, once established, this complex configuration becomes a barrier to change. To respond to a change in its external environment, it is not enough to make incremental changes to a few dimensions of strategy; it is likely that a firm will need to find a new configuration that involves a comprehensive set of changes.[24] The implication is that organizations tend to evolve through a process of punctuated equilibrium involving long periods of stability during which the widening misalignment between the organization and its environment ultimately forces radical and comprehensive change on the company.[25] Systematic changes that involve establishing a new configuration of activities that better matches the requirements of the external environment may require the appointment of a CEO from outside who is not wedded to the previous configuration.

Coping with technological change

When we examined the industry lifecycle earlier in this chapter, we noted how in the introductory phase new start-ups often compete with established firms diversifying from other industries. However, competition between new starts-ups and established firms is not limited to the early phases of industries' lifecycles; any change in the external environment of an industry offers opportunities for newcomers to challenge incumbents. In vacuum cleaners, Dyson displaced established leaders Hoover and Electrolux in several countries' markets. In financial information services, Bloomberg took leadership from Reuters and Dow Jones. The major stumbling block for established firms is technological change. What does research tell us about why technological change is such a problem for established firms?

COMPETENCE-ENHANCING AND COMPETENCE-DESTROYING TECHNOLOGICAL CHANGE Anderson and Tushman argue that some technological changes are 'competence destroying': they render obsolete the resources and capabilities of established firms. Other changes are 'competence enhancing': they preserve, even strengthen, the resources and capabilities of incumbent firms.[26] The quartz watch radically undermined the competence base of mechanical watchmakers, requiring transformation of the Swiss watch industry. Conversely, the turbofan, a major advance in jet engine technology, extended rather than weakened the capability base of existing jet engine manufacturers.

To determine the impact of a new technology on the competitive position of incumbent firms, it is necessary to look in detail at the implications of new technology for the individual resources and capabilities possessed by the established firms. In the typesetting industry, the ability of incumbent firms to withstand the transition to radically new technologies rested upon their strengths in certain key resources that were not undermined by new technology: customer relationships, sales and service networks and font libraries.[27]

ARCHITECTURAL AND COMPONENT INNOVATION A key factor determining the success of established firms in adapting to technological change is whether the technological innovation occurs at the component or the architectural level. Rebecca Henderson argues that innovations which change the overall architecture of a product create great difficulties for established firms because an architectural innovation requires a major reconfiguration of a company's strategy and organizational structure.[28] In automobiles, the hybrid engine was an important innovation, but it did not require a major reconfiguration of car design and engineering. The battery-powered electric motor is an architectural innovation: it requires redesign of the entire car and involves carmakers in creating systems for recharging. In many sectors of e-commerce – online grocery purchases and online banking – the Internet involved innovation at the component level (it provided a new channel of distribution for existing products). Hence, existing supermarket chains and established retail banks with their 'clicks 'n' bricks' business models have dominated online groceries and online financial services. However, with the transistor radio (outlined in Featured Example 5.1): although this innovation was based on a single component, it was an architectural innovation since it required established radio producers to radically change their approaches to product design, manufacturing and marketing.

Featured Example 5.1

In the mid-1950s, engineers at RCA's corporate R & D centre developed a prototype of a portable, transistorized radio receiver. The new product used technology in which RCA was accomplished (transistors, radio circuits, speakers, tuning devices), but RCA saw little reason to pursue such an apparently inferior technology. In contrast, Sony, a small, relatively new company, used the small, transistorized radio to gain entry into the US market. Even after Sony's success was apparent, RCA remained a follower in the market as Sony introduced successive models with improved sound quality and FM capability. The irony of the situation was not lost on the R & D engineers: for many years, Sony's radios were produced with technology licensed from RCA, yet RCA had great difficulty matching Sony's product in the marketplace.[29]

DISRUPTIVE TECHNOLOGIES Clayton Christensen of Harvard Business School has also questioned why established firms find it so difficult to adapt to new technology. He distinguishes between new technology that is sustaining – it augments existing performance attributes – and disruptive – it incorporates different performance attributes than the existing technology.[30]

In the disk-drive industry, some technological innovations – such as thin film heads and more finely dispersed ferrous oxide disk coatings – have enhanced the dominant performance criterion: recording density. Such innovation has typically been led by established industry leaders. Other disk-drive technologies – notably new product generations with smaller diameters – were disruptive in their impact: established companies were, on average, two years behind newcomers in launching the new disk sizes and typically lost their industry leadership.[31] Incumbents' resistance to the new disk sizes reflected two factors: inferior initial performance and customer resistance. In 1987, Connor Peripherals began shipping a 3.5-inch disk drive. Industry leader Seagate had developed a 3.5-inch drive but halted its development for two reasons: first, it was inferior to the existing 5.25-inch disk in terms of capacity and cost per megabyte of memory; second, Seagate's main customers, the manufacturers of desktop PCs, showed no interest in the 3.5-inch disks. The 3.5-inch disks were adopted by Compaq and laptop makers. By 1990, the rapid development of the 3.5-inch disk had rendered the 5.25-inch disk obsolete.[32]

Similarly with other technologies: steam-powered ships were initially slower, more expensive and less reliable than sailing ships. The leading shipbuilders failed to make the transition to steam power because their leading customers – the trans-ocean shipping companies – remained loyal to sail until after the turn of the 20th century. Steam power was used mainly for inland waters, which lacked constant winds. After several decades of gradual development for these niche markets, stream-powered ships were able to outperform sailing ships on ocean routes.

Managing strategic change

Given the many barriers to organizational change and the difficulties that companies experience in coping with disruptive technologies and architectural innovation, how can companies adapt to changes in their environment?

Just as the sources of organizational inertia are many, so too are the theories and methods of organizational change. Traditionally, the management of organizational change has been viewed as a distinct area of management. Organizational development comprises a set of methodologies through which an internal or external consultant acts as a catalyst for systemic change within a team or organizational unit.[33] Organizational development draws upon theories of psychology and sociology and is based upon a set of humanistic values. It emphasizes group processes as vehicles for organizational change. The emphasis of organizational development is upon individual organizational units and bottom-up change in larger organizations. Because our emphasis is on strategic change – the redirection and adaptation of the entire organization – our focus is on top-down change processes. Nevertheless, as political revolutions frequently demonstrate, the power of bottom-up change should not be underestimated.

Dual strategies and organizational ambidexterity

In Chapter 1, we learnt that strategy has two major dimensions: positioning for the present and adapting to the future. As we observed then, reconciling the two is difficult. Derek Abell argues that 'managing with dual strategies' is the most challenging dilemma that senior managers face:

> Running a successful business requires a clear strategy in terms of defining target markets and lavishing attention on those factors which are critical to success; changing a business in anticipation of the future requires a vision of how the future will look and a strategy for how the organization will have to adapt to meet future challenges.[34]

Abell argues that dual strategies require dual planning systems: short-term planning that focuses on strategic fit and performance over a one- or two-year period and longer-term planning to develop vision, reshape the corporate portfolio, redefine and reposition individual businesses, develop new capabilities and redesign organizational structures over periods of five years or more. Given the observation that companies are biased towards the exploitation of current resources and capabilities in relation to known opportunities, rather than exploration for new opportunities, most firms will emphasize short-term over long-term planning.

The challenges of reconciling 'mastering the present' with 'pre-empting the future' extend well beyond strategy formulation and the design of strategic planning systems. In recent years, Charles O'Reilly and Michael Tushman have stimulated interest in the **ambidextrous organization** that is 'capable of simultaneously exploiting existing competences and exploring new opportunities'.[35] Two types of organizational ambidexterity have been identified:

- Structural ambidexterity where different parts of the organization undertake exploratory and exploitative activities. It is usually easier to foster change initiatives in new organizational units rather than within the existing organization. For example, faced with the challenge of **disruptive technologies**, Christensen and Overdorf suggest that established companies develop products and businesses that embody the new technologies in organizationally separate units.[36] Such efforts show mixed results. In the opening case, we saw that IBM developed its PC in a separate unit in Florida – a thousand miles from IBM's corporate headquarters in New York.[37] Xerox's Palo Alto Research Center (PARC) pioneered many of the technologies that formed the basis of the microcomputer revolution of the 1980s. However, few of these innovations were exploited by Xerox's New York-based establishment; most flowed to nearby competitors Hewlett-Packard, Apple, Microsoft and Sun Microsystems.[38] Similarly, GM's Saturn subsidiary set up in Tennessee to pioneer new approaches to manufacturing and marketing did little to revitalize the parent organization.[39] Attempts by Continental, United, British Airways and several other legacy airlines to adapt to change by establishing budget airline subsidiaries were also costly failures.

- Contextual ambidexterity involves the same organizational units and the same organizational members pursuing both exploratory and exploitative activities. At Oticon, the Danish hearing aid company, employees were encouraged to sustain existing products while pursuing innovation and creativity.[40] Under the slogan 'Innovation from Everyone, Everywhere', Whirlpool sought to embed innovation throughout its existing organization: 'Innovation had been the responsibility of a couple of groups, engineering and marketing. Now, you have thousands of people involved.'[41]

Case Insight 5.6

Managing change within IBM

In the 1970s, IBM became the world's dominant supplier of mainframe computers. These computers, often costing as much as $9 million, required large air-conditioned rooms to house them and teams of up to 60 people to operate them. As IBM grew and developed its presence in this market, it naturally developed a 'mainframe mentality', that is to say it tended to view things in terms of the world it knew best. IBM's mainframe strategy comprised focusing upon a relatively small number of large customers with whom IBM established long-term relationships, high prices, high levels of technical support and vertical integration – IBM produced its own microprocessors and most other components and developed its own software.

The personal computer was a disruptive technology: its user base, its applications, its distribution and its price were radically different from the mainframes that were at the heart of IBM's business. It required a very different business strategy, based on high volumes, low margins and distribution through retail outlets. IBM's first foray into the PC market with its IBM 5100 was a dismal failure but, despite this setback, senior managers at IBM kept an eye on this emerging market and had the foresight to recognize its strategic significance. IBM realized that it needed to develop and launch its own personal computer quickly if it wanted to maintain its lead position in the computing industry and not lose out to smaller players.

William Lowe, the lab director at IBM's Boca Raton base in Florida, was assigned the seemingly impossible task of building a working IBM PC in a year. Lowe argued that the conventional 'ways of doing things' at IBM inhibited rapid development and persuaded the IBM board to set up, under his leadership, an independent business unit comprising a small group of technologists. This group was freed from the usual organizational constraints, controlled its own budget and had a degree of licence in the way it operated. Because of the time pressure, the group bought in some components of hardware and software from third-party suppliers rather than developing everything in-house. They also chose to make the PC's design details freely available to facilitate the rapid development of IBM-compatible hardware and software. The product was an immediate success and IBM developed a strong initial lead in the market.

Before the project was started, one analyst had commented that 'IBM bringing out a PC would be like teaching an elephant to tap dance'.[42] It seems that in the right environment and with skilful management even the largest of animals can become nimble.

Tools of strategic change management

If organizational change follows a process of punctuated equilibrium in which periods of stability are interspersed by periods of intense organizational upheaval, it follows that top management must play an active role in managing these interludes of strategic change. Most large companies exhibit periodic restructuring involving simultaneous changes in strategy, structure, management systems and top management personnel. Such restructuring typically follows declining performance caused either by a major external shock or by a growing misalignment between the firm and its external environment. For example, many of the major American car companies like General Motors and Ford went through major restructuring following the global downturn that followed the 2008 banking crisis.[43] A challenge for top management is to undertake large-scale change before the company is pressured by declining performance.

CREATING PERCEPTIONS OF CRISIS Change initiatives frequently fail because they become overwhelmed by the forces of inertia. A crisis sets up the conditions for strategic change by loosening the organization's attachment to the status quo. The problem is that by the time the organization is engulfed in crisis it is already too late, hence the merits of the CEO creating the perception of impending crisis within the company so that necessary changes can be implemented well before the real crisis emerges. At General Electric, even when the company was reporting record profits, Jack Welch was able to convince employees of the need for change in order to defend against emerging threats. Andy Grove's effectiveness at communicating his dictum 'Only the paranoid survive' helped Intel maintain a continual striving for improvement and development despite its dominance of the market for PC microprocessors.

ESTABLISHING STRETCH TARGETS Another approach to weakening the powers of organizational inertia is to continually pressure the organizations by means of ambitious performance targets. The idea is to set performance targets that are achievable, but only with an extension of employee effort, in order to motivate creativity and initiative while attacking complacency. Stretch targets are normally associated with short- and medium-term performance goals for individuals and organizational units. However, they also relate to long-term strategic goals. A key role of vision statements and ambitious strategic intent is to create a sustained sense of ambition and organizational purpose. These ideas are exemplified by Collins and Porras' notion of 'Big Hairy Ambitious Goals' that we discussed in Chapter 1.

CREATING ORGANIZATIONAL INITIATIVES Among the tools deployed by organizational leaders to influence their members, a potent one is an organization-wide initiative endorsed and communicated by the chief executive. Corporate initiatives sponsored by the CEO are effective for disseminating strategic changes, best practices and management innovations. At General Electric Jack Welch was an especially effective exponent of using corporate initiatives to drive organizational change. These were built around communicable and compelling slogans such as 'Be number 1 or number 2 in your industry', 'GE's growth engine', 'boundarylessness', 'six-sigma quality' and 'destroy-your-business-dot-com'.

REORGANIZATION AND NEW BLOOD By reorganizing the company structure, top management can create an opportunity for redistributing power, reshuffling top management and introducing new blood. Periodic changes in organizational structure can stimulate local initiatives, encourage searches for new solutions and result in a more effective exploitation of new ideas.[44] A typical pattern is to oscillate from periods of decentralization to periods of centralization.[45]

Organizational change is also stimulated by recruiting new managers from outside the organization. Externally recruited CEOs result in more strategic change than those promoted from within.[46] In many cases, boards of directors seek out an external CEO for the explicit purpose of leading strategic change, for example George Fisher (from Motorola) and Antonio Perez (from HP) at Eastman Kodak, Lou Gerstner (from RJR Nabisco) at IBM and Stephen Hester (from British Land) at Royal Bank of Scotland. Other members of the top management teams may also act as drivers of change: newcomers to top management hired outside the firms have been shown to be especially effective.[47]

Dynamic capabilities

The ability of some firms – IBM, General Electric, 3M, Shell and Toyota – to adapt to new circumstances while others ossify and fail implies differences in the capability base of different companies. David Teece and his colleagues introduced the term **dynamic capabilities** to refer to a 'firm's ability to integrate, build, and reconfigure internal and external competences to address rapidly changing environments'.[48]

The precise definition of a dynamic capability has proved contentious. Eisenhardt and Martin consider dynamic capabilities any capabilities that allow an organization to reconfigure its resources in order to adapt and change.[49] Winter and Zollo are more precise: a dynamic capability is a 'higher level' process through which the firm modifies its operating routines.[50] These differences are important. If dynamic capabilities are simply those that allow change to occur, they include product development capability, acquisition capability, research capability and HR recruitment capabilities. But if dynamic capability is restricted to higher-level capabilities that manage change in lower-level capabilities, we are referring to capabilities that are more strategic and embedded in top management practices. Winter emphasizes that these higher-order change capabilities are not simply ad hoc problem solving – they are approaches to strategic change that are routine, highly patterned and repetitious.[51]

Case Insight 5.7

Dynamic capabilities at IBM

IBM offers an example of these higher-level dynamic capabilities. Under the leadership of three CEOs – Lou Gerstner, Sam Palmisano and Ginni Rometty – IBM has developed a system for managing strategic change that comprises its Business Leadership Model, strategy processes such as its deep dive and Emerging Business Opportunities methodologies, its Strategic Leadership Forum and the Corporate Investment Fund.[52]

USING SCENARIOS TO PREPARE FOR THE FUTURE A company's ability to adapt to changes in its environment depends on its capacity to anticipate such changes. Yet predicting the future is hazardous, if not impossible. 'Only a fool would make predictions – especially about the future,' remarked movie mogul Samuel Goldwyn. But the inability to predict does not mean that it is not useful to think about what may happen in the future. Scenario analysis is a systematic way of thinking about how the future may unfold that builds on what we know about current trends and signals. Scenario analysis is not a forecasting technique but a process for thinking and communicating about the future.

Herman Kahn, who pioneered the use of scenarios first at the Rand Corporation and subsequently at the Hudson Institute, defined scenarios as 'hypothetical sequences of events constructed for the purpose of focusing attention on causal process and decision points'.[53] The multiple scenario approach constructs several distinct, internally consistent views of how the future may look five to 25 years ahead (shorter in the case of fast-moving sectors). Its key value is in combining the interrelated impacts of a wide range of economic, technological, demographic and political factors into a few distinct alternative stories of how the future may unfold. Scenario analysis can be either qualitative or quantitative, or involve some combination of the two. Quantitative scenario analysis models events and runs simulations to identify likely outcomes. Qualitative scenarios typically take the form of narratives and can be particularly useful in engaging the insight and imagination of decision makers.

For the purposes of strategy making, scenario analysis is used to explore likely paths of industry evolution, to examine developments in particular country markets, to think about the impact of new technologies and to analyse prospects for specific investment projects. Applied to industry evolution, scenarios can clarify and develop alternative views of how changing customer requirements, emerging technologies, government policies and competitor strategies can have an impact on industry structure and what the implications for competition and competitive advantage may be.

However, as with most strategy techniques, the value of scenario analysis is not in the results but in the process. Scenario analysis is a powerful tool for bringing together different ideas and insights, for surfacing deeply held beliefs and assumptions, for identifying possible threats and opportunities, for generating and evaluating alternative strategies, for encouraging more flexible thinking by managers and for building consensus. Evaluating the likely performance of different strategies under different scenarios can help identify which strategies are most robust and can assist in contingency planning by forcing managers to address 'What if?' questions. Featured Example 5.2 outlines the use of scenarios at Shell.

Featured Example 5.2

Multiple scenario development at Shell

Royal Dutch Shell has pioneered the use of scenarios as a basis for long-term strategic planning in an industry where the life of investment projects (up to 50 years) far exceeds the time horizon for forecasting (two or three years). In 1967, a 'Year 2000' study was inaugurated and scenario development soon became fundamental to Shell's planning process. Mike Pocock, Shell's former chairman, observed: 'We believe in basing planning not on single forecasts, but on deep thought that identifies a coherent pattern of economic, political, and social development.'

Shell views its scenarios as critical to its transition from planning towards strategic management, in which the role of the planning function is not so much to produce a plan but to manage a process, the outcome of which is improved decision making by managers. This involves continually challenging current thinking within the group, encouraging a wider look at external influences on the business, promoting learning and forging coordination among Shell's 200-odd subsidiaries.

Shell's global scenarios are prepared about every four years by a team comprising corporate planning staff, executives and outside experts. Economic, political, technological and demographic trends are analysed 20 years into the future. Shell's 2005–25 scenarios were based on three sets of forces – market incentives, community, and coercion and regulation – and three objectives – efficiency, social cohesion and security. Their interactions produced three scenarios, each embodying different social, political and economic conditions:

- *Low Trust Globalization:* A legalistic world where emphasis is on security and efficiency at the expense of social cohesion.
- *Open Doors:* A pragmatic world emphasizing social cohesion and efficiency with the market providing built-in solutions to crises of security and trust.
- *Flags:* A dogmatic world where community and security values are emphasized at the expense of efficiency.

Once approved by top management, the scenarios are disseminated by reports, presentations and workshops, where they form the basis for long-term strategy discussion by business sectors and operating companies.

Shell is adamant that its scenarios are not forecasts. They represent carefully thought-out stories of how the various forces shaping the global energy environment of the future may play out. Their value is in stimulating the social and cognitive processes through which managers envisage the future. CEO Van Der Veer commented: 'the imperative is to use this tool to gain deeper insights into our global business environment and to achieve the cultural change that is at the heart of our group strategy ... I know that they broaden one's mindset and stimulate discussions.'

Sources: Pierre Wack, 'Scenarios: Uncharted Waters Ahead', *Harvard Business Review* (September–October, 1985): 72 and 'Scenarios: Shooting the Rapids', *Harvard Business Review* (November–December 1985): 139; Arie De Geus, 'Planning as Learning', *Harvard Business Review* (March–April 1988): 70–4; Paul Schoemacher, 'Multiple Scenario Development: Its conceptual and behavioral foundation', *Strategic Management Journal* **14** (1993): 193–214; Shell Global Scenarios to 2025 (Shell International, 2005).

SHAPING THE FUTURE A succession of management gurus from Tom Peters to Gary Hamel have argued that the key to organizational change is not to adapt to external change but to create the future. Companies that adapt to change are doomed to play catch-up; competitive advantages accrue to those companies that act as leaders and initiate change. Hamel and Prahalad's 'new strategy paradigm' emphasizes the role of strategy as a systematic and concerted approach to redefining both the company and its industry environment in the future.[54]

According to Gary Hamel, in an age of revolution, 'the company that is evolving slowly is already on its way to extinction'.[55] The only option is to give up incremental improvement and adapt to a nonlinear world: revolution must be met by revolution. Achieving internal revolution requires changing the psychological and sociological norms of an organization that restrict innovation (Table 5.2).

Hamel's challenge for managers to cast off their bureaucratic chains and become revolutionaries is invigorating and inspiring. But is revolutionary change among established companies either feasible or desirable? Some established companies have achieved radical change:

- BMW survived the destruction of two world wars and in the process transformed itself from a producer of aero engines to a motorcycle company before emerging as one of the world's leading suppliers of luxury cars.
- Burberry, the British fashion house, was founded in 1856 as a manufacturer and retailer of gabardine raincoats. During the 20th century, it transformed itself from a supplier of rain and windproof outerwear to polar explorers, mountaineers and army officers into a global fashion brand.
- Amazon has only existed since 1995, yet during its first two decades of life it has demonstrated a remarkable capacity for change. Initially an online bookseller, it

Table 5.2 Shaking the foundations.

Old brick	New brick
Top management is responsible for setting strategy	Everyone is responsible for setting strategy
Getting better, getting faster is the way to win	Rule-busting innovation is the way to win
IT creates competitive advantage	Unconventional business concepts create competitive advantage
Being revolutionary is high risk	More of the same is high risk
We can merge our way to competitiveness	There's no correlation between size and competitiveness
Innovation equals new products and new technology	Innovation equals entirely new business concepts
Strategy is the easy part; implementation the hard part	Strategy is the easy part only if you're content to be an imitator
Change starts at the top	Change starts with activists
Our real problem is execution	Our real problem is incrementalism
Big companies can't innovate	Big companies can become gray-haired revolutionaries

Source: Adapted from G. Hamel, *Leading the Revolution* (Boston: Harvard Business School Press, 2000): 280–1. Adapted with permission.

expanded into an online supplier of almost every consumer good and then continued to diversify into book publishing, electronic hardware (Kindle), video streaming and cloud computing.

However, for most established companies, efforts at radical change have resulted in disaster:

- Enron's transformation from a utility and pipeline company to a trader and market-maker in energy futures and derivatives ended in its demise in 2001.
- Vivendi's multimedia empire built on the base of French water and waste utility fell apart in 2002.
- Nokia's metamorphosis from a forest products and cable manufacturer into the world's biggest supplier of wireless handsets is a remarkable tale of corporate change. Yet, ultimately, Nokia was unable to sustain corporate adaptation: in 2013, it sold its mobile phone business to Microsoft.
- RBS Group's transformation from a Scottish retail bank to the world's biggest commercial bank (as measured by total assets) through a series of cross-border acquisitions culminated in its rescue by the British government in 2008.

The perils of radical strategic change are not difficult to understand. At their core is the difficulty that established companies experience in developing the new organizational capabilities demanded by new circumstances or a new area of business. Let us turn to that issue now.

Developing new capabilities

Ultimately, adapting to a changing world is about developing the capabilities needed to renew competitive advantage. To get a glimpse into the challenges this presents, consider the distinctive capabilities (or 'core competencies') of some of today's leading companies and ask, 'Where did these capabilities come from?'

EARLY EXPERIENCES AND PATH DEPENDENCY In many, many instances distinctive capabilities can be traced back to the circumstances that prevailed during the founding and early development of these companies. In other words, organizational capability is **path dependent**: a company's capabilities today are the result of its history.[56] For example:

- How did Wal-Mart, Inc., the world's biggest retailer, develop its outstanding capability in supply chain logistics? As we saw in the closing case to Chapter 3, Walmart's super-efficient system of warehousing, distribution and vendor relationships was not the result of careful planning and design; it evolved from the circumstances that Walmart faced during its early years of existence. Its small-town locations in Arkansas and Oklahoma resulted in unreliable delivery from its suppliers. Consequently, Walmart established its own distribution system. What about the other capabilities that contribute to Walmart's remarkable cost efficiency? These too can be traced back to Walmart's origins in rural Arkansas and the values of its founder, Sam Walton.
- The world's leading oil and gas majors illustrate the same point (Table 5.3). Despite long histories of competing together in the same markets, with near-identical products and similar strategies, the majors display very different capability profiles. Industry leaders

Table 5.3 Distinctive capabilities as a consequence of childhood experiences: The oil majors.

Company	Distinctive capability	Early history
Exxon	Financial management	Exxon's predecessor, Standard Oil (NJ), was the holding company for Rockefeller's Standard Oil Trust
Royal Dutch Shell	Coordinating a decentralized global network of 200 operating companies	Shell Transport & Trading headquartered in London and founded to sell Russian oil in China and the Far East Royal Dutch Petroleum headquartered in The Hague and founded to exploit Indonesian reserves
BP	'Elephant hunting'	Discovered huge Persian reserves, went on to find Forties field (North Sea) and Prudhoe Bay (Alaska)
ENI	Deal making in politicized environments	The Enrico Mattei legacy; the challenge of managing government relations in post-war Italy
Mobil	Lubricants	Vacuum Oil Co. founded in 1866 to supply patented petroleum lubricants

Exxon and Royal Dutch Shell exemplify these differences. Exxon (now ExxonMobil) is known for its outstanding financial management capabilities exercised through rigorous investment controls and unrelenting cost efficiency. Royal Dutch Shell is known for its decentralized, international management capability, which allows it to adapt to different national environments and to become an 'insider' wherever it does business. These differences can be traced back to the companies' 19th-century origins. Exxon (then Standard Oil New Jersey) acted as holding company for Rockefeller's Standard Oil Trust, exercising responsibility for overall financial management. Shell was established to sell Russian oil in China and the Far East, while Royal Dutch was created to exploit Indonesian oil reserves. With head offices thousands of miles away in Europe, both parts of the group developed a decentralized, adaptable management style.

These observations are troubling for managers in established companies: if a firm's capabilities are determined during the early stages of its life, is it really possible to develop the new capabilities needed to adapt to current changes and the challenges of tomorrow? The presence of established capabilities and their embedding within an organizational structure and culture present formidable barriers to building new capabilities. Indeed, the more highly developed a firm's organizational capabilities, the greater the barrier they create. Because Dell Computer's direct-sales model was so highly developed, Dell found it difficult to adapt to selling though retail outlets as well, hence the argument that core capabilities are simultaneously core rigidities.[57]

INTEGRATING RESOURCES TO CREATE CAPABILITY The encouraging fact is that companies do develop new capabilities – all companies that have survived over periods of multiple decades have done so by creating capabilities that they did not possess before. To appreciate how this is done, let us look once more at the structure of organizational capability. In Chapter 3, we observed that organizational capability results from the combination of different resources, most importantly the skills of different organizational members. The effectiveness of this integration depends upon the presence of suitable processes, an appropriate organizational structure, motivation and overall organizational alignment, especially with the organization's culture.

Using each of these components, organizations can put in place the building blocks for developing new capabilities:

- *Processes:* Without processes, organizational capability will be completely dependent on individual skills. With processes (or organizational routines), we can ensure that task performance is efficient, repeatable and reliable. When Whirlpool launched its innovation drive, the emphasis was on creating processes: processes for training employees in the tools of innovation, processes for idea generation, processes for idea selection and development.[58] Once processes are in place, they are developed through routinization and learning; essential to capability development is the creation of mechanisms that facilitate 'learning by doing' and ensure the retention and sharing of learning.
- *Structure:* The people and processes that contribute to an organizational capability need to be located within the same organizational unit if they are to achieve the coordination needed to ensure a high performance capability. When Royal Dutch Shell wanted to develop capability in breakthrough innovation, it created a new organizational unit, Gamechanger. When Ducati wanted to create the capabilities needed for a successful MotoGP racing team, it established Ducati Corse as a separate subsidiary. At several of the business schools in which the authors have worked, a common complaint among students has been the lack of integration across courses, while a common aspiration of several MBA course directors has been to introduce multidisciplinary courses that involve students in cross-functional problem solving. However, little can be achieved if faculty members are located within specialist, discipline-defined departments and coordination across courses is limited to a single 'teachers' meeting' held each semester.
- *Motivation:* Again, we come back to the fundamental driver of performance in organizations: without motivation, not only will individuals give less than their best but also, equally important, they will not set aside their personal preferences and prejudices to integrate as a team. At Honda Motor, the development of automotive capabilities, especially in engine design, was driven by the passion of its founder Soichiro Honda for motorcycle racing.
- *Organizational alignment:* Finally, there is the issue of fit. Excellent capabilities require the components of capability to fit with one another and with the broader organizational context. As we saw in Chapter 3, Harley-Davidson's capabilities in delivering the 'Harley Experience' are the result of a close fit between the human resources, the brand, the traditions and the company's Milwaukie location. Imperfect alignment can stunt capability development: the failure of established airlines to launch low-cost subsidiaries (BA's Go, United's Ted, Continental's Continental Lite) reflects a misfit between the capabilities needed by a budget airline and the culture and management systems of legacy carriers. Corporate culture is a critical ingredient in this fit: in the privatized, competitive, deregulated telecom markets of the 21st century, former national monopolies such as British Telecom (BT), Deutsche Telekom and Verizon have had difficulty developing the capabilities needed to compete successfully outside their home markets.

DEVELOPING CAPABILITIES SEQUENTIALLY Developing new capabilities requires a systematic and long-term process of development that integrates the four components described above. For most organizations, the key challenge is not obtaining the underlying resources. Indeed, many examples of outstanding capabilities have resulted from the pressures of resource shortage. Toyota's lean production capability was born during a period of acute resource shortage in Japan.

If integrating resources into capabilities requires establishing processes, developing these processes through routinization and learning, putting in place the right structure, motivating the people involved and aligning the new capability with other aspects of the organization – the demands upon management are considerable. An organization must limit the number and scope of the capabilities that it is attempting to create at any point in time. One implication is that capabilities need to be developed sequentially rather than all at once.

The task of capability development is also complicated by the fact that we have limited knowledge about how to manage capability development. Hence, it may be helpful to focus not on the organizational capabilities themselves but on developing and supplying the products that use those capabilities. A trajectory through time of related, increasingly sophisticated products allows a firm to develop the 'integrative knowledge' that is at the heart of organizational capability.[59] Matsushita utilized this approach in developing operational capabilities in countries when establishing manufacturing in new countries:

> In every country batteries are a necessity, so they sell well. As long as we bring a few advanced automated pieces of equipment for the processes vital to final product quality, even unskilled labour can produce good products. As they work on this rather simple product, the workers get trained, and this increased skill level then permits us to gradually expand production to items with increasingly higher technology levels, first radios, then televisions.[60]

Where a company is developing an entirely new area of business, such a sequential approach can be effective. The key here is for each stage of development to be linked not just to a specific product (or part of a product) but also to a clearly defined set of capabilities. Featured Example 5.3 looks at the sequential approach to capability development followed by Hyundai Motor.

Featured Example 5.3

Hyundai Motor: Developing capabilities through product sequencing

Hyundai's emergence as a world-class automobile producer is a remarkable example of capability development over a sequence of compressed phases. Each phase of the development process was characterized by a clear objective in terms of product outcome, a tight time deadline, an empowered development team, a clear recognition of the capabilities that needed to be developed in each phase and an atmosphere of impending crisis should the project not succeed (Figure 5.5). The first phase was the construction of an assembly plant in the unprecedented time of 18 months in order to build Hyundai's first car – a Ford Cortina imported in semi-knocked down (SKD) form. Subsequent phases involved products of increasing sophistication and the development of more advanced capabilities.

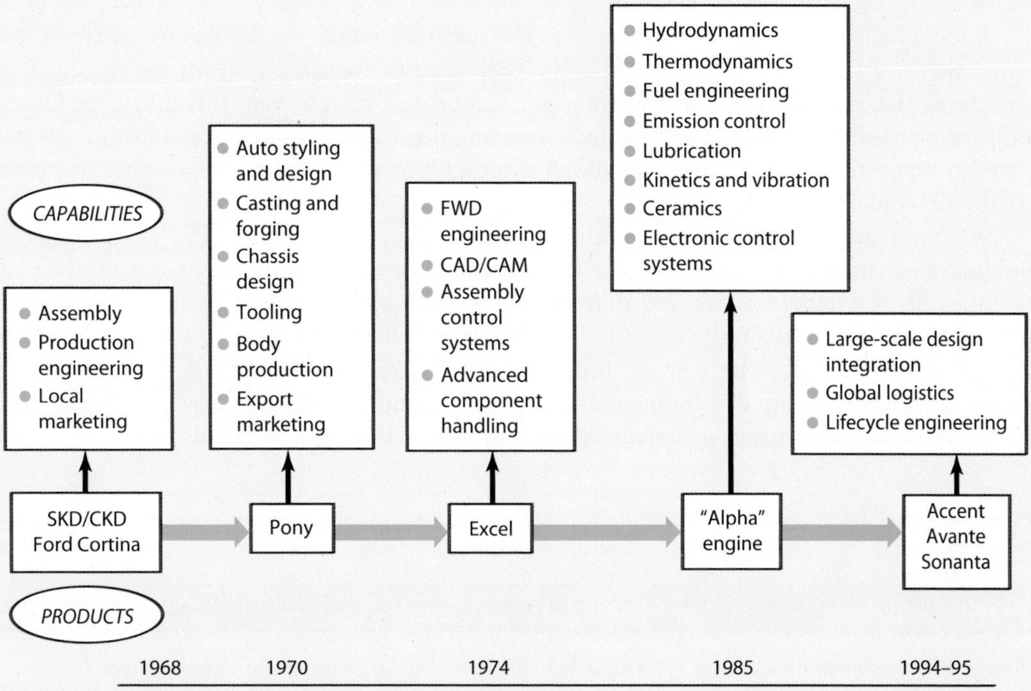

Figure 5.5 Phased development at Hyundai Motor.

Source: L. Kim, 'Crisis construction and organizational learning: Capability building and catching up at Hyundai Motor,' *Organizational Science* 9 (1998): 506–21. Reproduced with permission.

Summary

In this chapter, we have argued that some patterns are evident in the evolutionary paths that industries follow. The lifecycle model is a useful approach to exploring the impact of market maturity, technology development and knowledge dissemination on industry structure and the basis of competitive advantage. Classifying industries according to their stage of development can in itself be an insightful exercise because:

- It acts as a shortcut in strategy analysis. Categorizing an industry according to its stage of development can alert us to the type of competition likely to emerge and the kinds of strategy likely to be effective.
- It encourages comparison with other industries. By highlighting similarities and differences with other industries, such comparisons can help us gain a deeper understanding of the strategic characteristics of an industry.

- It directs attention to the forces of change and direction of industry evolution, thereby helping us to anticipate and manage change.

A key challenge of managing change is the need for managers to operate in two time zones: they need to optimize for today while preparing the organization for the future. The concept of the ambidextrous organization is an approach to resolving this dilemma. Other tools for managing strategic change include: creating perceptions of crisis, establishing stretch targets, corporate-wide initiatives, recruiting external managerial talent, developing dynamic capabilities and scenario planning.

Whatever approach or tools are adopted to manage change, strategic change requires building new capabilities. To the extent that an organization's capabilities are a product of its entire history, building new capabilities is a formidable challenge. To understand how organizations build capability we need to understand how resources are integrated into capability, in particular the role of processes, structure, motivation and alignment. The complexities of capability development and our limited understanding of how capabilities are built point to the advantages of sequential approaches to developing capabilities.

Summary table

Learning objectives	Summary
Recognize the different stages of industry development and understand the factors that drive the process of industry evolution	We have seen that some regular patterns exist in the evolutionary paths that many industries follow. Industry lifecycles typically comprise four stages: introduction, growth, maturity and decline. This evolution is driven by changes in industries' growth rates over time, changes in technology and the creation and diffusion of knowledge over time
Identify the key success factors associated with industries at different stages of their development and the strategies appropriate to different stages in the industry lifecycle	During the introduction phase, the emphasis is on product innovation and marketing, whereas during the growth phase the key to success is being able to scale up production efficiently and effectively. By the time a market reaches maturity, price competition tends to be intense and successful strategies involve cost efficiency through mass production and low input prices. In the decline phase, firms can still operate profitably if they can rationalize capacity in an orderly way, find protected market niches or innovate. The alternative is to exit at an appropriate time
Appreciate the sources of organizational inertia that act as barriers to change	We have explored a number of different sources of organizational inertia, including competency traps, social and political systems, bounded rationality and complex organizational configurations that act as barriers to change
Be familiar with different approaches to managing strategic change, including the quest for organizational ambidexterity and the use of tools of strategic change management	We have considered how firms seek to remain agile through the idea of organizational ambidexterity and have explored some of the tools of strategic change management, including creating perceptions of crisis, establishing stretch targets, creating organizational initiatives and reorganization

Learning objectives	Summary
Be familiar with the concept of 'dynamic capabilities' and how firms can anticipate change and shape their futures.	We have noted that precise definition of dynamic capabilities has proved contentious but that the concept encapsulates a firm's ability to reconfigure itself in order to adapt and change. We have also examined how scenario development can be used to anticipate change and how firms may be able, at least in part, to shape their own futures.
Be aware of different approaches that firms have taken in developing organizational capabilities	We have seen that new capabilities may be developed internally or through acquisition, but the main challenge is integrating resources into capabilities and aligning new capabilities with other aspects of the organization

Further reading

Seminal readings on strategy and industry lifecycle include:

Harrigan, K. R. and Porter, M. E. (1983). End-game strategies for declining industries. *Harvard Business Review*, July–August, 111–20 (a classic explanation of the strategies available to firms in declining markets).

Hoffer, C. (1975). Towards a contingency theory of business strategy. *Academy of Management Journal*, 18(4), 784–810.

The ambidextrous organization is discussed in:

O'Reilly, C. and Tushman, M. (2013). The Ambidextrous Organization: Past, present and future. *Academy of Management Perspectives* 27(4), 324–38.

The key features of scenario planning are covered in:

Schoemaker, P. (1995). Scenario Planning: A tool for strategic thinking. *Sloan Management Review* Winter, 25–40.

Self-study questions

1 Consider the changes that have occurred in a comparatively new industry (e.g. wireless communication services, wireless handsets, video game consoles, online auctions, bottled water, online book retailing). To what extent has the evolution of the industry followed the pattern predicted by the industry lifecycle model? What particular features does the industry have that have influenced its pattern of evolution? At what stage of development is the industry today? How is the industry likely to evolve in the future?

2 Select a product that has become a dominant design for its industry (e.g. the IBM PC in personal computers, McDonald's in fast food, Harvard in MBA education). What factors caused one firm's product architecture to become dominant? Why did other firms imitate this dominant design? To what extent has the dominant design evolved or been displaced?

3 Select a product the market for which is declining (e.g. video rental stores, photographic film, correction fluid for typed documents, floppy disks). What advice would you give to a firm that is continuing to operate in your selected industry? Justify your advice.

4 Track an organizational change process that you have experienced or have researched. What tools were used to manage the change? What else could have been done to generate a willingness to change?

5 Consider an industry facing fundamental technology change (e.g. the recorded music industry and digital technology, computer software and open-source, newspapers and the Internet, cars and alternative fuels, corporate IT services and cloud computing). Develop two alternative scenarios for the future evolution of your chosen industry. In relation to one leading player in the industry, identify the problems posed by the new technology and develop a strategy for how the company could adapt to and exploit the changes you envisage.

Closing Case

Cirque du Soleil

Cirque du Soleil (Circus of the Sun) was formed in 1984 by Guy Laliberté and a group of fellow street performers when they won a grant from the Canadian Arts Council to provide entertainment to mark the 450th anniversary of Cartier's discovery of Canada. From its modest beginnings the company has grown into the world's biggest theatrical performance company with over 5400 employees from 40 different counties; a corporate headquarters, training and development centre in Montreal; permanent companies in Las Vegas, Orlando and Riviera Maya, Mexico; and four separate touring companies. Cirque du Soleil's success is all the more remarkable since it has been achieved within an industry that was believed to be in terminal decline.

A brief history of the circus

The invention of the circus is commonly attributed to an Englishman, Philip Astley, in 1768. The early circus comprised of four main elements – equestrian events, clowns, acrobats and jugglers – and circus companies toured the country moving from place to place. Circus arenas were circular to facilitate the spectacle and to accommodate popular acts, such as riders standing on the backs of galloping horses. Astley's innovative form of entertainment was quickly copied and, over time, spread to many different countries, with showmen like P. T. Barnum and the Ringling Brothers becoming legendary names in the business. Promoters added human and animal curiosities and menageries to their repertoires to enhance the display, and during its heyday in the 19th century whole towns would turn out to see performances as the circus passed through.

The Depression of the 1920s and 1930s together with two world wars took its toll on the industry and by the 1950s audiences were beginning to decline. Other forms of popular entertainment like cinema, television and sporting events were beginning to come to the fore. Increasingly, the circus was seen as something for children rather than adults and as the decades progressed even children's interest in this form of entertainment began to wane, displaced by video games and other forms of amusement. At the same time, campaigns by animal welfare groups created bad publicity for circus companies and reduced the public's appetite for shows that used performing animals. By the 1980s, the main surviving circus companies were the state-owned circuses of the USSR, China and other communist countries.

The reinvention of the circus experience

In the West, the skills and traditions of the circus – acrobatics, juggling, clowning and the bohemian, carefree lifestyle of the performers – were kept alive mainly by street performers. Guy Laliberté's vision was the reinvention of the circus experience by building his troupe of acrobats, stilt-walkers, jugglers and musicians into an integrated, multisensory experience that would appeal to new groups of customers, including adults and corporate clients, who were more used to trips to the ballet and the opera. Cirque du Soleil preserved key elements of the circus experience – the tent, the clowns and the acrobats – but set out to enhance and transform each of them. The tent, long the main symbol of the circus, was redesigned for audience comfort and a sophisticated external image; the clowns shifted from slapstick to a more urbane style; animals were eliminated and the primary focus was shifted towards acrobatic displays of unprecedented grace, daring and sophistication. Cirque borrowed heavily from the theatre and developed its acts into multimedia spectacles with original musical scores and stunning lighting effects. Whereas in the past circus shows had comprised a series of disconnected displays, Cirque built its performances around story lines and, while it emphasized exceptional performances, eschewed celebrity acts.

The evolution of Cirque du Soleil

Cirque du Soleil's transformation from a group of street performers led by fire-breather and visionary Guy Laliberté and co-founder Daniel Gauthier, a computer programmer who became the company's business manager, into an international entertainment company involved risk taking and attention to building the resources and capabilities needed to realize Laliberté's vision. An invitation to perform at the Los Angeles Arts Festival in 1987 proved a turning point. The show received critical acclaim and allowed the company to display its work to a much wider audience. The North American tour that followed enabled the company to establish itself on a sound financial footing.

The next two decades saw almost continuous expansion of Cirque's activities. In 1990, Cirque travelled to Europe and two years later to Asia. In 1992, Laliberté sought a resident venue for Cirque's shows in Las Vegas. After having been turned down by the board of Caesar's Palace, who deemed the venture too risky, Cirque entered into an agreement with Mirage Resorts, which resulted in Cirque creating a resident show at Mirage's Las Vegas resorts. This was followed by a deal with Disney to produce a resident show for the Walt Disney Resort in Orlando, Florida. The quest for permanent venues encouraged Cirque to ally itself with property developers to create mixed-use complexes that would be based on Cirque-created environments. A plan to acquire and convert London's derelict Battersea Power station into a venue eventually failed – as did several other planned ventures. However, in 2014, Cirque announced an agreement with Grupo Vidanta to create its first resident show outside of North America at Riviera Maya, Mexico.

Expansion created tension and disagreement between the two founders. In 2000, Gauthier sold his 50% shareholding back to Laliberté for an undisclosed amount. In 2004, Laliberté stepped down from his roles as President and Chief Operating Officer and handed over control for day-to-day operations while retaining the titles of Founder, Chief Executor and 'Guide'. In 2008, he sold 20% of his shares to two Dubai-based investment groups for $600m but still retains 75% ownership.

By 2014, Cirque operated four touring companies and had three resident locations. At Las Vegas, Cirque had built a huge presence: in March 2014, it was offering eight different shows in eight separate MGM-owned resorts. Through partnerships with other organizations, it diversified into a number of activities beyond its core Cirque du Soleil shows. These included a tour based on the life and music of Elvis Presley and two on Michael Jackson. Cirque was involved in movie and TV productions; special events, which included corporate and private shows and entertainment for sporting events such as the Super Bowl and the opening ceremony for the 2015 Pan American Games; a range of fashion clothing designed in collaboration with Desigual and sold through Cirque's online boutique; and the design of restaurants, hotel lounges and nightclubs.

Cirque du Soleil's management combines anarchy and meticulous planning. Its creative, training and operational activities are concentrated at its international headquarters in Montreal, where almost 2000 of its employees are based. In addition, Cirque has regional offices in London, Las Vegas, Macau and Melbourne. Key headquarters functions include:

- *Product development:* New shows take two to three years to develop. One or two new shows are produced each year; a show may run for over a decade (*Alegría* ran for 19 years with more than 5000 performances). Each new show is developed by a creative team headed by an artistic director. The starting point is identification of a theme for a new show – an interactive process in which CEO Daniel Lamarre and founder Guy Laliberté are actively involved. The initial broad vision is developed through a process of creative friction in which team members are encouraged to challenge and contribute, sometimes as a single word, rather than a confined mandate, to allow others to have the flexibility to contribute during the creative process. The inspiration and creativity of the development teams are supplemented by input from researchers who feed information of cultural and artistic trends, which allows the creative directors to access the appeal of the new show's content and style. Lamarre and Laliberté review progress every six months and suggest changes to the creative director.
- *Human resource management:* Recruitment involves a global search led by the casting department, an international team of talent scouts. The HR database includes 24 giants, 466 contortionists, 14 pickpockets, 35 skateboarders, 1278 clowns, eight dislocation artists and 73 people classified as 'small' – including a one-metre tall Brazilian acrobat. Training, however, is concentrated at the Creative Centre within the International Headquarters, which includes three acrobatic training rooms, a dance studio, a studio theatre and weight-training facilities.
- *Logistics:* In March 2014, Cirque was performing in 11 different cities throughout the world and 10 of these were touring. Taking down, shipping and setting up a show typically requires between eight and 11 days and is an immensely complex process, especially when it involves moving the show across national borders. The process is managed by the tour planning team based in the Montreal headquarters and involves close collaboration with Cirque's logistics partner, DHL through DHL's Global Trade Fairs & Events unit.
- *Technology:* The Creative Centre also includes a design studio and production facilities for costumes and engineering workshops for designing and manufacturing sets. Information Technology and Knowledge Management play a central role in all of Cirque's development and operating activities from the development of initial storyboards for new shows, through set and costume design, to the management of logistics, artists' training and fitness programmes, productions, marketing and sales. An IT team is an integral part of each touring show. Knowledge management is critical to the development of new shows. Every aspect of the development of a new show generates documents and images that are stored in an interactive database which can then support learning, stimulate creativity and short-circuit development processes for subsequent processes.

Addressing the future

During 2014, Cirque du Soleil was forced into a painful reappraisal of its strategy. Cirque's reputation and finances had been dented by a series of setbacks. During 2012, it was forced to close four major touring shows incurring losses of around $250 million. During 2012 and 2013, Cirque launched only two new shows: *Amaluna* and *Michael Jackson One*. While the latter received critical and popular acclaim, many viewed Cirque's series of shows based round the lives of former rock stars (Elvis, the Beatles and Michael Jackson) as symptomatic of the company's abandoning creativity in favour of commercialism. *Amaluna* had received a lukewarm reception from reviewers. Other new productions were also disappointments – most notably Cirque's 3D movie *Worlds Away*, which flopped at the box office. In January 2013, the company laid off 400 members of its head office staff to streamline its operations in the light of rising costs and slowing revenue growth. Finally, the death of a female acrobat from a fall during a production of *Ka* at the MGM Grand was a blow to Cirque's morale and reputation.

Some observers viewed Cirque's problems as a consequence of over-expansion: during 2008–2011, it had launched 10 new shows and had diversified into a range of new ventures outside of live entertainment. Underlying the issue of Cirque's optimal size and diversity of activities was the underlying tension within Cirque between creative artistry and commercialism. Cirque's website extols its 'creative approach':

> Cirque du Soleil was built on values and deep convictions which rest on a foundation of audacity, creativity, imagination and our people: the backbone of our success.
>
> Cirque du Soleil places creativity at the core of all its endeavours so as to ensure limitless possibilities. This is why the creative challenge is of the utmost importance with each new business opportunity, whether it is a show or any other creative activity.
>
> Cirque du Soleil dream is also an integral part of its philosophy: To take the adventure further, step beyond its dreams and, above all, believe that our people are the engine of our enterprise. Cirque du Soleil offers its artists and creators the necessary freedom to imagine their most incredible dreams and bring them to life.
>
> The International Head Office, located in Montreal, wishes to be an international laboratory of creativity, where our world's best creative minds, craftsmen, experts on various domains and performers can collaborate on creative projects. By assuming the roles of catalyst and unifier, Cirque du Soleil is able to reinvent itself with each new chapter of its history.

However, the driving force behind Cirque's creativity was its co-founder, Guy Laliberté. By 2014, Laliberté's involvement in Cirque had been greatly reduced and his attention had shifted towards charity (notably the One Drop Foundations campaign to expand access to clean water in the developing world), spaceflight, and poker. At the same time, there was a question as to whether the excitement and wonder of Cirque performances had become diluted through overexposure. With 19 different shows simultaneously being performed throughout the globe together with Cirque du Soleil's presence on TK and movie theatres, and the Cirque du Soleil's brand appearing upon a widening variety of merchandise and entertainment experiences, was there a risk that that the brand would lose its cache?

Sources: www.cirquedusoleil.com; T. Delong and V. Vijayaraghavana, *Cirque du Soleil,* Harvard Business School Case 9-403-006, 2002; Avi Dan, 'The Secret That Inspires Cirque du Soleil's Culture of Innovation: Creative Friction', http://www.forbes.com/sites/avidan (29th May 2012); M.-H. Jobin and J. Talbot, 'Tour Planning at Cirque du Soleil', *International Journal of Case Studies in Management* **9** (March 2011).

Case questions

- To what extent has the evolution of the circus industry followed the pattern predicted by the industry life-cycle model?
- How would you account for Cirque du Soleil's success in a declining market?
- How has Cirque du Soleil changed over time? Outline some of the new capabilities you think it has developed as it has moved from a small touring company to an enterprise employing more than 5000 people with resident as well as touring shows.
- What strategy alternatives are available to Cirque du Soleil? Which would you recommend to CEO Daniel Lamarre and majority owner Guy Laliberté?

Notes

1 H. Landis Gabel, *Competitive Strategies for Product Standards* (New York: McGraw-Hill, 1991).

2 The term 'skunk works' refers to a group within an organization that has a high degree of autonomy, is unhampered by the normal corporate bureaucracy and is given the task of working on an important or secret project.

3 D. C. Wise, 'Can John H. Sculley clean up the mess at Apple? With Steve Jobs on the sidelines, the company will no longer go it alone', *Business Week* (29th July 1985): 70–2.

4 T. Levitt, 'Exploit the product life cycle', (November–December 1965): 81–94; G. Day, 'The product life cycle: Analysis and applications', *Journal of Marketing*, 45 (Autumn 1981): 60–7.

5 J. M. Utterback and F. F. Suarez, 'Patterns of industrial evolution, dominant designs and firms' survival', Working Paper (Sloan School of Management, MIT 1993): 3600–93.

6 P. Anderson and M. L. Tushman, 'Technological discontinuities and dominant designs', *Administrative Science Quarterly*, 35 (1990): 604–33.

7 M. A. Cusumano and D. B. Yoffie, *Competing on Internet Time: Lessons from Netscape and its battle with Microsoft* (New York: Free Press, 1998).

8 C. Arthur (2013) 'Future tablet market will outstrip PCs and reach 900m people, Forrester says', *The Guardian*, 7th August.

9 The first use of the term 'born global' is commonly attributed to M. W. Rennie, 'Global competitiveness: Born global', *McKinsey Quarterly*, 4 (1993): 45–52. The concept is developed by P. McDougall, P. Shane and B. Oviatt, 'Explaining the formation of international new ventures', *Journal of Business Venturing*, 9 (1994): 469–87.

10 M. Mazzucata, 'The PC industry: New economy or early life cycle', *Review of Economic Dynamics*, 5 (2002): 318–45.

11 High rates of entry and exit may continue well into maturity. In US manufacturing industries in any given year, it was found that 39% of larger companies were not industry participants five years earlier and 40% would not be participants five years later. See T. Dunne, M. J. Roberts and L. Samuelson, 'Patterns of firm entry and exit in US manufacturing industries', *Rand Journal of Economics*, 19 (1988): 495–515.

12 R. McGrath *The End of Competitive Advantage: How to keep your strategy moving as fast as your business* (Boston: Harvard Business Review Press, 2013).

13 See, for example, 'Dell and Hewlett Packard: Rebooting their systems' *The Economist* (12th March 2010).

14 See, for example, M. Jacobides, 'Industry change through vertical disintegration: How and why markets emerged in mortgage banking', *Academy of Management Journal*, 48 (2000): 465–98.

15 B. Levitt and J. G. March, 'Organizational Learning', *Annual Review of Sociology*, 14 (1988): 319–40.

16 D. Leonard-Barton, 'Core capabilities and core rigidities: A paradox in managing new product development', *Strategic Management Journal*, (Summer Special Issue 1992): 111–25.

17 M. T. Hannan, L. Polos and G. R. Carroll, 'Structural inertia and organizational change revisited III: The evolution of organizational inertia', *Stanford GSB Research Paper*, 1734 (April 2002).

18 P. J. DiMaggio and W. Powell, 'The Iron Cage Revisited': Institutional isomorphism and collective rationality in organizational fields', *American Sociological Review*, 48 (1983): 147–60.

19 J.-C. Spender, *Industry Recipes* (Oxford: Blackwell, 1989).

20 J. G. March, 'Exploration and exploitation in organizational learning', *Organizational Science*, 2 (1991): 71–87.

21 P. R. Milgrom and J. Roberts, 'Complementarities and fit: Strategy, structure, and organizational change in manufacturing', *Journal of Accounting and Economics*, 19 (1995): 179–208; M. E. Porter and N. Siggelkow, 'Contextual interactions within activity systems', *Academy of Management Perspectives*, 22 (May 2008): 34–56.

22 E. Trist, 'The sociotechnical perspective', in A. H. Van de Ven and W. Joyce (eds), *Perspectives on Organization Design and Behavior* (New York: John Wiley & Sons, Inc., 1984).

23 J. W. Rivkin, 'Imitation of complex strategies', *Management Science*, 46 (2000): 824–44.

24 M. E. Porter and N. Siggelkow, 'Contextual Interactions within Activity Systems', *Academy of Management Perspectives*, 22 (May 2008): 34–56.

25 M. L. Tushman and E. Romanelli, 'Organizational evolution: A metamorphosis model of convergence and reorientation', in L. L. Cummins and B. M. Staw (eds), *Research in Organizational Behavior* (1985): 171–26; E. Romanelli and M. L. Tushman, 'Organizational transformation as punctuated equilibrium: An empirical test', *Academy of Management Journal*, 37 (1994): 1141–66.

26 M. L. Tushman and P. Anderson, 'Technological discontinuities and organizational environments', *Administrative Science Quarterly*, 31 (1986): 439–65.

27 M. Tripsas, 'Unravelling the process of creative destruction: Complementary assets and incumbent survival in the typesetter industry', *Strategic Management Journal*, 18 (Summer Special Issue 1997): 119–42.

28 R. M. Henderson and K. B. Clark, 'Architectural innovation: The reconfiguration of existing systems and the failure of established firms', *Administrative Science Quarterly*, 35 (1990): 9–30.

29 Ibid.

30 J. Bower and C. M. Christensen, 'Disruptive technologies: Catching the wave', *Harvard Business Review* (January–February 1995): 43–53.

31 C. M. Christensen, *The Innovator's Dilemma* (Boston: Harvard Business School Press, 1997).

32 Ibid.

33 T. G. Cummins and C. G. Worley, *Organization Development and Change*, 8th edn (Cincinnati, OH: Southwestern College Publishing: 2005).

34 D. F. Abell, *Managing with Dual Strategies* (New York: Free Press, 1993): 3.

35 C. A. O'Reilly and M. L. Tushman, 'The ambidextrous organization', *Harvard Business Review* (April 2004): 74–81.

36 C. M. Christensen and M. Overdorf, 'Meeting the challenge of disruptive change', *Harvard Business Review* (March–April 2000): 66–76.

37 T. Elder, 'Lessons from Xerox and IBM', *Harvard Business Review* (July/August 1989): 66–71.

38 *Xerox PARC: Innovation without profit?* ICMR Case Study (2004).

39 J. O'Toole, *Forming the Future: Lessons from the Saturn Corporation* (New York: Harper, 1996).

40 G. Verona and D. Ravasi, 'Unbundling dynamic capabilities: An exploratory study of continuous product innovation', *Industrial and Corporate Change*, 12 (2002): 577–606.

41 Interview with Nancy Snyder, Whirlpool's vice-president of leadership and strategic competency development, *Business Week* (6th March 2006): 425.

42 http://www-03.ibm.com/ibm/history/exhibits/pc25/pc25_birth.html, accessed 29th September 2014.

43 T. Klier and J. Rubenstein 'The restructuring of the U.S. auto industry in the 2008–9 recession', *Economic Development Quarterly*, 27 (2013): 144–59.

44 N. Siggelkow and D. A. Levinthal, 'Escaping real (non-benign) competency traps: Linking the dynamics of organizational structure to the dynamics of search', *Strategic Organization*, 3 (2005): 85–115.

45 J. Nickerson and T. Zenger, 'Being efficiently fickle: A dynamic theory of organizational choice', *Organization Science*, 13 (1992): 73–94.

46 M. F. Wiersema, 'Strategic consequences of executive succession within diversified firms', *Journal of Management Studies*, 29 (September/October 2002): 547–67.

47 R. Agarwal, P.-L. Chen and C. Williams, *Renewal through Rookies: The growth effects of top management recruits from different levels, organizations, and industries*, Working Paper, Bocconi University, Milan (2011).

48 D. J. Teece, G. Pisano and A. Shuen, 'Dynamic capabilities and strategic management', *Strategic Management Journal*, 18 (1997): 509–33.

49 K. M. Eisenhardt and J. A. Martin, 'Dynamic capabilities: What are they?' *Strategic Management Journal*, 21 (2000): 1105–21. See also H. Volberda, *Building the Flexible Firm* (Oxford: OUP, 1998).

50 M. Zollo and S. G. Winter, 'Deliberate learning and the evolution of dynamic capabilities', *Organization Science*, 13 (2002): 339–51; S. G. Winter, 'Understanding dynamic capabilities', *Strategic Management Journal*, 24 (2003): 991–5.

51 Winter (2003), op. cit.

52 J. B. Harreld, C. A. O'Reilly and M. L. Tushman, 'Dynamic capabilities at IBM: Driving strategy into action', *California Management Review*, 49 (2007): 21–43.

53 H. Kahn, *The Next 200 Years: A scenario for America and the world* (New York: William Morrow, 1976). For a guide to the use of scenarios in strategy making, see K. van der Heijden, *Scenarios: The art of strategic conversation* (Chichester: John Wiley & Sons Ltd, 2005).

54 G. Hamel and C. K. Prahalad, *Competing for the Future* (Boston: Harvard Business School Press, 1995).

55 G. Hamel, *Leading the Revolution* (Boston: Harvard Business School Press, 2000): 5.

56 B. Wernerfelt, 'Why do firms tend to become different?' in C. E. Helfat (ed.), *Handbook of Organizational Capabilities* (Oxford: Blackwell, 2006): 121–33.

57 D. Leonard-Barton, 'Core capabilities and core rigidities', *Strategic Management Journal*, 13 (Summer 1992): 111–26.

58 N. T. Snyder and D. L. Duarte, *Unleashing Innovation: How Whirlpool transformed an industry* (San Francisco: Jossey-Bass, 2008).

59 C. E. Helfat and R. S. Raubitschek, 'Product sequencing: Co-evolution of knowledge, capabilities and products', *Strategic Management Journal*, 21 (2000): 961–79. The parallel development of capabilities and products has also been referred to as 'dynamic resource fit'. See: H. Itami, *Mobilizing Invisible Assets* (Boston: Harvard University Press, 1987): 125.

60 Takahashi, *What I Learned from Konosuke Matsushita* (Tokyo: Jitsugyo no Nihonsha, 1980); in Japanese, quoted by H. Itami, *Mobilizing Invisible Assets* (Boston: Harvard University Press, 1987): 25.

6

Technology-based industries and the management of innovation

Introduction and objectives

In the previous chapter, we saw that technology is the primary force that creates new industries and transforms existing ones. In the past quarter century, technology-based new industries have included wireless telephony, biotechnology, photovoltaic power, fibre optics, online financial services, nanotechnology and 3D printing. Industries transformed by technology include the telecom sector, which has been turned upside-down by wireless technology and the Internet; the pharmaceutical industry, where the molecular biology revolution has made it difficult for established firms to maintain their lead; and healthcare, where changes in diagnostic tools, medical equipment and surgical techniques have transformed the ways in which health services are delivered.

The impact of technology has not been limited to science-based industries. A key feature of the past decade has been the pervasive influence of digital technologies – including communication technologies and the Internet. The music and book publishing industries have been reshaped and the way we organize our social lives has been transformed by social networking services like Facebook and Twitter and online dating agencies such as eHarmony and Match.com.

Our focus in this chapter is on business environments where technology is a key driver of change and an important source of competitive advantage. These technology-intensive industries include both emerging industries (those in the introductory and growth phases of their lifecycle) and established industries where technology continues to be the major driver of competition (e.g. pharmaceuticals, chemicals, telecommunications and electronics). The issues we examine, however, are also relevant to a much broader range of industries where technology has the *potential* to create competitive advantage.

In this chapter, our primary concern is the use of technology as a tool of competitive strategy. How does the firm use technology to establish competitive advantage?

By the time you have completed this chapter, you will be able to:

- analyse how technology affects industry structure and competition;
- identify the factors that determine the returns to innovation and evaluate the potential for an innovation to establish competitive advantage;
- formulate strategies for exploiting innovation and managing technology, focusing in particular on:
  - the relative advantages of being a leader or a follower in innovation,
  - identifying and evaluating strategic options for exploiting innovation,
  - how to win standards battles,
  - how to manage risk;
- design the organizational conditions needed to implement such strategies successfully.

This chapter is organized as follows. First, we examine the links between technology and competition in technology-intensive industries. Second, we explore the potential for innovation to establish sustainable competitive advantage. Third, we deal with key issues in designing technology strategies, including timing (to lead or to follow), alternative strategies for exploiting an innovation, setting industry standards and managing risk. Finally, we examine the organizational conditions needed for the successful implementation of technology-based strategies.

Opening Case
eBook readers

The first commercial eBook reader (e-reader) was launched in 1997 by SoftBook Press, a California start-up. Like today's e-readers, the product displayed text and had a built-in modem that allowed purchasers to download content, but it was bulky, expensive ($599) and heavy (1.4 kg), so it had few immediate advantages over paper books. Nonetheless, the market potential of this electronic device was soon recognized and many established electronics firms, for example Hewlett-Packard and Sony, started to experiment with e-reader technologies. NuvoMedia, another Californian start-up, entered the market in 1998 with a slightly cheaper, smaller product, but this did not have a built-in modem and required content to be acquired using a personal computer and then transferred to the device.[1] At the beginning of 2000, both SoftBook Press and NuvoMedia were acquired by Gemstar International, a firm that provided interactive television programme technology (TV guides) to cable and satellite television providers and consumer electronics companies. This company had ambitious expansion plans to grow the eBook market.

Gemstar introduced two new products, the REB 1100 and 1200, with longer battery lives, easier-to-read screens and built-in copyright protection for digital content. The price of the readers remained reasonably high (between $299 and $699, depending on the model), but the company was confident it could reduce costs significantly as sales grew. To encourage take-up, Gemstar sought agreements with traditional book publishers to introduce new titles in the REB format and promoted the idea of launching some titles exclusively for their readers prior to more general publication. While, in public, publishers hailed the emergence of the e-reader as a welcome innovation, few actually offered their bestselling titles in the REB format. By January 2001, only five of the 15 titles listed in the *New York Times'* list of bestsellers were available in REB readers.[2] Unfortunately for Gemstar, its core business in television technology deteriorated in 2002 and, at the same time, the company became embroiled in legal challenges with regard to some of its accounting practices. As a consequence, Gemstar was not able to push ahead with its planned $100 million marketing campaign to popularize eBooks and its e-readers and the already wary publishers became even more reluctant to release their book content in an e-format. Without Gemstar's pioneering efforts, the market for eBook readers failed to take off and languished until Sony entered the market in September 2006 with its Personal Reader System (PRS 500).

The competition hots up

Sony's new e-reader utilized a display technology that made the screen easy to read even in full sunlight, used very little battery power and was cheaper than the early eBook readers. In addition, learning from Apple's success with its iPod music player and iTunes music library, Sony realized the critical importance of having reasonably priced content available to complement its reader. The company entered into agreements with HarperCollins, Simon Schuster and Random House to publish books, and sales of its e-reader began to grow. It wasn't long, however, before competition emerged. In 2007, Amazon launched the Kindle. The Kindle had two main advantages over the Sony reader; it incorporated technology that allowed users to surf the Internet as well as read text and it enabled users to purchase eBooks from its newly developed online Kindle store. Many users were already familiar with ordering goods and services online and Amazon had significant capability in, and a reputation for, online book retailing. Sony responded to Amazon's entry by bringing an upgraded, less expensive version of the PRS reader onto the market and in 2008 introduced touch-screen technology. Amazon, in turn, innovated with the Kindle 2, launched in February 2009, and followed up with the release of a range of Kindle 2 products later that year. In 2010, competition intensified further when Barnes & Noble entered the market with its Nook e-reader and the Toronto-based entrepreneur Mike Serbinis launched the Kobo as a low-cost, minimalist alternative to the more expensive devices on the market at the time. It was also the year in which Apple launched its iPad.

The arrival of the iPad

Apple's iPad was not, strictly speaking, an eBook reader; rather, it was a tablet computer positioned in the market space between a laptop computer and a smartphone. The iPad offered a wider range of functions than the available e-readers because it could be used to watch videos, surf the Internet, play games and view photographs as well as read books. The iPad's colour displays and backlit screen meant that it was better suited to display content with pictures, for example comic books, newspapers and magazines, but this additional functionality also imposed some constraints, like shorter battery life than rival products. The iPad was an immediate success with sales growing from three million in the second quarter of 2010 to 7.3 million in the fourth quarter and Apple soon established a dominant position in the tablet computer market.[3] Other firms were quick to copy and, according to *The Economist* magazine, by early 2011 there were '100 tablet devices from 60 different manufacturers scrambling for part of the tablet computer market.'[4]

The impact of tablet computers on e-reader sales was not felt immediately because tablets were more expensive than e-readers and, because they were multipurpose devices, didn't offer the same quality of reading experience for book lovers. Incremental innovation in e-reader design continued apace and the devices became sleeker, lighter, stored more books and allowed the reader to turn pages more quickly. E Ink Corporation, the company that provided the screen technologies incorporated in the majority of e-readers, continually improved their displays and improved readability in different lighting conditions. By 2011, shipments of e-readers had risen to 22.7 million but the expansion in demand proved very short-lived.[5]

The e-reader market in 2014

The demand for e-readers peaked in 2011 and went into sharp decline thereafter. Purchases of e-books were still rising but readers were making greater use of their existing devices or using multipurpose devices such as tablets and smartphones to access digital books. Competition drove down the price of tablets to the point where some models occupied the same price band as e-readers and more and more consumers turned to tablets, perceiving the benefits of multifunctionality to outweigh the disadvantages associated with non-dedicated devices. The leading players in the market – Amazon (Kindle), Barnes & Noble (Nook), Sony (PRS) and Kobo, Inc. (Kobo) – all suffered, but some players fared worse than others.

Amazon weathered the storm better that most: because Amazon had extended its reach in overseas markets such as China and India, sales of Kindles continued to increase in absolute terms, albeit at a lower rate than previously. Sales of Kindles and eBooks were estimated to constitute around 11% of Amazon's total revenue in 2013.[6] Success in the e-reader market depended on the availability of reasonably priced digital content that was device compatible. Amazon's strong existing relationships with content providers was, therefore, of critical importance. For Amazon, Kindle devices were primarily a vehicle for selling digital content including books, audiobooks, movies and games. This 'razor and blades' model involved cutting the price of its e-readers to grow the market for content.[7] The company invested large sums in improving its devices, adding functionality and narrowing the difference between tablet computers and e-readers.

Barnes & Noble, America's largest bookstore chain, was much less successful. Sales of Nook e-readers suffered significant year-on-year decline from 2011 onwards partly because competition forced prices down and partly because fewer units were sold. At the end of the 2013 fiscal year, the company posted losses of $475 million on its Nook operation and announced its intention to exit from the manufacture of colour readers, preferring instead to enter partnerships with consumer electronics manufacturers to co-brand devices. Despite negotiating deals with Microsoft and Pearson (a British education and publishing company), laying off staff and cutting costs, the Nook division continued to flounder, but for Barnes & Noble e-readers were a central plank in its efforts to stem the tide of sales losses from its physical bookstore. As the CEO put it: 'Your best chances of success for selling digital content is on your own dedicated devices which have your brand or co-brand on them', so the company continued to develop new devices albeit, where possible, in partnership with others.

Despite being an early mover in the market, in February 2014 Sony announced its exit from the US e-book market and the transfer of its business to the Kobo platform. The sales of its readers had failed to take off and its digital bookstore was small in comparison to that of its main rivals. Despite their fit with Sony's mission, e-reader sales constituted a tiny proportion of Sony's total revenues and incurred losses. However, Sony did not abandon the market altogether: soon after announcing its exit from consumer e-book readers, Sony launched a new document e-reader aimed at the corporate and professional market. The device, named Digital Paper, allowed users to annotate documents and write on a digital screen in much the same way as they would on paper but with the added advantage that documents could be uploaded, downloaded, stored and shared digitally. The product incorporated Sony's latest proprietary technology together with innovative display technology developed by E Ink Corporation. Priced at $1100, the product was positioned at the top end of the e-reader market but presented the same challenge for Sony' as its e-book predecessors, namely how could the company move Digital Paper from a niche product to a 'must have' device in order to profit from its innovation?

With the exit of Sony, Kobo was able to position itself as the world's no. 2 supplier of eBook readers. It had followed a distinctive strategy: in addition to its low prices, it developed apps for Windows, Blackberry and Android devices that gave users easy access to the Kobo digital bookstore. Despite a small US market share, its 'multilocal strategy' involved Kobo entering new countries by establishing partnerships with leading physical bookstore chains, for example Fnac in France, WHSmith in the UK and offering a 'Kobo experience' tailored to local market needs. Books were available in local languages and care was taken to make sure users in different countries could easily access their favourite authors and favourite genres. Within these markets, Kobo targeted heavy readers: those reading ten or more books a year, compared to the average of three of four. Kobo also offered a self-publishing platform that allowed authors to publish their own work and gave readers access to unique content. In 2011, Kobo was acquired by Rakuten, a Japanese company offering a wide range of Internet-delivered content and services. By 2014, the company claimed to have more than 18 million users in 190 countries with a digital book library of more than four million titles in 68 languages. Although Rakuten did not separate its Kobo activities from its other businesses in its public financial statements, in his statement to investors the chairman and CEO, Hiroshi Mikitani, indicated that Kobo was growing nicely but had yet to return a profit.[8]

In 2014, predictions for the industry were gloomy. Commentators suggested that demand for e-books had tapered off and that there was little future for stand-alone devices like e-readers. Firms like E Ink were diversifying away from e-reader technology and Sony and others looked poised to exit the market. If the predictions of sharp decline are correct the product lifecycle of e-readers will have been very short indeed even by the standards of the volatile consumer electronics industry.[9]

Competitive advantage in technology-intensive industries

Innovation forms the key link between technology and competitive advantage. It is the quest for competitive advantage that causes firms to invest in innovation; it is innovation that is responsible for new industries coming into being; and it is innovation that is the main reason why some firms are able to dominate their industries. Let us begin by exploring what we mean by 'innovation' and the conditions under which innovation generates profitability.

The innovation process

Invention is the creation of new products and processes through the development of new knowledge or from new combinations of existing knowledge. Most inventions are the result of novel applications of existing knowledge. Samuel Morse's telegraph, patented in 1840, was based on several decades of research into electromagnetism from Ben Franklin to Ørsted, Ampère and Sturgeon. Current eBook readers utilize touch-screen technology that was pioneered by Dr Samuel C. Hurst in 1971.

Innovation is the initial commercialization of invention by producing and marketing a new good or service or by using a new method of production. Once introduced, innovation diffuses: on the demand side, through customers purchasing the good or service; on the supply side, through imitation by competitors. An innovation may be the result of a single invention (most product innovations in chemicals and pharmaceuticals involve discoveries of new chemical compounds) or it may combine many inventions (the development of light-emitting diodes, LEDs, involved a number of linked breakthroughs in physics and materials science). Not all invention progresses into innovation: among the patent portfolios of most technology-intensive firms are inventions that have yet to find a viable commercial application. Similarly,

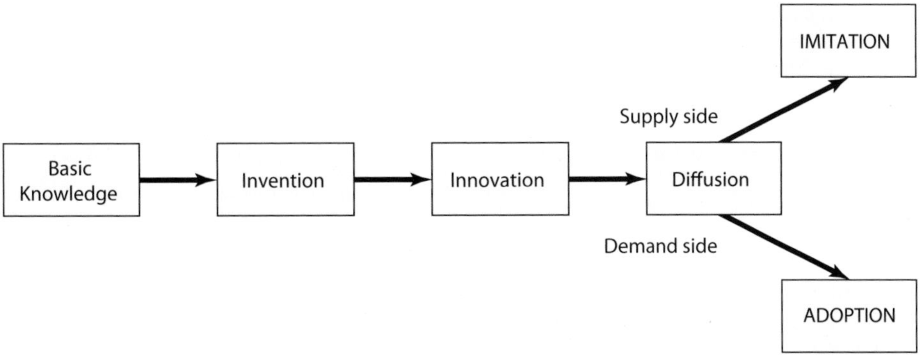

Figure 6.1 The development of technology: From knowledge creation to diffusion.

many innovations may involve little or no new technology: eBooks have brought together a number of existing technologies such as e-ink, fingerprint-resistant coatings and lithium polymer batteries; most new types of packaging – including the vast array of tamper-proof packages – involve novel design but no new technology.

Figure 6.1 shows the pattern of development from knowledge creation to invention and innovation. Historically, the lags between knowledge creation and innovation have been long; however, recently the innovation cycle has speeded up.

Chester F. Carlson invented xerography in 1938 by combining established knowledge about electrostatics and printing. The first patents were awarded in 1940. Xerox purchased the patent rights and launched its first office copier in 1958. By 1974, the first competitive machines were introduced by IBM, Kodak, Ricoh and Canon.

The jet engine, employing Newtonian principles of forces, was patented by Frank Whittle in 1930. The first commercial jet airliner, the De Havilland Comet, flew in 1957. Two years later, the Boeing 707 was introduced.

The mathematics of 'fuzzy logic' was developed by Lotfi A. Zadeh at Berkeley during the 1960s. By the early 1980s, Dr Takeshi Yamakawa of the Kyushu Institute of Technology had registered patents for integrated circuits embodying fuzzy logic, and in 1987 a series of fuzzy logic controllers for industrial machines was launched by Omron of Kyoto. By 1991, the world market for fuzzy logic controllers was estimated to be worth $2 billion.[10]

MP3, the audio file compression software, was developed at the Fraunhofer Institute in Germany in 1987; by the mid-1990s, the swapping of MP3 music files had taken off in US college campuses and in 1998 the first MP3 player, Diamond Multimedia's Rio, was launched. Apple's iPod was introduced in 2001.

The profitability of innovation

'If a man … make a better mousetrap than his neighbor, though he build his house in the woods, the world will make a beaten path to his door,' claimed Ralph Waldo Emerson. Yet,

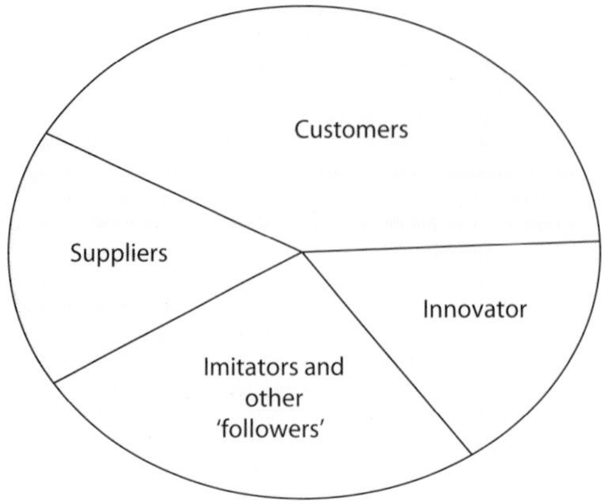

Figure 6.2 Appropriation of value: Who gets the benefits from innovation?

the inventors of new mousetraps and other gadgets, too, are more likely to be found at the bankruptcy courts than in the millionaires' playgrounds of the Caribbean. Certainly, innovation is no guarantor of fame and fortune, either for individuals or for companies. There is no consistent evidence that either R & D intensity or frequency of new product introductions are positively associated with profitability.[11]

The profitability of an innovation to the innovator depends on the value created by the innovation and the share of that value that the innovator is able to appropriate. The value created by an innovation is distributed among a number of different parties (Figure 6.2). In the case of the personal computer industry (the opening case in Chapter 5), the innovators – Tandy, Commodore and Apple – earned modest profits from their innovation. The imitators – IBM, Dell, Compaq, Acer, Toshiba and a host of other later entrants – did somewhat better, but their returns were overshadowed by the huge profits earned by the suppliers to the industry: Intel in microprocessors, Seagate in disk drives, Sharp in flat-panel displays and Microsoft in operating systems. However, because of strong competition in the industry, the greatest part of the value created by the personal computer was appropriated by customers, who typically paid prices for their PCs that were far below the value that they derived.

The term **regime of appropriability** is used to describe the conditions that influence the distribution of returns to innovation. In a strong regime of appropriability, the innovator is able to capture a substantial share of the value created: NutraSweet artificial sweetener (developed by Searle, subsequently acquired by Monsanto), Pfizer's Viagra and Pilkington's float glass process generated huge profits for their owners. In a weak regime of appropriability, other parties derive most of the value. In Internet telephony (VoIP), ownership of technologies is diffused and standards are public, with the result that no players are likely to earn massive profits. Four factors are critical in determining the extent to which innovators are able to appropriate the value of their innovation: property rights, the tacitness and complexity of the technology, lead-time and complementary resources.

PROPERTY RIGHTS IN INNOVATION Appropriating the returns to innovation depends, to a great extent, on the ability to establish property rights in the innovation. It was the desire to protect the returns to inventors that prompted the English Parliament to pass the

1623 Statute of Monopolies, which established the basis of patent law. Since then, the law has been extended to several areas of intellectual property, including:

- *Patents:* exclusive rights to a new and useful product, process, substance or design. Obtaining a patent requires that the invention is novel, useful and not excessively obvious. Patent law varies from country to country. In the US, a patent is valid for 17 years (14 for a design).
- *Copyrights:* exclusive production, publication or sales rights to the creators of artistic, literary, dramatic or musical works. Examples include articles, books, drawings, maps, photographs and musical compositions.
- *Trademarks:* words, symbols or other marks used to distinguish the goods or services supplied by a firm. In the US and UK, they are registered with the Patent Office. Trademarks provide the basis for brand identification.
- *Trade secrets:* offer a modest degree of legal protection for recipes, formulae, industrial processes, customer lists and other knowledge acquired in the course of business.

The effectiveness of intellectual property law depends on the type of innovation being protected. For new chemical products (e.g. a drug or plastic), patents can provide effective protection. For products that involve new configurations of existing components or new manufacturing processes, patents may fail to prevent rivals from innovating around them. The scope of the patent law has been extended to include life forms created by biotechnology, computer software and business methods. Business method patents have generated considerable controversy, especially Amazon's patent of 'one-click-to-buy' Internet purchasing.[12] While patents and copyright establish property rights, their disadvantage (from the inventor's viewpoint) is that they make information public. Hence, companies may prefer secrecy to patenting as a means of protecting innovations.

In recent decades, companies have devoted increasing attention to protecting and exploiting the economic value of their intellectual property. When Texas Instruments (TI) began exploiting its patent portfolio as a revenue source during the 1980s, the technology sector as a whole woke up to the value of its knowledge assets. During the 1990s, TI's royalty income exceeded its operating income from other sources. One outcome has been an upsurge in patenting. An average of 231 000 patents were granted by the US Patent Office in each year between 2009 and 2011 – well over double the annual rate during the 1980s.

TACITNESS AND COMPLEXITY OF THE TECHNOLOGY In the absence of effective legal protection, the extent to which an innovation can be imitated by a competitor depends on the ease with which the technology can be comprehended and replicated. This depends, first, on the extent to which the technical knowledge is codifiable. Codifiable knowledge, by definition, is that which can be written down. Hence, if it is not effectively protected by patents or copyright, diffusion is likely to be rapid and the competitive advantage not sustainable. Financial innovations such as mortgage-backed securities and credit default swaps embody readily codifiable knowledge that can be copied very quickly. Similarly, Coca-Cola's recipe is codifiable and, in the absence of trade secret protection, is easily copied. Intel's designs for advanced microprocessors are codified and copyable; however, the processes for manufacturing these integrated circuits are based on deeply tacit knowledge.

The second key factor is complexity. Every new fashion, from the Mary Quant miniskirt of 1962 to Stella McCartney's shift dresses of 2013, involves simple, easy-to-copy ideas. Airbus's A380 and the Altera Corporation's Stratix V FPGA chip (one of the world's most complex integrated circuits) represent entirely different challenges for the would-be imitator.

LEAD-TIME Tacitness and complexity do not provide lasting barriers to imitation, but they do offer the innovator *time*. Innovation creates a *temporary* competitive advantage that offers a window of opportunity for the innovator to build on the initial advantage.

The innovator's **lead time** is the time it will take followers to catch up. The challenge for the innovator is to use initial lead-time advantages to build the capabilities and market position to entrench industry leadership. Microsoft, Intel and Cisco Systems were brilliant at exploiting lead-time to build advantages in efficient manufacture, quality and market presence. Conversely, British companies are notorious for having squandered their lead-time advantage in jet planes, radars, CT scanners and genomics.

Lead-time allows a firm to move down its learning curve ahead of followers.[13] In new generations of microprocessors, Intel has traditionally been first to market, allowing it to move quickly down its experience curve, cut prices and so pressure the profit margins of its rival AMD.

COMPLEMENTARY RESOURCES Bringing new products and processes to market requires not just invention but also the diverse resources and capabilities needed to finance, produce and market the innovation. These are referred to as **complementary resources** (Figure 6.3). Chester Carlson invented xerography, but was unable for many years to bring his product to market because he lacked the complementary resources needed to develop, manufacture, market, distribute and service his invention. Conversely, Searle (and Monsanto, its later parent company) was able to provide almost all the development, manufacturing, marketing and distribution resources needed to exploit its NutraSweet innovation. As a result, Carlson was able to appropriate only a tiny part of the value created by his invention of the plain-paper Xerox copier, while Searle/Monsanto was successful in appropriating a major part of the value created by its new artificial sweetener.

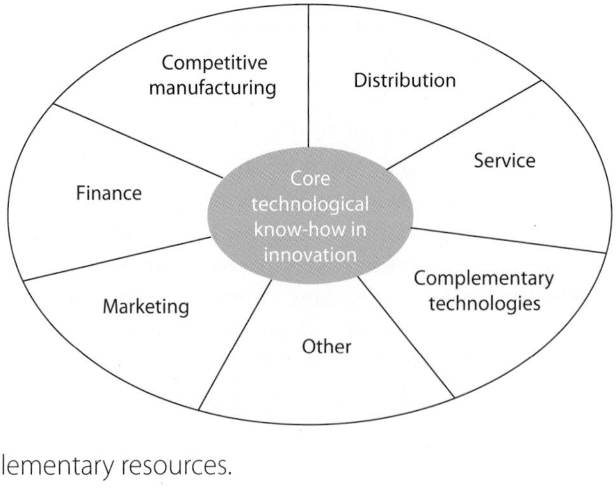

Figure 6.3 Complementary resources.

Complementary resources may be accessed through alliances with other firms, for example biotech firms ally with large pharmaceutical companies for clinical testing, manufacture and marketing.[14] When an innovation and the complementary resources that support it are supplied by different firms, the division of value between them depends on their relative power. A key determinant of this is whether the complementary resources are *specialized* or *unspecialized*. Fuel cells may eventually displace internal combustion engines in many of the world's cars. However, the problem for the developers of fuel cells is that their success depends on car manufacturers making specialized investments in designing a new range of cars, oil companies providing specialized refuelling facilities and service and repair firms investing in training and new equipment. The widespread adoption of fuel cells will require the benefits of the innovation to be shared widely with the different providers of these complementary resources.

Where complementary resources are generic, the innovator is in a much stronger position to capture value. Because Adobe Systems' Acrobat Portable Document Format (pdf) works with files created in almost any software application, Adobe is well positioned to capture most of the value created by its innovatory software product. However, one advantage of co-specialized complementary resources is that they raise barriers to imitation. Consider the threat that Linux presents to Microsoft Windows' dominance of PC operating systems. Because Intel has adapted its microprocessors to the needs of Windows and most applications software is written to run on Windows, the challenge for the Linux community is not just to develop a workable operating system but also to encourage the development of applications software and hardware that are compatible with the Linux operating system.

Case Insight 6.1

Who will appropriate the value of eBook readers?

We have noted that the extent to which innovators are able to appropriate the value of their innovation depends on property rights, the tacitness and complexity of the technology, lead-times and complementary resources. We can use this framework to speculate on who could capture the value created by the innovations in e-readers.

Intellectual property issues loom large in this market with all the major players seeking to obtain and defend patents, enforce copyright and establish trademarks. Intellectual property rights have often been acquired through mergers and acquisitions, for example Gemstar took over SoftBook Press and NuvoMedia to gain those companies' intellectual property and, more recently, Google acquired a company called eBook Technologies in 2011 to gain access to its patents.[15] Disputes over patents have also been common, for example in March 2009 Discovery Patent Holdings filed a suit against Amazon claiming that Amazon's Kindle violated its 'Electronic Book Security and Copyright Protection System' patent and in November of the same year Spring Design brought a suit against Barnes & Noble regarding the technology used in the Nook 3G e-reader.

While recognizing that intellectual property rights are of tactical significance to firms operating in this market, the codified nature of the technology together with the wide range of different technologies in use and the rapid pace of innovation make it unlikely that competitors will be able to establish strong property rights with regard to e-readers.

The exceptions here are ARM Holdings and E Ink Corporation. ARM is a British company that owns and licenses semiconductor intellectual property to a network of manufacturers. ARM central processing units are estimated to be used in 90% of all e-readers and 95% of tablet computers.[16] ARM does not manufacture or sell central processing units based on its own designs but licenses the architecture to third parties. E Ink was founded in 1997 as a spin-off of the MIT Media Lab. E Ink owns the intellectual property on the electronic paper displays that are incorporated into the majority of e-readers.

While e-readers utilize an array of sophisticated technologies, innovations in this market are rapidly disseminated and easily copied by manufacturers of electronic devices. The lead-times between new product introductions in this market have been very short. For these reasons e-readers have become commodities in much the same way as PCs. There is strong price competition between vendors, which is good news for consumers but means that manufacturers' profit margins are slim.[17] Few of the major players have managed to profit from sales of e-readers. However, complementary resources, particularly the availability of a wide range of affordable digital content, play a key role in this market. To expand the range of material available to users, many of the e-reader suppliers have made copyright-expired books available free of charge. Others have provided the opportunity for authors, who have had difficulty finding an outlet for their work through leading publishers, to distribute their books digitally, bypassing the traditional channels.

Overall, greater profits are captured from the sales of eBooks than eBook readers and the winners are those organizations that have succeeded in developing linkages across the value chain rather than those who have focused on a narrower subset of activities. Amazon, for example, has been more successful than Sony in the e-reader market because Kindle is supported by a large online store of books and other digital content and many customers are familiar with Amazon's 1-Click purchase facility. Publishers have been unable to capture the lion's share of the value created by eBooks because of the bargaining power established by the book retailers that have developed strong positions in the e-reader market.

Strategies to exploit innovation: How and when to enter

Having established some of the key factors that determine the returns to innovation, let us consider a few of the main questions concerning the formulation of strategies to manage technology and exploit innovation.

Alternative strategies to exploit innovation

How should a firm maximize the returns to its innovation? A number of alternative strategies are available. Figure 6.4 orders them according to the size of the commitment of resources and capabilities that each requires. Thus, licensing requires little involvement by the innovator in subsequent commercialization, hence a limited investment. Internal commercialization, possibly through creating a new enterprise or business unit, involves a much greater investment of resources and capabilities. In between, there are various opportunities for collaboration with other companies. Joint ventures and strategic alliances typically involve substantial resource sharing between companies. On a more limited scale, specific activities may be outsourced to other companies.

	Licensing	Outsourcing certain functions	Strategic alliance	Joint venture	Internal commercialization
Risk and return	Little investment risk but returns also limited. Risk that the licensee either lacks motivation or steals the innovation	Limits capital investment, but may create dependence on suppliers/partners	Benefits of flexibility. Risks of informal structure	Shares investment and risk. Risk of partner disagreement and culture clash	Biggest investment requirement and corresponding risks. Benefits of control
Resources requirements	Few	Permits external resources and capabilities to be accessed	Permits pooling of the resources and capabilities of more than one firm		Substantial requirements in terms of finance, production capability, marketing capability, distribution, etc.
Examples	Ericsson with its Bluetooth wireless technology; Dolby Labs with its sound reduction technology; Qualcomm and CDMA	Microsoft's Xbox was largely designed by other companies and Flextronics does the manufacturing	Ballard's strategic alliance with Daimler Chrysler to develop fuel cells	Psion created Symbian as a joint venture with Ericsson, Nokia and Motorola to develop the Symbian mobile phone operating system	Larry Page and Sergey Brin established Google Inc. to develop and market their Internet search technology

Figure 6.4 Alternative strategies for exploiting innovation.

The choice of strategy mode depends on two main sets of factors: the characteristics of the innovation and the resources and capabilities of the firm.

CHARACTERISTICS OF THE INNOVATION The extent to which a firm can establish clear property rights in an innovation critically determines the choice of strategy options. Licensing is only viable where ownership in an innovation is clearly defined by patent or copyrights. Thus, in pharmaceuticals, licensing is widespread because patents are clear and defensible. Many biotech companies engage only in R & D and license their drug discoveries to large pharmaceutical companies that possess the necessary complementary resources. Royalties from licensing its sound-reduction technologies accounted for 89% of Dolby Laboratories' 2013 revenues. Conversely, Steve Jobs and Steve Wozniak, developers of the Apple I and Apple II computers, had little option other than to go into business themselves – the absence of proprietary technology ruled out licensing as an option.

The advantages of licensing are, first, that it relieves the company of the need to develop the full range of complementary resources and capabilities needed for commercialization and, second, that it can allow the innovation to be commercialized quickly. If the lead-time offered by the innovation is short, multiple licensing can allow for a fast global rollout. The problem, however, is that the success of the innovation in the market is totally dependent on the commitment and effectiveness of the licensees. James Dyson, the British inventor of the bagless vacuum cleaner, created his own company to manufacture and market his 'dual cyclone' vacuum cleaners after failing to interest any major appliance company in a licensing deal for his technology.

RESOURCES AND CAPABILITIES OF THE FIRM As Figure 6.4 shows, different strategies require very different resources and capabilities. Hence, the choice of how to exploit an innovation depends critically upon the resources and capabilities that the innovator brings to the party. Start-up firms possess few of the complementary resources and capabilities needed to commercialize their innovations. Inevitably, they will be attracted to licensing or to accessing the resources of larger firms through outsourcing, alliances or joint ventures. New industries often follow a two-stage evolution where 'innovators' do the pioneering and 'consolidators' with their complementary resources do the developing. In biotechnology and electronics, technology is typically developed initially by a small, technology-intensive start-up, which then licenses to, or is acquired by, a larger, established firm.

Conversely, large, established corporations that can draw on their wealth of resources and capabilities are better placed for internal commercialization. Companies such as Sony, DuPont, Siemens, Hitachi and IBM have traditionally developed innovations internally – yet, as technologies evolve, converge and splinter, even these companies have increasingly resorted to joint ventures, strategic alliances and outsourcing arrangements to access technical capabilities outside their corporate boundaries.

Ron Adner observes that innovation increasingly requires coordinated responses by multiple companies. Innovating firms need to identify and map their innovation ecosystem, then manage the interdependencies within it. The failed introduction of HDTV can be attributed to inadequate coordination among TV manufacturers, production studios and broadcasters.[18] The initial slow take-up of e-readers could also be attributed to the lack of a coordinated response between device manufacturers and publishers.

Timing innovation: To lead or to follow?

To gain competitive advantage in emerging and technologically intensive industries, is it best to be a leader or a follower in innovation? As Table 6.1 shows, the evidence is mixed: in some products, the leader has been the first to grab the prize; in others, the leader has succumbed to the risks and costs of pioneering. Optimal timing of entry into an emerging industry and the introduction of new technology are complex issues. The advantage of being an early mover depends on the following factors:

- *The extent to which innovation can be protected by property rights or lead-time advantages.* If an innovation is appropriable through a patent, copyright or lead-time advantage, there is advantage in being an early mover. This is especially the case where patent protection is important, as in pharmaceuticals. Notable patent races include that between Alexander Graham Bell and Elisha Gray to patent the telephone (Bell got to the Patent Office a few hours before Gray),[19] and Celera Inc and the National Institute of Health to patent the sequence of the human genome.[20]
- *The importance of complementary resources.* The more important are complementary resources in exploiting an innovation, the greater the costs and risks of pioneering. Several firms – from Clive Sinclair with a battery-driven car to General Motors with a fuel-cell car – have already failed in their attempts to develop and market an electric car. The problem for the pioneer is that the development costs are huge because of the need to orchestrate multiple technologies and establish self-sufficiency across a range of business functions. Followers are also favoured by the fact that, as an industry develops, specialist firms emerge as suppliers of complementary resources. Thus, in pioneering the development of the British frozen foods industry, Unilever's Bird's Eye subsidiary had to set up an entire chain of cold stores and frozen distribution facilities.

Table 6.1 Leaders, followers and winners in emerging industries.

Product	Leader	Follower	The winner
Jet airliner	De Havilland (Comet)	Boeing (707)	Follower
Float glass	Pilkington	Corning	Leader
X-ray scanner	EMI	General Electric	Follower
Office PC	Xerox	IBM	Follower
VCRs	Ampex/Sony	Matsushita	Follower
Instant camera	Polaroid	Kodak	Leader
Pocket calculator	Bowmar	Texas Instruments	Follower
Microwave oven	Raytheon	Samsung	Follower
Fibre-optic cable	Corning	Many companies	Leader
Videogames console	Atari	Nintendo/Sony	Followers
Disposable diaper	Procter & Gamble	Kimberley-Clark	Leader
Inkjet printer	IBM and Siemens	Hewlett-Packard	Follower
Web browser	Netscape	Microsoft	Follower
MP3 music players	Diamond Multimedia	Apple (iPod)	Follower
Operating systems for mobile phones	Symbian	Microsoft	Leader (until 2010)
Laser printer	Xerox, IBM	Canon	Follower
Flash memory	Toshiba	Samsung, Intel	Followers
eBook reader	Sony (Digital Reader)	Amazon (Kindle)	Follower

Source: Based in part on D. Teece, *The Competitive Challenge: Strategies for industrial innovation and renewal* (Cambridge: Ballinger, 1987): 186–8.

Later entrants were able to rely on the services of public cold stores and refrigerated trucking companies.

- *The potential to establish a standard.* As we shall see later in this chapter, some markets converge on a technical standard. The greater the importance of technical standards, the greater the advantages of being an early mover in order to influence those standards and gain the market momentum needed to establish leadership. Once a standard has been set, displacing it becomes exceptionally difficult. IBM had little success with its OS/2 operating system against the entrenched position of Microsoft Windows. Linux has succeeded in taking market share from Windows; however, the main reason is that Linux is free!

Optimal timing depends also on the resources and capabilities that the individual firm has at its disposal. Different companies have different strategic windows, periods in time when their resources and capabilities are aligned with the opportunities available in the market. A small, technology-based firm may have no choice but to pioneer innovation: its opportunity is to grab first-mover advantage and then develop the necessary complementary resources before more powerful rivals appear. For the large, established firm with financial resources and strong production, marketing and distribution capabilities, the strategic window is likely to be both longer and later. The risks of pioneering are greater for an established firm with a reputation and brands to protect, while to exploit its complementary resources effectively typically requires a more developed market.

In personal computers, Apple was a pioneer; IBM a follower. The timing of entry was probably optimal for each. Apple's resources were its vision and its technology: only by pioneering could it hope to become a leading player. IBM had enormous strengths in manufacturing, distribution and reputation. It could build competitive advantage even without a clear technological advantage. The key for IBM was to delay its entry until the time when the market had developed to the point where IBM's strengths could have their maximum impact.

In the browser war between Netscape and Microsoft, Microsoft had the luxury of being able to follow the pioneer, Netscape. Microsoft's huge product development, marketing and distribution capabilities and, most important, its vast installed base of the Windows operating system allowed it to overhaul Netscape's initial lead.

Although General Electric entered the market for CT scanners some four years after EMI, GE was able to overtake EMI within a few years because of its ability to apply vast technological, manufacturing, sales and customer service capabilities within the field of medical electronics.

The most effective follower strategies are those that initiate a new product's transition from niche market to mass market. According to Markides and Geroski, successful first movers pioneer new products that embody new technologies and new functionality.[21] The opportunity for the fast-second entrant is to grow the niche market into a mass market by lowering cost and increasing quality. In the opening case, we saw that Amazon's Kindle fulfilled this function and created momentum in the e-reader market. Timing is critical. Sull argues a successful follower strategy requires 'active waiting': a company needs to monitor market developments and assemble resources and capabilities while it prepares for large-scale market entry.[22]

Case Insight 6.2

How and when to enter the e-reader market

The opening case highlighted the fact that lead innovators do not always gain competitive advantage in technologically intensive industries. Pioneers such as SoftBook Press, NuvoMedia and Gemstar were unable to generate much demand: their e-readers were bulky and underpowered, few e-books were available and slow Internet connections hampered their online distribution. Despite the early-movers' patents, these were easily circumvented by followers. Moreover, these early pioneers lacked the complementary resources, particularly the digital content, needed to gain critical mass quickly. Sony reinvigorated the market but it was Amazon as a fast follower that managed to transform what hitherto had been a niche market to one with more mass appeal. It is a matter of debate whether, in this context, Apple with its iPad was a follower or a leader. On the one hand, when Apple initially launched its iPad it positioned the product as an e-reader but the device had a much broader functionality than the e-readers on the market at that time and Apple is now referred to by many commentators as the first mover in tablet computing.[23] It will be interesting to see whether Sony's pioneering moves in digital document readers targeted at business users will be successful or whether profits will elude Sony in this market too.

Managing risks

Emerging industries are risky. There are two main sources of uncertainty:

- *Technological uncertainty* arises from the unpredictability of technological evolution and the complex dynamics through which technical standards and dominant designs are selected. Hindsight is always 20/20, but before the event it is difficult to predict how technologies and the industries that deploy them will evolve.
- *Market uncertainty* relates to the size and growth rates of the markets for new products. When Xerox introduced its first plain-paper copier in 1959, Apple its first personal computer in 1977 or Sony its Walkman in 1979, none had any idea of the size of the potential market. Forecasting demand for new products is hazardous since all forecasting is based on some form of extrapolation or modelling based on past data. One approach is to use analogies.[24] Another is to draw on the combined insight and experience of a panel of experts.

If reliable forecasting is impossible, the keys to managing risk are alertness and responsiveness to emerging trends together with limiting vulnerability to mistakes through avoiding large-scale commitments. Useful strategies for limiting risk include:

- *Cooperating with lead users*. During the early phases of industry development, careful monitoring of and response to market trends and customer requirements is essential to avoid major errors in technology and design. Von Hippel argues that lead users provide a source of leading market indicators, they can assist in developing new products and processes and offer an early cash flow to fund development expenditures.[25] In computer software, 'beta versions' are released to computer enthusiasts for testing. Nike has two sets of lead users: professional athletes who are trendsetters for athletic footwear and gang members and hip-hop artists who are at the leading edge of urban fashion trends. In communications and aerospace, government defence contracts play a crucial role in developing new technologies.[26]
- *Limiting risk exposure*. The financial risks of emerging industries can be mitigated by financial and operational practices that minimize a firm's exposure to adversity. By avoiding debt and keeping fixed costs low, a firm can lower its financial and operational gearing. Outsourcing and strategic alliance can also hold down capital investment and fixed costs.
- *Flexibility*. Uncertainty necessitates rapid responses to unpredicted events. Achieving such flexibility means keeping options open and delaying commitment to a specific technology until its potential becomes clear. Large, well-resourced companies have the luxury of pursuing multiple strategic options.

Case Insight 6.3

Managing risks in the eBook market

Firms in the e-reader market faced both technological and market uncertainty. In the early years of development it was not clear what screen and power technologies would dominate; on the market side it was not clear whether readers would move away from traditional, paper books, whether they would prefer to read digital books on dedicated-use (e-reader) or multiple-use (e-tablet) devices and which of the competing eco-systems would prove most popular. Key players tried to manage these risks in different ways. Kobo entered new markets by entering partnership agreements with leading book retailers, Barnes & Noble sought to develop and co-brand its Nook devices with electronic goods manufacturers and Amazon made a Kindle app available to a wide range of tablet and smartphone users.

Competing for standards

In the previous chapter, we noted that the establishment of standards is a key event in industry evolution. The emergence of the digital, networked economy has made standards increasingly important and companies that own and influence industry standards are capable of earning returns that are unmatched by any other type of competitive advantage. The shareholder value generated by Microsoft and Intel from the 'Wintel' PC standard, by Qualcomm from its CDMA digital wireless communications technology and Cisco from its leadership role in setting Internet protocol standards are examples of this potential. Table 6.2 lists several companies whose success is closely associated with their control of standards within a particular product category.

Table 6.2 Examples of companies that own de facto industry standards.

Company	Product category	Standard
Microsoft	PC operating systems	Windows
Intel	PC microprocessors	x86 series
Matsushita	Videocassette recorders	VHS system
Sony/Philips	Compact disks	CD-ROM format
ARM (Holdings)	Microprocessors for mobile devices	ARM architecture
Sun Microsystems	Programming language for Web apps	Java
Rockwell and 3Com	56K modems	V90
Qualcomm	Digital cellular wireless communication	CDMA
Adobe Systems	Common file format for creating and viewing documents	Acrobat Portable Document Format
Bosch	Antilock braking systems	ABS and TCS (Traction Control System)
Symbian	Operating systems for mobile phones	Symbian OS
Sony	High-definition DVD	Blu-ray

Types of standard

A **standard** is a format, an interface or a system that allows interoperability. It is adherence to standards that allows us to browse millions of different Web pages, that ensures the light bulbs made by any manufacturer will fit any manufacturer's lamps and that keeps the traffic moving in Los Angeles (most of the time). Standards can be *public* or *private*.

- Public (or *open*) standards are those that are available to all either free or for a nominal charge. Typically, they do not involve any privately owned intellectual property or the IP owners make access free (e.g. Linux). Public standards are set by public bodies and industry associations. Thus, the GSM mobile phone standard was set by the European Telecom Standards Institute. Internet protocols – standards governing Internet addressing and routing – are mostly public. They are governed by several international bodies, including the Internet Engineering Task Force.
- Private (*proprietary*) standards are those where the technologies and designs are owned by companies or individuals. If I own the technology that becomes a standard, I can embody the technology in a product that others buy (Microsoft Windows) or license the technology to others who wish to use it (Qualcomm's CDMA).

Standards can also be classified according to who sets them. *Mandatory standards* are set by government and have the force of law behind them. They include standards relating to car safety and construction specifications and to TV broadcasting. *De facto standards* emerge through voluntary adoption by producers and users. Table 6.2 gives examples.

A problem with de facto standards is that they may take a long time to emerge, resulting in duplication of investments and delayed development of the market. It was 40 years before a standard railroad gauge was agreed in the US.[27] The delayed emergence of a standard may kill a technology altogether. The failure of quadraphonic sound to displace stereophonic sound during the 1970s resulted from incompatible technical standards which inhibited audio manufacturers, record companies and consumers from investing in the technology.[28]

Why standards appear: Network externalities

Standards emerge in markets that are subject to **network externalities**. A network externality exists whenever the value of a product to an individual customer depends on the number of other users of that product. The classic example of network externality is the telephone. Since there is little satisfaction to be gained from talking to oneself on the telephone, the value of a telephone to each user depends on the number of other users connected to the same telephone system. This is different from most products. When one of the authors pours himself a glass of Glenlivet after teaching a couple of exhausting classes, his enjoyment is independent of how many other people in the world are also drinking Glenlivet. Indeed, some products may have *negative* network externalities – the value of the product is less if many other people purchase the same product. If a professor spends £3000 on an Armani dress and finds that another female colleague at the faculty Christmas party is wearing the same garment, her satisfaction is significantly reduced.

Network externalities do not require everyone to use the same product or even the same technology, but rather that the different products are *compatible* with one another through some form of common interface. In the case of a wireless telephone service, it does not matter (as far as network access is concerned) whether the customer purchases the service from Orange or T-Mobile, because compatibility between each network allows connectivity. Similarly with railways, if a company is transporting coal from a mine to a power station, their choice of rail company is not critical, as, unlike in the 1800s, the whole railway now uses a standard gauge.

Network externalities arise from several sources:

- *Products where users are linked to a network.* Telephones, railways and email instant messaging groups are networks where users are linked together. Applications software, whether spreadsheet programs or videogames, also link users – they can share files and play games interactively. User-level externalities may also arise through social identification. You may watch CSI or the Oscar ceremony on TV not because you enjoy them but so that you have something to talk to friends about at work or at university.[29]
- *Availability of complementary products and services.* Where products are consumed as systems, the availability of complementary products and services depends on the number of customers for that system. You may choose to drive a Ford Focus rather than a Ferrari Testarossa because you know that, should you break down 200 miles from the nearest town, spare parts and a repair service will be more readily available.
- *Economizing on switching costs.* By purchasing the product or system that is most widely used, there is less chance that I shall have to bear the costs of switching. By using Microsoft Office rather than Apple iWork, it is more likely that we will avoid the costs of retraining and file conversion when we become visiting professors at other universities.

The implication of network externalities is that they create **positive feedback**. Once a technology or system gains market leadership, it attracts a growing proportion of new buyers. Conversely, once market leadership is lost, a downward spiral is likely. This process is called **tipping**: once a certain threshold is reached, cumulative forces become unstoppable.[30] The result is a tendency towards a winner-takes-all market. The markets subject to significant network externalities tend to be dominated by a single supplier (Microsoft in PC operating systems and office applications, eBay in Internet auctions).

Once established, technical and design standards tend to be highly resilient. Standards are difficult to displace, owing to learning effects and collective lock-in. Learning effects cause the dominant technology and design to be continually improved and refined. Even where the existing standard is inherently inferior, switching to a superior technology may not occur because of collective lock-in. The classic case is the QWERTY typewriter layout. Its 1873 design was based on the need to *slow* the speed of typing to prevent typewriter keys from jamming. Although the jamming problem was soon solved, the QWERTY layout has persisted, despite the patenting in 1932 of the more ergonomic Dvorak Simplified Keyboard (DSK).[31]

Winning standards wars

In markets subject to network externalities, control over standards is the primary basis for competitive advantage. Sony and Apple are unusual in that they lost their standards wars (in VCRs and personal computers, respectively) but returned as winners in other markets.

Most of the losers in standards wars – Lotus in spreadsheet software, Netscape in browsers, WordPerfect in word processing software – become mere footnotes in the history of technology. What can we learn from these and other standards wars about designing a winning strategy in markets subject to network externalities?

The first key issue is to determine whether we are competing in a market that will converge on a single technical standard. This requires a careful analysis of the presence and sources of network externalities.

The second strategic issue in standards setting is recognizing the role of positive feedback: the technology that can establish early leadership will rapidly gain momentum. Building a 'bigger bandwagon', according to Shapiro and Varian, requires the following:[32]

- *Before you go to war, assemble allies.* You'll need the support of consumers, suppliers of complements, even your competitors. Not even the strongest companies can afford to go it alone in a standards war.
- *Pre-empt the market.* Enter early, achieve fast-cycle product development, make early deals with key customers and adopt penetration pricing.
- *Manage expectations.* The key to managing positive feedback is to convince customers, suppliers and the producers of complementary goods that you will emerge as the victor. These expectations become a self-fulfilling prophecy. The massive pre-launch promotion and publicity built up by Sony prior to the American and European launch of PlayStation 2 in October 2000 was an effort to convince consumers, retailers and game developers that the product would be the blockbuster consumer electronics product of the new decade, thereby upsetting Sega and Nintendo's efforts to establish their rival systems.

The lesson that has emerged from the classic standards battles of the past is that in order to create initial leadership and maximize positive feedback effects, a company must share the value created by the technology with other parties (customers, competitors, complementors and suppliers). If a company attempts to appropriate too great a share of the value created, it may well fail to build a big enough bandwagon to gain market leadership. Thus, recent standards battles involve broad alliances, where the owner enlists the support of complementors and would-be competitors. In the 2006–2008 struggle between Sony (Blu-ray) and Toshiba (HD-DVD), each camp recruited movie studios, software firms and producers of computers and consumer electronics using various inducements, including direct cash payments. The defection of Warner Brothers to the Sony camp was critical to the market tipping suddenly in Sony's favour. However, it appears that all the financial gains from owning the winner DVD standard were dissipated by the costs of the war.[33]

Achieving compatibility with existing products is a critical issue in standards battles. Advantage typically goes to the competitor that adopts an **evolutionary strategy** (i.e. offers backward compatibility) rather than one that adopts a **revolutionary strategy**.[34] Microsoft Windows won the PC war against the Apple Macintosh for many reasons. Both companies offered an operating system with a graphical user interface. However, while Windows was designed for compatibility with the DOS operating system, the Apple Mac was incompatible both with DOS and the Apple II. Similarly, a key advantage of the Sony PlayStation 2 over the Sega Dreamcast and Nintendo Cube was its compatibility with the PlayStation 1. However, the limited compatibility of PlayStation 3 with PlayStation 2 was one of the many problems that limited the success of PlayStation 3.

What are the key resources needed to win a standards war? Shapiro and Varian emphasize:[35]

- control over an installed base of customers;
- owning intellectual property rights in the new technology;
- the ability to innovate in order to extend and adapt the initial technological advance;
- first-mover advantage;
- strength in complements (e.g. Intel has preserved its standard in microprocessors by promoting standards in buses, chipsets, graphics controllers and interfaces between motherboards and CPUs);
- reputation and brand name.

As companies become more familiar with the dynamics of standards competition, they are launching their strategic initiatives earlier – long before product release dates. As a result, standards wars are increasingly about the management of expectations. Companies are also more alert to the emergence of tipping points. As a result, standards wars are being resolved quicker: in high-definition DVDs a mere 19 months elapsed between Toshiba's launch of its HD-DVD and its withdrawal announcement.

Case Insight 6.4
Winning standards battles

As anyone who has tried to download an eBook will know, compatibility issues remain a source of frustration for consumers wishing to download digital content to their e-readers and for publishers who are required to provide content in a range of different formats. The majority of e-readers are designed to work with their own proprietary eBook formats and as e-readers have gained in popularity so new formats have emerged and proliferated. In addition to the proprietary e-reader formats, software has been developed by major software companies that is not specific to particular devices, for example Adobe's .pdf format. Nucci describes the situation of the e-reader market as follows: 'imagine having to decide which CD player to buy based not only on features and price but also on what music you'd be able to play on it. Music labels would publish music in one or more formats and pay commissions to the CD player manufacturers based on the sales of each CD issued in its format. If you didn't own the device(s) that supported discs by your favourite artist you'd be out of luck.'[36]

While the major players have recognized the problem, a common format has yet to emerge. The International Digital Publishing Forum (www.idpf.org), a trade and standards association for digital publishing, has developed and maintained a voluntary standard called EPub. While a number of reading devices support EPub in addition to their own proprietary formats, there has been no large-scale convergence on this standard. Paradoxically, while it has become much easier to print a book, it has become much more difficult to publish an electronic version of a book that can be read on a variety of e-readers. Problems of compatibility have resulted in the production of numerous apps that allow readers to convert content from one format to another. The existence of these converters means that a standard format is unlikely to emerge quickly and that the industry will continue to support a variety of different standards despite the frustration this causes for both readers and publishers.

Implementing technology strategies: Creating the conditions for innovation

Our analysis so far has taught us about the potential for generating competitive advantage from innovation and about the design of technology-based strategies, but it has said little about the conditions under which innovation is achieved. The danger is that strategic analysis can tell us a great deal about making money out of innovation, but this isn't much use if we cannot generate innovation in the first place. While innovation requires certain resources – people, facilities, information and time – there is no predetermined relationship between R & D input and innovation output.[37] Clearly, the productivity of R & D depends heavily on the organizational conditions that foster innovation. Hence, the crucial challenge facing firms in emerging and technology-based industries is to create the conditions conducive to innovation.

To address this question, we must return to the critical distinction between invention and innovation. While these activities are complementary, they require different resources and different organizational conditions. While invention depends on creativity, innovation requires collaboration and cross-functional integration.

Managing creativity

THE CONDITIONS FOR CREATIVITY Invention is an act of creativity requiring knowledge and imagination. The creativity that drives invention is typically an individual act that establishes a meaningful relationship between concepts or objects that had not previously been related. This reconceptualizing can be triggered by accidents: an apple falling on Isaac Newton's head or James Watt observing a kettle boiling. Creativity is associated with particular personality traits. Creative people tend to be curious, imaginative, adventurous, assertive, playful, self-confident, risk taking, reflective and uninhibited.[38]

Individual creativity also depends on the organizational environment in which people work – this is as true for the researchers and engineers at Amgen and Google as it was for the painters and sculptors of the Florentine and Venetian schools. Few great works of art or outstanding inventions are the products of solitary geniuses. Creativity is stimulated by human interaction: the productivity of R & D laboratories depends critically on the communication networks that the engineers and scientists establish.[39] An important catalyst of interaction is *play*, which creates an environment of enquiry, liberates thought from conventional constraints and provides the opportunity to establish new relationships by rearranging ideas and structures at a safe distance from reality. The essence of play is that it permits unconstrained forms of experimentation.[40] The potential for low-cost experimentation has expanded vastly, thanks to advances in computer modelling and simulation that permit prototyping and market research to be undertaken speedily and virtually.[41]

Featured Example 6.1
Using 3D printing to stimulate creativity

Engineers and designers have been using 3D printers for more than a decade to create prototypes and designs for new products but recent innovations are making these technologies cheaper to use and more widely available. 3D printing is much like printing a document from a computer file but instead of ink the printer deposits successive layers of thin material onto a tray and gradually builds a solid object by fusing the deposited material with a laser or electronic beam. These printers can now work with a wide range of materials, including industrial-grade plastics and metals that can be used to make objects quickly and cheaply. This technology is being used by firms in sectors as diverse as aerospace, jewellery, orthodontics, mobile phones and football boots. Perhaps one of the most exciting aspects of the technology, however, is the possibilities it opens up to experiment and play with ideas. A would-be entrepreneur could run off one or two prototypes to see whether their ideas work and could adjust the design based on feedback.[42]

ORGANIZING FOR CREATIVITY Creativity requires management systems that are quite different from those appropriate for efficiency. In particular, creatively oriented people tend to be responsive to distinctive types of incentive. They desire to work in an egalitarian culture with enough space and resources to provide the opportunity to be spontaneous, experience freedom and have fun in the performance of a task that, they feel, makes a difference to the strategic performance of the firm. Praise, recognition and opportunities for education and professional growth are also more important than assuming managerial responsibilities.[43] Nurturing the drive to create may require a degree of freedom and flexibility that conflicts with conventional HR practices. At Google, engineers have considerable discretion as to which project to join.

Organizational environments conducive to creativity tend to be both nurturing and competitive. Creativity requires a work context that is secure but not cosy. Dorothy Leonard points to the merits of creative abrasion within innovative teams – fostering innovation through the interaction of different personalities and perspectives. Managers must resist the temptation to clone in favour of embracing diversity of cognitive and behavioural characteristics within work groups, creating 'whole brain teams'.[44] Exploiting diversity may require constructive conflict. Microsoft's development team meetings are renowned for open criticism and intense disagreement. Such conflict can spur progress towards better solutions.

Table 6.3 contrasts some characteristics of innovative organizations compared with those designed for operational efficiency.

From invention to innovation: The challenge of integration

BALANCING CREATIVITY AND COMMERCIAL DIRECTION For creativity to create value, both for the company and for society, it must be directed and harnessed. Balancing creative freedom with discipline and integration is a key issue of companies such as Apple and Google, who position themselves on the leading edge of innovation. The problem is especially acute in

Table 6.3 The characteristics of 'operating' and 'innovating' organizations.

	Operating organization	Innovating organization
Structure	Bureaucratic Specialization and division of labour Hierarchical control Defined organizational boundaries	Flat organization without hierarchical control Task-oriented project teams Fuzzy organizational boundaries
Processes	Emphasis on eliminating variation (e.g. Six Sigma) Top-down control Tight financial controls	Emphasis on enhancing variation Loose controls to foster idea generation Flexible strategic planning and financial control
Reward systems	Financial compensation Promotion up the hierarchy Power and status symbols	Autonomy Recognition Equity participation in new ventures
People	Recruitment and selection based on the needs of the organization structure for specific skills: functional and staff specialists, general managers and operatives	Key need is for idea generators that combine required technical knowledge with creative personality traits Managers must act as sponsors and orchestrators

Source: Based on J. K. Galbraith and R. K. Kazanjian, *Strategy Implementation: Structure, systems and processes*, 2nd edn (St Paul, MN: West, 1986).

media companies: 'The two cultures – of the ponytail and the suit – are a world apart and combustible together.'[45] Many creative companies have been formed by frustrated innovators leaving established companies. Disney's 2006 acquisition of Pixar was motivated by its desire to reinvigorate its animated movies. Yet Pixar's John Lasseter, who was appointed creative head of Disney's animation studio, had been fired from Disney 20 years earlier for his advocacy of computer animation![46] Conversely, HBO's remarkable run of successful TV series between 1999 and 2007 (*The Sopranos*, *Sex and the City*, *The Wire* and *Six Feet Under*) reveals a remarkable ability to mesh creativity with commercial acuity.

Featured Example 6.2

Being creative in orthodontics

In 2001, Chishti and Wirth, two Stanford University MBA graduates, came up with a new system for realigning teeth. Their Invisalign system involved patients wearing a series of clear plastic retainers rather than metal braces to realign teeth. The original idea came from Chishti, who had undergone conventional orthodontic treatment and found metal braces to be both unattractive and uncomfortable. The orthodontist takes dental impressions and X-rays and sends them to Invisalign, which through the use of 3D computer modelling creates sets of retainers that move teeth to the final position recommended by the orthodontist. This technique has proved very popular, particularly with adults who want to avoid the look of metal braces. The system does, however, have strategic implications because the technology, in part, substitutes capital (computer systems operated by staff who do not require training in dentistry) for skilled labour (orthodontists) and changes the cost structure of this business.

The critical linkage between creative flair and commercial success is market need. Few important inventions have been the result of spontaneous creation by technologists; almost all have resulted from grappling with practical problems.

The old adage that 'necessity is the mother of invention' explains why customers are such fertile sources of innovation: they are most acutely involved with matching existing products and services to their needs.[47] Involving customers in the innovation process is an initial stage in the move towards open innovation (described in more detail in the next section).

ORGANIZATIONAL APPROACHES TO THE MANAGEMENT OF INNOVATION Creative activities require different organizational structures and management systems than operational activities do. Yet, the commercialization of new technology – developing and introducing new products and implementing new processes – requires the integration of creativity and technological expertise with capabilities in production, marketing, finance, distribution and customer support. Achieving such integration is difficult. Tension between the operating and the innovating parts of organizations is inevitable. Innovation upsets established routines and threatens the status quo. The more stable the operating and administrative side of the organization, the greater the resistance to innovation. A classic example was the opposition by the US naval establishment to continuous-aim firing, a process that offered huge improvements in gunnery accuracy.[48]

As innovation has become an increasing priority for established corporations, so chief executives have sought to emulate the flexibility, creativity and entrepreneurial spirit of technology-based start-ups. Organizational initiatives aimed at stimulating new product development and the exploitation of new technologies include:

- *Cross-functional product development teams:* Cross-functional product development teams have proven to be highly effective mechanisms for integrating creativity with functional effectiveness. Conventional approaches to new product development involved a sequential process that began in the corporate research lab then went 'over the wall' to engineering, manufacturing, finance and so on. Japanese companies pioneered autonomous product development teams staffed by specialists seconded from different departments with leadership from a 'heavyweight' team manager who was able to protect the team from undue corporate influence.[49] Such teams have proven effective in deploying a broad range of specialist knowledge and, most importantly, integrating that knowledge flexibility quickly (e.g. through rapid prototyping and concurrent engineering).[50]

- *Product champions* provide a means, first, for incorporating individual creativity within organizational processes and, second, for linking invention to subsequent commercialization. The key is to permit individuals who are sources of creative ideas to lead the teams which develop those ideas – but also to allow this leadership to continue through into the commercialization phases. Companies that are consistently successful in innovation have the ability to design organizational processes that capture, direct and exploit individuals' drive for achievement and success and their commitment to their innovations. The rationale for creating product champions is that these committed individuals can overcome resistance to change within the organization and generate enthusiasm that attracts the involvement of others and forges cross-functional integration. Schön's study of 15 major innovations concludes: 'the new idea either finds a champion or dies'.[51] A British study of 43 matched pairs of successful and unsuccessful innovations similarly concludes that a key factor distinguishing successful innovation is the presence of a 'business innovator' to exert entrepreneurial leadership.[52] 3M Corporation has a long tradition of using product champions to develop new product ideas and grow them into new businesses.

Featured Example 6.3

Innovation at 3M: The role of the product champion

Start little and build

We don't look to the president or the vice president for R & D to say, all right, on Monday morning 3M is going to get into such-and-such a business. Rather, we prefer to see someone in one of our laboratories, or marketing or manufacturing units bring forward a new idea that he's been thinking about. Then, when he can convince people around him, including his supervisor, that he's got something interesting, we'll make him what we call a 'project manager' with a small budget of money and talent and let him run with it. Throughout all our 60 years of history here, that has been the mark of success. Did you develop a new business? The incentive? Money, of course. But that's not the key. The key ... is becoming the general manager of a new business ... having such a hot project that management just has to become involved whether it wants to or not (Bob Adams, Vice-President for R & D, 3M Corporation).

Scotchlite

Someone asked the question, 'Why didn't 3M make glass beads, because glass beads were going to find increasing use on the highways?' ... I had done a little working in the mineral department on trying to color glass beads and had learned a little about their reflecting properties. And, as a little extra-curricular activity, I'd been trying to make luminous house numbers.

Well, this question and my free-time lab project combined to stimulate me to search out where glass beads were being used on the highway. We found a place where beads had been sprinkled on the highway and we saw that they did provide a more visible line at night ...

From there, it was only natural for us to conclude that, since we were a coating company and probably knew more than anyone else about putting particles onto a web, we ought to be able to coat glass beads very accurately on a piece of paper.

So, that's what we did. The first reflective tape we made was simply a double-coated tape – glass beads sprinkled on one side and an adhesive on the other. We took some out here in St. Paul and, with the cooperation of the highway department, put some down. After the first frost came and then a thaw, we found we didn't know as much about adhesives under all weather conditions as we thought …

We looked around inside the company for skills in related areas. We tapped knowledge that existed in our sandpaper business on how to make waterproof sandpaper. We drew on the expertise of our roofing people who knew something about exposure. We reached into our adhesive and tape division to see how we could make the tape stick to the highway better.

The resulting product became known as 'Scotchlite'. Its principal application was in reflective signs; only later did 3M develop the market for highway marking. The originator of the product, Harry Heltzer, interested the head of the New Products Division in the product and he encouraged Heltzer to go out and sell it. Scotchlite was a success and Heltzer became the general manager of the division set up to produce and market it.

Source: 'The technical strategy of 3M: Start more little businesses and more little businesses', *Innovation* **5** (1969).

- *Buying innovation:* Recognition that small, technology-intensive start-ups have advantages in the early stages of the innovation process, while large corporations have superior capabilities, has encouraged large companies to enhance their technological performance by acquiring innovation from other firms. Such acquisition may involve licensing, outright purchase of patents or acquiring the whole company. In biotechnology, pharmaceutical companies have pioneered this outsourcing of innovation. In addition to licensing drug patents, signing marketing agreements and acquiring specialist biotech firms (these include Genentech by Roche in 2009, ICOS by Eli Lilly in 2007, Chiron by Novartis in 2006, Scious by Johnson & Johnson in 2003), pharmaceutical companies have formed research alliances with biotech specialists.[53] In our opening case, we noted a number of similar moves in the e-reader market. Amazon has acquired Mobipocket.com, a French software company that produces publishing and reading tools for handheld devices.

- *Open innovation:* The shift from vertically integrated systems of innovation where companies develop their own technologies in-house, then exploit them internally, to more market-based systems where companies buy in technology while also licensing out their own technologies, has given way to ideas of **open innovation**. As innovation increasingly requires the integration of multiple technologies often from traditionally separate scientific areas, so firms have been forced to look wider in their sourcing technology and in sharing knowhow and ideas. Evidence that external linkages promote innovation has reinforced firms' desire to seek technological knowledge from beyond their own borders.[54] Open innovation requires creating a network of collaborative relationships that comprises licensing deals, component outsourcing, joint research, collaborative product development and informal problem solving and exchanges of ideas. Featured Example 6.4 outlines Procter & Gamble's approach to open innovation.

Featured Example 6.4

Procter & Gamble's open innovation initiative

In 2000 it became clear that P&G's internally focused approach to innovation and new product development was incapable of delivering the growth targets that the company had set itself. Despite a research staff numbering 7500 P&G estimated that for every one of its own research scientists there were probably 200 outside the company with the potential to contribute to P&G's development efforts. When CEO A. G. Laffey challenged the company to acquire 50% of its innovations from outside the company, the quest for a new innovation model began.

P&G's *Connect and Develop* innovation model seeks to 'identify promising ideas throughout the world and apply our own R&D, manufacturing, marketing and purchasing capabilities to them to create better and cheaper products, faster'.

The starting point is to identify what P&G is looking for. The approach is to avoid 'blue sky' innovation and seek ideas that have already been successfully embodied in a product, a prototype or a technology. To focus the search, each business is asked to identify its top 10 customer needs. These include: 'reduce wrinkles, improve skin texture and tone … softer paper products with higher wet strength'. These needs are then translated into specific technical requirements, e.g. biotechnology solutions that permit detergents to perform well at low temperatures. Priorities are then reordered by identifying initiatives which fit with existing areas of brand strength ('adjacencies') and those which permit strengthening of P&G's strategically important areas of technology ('technology game boards').

P&G's innovation network comprises a number of organisations:

- Within P&G, 70 *technology entrepreneurs* are responsible for developing external contacts and exploring for innovation in particular localities and with a focus around a particular product or technology area.
- *Suppliers.* P&G has an IT platform that allows it to share technology briefs with its suppliers. This is complemented by regular meetings between senior P&G executives and senior executives at individual suppliers which explore mutual development opportunities.
- *Technology brokers.* P&G is a member (in some cases a founder member) of several prominent technology brokering networks. These include *NineSigma* which links companies with universities, private labs, government bodies, consultants and other potential solutions providers; *Innocentive* which brokers solutions to science-based problems; *YourEncore* a network of retired scientists and engineers; and *Yet2.com* an online marketplace for intellectual capital.

These networks generate an enormous flow of suggestions and proposals that are initially screened and disseminated through P&G's *Eureka* online catalogue. It is then up to executives within the business groups to identify interesting proposals, to pursue these with the external provider through P&G's External Business Development group and to then move the initiative into their own product development process.

By 2005, 35% of P&G's new product launches had their origins outside the company. Some of P&G's most successful new products – including Swiffer cleaning cloths, Olay Regeneration and Crest Spinbrush – had been initiated by outsiders.

Source: L. Huston and N. Sakkab, 'Connect and develop: Inside Procter & Gamble's new model for innovation', *Harvard Business Review* (March 2006): 58–66. Reproduced by permission of Harvard Business Publishing.

- *Corporate incubators* are business developments established to fund and nurture new businesses, based upon technologies that have been developed internally but have limited applications within a company's established businesses. **Corporate incubators** became very popular during the IT boom at the end of the 1990s when companies saw the potential to generate substantial value from establishing then spinning off new tech-based ventures.[55] Despite a sound strategic and organizational logic, few major companies have achieved sustained success from the incubator units that they established, and, among the successful ones, many have been sold to venture capital firms. A key problem, according to Gary Hamel is that: 'Many corporate incubators became orphanages for unloved ideas that had no internal support or in-house sponsorship'.[56] Despite their uneven track record, several leading companies have experienced considerable success in introducing company-wide processes for developing new businesses based upon internally generated innovations. Featured Example 6.5 outlines the approaches of IBM and Cisco Systems.

Featured Example 6.5

Incubating innovation at IBM and Cisco systems

IBM uses Innovation Jam – a massive online brainstorming process – to generate, select and develop new business ideas. The 2006 Jam was based upon an initial identification of 25 technology clusters grouped into six broad categories. Websites were built for each technology cluster and for a 72-hour period IBM employees, their families and friends, suppliers and customers from all around the world were invited to contribute ideas for innovations based on these technologies. The 150 000 participants generated vast and diverse sets of suggestions that were subject to text-mining software and review by 50 senior executives and technical specialists who worked in nine separate teams to identify promising ideas. The next phase of the Jam subjected the selected innovation ideas to comments and review by the online community. This was followed by a further review process in which the 10 best proposals were selected and a budget of $100 million was allocated to their development. The selected business included a real-time foreign language translation service, smart healthcare payment systems, IT applications to environmental projects and 3D Internet. The new businesses were begun as incubator projects and were then transferred to one or other of IBM's business groups. As well as divisional links, the new ventures were also subject to monthly review by IBM's corporate top management.

Cisco Systems created its Emerging Technology Business Group with the goal of creating 20 new ventures by 2012. Within 18 months, 400 ideas for new businesses had been posted on the Cisco wiki and the Emerging Technology Business Group had begun developing several of these suggestions, including TelePresence, a video surveillance security system and an IP interoperability and collaboration systems server for emergency services. By 2008, TelePresence was established as a regular business group. Like IBM's Innovation Jam, a key feature of Cisco's incubator model is its close linkage with the rest of the company: the emerging technology group is part of Cisco's R & D organization and is subject to close involvement by Cisco's senior management, including CEO John Chambers.

Sources: O. M. Bjelland and R. C. Wood, 'An inside view of IBM's Innovation Jam', *MIT Sloan Management Review* (Fall 2008): 32–43; T. Sanders, 'Cisco reinvents the corporate incubator' (27 July 2007), www.vnunet.com/vnunet/news/2194961/cisco-reinvents-corporate.

Summary

In emerging and technology-based industries, nurturing and exploiting innovation is the fundamental source of competitive advantage and the focus of strategy formulation. Yet the basic tools of strategy analysis are the same as those that we have already encountered in this book. The fundamental strategic issues we are concerned with are the drivers of competition in these markets, in resources and capabilities through which a firm can establish competitive advantage and the design of structures and systems to implement strategy.

Yet, the unpredictability and instability of these industries mean that strategic decisions in technology-driven industries have a very special character. The remarkable dynamics of these industries mean that the difference between massive value creation and ignominious failure may be the result of small errors of timing or technological choices.

It is in these industries that traditional approaches to strategy based upon forecasting and detailed planning are so obviously inadequate. The combination of speed and unpredictability of change means that effective strategies are those which combine clarity of vision with flexibility and responsiveness. The companies that have succeeded in emerging and technology-based industries are those which have recognized most clearly the strategic characteristics of their industries and adapted most effectively to them. In industries that have been turned upside-down by technological change – whether telecommunications equipment, medical imaging, information storage or sports equipment – it is companies that have understood the sources of competitive advantage and assembled the resources and capabilities needed to exploit them that have emerged as winners.

We hope to have persuaded you that, despite the turbulence and uncertainty of these industries, there are analytic principles which can guide us towards strategies that, although they do not guarantee us success, certainly improve the odds. For example, our learning has included:

- evaluating an innovation's potential to generate profit;
- assessing the relative merits of licensing, alliances, joint ventures and internal development as alternative strategies for exploiting an innovation;
- identifying the factors that determine the comparative advantages of being a leader or a follower in innovation.

This chapter also pointed to the central importance of strategy implementation in determining success, a theme we return to in Chapter 9. The key to successful innovation is not resource allocation decisions but creating the structure, integration mechanisms and organizational climate conducive to innovation. Strategies aimed at the exploitation of innovation, choices of whether to be a leader or a follower and the management of risk must take careful account of organizational characteristics.

Technology-based industries also reveal some of the dilemmas that are a critical feature of strategic management in complex organizations and complex business environments. For example, technology-based industries are unpredictable, yet some investments in technology have time horizons of a decade or more. Successful strategies must be responsive to changing market conditions, but successful strategies also require long-term commitment. The fundamental dilemma is that innovation is an unpredictable process that requires creating a nurturing organizational context, whereas strategy is about resource-allocation decisions. How can a company create the conditions for nurturing innovation while planning the course of its development? John Scully, a former CEO of Apple, observed: 'Management and creativity might even be considered antithetical [mutually contrasting] states. While management demands consensus, control, certainty and the status quo, creativity thrives on the opposite: instinct, uncertainty, freedom and iconoclasm.'[57]

Fortunately, the experiences of companies such as 3M, Cisco Systems, Google and Nintendo point to solutions to these dilemmas. The need for innovation to reconcile individual creativity with coordination points towards the advantages of cross-functional team-based approaches over the isolation of R & D in a separate 'creative' environment. Moreover, the need to reconcile innovation with efficiency points towards the advantage of parallel organizational structures where, in addition to the 'formal' structure geared to the needs of existing businesses and products, an informal structure exists, which is the source of new products and businesses. The role of top management in balancing creativity with order and innovation with efficiency becomes critical – such reconciliation requires senior executives who are not necessarily experts in technology, but certainly literate in it to the point of appreciating its strategic implications.

The increasing pace of technological change and intensifying international competition suggests that the advanced, industrialized countries will be forced to rely increasingly on their technological capabilities as the basis for international competitiveness. Strategies for promoting innovation and managing technology will become more important in the future.

Summary table

Learning objectives	Summary
Analyse how technology affects industry structure and competition	Technological change often changes industry dynamics, altering amongst other things cost structures, models of revenue generation, rivalry, entry barriers and the relative bargaining strength of buyers and suppliers. Firms that succeed in technologically intensive industries recognize the strategic characteristic of their markets and adapt effectively
Identify the factors that determine the returns to innovation and evaluate the potential for an innovation to establish competitive advantage	Four factors are critical in determining the extent to which innovators are able to appropriate the value of their innovation: property rights, the tacitness and complexity of the technology, lead-time and complementary resources
Formulate strategies for exploiting innovation and managing technology, focusing in particular on: • the relative advantages of being a leader or a follower in innovation • identifying and evaluating strategic options for exploiting innovation • how to win standards battles • how to manage risk	The choice of strategy to exploit innovation depends on the characteristics of the innovation and the resources and capabilities of the firm. Deciding on the optimal strategy is complex but we have reviewed a range of analytical principles that improve the chances of success
Design the organizational conditions needed to implement such strategies successfully	Organizing for innovation requires different organizational structures and management systems than mainstream operational activities. We have considered a range of approaches and practices that enhance creativity and the likelihood of innovation success

Further reading

David Teece's 1986 article – 'Profiting from technological innovation', *Research Policy* 15(6) 285–305 – remains a seminal work in this area and he has followed this more recently with an article written with Gary Pisano:

Pisano, G. and Teece, D. (2007). How to capture value from innovation: Shaping intellectual property and industry architecture. *California Management Review*, 50(1): 278–96.

Shapiro and Varian provide an excellent exposition of the strategic issues surrounding the establishment of standards and the routes to success in standards wars in:

Shapiro, C. and Varian, H. (1999). The art of standards wars. *California Management Review*, 41(2), 8–32.

In an article published in 2008, Teresa Amabile and Mukti Khaire report on a two-day colloquium held at Harvard Business School with invited leaders from businesses whose success depends on creativity and scholars specializing in the study of creativity. Their conclusions from this event are written up in the following article:

Amabile, T. and Khaire, M. (2008). Creativity and the role of the leader. *Harvard Business Review*, October, 101–9.

Self-study questions

1 Trevor Baylis, a British inventor, submitted a patent application in November 1992 for a wind-up radio for use in Africa in areas where there was no electricity supply and people were too poor to afford batteries. He was excited by the prospects for radio broadcasts as a means of disseminating health education in areas of Africa devastated by AIDS. After appearances on British and South African TV, Baylis attracted a number of entrepreneurs and companies interested in manufacturing and marketing his clockwork radio. However, Baylis was concerned by the fact that his patent provided only limited protection for his invention: most of the main components – a clockwork generator and transistor radio – were long-established technologies. What advice would you offer Baylis as to how he could best protect and exploit his invention?

2 There have been several efforts to develop 3D printers suitable for desktop use by individual households. What are the main risks facing a start-up company intending to develop such a product?

3 From the evidence presented in Table 6.1, what conclusions can you draw regarding the factors that determine whether leaders or followers win out in the markets for new products?

4 What are the sources of network externalities in the e-book reader market? Will e-book readers become a winner-takes-all market? Why has Amazon been able to gain a lead over rivals? Can Kobo and Nook fight back? If so, how?

5 'Creativity is just connecting things. When you ask creative people how they did something they feel a little guilty because they didn't really do it, they just saw something. It seemed obvious to them after a while.' Steve Jobs.

Discuss the quote and consider its implications for organizations that wish to innovate.

Closing Case
Nespresso

Nespresso is the brand name of a coffee brewing system developed in the late 1970s by Nestlé, the multinational food company founded and headquartered in Switzerland. Nespresso allows consumers to brew high-quality coffee at the push of a button by placing hermetically sealed, aluminium covered, coffee capsules into a specially designed machine. While the idea sounds simple, the technology behind Nespresso is, in fact, complex because it requires air and water to be passed through ground coffee at the right temperature and pressure. At the time of its development, Nespresso constituted a major departure for Nestlé from its core operations that were based on the large-scale production and mass marketing of food products. In the late 1970s Nestlé's presence in the coffee market centred on instant coffees with products like Nescafé accounting for 80% of its revenue from coffee sales.

Early development

The original technology underpinning Nespresso was developed by the Battelle Institute, an independent research organization based in Geneva,[58] but Nestlé acquired the rights to develop the idea commercially in 1974 and went on to file a large number of patents on the product.[59] Camillo Pagano, who was at that time the senior executive in charge, felt that the product had potential despite the fact that sales in the coffee market were sluggish. At the time, the gourmet coffee market was beginning to expand and Nestlé saw Nespresso as a vehicle by which it could expand coffee sales by moving into the restaurant market. Many of Pagano's colleagues were sceptical about the innovation, questioning whether Nespresso could be commercialized and expressing concern about the amount of time and effort that would be taken up in launching such a niche product that had a poor fit with Nestlé's mainstream operations. Pagano felt that in order to flourish the Nespresso project needed to be taken outside Nestlé's day-to-day operations so, in 1984, he established Nespresso as a separate company (100% owned by Nestlé) which was free to develop its own marketing, operations and personnel policies.

Nespresso developed its system in conjunction with a number of partners: it collaborated with a Swiss company to improve the design of the machines; it licensed the manufacture of the machines to Turmix, a Swiss domestic appliance manufacturer; it partnered with Sobal, a distributor, to sell the product to end-users. The Nespresso system was launched in 1986 in Italy, Switzerland and Japan but the product flopped. By the end of 1987, only half the machines that had been manufactured had been sold and without sales of machines there could be no sales of the specially designed capsules. It looked very likely that Nestlé headquarters would kill off the project but it was decided to give it a further chance by bringing in an outsider to see whether a turnaround could be effected. The person selected for this role was Jean-Paul Gaillard, a former executive with Philip Morris, the tobacco company.[60]

The turnaround

Rupert Gasser, head of research at Nestlé, described Gaillard as 'ambitious and strong headed. He wanted to do something outstanding. [Gaillard] had personality; he was a force. And ▶

importantly, he did not carry all the trappings of the company history.'[61] Gaillard made a number of changes, the most important of which were:

- *Changing the customer focus:* Gaillard reasoned that the Nespresso system was more suited to the household than the restaurant market. Although his intuition was not supported by explicit market research, market trends in the late 1980s pointed in that direction. Gaillard's strategy was to target high-income households and, in line with that strategy, he sought to ensure that the coffee machines were retailed through high-end stores.
- *Establishing a direct channel to the end-users through the establishment of Nespresso Clubs:* selling Nespresso coffee capsules through supermarkets did not fit well with the exclusive brand image Gaillard wished to create, and so he had the idea of establishing the Nespresso Club. When households bought a machine, they automatically became members of the Club that offered around-the-clock ordering of coffee capsules, prompt delivery of orders and advice on coffee making and machine maintenance. The Club had the additional advantage of providing the company with up-to-date customer information.
- *Positioning the brand at the top end of the market:* the company developed partnerships with kitchen appliance makers such as Alessi, Krups, Magimix and Philips to produce well-designed machines sold through upmarket retail outlets.

By the time Gaillard left Nespresso in 1996, sales had taken off and there were 220 000 club members across Europe.

After Gaillard's departure, Nespresso continued to grow as it expanded geographically, extending its target market into small offices and businesses and widening it range of coffee capsules. The range of machines was increased to offer a number of sophisticated design options and the company opened a number of retail outlets – Nespresso boutiques – that sold coffee-related paraphernalia as well as the Nespresso system. Augmenting a marketing campaign that relied heavily on social media, Nespresso launched a long-running and successful television and billboard advertising campaign featuring George Clooney to further promote the product. By 2014, Nespresso had estimated annual sales of SFr 4 billion (US$4.5 billion), margins on earnings before interest and tax (most of which came from pods rather than machines) of more than 30% and accounted for around 8% of Nestlé's total operating profit.[62]

More recent challenges

As might be expected, the success of Nespresso paved the way for new competitors to enter the market. Despite having more than 1700 patents on Nespresso capsules and machinery, more than 20 years had elapsed since the product was first developed and early patents were beginning to expire. In addition, the product had proved relatively simple for new players to re-engineer without infringing Nestlé's patents. Nonetheless, Nestlé had built a strong brand and was the global market leader (Table 6.4). However, in the US Keurig, part of Keurig Green Mountain, and its K-Cup system dominated the market, with several other players, including both Starbucks and Walmart entering this market. In 2014, Nespresso

Table 6.4 Suppliers of single-serve coffee systems.

Parent company	Brand	Estimated global market share 2014 (%)
Nestlé	Nespresso	35
Sara Lee	Senseo	18
Keurig Green Mountain	Keurig (K-Cup system)	8
Kraft	Tassimo	8

launched its VertuoLine range designed to make the larger coffee servings preferred by Americans.

The bulk of the profit from single-serve pod coffee makers came from selling capsules rather than the machines themselves and this opened up a second route for new entrants. A number of companies, including one set up by Nespresso's former head, John-Paul Galliard, started selling substitute coffee pods for Nespresso machines. Nestlé robustly defended its property rights but in a landmark case in 2013 the UK High Court ruled that Dualit, a UK manufacturer of small domestic appliances, had not infringed Nestlé's patents by making substitute capsules for its Nespresso regime. Similar rulings followed in test cases in other European countries with significant repercussions for the viability of Nespresso's business model.

Nespresso and other makers of pod coffee machines also found themselves under increasing pressure from environmental campaigners, who highlighted the fact that capsules were difficult to recycle and added to waste and environmental damage. Nespresso launched a recycling campaign allowing consumers to return the single-use aluminium containers in special bags but this did little to dampen criticism.

By 2014, Nespresso was faced with a number of dilemmas with regard to its future direction. Could it sustain rapid growth in the face of increasing competition? Was it possible for Nespresso to retain and develop its exclusive image or should it move downmarket to increase its target market? Should Nestle re-integrate Nespresso into its mainstream organization to stimulate a new wave of innovation?

Case questions

- What insights into the innovation process can be gained from this case?
- The Nespresso innovation took more than 20 years to come to fruition. How would you account for the slow commercialization of this product?
- Nespresso's patents have not prevented competitors from offering coffee pods which fit Nespresso machines. How big a problem is this for Nespresso?
- Do you think that Nespresso has a sustainable competitive advantage? What suggestions would you make to Nespresso's management regarding future strategy?

Notes

1 K. Cool, P. Paranika and T. Cool, 'iPad vs. Kindle: e-Books in the US in 2010', (INSEAD Case Study, 2011).

2 Ibid.: 2.

3 C. Foresman, 'Apple way ahead of tablet competitors', *Ars Technica* (11th March 2011), http://www.wired.com/2011/03/apple-tablet-80-share/, accessed 29th September 2014.

4 *The Economist*, 'The difference engine: send in the clones' (11th March 2011), http://www.economist.com/blogs/babbage/2011/03/tablet_computers_0, accessed 29th September 2013.

5 See, for example, G. A. Fowler, 'Price cuts electrify the e-reader market', *Wall Street Journal* (22nd June 2010).

6 Morgan Stanley research.

7 The 'razor and blades' strategy refers to a business model that involves selling an item at a low price, sometimes even at a loss, in order to sell complementary products at a much higher margin. The name refers to the original Gillette company, which sold razors at cost and made a high margin on selling its razorblades.

8 http://seekingalpha.com/article/2376765-rakutens-rknuf-ceo-hiroshi-mikitani-on-q2-2014-results-earnings-call-transcript, accessed 29th September 2014.

9 See, for example, https://technology.ihs.com/417568/ebook-readers-device-to-go-the-way-of-dinosaurs, accessed 15th April 2014; and http://247wallst.com/special-report/2013/05/23/ten-brands-that-will-disappear-in-2014/, accessed 15th April 2014.

10 'The logic that dares not speak its name,' *The Economist* (16th April 1994): 89–91.

11 In the US, the return to R & D spending was estimated at between 3.7 and 5.5%. See M. Warusawitharana, 'Research and development, profits and firm value: A structural estimation', Discussion Paper (Washington, DC: Federal Reserve Board, September 2008).

12 *The Economist*, 'Knowledge monopolies: Patent wars', (8th April 2000): 95–9.

13 F. T. Rothermael, 'Incumbent advantage through exploiting complementary assets via interfirm cooperation', *Strategic Management Journal*, 22 (2001): 687–99.

14 R. C. Levin, A. K. Klevorick, R. R. Nelson and S. G. Winter, 'Appropriating the returns from industrial research and development', *Brookings Papers on Economic Activity*, 3 (1987).

15 'Why Google acquired eBook technologies', http://mashable.com/2011/01/13/why-google-acquired-ebook-technologies/, accessed 29th September 2014.

16 Matt Phillips, 'Tablet glut won't matter for ARM Holdings analyst says', *Wall Street Journal* (11th March 2011).

17 'The semi-conductor industry: Space Invaders', *Economist* (7th January 2012).

18 R. Adner, 'Match your innovation strategy to your innovation ecosystem', *Harvard Business Review* (April 2006): 17–37.

19 S. Shulman, *The Telephone Gambit* (New York: W. W. Norton, 2008).

20 'The Human Genome Race', *Scientific American* (24th April 2000).

21 C. Markides and P. A. Geroski, *Fast Second* (San Francisco: Jossey-Bass, 2005).

22 D. Sull, 'Strategy as active waiting', *Harvard Business Review* (September 2005): 120–9.

23 See, for example, C. Beaumont, 'Apple launches iPad tablet computer', *The Telegraph* (27th January 2010).

24 For example, data on penetration rates for electric toothbrushes and CD players were used to forecast the market demand for HD TVs in the United States. See B. L. Bayus, 'High-definition television: Assessing demand forecasts for the next generation consumer durable', *Management Science*, 39 (1993): 1319–33.

25 E. Von Hippel, 'Lead users: A source of novel product concepts', *Management Science*, 32 (July 1986): 791–805.

26 In electronic instruments, customers' ideas initiated most of the successful new products introduced by manufacturers. See E. Von Hippel, 'Users as innovators', *Technology Review*, 5 (1976): 212–39.

27 A. Friedlander, *The Growth of Railroads* (Arlington, VA: CNRI, 1995).

28 S. Postrel, 'Competing networks and proprietary standards: The case of quadraphonic sound', *Journal of Industrial Economics*, 24 (December 1990): 169–86.

29 S. J. Liebowitz and S. E. Margolis, 'Network externality: An uncommon tragedy', *Journal of Economic Perspectives*, 8, (Spring 1994): 133–50) refer to these user-to-user externalities as 'direct externalities'.

30 M. Gladwell, *The Tipping Point* (Boston: Little Brown, 2000).

31 P. David, 'Clio and the economics of QWERTY', *American Economic Review*, 75 (May 1985): 332–7; S. J. Gould, 'The panda's thumb of technology', *Natural History*, 96 (1986). For an alternative view see S. J. Leibowitz and S. Margolis, 'The fable of the keys', *Journal of Law and Economics*, 33 (1990): 1–26.

32 C. Shapiro and H. R. Varian, 'The art of standards wars', *California Management Review*, 41 (Winter 1999): 8–32.

33 R. M. Grant 'The DVD war of 2006–8: Blu-ray vs. HD-DVD', *Contemporary Strategic Analysis*, 7th edn (Chichester: John Wiley & Sons Ltd, 2009): 692–7.

34 Shapiro and Varian (1999), op. cit.: 15–16.

35 Ibid.: 16–18.

36 C. Nucci, 'E-book dilemma: Potboiler of the digital age', *TechWeb* (5th February 2001).

37 S. Ahn, *Firm dynamics and productivity growth: A review of micro evidence from OECD countries*, Economics Department Working Paper 297 (OECD, 2001).

38 J. M. George, 'Creativity in organisations', *Academy of Management Annals*, 1 (2007): 439–77.

39 M. L. Tushman, 'Managing communication networks in R&D laboratories', *Sloan Management Review* (Winter 1979): 37–49.

40 D. Dougherty and C. H. Takacs, 'Team play: Heedful interrelating as the boundary for innovation', *Long Range Planning*, 37 (December 2004): 569–90.

41 S. Thomke, 'Enlightened experimentation: The new imperative for innovation', *Harvard Business Review* (February 2001): 66–75.

42 'The printed world', *The Economist* (12th February 2011): 75–7.

43 R. Florida and J. Goodnight, 'Managing for creativity', *Harvard Business Review* (July–August 2005).

44 D. Leonard and S. Straus, 'Putting your company's whole brain to work', *Harvard Business Review* (July–August 1997): 111–21; D. Leonard and P. Swap, *When Sparks Fly: Igniting creativity in groups* (Boston: Harvard Business School Press, 1999).

45 'How to manage a dream factory', *The Economist* (16th January 2003).

46 'Lunch with the FT: John Lasseter', *Financial Times* (17th January 2009).

47 E. Von Hippel, *The Sources of Innovation* (New York: Oxford University Press, 1988) provides strong evidence of the dominant role of users in the innovation process.

48 E. Morrison, 'Gunfire at sea: A case study of innovation', in M. Tushman and W. L. Moore (eds), *Readings in the Management of Innovation* (Cambridge, MA: Ballinger, 1988): 165–78.

49 K. Clark and T. Fujimoto, *Product Development Performance: Strategy, organisation and management in the world car industry* (Boston: Harvard Business School Press, 1991).

50 K. Imai, I. Nonaka and H. Takeuchi, 'Managing the new product development process: How Japanese companies learn and unlearn', in K. Clark, R. Hayes and C. Lorenz (eds), *The Uneasy Alliance* (Boston: Harvard Business School Press, 1985).

51 D. A. Schön, 'Champions for radical new inventions', *Harvard Business Review* (March–April, 1963): 84.

52 R. Rothwell, C. Freeman, A. Horsley *et al.*, 'SAPPHO updated – Project SAPPHO Phase II', *Research Policy* 3 (1974): 258–91.

53 G. P. Pisano, *Science Business: The Promise, the reality and the future of biotech* (Boston: Harvard Business School Press, 2006).

54 A. Arora, A. Fosfur and A. Gambardella, *Markets for Technology* (Cambridge, MA: MIT Press, 2001); S. Breschi and F. Malerba, *Clusters, Networks and Innovation* (Oxford: Oxford University Press, 2005).

55 M. T. Hansen, H. W. Chesborough, N. Nohria and D. N. Sull, 'Networked Incubators: Hothouse of the new economy', *Harvard Business Review* (September–October, 2000): 74–88.

56 G. Hamel and C. K Prahalad, 'Nurturing creativity: Putting passions to work', *Shell World* (Royal Dutch Shell, 14th September 2007): 1–12.

57 J. Sculley, *Odyssey: Pepsi to Apple: A journey of adventure, ideas and the future* (New York: Harper & Row, 1987).

58 J. Miller, *Innovation and Renovation: The Nespresso story*, Case 543 (Lausanne: IMD, 2003).

59 Nespresso. Wikipedia [online]. Last updated 26th September 2014, http://en.wikipedia/wiki/nespresso, accessed 29th September 2014.

60 Jean-Paul Gaillard is referred to as Yannick Lang in the IMD case, see P. Silberzahn, 'Nespresso: Victim of low-end disruption?' *The Management of Innovation* [blog] (13th April 2010), http://philippesilberzahneng.wordpress.com/tag/jean-paul-gaillard/, accessed 29th September 2014.

61 IMD case study (2003), op. cit.: 6.

62 J. Shotter, 'Nespresso brews plans to see off rivals', *Financial Times* (1st January 2014); L. Ludes 'Nespresso's bitter taste of defeat', *Financial Times* (24th April 2013).

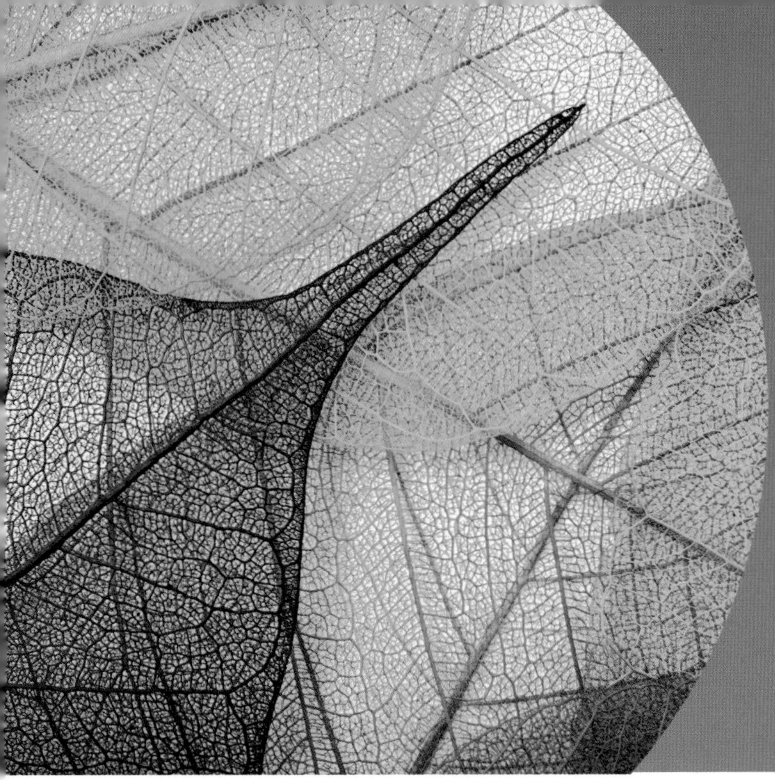

7

Corporate strategy

Introduction and objectives

In Chapter 1, we introduced the distinction between corporate and business strategy. Corporate strategy is concerned with *where* a firm competes, whereas business strategy is concerned with *how* a firm competes in a particular area of business. The major part of this book so far has been about business strategy but in the next two chapters we turn our attention to corporate strategy and the scope of the firm's activities. When we refer to the scope of the firm, we are directing our attention to the range of product/market activities the firm undertakes. This includes the firm's:

- *Product scope:* how specialized the firm is in terms of the range of products it supplies. Coca-Cola (soft drinks), Gap (fashion retailing) and SAP (software) are specialized companies: each is engaged in a single industry sector. Sony Corporation, General Electric and Tata Group are diversified companies: each spans multiple industries. In our opening case, we see that Tesco, a grocery retailer, has extended the range of its activities into retail banking and telecommunication services.
- *Vertical scope:* the range of vertically linked activities the firm encompasses. Most oil companies such as Shell and Exxon are active along the whole supply chain. They prospect for new oil deposits, drill and extract crude oil, transport it through pipelines and specialized shipping, refine it and distribute it through their retail outlets. Nike is much more vertically specialized: it designs and markets footwear and apparel, but outsources most activities in its value chain, including manufacturing, distribution and retailing. In our opening case we see that, although Tesco has developed long-term relationships with its suppliers, it rarely undertakes food processing or product manufacture.
- *Geographical scope:* the geographical spread of activities of the firm. In the advertising business, Saatchi & Saatchi is a global company operating in 80 countries, whereas StrawberryFrog is an independent agency with offices in three main centres: Amsterdam, New York and São Paulo. In the case of Tesco, while the UK still dominates its sales of groceries, 65% of its selling space is now outside the UK.

In this chapter, we consider the first two of these dimensions of corporate scope – product scope and vertical scope – and the key challenges managers face in developing and implementing corporate strategy. We begin by considering the overall scope of the firm and introduce a number of important analytical concepts that help us to understand what shapes firm boundaries. We devote the remainder of the chapter to consideration of the rationale for operating multiple businesses and the costs and benefits to firms of extending vertical and product scope. The strategic issues associated with a firm's geographical scope are discussed in Chapter 8.

By the time you have completed this chapter, you will:

- be familiar with the concepts of economies of scope, transaction costs and the costs of managing complexity, and understand how these ideas help to explain firm boundaries and the shifts in firm boundaries over time;
- understand the rationale behind multibusiness activity and the potential benefits and costs of extending the horizontal or vertical scope of a firm;
- be able to evaluate the advantages and disadvantages of changing a firm's scope and the different ways of exploiting opportunities for value creation;
- appreciate the trends in diversification and vertical integration over time;
- be familiar with the techniques of portfolio analysis and be able to apply these to corporate strategic decisions.

Opening Case

Tesco plc.: From food to finance

Tesco is a global supermarket chain headquartered in London. It is Britain's biggest retailer, employing more than 530 000 people in 6784 stores, 3146 of them in the UK, 2131 in Asia and 1507 in continental Europe. In 2014, it reported sales revenues of £70.9 billion, about the same as in the previous year, but its pre-tax profit was down 7%, after a 14.5% decline in the previous year.[1] After hitting an all-time high in April 2010, Tesco's share price declined by 40% during the next four years. With declining profits, then CEO Philip Clarke was forced to reconsider Tesco's corporate strategy. Tesco had already withdrawn from the US (it sold its Fresh & Easy chain in November 2013), but, faced with an increasingly competitive UK grocery market, should Tesco go further in narrowing its corporate scope or should it continue to diversify into related fields?

A brief history

In 1919, Jack Cohen, the son of a Polish shopkeeper, started with a market stall in the East End of London. He adopted the name Tesco when he had labels made up for a shipment of tea he had bought from the supplier T. E. Stockwell.[2] 'Tesco' combined his supplier's initials (TES) and the first two letters from his surname (CO). In the 1950s and 1960s, Tesco grew, primarily through acquisitions and a strategy of 'piling it high and selling it cheap', to become one of Britain's leading grocery chains. But, as consumers grew more sophisticated and demanded higher quality and greater choice, results slipped. Jack stepped down in 1973 and handed control to Leslie Porter (chairman and Jack's son-in-law) and Ian MacLaurin (managing director). The new management team repositioned Tesco to put the emphasis on quality rather than low prices, introduced several new store formats, including Tesco Extra (out-of-town hypermarkets) and Tesco Express (neighbourhood convenience stores) and invested heavily in information technology. The new strategy, together with continued acquisitions resulted in Tesco overtaking Sainsbury to become Britain's largest supermarket chain.

In the 1990s, Tesco became the first UK supermarket to introduce loyalty cards. Its Clubcard offered customers points for every pound spent and proved very popular, despite criticisms that each point was of low monetary value. The loyalty card provided Tesco with valuable information about its customers, including age, gender, postcode and purchasing behaviour. This information allowed Tesco to segment its customer base more accurately and to target promotions and cross-selling initiatives in a more focused way. The collection and analysis of the data generated by Clubcards was undertaken by dunnhumby, a company founded by the husband-and-wife team Edwina Dunn and Clive Humby. After acquiring a minority interest in the firm, Tesco eventually purchased dunnhumby in 2010.

Broadening the company's scope

In 1997, Terry Leahy took over from MacLaurin as CEO. Recognizing the limited growth opportunities in the highly competitive UK grocery market, Leahy broadened Tesco's scope, transforming it from a British supermarket chain into a diversified, international retailer. The company had already diversified into non-food retailing, offering products such as discount clothing, consumer electronics, homeware and fuel. Non-food products tended to have much bigger profit margins than traditional groceries but drew on the same retailing capabilities that Tesco had developed in its grocery business. Tesco also entered online grocery shopping in 1997 and online non-food shopping the following year. The fulfilment of online customers' orders for non-food items was achieved through a profit-sharing joint venture with Grattan, a well-established mail-order company. The joint venture lasted until 2006, when Tesco decided to go it alone and launched Tesco Direct.

At the same time as developing its online business, Tesco decided to move into retail banking. Tesco Personal Finance was launched in 1997 as a 50/50 joint venture with the Royal Bank of Scotland (RBS). The company offered a range of simple, easy-to-understand products that included credit cards, savings accounts and several types of insurance. Financial services were attractive to Tesco for a number of reasons. First, the sheer size of the potential market that could be tapped made the prospect interesting. Tesco already had a large established customer base and a deep knowledge of its customers through its Clubcard database. By combining in-store offers, particularly on non-food items, with financing options, the company could extend its reach. Second, Tesco was in a strong position in terms of its financial and physical assets. The resources of the company meant that it was able to meet the capital requirement necessary for the award of a banking licence and its large numbers of stores obviated the need to establish a branch network.[3] Customers were already familiar with using supermarkets for simple financial transactions, for example withdrawing cash at supermarket checkouts, and the company felt that there were strong synergies between retailing and financial services. For example, simple, financial products could be purchased as a standard pack from the supermarket shelf and swiped through the checkout, Clubcard points could be used to attract customers to the Tesco Bank and, by combining data on financial as well as physical transactions, Tesco could gain an even deeper knowledge of its customer base, which could be used to fine-tune its marketing and promotional efforts.

Tesco's plans to develop into a full-scale bank were given an unanticipated boost by the 2008 financial crisis. Consumers were increasingly disillusioned with the large High Street banks but were thought to trust supermarket brands. Tesco's joint venture partner, RBS, was in severe difficulty so Tesco seized the opportunity to acquire RBS's shares in Tesco Personal Finance and launched a wholly owned subsidiary, Tesco Bank. Tesco announced that its intention was to move into full-service retail banking, offering current accounts, mortgages and small business loans in addition to the 'off the shelf' financial products it supplied in partnership with RBS. Five years on, however, Tesco had yet to launch its planned current account and mortgage services despite having spent large sums on information systems and other investments related to financial services. The move into banking had evidently proved more challenging than anticipated. Commentators questioned whether synergies between retailing and banking were more imagined than real. While supermarket stores had some advantages over bank branches, for example accessibility and ease of parking, not everyone thought they provided an environment conducive to financial transactions. Many aspects of full service banking involve face-to-face discussions and the exchange of confidential information. Customers may not want to arrange a mortgage or sort out a loan against a background of ringing tills and promotional announcements. Similarly, the notion that consumers placed more trust in supermarkets than banks was potentially overstated. If store groups began behaving like banks, for example calling in loans or, in the extreme, repossessing the houses of mortgage defaulters, then the supermarket's reputation would undoubtedly be affected. In the light of these uncertainties, Tesco's cautious approach seemed sensible.

Reinvigorating the core business

Over time, Tesco had added a plethora of new businesses to its portfolio. For example, in 2003, it established Tesco Mobile, a virtual network service operated in conjunction with O2, a UK mobile telecommunication provider; in 2008, it acquired Dobbies, a UK chain of garden centres; in 2010, it rolled out Tesco Home Services, offering home maintenance and repair services. Yet, despite this expanding scope, the core of Tesco's business remained in UK food retailing, which accounted for the majority of the group's revenue and profits. Indeed, under Leahy, Tesco expanded the number of its UK stores from 625 to 3285.

By the time Philip Clarke took over from Terry Leahy in 2011, fault lines were beginning to emerge. Tesco had started to lose ground, on the one hand, to heavy discounters like Aldi and Lidl who offered a narrow range of products at very low prices and, on the other, to more upmarket chains like Waitrose and Marks & Spencer. Both sales and profits began to slip and many complained that Tesco's rapid expansion both at home and abroad had caused it to take its eye off the UK ball. Tesco failed to convince UK consumers that its prices were competitive and shoppers complained about the lack of consistency between stores. While some offered an excellent shopping experience, others were considered mediocre and lacking in investment, leading analysts to suggest that Tesco had diverted too many resources away from its traditional heartland into more risky ventures.

Central to Clarke's strategy to reinvigorate Tesco was improving the shopping experience of UK customers. This was to be achieved, in large part, by making its stores more desirable locations to visit. At the same time, Clarke continued to diversify Tesco's business interests beyond food retailing: it acquired Giraffe, an restaurant chain with 46 outlets; a controlling stake in Harris + Hoole, a chain of coffee shops with an artisan look and feel; and Euphorium Bakery, allowing Tesco to open craft bakeries within its stores. At the same time, Tesco continued to expand its online presence through its acquisition of Blinkbox, a video-streaming service that also offered e-books and music streaming. This was followed by the launch of Hudl, a low-priced tablet computer with a pre-installed Tesco button.

By 2014, Tesco had a complex array of brands and business activities that extended beyond retailing. For example, one of the consequences of Tesco's expansion into online shopping and neighbourhood stores was that it no longer needed as many very large stores. Tesco's engagement in an aggressive 'space race' with other retailers had resulted in it becoming one of the largest property companies in Europe. Tesco's surplus land holdings encouraged it to engage in house building and property development.[4]

Each of Tesco's diversifications beyond UK grocery retailing could be justified in terms of exploiting its brand, its customer relationships or its retailing capabilities in related markets. Yet, as it added new lines of business, it greatly increased its internal complexity. As Tesco struggled to maintain its market share and profit margins in an increasingly competitive UK grocery trade, the fear was that the burden of managing a diversified, multinational corporation blunted Tesco's edge in its core business by impeding its nimbleness and responsiveness.

The scope of the firm

Deciding 'What business are we in?' is the starting point of strategy and the basis for defining the firm's identity. Corporate strategic decisions encompass choices over all three dimensions of a firm's scope: its product range (product scope), its presence along the industry value chain (vertical scope) and the geographical markets in which it will compete (geographical scope). In their statements of vision and mission, some companies define their businesses broadly. Shell's objective is 'to engage efficiently, responsibly and profitably in oil, oil products, gas, chemicals and other selected businesses'. Other companies define their businesses more narrowly: McDonald's vision is 'to be the world's best quick-service restaurant chain'; Caterpillar will 'be leader in providing the best value in machines, engines and support services for companies dedicated to building the world's infrastructure and developing and transporting its resources'. Some companies focus exclusively on a narrow part of the supply chain; others extend their reach across many supply chain activities. For example, in the travel market some tour operators, like Kuoni, focus exclusively on coordinating tour and travel arrangements for holidaymakers, whereas other companies, such as First Choice, have extended their activities and have their own airline.

The scope of a firm's business is likely to change over time. The dominant trend of the past two decades has been 'refocusing on core businesses'. Between 2000 and 2014, Philips, the Dutch-based electrical and electronics conglomerate, has divested its semiconductors, computer software and mobile phone businesses and most of its consumer electronics and domestic appliances activities to focus on just three areas: healthcare, lighting and consumer well-being. Most US and European conglomerates – notably ITT, Hanson, Gulf & Western, Cendant, Vivendi Universal and Tyco – have broken up altogether.

Some companies have moved in the opposite direction. Microsoft, once a supplier of operating systems, expanded into application and networking software, information services, entertainment systems and video games consoles. Google has diversified from search engines into a bewildering array of software products – including Internet browsers, operating system and applications software – and even into hardware (smartphones, intelligent eyeware, driverless cars). In our opening case, we have seen how Tesco, once a UK grocery chain, has diversified into a variety of goods and services as well as expanding internationally (Case Insight 7.1).

Similar trends are evident with respect to the vertical reach of business organizations. **Vertical integration**, a firm's extension of its activities into the preceding (or succeeding) stages of the production process, was seen as a way of improving coordination and reducing risk. More recently, the trend has been towards outsourcing and de-integration. In the pharmaceutical industry, for example, firms were traditionally highly vertically integrated and involved in all stages of the production process from basic research on drug formulation through the manufacture of the active chemical ingredients to packaging and marketing of the product. From the 1980s onwards, the industry started to de-integrate with pharmaceutical companies initially outsourcing chemical manufacture, then product formulation and more recently clinical trials and some basic research.

Case Insight 7.1

The scope of Tesco's activities

In its 2010 annual report, Tesco declared it had a well-established and consistent strategy for growth. By broadening the scope of its business, Tesco would deliver strong, sustainable, long-term growth by following customers into large expanding markets – such as financial services, non-food and telecoms – and new markets abroad, including Central Europe, Asia and America. By 2014, under new leadership, the company had withdrawn from America and Japan, delayed its move into full-service banking and declared its desire to pursue a more focused growth strategy. Yet, despite the retrenchment, the scope of Tesco's activities in the 21st century was much broader and deeper than the company's founder could ever have imagined.

In terms of its product offering, in 2014 Tesco's scope extended far beyond the usual range of household food and non-food items to include, amongst other things, telecommunication services (Tesco Mobile), entertainment (Blinkbox), financial services (Tesco Bank), customer relationship management services (dunnhumby) and family restaurants (Giraffe). It also delivered its retail services through multiple channels which included a range of different store formats (Tesco Metro, Tesco Express and Tesco Superstores), online delivery (Tesco grocery and Tesco Direct) and 'Click and Collect' services.

Tesco activities extend backwards along its supply chain. It owns and operates warehouses, distribution centres and fleets of lorries but has stopped short of some of its rivals, like Morrison's, who owns some food production and processing facilities.

In addition to product diversification and vertical integration, a further feature of Tesco's strategy under CEO Terry Leahy (1997–2011) was the broadening of its geographical scope. By 2014, 32% of group sales and 29% of the company's profits were generated outside the UK. Although the company had withdrawn from Japan and the US, it owned market-leading businesses in eight of the 11 international markets in which it operated and, operated partnerships, with local firms in China, Thailand and India.

Key concepts for analysing firm scope

Firms extend (or reduce) their scope because they perceive this to be in the organization's best interest. In the case of for-profit firms, it is reasonable to assume that changes in firm boundaries are designed to create value for shareholders, either by increasing revenue or by reducing costs (hopefully both). In this section, we introduce three concepts that are key to analysing corporate strategic decisions and shifts in the scope of firms' activities over time:

- *Economies of scope:* While most students are familiar with the notion of economies of scale, the equally important notion of **economies of scope** is often less well understood. Whereas 'economies of scale' refers to the reductions in unit costs that result from an increase in the output of a single product, economies of scope are cost economies that arise from increasing the output of multiple products.[5] Economies of scope exist when using a resource across multiple activities uses less of that resource than when the activities are carried out independently. The existence of economies of scope creates the potential for multibusiness firms to gain cost advantages over more specialized businesses.

- *Transaction costs:* Firms acquire inputs from markets and sell their output on markets. Markets are not costless: finding a supplier or a buyer entails search costs, making an agreement involves negotiating, drawing up a contract, monitoring that what was promised is being delivered and, if necessary, enforcing the contract through arbitration or litigation. All these costs are types of **transaction costs**. Can these transaction costs be avoided? In many instances, yes. When the firm extends its activities to encompass the activity undertaken by the seller or buyer, what was a market transaction becomes a transfer within the firm. Hence, the greater the transaction costs of markets, the more likely the firm is to extend its corporate scope.
- *The costs of corporate complexity:* Extending the boundaries of the firm can eliminate the transaction costs of the market, but internalizing business transactions imposes its own costs: the costs of corporate complexity. As the number and diversity of transactions managed internally grows, so the demands on managers and management systems grow, imposing costs that may well outweigh the savings from economies of scope and the elimination of transaction costs. The more the firm spreads itself over different types of business activity, the more these costs of corporate complexity escalate.

These three concepts allow us to evaluate the merits of specialization as compared to broad corporate scope. Consider the situations depicted in Figure 7.1. In the case of product scope, which is more efficient: to have metal cans, plastic containers and glass bottles produced by three separate companies or to have a single diversified packaging company produce all three? With regard to vertical scope, which is more efficient: three independent companies – one producing steel, the next rolling the steel into sheet and the third producing steel cans – or having a single company operating across all three stages of production? In the case of geographical scope, is it better to separate companies producing cans to serve the US, UK and German markets or to have a single multinational company supplying all three countries? In simple terms, it depends on whether the benefits of integration in terms of exploiting economies of scope and avoiding the transaction costs are sufficient to offset the costs associated with increased complexity of integrated firms.

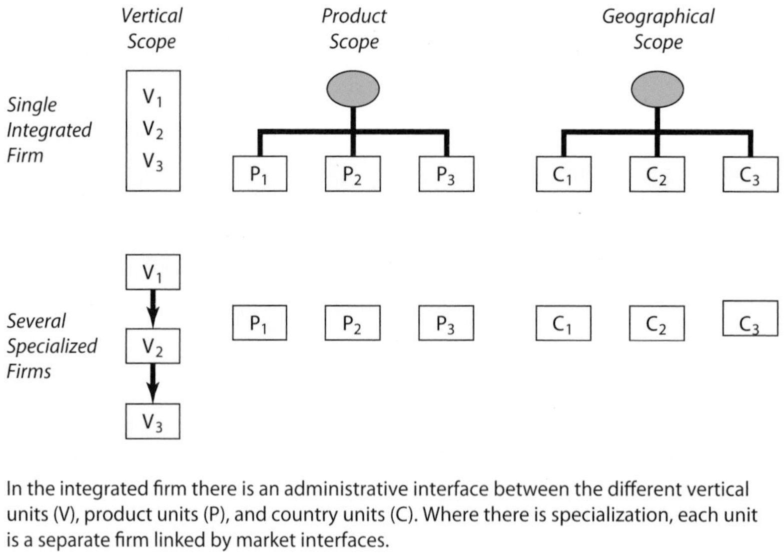
Vertical Scope
Product Scope
Geographical Scope
Single Integrated Firm
Several Specialized Firms
V1 V2 V3
P1 P2 P3
C1 C2 C3
In the integrated firm there is an administrative interface between the different vertical units (V), product units (P), and country units (C). Where there is specialization, each unit is a separate firm linked by market interfaces.

Figure 7.1 The scope of the firm: Specialization versus integration.

The roles of these three factors have changed over time. During most of the 20th century, companies grew in size and scope, absorbing transactions that had previously taken place across markets. A major factor encouraging firms to extend their boundaries was the fall in the administrative costs of firms relative to the transaction costs of markets. Technological innovation was a major source of falling administrative costs: the telegraph, telephone and computer greatly increased the efficiency of coordination and decision making within large, complex firms. The increasing capital and knowledge intensity of production processes also increased the importance of economies of scale and scope.

However, during the 1980s and 1990s, the trend towards increased corporate scope reversed. Instead of vertically integrating, firms outsourced more and more activities within their value chains. Instead of diversifying, firms began divesting diversified businesses in order to refocus on their core businesses. Two factors contributed to specialized firms increasing their efficiency relative to broad-based firms. First, increased turbulence of the business environment increased the costs of corporate complexity. Second, developments in information and communications technology (ICT) have favoured small firms linked by markets. While the mainframes of the 1970s reinforced the advantages of giant corporations, personal computers, the Internet and mobile communications have eliminated the disadvantages of small firms and reduced the transaction costs of markets.

Diversification

Defining diversification

Diversification refers to the expansion of an existing firm into another product line or field of operation. Diversification may be related or unrelated. Related diversification – also referred to as 'concentric diversification' – occurs when a firm expands into a similar field of operation, for example Honda extending its product line from motorcycles to cars. Unrelated diversification – also referred to as 'conglomerate diversification' – takes place when the additional product line is very different from the firm's core business, for example Japan Tobacco's acquisition of Katokichi, a supplier of frozen foods.

The distinction between related and unrelated diversification is, however, not as straightforward as it may at first seem. It depends upon what we mean by relatedness. For example, we could argue that Honda's decision to extend the scope of its business from motorcycles to cars constitutes related diversification, because motorcycles and cars use similar manufacturing processes. Hence, we are defining relatedness at an operational level, but this is not the only, or necessarily the most useful, way of viewing relatedness.

As we have already noted, economies of scope offer an important rationale for a firm to extend its corporate scope. While at first glance cigarettes and frozen foods appear to be very different, unrelated businesses, closer investigation may reveal that they involve similar organizational capabilities such as marketing and distribution. Whereas the opportunities for economies of scope derived from exploiting joint inputs may be relatively easy to identify at an operational level, strategic relatedness is more elusive. Richard Branson's Virgin Group covers a huge array of businesses from airlines to music stores, yet they share certain strategic similarities: almost all are start-up companies that benefit from Branson's entrepreneurial zeal and expertise; almost all sell to final consumers and are in sectors that offer opportunities for innovative approaches to differentiation. Classifying diversification as related or unrelated requires an understanding of the overall strategic approach of the company and recognition of its corporate-level management capabilities.

The benefits and costs of diversification

Diversification is beneficial if it helps a firm to achieve its objectives. Our main focus is on for-profit firms, so we concentrate on the ways in which diversification can assist firms to improve profitability and shareholder value, but it is important to recognize that diversification can be undertaken for other motives. Much corporate diversification appears to have been motivated by the desire for growth or risk reduction, which is not always in shareholders' interests. Alternative motives may also drive diversification by not-for-profit organizations. However, organizations that operate in the public and not-for-profit sectors may have their options for diversification restricted by statute or their focused missions. Let us consider whether growth and risk reduction are valid goals for profit-oriented firms.

GROWTH In the absence of diversification, firms are prisoners of their industry. For firms in stagnant or declining industries, this is a daunting prospect and makes diversification an appealing prospect for managers. Companies in low-growth, cash-flow-rich industries such as tobacco and oil have been especially susceptible to the temptations of diversification. During the 1980s, Exxon diversified into copper and coal mining, electric motors, computers and office equipment; RJR Nabisco transformed itself from a tobacco company into a diversified consumer products company. In both cases, diversification was highly destructive of shareholder value. Shareholders are quite happy to invest in companies in low-growth, even declining, industries, so long as these companies throw off plenty of cash flow that shareholders can invest in promising growth companies.

RISK REDUCTION The rationale for diversifying to reduce risk is captured by the familiar advice 'Don't put all your eggs in one basket.' If the cash flows of different businesses are imperfectly correlated, bringing them together under common ownership results in more stable profit earnings. But does such risk reduction create value for shareholders? Shareholders can diversify risk by holding diversified portfolios of shares rather than shares in diversified companies, and portfolio diversification by individual shareholders is typically cheaper than business diversification by companies. Not only do acquiring firms incur the heavy costs of using investment banks and legal advisers, they must also pay an acquisition premium to gain control of an independent company. The primary beneficiaries of risk reduction through diversification tend to be managers: stable profits are likely to mean job security.

VALUE CREATION: PORTER'S 'ESSENTIAL TESTS' In order to ensure that diversification creates value for shareholders through increasing the long-run profitability of the firm, Michael Porter proposes three 'essential tests':[6]

- *The attractiveness test:* The industries chosen for diversification must be structurally attractive or capable of being made attractive.
- *The cost-of-entry test:* The cost of entry must not outweigh all the future profits.
- *The better-off test:* Either the new unit must gain competitive advantage from its link with the corporation or vice versa.

A key feature of Porter's 'essential tests' is that industry attractiveness is insufficient on its own. Although diversification allows a firm to access more attractive investment opportunities than are available in its own industry, it faces the challenge of entering the new industry. The second test, cost of entry, recognizes that an industry offers above-average profitability to its participants because it is protected by barriers to entry. For a firm seeking to enter that industry, the cost of entry may eat up the benefits of being in that industry. Firms seeking to enter a high-profit industry such as pharmaceuticals or soft drinks can do so in two ways. They may acquire an established player, in which case the acquisition price will almost certainly fully capitalize the target firm's profit prospects (especially given the need to pay an acquisition premium over the market price of the target).[7] Alternatively, they may enter through establishing a new venture. In this case, the diversifying firm must directly confront the barriers to entry protecting that industry.[8]

Hence, in most diversification decisions, it is the better-off test that dominates. Industry attractiveness cannot be relied on as an ongoing source of superior profitability; and the attractiveness test and the cost-of-entry test tend to cancel each other out: attractive industries tend to be those that are costly to enter. So what determines whether diversification makes the diversifying firm better off? We are back to the three core factors that we identified as determining whether corporate strategy decisions create value for the firm: economies of scope, transaction costs and the costs of corporate complexity. In short, diversification can create value when it exploits economies of scope in shared resources and capabilities and economizes on the transaction costs of markets, while avoiding the impediments of increased complexity. Let us consider each of these in turn.

EXPLOITING ECONOMIES OF SCOPE Diversification offers the potential to exploit economies of scope wherever different businesses use the same resources and capabilities. Different resources and capabilities give rise to different opportunities for exploiting economies of scope.

Tangible resources – such as distribution networks, information technology systems, sales forces and research laboratories – offer economies of scope by creating a single shared facility thereby eliminating duplication between businesses. The greater the fixed costs of these items, the greater the economies of scope that can be exploited through diversification. Entry by cable TV companies into telephone services and telephone companies into cable TV are motivated by the desire to spread the costs of networks and billing systems over as great a volume of business as possible. Common resources such as customer databases, customer service centres and billing systems have encouraged British Gas, a former publicly owned gas utility, to diversify into supplying electricity, fixed-line and mobile telephone services, broadband Internet connections, home security systems, home insurance and home appliance repair.

Economies of scope also arise from the centralized provision of administrative and support services to the different businesses of the corporation. Within diversified companies, accounting, legal services, government relations and information technology tend to be centralized – often through **shared service organizations** that supply common administrative and technical services to the operating businesses. Similar economies arise from centralizing research activities in a corporate R & D lab.

Intangible resources – such as brands, corporate reputation and technology – offer economies of scope from the ability to extend them to additional businesses at low marginal cost. Exploiting a strong brand across additional products is called **brand extension**. Starbucks has extended its brand to ice cream, packaged cold drinks, home espresso machines, audio CDs and books. Tesco's diversification from groceries to a broad range of goods and services has similarly benefited from a trusted and well-known brand (Case Insight 7.2).

Organizational capabilities are also subject to economies of scope. These economies result from the ability to transfer capabilities between businesses within the diversified company.[9] For example:

- LVMH is the world's biggest and most diversified supplier of branded luxury goods. Its distinctive capability is marketing, specifically the management of luxury brands. This capability comprises market analysis, advertising, promotion, retail management and quality assurance. These capabilities are deployed across Louis Vuitton (accessories and leather goods), Hennessey (cognac), Moët & Chandon, Dom Pérignon, Veuve Clicquot and Krug (champagne), Céline, Givenchy, Kenzo, Dior, Guerlain and Donna Karan (fashion clothing and perfumes), TAG Heuer and Chaumet (watches), Sephora and La Samaritaine (retailing) and some 25 other branded businesses.
- W. L. Gore & Associates was founded to produce Gore-Tex, a synthetic fabric based upon DuPont's Teflon. W. L. Gore's has used technological capability in specialized synthetic fibres to diversify from fabrics for protective clothing into medical products, such as heart patches and synthetic blood vessels, industrial products such as high-tech air filters, guitar strings and a number of other products.

Some of the most important capabilities offering economies of scope to diversified companies are general management capabilities. Consider General Electric, one of the world's biggest and most successful diversified companies. GE possesses strong technological and operational capabilities and is good at sharing these capabilities across businesses (e.g. turbine know-how between jet engines and electrical-generating equipment). However, GE's most important core capabilities are its general management capabilities that reside primarily at the corporate level. These include its management development capabilities, its strategic management capabilities and its financial management capabilities.[10]

Case Insight 7.2

Economies of scope at Tesco

In the opening case, we saw that Tesco has diversified into areas that have allowed it to make shared use of both its tangible and intangible resources and its organizational capabilities:

- Its network of retail stores has provided the platform for diversification into non-food retailing and banking.
- The customer data generated by its Clubcard holders assists Tesco in 'following its customers into new markets'.
- Tesco's brand name and established reputation transfers from one line of business to another, although there is a risk that problems in one area of business could adversely affect other parts.
- Tesco's capabilities in market analytics and information processing, via dunnhumby, have allowed it to provide market and customer analysis services to other companies. Similarly, Tesco's capabilities in land and property management have facilitated its entry into house building and property development.

TRANSACTION COSTS OF MARKETS VERSUS THE COSTS OF CORPORATE COMPLEXITY

Economies of scope offer a powerful incentive for firms to enter related businesses, but do firms need to diversify in order to exploit these economies of scope? Economies of scope can also be exploited simply by selling or licensing the use of the resource or capability to another company. For example, Starbucks extends its brand to other products by licensing other companies to produce Starbucks-branded products: Pepsi produces and distributes Starbucks' Frappuccino, Unilever produces Tazo Tea beverages and Dreyer's produces Starbucks' ice cream. Even tangible resources can be shared across different businesses through market transactions. Airport and railway station operators exploit economies of scope in their facilities not by diversifying into catering and retailing but by leasing out space to specialist retailers and restaurants. As our opening case illustrated, Tesco decided to exploit its retail store assets by diversifying into new lines of business but it could have chosen to lease space to third parties, for example entering agreements with established clothing retailers rather than offering its own range of discount clothing, licensing Giraffe to provide within-store restaurants rather than acquiring the company. To explain why firms sometimes diversify in order to exploit economies of scope in shared resources and capabilities and sometimes exploit them externally through market contracts, we must consider the cost involved, specifically the costs of market transactions relative to the costs of corporate complexity.

For intellectual property such as patents or trademarks, licensing typically allows the firm to exploit the value that its resource generates in the diversified activity while avoiding the complexities that diversification would entail. Thus, Starbuck's licensing agreement with PepsiCo for the latter to produce Frappuccino bottled drinks involved relatively modest costs of negotiation and enforcement while avoiding the administrative and operational complexities of Starbucks entering into the bottling and distribution of soft drinks. In other cases, however, the transaction costs of licensing may be much higher. Virgin has a separate licensing company but only licenses its brand to companies within the Virgin group. So why doesn't Virgin license its brand to companies it does not own? The answer presumably is that the brand is an integral part of a package of resources and capabilities that Virgin possesses, including marketing skills through which the brand is promoted and the role of Richard Branson as a publicist and brand champion. A simple brand licensing arrangement is unlikely to fully exploit this package of resources and capabilities.

In general, organizational capabilities cannot be easily exploited through market contracts. When Apple sought to exploit its design and product development capabilities outside of its core computer business, it chose to diversify into MP3 music players and smartphones; it is difficult to imagine that it could have effectively exploited these capabilities by licensing arrangements with existing consumer electronics firms and mobile handset makers.

The ability of diversified firms to economize on the transaction costs of markets can provide a rationale for diversification even where economies of scope are negligible. In the case of two key resources, finance and labour, the diversified firm allocates these across its different businesses, whereas among specialized firms it is external capital and labour markets that allocate these resources.

In the case of finance, the diversified firm represents an **internal capital market**: the corporate headquarters allocates funds to different businesses through the capital expenditure budget. This internal allocation has two key advantages over the external capital market:

- By maintaining a balanced portfolio of cash-generating and cash-using businesses, diversified firms can avoid the costs of issuing new debt and equity.

- Diversified companies have better access to information on the financial prospects of their different businesses than that typically available to external financial markets.[11]

Against these advantages is the critical disadvantage that investment allocation within the diversified companies is a politicized process in which strategic and financial considerations are subordinated by turf wars and ego building. Evidence suggests that diversified firms sometimes cross-subsidize poorly performing divisions and are reluctant to transfer cash flows to the divisions with the best prospects.[12]

Diversified firms can derive similar advantages from internally transferring employees, especially managers and technical specialists, between their businesses. For specialized firms, the costs of hiring and firing can be substantial. The costs of hiring include advertising, the time spent in interviewing and selection and the costs of headhunting agencies. The costs of terminating employees can be very high, especially when severance payments must be offered. A diversified corporation can operate an **internal labour market** (its pool of employees) and can respond to the specific needs of any one business through transfer from elsewhere within the corporation. Also, the broader set of career opportunities available in the diversified corporation as a result of internal transfer may also result in attracting a higher calibre of employee. Graduating students compete intensely for entry-level positions in diversified corporations, such as Siemens, General Electric, Unilever and Nestlé, in the belief that these companies can offer richer career development than more specialized companies.

The informational advantages of diversified firms are especially important in relation to internal labour markets. A key problem of hiring from the external labour market is limited information. A CV, references and a day of interviews are poor indicators of how a new hire will perform in a particular job. The diversified firm can build detailed information on the performance and competencies of its employees in a range of different job roles.

Case Insight 7.3

Assessing the pros and cons for Tesco of entry into the financial services market

To evaluate whether Tesco's decision to enter full-service retail banking is in its shareholders' interest, Michael Porter proposes three essential tests:

- the attractiveness test
- the cost-of-entry test
- the better-off test.[13]

The attractiveness test invites us to ask whether the retail financial services market is attractive or capable of being made attractive. For many years, retail banking in the UK has been dominated by a few large players, such as RBS, Barclays and Lloyds. Until 2008, British banks were argued to be the envy of Europe for their high returns on equity which were thought to be around 20% compared to levels of 12% elsewhere. However, the financial collapse and the subsequent credit crunch severely dented industry prospects. Bad debts and the increased cost and difficulty of obtaining wholesale funds reduced profitability and contributed to a number of banks being rescued by the government. In addition, the high levels of competition between existing players, the recent entry of new ambitious new players like Santander and

Metro Bank and the well-documented reluctance of UK bank customers to switch their current accounts all combined to reduce the attractiveness of the market to newcomers.

Tesco recognized that particular segments of the retail banking market had become unattractive. Andrew Higginson, the CEO of Tesco speaking in 2009 about the company's earlier decision to hold back on its entry into retail banking, suggested this was a positive decision and not an accident. He argued: 'We couldn't see a way of making money and didn't know how the banks were doing so. We were happy to leave it alone.'[14] On the other hand, financial turmoil has also created the opportunity for Tesco to make the most of its trusted brand and customer relationships at a time when the status of High Street banks has been diminished.

The cost-of-entry test requires that future profits are not negated by the cost of gaining a position in the market. Two of the most significant costs of entry into retail banking are the costs of setting up a branch network and of establishing an appropriate IT infrastructure. Tesco, like a number of other retail chains, can use its existing stores as the basis for banking operations. While it already has a good capital base and a sophisticated IT system in place, the company has been required to make significant further IT investments following its purchase of the RBS interests in Tesco Bank.[15]

The better-off test requires the new business to provide the parent company with a competitive advantage. Tesco has a number of resources and capabilities that can be extended to retail financial services and benefits from an absence of some of the legacies that constrain established banks. Tesco stores are open for longer hours than bank branches, are located in places that provide free parking and allow customers to combine banking with weekly shopping. Simple savings products and general insurance have characteristics that lend themselves to off-the-shelf retailing and Tesco already has a large Internet operation. The company has strong capabilities in building and integrating IT systems and in customer relationship management as well as a significant presence in markets such as Eastern Europe and Asia that currently lack mature retail banking services. However, some analysts have suggested that some of the suggested synergies may be more illusory than real. Consumers may not wish to manage their finances in a store environment and the fallout from the financial crisis may mean they are distrustful of all big businesses, not just banks.

By broadening its corporate scope through its move into financial services Tesco also increased the complexity of its operations and its administrative and communication costs. At the start of 2014, Tesco reported a second consecutive fall in full-year profits and a continued loss in market share to rivals. Some commentators accused Tesco's management of taking its eye off the ball because it was distracted from its core UK grocery market by its ever more diverse range of activities. By going off in so many directions, they argued, Tesco diluted its efforts, stretched its capabilities too far and reduced the quality of its decision making.

Does diversification enhance corporate performance?

Empirical research into diversification has concentrated on two major issues: first, how do diversified firms perform relative to specialized firms and, second, does related diversification outperform unrelated diversification?

Despite many empirical studies over the past four decades, consistent, systematic relationships between diversification and performance are lacking. Beyond a certain threshold, high levels of diversification appear to be associated with lower profitability, probably because of the organizational complexity that diversification creates. Among British companies, diversification was associated with increased profitability up to a point, after which further diversification was accompanied by declining profitability.[16] Several other studies have detected a similar curvilinear relationship between diversification and profitability.[17] McKinsey & Company also points to the benefits of moderate diversification: 'a strategic sweet spot between focus and broader diversification'. Diversification, it argues, makes most sense when a company has exhausted growth opportunities in its existing markets and can match its existing capabilities to emerging external opportunities.[18]

A key problem is distinguishing *association* from *causation*. If moderately diversified companies are generally more profitable than specialized firms, is it because diversification increases profitability or because profitable firms channel their cash flows into diversifying investments? The performance effects of diversification depend on the mode of diversification. Mergers and acquisitions involving companies in different industries appear to perform especially poorly.[19]

More consistent evidence concerns the performance results of refocusing initiatives by North American and European companies: when companies divest diversified businesses and concentrate more on their core businesses, the result is typically increased profitability and higher stock market valuation.[20] These findings may reflect a changing relationship between diversification and profitability over time: growing turbulence of the business environment may have increased the costs of managing diversified corporations.

Given the importance of economies of scope in shared resources and capabilities, it seems likely that diversification into *related* industries should be more profitable than diversification into *unrelated* industries. Yet the findings of empirical research have been inconsistent. Initial findings[21] which appeared to show that closely related diversification was more profitable than unrelated diversification were contradicted by some subsequent studies.[22] Several factors may be confusing the relationship. First, related diversification offers greater potential benefits than unrelated diversification, but managing these linkages also creates greater management complexity. Second, the distinction between related and unrelated diversification is not always clear: it may depend upon the strategy and characteristics of individual firms. Champagne and luggage are not obviously related products, but LVMH applies similar brand management capabilities to them both.

Recent trends in diversification

When considering 'The scope of the firm' earlier in this chapter, we observed that, since the 1980s, the trend towards diversification has reversed and diversified companies have been refocusing their business portfolios through divesting non-core businesses. Equally significant, *conglomerate firms* – highly diversified companies created from multiple, unrelated acquisitions – have almost disappeared as a distinctive corporate form. In the UK, Hanson split into eight separate companies, including Imperial Tobacco, and BTR became a specialized engineering company. In the US, similar dismemberment occurred at ITT, Textron and Allied Signal. The divestment trend among large US companies meant that between 1980 and 1990 the average index of diversification for the Fortune 500 declined from 1.00 to 0.67.[23]

Outside of North America and Western Europe and the mature industrialized countries, the situation is very different. Highly diversified business groups dominate the industrial sectors of many emerging countries: Tata Group and Reliance in India, Charoen Pokphand (CP) in Thailand, Astra International in Indonesia, Sime Darby in Malaysia, ALFA and Grupo

Carso in Mexico. One reason for the continued dominance of large conglomerates in emerging market countries may be the higher transaction costs associated with their less sophisticated markets for finance, information and labour that offer diversified companies advantages over their specialized competitors.[24]

There are also signs that diversification may be making a comeback in the advanced industrial nations. In the technology sector, digitization is tending to break down conventional market boundaries. Simultaneously, complementarities are becoming more important between different products. Apple's diversification from personal computers into MP3 players, content download services, smartphones and tablet computers reflects increasing linkages between them. Similarly, Google has diversified from its core search engine into a bewildering variety of search and software products, including an operating system for mobile devices (Android) and an Internet browser (Chrome). As the rate at which technologies and products become obsolete increases and competitive advantage in core businesses erodes, so firms are finding it desirable to create (or acquire) 'growth options' in other industries.

Vertical integration

Defining vertical integration

'Vertical integration' refers to a firm's ownership of vertically related activities. The greater the span of vertical activities over which a firm's ownership extends, the greater its degree of vertical integration. The degree of a firm's vertical integration is indicated by the *ratio of its value added to its sales revenue*: the more a firm makes rather than buys, the lower are its costs of bought-in goods and services relative to its final sales revenue.

Vertical integration can be either *backward*, where the firm acquires ownership and control over the production of its own inputs, or *forward*, where the firm acquires ownership and control of activities previously undertaken by its customers.

Vertical integration may be *full* or *partial*. Some Australian wineries are fully integrated: they produce wine only from the grapes they grow and sell it all directly to final customers. Most are partially integrated: their home-grown grapes are supplemented with purchased grapes and they sell some wine through their own tasting rooms with independent distributors taking the rest.

The benefits and costs of vertical integration

Strategies towards vertical integration have been subject to shifting fashions. For most of the 20th century, the prevailing wisdom was that vertical integration was generally beneficial because it allowed superior coordination and reduced risk. During the past 25 years, there has been a profound change of opinion: outsourcing, it is claimed, enhances flexibility and allows firms to focus on their 'core competencies'. Moreover, many of the coordination benefits traditionally associated with vertical integration can be achieved through collaboration between vertically related companies.

However, as in other areas of management, fashion is fickle. As we saw in the opening case to Chapter 5 on the evolution of the computer industry and Chapter 6 on e-readers, the vertical integration of software devices and content is viewed as a critical advantage in the face of rapid technological change in a number of high-tech industries. Our task is to go beyond fads and fashions to uncover the factors that determine whether vertical integration enhances or weakens performance. On the positive side, vertical integration offers cost savings from the physical integration of processes, the elimination of certain transaction costs and the facilitation of transaction-specific investments. On the negative side, vertical integration may restrict a firm's ability to benefit from scale economies, reduce its flexibility and increase its risk.

TECHNICAL ECONOMIES FROM THE PHYSICAL INTEGRATION OF PROCESSES Analysis of the benefits of vertical integration has traditionally emphasized the **technical economies** of vertical integration: cost savings that arise from the physical integration of processes. Thus, most steel sheet is produced by integrated producers in plants that first produce steel and then roll the hot steel into sheet. Linking the two stages of production at a single location reduces transportation and energy costs. Similar technical economies arise from integrating pulp and paper production and linking oil refining with petrochemical production.

However, although these considerations explain the need for the co-location of plants, they do not explain why vertical integration in terms of common ownership is necessary. Why can't steel and steel strip production or pulp and paper production be undertaken by separate firms that own physically integrated plants? To answer this question, we must look beyond technical economies and consider the implications of linked processes for transaction costs.

TRANSACTION COSTS IN VERTICAL EXCHANGES Consider the value chain for steel cans, which extends from mining iron ore to delivering cans to food-processing companies (Figure 7.2). There is vertical integration between some stages; between others, there are mostly market contracts between specialist firms. In the final linkage – between can producing and canning – most cans are produced by specialist packaging companies (such as Crown Holdings and Ball Corporation); others are produced by food processors (such as Campbell's Soup and H. J. Heinz) that have backward integrated into can-making.[25]

The predominance of market contracts between steel strip production and can production is the result of low transaction costs in the market for steel strip: there are many buyers and sellers, information is readily available and the switching costs for buyers and suppliers are low. The same is true for many other commodity products: few jewellery companies own gold mines; few bakeries own wheat farms.

To understand why vertical integration predominates across steel production and steel strip production, let us see what would happen if the two stages were owned by separate companies.

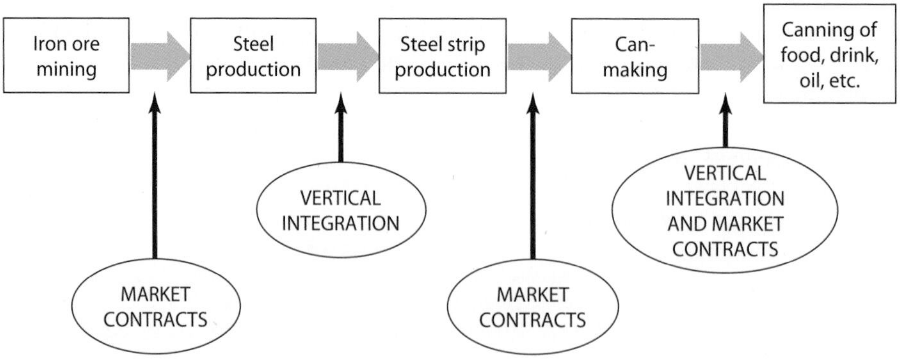

Figure 7.2 The value chain for steel cans.

Because there are technical economies from hot-rolling steel as soon as it is poured from the furnace, steel makers and strip producers must invest in integrated facilities. A competitive market between the two stages is impossible; each steel strip producer is tied to its adjacent steel producer. In other words, the market becomes a series of **bilateral monopolies**.

Why are these relationships between steel producers and strip producers problematic? To begin with, where a single supplier negotiates with a single buyer, there is no market price: it all depends on relative bargaining power. Such bargaining is likely to be costly: the mutual dependency of the two parties is likely to give rise to opportunism and strategic misrepresentation as each company seeks to both enhance and exploit its bargaining power at the expense of the other. Hence, once we move from a competitive market situation to one where individual buyers and sellers are locked together in close bilateral relationships, the efficiencies of the market system are lost.

The culprits in this situation are transaction-specific investments. When a can-maker buys steel strip, neither the steel strip producer nor the can-maker needs to invest in equipment or technology that is specific to the needs of the other party. In the case of the steel producer and the steel roller, each company's plant is built to match the other party's plant. Once built, the plant's value depends upon the availability of the other party's complementary facilities – each seller is tied to a single buyer, which gives each the opportunity to hold up the other.

Thus, transaction-specific investments result in transaction costs arising from the difficulties of framing a comprehensive contract and the risks of disputes and opportunism that arise from contracts that do not cover every possible eventuality. Empirical research confirms the likelihood of vertical integration where transaction-specific investments are required:[26]

- Among automakers, specialized components are more likely to be manufactured in-house than commodity items such as tyres and spark plugs.[27] Similarly, in aerospace, company-specific components are more likely to be produced in-house rather than purchased externally.[28]
- In semiconductors some companies, like Intel and ST Microelectronics, are integrated across design and fabrication; others are specialists in either chip design (e.g. ARM) or in fabrication (e.g. Taiwan Semiconductor Manufacturing Company). The more technically complex the integrated circuit and hence the greater the need for the designer and fabricator to invest in technical collaboration and adapt processes to the needs of the other, the better the relative performance of integrated producers.[29]

The problem of hold up could be eliminated by contracts that fully specify prices, quality, quantities and other terms of supply under all possible circumstances. The problem is uncertainty about the future – it is impossible to anticipate all eventualities during the contract period – hence contracts are inevitably incomplete.

DIFFERENCES IN OPTIMAL SCALE BETWEEN DIFFERENT STAGES OF PRODUCTION United Parcel Services (UPS) requires parcel delivery vans that are designed and manufactured to meet its specific needs. This requires its supplier, Morgan Olson, to make transaction-specific investments in producing vans for UPS. As a result, UPS is dependent upon Morgan Olson for its supply of vans and Morgan Olson is dependent upon UPS buying these vans. To avoid the difficulties of this situation, UPS has an incentive to manufacture its own vans. Would this be an efficient solution? Almost certainly not: the transaction costs avoided by UPS are likely to be trivial compared with the inefficiencies incurred in manufacturing its own vans.

UPS purchases about 20 000 trucks and vans each year, Morgan Olson manufactures over 500 000 trucks and vans annually.

The same logic explains why specialist brewers such as Adnams of Suffolk, England or Leffe of Belgium are not backward integrated into cans and bottles like Anheuser-Busch InBev or SABMiller – they simply do not possess the scale needed for efficiency in bottle and can manufacture.

THE INCENTIVE PROBLEM Vertical integration changes the incentives between vertically related businesses. Where a market interface exists between a buyer and a seller, profit incentives ensure that the buyer is motivated to secure the best possible deal and the seller is motivated to pursue efficiency and service in order to attract and retain the buyer: these are termed 'high-powered incentives'. With vertical integration, internal supplier–customer relationships are subject to 'low-powered incentives': if Shell's tanker fleet is inefficient, employees will lose their bonuses and the head of shipping may be fired. However, these consequences tend to be slow and undramatic. Most of us who have worked in large organizations have found that external contractors are often more responsive to our requests than internal service providers.

One approach to creating stronger performance incentives within vertically integrated companies is to open internal divisions to external competition. Many large corporations have created 'shared service organizations', where internal suppliers of corporate services such as IT, training and engineering compete with external suppliers of the same services to serve internal operating divisions.

FLEXIBILITY Both vertical integration and market transactions can claim advantage with regard to different types of flexibility. Where the required flexibility is rapid responsiveness to uncertain demand, there may be advantages in market transactions. The lack of vertical integration in the construction industry reflects, in part, the need for flexibility in adjusting both to cyclical patterns of demand and to the different requirements of each project. Vertical integration may also be disadvantageous in responding quickly to new product development opportunities that require new combinations of technical capabilities. Some of the most successful new electronic products of recent years – Apple's iPod, Microsoft's Xbox, Dell's range of notebook computers – have been produced by contract manufacturers. Extensive outsourcing has been a key feature of fast-cycle product development throughout the electronics sector.

Yet, where system-wide flexibility is required, vertical integration may allow for speed and coordination in achieving simultaneous adjustment throughout the vertical chain. The value chain for T-shirts typically involves specialist companies that undertake knitting, cut-and-sew operations, printing and retailing. Yet, American Apparel operates a tightly coordinated integrated chain that extends from its Los Angeles design and manufacturing centre to its 160 retail stores across 10 countries. This vertical integration allows a super-fast, highly responsive, design-to-distribution cycle.

COMPOUNDING RISK To the extent that vertical integration ties a company to its internal suppliers, vertical integration represents a compounding of risk in so far as problems at any one stage of production threaten production and profitability at all other stages. When union workers at a GM brake plant went on strike in 1998, GM's 24 US assembly plants were quickly brought to a halt. If Disney animation studios fail to produce blockbuster animation movies with new characters, the knock-on effects are felt through DVD sales, merchandise sales in Disney Stores and lack of new attractions at Disney theme parks.

Assessing the pros and cons of vertical integration

Vertical integration, as we have seen, is neither good nor bad. As with most questions of strategy: it all depends. The value of our analysis is that we are now able to identify the factors that determine the relative advantages of the market transactions versus internalization within the firm. Table 7.1 summarizes some of the key criteria. However, our analysis is not yet complete; we must consider some additional factors that influence the choice of vertical strategy, in particular the fact that vertical relationships are not limited to the simple choice of make or buy.

Table 7.1 Vertical integration (VI) versus outsourcing: Some key considerations.

Characteristics of the vertical relationship	Implication
How many firms are there in the vertically adjacent activity?	The fewer the number of firms, the greater the transaction costs and the bigger the advantages of VI
Do transaction-specific investments need to be made by either party?	Transaction-specific investments give rise to transaction costs increasing the advantages of VI
How evenly distributed is information between the vertical stages?	The greater the information asymmetries, the more likely is opportunistic behaviour and the greater the advantages of VI
Are market transactions in intermediate products subject to taxes or regulations?	Taxes and regulations are a form of transaction cost that can be avoided by VI
How uncertain are the circumstances of the transactions over the period of the relationship?	The greater the uncertainties over costs, technologies and demand, the greater the difficulty of writing contracts and the greater the advantages of VI
Are two stages similar in terms of the optimal scale of operation?	The greater the dissimilarity, the greater the advantages of market contracts as compared with VI
Are the two stages strategically similar (e.g. similar key success factors, common resources/capabilities)?	The greater the strategic similarity, the greater the advantages of VI over outsourcing
How great is the need for continual investment in upgrading and extending capabilities within individual activities?	The greater the need to invest in capability development, the greater the advantages of outsourcing over VI
How great is the need for entrepreneurial flexibility and drive in the separate vertical activities?	The greater the need for entrepreneurial flexibility, the greater the advantages of high-powered incentives from market contracts and the greater disadvantages of VI
How uncertain is market demand?	The greater the unpredictability of demand, the greater the flexibility advantages of outsourcing
Does vertical integration compound risk, exposing the entire value chain risks affecting individual stages?	The heavier the investment requirements and the greater the independent risks at each stage, the more risky is VI

Designing vertical relationships

Our discussion so far has compared vertical integration with arm's-length market contracts. In practice, there are a variety of relationships through which buyers and sellers can interact and coordinate their interests. Figure 7.3 shows a number of different types of relationship between buyers and sellers. These relationships may be classified in relation to two characteristics. First, the extent to which the buyer and seller commit resources to the relationship: arm's-length, spot contracts involve no resource commitment beyond the single deal; vertical integration typically involves a substantial investment. Second, the formality of the relationship: long-term contracts and franchises are formalized by the complex written agreements they entail; spot contracts may involve little or no documentation but are bound by the formalities of common law; collaborative agreements between buyers and sellers are usually informal, while the formality of vertical integration is at the discretion of the firm's management.

These different types of vertical relationship offer different combinations of advantages and disadvantages. For example:

- *Long-term contracts:* Market transactions can be either spot contracts – buying a cargo of crude oil on the Rotterdam petroleum market – or long-term contracts – involving a series of transactions over a period of time and specifying the terms of sales and the responsibilities of each party. Spot transactions work well under competitive conditions (many buyers and sellers and a standard product) where there is no need for transaction-specific investments by either party. Where closer supplier–customer ties are needed, particularly when one or both parties need to make transaction-specific investments, a longer-term contract can help avoid opportunism and provide the security needed to make the necessary investment. However, long-term contracts face the problem of anticipating the circumstances that may arise during the life of the contract: either they are too restrictive or they are so loose that they give rise to opportunism and conflicting interpretation. Long-term contracts often include provisions for the arbitration of contract disputes.
- *Vendor partnerships:* The greater the difficulties of specifying complete contracts for long-term supplier–customer deals, the greater the advantage of vertical relationships

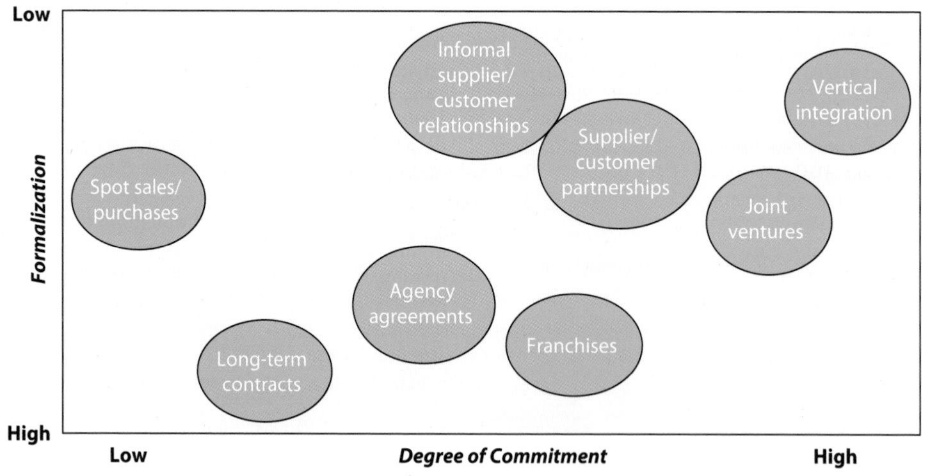

Figure 7.3 Different types of vertical relationship.

being based on trust and mutual understanding. Such relationships can provide the security needed for transaction-specific investments, the flexibility to meet changing circumstances and the incentives to avoid opportunism. Such arrangements may be entirely **relational contracts** with no written contract at all. The model for vendor partnerships has been the close collaborative relationships that many Japanese companies have with their suppliers. Japanese automakers have been much less backward integrated than their US or European counterparts, but have also achieved close collaboration with component makers in technology, design, quality and production scheduling.[30]

- *Franchising:* A **franchise** is a contractual agreement between the owner of a business system and trademark (the franchiser) and a licensee (franchisee) that permits the franchisee to produce and market the franchiser's product or service in a specified area. Franchising brings together the brand, marketing capabilities and business systems of the large corporation with the entrepreneurship and local knowledge of small firms. The franchising systems of companies such as McDonald's, Hilton Hotels and 7-Eleven convenience stores facilitate the close coordination and investment in transaction-specific assets that vertical integration permits with the high-powered incentives, flexibility and cooperation between strategically dissimilar businesses that market contracts make possible.

Recent trends in vertical integration

The main feature of recent years has been a growing diversity of hybrid vertical relationships that have attempted to reconcile the flexibility and incentives of market transactions with the close collaboration provided by vertical integration. Although collaborative vertical relationships are viewed as a recent phenomenon – associated with microelectronics, biotechnology and other hi-tech sectors – local groupings of vertically collaborating firms are a long-time feature of the craft industries of Europe. This is especially true of northern Italy – both in traditional sectors such as textiles[31] and newer sectors such as packaging equipment[32] and motorcycles.[33]

The supplier networks of Japanese manufacturers with their knowledge sharing and collaborative new product development have become models for many large American and European companies.[34] There has been a massive shift from arm's-length supplier relationships to long-term collaboration with fewer suppliers. In many instances, competitive tendering and multiple sourcing have been replaced by single-supplier arrangements. Vendor relationships frequently involve supplier certification and quality management programmes and technical collaboration.

The mutual dependence that results from close, long-term supplier–buyer relationships creates vulnerability for both parties. While trust may alleviate some of the risks of opportunism, companies can also reinforce their vertical relationships and discourage opportunism through equity stakes and profit-sharing arrangements. For example: Commonwealth Bank of Australia took an equity stake in its IT supplier, EDS Australia; pharmaceutical companies often acquire equity stakes in the biotech companies that undertake much of their R & D; and oil field services companies are increasingly equity partners in upstream projects.

However, in this world of closer vertical relationships, some trends have been in the opposite direction. The Internet has radically reduced the transaction costs of markets, particularly in pruning search costs and facilitating electronic payments. The result has been a revival in arm's-length competitive contracting through business-to-business e-commerce hubs such as Covisint (car parts), Elemica (chemicals) and Rock & Dirt (construction equipment).[35] At the same time, enthusiasm for exploiting lower labour costs in emerging countries has intensified outsourcing among companies in North America, Europe and Japan. In the electronics sector, companies such as Nokia, Hewlett-Packard and Sony have outsourced manufacturing to China and services (including call centres and software development) to India.

The scope of outsourcing has extended from basic components to a wide range of business services, including payroll, IT, training and customer service and support. Increasingly, outsourcing involves not just individual components and services but also whole chunks of the value chain. In electronics, the design and manufacture of entire products are often outsourced to contract manufacturers such as Hon Hai Precision Industry Co., Ltd, which makes Apple iPods, Nokia phones and Sony's PlayStation.

Extreme levels of outsourcing have given rise to the concept of the **virtual corporation**: a firm whose primary function is to coordinate the activities of a network of suppliers and downstream partners. Coordination typically takes place through the use of information and communication technologies: a firm whose primary function is to coordinate the activities of a network of suppliers and downstream partners.[36] In this organizational form, the hub company has the role of 'systems integrator'. The critical issue is whether a company that outsources most functions can retain the **architectural capabilities** needed to manage the **component capabilities** of the various partners and contractors. The risk is that the virtual corporation may degenerate into a 'hollow corporation', where it loses the capability to evolve and adapt to changing circumstances.[37] If, as Prahalad and Hamel argue, core competencies are embodied in 'core products' then the more these core products are outsourced, the greater the potential for the erosion of core competence.[38] Andrea Prencipe's research into aero engines points to the complementarity between architectural capabilities and component capabilities. Thus, even when the aero engine manufacturers outsource key components, they typically maintain R & D in those component technologies.[39] The problems experienced by Boeing in managing the outsourced network model it adopted for its 787 Dreamliner point to the complexity of the system integrator role.[40]

Case Insight 7.4

Should Tesco own and operate its own fleet of lorries?

Tesco's corporate scope is broad in terms of products and geographical markets, but vertically Tesco's scope is narrow: it is primarily a retailer. Tesco has many thousands of suppliers and these supplier relationships involve significant transaction costs relating to search, negotiation, monitoring and contract enforcement. Yet, Tesco has chosen not to backward integrate into food processing, agriculture and the many other industries that supply it with goods and services. It would appear that the benefits from avoiding transactions costs are offset by the disadvantages of such backward integration, notably Tesco's lack of capabilities in manufacturing and added complexity of engaging in these activities.

One area where Tesco is backward integrated is in operating its own supply chain logistics, notably its own transport fleet. Is this beneficial or would Tesco be better off outsourcing this to a specialist transportation company? Table 7.2 applies the considerations listed in Table 7.1 to this issue. The nature of the relationship between distribution logistics and supermarket retailing means that the transactions costs of outsourcing distribution are likely to be high, while the integration of distribution logistics and retailing in a single company is likely to facilitate coordination, responsiveness and innovation.

Table 7.2 Key considerations in outsourcing transport for Tesco.

Characteristics of the vertical relationship	Implications for Tesco's choice between integration vs. outsourcing
How many firms are there in the vertically adjacent activity?	There are many logistics firms, but few have the scale needed to service Tesco's requirements. The fewer the firms available to Tesco, the more vulnerable is Tesco to potential hold up
Do transaction-specific investments need to be made by either party?	Yes. Supplying Tesco stores may not require specialized types of vehicle but will require investment in highly specific information systems and tracking technologies
How evenly distributed is information between the vertical stages?	Tesco has total access to customer and store data that would be difficult and costly to share with third parties. Keeping logistics in-house is less risky for Tesco
How uncertain are the circumstances of the transactions over the period of the relationship?	Tesco's transportation requirements cannot be precisely predicted over the period of the outsourcing contract. Hence, contracts with logistics firms will need to be flexible, giving scope for disagreements and differences in interpretation
Are two stages similar in terms of the optimal scale of operation?	Supermarkets and road transportation are both subject to continuing scale economies. But in some overseas markets, Tesco is too small to justify operating its own fleet of trucks
Are the two stages strategically similar (e.g. similar key success factors, common resources/capabilities)?	Logistical capabilities and use of IT for national coordination of local activities are critical to success both in retailing and transportation
How great is the need for continual investment in upgrading and extending capabilities within individual activities?	Brutal competition in supermarket retailing requires continual adaptation and upgrading of capabilities. The key here is that this adaptation and upgrading needs to be coordinated with adaptation in supply chain logistics (e.g. the shift towards more small, local stores requires more frequent deliveries). Such close coordination favours integration
How great is the need for entrepreneurial flexibility and drive in the separate vertical activities?	Not a key consideration: both supermarkets and transportation are businesses where centralized decision making and operational planning are the keys: entrepreneurial flexibility by local units is not essential to success
How uncertain is market demand?	The greater the unpredictability of demand, the greater the flexibility advantages of outsourcing. Although consumer tastes change over time, there is a great deal of stability with regard to regular purchases of food products
Does vertical integration compound risk, exposing the entire value chain to risks affecting individual stages?	Any disruption in transportation, e.g. due to strikes, will have dire implications for Tesco's supermarket business. However, it is not obvious that this risk is much different whether transportation is insourced or outsourced

Managing the corporate portfolio

If opportunities exist to create value through diversification or vertical integration, managers are confronted by another question: 'How do we manage a multibusiness firm in ways that generate as much value as possible?' Portfolio planning models can be a helpful way of starting to address this question.

The GE/McKinsey matrix

The basic idea of a portfolio planning model is to represent graphically the individual businesses of a multibusiness company in terms of key strategic variables that determine their potential for profit. These strategic variables typically relate to the attractiveness of their market and their competitive advantage within that market. This analysis can guide:

- allocating resources between the businesses on the basis of each business's market attractiveness and competitive position;
- formulating business unit strategy – by comparing the strategic positioning of different businesses, opportunities for repositioning (including divestment) can be identified;
- analysing portfolio balance – a single display of all the company's businesses permits assessment of the overall balance of the portfolio in terms of cash flow generation and growth prospects;
- setting performance targets on the basis of each business's market attractiveness and its competitive position.

In the GE/McKinsey matrix (Figure 7.4) the industry attractiveness axis combines: market size, market growth rate, market profitability (return on sales over three years); cyclicality, 'inflation recovery' (potential to increase productivity and product prices) and international potential (ratio of foreign to domestic sales). Business unit competitive advantage combines: market share; return on sales relative to competitors; and relative position with regard to quality, technology, manufacturing, distribution, marketing and cost.[41] The strategy implications are shown by the three regions of Figure 7.4.

BCG's growth–share matrix

The Boston Consulting Group's growth–share matrix also uses industry attractiveness and competitive position to compare the strategic positions of different businesses. However, it uses

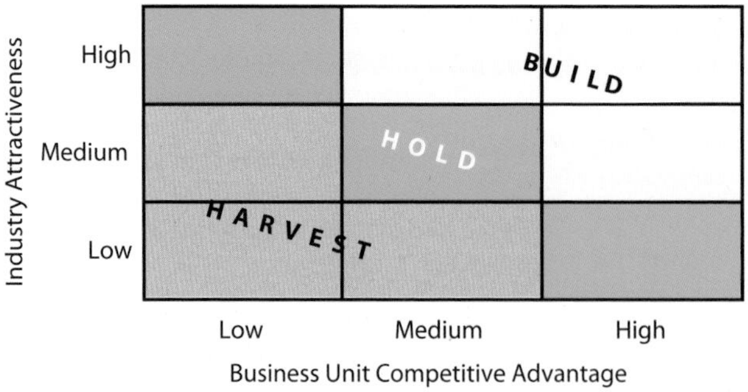

Figure 7.4 The GE/McKinsey portfolio planning matrix.

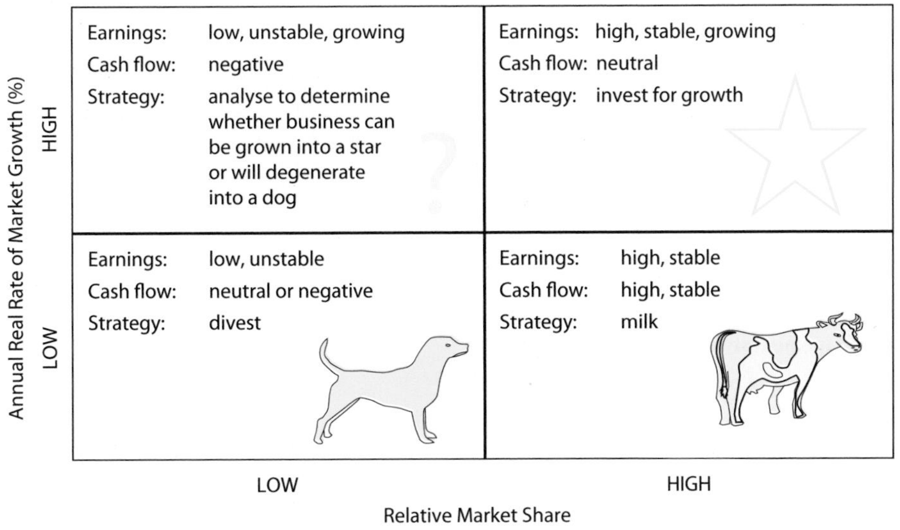

Figure 7.5 The BCG growth–share matrix.

a single indicator as a proxy for each of these dimensions: industry attractiveness is measured by *rate of market growth* and competitive advantage by *relative market share* (the business unit's market share relative to that of its largest competitor). The four quadrants of the BCG matrix predict patterns of profits and cash flow and indicate strategies to be adopted (Figure 7.5).[42]

The simplicity of the BCG matrix is both its limitation and its usefulness. It can be prepared very easily and offers a clear picture of a firm's business portfolio in relation to some important strategic characteristics. But the simplicity also masks some problems, for example with respect to market definition. For instance, in the BCG matrix, is BMW's car business a 'dog', because it holds less than 2% of the world car market, or a 'cash cow', because it is market leader in the luxury car segment? An even greater problem is the implicit assumption that every business in the portfolio is independent – a direct denial of the basic rationale for the multibusiness corporation: the synergistic linkages between businesses.[43]

The Heartland Matrix

The Heartland Matrix is based upon Campbell *et al's* parenting advantage framework.[44] It takes account of the fact that the value-creating potential of a business within a company's business portfolio depends not just on the characteristics of the business (as assumed by the McKinsey and BCG matrices) but also on the characteristics of the parent. The focus, therefore, is on the fit between a business and its parent company. The horizontal axis of Figure 7.6 shows the parent's potential for creating additional profit within the business, for example from applying corporate-level management capabilities to the business, from sharing resources and capabilities with other businesses and from economizing on transaction costs. The vertical axis measures the risk of subtracting value by the parent. This could result from the parent misunderstanding or failing to adjust to the situation in the business and could include bureaucratic rigidity, incompatibility with the top management's mindset, politicization of decision making and risks of inappropriate strategic guidance.

The need for assessment of complex issues of fit between the business and the parent and the fact that these assessments inevitably require subjective judgements mean that the Heartland

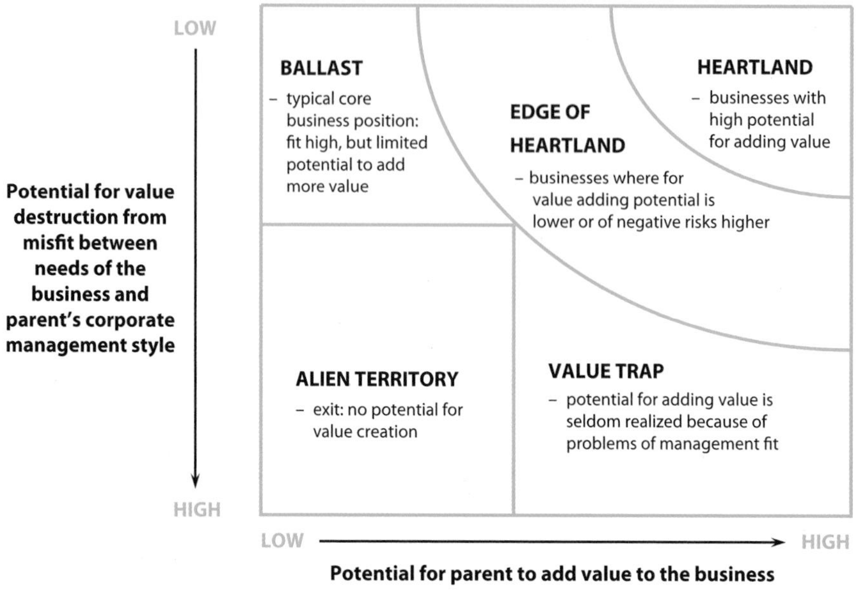

Figure 7.6 The Heartland Matrix: The potential for parenting advantage.
Source: A. Campbell, M. Goold, M. Alexander and J. Whitehead, *Strategy for the Corporate Level: Where to invest, what to cut back and how to grow organisations with multiple divisions* (Jossey-Bass, 2014).

Matrix is more difficult to use than the GE/McKinsey or BCG matrices. However, this is the reality of the subject matter: creating value from the configuration and reconfiguration of a portfolio of business involves complex issues of fit that require insight into the fundamental strategic characteristics of the businesses and the nature of corporate management systems and style.

Summary

Corporate strategy is about deciding in which businesses to engage and, for top management, often represents some of the most important and difficult decisions they are likely to take. Mistakes can be very expensive, both financially and strategically, and the business press is littered with examples of large companies who have made such errors. Nevertheless, for firms to prosper in the long term, they must change, and inevitably this involves redefining the business in which they operate. Whenever we look at firms that have long histories, we see that they have changed their product lines, acquired new resources and developed new capabilities in line with market opportunities.

Long-term adaptation to market conditions through diversification is likely to be much more successful if it is based on sound strategic analysis. The objectives of diversification need to be clear and, although some top managers may be tempted to use diversification as a means of growing their own empire, such empires are unlikely to endure unless they are based on genuine value creation. In the late 1980s, diversification decisions were often based on vague notions of synergy that involved identifying linkages (sometimes rather tenuous) between industries. We are now able to be much more precise about the need for economies of scope in resources and capabilities and 'economies of internalization'[45] if diversification is to add value.

Similarly, deciding what parts of the value chain to engage in requires systematic thought. Managers need to decide not only what activities they will undertake internally and what they will outsource but also how best to organize their arrangements with external and internal buyers and suppliers. Possible arrangements include arm's-length contracts, long-term agreements and strategic alliances. To decide what constitutes the best option, each firm needs to evaluate its strategic needs, its resources and capabilities at different stages of the value chain, the relative attractiveness of different parts of the value chain and the characteristics of the transactions involved.

Having determined the potential for diversification or vertical integration to add value, the challenge is then how to manage the multibusiness firm to extract this potential value. Portfolio planning models can aid managers to make sense of the complexity and to start to develop a degree of consistency in the firm's activities to produce coherence and fit.

Summary table

Learning objectives	Summary
Be familiar with the concepts of economies of scope, transaction costs and the costs of managing complexity, and understand how these ideas help to explain firm boundaries and the shifts in firm boundaries over time	'Economies of scope' refers to the cost savings that arise from sharing and transferring resources and capabilities, but those cost savings can be exploited within the firm or by simply selling or licensing the use of resources and capabilities to other companies. If the firm chooses to take advantage of synergies by internalizing transactions, it incurs the costs of coordination and controlling activities. If instead the firm chooses to enter into deals with outside parties, it incurs transaction costs. We would expect profit-seeking firms to select the least-cost options and for the boundaries of the firm to reflect this. Over time, firm boundaries change because the transaction costs of market contracts and the administrative costs of diversified activities change relative to each other
Understand the rationale behind multibusiness activity and the potential benefits and costs of extending the horizontal or vertical scope of a firm	We have primarily looked at the ways in which extensions to product and vertical scope can create (or destroy) value by reducing (or increasing) costs and by creating (or destroying) competitive advantage, but we also noted that managers sometimes act in their own self-interest rather than that of shareholders. Managers may pursue multiple business activities for reasons of growth or risk reduction rather than profit
Be able to evaluate the advantages and disadvantages of changing a firm's scope and the different ways of exploiting opportunities for value creation	Porter suggests that there are three essential tests to be applied to diversification: the attractiveness test, the cost-of-entry test and the better-off test
Appreciate the trends in diversification and vertical integration over time	In recent years, the dominant trend in terms of product scope has been refocusing on the core business. Many large, diversified conglomerates have been broken up. The picture with regard to vertical scope has been more complex with a trend towards more hybrid collaborative arrangements
Be familiar with the techniques of portfolio analysis and be able to apply these to corporate strategic decisions	Three portfolio approaches have been outlined: the GE/McKinsey matrix, the BCG matrix and the Heartland matrix display. All three approaches assist managers to make sense of complex multibusiness activities but all require some element of subjective judgement and insight into the fundamental strategic characteristics of the businesses

Further reading

Two of the classic texts on corporate strategy are:

Porter, M. (1987). From competitive advantage to corporate strategy. *Harvard Business Review*, 65(3), 43–59.

Teece, D (1980) Economies of scope and the scope of the enterprise. *Journal of Economic Behavior and Organization* 1, 223–47.

The paper by Constantinos Markides also provides a nice introduction to the diversification debate:

Markides, C. (1997). To diversify or not to diversify? *Harvard Business Review*, Nov/Dec, 93–9.

as does the book by Campbell *et al.*:

Campbell, A., Goold, M., Alexander, M. and Whitehead, J. (2014). *Strategy for the Corporate Level: Where to invest, what to cut back and how to grow organizations.* Jossey-Bass.

Professor Rita McGrath of Harvard Business School argues that vertical integration is making a comeback. The blog 'Why vertical integration is making a come-back' can be found on the Harvard Business Review website (http://blogs.hbr.org/2009/12/vertical-integration-can-work):

With respect to portfolio planning techniques, Untiedt *et al.* have undertaken a literature review in which they revisit corporate portfolio analysis tools and ask why they have become unpopular:

Untiedt, R., Nippa, M. and Pidun, U. (2012). Corporate portfolio analysis tools revisited: Assess causes that may explain scholarly disdain. *International Journal of Management Reviews*, 14(3), 63–279.

Self-study questions

1 It has been argued that the developments in information and communication technology (e.g. telephone and computer) during most of the 20th century tended to lower the costs of administration within the firm relative to the costs of market transactions, thereby increasing the size and scope of firms. What about the Internet? How has this influenced the efficiency of large, integrated firms relative to small, specialized firms coordinated by markets?

2 Minor International plc (MINT) is a large Thai conglomerate that owns and operates over 70 hotels and resorts, runs a range of fast-food outlets and is one of Thailand's largest distributors of fashion and cosmetics brands. What are the main advantages and disadvantages for MINT of engaging in such a wide portfolio of activities?

3 Tata Group is one of India's largest companies, employing 424 000 people in many different industries, including steel, motor vehicles, watches and jewellery, telecommunications, financial services, management consulting, food products, tea, chemicals and fertilizers, satellite TV, hotels, motor vehicles, energy, IT and construction. Such diversity far exceeds

that of any North American and Western European company. What are the conditions in India that make such broad-based diversification both feasible and profitable?

4 A large proportion of major corporations outsource their IT function to specialist suppliers of IT services such as IBM, EDS (now owned by Hewlett-Packard), Accenture and Capgemini. What transaction costs are incurred by these outsourcing arrangements and why do they arise? What are the offsetting benefits from IT outsourcing?

5 Electro, a multinational electronics company, operates in four broad product markets. It produces personal computers, printers and scanners, server computers (basic infrastructure for corporate IT) and provides IT services. Its position in each of these markets is as follows:

   a The company is currently the leading manufacturer of personal computers, with a market share of 20% of the global market. It is, however, facing strong competition from rival manufacturers whose cost bases appear to be lower than Electro's.

   b The company has long regarded its printer and scanning business as its crown jewel. The profits made by this unit are regularly used to subsidize other parts of the business.

   c The company is the third-largest supplier of server computers, but in recent years it has lost ground to other established competitors.

   d IT services represent a new venture for the company, and it has met with some initial success in this market. Its current capabilities in this area are, however, limited and it will need to invest heavily and recruit more specialist staff if it wishes to build this part of the business.

Use a portfolio planning model of your choice to analyse Electro's position. What challenges do you face in trying to apply your selected model? What additional information do you need to make a proper evaluation? What advice may you be able to offer Electro on managing its portfolio? What are the limitations of the portfolio approach you have selected?

Closing Case

Diversification at Disney

In his 2014 annual statement, Robert Iger, chairman and chief executive officer of the Walt Disney Company, took pleasure in announcing that the company had, for the third year running, surpassed its previous performance records and that its share price was hovering at an all-time high.[46] In recent years, the company has had a stream of hit movies including *Tangled*, *Frozen*, *The Avengers* and its acquisition of Lucasfilm in 2012 had added further creative momentum with fans eagerly awaiting the release of a new *Star Wars* movie that was scheduled for 2015. Success in the movie business was having positive spin-off effects for Disney consumer products and theme parks and its new TV channel, Disney Junior, and games platform, Disney Infinity, were also riding high. This was quite an achievement for the leader of such a large and complex organization, particularly given that Disney had been a troubled company when Iger took over from his predecessor, Michael Eisner, in 2006.

The background to the Walt Disney Company

The Walt Disney Company, founded by Walt and Roy Disney, started life as The Disney Brothers Cartoon Studio producing the cartoon series which brought the world such memorable characters as Mickey Mouse and Donald Duck. Having achieved success with short films, the Disney Studio quickly moved into the production of feature-length animated films, including *Snow White and the Seven Dwarves*, *Pinocchio* and *Fantasia*. The brothers were introduced early in the company's existence to opportunities for diversification when a businessman, who wanted to use the image of Mickey Mouse to promote sales of a drawing tablet for children, approached them. The establishment of the Mickey Mouse Club for fans soon after this encounter suggests that the Disney brothers recognized immediately the potential for selling toys, books and other products linked to their animated characters. Over time, Disney added more and more businesses to its portfolio and by 2014 had transformed itself into a multinational media and entertainment company, ranked in *Fortune* magazine's top 50 companies.

The scope of the firm's business activities in 2014

The Walt Disney Company grouped its activities into five main areas: Media Networks, Parks and Resorts, Studio Entertainment, Consumer Products and Interactive Media, but beneath these five titles lay a multiplicity of different business activities.

Table 7.3 indicates the size of these different parts of the business by revenue in 2012/13.

Table 7.3 Disney's revenue 2012/13.

Business group	Revenue $million	Revenue as % of the total
Media Networks	20356	45
Parks and Resorts	14087	31
Studio Entertainment	5979	13
Consumer Products	3555	9
Interactive Media	1064	2
Total	45041	100

- *Media Networks:* Disney's Media Network segment comprised the US television and radio stations, international cable networks and distribution and publishing operations through which it distributed its media content to households. Having access to distribution channels was (and remains) a key success factor in the media industry because the high fixed costs of making films and television programmes mean that profitability depends on gaining as broad an audience as possible. If a company controls both content and distribution, it can promote its own content and shape how and when its content is broadcast. As the media industry became more concentrated with large conglomerates like Time Warner and Bertelsmann dominating scheduling, the position of independent content providers became more precarious. In 1995, Disney acquired the TV and radio broadcasting company Capital Cities/ABC for the sum of $19 billion. Disney paid a lot to acquire the company but the deal was of particular strategic importance because it secured Disney's access to media channels for its creative content.
- *Parks and Resorts:* Amongst the first areas of business developed by Disney outside its animation and merchandising base were theme parks. The company opened Disneyland in California in 1955 and went on to establish the Walt Disney World Resort in Orlando, Florida in 1971. Disneyland resorts were subsequently developed in Tokyo (Japan in 1983), Paris (France in 1993), Hong Kong (in 2005) and most recently Shanghai (China, currently under construction). The theme parks were a natural extension of Disney's core business because the themes and characters that appeared in its films provided the basis for the rides and fantasy settings. A virtuous circle was created whereby the films promoted the parks and the parks promoted the films. Over time, the development of the theme parks took Disney into a new area. Visitors to the theme parks needed accommodation so Disney built and ran hotels; Disney became skilful in managing travel arrangements and the tourist experience and subsequently founded the Disney Vacation Club and the Disney Cruise Line. Disney also planned and built retail, entertainment and dining complexes, which led to the establishment of the Disney Development Company.
- *Studio Entertainment:* At the heart of the Disney operation lay its creative content. The early success of the company was based on its animated cartoons and the characters who populated them, but as audiences' tastes changed so Disney needed to move with the times by acquiring new content and embracing new animation technologies. To that end, in 2006, it acquired Pixar, a computer animation studio best known for films such as *Toy Story* and *Finding Nemo*. It purchased Marvel Entertainment, the owner of comic book characters

Credit: Bloomberg via Getty Images

such as Spider Man and the Hulk, in 2009, and, in 2012, bought Lucasfilm, the production company behind the *Star Wars* movies. In addition, Disney acquired the rights to other film, direct-to-video, musical and theatrical content.

- *Consumer Products:* the consumer products division was the vehicle that Disney used to exploit its intellectual property by awarding licences to third parties to produce and sell merchandise based on its characters; publishing children's book, magazines and learning devices; and operating both physical and online Disney Stores. Its stores were generally located in shopping malls or retail complexes; by 2014, Disney owned and operated 214 stores in the US, 88 in Europe and 46 in Japan.
- *Interactive Media:* this division focused on developing console, mobile, social and virtual world games that were marketed on a worldwide basis. While most of the game development activity took place in-house, Disney also licensed some third-party developers to develop games based on Disney material. From small beginnings the division grew relatively rapidly.

What drives success?

Unlike many other large conglomerates, Disney has, in recent years, been able to maintain momentum and improve its performance in all its major segments, raising the question of what drives success. Iger has suggested that there are three main elements underlying Disney's performance. First, he argues that, under his leadership, the company has made the production of high-quality, family-orientated content its priority with the ongoing development of creative content driving all parts of the business. Much of the creative impetus has come from acquiring companies but, once acquired, Disney has allowed these businesses to operate quasi-autonomously and has encouraged innovation. Second, he suggests that Disney is future-orientated and has succeeded by making its content more accessible and engaging through the use of digital technology. The company has been willing to learn from its mistakes, for example restructuring its interactive division and moving away from console games when this segment failed to make money. Finally, he places emphasis on building a portfolio of brands.

Disney's continuing success depends on its ability to consistently create and distribute films, broadcast and cable programmes, online material, electronic games, theme park attractions, hotel and other resort facilities, travel experiences and consumer products that meet the changing preferences of a wide range of consumers, a growing number of whom are located outside the US. The linkages between businesses mean that success or failure in one part of the business can affect other parts. For example, if entertainment offerings like *Who Wants to be a Millionaire* or *High School Musical* cease to be popular with audiences then revenue from advertising, which is based in part on programme ratings, falls and so does revenue from merchandising. In the worst-case scenario if the firm experiences successive content failures then viewers might cancel their subscriptions to cable channels or reduce their visits to entertainment parks where the themed rides are seen as passé. Disney has had its fair share of flops as well as hits, for example the *Lone Ranger* and *John Carter* failed to make it at the box office. At the same time, changes in technology and different delivery formats such as television, DVDs, computer and Web-based formats are affecting not only the demand for the company's entertainment products but also the cost of producing and distributing them.

Disney faces a fundamental tension, namely in expanding to exploit the benefits of scale and scope present in its business activities, the size and complexity of its organization increases and makes it more difficult for the company to be agile and innovative. The challenge for Iger remains that of maintaining creative impetus while putting in place the structures and systems necessary to manage such a large and complex organization.

Case questions

- How does the concept of 'economies of scope' help to explain Disney's diversification strategy?
- What are the pros and cons for Disney of operating television and cable networks?
- In 2009, Disney announced that it had acquired Marvel Entertainment, a comic book and action hero company for $4 billion. How would you evaluate the value-creating potential of this decision?
- What are the key challenges Disney's senior managers face in running such a diverse set of businesses?

Notes

1 Tesco PLC Annual Report and Financial Statements 2013.

2 S. Mauch, *From A(pples) to Z(oom lenses): Extending the boundaries of multi-channel retailing at Tesco.com*, INSEAD Case Study (2007).

3 Tesco was awarded a banking licence in 1997.

4 Butler, S., 'Now supermarkets want you to live over their shops', *Observer* (1st September 2013).

5 Economies of scope can arise in consumption as well as in production: Customers may prefer to buy different products from the same supplier. See T. Cottrell and B. R. Nault, 'Product variety and firm survival in microcomputer software', *Strategic Management Journal*, 25 (2004): 1005–26.

6 M. E. Porter, 'From competitive advantage to corporate strategy', *Harvard Business Review* (May–June 1987): 46.

7 M. Hayward and D. C. Hambrick, 'Explaining the premiums paid for large acquisitions', *Administrative Science Quarterly*, 42 (1997): 103–27.

8 A study of 68 diversifying ventures by established companies found that, on average, breakeven was not attained until the seventh or eighth years of operation: R. Biggadike, 'The risky business of diversification', *Harvard Business Review* (May–June, 1979): 103–11.

9 The role of capabilities in diversification is discussed in C. C. Markides and P. J. Williamson, 'Related diversification, core competencies and corporate performance', *Strategic Management Journal*, 15 (Special Issue, 1994): 149–65.

10 'Jeff Immelt and the reinventing of General Electric', in R. M. Grant, *Contemporary Strategy Analysis: Text and cases*, 8th edition (John Wiley & Sons Ltd, 2013).

11 J. P. Liebeskind, 'Internal capital markets: Benefits, costs and organizational arrangements', *Organization Science*, 11 (2000): 58–76.

12 D. Scharfstein and J. Stein, 'The dark side of internal capital markets: Divisional rent seeking and inefficient investment', *Journal of Finance*, 55 (2000): 2537–64; V. Maksimovic and G. Phillips, 'Do conglomerate firms allocate resources inefficiently across industries?' *Journal of Finance*, 57 (2002): 721–67; R. Rajan, H. Servaes and L. Zingales, 'The cost of diversity: The diversification discount and inefficient investment', *Journal of Finance*, 55 (2000): 35–84.

13 M. E. Porter, 'From competitive advantage to corporate strategy', *Harvard Business Review* (May–June 1987): 46.

14 S. Butler, 'Do Britain's biggest retailers have the know-how to cash in on our lack of trust of high street banks?' *Management Today* (1st July 2009).

15 In 2011, Tesco announced that it was spending an additional £200 million on upgrading its banking IT systems (A. Mari, 'Tesco increases spend on banking IT', *Computer Weekly* (19th April 2011)).

16 R. M. Grant, A. P. Jammine and H. Thomas, 'Diversity, diversification and performance in the British manufacturing industry', *Academy of Management Journal*, 31 (1988): 771–801.

17 L. E. Palich, L. B. Cardinal and C. C. Miller, 'Curvi-linearity in the diversification-performance linkage: An examination of over three decades of research', *Strategic Management Journal*, 22 (2000): 155–74.

18 N. Harper and S. P. Viguerie, 'Are you too focused?' *McKinsey Quarterly* (2002 Special Edition): 29–37.

19 J. D. Martin and A. Sayrak, 'Corporate diversification and shareholder value: A survey of recent literature', *Journal of Corporate Finance*, 9 (2003): 37–57.

20 C. C. Markides, 'Consequences of corporate refocusing: Ex ante evidence', *Academy of Management Journal*, 35 (1992): 398–412; C. C. Markides, 'Diversification, restructuring and economic performance', *Strategic Management Journal*, 16 (1995): 101–18.

21 R. P. Rumelt, *Strategy, Structure and Economic Performance* (Cambridge, MA: Harvard University Press, 1974).

22 See, for example, A. Michel and I. Shaked, 'Does business diversification affect performance?' *Financial Management*, 13 (1984): 18–24; G. A. Luffman and R. Reed, *The Strategy and Performance of British Industry: 1970–80* (London: Macmillan, 1984).

23 G. F. Davis, K. A. Diekman and C. F. Tinsley, 'The decline and fall of the conglomerate firm in the 1980s: A study in the de-institutionalization of an organizational form', *American Sociological Review*, 49 (1994): 547–70.

24 T. Khanna and K. Palepu, 'Why focused strategies may be wrong for emerging markets', *Harvard Business Review* (July–August, 1997): 41–51; D. Kim, D. Kandemir and S. T. Cavusgil, 'The role of family conglomerates in emerging markets', *Thunderbird International Business Review*, 46 (January, 2004): 7–20.

25 The situation is different in aluminium cans, where aluminium producers such as Alcoa and Pechiney and users such as Coca-Cola and Anheuser-Busch are major producers of beverage cans.

26 For a review of empirical evidence on transaction costs and vertical integration, see J. T. Macher and B. D. Richman. 'Transaction cost economics: An assessment of empirical research in the social sciences', *Business and Politics*, 10 (2008): Article 1; and M. D. Whinston, 'On the transaction cost determinants of vertical integration', *Journal of Law Economics and Organization*, 19 (2003): 1–23.

27 K. Monteverde and J. J. Teece, 'Supplier switching costs and vertical integration in the car industry', *Bell Journal of Economics*, 13 (Spring 1982): 206–13.

28 S. Masten, 'The organisation of production: Evidence from the aerospace industry', *Journal of Law and Economics*, 27 (October 1984): 403–17.

29 J. T. Macher, 'Technological development and the boundaries of the firm: A knowledge-based examination in semiconductor manufacturing', *Management Science*, 52 (2006): 826–43;

K. Monteverde, 'Technical dialogue as an incentive for vertical integration in the semiconductor industry', *Management Science*, 41 (1995): 1624–38.

30 J. H. Dyer, 'Effective interfirm collaboration: How firms minimise transaction costs and maximize transaction value', *Strategic Management Journal*, 18 (1997): 535–56; J. H. Dyer, 'Specialised supplier networks as a source of competitive advantage: Evidence from the car industry', *Strategic Management Journal*, 17 (1996): 271–92.

31 N. Owen and A. C. Jones, 'A comparative study of the British and Italian textile and clothing industries', (2003), http://cep.lse.ac.uk/seminarpapers/20-10-03-OWE.pdf, accessed 29th September 2014.

32 G. Lorenzoni and A. Lipparini, 'The leveraging of interfirm relationships as distinctive organisational capabilities: A longitudinal study', *Strategic Management Journal*, 20 (1999): 317–38.

33 G. Lorenzoni and A. Lipparini, 'Organising around strategic relationships: Networks of suppliers in the Italian motorcycle industry', in K. O. Cool *et al.* (eds), *Restructuring Strategy* (Oxford: Blackwell, 2005): 44–67.

34 J. H. Dyer and K. Nobeoka, 'Creating and managing a high-performance knowledge-sharing network: The Toyota case', *Strategic Management Journal*, 21 (2000): 345–68.

35 www.covisint.com; www.elemica.com; www.rockanddirt.com.

36 'The virtual corporation', *Business Week* (8th February 1993): 98–104; W. H. Davidow and M. S. Malone, *The Virtual Corporation* (New York: HarperCollins, 1992).

37 H. W. Chesborough and D. J. Teece, 'When is virtual virtuous? Organising for innovation', *Harvard Business Review* (May–June 1996): 68–79.

38 C. K. Prahalad and G. Hamel, 'The core competences of the corporation', *Harvard Business Review* (May–June 1990): 79–91.

39 S. Brusoni, A. Prencipe and K. Pavitt, 'Knowledge specialization, organizational coupling and the boundaries of the firm: Why do firms know more than they make?' *Administrative Science Quarterly*, 46 (2001): 597–621.

40 'Boeing's Dreamliner delays are a nightmare', http://seekingalpha.com/article/110735-boeings-dreamliner-delays-are-a-nightmare, accessed 29th September 2014.

41 For a fuller discussion of the GE/McKinsey matrix see: 'Enduring Ideas: The GE-McKinsey nine-box matrix', *McKinsey Quarterly* (September 2008).

42 For a fuller discussion of the BCG matrix see: B. Henderson, 'The experience curve reviewed: IV: The growth share matrix or product portfolio', (1973), https://www.bcgperspectives.com/content/Classics/corporate_finance_corporate_strategy_portfolio_management_experience_curve_reviewed_growth_share_matrix_product_portfolio/, accessed 29th September 2014.

43 Booz Allen Hamilton claims that 'dog' businesses can offer promising potential (H. Quarls, T. Pernsteiner and K. Rangan, 'Love your dogs', *strategy+business* (15th March 2005)).

44 A. Campbell, M. Goold, M. Alexander and J. Whitehead, *Strategy for the Corporate Level: Where to invest, what to cut back and how to grow organisations with multiple divisions* (San Francisco: Jossey-Bass, 2014).

45 The 'economies of internalization' is merely a shorthand way of referring to the cost savings that result from undertaking activities and associated transactions within the firm rather than externally with third parties.

46 The Walt Disney Company Annual Report 2014.

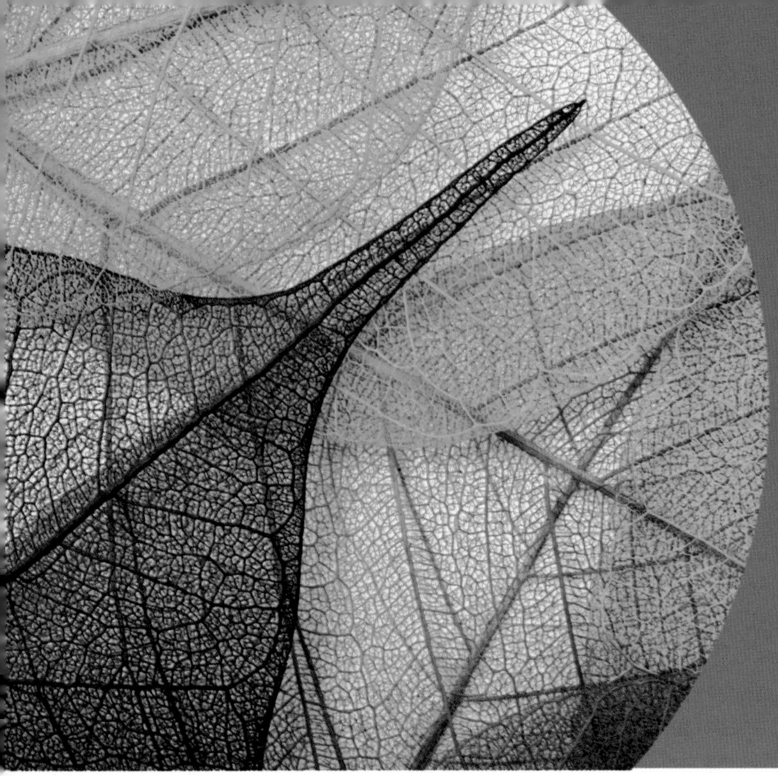

8

Global strategies and the multinational corporation

Introduction and objectives

There have been two primary forces driving change in business environment during the past half century. One is technology; the other is internationalization. Internationalization is a source of huge opportunity. In 1981, Infosys, with just six employees, was established in Pune, India. By supplying IT services to corporations throughout the world, Infosys had 160 405 employees in April 2014. It was the world's 10th-biggest IT services company (in terms of revenues) a few places behind its close neighbour, Tata Consultancy Services.

Internationalization is also a potent destroyer. For centuries, Sheffield, England was the world's leading centre of cutlery manufacture. By 2014, only a few hundred people were employed making cutlery in Sheffield. The industry had been devastated by cheap imports first from South Korea and then from China. Nor is it just the industries in the mature industrial nations that have been ravaged by imports. Bulk imports of second-hand clothing from Europe and North America (much of it from charities and churches) have been ruinous for Kenya's textile and apparel sector.

Internationalization occurs through two mechanisms: trade and direct investment. The growth of world trade has consistently outstripped the growth of world output, increasing export/sales and import penetration ratios for all countries and all industries. For the OECD countries, total trade (imports and exports) rose from 11% of GDP in 1960 to 52% in 2011. Flows of foreign direct investment have risen even faster, reaching $1.5 trillion in 2013.[1]

The forces driving both trade and direct investment are, first, the quest to exploit market opportunities in other countries and, second, the desire to exploit resources and capabilities located in other countries. The resulting 'globalization of business' has created vast flows of international transactions comprising payments for trade and services, flows of factor payments (interest, profits and licensing fees) and flows of capital.

What does the internationalization of the world economy mean for our strategy analysis? As we have already noted, internationalization is both a threat and an opportunity. However, in terms of analysis, the primary implication of introducing the international dimension is that it adds considerable complexity to our strategy analysis, not just in broadening the scope of markets (and competition) but also in complicating the analysis of competitive advantage.

By the time you have completed this chapter, you will:

- be aware of the impact of internationalization on industry structure and competition;
- be able to analyse the implications of a firm's national environment for its competitive advantage;

- be able to formulate strategies for exploiting overseas business opportunities, including overseas market entry strategies and overseas production strategies;
- appreciate how international strategies can be shaped to achieve an optimal balance between global integration and national differentiation;
- be able to design organizational structures and management systems appropriate to the pursuit of international strategies.

Opening Case
IKEA's international strategy

© IKEA

IKEA is one of the largest furniture makers and retailers in the world and is well known for its low-cost, stylish furniture and bold, sometimes controversial, advertising campaigns. Established by Swedish entrepreneur Ingvar Kamprad in 1943, by 2013 the company had an estimated turnover of €27.9 billion, net profits of €3.3 billion and around 300 stores in 26 countries.[2] While IKEA has undoubtedly succeeded in foreign markets, establishing stores in countries as far apart as Australia and Romania, around 70% of its sales still come from Europe and its overseas expansion has not always progressed as smoothly as it would have liked. Adapting the company's culture to national norms has proved challenging and there have been mistakes along the way.

A brief company history

Brought up in a small farming community in southern Sweden, Kamprad was an enterprising individual who even as a boy sold small items like matches and Christmas cards to his neighbours. He came up with the name IKEA by combining his initials (IK) with the first letters of the name of the farm and village in which he grew up (Elmtaryd, Agunnaryd). At first, IKEA was a vehicle for Kamprad's trading and mail-order activities. He added furniture to his product lines in 1947, mainly by accident, but quickly recognized that there was a growing demand in post-war Sweden for inexpensive household goods. Owing to problems with Swedish manufacturers, the company started to procure furniture from Poland and found this to be a cost-effective strategy. By 1951, Kamprad had decided to focus exclusively on furniture and the first IKEA showroom was opened in Sweden in 1953 to allow mail-order customers to establish the quality of the items they were ordering by seeing and touching them. In 1955, the company started designing its own products and a few years later opened retail stores.

The company offered well-designed, stylish items that drew on Swedish design traditions at inexpensive prices. Costs were kept down by designing furniture with a target price in mind. Furniture was flat-packed to minimize transportation costs, assembled by the customer to keep operating costs low and production was sourced from low-cost locations. IKEA became known for its cost-minimizing approach and its associated capabilities in cost-efficient design, sourcing and logistics. Kamprad, reflecting his upbringing in a Southern Swedish farming community, placed a high value on thriftiness and morality and shaped IKEA's culture accordingly. The company's stated mission was to 'offer a wide range of well-designed, functional home furnishing products at prices so low that as many people as possible will be able to afford them'[3] and co-workers were recruited as much on the basis of their values and beliefs as on their experience and skills. In 1976, Kamprad published his

Testament of a Furniture Dealer, which contained slogans like 'expensive solutions to any kind of problem are usually the work of mediocrity'; in many respects this document represented the credo of the company.

The pattern of IKEA's internationalization

The company's forays into international markets began first by opening stores in other Scandinavian countries but the company quickly moved farther afield. In the early years, the formula for international expansion was a simple one. The company identified markets with the potential for high sales volumes and then purchased cheap land on the outskirts of a big city to establish a base. A tight-knit team of trusted and experienced Swedish managers (sometimes referred to as 'IKEA missionaries') relocated to the country in question and supervised the building of the new store, led the operational team and ran the business until it was deemed mature and could be handed over to local managers. Once a beachhead was established, IKEA tended to cluster further stores in the same geographical area. By 2014, IKEA operated 290 stores in 26 countries.

In its first phase of internationalization, IKEA entered new markets by keeping its product catalogue and its management processes the same. There were sometimes minor adjustments to items to reflect national differences, for example standard bed sizes tended to differ between countries, but the overwhelming majority of the products sold by IKEA were common across countries. The Swedish roots of the company were celebrated as a source of distinctiveness not only in the design of the firm's products but also in its management style. Managers across the organization were strongly encouraged to adopt a Swedish, open and non-hierarchical management style because Kamprad felt that this mode motivated employees and had universal appeal. A pragmatic problem-solving style and egalitarian approach to decision making became the cornerstone of IKEA's unique culture and was referred to by the founder and his team as the 'IKEA way'.[4]

The challenges of internationalization

As the company moved further from its Scandinavian base and became more dependent on overseas operations so the pressure for the company to be more nationally responsive grew. One of IKEA's first challenges came when it entered the US market. The company expected its standard range to sell as well as it did in Europe but instead faced some unexpected problems. IKEA executives were, for example, initially perplexed by the number of vases they were selling until they realized that Americans were buying vases to drink from rather than put flowers in because European style glasses were too small for American tastes. Conversely, IKEA's first forays into Japan were unsuccessful, partly because its furniture products were viewed as too large to fit into small, Japanese living spaces.

While recognizing the need to adapt some of its products to local demands, IKEA's low-cost business model depended on the high volume sales that came from standardization. The IKEA headquarters team recognized the need for some country-specific adaptations and made it possible for area managers to put forward suggestions, but to achieve economies of scale, the extent of adaptation was limited to 5–10% of the product range.

As well as adapting the company's product lines, there was also pressure to adapt the management style. The democratic approach to management characteristic of Swedish organizations was not perceived universally to be as favourable as the top team expected. Grol and Schoch, for example, point out that in Germany Swedish management was considered peculiar.[5] Older workers felt uncomfortable calling managers by their first names and employees, in general, disliked the lack of formality. Similarly, in France, rather than seeing IKEA's flat organization structure as enabling, many employees saw it as stripping them of status and removing opportunities for promotion. The fact that the key decision-making and training centres were located in Sweden (and required managers to be fluent in Swedish) made it very difficult for non-Scandinavians to progress to the higher echelons of management.

IKEA faced a different set of challenges in Asia, particularly when it entered the Chinese market.[6] The company had always positioned itself as a low-cost provider, but in China it was seen as an expensive brand by its target market of young professionals. Import duties and exchange rate fluctuations made it difficult for IKEA to compete with domestic furniture producers on cost and IKEA's designs were quickly copied and prices undercut by local producers. China had huge market potential for IKEA because its population was growing more affluent and home ownership was increasing rapidly, but it was very difficult to maintain a low-cost market position in this environment. Faced with this dilemma, IKEA chose to maintain its competitive positioning and cut its prices significantly, with some of its products selling at prices 70% lower in China than in other countries. The decision to sacrifice short-term profits in order to gain a foothold in the market and achieve long-term growth seemed to pay off: 12 years after its initial entry, IKEA's Chinese retail stores began to show a profit.

The move into Asia also highlighted for IKEA the fact that one size did not fit all in other aspects of its strategy. In Europe and the US, most customers used private transport to get to IKEA stores, but in China the majority of customers used public transport. As a result, IKEA had to alter its location strategy, situating its retail stores near rail and metro hubs on the outskirts of cities rather than opting for more out-of-town sites. Similarly, the company had to adapt its environmental strategy. Like many other European retailers, IKEA sought to improve its green credentials by charging for plastic bags and requiring its suppliers to provide environmentally friendly products. The majority of Chinese suppliers were unable to provide products that met IKEA environmental standards and, rather than welcoming IKEA's environment-friendly approach, price-sensitive Chinese customers were irritated by charges for plastic bags. Consumers were unfamiliar with the concept of flat-pack furniture, lacked the means of transporting furniture to their homes and did not own the tools necessary for assembling flat packs. IKEA, inadvertently, created a new industry comprised of enterprising individuals who set up in business delivering and making up IKEA furniture but, unfortunately for IKEA, they also created the impression that there were hidden charges associated with the purchase of IKEA products.

Internationalization has presented IKEA with challenges but it has also opened up opportunities for innovation and learning. While much of the information flow within IKEA is from the headquarters to the stores, knowledge also flows in the reverse direction. The centre issues retail stores with detailed instructions about operating practices that need to be copied exactly, including how stores should be laid out, how the IKEA catalogue should be presented, what the product range should contain and what colours bags and staff uniforms should be, but operatives are also encouraged to explore new work methods and new product ideas. For example, the layout of each IKEA store needs to include the presentation of five living rooms for customers to view but the specific content and design of those rooms can be tailored to local tastes. New ideas emanating from employees are passed first to the service office in the relevant store, then to the service office in the relevant market and finally to the global service office. At each stage, new ideas can be rejected or passed on but, in all cases, the rationale for acceptance or rejection is articulated via the company's intranet. A formal system of store audits monitors individual stores' adherence to the IKEA concept but also identifies good practices and new ideas that are shared across the organization. Expatriates play an important role as mentors and, when IKEA enters a new country, co-workers are sent to other countries to learn about IKEA.

IKEA, like most other multinationals, struggles to balance global and local pressures but, over time, has found ways of replicating its core business model and operating practices in flexible ways.

The implications of international competition for industry analysis

Patterns of internationalization

Internationalization occurs through *trade* – the sale and shipment of goods and services from one country to another – and *direct investment* – building or acquiring productive assets in another country. On this basis we can identify different types of industry according to the extent and mode of their internationalization (Figure 8.1):

- Sheltered industries are served exclusively by indigenous firms. They are sheltered from both imports and inward direct investment by regulation, trade barriers or because of the localized nature of the goods and services they offer. The forces of internationalization have made this category progressively smaller over time, as the Featured Example 8.1 on Toni & Guy illustrates. Sheltered industries are primarily fragmented service industries (dry cleaning, car repair, funeral services), some small-scale manufacturing (handicrafts, residential construction) and industries producing products that are non-tradable because they are perishable (fresh milk, bread) or difficult to move (four-poster beds, garden sheds).
- Trading industries are those where internationalization occurs primarily through imports and exports. If a product is transportable, not nationally differentiated and subject to substantial scale economies, exporting from a single location is the most efficient means to exploit overseas markets. This would apply, for example, to commercial aircraft, shipbuilding and defence equipment. Trading industries also include products whose inputs are available only in a few locations: diamonds from South Africa or caviar from Iran and Azerbaijan.
- Multidomestic industries are those that internationalize through direct investment, either because trade is unfeasible (as in the case of service industries such as retail banking, consulting or hotels) or because products are nationally differentiated (e.g. frozen meals, recorded music).
- Global industries are those in which both trade and direct investment are important. Most large-scale manufacturing industries tend to evolve towards global structures: in cars, consumer electronics, semiconductors, pharmaceuticals and beer, levels of trade and direct investment are high.

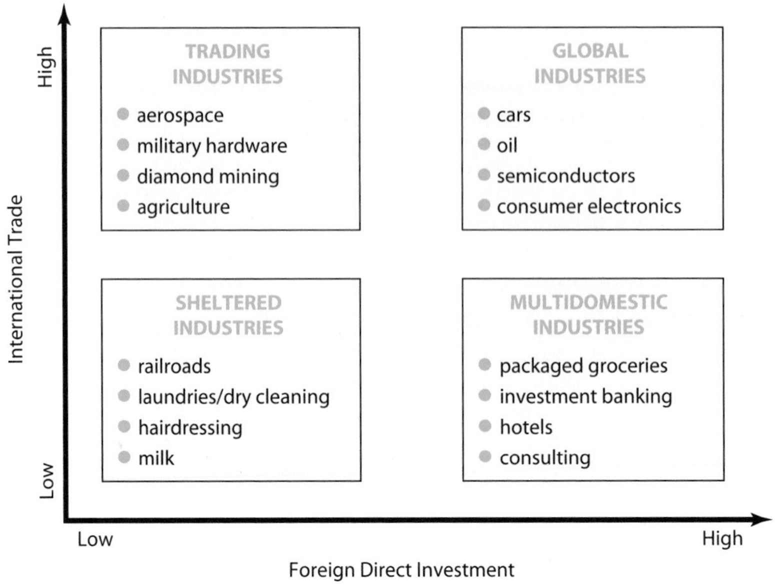

Figure 8.1 Patterns of industry internationalization.

By which route does internationalization typically occur? In the case of manufacturing companies, internationalization typically begins with exports – mostly to countries with the least 'psychic distance' from the home country. Later, a sales and distribution subsidiary is established in the overseas country. Eventually, the company develops a more integrated overseas subsidiary that undertakes manufacturing and product development as well.[7] In service industries, internationalization may involve replication (McKinsey & Company), acquisition (HSBC) or franchising (McDonald's).[8] However, with the advent of the Internet, some companies have gone global from their inception.[9]

Featured Example 8.1

Are sheltered industries shrinking?

Hairdressing has always been a good example of a sheltered industry. The relative ease with which newcomers can start up a hairdressing business together with the personal nature of the service has resulted in an industry made up of a large number of localized small firms, each catering for the needs of a slightly different clientele but essentially offering a very similar service. In recent years, however, even industries like hairdressing have begun to feel the force of internationalization. Toni & Guy is a British hairdressing chain set up by two Italian brothers, Giuseppe (Toni) and Gaetano (Guy) Mascolo, who immigrated to the UK with their parents in the early 1960s. From a humble start, the brothers have managed to build a business with an annual turnover of £175 million and over 500 salons in 42 countries.[10]

The brothers have achieved this success by creating a standardized service and a brand that they have franchised across the globe. While everyone's hair is different and there have always been recognizable national and local differences in hairstyles and treatments, the advent of mass media and the Internet has resulted in the rapid transmission of fashion trends between countries. This has resulted in a degree of convergence in consumer preferences, particularly of young adults, around appearance. This convergence has created the opportunity for Toni & Guy to create an international brand.

To achieve consistency in hairdressing services, all Toni & Guy hairdressers are trained at one of the company's 24 academies around the world. The salons are designed to a common template and use the range of haircare products developed by the firm. The growth of the firm has provided the resources necessary to undertake advertising campaigns, to develop online booking systems and style galleries for clients and to extend its product range. The success of the firm has spawned a number of imitators, and, though it is unlikely that international chains will replace local independent businesses in the near future, the nature of competition in the industry is changing. An industry that was once sheltered is beginning to see the growth of international competition.

Implications for competition

Internationalization usually means more competition and lower industry profitability. In 1976, the US automobile market was dominated by GM, Ford and Chrysler, with 84% of the market. By 2011, there were 14 companies with auto plants within the US; GM and Ford were the remaining indigenous producers accounting for just 35.7% of auto sales.

We can use Porter's five forces of competition framework to analyse the impact of internationalization on competition and industry profitability. If we define the industry in terms of the national market, internationalization directly influences three of the five forces of competition:

- *Competition from potential entrants:* Internationalization is a cause and a consequence of falling barriers to entry into most national markets. Tariff reductions, falling real costs of transportation, foreign-exchange convertibility, the removal of exchange controls, internationalization of standards and convergence of customer preferences have made it much easier for producers in one country to supply customers in another. Entry barriers that are effective against domestic entrants may be ineffective against potential entrants that are established producers overseas.

- *Rivalry among existing firms:* Internationalization increases internal rivalry primarily because it increases the number of firms competing within each national market – it *lowers seller concentration*. The European market for motor scooters was once dominated by Piaggio (Vespa) and Innocenti (Lambretta). There are now over 25 suppliers of scooters to the European market, including BMW from Germany; Honda, Yamaha and Suzuki from Japan; KYMCO from Taiwan; BenZhou/Yiying, Baotian and

Xingyue from China; Bajaj from India; and Baron and Vectrix from the US. Although internationalization has involved a massive wave of mergers and acquisitions, Ghemawat and Ghadar show that global concentration has declined as a result of national producers entering the global market.[11] In addition, internationalization stimulates competition by increasing investments in capacity and increasing the diversity of competitors.

- *Increasing the bargaining power of buyers:* The option of sourcing from overseas greatly enhances the power of industrial buyers. It also allows distributors to engage in international arbitrage: pharmaceutical distributors have become adept at searching the world for low-price pharmaceuticals then importing them for the domestic market.

Analysing competitive advantage in an international context

The growth of international competition over the past 20 years has been associated with some stunning reversals in the competitive positions of different companies. In 1989, US Steel was the world's biggest steel company; in 2014, ArcelorMittal based in Luxemburg and India was the new global giant. In 1990, Motorola, Ericsson and Siemens were the world leaders in wireless handsets. By 2014, Samsung and Apple had taken their places.

To understand how internationalization has shifted the basis of competition, we need to extend our framework for analysing competitive advantage to include the influence of firms' national environments. Competitive advantage, we have noted, is achieved when a firm matches its internal strengths in resources and capabilities to the key success factors of the industry. In international industries, competitive advantage depends not just on a firm's internal resources and capabilities but also its national environment, and in particular the availability of resources within the countries where it does business. Figure 8.2 summarizes the implications of internationalization for our basic strategy model in terms of the impact both on industry conditions and on firms' access to resources and capabilities.

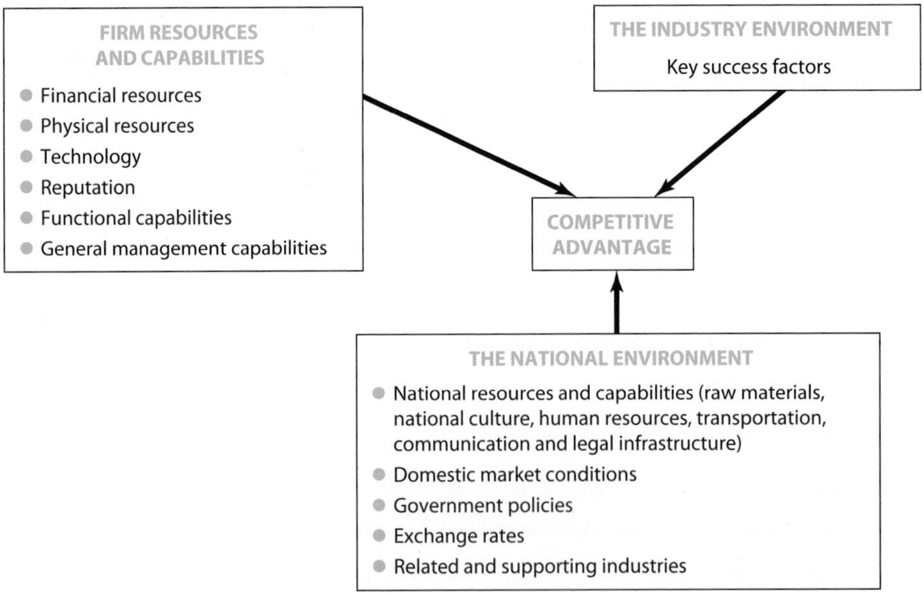

Figure 8.2 Competitive advantage in an international context.

National influences on competitiveness: Comparative advantage

The role of national resource availability on international competitiveness is the subject of the theory of **comparative advantage**. The theory of comparative advantage states that a country has a comparative advantage in those products that make intensive use of those resources available in abundance within that country. Thus, Bangladesh has an abundant supply of unskilled labour. The US has an abundant supply of technological resources: trained scientists and engineers, research facilities and universities. Bangladesh has a comparative advantage in products that make intensive use of unskilled labour, such as clothing, handicrafts, leather goods and the assembly of consumer electronic products. The US has a comparative advantage in technology-intensive products, such as microprocessors, computer software, pharmaceuticals, medical diagnostic equipment and management consulting services.

The term 'comparative advantage' refers to the *relative* efficiencies of producing different products. So long as exchange rates are well behaved, comparative advantage translates into competitive advantage. Trade theory initially emphasized the role of natural resource endowments, labour supply and capital stock in determining comparative advantage. More recently, emphasis has shifted to the central role of knowledge (including technology, human skills and management capability) and the resources needed to commercialize knowledge (capital markets, communications facilities and a legal system).[12] For industries where scale economies are important, a large home market is an additional source of comparative advantage (e.g. the US in aerospace).[13]

A country has a comparative advantage in those products that make intensive use of those resources available in abundance within that country.

Research and development (R & D) activities have tended historically to be undertaken in a firm's home country so we would typically expect the research centre of a Dutch company like Philips to be located in the Netherlands and the research centre for Apple to be located in the US. However, reductions in communication and travel costs together with the growing economic importance of new industrialized and emerging economies have caused companies to rethink their location strategies. Tellis *et al.* investigated where the world's top companies located their R & D centres.[14] They took the country where a firm's headquarters was located to be its home country. They found significant and widespread globalization of innovation with firms headquartered in developed economies having 50% or more of their R & D centres located offshore.

Porter's national diamond

Michael Porter has extended our understanding of comparative advantage by examining the dynamics through which particular industries within a country develop the resources and capabilities that confer international competitive advantage. Porter's national diamond framework identifies four key factors which determine a country's competitive advantage within a particular sector (Figure 8.3):[15]

FACTOR CONDITIONS Whereas the conventional analysis of comparative advantage focuses on endowments of broad categories of resource, Porter emphasizes the role of highly specialized resources, many of which are home-grown rather than endowed. For example, in analysing

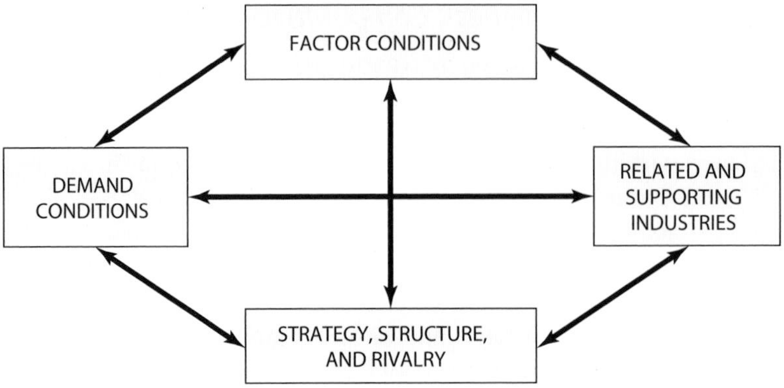

Figure 8.3 Porter's national diamond framework.

Source: Adapted with the permission of Simon & Schuster Publishing Group from the Free Press edition of *The Competitive Advantage of Nations* by Michael E. Porter. Copyright © 1990, 1998 by Michael E. Porter. All rights reserved.

Hollywood's superiority in film production, Porter points to the local concentration of highly skilled labour, including the roles of UCLA and USC film schools. He also suggests that resource constraints may encourage the development of substitute capabilities: in post-war Japan, raw material shortages spurred miniaturization and low-defect manufacturing; in Italy, restrictive labour laws have stimulated automation.

RELATED AND SUPPORTING INDUSTRIES One of Porter's most striking empirical findings is that national competitive strengths tend to be associated **clusters** of industries. Silicon Valley's cluster comprises semiconductor, computer, software and venture capital firms. For each industry, closely related industries are sources of critical resources and capabilities. Denmark's global leadership in wind power is based upon a cluster comprising wind turbine manufacturers, offshore wind farm developers and operators and utilities.

DEMAND CONDITIONS Demand conditions in the domestic market provide the primary driver of innovation and quality improvement. For example, Switzerland's pre-eminence in watches is supported by the obsessive punctuality of the Swiss. Japan's dominant share of the world market for cameras by companies owes much to Japanese enthusiasm for amateur photography and their eager adoption of innovation in cameras. German dominance of the high-performance segment of the world car industry through Daimler, BMW, Porsche and VW-Audi reflects German motorists' love of quality engineering and their irrepressible urge to drive on autobahns at terrifying speeds.

STRATEGY, STRUCTURE AND RIVALRY National competitive performance in particular sectors is inevitably related to the strategies and structures of firms in those industries. Porter puts particular emphasis on the role of intense domestic competition in driving innovation, efficiency and the upgrading of competitive advantage. The international success of the Japanese in cars, cameras, consumer electronics and office equipment is based upon domestic industries that feature at least six major producers that are strongly competitive with one another.

Consistency between strategy and national conditions

Establishing competitive advantage in global industries requires congruence between business strategy and the pattern of the country's comparative advantage. In wireless handsets, it is sensible for Chinese producers, such as ZTE and Huawei, to use their cost advantages to concentrate on the mass market and supply under distributors' brands; for Apple, Samsung, Sony and RIM the emphasis needs to be on differentiation through technology and design.

Achieving congruence between firm strategy and national conditions also extends to the embodiment of national culture within strategy and management systems. The success of US companies in many areas of high technology, including computer software and biotechnology, owes much to a business system of entrepreneurial capitalism which exploits a national culture that emphasizes individuality, opportunity and wealth acquisition. The global success of Korean corporate giants such as Samsung and LG reflects organizational structures and management systems that embody Korean cultural characteristics such as loyalty, respect for authority, conformity to group norms, commitment to organizational goals and having a strong work ethic – what has come to be referred to as 'dynamic collectivism'.[16]

The limitations of the diamond model

Since it was published in 1990, Porter's diamond framework has had a significant influence on business practitioners and government policy-makers but it has also been the source of much debate.[17] Criticism of the model has mainly come from two different perspectives. The first perspective (associated with the work of academics such as Rugman and Dunning) sees the diamond model as omitting key factors.[18] In particular, it is argued that the model fails to consider the attributes of the home country's largest trading partners, isn't applicable to most of the world's smallest nations and ignores the role of multinational corporations in influencing the competitive success of nations. These critics suggest that the diamond framework needs to be expanded and amended, for example Rugman and D'Cruz propose a 'double diamond' framework, which incorporates both a national and a global diamond.[19] The argument they put forward is that small countries like Korea and Singapore don't target markets and resources in a domestic context but in a global context too.[20]

Singapore, for example, has been the recipient of inbound foreign direct investment by foreign multinationals attracted by the country's well-educated workforce and efficient infrastructure of roads, airports and telecommunications. Singaporean firms have also invested directly in other countries that have provided access to cheap labour and natural resources. In other words, the competitive advantage of many Singaporean firms depends not only on their domestic diamond (the factor and demand conditions, related and supporting industries, etc. in Singapore) but also on the international diamond relevant to its firms (the factor and demand conditions, related and supporting industries, etc. in countries in which its firms operate).

The second perspective (associated with the work of academics such as Waverman[21] and Davies and Ellis[22]) suggests that the diamond model is so general that it lacks value. These critics argue that by trying to explain all aspects of trade and competition the model ends up explaining nothing because it is insufficiently precise to generate testable predictions.

Case Insight 8.1

Does IKEA gain a competitive advantage from being Swedish?

Porter's diamond model explains why some nations have an international competitive advantage with respect to particular industries. We can use this model to explore whether the national home base of IKEA has provided it with some advantages that it has been able to exploit on a global scale.

Factor conditions – Sweden has always had a plentiful supply of timber. It is Europe's second-biggest afforested area after Russia and today the forestry business accounts for around 12% of the country's exports.[23] Until the 1900s, Sweden was predominantly an agriculture society and its proximity to the Arctic Circle meant its farming communities faced long, harsh winters. Farmers had to be independent and self-sufficient and during the winter months, when little could be done on the land, they would make furniture and utensils, using the timber that was readily available. As skills and craftsmanship improved, supplying furniture to nearby towns became a way of supplementing income and Sweden developed a strong base of skilled furniture makers. In addition, Sweden has a long tradition of design appreciation. Swedish designs are known for their simplicity, clean lines and light minimalist look. The country boasts many design schools and university courses in furniture design.

Related and supporting industries – the favourable conditions for furniture making have produced a number of furniture clusters in Sweden. For example, the Tibro cluster in Västra Götaland comprises more than 70 furniture companies and includes producers of kitchen and office furniture, design and handicraft firms and centres for wood technology. The geographical proximity of companies facilitates the exchange of information and means that innovative ideas are quickly disseminated. Firms pool resources like marketing and logistics, and work in partnership with the regional government. In its early years, IKEA benefited from the presence of these regional clusters and even today seeks to produce its own clusters in the markets it enters.

Demand conditions – firms are generally sensitive to their closest customers and the design preferences of Swedish consumers have been particularly important in shaping the type of furniture produced. Swedish customers are sensitive to environmental considerations and are concerned with sustainability. Waste wood and cellulose matter from furniture production is incinerated to produce energy and strict codes of conduct are in place to make sure that forests are managed in a responsible manner. The environmental concerns of IKEA's Swedish customers are reflected in the company's commitment to environmental stewardship. IKEA argues that its goes for low cost but not at a cost to the environment and this is a message that is increasingly appreciated by consumers around the world. It has also been suggested that the values of IKEA's founder, who was brought up in Småland, a poor rural community in southern Sweden, have shaped the firm's ethos. Smålanders are known for working hard and making the best possible use of limited resources; they demand value for money. This frugality is seen by many as the basis of the 'IKEA way'.

Local firm strategy, structure and rivalry – historically, furniture manufacturing was highly localized because furniture is bulky and costly to transport over long distances and in Sweden there was significant competition between small local producers. IKEA's development of flat-pack, non-assembled furniture together with reductions in transportation costs moved competition beyond regional and national boundaries. It is estimated that the Swedish furniture industry comprises around 800 firms, most of whom make intensive use of technology to produce their finished products. They face significant rivalry from other Scandinavian producers located in Denmark, Finland and Norway, but increasingly Swedish manufacturers, including IKEA, face competition from low-cost manufacturers in China and other parts of Asia. This rivalry has been a stimulus to IKEA to redouble its efforts to reduce costs. For example, even something as small as one of IKEA's mugs has been redesigned several times to fit more into pallets and reduce transportation costs.

The international location of production

To examine how national resource conditions influence international strategies, we look at two types of strategic decision in international business: first, where to locate production activities and, second, how to enter a foreign market. Let us begin with the first of these.

Firms move beyond their national borders not only to seek foreign markets but also to access the resources and capabilities available in other countries. Traditionally, multinationals established plants to serve local markets. Increasingly, decisions concerning where to produce are being separated from decisions over where to sell. For example, STMicroelectronics, the world leader in application-specific integrated circuits (ASICs) is headquartered in Switzerland; production is mainly in France, Italy and Singapore; R & D is conducted mainly in France, Italy and the US; and its biggest markets are Singapore, the Netherlands, the US and Japan.

Choosing where to locate production

The decision of where to locate production requires consideration of four sets of factors:

- *National resource availability:* Where key resources differ between countries in their availability or cost, firms should manufacture in countries where resource supplies are favourable. For the oil industry, this means exploring in Kazakhstan, offshore Angola and the Gulf of Mexico. In most areas of manufacturing, offshoring by companies in the older industrial nations has been driven primarily by the quest to lower wage costs. Table 8.1 shows differences in employment costs between countries. However, for many industries, gaining access to specialized know-how is a critical consideration.
- *Firm-specific competitive advantages:* For firms whose competitive advantage is based on internal resources and capabilities, optimal location depends on where those resources and capabilities are situated and how mobile they are. Walmart has experienced difficulty recreating its capabilities outside of the US. Conversely, Toyota and Goldman Sachs have successfully transferred their operational capabilities to their overseas subsidiaries.
- *Tradability:* The more difficult it is to transport a product and the more it is subject to trade barriers (such as tariffs and quotas) or government restrictions (such as import

Table 8.1 Hourly compensation costs for production workers in manufacturing (US$).

	1975	2000	2012
Switzerland	6.09	21.24	57.79
Germany	6.31	24.42	45.79
Australia	5.62	14.47	47.68
France	4.52	15.70	39.81
US	6.36	19.76	35.67
Italy	4.67	14.01	34.18
Japan	3.00	22.27	35.34
UK	3.37	16.45	31.23
Spain	2.53	10.78	26.83
Korea	0.32	8.19	20.72
Taiwan	0.40	5.85	9.46
Mexico	1.47	2.08	6.36
Philippines	0.62	1.30	2.10

Source: US Department of Labor, Bureau of Labor Statistics.

licences), the more production will need to take place within the local market. Services – hairdressing, restaurant meals and banking – typically need to be produced in close proximity to where they are consumed.

- *Political considerations:* Government incentives, penalties and restrictions affect location decisions.

Location and the value chain

The production of most goods and services comprises a vertical chain of activities where the input requirements of each stage vary considerably. Hence, different countries offer advantages at different stages of the value chain. In the consumer electronics industry: component production is research- and capital-intensive and is concentrated in the US, Japan, Korea and Taiwan; assembly is labour-intensive and is concentrated in China, Thailand and Latin America.

A key feature of recent internationalization has been the international division of value chains as firms seek to locate to countries whose resource availability and cost best match each stage of the value chain.[24] The globally dispersed value chain of the Apple iPhone 4 is illustrated in Table 8.2.

However, cost is just one factor in offshoring decisions: because cost advantages are vulnerable to exchange rate changes, it is important to consider underlying issues concerning the availability and quality of resources and capabilities. For most Western and Japanese companies, it is the potential for overall operational efficiency rather than local wage rates that is the key criterion influencing choice of location. The modern laptop is the epitome of a globally dispersed value chain where every component and every process is located according to the best combination of cost and technical know-how. Figure 8.4 summarizes the relevant criteria in location decisions.

Table 8.2 Where does the iPhone come from? The location of iPhone suppliers.

Item	Supplier	Location
Design and operating system	Apple	US
Flash memory	Samsung Electronics	S. Korea
DRAM memory	Samsung Electronics Micron Technology	S. Korea US
Application processor	Murata	Japan/Taiwan
Baseband	Infineon Skyworks TriQuint	Taiwan US
Power management	Dialog Semiconductor	Taiwan
Audio	Texas Instruments	US
Touchscreen control	Cirrus Logic	US
Accel and gyroscope	STMicroelectronics	Italy
E-compass	AKM Semiconductor	Japan
Assembly	Foxconn	China

Source: 'Slicing an Apple', *Economist* (10th August 2011), http://www.economist.com/node/21525685, accessed 29th September 2014.

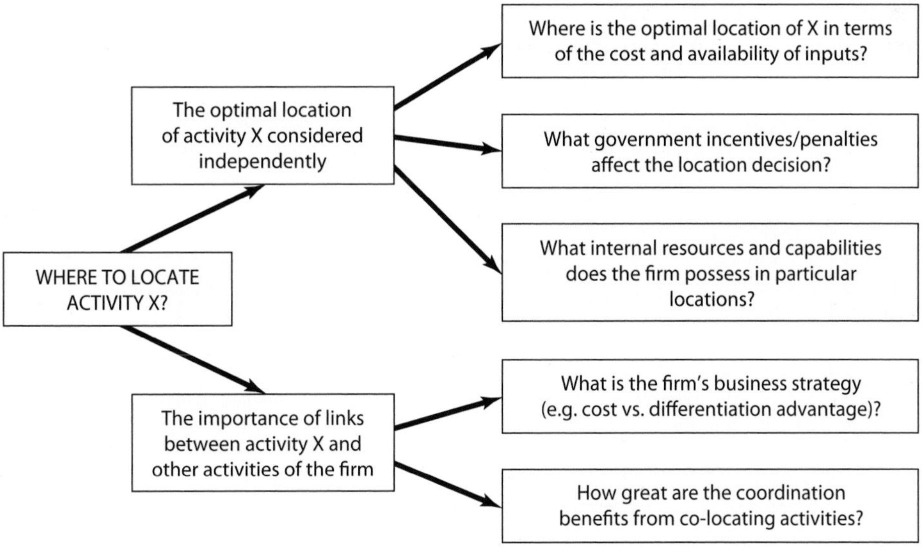

Figure 8.4 Determining the optimal location of value chain activities.

Case Insight 8.2

The globalization of IKEA's supply chain

IKEA's founder, Ingvar Kamprad, recognized the benefit of an internationally distributed supply chain very early on when he changed from Swedish to Polish sources of supply in order to cut costs. As the company grew and entered new markets, its value chain became more distributed. While product design remained in Sweden, the company moved its headquarters to the Netherlands in 2001 and located its European logistics centre in Germany. IKEA has its own manufacturing subsidiary, IKEA Industry, which manufactures and distributes wooden furniture and controls the entire value chain by managing and operating long-term forest contracts, sawmills, board factories as well as producing and distributing self-assembly furniture. IKEA Industry itself has internationalized and now owns and operates facilities in a number of countries, including the US and Russia. In addition, IKEA has a network of about 2000 other suppliers around the globe. Suppliers are chosen primarily for their ability to provide specific products at low cost and IKEA closely monitors their adherence to its product and process specifications.

How should firms enter foreign markets?

Firms enter foreign markets in pursuit of profitability. The profitability of entering a foreign market depends upon the attractiveness of that market and whether the firm can establish a competitive advantage within it. While market attractiveness can be a magnet for foreign multinationals – the size and growth of the Chinese economy has been irresistible to many Western companies – over the longer term, the key determinant of profitability is likely to be the ability to establish competitive advantage vis-à-vis local firms and other multinationals.

A firm's potential for establishing competitive advantage has important implications for the means by which it enters a foreign market. The basic distinction is between market entry by means of *transactions* and market entry by means of *direct investment*. Figure 8.5 shows a spectrum of market entry options arranged according to the degree of resource commitment by

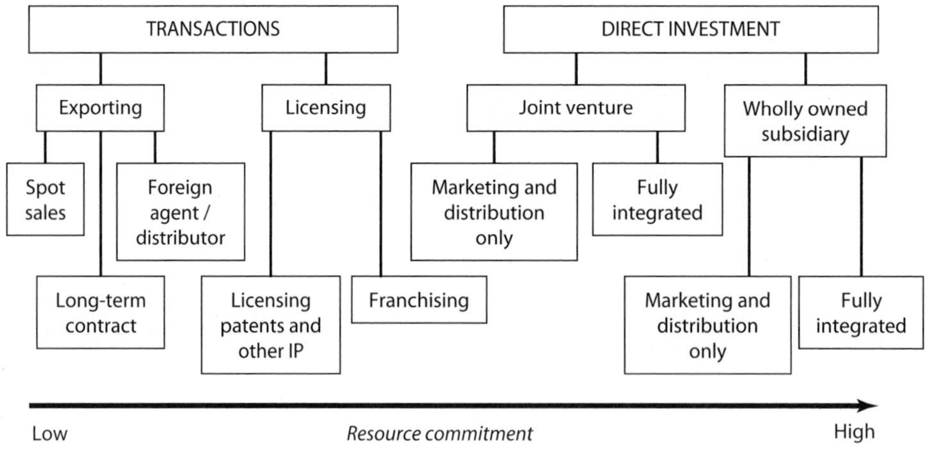

Figure 8.5 Alternative modes of overseas market entry.

the firm. Thus, at one extreme there is exporting through individual spot-market transactions; at the other, there is the establishment of a wholly owned, fully integrated subsidiary.

How does a firm weigh the merits of different market entry modes? Five key factors are relevant.

- *Is the firm's competitive advantage based on firm-specific or country-specific resources?* If the firm's competitive advantage is country based, the firm must exploit an overseas market by exporting. Thus, to the extent that Tata Motors' competitive advantage in Western car markets is its low domestic cost base, it must produce in India and export to foreign markets. If Toyota's competitive advantage is its production and management capabilities, then, as long as it can transfer and replicate these capabilities, Toyota can exploit foreign markets either by exports or by direct investment.[25]
- *Is the product tradable and what are the barriers to trade?* If the product is not tradable because of transportation constraints or import restrictions, accessing that market requires entry either by investing in overseas production facilities or by licensing the use of key resources to local companies within the overseas market.
- *Does the firm possess the full range of resources and capabilities for establishing a competitive advantage in the overseas market?* Competing in an overseas market is likely to require the firm to acquire additional resources and capabilities, particularly those related to marketing and distributing in an unfamiliar market. Accessing such country-specific resources is most easily achieved by establishing a relationship with firms in the overseas market. The form of relationship depends, in part, on the resources and capabilities required. If a firm needs marketing and distribution, it may appoint a distributor or agent with exclusive territorial rights. If a wide range of manufacturing and marketing capabilities is needed, the firm may license its product and/or its technology to a local manufacturer. In technology-based industries, licensing technology to local companies is common. In marketing-intensive industries, firms with strong brands can license their trademarks to local companies. Alternatively, a joint venture may be sought with a local manufacturing company. US companies entered the Japanese market by joint ventures with local companies (e.g. Fuji–Xerox, Caterpillar–Mitsubishi). These combined the technology and brand names of the US partner with the market knowledge and manufacturing and distribution facilities of the Japanese firm.
- *Can the firm directly appropriate the returns to its resources?* Whether a firm licenses the use of its resources or chooses to exploit them directly (either through exporting or direct investment) depends partly on appropriability considerations. In chemicals and pharmaceuticals, the patents protecting product innovations tend to offer strong legal protection, in which case patent licences to local producers can be an effective means of appropriating their returns. In computer software and computer equipment, the protection offered by patents and copyrights is looser, which encourages exporting rather than licensing as a means of exploiting overseas markets. With all licensing arrangements, key considerations are the capabilities and reliability of the local licensee. This is particularly important in licensing brand names, where the licenser must carefully protect the brand's reputation. Thus, San Miguel Corporation, based in the Philippines, licenses Carlsberg, the Danish brewer, to produce its San Miguel beer in Northampton, UK. This arrangement reflects the fact that Carlsberg has production and distribution facilities in Europe that San Miguel cannot match and San Miguel's confidence in Carlsberg as a reliable business partner.

- *What transaction costs are involved?* A key issue that arises in the licensing of a firm's trademarks or technology concerns the transaction costs of negotiating, monitoring and enforcing the terms of such agreements as compared with internationalization through a fully owned subsidiary. In expanding overseas, Starbucks owns and operates most of its coffee shops, while McDonald's franchises its burger restaurants. McDonald's competitive advantage depends primarily upon the franchisee faithfully replicating the McDonald's system. This can be enforced effectively by means of franchise contracts. Starbucks believes that its success is achieved through creating the 'Starbucks experience', which is as much about ambiance as it is about coffee. It is difficult to articulate the ingredients of this experience, let alone write it into a contract.

Issues of transaction costs are fundamental to the choices between alternative market entry modes. Barriers to exporting in the form of transport costs and tariffs are forms of transaction costs; other costs include exchange rate risk and information costs. Transaction cost analysis has been central to theories of the existence of multinational corporations. In the absence of transaction costs in the markets either for goods or for resources, companies exploit overseas markets either by exporting their goods and services or by selling the use of their resources to local firms in the overseas markets.[26] Thus, multinationals tend to predominate in industries where:

- firm-specific intangible resources such as brands and technology are important (transaction costs in licensing the use of these resources favour direct investment);
- exporting is subject to transaction costs (e.g. through tariffs or import restrictions);
- customer preferences are reasonably similar between countries.

International alliances and joint ventures

Strategic alliances – collaborative arrangements between firms – have become an increasingly popular means of accessing foreign markets. International strategic alliances take many forms: some are information collaborative arrangements; some involve one partner taking an equity stake in the other; others may involve equity cross-holdings. An international venture is where partners from different counties form a new company that they jointly own.

The traditional reason for cross-border alliances and joint ventures was the desire by multinational corporations to access the market knowledge and distribution capabilities of a local company, together with the desire by local companies to access the technology, brands and product development of the multinationals. Western banks entering China's booming credit card market have usually formed marketing alliances with local banks, often reinforced with an equity stake.[27] Governments in emerging market countries often oblige foreign companies to take a local partner in order to encourage the flow of technology and management capabilities to the host country.

By sharing resources and capabilities between the partners, alliances not only economize on investment but also allow access to more highly developed resources and capabilities than a firm could create for itself. Thus, the Freemove alliance formed by Telefónica Móviles (Spain), TIM (Italy), T-Mobile (Germany) and Orange (France) created a seamless third-generation, wireless communication network across Europe at a fraction of the cost incurred by Vodafone; it also allowed each firm access to the mobile network of the leading operator in at least five major European markets.[28] In building an international presence, some business schools have established sister schools in foreign countries (e.g. INSEAD, based near Paris, created a new campus in Singapore), but most have sought strategic alliances with local schools. Thus, London Business School has a joint Executive MBA programme with Columbia Business School and Hong Kong University, a faculty-sharing arrangement with the Indian Business School and student exchange agreements with 35 different overseas schools.

Some companies have based their international strategies almost entirely on alliances with foreign partners. For Gazprom, the Russian gas giant, alliances relate to shared pipeline projects with Eni (Italy), CNPC (China), Eon (Germany), PDVSA (Venezuela) and MOL (Hungary); liquefied natural gas projects with Petro-Canada and Sonatrach (Algeria); and long-term supply arrangements with Gaz de France.

While the strategic rationale is strong, the success of cross-border alliances (including joint ventures) has been mixed. The Fuji–Xerox copier joint venture, the Sony–Ericsson mobile phone joint venture, the Renault–Nissan alliance and the collaboration between Hewlett-Packard and Canon in printers have been very successful. Conversely, BT and AT&T's Concert alliance, the GM–Fiat alliance and Swissair's network of airline alliances were all disasters. Disagreements over the sharing of the contributions to and returns from an alliance are a frequent source of friction, particularly in alliances between firms that are also competitors. When each partner seeks to access the other's capabilities, 'competition for competence' results.[29] In several of the alliances between Japanese and Western firms, the Japanese partner was better at appropriating the benefits of the alliance.[30]

Case Insight 8.3
IKEA's foreign entry strategy

IKEA is a private company with a complex ownership and control structure. INGKA Holding is the parent organization that controls the IKEA Group of companies. IKEA Systems BV, one of the companies under the INGKA Holding umbrella, owns the IKEA concept and trademark, and designs and controls its strategy for entering foreign markets. The decision to enter a new market is based on very detailed market research. In 2014, there were 355 IKEA stores in 44 countries.

All IKEA retailers are technically franchisees, that is to say they have entered into a formal franchise agreement with Inter IKEA Systems BV, the entity that owns, operates and develops the 'IKEA concept', but over 300 of IKEA stores worldwide are owned and operated within the IKEA group and so, to all intents and purposes, are wholly owned subsidiaries. In a few countries (e.g. China, Israel, United Arab Emirates and Qatar), IKEA has adopted a more conventional franchise model. Conventional franchising has the advantage of raising capital, providing a stream of income from royalties and tapping into local knowledge, but the IKEA Group tends to franchise to third parties only when compliance with government regulations forces it to work with a local partner or where local knowledge is key to success. Potential franchisees go through a rigorous selection process in which they are required to demonstrate that they have a presence in the local market, possess the requisite knowledge and experience to be successful in the local context, subscribe to IKEA's values and culture and have the financial strength to invest at a level that allows full country penetration with large-scale retail units. The IKEA group carefully monitors the performance of each of its stores through regular audits and has a well-developed system for transmitting good practice from one store to another.

Multinational strategies: Global integration vs. national differentiation

So far, we have viewed international expansion, whether by export or by direct investment, as a means by which a company can exploit its competitive advantages, not just in its home market but also in foreign markets. However, international scope may itself be a source of competitive advantage over geographically focused competitors. In this section, we explore whether, and under what conditions, firms that operate on an international basis are able to gain a competitive advantage over nationally focused firms. What is the potential for such global strategies to create competitive advantage? In what types of industry are they likely to be most effective? And how should they be designed and deployed in order to maximize their potential?

The benefits of a global strategy

A global strategy is one that views the world as a single, if segmented, market. There are five major sources of value from operating internationally.

COST BENEFITS OF SCALE AND REPLICATION Fifty years ago, Ted Levitt pointed out the advantage companies that compete globally have over their local rivals.[31] Supplying the world market allows access to scale economies in product development, manufacturing and marketing. (Ghemawat refers to these as benefits from 'cross-border aggregation'.)[32] Exploiting these scale economies has been facilitated by the growing uniformity imposed by technology, communication and travel: 'Everywhere everything gets more and more like everything else as the world's preference structure is relentlessly homogenized,' observed Levitt.[33] In many industries – commercial aircraft, semiconductors, consumer electronics, video games – firms have no choice: they must market globally to amortize the huge costs of product development. In service industries, the cost efficiencies from international operation derive primarily from economies in the replication of knowledge-based assets, including organizational capabilities.[34] Once a company has created a knowledge-based asset or product – be it a recipe, a piece of software or an organizational system – it can be replicated in additional national markets at a fraction of the cost of creating the original. Disneyland theme parks in Tokyo, Paris, Hong Kong and Shanghai replicate the rides and management systems that Disney develops for its parks in Anaheim and Orlando. This is the appeal of franchising: if you create a brilliantly innovative business offering dental care for dogs, why limit yourself to Santa Monica, California? Why not try to emulate McDonald's with its 67 000 outlets across 200 countries of the world?

SERVING GLOBAL CUSTOMERS In several industries – investment banking, audit services, advertising – the primary driver of globalization has been the need to service global customers.[35] Hence, car parts manufacturers have internationalized as they have followed the major car producers. Law firms such as Clifford Chance and Linklaters have internationalized to better serve their multinational clients.

EXPLOITING NATIONAL RESOURCES: ARBITRAGE BENEFITS As we have already seen, global strategy does not necessarily involve production in one location and then distributing globally. Global strategies also involve exploiting the efficiencies from locating different activities in different places. As we have seen, companies internationalize not just in search of market opportunities but also in search of resource opportunities. Traditionally, this has meant a quest for raw materials and low-cost labour. Increasingly, it means a quest for knowledge. For example, among semiconductor firms, a critical factor determining the location of overseas subsidiaries is the desire to access knowledge within the host country.[36]

LEARNING BENEFITS The learning benefits of multinational operation refer not only to multinational corporations' ability to access and transfer localized knowledge but also to the integration of knowledge from different locations and the creation of new knowledge through interacting with different national environments. IKEA's expansion has required it to adjust to the Japanese style and design preferences, Japanese modes of living and Japanese fanatical quality-consciousness. As a result, IKEA has developed its capabilities with regard to both quality and design that it believes will enhance its competitiveness worldwide. According to the CEO of IKEA Japan, 'One reason for us to enter the Japanese market, apart from hopefully doing very good business, is to expose ourselves to the toughest competition in the world. By doing so, we feel that we are expanding the quality issues for IKEA all over the world.'[37]

Recent contributions to the international business literature suggest that this ability of multinational corporations to develop knowledge in multiple locations, to synthesize that knowledge and transfer it across national borders may be their greatest advantage over nationally focused companies.[38]

The critical requirement for exploiting these learning benefits is that the company possesses some form of global infrastructure for managing knowledge that permits new experiences, new ideas and new practices to be diffused and integrated.

COMPETING STRATEGICALLY A major advantage of the Romans over the Gauls, Goths and other barbarian tribes was the Romans' ability to draw upon the military and economic resources of the Roman Empire to fight local wars. Similarly, multinational corporations possess a key strategic advantage over their nationally focused competitors: multinationals can fight aggressive competitive battles in individual national markets using their resources (cash flows in particular) from other national markets. At its most simple, this **cross-subsidization** of competitive initiatives in one market using profits from other markets involves 'predatory pricing' – cutting prices to a level that drives competitors out of business. Such pricing practices are likely to contravene both the World Trade Organization's antidumping rules and national antitrust laws. More usually, cross-subsidization involves using cash flows from other markets to finance aggressive sales and marketing campaigns.[39] There is some evidence that Asian electronics firms use the profits from higher prices at home to subsidize expansion in Western markets.[40]

Strategic competition between multinational corporations presents more complex opportunities for attack, retaliation and containment.[41] The most effective response to competition in one's home market may be to retaliate in the foreign multinational corporation's home market. Fuji Film's incursion into Kodak's backyard was symbolized by Fuji's sponsorship of the 1984 Olympic Games in Los Angeles. Kodak responded by expanding its marketing efforts in Japan.[42] To effectively exploit such opportunities for national leveraging, some overall global coordination of competitive strategies in individual national markets is required.

Kenichi Ohmae argues that to become effective global competitors multinationals must become true insiders in all of the world's leading economic centres. This used to mean positioning within the 'triad': North America, Europe and Japan.[43] This doctrine has been weakened, first, by the rise of new industrial powers (notably China and India) and, second, the disappointing outcomes of several attempts to build 'triad power', for example Daimler-Benz's acquisitions of Chrysler in the US and Mitsubishi in Japan.

The need for national differentiation

For all the advantages of global strategy, the evidence of the past decade is that national differences in customer preferences continue to exert a powerful influence in most markets:

products designed to meet the needs of the 'global customer' tend to be unappealing to most consumers. Moreover, costs of national differentiation can be surprisingly low if common basic designs and common major components are used. Most car firms have abandoned attempts to create global car models in favour of common platforms.[44] Flexible manufacturing systems have reduced the costs of customizing products to meet the preferences of particular customer groups.

Domestic appliances provide an interesting refutation of the globalization hypothesis. In washing machines, national preferences have shown remarkable resilience: French and US washing machines are primarily top loading, elsewhere in Europe they are mainly front loading; the Germans prefer higher spin speeds than the Italians; US machines feature agitators rather than revolving drums; and Japanese machines are small. The pioneers of globalization in domestic appliances, such as Electrolux and Whirlpool, still struggle to outperform national and regional specialists.[45] Similarly in retail banking, despite some examples of successful internationalization (Banco Santander, HSBC), most of the evidence points to few economies from cross-border integration and the critical need to adapt to local market conditions.[46]

Every nation represents a unique combination of distinctive characteristics. How can we recognize and assess the extent of similarities and differences between countries? Pankaj Ghemawat proposes four key components: cultural distance, administrative and political distance, geographical distance and economic distance – his 'CAGE' framework (Table 8.3).[47]

Ghemawat's broad categories are only a starting point for exploring the national idiosyncrasies that make international expansion such a minefield. For consumer products firms, the structure

Table 8.3 Ghemawat's CAGE framework for assessing country differences.

	Cultural distance	Administrative and political distance	Geographical distance	Economic distance
Distance between two countries increases with	Different languages, ethnicities, religions, social norms Lack of connective ethnic or social networks	Absence of shared political or monetary association Political hostility Weak legal and financial institutions	Lack of common border, water way access, adequate transportation or communication links Physical remoteness	Different consumer incomes Different costs and quality of natural, financial and human resources Different information or knowledge
Industries most affected by source of distance	Industries with high linguistic content (TV, publishing) and cultural content (food, wine, music)	Industries viewed by government as strategically important (e.g. energy, defence, telecommunications)	Product with low value-to-weight (cement) that are fragile or perishable (glass, milk) or where communications are vital (financial services)	Products whose demand is sensitive to consumer income levels (luxury goods) Labour-intensive products (clothing)

Source: Adapted from P. Ghemawat, 'Distance still matters: The hard reality of global expansion', *Harvard Business Review* (September 2001). Adapted with permission.

of distribution channels is likely to be a critical barrier to global marketing and distribution. P&G must adapt its marketing, promotion and distribution of toiletries and household products to take account of the fact that, in the US, a few chains account for a major share of its US sales; in southern Europe, most sales are through small, independent retailers; while in Japan, P&G must sell through a multi-tiered hierarchy of distributors. The closer an industry to the final consumer, the more important cultural factors are likely to be. It is notable that so few retailers have become successful abroad. With the exception of IKEA, H&M and a handful of others, few international retailers are truly global and few have been as successful overseas as at home. For many, franchising has provided a lower-risk internationalization strategy.

Reconciling global integration with national differentiation

Choices about internationalization strategy have been viewed as a trade-off between the benefits of global integration and those of national adaptation (Figure 8.6).[48] Industries where scale economies are huge and customer preferences homogeneous call for a global strategy (e.g. jet engines). Industries where national preferences are pronounced and where customization is not prohibitively expensive favour a 'multidomestic' strategy (e.g. retail banking). Indeed, if there are no significant benefits from global integration, we may see these industries supplied almost entirely by locally specialized firms (as in funeral services and hairdressing). However, some industries may be low on most dimensions: cement and car repair services are fairly homogeneous worldwide but also lack significant scale economies or other major benefits from global presence. Conversely, other industries offer substantial benefits from operating at global scale (telecommunications equipment, military hardware), but national preferences and standards may also necessitate considerable adaptation to the needs of specific national markets.

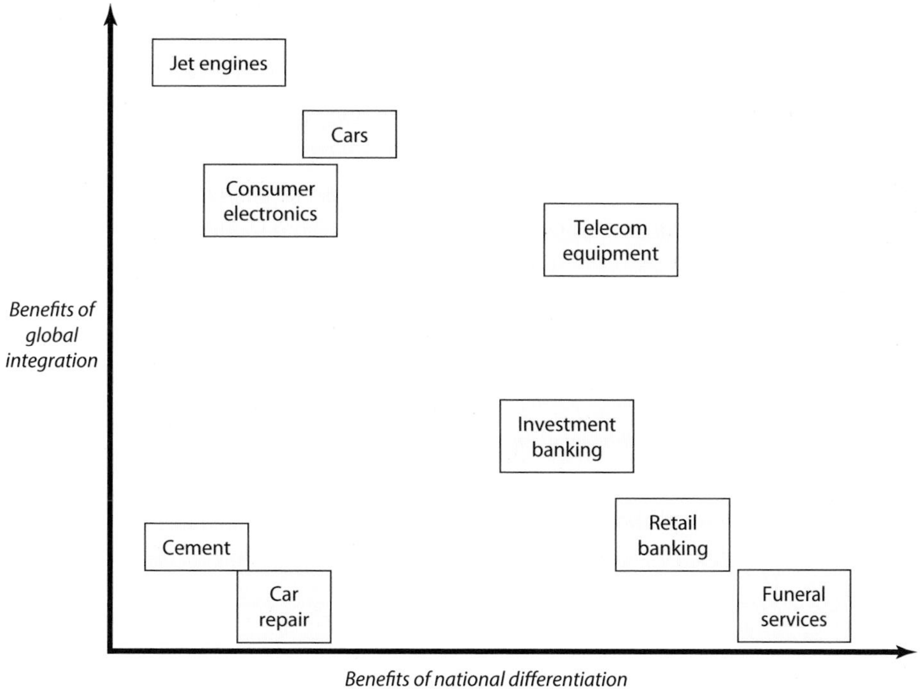

Figure 8.6 Benefits of global integration versus national differentiation.

Reconciling conflicting forces for global efficiency and national differentiation represents one of the greatest strategic challenges facing multinational corporations. Achieving 'global localization' involves standardizing product features and company activities where scale economies are substantial and differentiating them where national preferences are strongest and where achieving differentiation is not over-costly. Thus, a global car such as the Honda Civic (introduced in 1972 and sold in 110 countries of the world) now embodies considerable local adaptations – not just to meet national safety and environmental standards but also to meet local preferences for legroom, seat specifications, accessories, colour and trim. McDonald's, too, meshes global standardization with local adaptation, for example introducing more vegetarian and spicy options in India (e.g. McSpicy Paneer and McAloo Tikki) and a range of wraps in Australia (e.g. the Chicken and Aioli McWrap).

Case Insight 8.4

IKEA goes glocal

IKEA has sought to introduce its Swedish-style home decor to the world by standardizing not only its stores and its product range but also its management practices in all the countries in which it operates. On the outside, IKEA stores look the same regardless of where they are. They are all painted blue and yellow, reflecting the colours of the Swedish flag and all offer much the same retail experience. Nonetheless, IKEA has had to adapt to some local conditions. In Japan, for example, space is at a premium. IKEA has had to reduce the size of many of its furniture items so that they fit Japanese rooms, which are typically smaller than those in other countries.[49] Similarly, it has had to ensure that its kitchen cabinets comply with Japanese earthquake standards by fitting them with automatic locking systems. In contrast, IKEA has had to increase the size of its furniture in the US. European beds are narrower than Americans are used to and cabinet drawers too shallow to take bulky sweaters.

IKEA has also faced pressure to make adjustments to its management practices, which have met with different responses in different countries. While many European employees may be comfortable with the company's somewhat paternalistic style, flat structure and informality, employees in some parts of the world have been less happy with these arrangements and see the flat structure as limiting opportunities for progression.

Reconciling global efficiency with national differentiation involves disaggregating the company by product and function. In retail banking, different products and services have different potential for globalization. Credit cards and basic savings products such as certificates of deposit tend to be globally standardized; current accounts[50] and mortgage lending are much more nationally differentiated. Similarly with business functions: R & D, purchasing, IT and manufacturing have strong globalization potential; sales, marketing, customer service and human resource management need to be much more nationally differentiated. These differences have important implications for how the multinational corporation is organized.

Strategy and organization within the multinational corporation

The same issues (the benefits from global integration and need for national differentiation) that influence the design of international strategies also have critical implications for the design of organizational structures and management systems to implement these strategies. As we shall see, one of the greatest challenges facing the senior managers of multinational corporations is aligning organizational structures and management systems and their fit with the strategies being pursued.

The evolution of multinational strategies and structures

Over the past 100 years, the forces driving the internationalization of companies have changed considerably; the trade-off between the benefits of global integration and those of national differentiation has shifted markedly. During different periods, international firms have adopted different strategies and different structural configurations. Yet, even though some firms have adapted to change, many others have maintained their old structures. Structural configurations have tended to persist over time not only because organizations are subject to some inertia but also because of the complexity multinational corporations face in trying to execute structural change. To a large extent, multinational corporations are captives of their history: their strategy–structure configurations today reflect choices they made at the time of their international expansion. Radical changes in strategy and structure are difficult: once an international distribution of functions, operations and decision-making authority has been determined, reorganization is slow, difficult and costly, particularly when host governments become involved. Bartlett and Ghoshal argue that the 'administrative heritage' of a multinational corporation – its configuration of assets and capabilities, its distribution of managerial responsibilities and its network of relationships – is a critical determinant of its current capabilities and a key constraint upon its ability to build new strategic capabilities.[51]

Bartlett and Ghoshal identify three eras in the development of the multinational corporation (Figure 8.7):

- *Early 20th century: Era of the European multinational:* European companies such as Unilever, Shell, ICI and Philips were pioneers of multinational expansion. Because of the conditions at the time of internationalization (poor transportation and communications, highly differentiated national markets) the companies created 'multinational federations': each national subsidiary was operationally autonomous and undertook the full range of functions, including product development, manufacturing and marketing.
- *Post-World War II: Era of the American multinational:* US economic dominance was the basis for the pre-eminence of US multinationals such as GM, Ford, IBM, Coca-Cola, Caterpillar and P&G. While their overseas subsidiaries were allowed considerable autonomy, this was within the context of the dominant position of their US parent in terms of capital, new product and process technology, management capabilities and management systems. US-based resources and capabilities were their primary competitive advantages in world markets.
- *The 1970s and 1980s: The Japanese challenge:* Japanese multinational corporations – Honda, Toyota, Matsushita, NEC and YKK – pursued global strategies from centralized domestic bases. R & D and manufacturing were concentrated in Japan; overseas subsidiaries were responsible for sales and distribution. Globally standardized products manufactured in large-scale plants provided the basis for unrivalled cost and quality advantages. Over time, manufacturing and R & D were dispersed, initially because of trade protection by consumer countries and the rising value of the yen against other currencies.

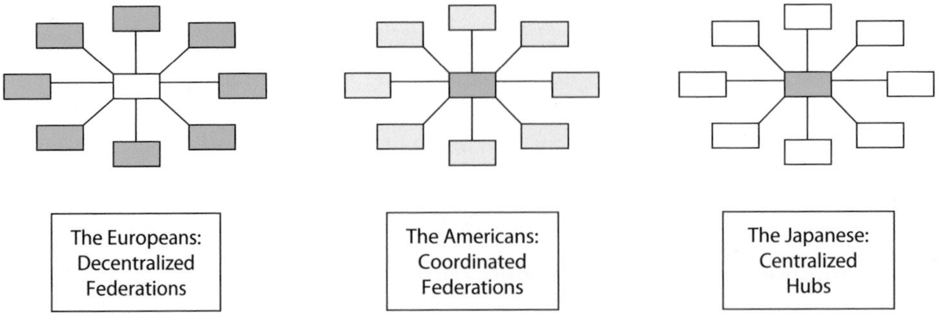

Figure 8.7 The development of the multinational corporation: Alternative parent–subsidiaries relations.

Source: C. A. Bartlett and S. Ghoshal, *Managing Across Borders: The Transnational Solution* (Boston: Harvard Business School Press, 1998). Reproduced with permission.

The different administrative heritage of these different groups of multinational corporations continues to shape their organizational capabilities today. The strength of European multinationals is adaptation to the conditions and requirements of individual national markets. The strength of the US multinationals is their ability to transfer technology and proven new products from their domestic strongholds to their national subsidiaries. That of the Japanese multinational corporations is the efficiency of global production and new product development. Yet, these core capabilities are also core rigidities. The challenge for European multinational corporations has been to achieve greater integration of their sprawling international empires. For Shell and Philips, this has involved reorganizations lasting more than two decades. For US multinational corporations, such as Ford and P&G, it has involved nurturing the ability to tap their foreign subsidiaries for technology, design and new product ideas. For Japanese multinational corporations, such as Nomura, Hitachi and NEC, the challenge is to become true insiders in the overseas countries where they do business.

Reconfiguring the multinational corporation: The transnational corporation

CHANGING ORGANIZATION STRUCTURE For North American and European-based multinational corporations, the principal structural changes of recent decades have been a shift from organization around national subsidiaries and regional groupings to the creation of worldwide product divisions. For most multinational corporations, country and regional organizations are retained, but primarily for the purposes of national compliance and customer relationships. Thus, Hewlett-Packard, the world's biggest IT company, conducts its business through five global product groups: Enterprise Servers, Storage and Networking; Enterprise Services; Software; Personal Systems; and Imaging and Printing. Each of these product groups and each of HP's functions has activities in multiple countries. For example, HP Labs are in Palo Alto, California; Singapore; Bristol, UK; Haifa, Israel; St Petersburg, Russia; Bangalore, India; and Beijing, China. To assist geographical coordination, HP has regional headquarters for the Americas (in Houston); for Europe, the Middle East and Africa (in Geneva); and for Asia Pacific (in Singapore). Because of the special importance of China and India, its head of the Personal Systems Group also has special responsibility for China and the head of the Imaging and Printing Group has special responsibility for India.

RECONCILING LOCALIZATION AND GLOBAL INTEGRATION: THE TRANSNATIONAL However, the formal changes in structure are less important than the changes in responsibilities, decision-making powers and modes of coordination within these structures. Escalating costs of research and new product development have made global strategies with global product platforms essential. At the same time, meeting consumer needs in each national market and responding swiftly to changing local circumstances requires greater decentralization. Accelerating technological change further exacerbates these contradictory forces: despite the cost and 'critical mass' benefits of centralizing research and new product development, innovation occurs at multiple locations within the multinational corporation and requires nurturing of creativity and initiative throughout the organization. 'It's the corporate equivalent of being able to walk, chew gum and whistle at the same time,' notes Chris Bartlett.

According to Bartlett, the simultaneous pursuit of responsiveness to national markets and global coordination requires 'a very different kind of internal management process than existed in the relatively simple multinational or global organizations. This is the *transnational organization*.'[52] The distinguishing characteristic of the transnational is that it becomes an integrated network of distributed and interdependent resources and capabilities (Figure 8.8). This necessitates that:

- Each national unit is a source of ideas, skills and capabilities that can be harnessed for the benefit of the total organization.
- National units access global scale economies by designating them the company's world source for a particular product, component or activity.
- The centre must establish a new, highly complex managing role that coordinates relationships among units but does so in a highly flexible way. The key is to focus less on managing activities directly and more on creating an organizational context that is conducive to the coordination and resolution of differences. Creating the right organizational context involves 'establishing clear corporate objectives, developing managers with broadly based perspectives and relationships and fostering supportive organizational norms and values'.[53]

Balancing global integration and national differentiation requires a company to adapt to the differential requirements of different products, different functions and different countries. P&G adopts global standardization for some of its products (Pringles potato chips and high-end perfumes, for example); for others (hair care products and laundry detergent, for example), it allows significant national differentiation. Across countries, P&G organizes global product divisions to serve most of the industrialized world because of the similarities between their markets, while for emerging market countries (such as China and India) it operates through country subsidiaries in order to adapt to the distinctive features of these markets. Among

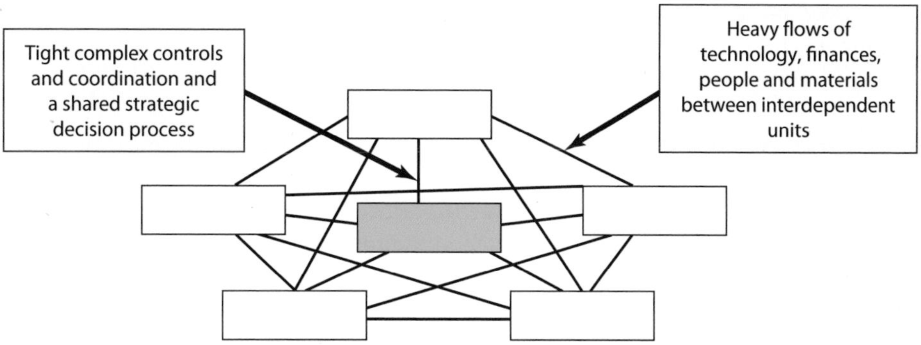

Figure 8.8 The transnational corporation.

functions, R & D is globally integrated while sales are organized by national units that are differentiated to meet local market characteristics.

The transnational firm is a concept and direction of development rather than a distinct organizational archetype. It involves convergence of the different strategy configurations of multinational corporations. Thus, companies such as Philips, Unilever and Siemens have reassigned roles and responsibilities to achieve greater integration within their traditional 'decentralized federations' of national subsidiaries. Japanese global corporations such as Toyota and Matsushita have drastically reduced the roles of their Japanese headquarters. American multinationals such as Citigroup and IBM are moving in two directions: reducing the role of their US bases while increasing integration among their different national subsidiaries.

Multinational corporations are increasingly locating management control of their global product divisions outside their home countries. When Philips adopted a product division structure, it located responsibility for medical electronics in its US subsidiary and leadership in consumer electronics in Japan. Nexans, the world's biggest manufacturer of electric cables, has moved the head office of five of its 20 product divisions outside of France. For example, the head of ships' cables is based in South Korea, the world leader in shipbuilding.[54] Aligning structure, strategy and national resources may even require shifting the corporate headquarters – HSBC moved from Hong Kong to London, Tetra Pak from Lund, Sweden to Lausanne, Switzerland.[55]

ORGANIZING R & D AND NEW PRODUCT DEVELOPMENT Probably the greatest challenges facing the top managers of multinational corporations are organizing, fostering and exploiting innovation and new product development. Innovation is stimulated by diversity and autonomy, while its exploitation and diffusion require critical mass and coordination. The traditional European decentralized model is conducive to local initiatives – but not to their global exploitation. Philips has an outstanding record of innovation in consumer electronics. In its TV business, its Canadian subsidiary developed its first colour TV; its Australian subsidiary developed its first stereo-sound TV and its British subsidiary developed teletext TVs. However, lack of global integration constrained their success on a global scale. Building a globally integrated approach to new product development has been a major priority of the past two decades.

Assigning national subsidiaries global mandates allows them to take advantage of local resources and develop distinctive capabilities while exploiting globally the results of their initiatives. [56] For example, P&G, recognizing Japanese obsessiveness over cleanliness, assigned increasing responsibility to its Japanese subsidiary for developing household cleaning products. Its 'Swiffer' dust-collecting products were developed in Japan (using technology developed by other firms) before being introduced into other markets. Where a local unit possesses unique capabilities, it can be designated a 'centre of excellence'.[57]

Summary

Moving from a national to an international business environment represents a quantum leap in complexity. In an international environment, a firm's potential for competitive advantage is determined not just by its own resources and capabilities but also by the conditions of the national environment in which it operates. The extent to which a firm is positioned in a single market or multiple national markets also influences its competitive position.

Our approach in this chapter is to simplify the complexities of international strategy by applying the same basic tools of strategy analysis that we developed in earlier chapters.

For example, to determine whether a firm should enter an overseas market, our focus has been the profit implications of such an entry. However, establishing the potential for a firm to create value from internationalization is only a beginning. Subsequent analysis needs to design an international strategy: do we enter an overseas market by exporting, licensing or direct investment? If the latter, should we set up a wholly owned subsidiary or a joint venture? Once the strategy has been established, a suitable organizational structure needs to be designed.

The fact that so many companies which have been outstandingly successful in their home market have failed so miserably in their overseas expansion demonstrates the complexity of international management. In some cases, the companies have failed to recognize that the resources and capabilities which underpinned their competitive advantages in their home market could not be readily transferred or replicated in overseas markets. In others, the problems were in designing the structures and systems that could effectively implement the international strategy.

As the lessons of success and failure from international business become recognized and distilled into better theories and analytical frameworks, so we advance our understanding of how to design and implement strategies for competing globally. We are at the stage where we recognize the issues and the key determinants of competitive advantage in an international environment. However, there is much that we do not fully understand. Designing strategies and organizational structures that can reconcile critical trade-offs remains a key challenge for senior managers. Trade-offs include global scale economies versus local differentiation, decentralized learning and innovation versus worldwide diffusion and replication and localized flexibilities versus international standardization.

Summary table

Learning objectives	Summary
Be aware of the impact of internationalization on industry structure and competition	Industry can be categorized on the basis of their internationalization – sheltered, trading, multidomestic and global – and also on the basis of the different routes by which firms internationalize. Internationalization usually means more competition and lower industry profitability
Be able to analyse the implications of a firm's national environment for its competitive advantage	Porter's diamond model explores the processes through which particular industries within a country develop the resources and capabilities that confer an international competitive advantage. The four key factors highlighted by Porter are factor conditions, related and supporting industries, demand conditions and strategy, and structure and rivalry. There needs to be consistency between firm strategy and national conditions for firms to exploit national strengths
Be able to formulate strategies for exploiting overseas business opportunities, including overseas market entry strategies and overseas production strategies	Firms move across national borders to seek foreign markets and to access the resources and capabilities available in other countries. Increasingly, decisions of where to produce are made independently of decisions about where to sell. Decisions on location depend on national resource availability, firm-specific advantages and tradability. Firms moving into new geographical markets also need to decide on their mode of entry, e.g. licensing, joint ventures, direct investment. There are advantages and disadvantages of each approach

Learning objectives	Summary
Appreciate how international strategies can be shaped to achieve an optimal balance between global integration and national differentiation	A global strategy views the world as a single market and confers a number of benefits. But national differences in consumer preferences exert a powerful pressure for firms to adapt their products to local needs. Reconciling these conflicting forces represents a significant challenge for most international firms, and achieving an optimal balance depends on standardizing product features and company activities where scale economies are substantial and differentiating where national preferences are strongest
Be able to design organizational structures and management systems appropriate to the pursuit of international strategies	The trade-offs that firms make with respect to global integration versus local responsiveness influence firm structure. During different periods of time, international firms have adopted different organizational structures and even when circumstances change they can be slow to change. Bartlett and Ghoshal suggest that the simultaneous pursuit of global integration and local responsiveness requires firms to adopt very different kinds of internal management processes and to become 'transnational'

Further reading

To gain a deeper understanding of the models and frameworks that help us to understand the challenges of formulating and implementing global strategies, it is well worth reading the original work by authors such as Christopher Bartlett and Sumantra Ghoshal, Ted Levitt and Michael Porter. If time pressures prevent you from reading their books, many of their key ideas are captured in journal articles, for example:

Bartlett, C. and Ghoshal, S. (2003). What is a global manager? *Harvard Business Review*, 81(8), 101–8.

Levitt, T. (1983). The globalization of markets. *Harvard Business Review*, May–June, 92–102.

Porter, M. (1990). The competitive advantage of nations. *Harvard Business Review*, 68(2), 73–93.

Grant provides a useful critique of Porter's diamond model in:

Grant, R. C. (1991). Porter's competitive advantage of nations: An assessment. *Strategic Management*, 12(7), 535–54.

Ghemawat explores the central tension between global integration and national responsiveness in:

Ghemawat, P. (2007). Managing difference: The central challenge of global strategy. *Harvard Business Review*, March, 59–68.

Self-study questions

1. With reference to Figure 8.1 identify a 'sheltered industry' (i.e. one that has been subject to little penetration either by imports or by foreign direct investment). Explain why this industry has escaped internationalization. Explore whether there are opportunities for profitable internationalization within the industry and, if so, the strategy that would offer the best chance of success.

2. According to Michael Porter's *Competitive Advantage of Nations*, some of the industries where British companies have an international advantage are advertising, auctioneering of antiques and artwork, distilled alcoholic beverages, hand tools and chemical preparations for gardening and horticulture. Some of the industries where US companies have an international competitive advantage are: photo film, aircraft and helicopters, computer hardware and software, oilfield services, management consulting, cinema films and TV programmes, healthcare products and services and financial services. For either the UK or the US, use Porter's national diamond framework (Figure 8.3) to explain the observed pattern of international competitive advantage.

3. How does McDonald's balance global standardization and national differentiation? Should it offer its franchisees in overseas countries greater initiative in introducing products that meet national preferences? Should it also allow greater flexibility for its overseas franchisees to adapt store layout, operating practices and marketing? What aspects of the McDonald's system should McDonald's top management insist on keeping globally standardized?

4. You are the founder of an Internet service in the US that helps people to rent rooms. You are thinking of extending your service to clients in Germany and then other parts of Europe. What are the key challenges you are likely to face in internationalizing your business?

5. Visit the website www.nestle.com and consider the way in which the company is organized (see the General Organization of Nestlé SA diagram in the company's *Corporate Governance Report*). What additional information would you need to be able to judge whether Nestlé could be considered a transnational organization?

Closing Case

Sharp and the production of liquid crystal displays

The Sharp Corporation is one of the world's leading manufacturers of electronic products and components. Founded in 1915 by Tokuji Hayakawa, who invented the 'Ever-Sharp Pencil', the company had net sales of just under ¥3 billion in 2013 and produced a wide range of products, including television sets, electronic calculators, microwave ovens, solar panels and LED lights. The company first experimented with liquid crystal displays (LCDs) in the 1960s when it licensed the technology from RCA. LCD technology seemed unpromising at first because displays were expensive to produce and small, but Sharp, along with a number of other firms in the industry, invested in R & D and over time barriers were overcome. By the turn of the century, LCD technology had become the dominant technology in flat-screen television displays and Sharp had developed a strong reputation for capability in the broad area of optoelectronics (the fusion of light and electronics).

In the early days of development, the major players in the electronics industry had collaborated on LCD technology and breakthroughs were disseminated quickly but as the technology matured, competition intensified. Lehmberg points out: 'By the time production technology reached its fifth generation, it had been improved to the point that firms with little LCD experience could buy a new plant and get it to function well with limited outside help.'[58] Firms based in countries with lower labour costs, such as Taiwan and Korea, started to compete. In response, Sharp, afraid that its core technology might be at risk, sought to wall off its proprietary knowledge. The company implemented a policy of secrecy; no outsiders, even suppliers, were allowed to visit Sharp's LCD plants.

Sharp's business model was based on manufacturing in Japan and selling overseas. For a long time, this strategy served the company well. Prior to 2000, the main market for Sharp's electronics products was Japan and a significant proportion of its LEDs went into its own products, the remainder being sold to other producers of electronic goods. The company was able to benefit from the geographical closeness of its plants and its proximity to a cluster of small and medium-sized suppliers in an area known as Crystal Valley. These firms supplied key inputs into the LCD production process, for example 'steppers' – machines that etch circuitry into LCD panels – and specialized adhesives and films. Sharp's 'make in Japan' policy meant that it was able to consolidate production and exploit available economies of scale. Successive generations of LCD technologies required larger and larger investments and Sharp achieved efficiency gains by investing in new plants. In 2009, it opened its ¥430 billion, state-of-the-art factory at Sakai in Japan, which produced large tenth-generation LCDs that were primarily used in flat-screen television sets.[59]

As Sharp internationalized, however, the drawbacks of its 'export' model became evident. While in 2004, 34% of sales had been in overseas markets, by 2009 that figure was 54%, dropping back to 48% in 2010. LCDs were expensive to ship by air and transport by sea was slow. The LCD market was very competitive and prone to significant fluctuations in demand and supply, causing price volatility. Sharp faced higher taxes and labour costs than many of its non-Japanese rivals and the rapid appreciation of the yen in the latter part of the 2000s meant that Sharp received less revenue from overseas sales designated in foreign currencies. At the same time, the Korean won depreciated, giving an advantage to Korean competitors such as Samsung. To add to the company's problems, sales of electronic products like televisions that utilized LCDs were severely affected by the global recession. The combination of new competition and weak sales drove prices down, for example between 2004 and 2012 the price of 40-inch LCD panels fell from $2,700 to $250. Sharp moved from profit to loss with a consequent drop in its share price.

In 2009, Sharp's president, Mikio Katayama, announced a change in business strategy.[60] He declared that Sharp was moving away from its Japanese-centric policy to one based more on the concept of *chisan chishou* – local production for local consumption. Following the example of Japanese car-makers, Sharp planned to change its global production strategy to one based more on the establishment of LCD and TV assembly plants abroad. He argued that Sharp's core technology wasn't making LCD panels or assembling LCD TVs: it was production technology. By inference, the company was beginning to place less emphasis on investment in big production plants and to give greater emphasis to its intellectual property and specialized knowledge.

The most obvious location for offshore production was China. As the global economy came out of recession, the strongest market growth was in China, and Sharp had received approaches from several Chinese electronics firms who were interested in entering into agreements with them to produce LCDs. Sharp entered into negotiations with the China Electronics Group but these stalled because the Chinese authorities were only prepared to approve tenth-generation LCD plants whereas Sharp wished to license eighth-generation plants and was not willing to export its latest technology. At the same time, Sharp found itself caught up in a wave of anti-Japanese sentiment that swept through China following the Japanese government's decision to purchase three islands located in the East China sea from a private owner. China disputed the ownership of these islands and the incident fuelled already deep-rooted anti-Japanese nationalism, resulting in attacks by Chinese nationals on Japanese-owned businesses and brands.

Before the new strategy could be put in place, Sharp's position deteriorated further and President Katayama was replaced by Okuda and shortly afterwards by Takahashi. In 2012, the year that the company celebrated its 100th anniversary, it also announced its greatest ever losses of ¥545 billion, and even its senior executives started to question the company's ability to survive. In its scramble to stay afloat, it was forced to turn to rivals such as Taiwan's Hon Hai Precision Industry Co. (also known as Foxconn) and Samsung for capital. The new president (Takahashi) blamed some of the company's failure on its inward-looking culture, which, he argued, had resulted in excessive numbers of meetings, a time-consuming consensus-based approach to decision making and greater attention to managing the organization chart than to doing what was best for the business and its customers.

Case questions

- What factors did the Sharp Corporation need to consider when deciding where to locate its LCD production? What are the advantages and disadvantages of changing its 'make in Japan, sell overseas' strategy?
- What are the potential costs and benefits to Sharp of engaging in joint ventures with Chinese and Taiwanese electronics manufacturers?
- Critically evaluate President Katayama's suggestion that Sharp should have placed greater emphasis on its knowledge assets rather than its physical resources.
- What impact has national culture had on Sharp's strategy and performance?

Notes

1 *OECD in Figures 2013* (OECD, 2013) and *Global Investment Trends* (UNCTAD, 2013).

2 IKEA Annual Report 2013.

3 www.ikea.com, accessed 29th September 2014.

4 I. Kamprad and B. Torekull, *Leading by Design: The IKEA story* (New York: HarperBusiness, 1999).

5 P. Grol and C. Schoch, *IKEA: Culture as competitive advantage* (Paris: Group ICPA Case Study, 1998).

6 See, for example, P. Girija and S. Chaudhuri, *IKEA in China: Competing through low-cost strategies* (IBSCDC Case Study, 2006).

7 This process was proposed by J. Johanson and J.-E. Vahlne, 'The internationalisation process of the firm', *Journal of International Business Studies*, 8 (1977): 23–32. See also L. Melin, 'Internationalisation as a strategy process', *Strategic Management Journal*, 13 (1992 Special Issue): 99–118.

8 S. L. Segal-Horn, 'Globalisation of service industries', in J. McGee (ed.) *The Blackwell Encyclopedia of Management: Strategic management* (Oxford: Blackwell Publishing, 2005): 147–54.

9 A. Kundna, G. Yip and H. Barkema, 'Born global', *Business Strategy Review* Winter (2008): 38–44.

10 'City Interview: Toni Mascolo still a cut above at hairdressing empire Toni & Guy', www.thisismoney.co.uk/money/markets/article-2034792/CITY-INTERVIEW-Toni-Mascolocut-hairdressing-empire-Toni–Guy.html, accessed 29th September 2014.

11 P. Ghemawat and F. Ghadar, 'Global integration and global concentration', *Industrial and Corporate Change*, 15 (2006): 595–624.

12 A key finding was that 'human capital' (knowledge and skills) was more important than 'physical capital' in explaining US comparative advantage. See W. W. Leontief, 'Domestic production and foreign trade', in R. Caves and H. Johnson (eds), *Readings in International Economics* (Homewood, IL: Irwin, 1968).

13 P. Krugman, 'Increasing returns, monopolistic competition and international trade', *Journal of International Economics*, 9 (November 1979): 469–79.

14 G. Tellis, A. Eisingerich, R. Chandy and J. Prabhu, 'Competing for the future: Patterns of global location of R&D centres by the world's largest firms', *AIM Working Paper* (2009).

15 M. E. Porter, *The Competitive Advantage of Nations* (New York: Free Press, 1990).

16 Y.-H. Cho and J. Yoon 'The origin and function of dynamic collectivism: An analysis of Korean corporate culture', *Asia Pacific Business Review*, 7 (2001): 70–88.

17 For a review of the Porter analysis, see R. M. Grant, 'Porter's Competitive Advantage of Nations: An assessment', *Strategic Management Journal*, 12 (1991): 535–48.

18 A. M. Rugman, 'Porter takes the wrong turn', *Business Quarterly*, 56 (1992): 59–64; J. H. Dunning, 'The competitive advantage of nations and TNC activities: A review article', *Transnational Corporations*, 191 (1992): 135–68.

19 A. M. Rugman and J. R. D'Cruz, 'The double diamond model of international competitiveness: Canada's experience', *Management International Review*, 33 (1993): 17–39.

20 H. Moon, A. M. Rugman and A. Verbeke, 'A generalized double diamond approach to the global competitiveness of Korea and Singapore', *International Business Review*, 7 (1998): 135–50.

21 L. Waverman, 'A critical analysis of Porter's framework on the competitive advantage of nations', in A. M. Rugman, J. Van den Broeck and A. Verbeke (eds), *Research in Global Strategic Management: Volume V: Beyond the diamond* (Greenwich, CT: JAI Press, 1995).

22 H. Davies and P. Ellis, 'Porter's *Competitive Advantage of Nations*: Time for the final judgement', *Journal of Management Studies*, 37 (2000): 1189–213.

23 Statistics Sweden 2013, http://www.scb.se/en_/, accessed 29th September 2014.

24 The linking of value-added chains to national comparative advantages is explained in B. Kogut, 'Designing global strategies and competitive value-added chains', *Sloan Management Review* (Summer 1985): 15–38.

25 The role of firm-specific assets in explaining the multinational expansion is analysed in R. Caves, 'International corporations: The industrial economics of foreign investment', *Economica*, 38 (1971): 1–27.

26 D. J. Teece, 'Transactions cost economics and multinational enterprise', *Journal of Economic Behavior and Organisation*, 7 (1986): 21–45. See also 'Creatures of imperfection', in 'Multinationals: A survey', *The Economist* (27th March 1993): 8–10.

27 D. von Emloh and Y. Wang, 'Competing for China's credit card market', *McKinsey Quarterly Reports* (November 2005).

28 'Freemove: Creating value through strategic alliance in the mobile telecommunications industry', IESE Case 0-305-013 (2004).

29 'Fiat nears stake in Chrysler that could lead to takeover', *Wall Street Journal* (20th January 2009).

30 G. Hamel, 'Competition for competence and inter-partner learning within international strategic alliances', *Strategic Management Journal*, 12 (1991): 83–103.

31 T. Levitt, 'The Globalization of Markets', *Harvard Business Review* (May/June 1983): 92–102.

32 P. Ghemawat, *Redefining Global Strategy: Crossing borders in a world where differences still matter* (Boston: Harvard Business School, 2007).

33 Levitt (1983) op. cit.: 94.

34 S. G. Winter and G. Szulanski, 'Replication as Strategy', *Organization Science*, 12 (2001): 730–43.

35 D. B. Montgomery, G. S. Yip and B. Villalonga, 'Explaining supplier behavior on global account management', Stanford Research Paper No. 1767 (November 2002). Available at SSRN: http://ssrn.com/abstract=355240, accessed 29th September 2014.

36 P. Almeida, 'Knowledge sourcing by foreign multinationals: Patent citation analysis in the US semiconductor industry', *Strategic Management Journal* 17, Winter Special Issue (1996): 155–65. See the McDonald's individual country websites, e.g. www.mcdonalds.com (US), www.mcdonalds.co.uk (UK), www.mcdonalds.fr (France).

37 Comments by Tommy Kullberg (IKEA Japan) in 'The Japan paradox', Conference organized by the European Commission, Director General for External Affairs (December 2003): 62–3, http://www.deljpn.ec.europa.eu/data/current/japan-paradox.pdf, accessed 29th September 2014.

38 A. K. Gupta and P. Govindarajan, 'Knowledge flows within multinational corporations', *Strategic Management Journal*, 21 (April 2000): 473–96; P. Almeida, J. Song and R. M. Grant, 'Are firms superior to alliances and markets? An empirical test of cross-border knowledge building', *Organisation Science*, 13 (March–April 2002): 147–61.

39 G. Hamel and C. K. Prahalad, 'Do you really have a global strategy?' *Harvard Business Review* (July–August 1985): 139–48.

40 H. Simon and Y. Eriguchi, 'Pricing challenges for Japanese companies in the 21st century', *Journal of Professional Pricing*, 14 (2005), www.pricingsociety.com; B. Y. Aw, G. Batra and M. J. Roberts, 'Firm heterogeneity and export–domestic price differentials: A study of Taiwanese electrical products', *Journal of International Economics*, 54 (2001): 149–69.

41 I. C. Macmillan, A. van Ritten and R. G. McGrath, 'Global gamesmanship', *Harvard Business Review* (May 2003): 62–71.

42 R. C. Christopher, *Second to None: American companies in Japan* (New York: Crown, 1986).

43 K. Ohmae, *Triad Power: The coming shape of global competition* (New York: Free Press, 1985).

44 The Ford Mondeo/Contour is a classic example of a global product that failed to appeal strongly to any national market. See M. J. Moi, 'Ford Mondeo: A Model T world car?' *Idea Group* (2001).

45 C. Baden-Fuller and J. Stopford, 'Globalisation frustrated', *Strategic Management Journal*, 12 (1991): 493–507.

46 M. Venzin, *Building an International Financial Services Firm: How successful firms design and execute cross-border strategies* (Oxford: Oxford University Press, 2009).

47 P. Ghemawat, 'Distance still matters: The hard reality of global expansion', *Harvard Business Review* (September 2001).

48 Ghemawat (2007, op. cit.) proposes a three-way rather than a two-way analysis. In his Adaptation–Aggregation–Arbitrage (AAA) framework, he divides integration into aggregation and arbitrage.

49 P. Indu and D. Purkayastha, *IKEA: The Japanese misadventure and successful re-entry*, Case study: ICMR Center for Management Research (2008).

50 Referred to as 'checking accounts' in some parts of the world.

51 C. A. Bartlett and S. Ghoshal, *Managing across Borders: The transnational solution*, 2nd edn (Boston: Harvard Business School Press, 1998).

52 C. Bartlett, 'Building and managing the transnational: The new organisational challenge', in Michael E. Porter (ed.), *Competition in Global Industries* (Boston: Harvard Business School Press, 1986): 377.

53 Ibid.: 388.

54 'The country prince comes of age', *Financial Times* (9th August 2005).

55 J. Birkinshaw, P. Braunerhjelm, U. Holm and S. Terjesen, 'Why do some multinational corporations relocate their headquarters overseas?' *Strategic Management Journal*, 27 (2006): 681–700.

56 J. Birkinshaw, N. Hood and S. Jonsson, 'Building firm-specific advantages in multinational corporations: The role of subsidiary initiative', *Strategic Management Journal*, 19 (1998): 221–42.

57 T. S. Frost, J. M. Birkinshaw and P. C. Ensign, 'Centers of excellence in multinational corporations', *Strategic Management Journal*, 23 (2002): 997–1018.

58 D. Lehmberg, *Sharp Corporation: Beyond Japan*, Case Study, Richard Ivey School of Business (2011).

59 M. Williams, 'Inside the world's most advanced LCD factory', *PC World* (1st December 2009), http://www.pcworld.com/article/183422, accessed 29th September 2014.

60 'Sharp adopts global production model', *Bloomberg Business Week* (8th April 2009). http://www.businessweek.com/globalbiz/content/apr2009/gb2009048_640568.htm, accessed 29th September 2014.

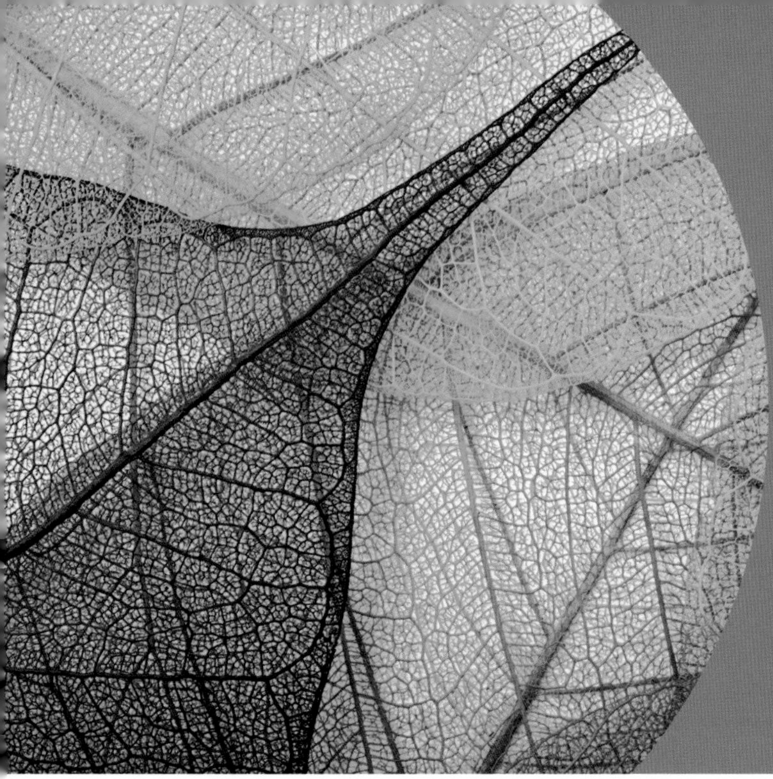

9

Realizing strategy

www.foundationsofstrategy.com

Introduction and objectives

We spend a lot of our time strategizing: working out how we can best develop our careers, making plans for a summer vacation, thinking about how to improve our attractiveness to members of the opposite sex. Most of these strategies remain just wishful thinking: if strategy is to yield results, it must be backed by commitment and translated into action.

Realizing strategy presents organizations with even more challenges than those faced by individuals, because strategy implementation requires the combined efforts of all the members of the organization. Many of those implementing strategy will have played no role in its formulation; others will find that the strategy conflicts with their own personal interests; some may not believe in the strategy. Even without these impediments, there is the simple truth that implementation tends to be neglected because it requires commitment, persistence, and hard work. 'How many meetings have you attended where people left without firm conclusions about who would do what and when?' asks consultant, Ram Charan.[1]

We begin this chapter by considering the management systems through which strategy is linked to action and performance. As we shall see, formal strategic planning systems may not be particularly effective at formulating strategy; their primary value is in creating a mechanism for linking strategy to a system of implementation that involves operational planning, target setting and resource allocation.

However, the challenge of strategy implementation goes beyond the tasks of operationalizing strategic decisions. The way in which a company organizes itself is fundamental to the effectiveness of its strategic management. Hence, a wider goal of this chapter is to introduce the concepts needed to understand the challenge of organizing and to provide a framework for designing organizational structure. We consider not just the role of organizational structure but also the informal aspects of an organization's social structure, namely its organizational culture.

The broad aim of this chapter is to introduce you to the fundamentals of strategy implementation: the basic aspects of organizational structure, systems and culture that determine the effectiveness with which strategy is executed. There are obvious links with Chapter 5, where we discussed the management of strategic change; Chapter 6, where we considered the organizational conditions conducive to innovation; Chapter 7, where we examined the structure and systems of the multibusiness corporations; and Chapter 8, where we considered organizing the multinational business.

By the time you have completed this chapter, you will be able to:

- understand how strategic planning links to operational planning, performance management and resource allocation in implementing strategy;
- appreciate the basic principles that determine the structural characteristics of complex human organizations;
- select the organizational structure best suited to a particular business context;
- recognize how companies have been changing their organizational structures in recent years and the forces that have been driving these changes;
- appreciate the role an organization's culture plays in realizing strategy.

Opening Case

BP's environmental disasters

In 2006, BP came 23rd on *Fortune* magazine's list of the World's Most Admired Companies and third among European companies; by 2014, BP had dropped off the top-50 list and ranked behind all the other international oil majors. Over the same period, its market capitalization had declined by $37.4 billion.

Deepwater Horizon, Texas City and more

The reason for BP's fall from grace was not hard to fathom. In April 2010, Transocean's *Deepwater Horizon* offshore oilrig drilling BP's Macondo oil well in the Gulf of Mexico exploded and caught fire, killing 11 workers and triggering one of the worst environmental disasters in US history. The company took an accounting charge of $37.2 billion – its estimate of the likely costs of clean-up, compensation and legal penalties.

However, the Macondo disaster was not an isolated event. In 2000, a series of major safety failures at BP's Grangemouth refinery in Scotland had prompted an investigation by Britain's Health and Safety Executive. In 2005, a massive explosion ripped through BP's Texas City refinery in the US, killing 15 workers and injuring 170 others. The following year, 4800 barrels of oil leaked from a corroded section of BP's pipeline from its massive Prudhoe Bay oilfield in Alaska and, shortly before the Macondo blow-out, BP was fined $3 million for safety violations at its Toledo, Ohio refinery.

While the civil and criminal legal proceedings that followed the Macondo disaster focused on issues of negligence and the allocation of responsibility between BP and its contractors, Transocean, Cameron International and Halliburton, attention was also drawn to BP's corporate strategy and to the organizational structure, management systems and corporate culture through which that strategy was implemented.

Strategy, structure, systems and culture

From 1913 to 1979, BP was majority owned by the British government. Between 1979 and 1987, BP was privatized, inaugurating a new era of growth and regeneration. As a shareholder-owned company, BP shed its bureaucratic culture and became an industry leader in innovation and entrepreneurial dynamism. Its acquisitions of Amoco, Atlantic Richfield and Burmah Castrol made BP the world's third-biggest petroleum major and precipitated an industry-wide wave of consolidation.

Under John Browne, CEO from 1995 to 2007, BP underwent a profound strategic and organizational transformation. Committed to the creation of shareholder value, he restructured its business portfolio, shedding poorly performing downstream businesses, outsourcing non-core activities, shifting resources towards exploration in frontier regions (such as Russia, Azerbaijan, Vietnam and deep-sea locations in the Gulf of Mexico and elsewhere) and engaging in vigorous cost cutting.

The pursuit of shareholder value was accompanied by a radical decentralization of the company. Browne's concept of an 'atomic structure' was based upon the premise that 'people work better in small units because the closer you can identify people to objectives and targets, the better things happen'.[2] Instead of BP's business units being combined into divisions, each of the 150 business units reported directly to the corporate centre, where the relationship was governed by a 'performance contract': an agreement between the head of the business unit and the corporate centre over the performance that the business would deliver in the year ahead. While the performance targets included strategic and operational goals – including health, safety and environmental (HSE) objectives – the primary emphasis was on financial performance (including net income and net cash flow). To help them attain their stretch targets, the 150 business units were divided into 15 'peer groups' – networks of similar businesses that could collaborate in sharing knowledge and matters of common interest while also challenging one another. In the process headquarters staff was cut from 2000 to 350. Business unit and peer group performance became major determinants of managers' compensation. Browne believed that the new management system would release creativity and empower the talented people within the company, allowing them to be 'entrepreneurs not bureaucrats'.

Browne also envisaged the new BP as being more open and responsive to the needs of society, particularly in recognizing and responding to climate change. As the *Oil & Gas Journal* reported:

> Among the top 10 [oil and gas companies] there is one striking example of a company driven by a different vision. BP has designated corporate citizenship and being forward-thinking about the environment, human rights and dealing with people and ethics and as the new fulcrum of competition between the oil companies.[3]

In 2007, Tony Hayward took over from Browne as CEO and instigated further changes to BP's management model. A consulting report from Bain and Co. declared that BP was the most complicated organization they had ever come across with more than 10 000 organizational interfaces and encouraged Hayward to introduce his 'forward agenda', which emphasized cost cutting and simplification. Hayward eliminated regional structures, streamlined functional structures and reduced the number of senior executives from 650 to 500 – 50% of whom were new to their roles. Hayward also cited safety as a key priority within BP.[4]

Were BP's structure, systems and culture to blame?

Investigation of the causes of BP's environmental and safety incidents have focused on the decision and management systems of the particular units involved, notably the *Deepwater Horizon* rig and the Texas City refinery.[5] However, all the official inquiries have commented on the role of BP's corporate management in these failures. Several features of BP's management system compromised safety and raised wider issues over its fit with the requirements of the petroleum business:

- *Corporate goals:* Under Browne's leadership, BP committed to delivering superior returns to shareholders. For the business units this translated into short-term targets for profits and cash flows. Yet, the petroleum business comprises long-term projects: a deep-water oilfield such as Macondo may take 10 years to develop and may continue producing for over 20 years. Short-term financial targets may encourage decisions that conflict with creating shareholder value over the long term.
- *Performance metrics:* Establishing and monitoring performance targets can reconcile decentralized decision making with overall coordination, but only if the targets

encourage the right decisions. In safety, BP's key performance metric was number of days lost through injury. While conducive to improvements in personal safety, this metric did not help BP in improving its process safety.

- *Systems and culture:* Decentralization is suited to businesses where success depends on the effectiveness of local decisions and their implementation (e.g. a retail chain). At high levels of complexity, especially where the costs of failure are very high, management based upon centralized rules and standardized procedures may be more appropriate. The entrepreneurial culture that Browne sought for BP owed much to his admiration for Silicon Valley and his experience as a board member at Intel and Goldman Sachs. But how appropriate was such a culture for a company engaged in multi-billion-dollar projects, operating in a high-risk environment where major deals were negotiated with heads of state and their ministers?

From strategy to execution

Strategic management has conventionally been viewed as a two-stage process: first formulation and then implementation. As we observed in Chapter 1, the notion of strategic management as a top-down process in which top management formulates then the lower levels of the organization implement has been challenged by Henry Mintzberg. His strategy-as-process view recognized that in the process of implementation the 'intended strategy' is reformulated and redirected by the 'emergent strategy'.[6]

The notion that strategic management can be separated into self-contained formulation and implementation stages is wrong. The intended strategy of any organization is inevitably incomplete: it comprises goals, directions and priorities, but it can never be a comprehensive plan. It is during the implementation phase that the gaps are filled in and, because circumstances change and unforeseen issues arise, inevitably the strategy changes. At the same time, strategy formulation must take account of the conditions of implementation. The observation 'Great strategy; lousy implementation' is typically a misdiagnosis of strategic failure: a strategy that has been formulated without taking account of its ability to be implemented is a poorly formulated strategy. The conventional formulation–implementation sequence is summed up in the adage 'Structure follows strategy'. Yet, management guru Tom Peters argues the reverse: for Domino's Pizza, with its global network of 8000 franchised outlets, or Amway, with its pyramid of commission-based, independent distributors, the structure *is* the strategy.

Clearly, strategy formulation and implementation are interdependent. Nevertheless, the fact remains that purposeful behaviour requires action to be preceded by intention. Hence, a feature of all the strategic planning systems that we have encountered is recognition that a strategy cannot be implemented until it has been formulated. In this strategy process, formulation is linked to implementation by systems of operational planning, performance management and resource allocation.

The strategic planning system: Linking strategy to action

Small enterprises can operate successfully without an explicit strategy. If the business comprises a sole owner or a single family, the firm's strategy may exist only in the head of the owner-manager. Unless that owner-manager needs to write a business plan in order to attract outside financing, the strategy may never be articulated. There is no need to articulate the strategy because implementation is by the owner-manager, who knows what is in his/her own head.

Once the top management of a business comprises more than one person, strategy formulation has to become explicit. When they founded Apple Computer, Steve Jobs and Steve Wozniak each had ideas about what Apple II should be like and how it would be built and marketed. Agreeing a strategy required discussion between them. At many family firms, strategy is decided at the kitchen table.

As companies get larger, so the process of strategy making needs to be more formalized. Meetings must be held to allow managers to bring their different areas of knowledge, ideas and perceptions together and to make decisions. Documents need to be created in order to communicate analysis and decisions from one part of the organization to another. A procedure needs to be established so that individuals and groups commit to the strategies that have been agreed.

THE ANNUAL STRATEGIC PLANNING CYCLE Most large companies have a regular (normally annual, sometime bi-annual) strategic planning process that results in a document that is endorsed at the highest level of the company, normally the board of directors. The strategic planning process is a systematized approach that assembles information, shares perceptions, conducts analysis, reaches decisions, ensures consistency among those decisions and commits managers to courses of action and performance targets.

Strategic planning processes vary between organizations. At some it is highly centralized. Even after the entrepreneurial start-up has grown into a large company, strategy making may remain the preserve of the chief executive. At MCI Communications, former CEO Orville Wright observed: 'We do it strictly top-down at MCI.'[7] At General Electric Company, Inc. and BP plc, the strategic planning process is more decentralized, driven primarily by bottom-up initiatives.

As companies mature, their strategic planning processes become more systematized and typically follow an annual cycle. Strategic plans tend to be for three to five years and combine top-down initiatives and directives and bottom-up strategy proposals. Figure 9.1 shows a typical strategic planning cycle. The principal stages are:

- The CEO typically initiates the process with some clear indications of strategic priorities – these will be influenced by the outcome of the previous performance reviews. In addition, the strategic planning unit may also offer input into the process in the form of assumptions or forecasts that provide a common basis for strategic planning by different units and levels within the organization. (Shell's 2011–2014 planning was undertaken as one of two alternative oil market scenarios: $60 a barrel and $80 a barrel.)
- On the basis of this framework of priorities and planning assumptions, the different organizational units (divisions and functional departments) create their strategic plans, which are then presented at a series of review meetings (usually typically each involving a half-day or full day). On the basis of commentary from the CEO, CFO and head of strategy (typically), the business plans are then revised.

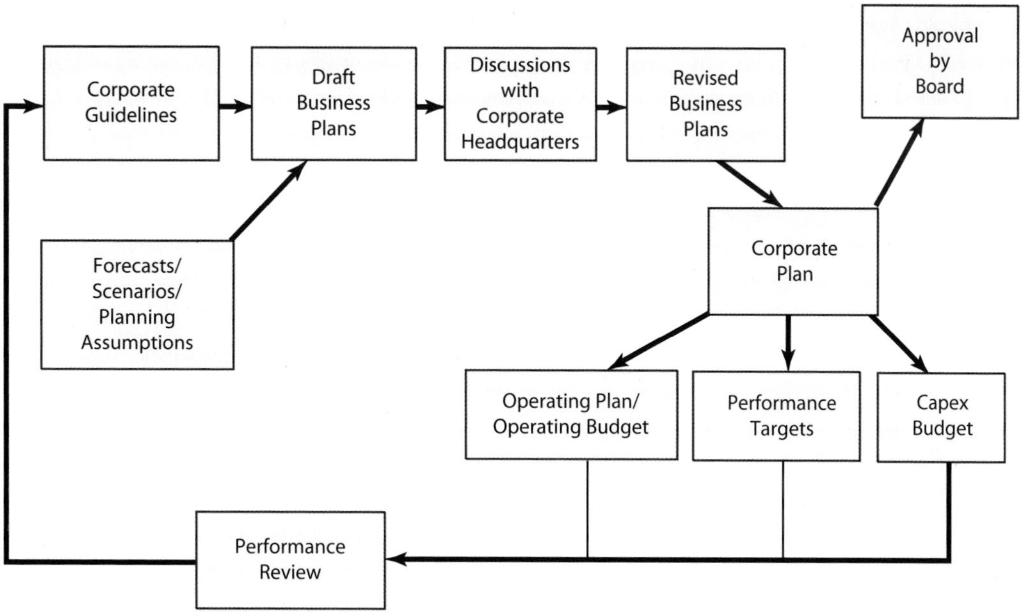

Figure 9.1 The generic annual strategic planning cycle.

Once agreed, the business plans are integrated to create the corporate strategic plan that is then presented to the board for approval.

THE CONTENT OF STRATEGIC PLANS A strategic plan typically comprises the elements shown in Case Insight 9.1.

Case Insight 9.1

The contents of a strategic plan: Illustrations from BP

Main components of a strategic plan	Examples from BP's strategic plan for 2012–2014
Corporate priorities: both strategic (e.g. gaining market leadership, portfolio rebalancing, competitive repositioning, new business development) and financial (e.g. sales growth, boosting profitability, debt reduction)	Goals: to be a focused oil and gas company that delivers value over volume; to create shareholder value by generating sustainable free cash flow (operating cash flow less net investment), which will enable the company to invest for the future while aiming to increase distributions to its investors. Key differentiators: advanced technology, strong relationships with governments, customers and suppliers, and proven expertise, maintained by attracting and developing talented people

Main components of a strategic plan	Examples from BP's strategic plan for 2012–2014
Priorities of business strategies in terms of primary basis for competitive advantage (e.g. cost-reduction initiatives, innovation goals)	Safe, reliable and compliant operations Disciplined financial choices Competitive project delivery
Strategic milestones: target dates for initiating or completing specific targets or for reaching certain performance goals	A 10-point plan which includes, amongst other things: a relentless focus on safety and managing risks through the systematic application of global standards; playing to company strengths in exploration, deep water, giant fields and gas value chains; simpler and more standardized with fewer assets and operations in fewer countries; more streamlined internal reward and performance management processes
Resource commitments	Annual capital expenditure $24–$25 billion 2012–14, rising to $26 billion 2015–2018. Upstream investments in exploration for gas in India, increasing oil production in Azerbaijan, major projects in the North Sea and Gulf of Mexico.
Performance targets and financial projections	*Financial*: Gearing target of 10–20% $10 billion of planned divestment by end of 2014 *Exploration*: 15 new exploration wells by end of 2014 *Production*: Improving refining availability *Downstream*: Increase crude processing at Whiting refinery to 280 000 barrels a day. Cease operations at Bulwer Island refinery, Australia by end of 2015 *Safety*: Year-on-year reductions in injury frequency. Year-on-year reductions in Tier 1 process safety events (loss of primary containment of the greatest consequence – causing harm to a member of the workforce, costly damage to equipment or exceeding defined quantities).

Although strategic planning tends to emphasize the specific commitments and decisions that are documented in written strategic plans, the most important aspect of strategic planning is the strategy process: the dialogue through which knowledge is shared and ideas communicated, and a consensus established. As General (later President) Dwight Eisenhower observed: 'Plans are nothing; planning is everything.' General von Moltke of Prussia made a similar point a century earlier: 'No battle plan survives contact with the enemy.'

Changes in strategic planning processes in recent decades have taken account of the need for flexibility and adaptation. Companies recognized the impossibility of forecasting the future and based their strategies less on medium- and long-term economic and market forecasts and more on general issues of strategic direction (in the form of vision, mission and strategic intent) and alternative views of the future (e.g. using scenario analysis). Planning horizons have also shortened (two to five years is the typical planning period). The plans themselves have become less concerned with specific actions and more heavily oriented towards establishing overall performance goals.

In terms of process, strategic planning shifted from a control perspective, in which senior management used the strategic planning mechanisms as a means of controlling decisions and resource deployments by organizational units towards a coordination perspective emphasizing dialogue, knowledge sharing and consensus building. The result has been, first, that the strategic planning process has become increasingly informal with less emphasis on written documents and, second, that the role of strategic planning staff has diminished: responsibility for strategy making has been placed on the shoulders of line managers.[8]

THE LINK WITH IMPLEMENTATION The strategy process achieves nothing unless the strategy is implemented. The key to strategy execution is achieved by linking the strategy process to action, through the operating plan; to motivation and accountability, through performance management; and to resource allocation, through capital budgeting. These implementation phases of the strategic planning process are shown in Figure 9.1.

Operating plans

Implementing a strategy requires breaking down medium-term planning into a series of short-term plans that can be a focus for action and a basis for performance monitoring. At the basis of the annual operating plan are a set of performance targets that are derived from the series of annual plans. These performance targets are both financial (sales growth, margins, returns on capital) and operational (inventory turns, defect rates, number of new outlets opened). Goal setting typically starts with the overall goals of the organization, which are disaggregated into more specific performance goals as we move down the organization. This approach to implementing strategy through establishing performance targets (not just for every organizational unit but also for every employee) has been widely used for over a half a century: 'management by objectives' (the process of participative goal setting) was proposed by Peter Drucker in 1954.[9]

These performance targets become built into the annual operating budget. The **operating budget** is a pro forma profit-and-loss statement for the company as a whole and for individual divisions and business units for the upcoming year. It is usually divided into quarters and months to permit continual monitoring and the early identification of variances. The operating budget is part forecast and part target: it is set within the context of the performance targets established by the strategic plan. Each business typically prepares an operating budget for the following year that is then discussed with the top management committee and, if acceptable, approved. In some organizations the budgeting process is part of the strategic planning system: the operating budget is used as the basis for the first year of the strategic plan; in others, budgeting follows strategic planning.

Operational planning is more than setting performance targets and agreeing budgets; it also involves planning specific activities. As Bossidy and Charan explain: 'An operating plan includes the programs your business is going to complete within one year ... Among these programs are product launches; the marketing plan; a sales plan that takes advantage of market opportunities; a manufacturing plan that stipulates production outputs; and a productivity plan that improves efficiency.'[10]

Allocating resources: Capital expenditure budgeting

Capital expenditure budgets are established through both top-down and bottom-up processes. When organizational units prepare their business plans, they will indicate the major projects they plan to undertake during the strategic planning period and the capital expenditures involved. When top management aggregates business plans to create the corporate plan, it establishes capital expenditure budgets both for the company as a whole and for the individual business units.

It is then up to the individual units to submit capital expenditure requests for specific projects. Companies have standardized processes for evaluating and approving projects. Requests for funding are prepared according to a standardized methodology, typically based on a forecast of cash flows, which are then discounted at the company's cost of capital (adjusted to take account of the project's level of risk). The extent to which the project's returns are sensitive to key environmental uncertainties is also estimated. Capital expenditure approvals take place at different levels of a company according to their size. Projects of up to $5 million may be approved by a business unit head; projects up to $25 million may be approved by divisional top management; larger projects may need to be approved by the top management committee, while the biggest projects require approval by the board of directors.

Organizational design: The fundamentals of organizing

Implementing strategy is not just about strategic planning processes and linking them to goal setting, operational activities and resource allocation. Strategy implementation encompasses the entire design of the organization. How a firm is organized determines its capacity for action. We saw in Chapter 3 that the design of processes and structures is fundamental to organizational capabilities. The same is true in war: from the conquests of the Roman legions, to the one-sided outcome of the Franco-Prussian War (1870–1871) and the Israeli victories in the Six-Day War (1967) and Yom Kippur War (1973), organizational superiority has played a critical role in military success.

Business enterprises come in many shapes and sizes. Samsung Corporation and Louie's Sandwich Bar on 32nd Street, New York share few organizational commonalities. When we include social enterprises, we expand the range of organizations even further. Despite their diversity, all business enterprises face the same challenge of designing structures and systems that match the particular circumstances of their own situation. In the same way that strategic management is a quest for unique solutions to the matching of internal resources and capabilities to external business opportunity, so organizational design is about selecting structures, systems and management styles that can best implement such strategies. To establish principles, guidelines and criteria for designing business organizations we need to consider the fundamental challenges of organizing.

To design a firm we must first recognize what it is supposed to do. According to Henry Mintzberg:

> Every organized human activity – from making pots to placing a man on the moon – gives rise to two fundamental and opposing requirements: the division of labor into various tasks, and the coordination of these tasks to accomplish the activity. The structure of the organization can be defined simply as the ways in which labor is divided into distinct tasks and coordination is achieved among these tasks.[11]

Specialization and division of labour

Firms exist because of their efficiency advantages in producing goods and services. The fundamental source of efficiency in production is specialization through the division of labour into separate tasks. The classic statement on the gains due to specialization is Adam Smith's description of pin manufacture:

> One man draws out the wire, another straightens it, a third cuts it, a fourth points it, a fifth grinds it at the top for receiving the head; to make the head requires two or three distinct operations; to put it on is a peculiar business, to whiten the pins is another; it is even a trade by itself to put them into the papers.[12]

Smith's pin makers produced about 4800 pins per person each day. 'But if they had all wrought separately and independently and without any of them having been educated to this peculiar business, they certainly could not each have made 20, perhaps not one pin, in a day.' Similarly, Henry Ford achieved huge productivity gains by his assembly line system that assigned individuals to highly specific tasks. Between the end of 1912 and early 1914, the time taken to assemble a Model T fell from 106 hours to six hours.

But specialization comes at a cost. The more a production process is divided between different specialists, the more complex is the challenge of integrating the efforts of individual specialists. Integrating the efforts of specialist individuals involves two organizational problems: there is the *cooperation problem* – that of aligning the interests of individuals who have divergent goals – and the *coordination problem* – even in the absence of goal conflict, how do individuals harmonize their different activities?

The cooperation problem

The economics literature analyses cooperation problems arising from differing goals in terms of the concept of 'agency'.[13] An **agency relationship** exists when one party (the principal) contracts with another party (the agent) to act on behalf of the principal. The problem for the principal is ensuring that the agent acts in his or her interest. Economics scholars usually focus on the agency problem between owners (shareholders) and managers and see the main issue for today's businesses as ensuring that professional managers run companies in ways that maximize shareholder wealth. During the 1990s, changes in the ways top management were rewarded – in particular placing greater emphasis on share options – were intended to align the interests of managers with those of shareholders.[14] However, at Enron, WorldCom and other companies, these incentives induced managers to manipulate reported earnings rather than to work for long-term profitability.

Agency problems do not just exist between managers and owners of firms. For individual employees, systems of incentives, monitoring and appraisal are designed to encourage the pursuit of organizational objectives and overcome employees' tendency to do their own thing or simply to take it easy. The way an organization is structured can add to the challenge. Organizational departments frequently have their own subgoals and these can be at odds with those of other departments. The classic conflicts are between different functions: sales wishes to please customers, production wishes to maximize output, R & D wants to introduce mind-blowing new products while finance worries about profit and loss.

Several mechanisms are available to managers to try to align the goals of different individuals and groups within organizations:

- Control mechanisms typically operate through hierarchical supervision. Managers supervise the behaviour and performance of subordinates who must seek approval for their actions that lie outside their defined area of discretion. Control is enforced through positive and negative incentives: the primary positive incentive is the opportunity for promotion up the hierarchy; negative incentives are dismissal and demotion.

- Performance incentives link rewards to outputs: these kinds of incentives include piece-rates for production workers and profit bonuses for executives. Such performance-related incentives are seen as having two main benefits: first, they are high powered – that is to say they relate rewards directly to output – and second, they economize on the need for costly monitoring and supervision. Pay-for-performance becomes more difficult when output is difficult to measure.
- Shared values. Some organizations are able to achieve high levels of cooperation and low levels of goal conflict without extensive explicit control mechanisms or performance-related incentives. Churches, charities, clubs and voluntary organizations typically display a commonality of purpose and values among members. Shared values encourage the perceptions and views of organizational members to converge, which facilitates consensus and avoids conflict. In doing so, shared values can act as a control mechanism that is an alternative to bureaucratic control or financial incentives – Bill Ouchi refers to this as 'clan control'.[15] An organization's values are one component of its culture.

The coordination problem

The desire to cooperate is not enough to ensure that organizational members integrate their efforts – it is not lack of a common goal that causes Olympic sprint teams to drop the baton. Unless individuals can find ways of coordinating their efforts, production doesn't happen. Among the mechanisms for coordination, the following can be found in all firms:

- *Rules and instructions:* A basic feature of the firm is the existence of general employment contracts under which individuals agree to perform a range of duties as required by their employer. This allows managers to exercise authority by means of 'general rules' ('Secret agents on overseas missions will have essential expenses reimbursed only on production of original receipts') and 'specific instructions' ('Miss Moneypenny, show Mr Bond his new cigarette case with 4G communication and a concealed death ray').
- *Routines:* Where activities are performed recurrently, coordination based on mutual adjustment and rules becomes institutionalized within organizational routines. As we noted in Chapter 3, these regular and predictable sequences of coordinated actions by individuals are the foundation of organizational capability. If organizations are to perform complex activities at extreme levels of efficiency and reliability, coordination by rules, directives or mutual adjustment is not enough: coordination must become embedded in routines.
- *Mutual adjustment:* The simplest form of coordination involves the mutual adjustment of individuals engaged in related tasks. In soccer, each player coordinates with fellow team members without any authority relationship among them. Such mutual adjustment occurs in leaderless teams and is especially suited to novel tasks where routinization is not feasible.

The relative roles of these different coordination devices depend on the types of activity being performed and the intensity of collaboration required. Rules tend to work well for activities where standardized outcomes are required – most quality control procedures involve the application of simple rules. Routines form the basis for coordination in most activities where close interdependence exists between individuals, whether a basic production task (supplying customers at Starbucks) or a more complex activity (performing a heart bypass operation or implementing a systems integration project for a multinational corporation).

Case Insight 9.2

Co-ordination and control

With 84 000 employees in 80 countries spread across several hundred occupational categories, BP, like all companies, faces significant challenges in ensuring cooperation and coordination to achieve corporate goals.

Cooperation problems arise because employees' interests do not align with those of shareholders (as represented by a company's board of directors). In the case of health, safety and environmental policies (HSE), such a conflict of interest is not apparent: employees do not wish to be killed, injured or blamed for mishaps; shareholders do not want to bear the massive costs accidents impose. (A key lesson from the *Exxon Valdez* and BP Macondo oil spillages is their huge impact on the companies' profits and share prices.) However, this community of interest needs to be reflected in the controls and incentives that determine employee behaviour. Traditionally, HSE goals are enforced through bureaucratic means – directives and procedures imposed from above. However, in the decentralized, performance-based management system created by Browne, cooperation was achieved primarily through performance targets reinforced through financial incentives. Such a system did not lend itself to excellence in safety management, particularly since it was difficult to select performance targets that encouraged appropriate risk management behaviour. At the same time, the cultural changes introduced at BP shifted the value system: encouragement to entrepreneurship, initiative and innovation implies a very different attitude towards risk than that required for accident prevention,

In terms of coordination, BP's shift from a vertical structure based on hierarchy and bureaucracy to a horizontal structure based on teams and peer groups meant that coordination was achieved less through rules and instructions and more through mutual adjustment. Yet, achieving risk prevention in complex processes such as drilling oil wells and operating refineries is likely to require precise, highly systematized processes where adherence can only be ensured through meticulous attention to rules. A report into *Deepwater Horizon* pointed to the limits of mutual adjustment and collaborative decision making: a lack of coordination of critical procedures and the failure to refer decisions to higher authorities resulted in warning signs of imminent danger going undetected.[16] Ultimately, rules and procedures become embodied in routines. However, the evidence from both the Texas City and *Deepwater Horizon* inquiries suggests that the constant flow of new corporate initiatives together with BP's outsourcing (which meant that safety procedures required coordination among the employees of different firms) impeded the development of high-reliability operating routines.

Hierarchy in organizational design

Hierarchy is the fundamental feature of organizational structure. It is the primary means by which companies achieve specialization, coordination and cooperation. Despite the negative images hierarchy often stimulates, it is a feature of all complex human organizations and is essential for efficiency and flexibility. The critical issue is not whether to organize by hierarchy – there is little alternative – but how the hierarchy should be structured and how the various parts should be linked.

HIERARCHY AS CONTROL: BUREAUCRACY Hierarchy is an organizational form in which members of the organization are arranged in vertical layers; at intermediate layers, each individual reports to a superior and has subordinates to supervise and monitor. Hierarchy offers a solution to the problem of cooperation through the imposition of top-down control.

As an administrative mechanism for exercising centralized power, hierarchy was a feature of the government system of the Ch'in dynasty of China in the late third century BC and has been a feature of all large organizations in the fields of public administration, religion and the military. For Max Weber, 'the father of organizational theory', hierarchy was the central feature of his system of bureaucracy, which involved: 'each lower office under the control and supervision of a higher one'; a 'systematic division of labor'; formalization in writing of 'administrative acts, decisions, and rules'; and work governed by standardized rules and operating procedures, where authority is based on 'belief in the legality of enacted rules and the right of those elevated to authority under such rules to issue commands'.[17]

Weber's preference for rationality and efficiency over cronyism and personal use of hierarchical authority typical of his time encouraged organizational designs that sought safeguards against human traits such as emotion, creativity, fellowship and idiosyncrasies of personality. As a result bureaucratic organizations have been referred to as 'mechanistic'[18] or as 'machine bureaucracies'.[19]

HIERARCHY AS COORDINATION: MODULARITY In a general sense, hierarchy is a feature of almost all complex systems, for example:[20]

- Political systems are often organized as hierarchies, with authority running from federal government down to state, city, town and then borough or municipality, depending on the place.
- The military is developed as a hierarchy. In the British Army, for example, a field marshal ranks above a general, a general above a major and a major above a captain.
- Religious organizations are frequently hierarchical. The pope, for example, heads the Catholic Church and is served by bishops, who in turn are assisted by priests.

The advantages of hierarchical structures in coordinating include:

- *Economizing on coordination:* Suppose we launch a consulting firm with five partners. If we structure the firm as a 'self-organized team' where coordination is by mutual adjustment (Figure 9.2a), 10 bilateral interactions must be managed. Alternatively, if we appoint the partner with the biggest feet as managing partner (Figure 9.2b), there are only four relationships to be managed. Of course, this says nothing about the quality of the coordination: for routine tasks such as assigning partners to projects, the hierarchical

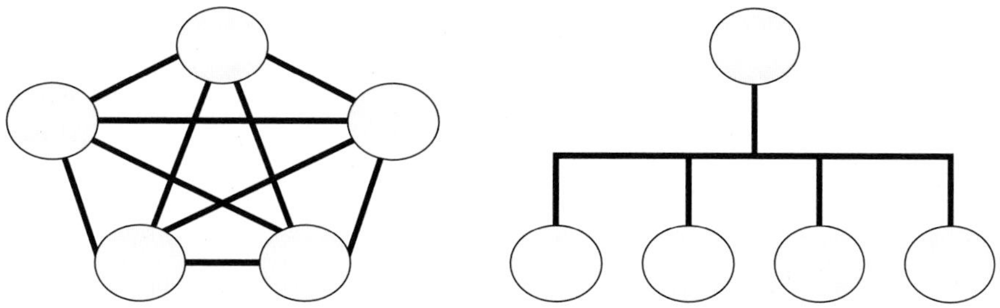

Figure 9.2 How hierarchy economizes on coordination.

structure is clearly advantageous; for complex problem solving, the partners are better reverting to a self-organizing team to thrash out a solution. The larger the number of organizational members, the greater the efficiency benefits from organizing hierarchically. Microsoft's Windows 8 development team involved about 3200 software development engineers, test engineers and program managers. These were organized into 35 'feature teams', each of which was divided into a number of component teams. As a result, each engineer needed to coordinate only with the members of his or her immediate team. The modular structure of the Windows 8 development team mirrors the modular structure of the product.

- *Adaptability:* Hierarchical, modular systems can evolve more rapidly than unitary systems. This adaptability requires 'decomposability': the ability of each component subsystem to operate with some measure of independence from the other subsystems. Modular systems that allow significant independence for each module are referred to as 'loosely coupled'.[21] The modular structure of Windows 8 allows a single feature team to introduce innovative product features and innovative software solutions without the need to coordinate with all 34 other teams. The key requirement is that the different modules must fit together – this requires a standardized interface. The multidivisional firm is a modular structure. At Procter & Gamble, decisions about developing new shampoos can be made by the Global Hair Care division without involving the Global Fabric Care, Global Health Care or Duracell divisions. A divisional structure also makes it easier for Procter & Gamble to add new businesses (Gillette, Wella) or to divest them (Folgers Coffee, Pringles).[22]

Contingency approaches to organizational design

Like strategy, organizational design has been afflicted by the desire to find the 'best' way of organizing. During the first half of the 20th century, bureaucracy and scientific management were believed to be the best way of organizing. During the 1950s and 1960s, the human relations school recognized that cooperation and coordination within organizations was about social relationships, which bureaucracy stifled through inertia and alienation: Theory X had been challenged by Theory Y.

However, empirical studies pointed to different organizational characteristics being suited to different circumstances. Among Scottish engineering companies, Burns and Stalker found

Table 9.1 Mechanistic versus organic organizational forms.

Feature	Mechanistic forms	Organic forms
Task definition	Rigid and highly specialized	Flexible and broadly defined
Coordination and control	Rules and directives vertically imposed	Mutual adjustment, common culture
Communication	Vertical	Vertical and horizontal
Knowledge	Centralized	Dispersed
Commitment and loyalty	To immediate superior	To the organization and its goals
Environmental context	Stable with low technological uncertainty	Dynamic with significant technological uncertainty and ambiguity

Source: Adapted from Richard Butler, *Designing Organizations: A Decision-Making Perspective* (London: Routledge, 1991): 76 with permission from Taylor and Francis.

that firms in stable environments had 'mechanistic forms', characterized by bureaucracy; those in less stable markets had 'organic forms' that were less formal and more flexible.[23] Table 9.1 contrasts key characteristics of the two forms.

By the 1970s, 'contingency theory' – the idea there was no one best way to organize; it depended upon the strategy being pursued, the technology employed and the surrounding environment – had become widely accepted.[24] Although Google and McDonald's are of similar sizes in terms of revenue, their structures and systems are very different. McDonald's is highly bureaucratized, with high levels of job specialization, formal systems and a strong emphasis on rules and procedures. Google emphasizes informality, low job specialization, horizontal communication and the importance of principles over rules. These differences reflect differences in strategy, technology, human resources and the dynamism of the business environments that each firm occupies. In general, the more standardized goods or services (beverage cans, blood tests, or haircuts for army inductees) are and the more stable the environment is, the greater are the efficiency advantages of the bureaucratic model with its standard operating procedures and high levels of specialization. Once markets become turbulent, innovation becomes desirable or buyers require customized products, the bureaucratic model breaks down.

These contingency factors also cause functions within companies to be organized differently. Stable, standardized activities such as payroll, treasury, taxation, customer support and purchasing activities tend to operate well when organized along bureaucratic principles; research, new product development, marketing and strategic planning require more organic modes of organization.

As the business environment has become increasingly turbulent, the trend has been towards organic approaches to organizing, which have tended to displace more bureaucratic approaches. Since the mid-1980s, almost all large companies have made strenuous efforts to restructure and reorganize in order to achieve greater flexibility and responsiveness. Within their multidivisional structures, companies have decentralized decision making, reduced their number of hierarchical layers, shrunk headquarters staffs, emphasized horizontal rather than vertical communication and shifted the emphasis of control from supervision to accountability.

However, the trend has not been one way. The financial crisis of 2008 and its aftermath have caused many companies to re-impose top-down control. Greater awareness of the need to manage financial, environmental and political risks in sectors such as financial services, petroleum and mining have also reinforced centralized control and reliance on rules. It is possible that the cycles of centralization and decentralization many companies exhibit are a means of managing the trade-off between integration and flexible responsiveness.[25]

Developments in ICT have worked in different directions. In some cases, the automation of processes has permitted their centralization and bureaucratization (think of the customer service activities of your bank or telecom supplier). In other areas, ICT has encouraged informal approaches to coordination. The huge leaps in the availability of information available to organizational members and the ease with which they can communicate with one another has increased vastly the capacity for mutual adjustment without the need for intensive hierarchical guidance and leadership.

Organizational design: Choosing the right structure

We have established that the basic feature of organizations is hierarchy. In order to undertake complex tasks, people need to be grouped into organizational units, and cooperation and coordination need to be established among these units. The key organizational questions are now:

- On what basis should specialized units be defined?
- How should decision-making authority be allocated?
- How should the different organizational units be assembled for the purposes of coordination and control?

In this section, we tackle two central issues in the design of organizations. First, on what basis should individuals be grouped into organizational units? Second, how should organizational units be configured into overall organizational structures?

Defining organizational units

In creating a hierarchical structure, on what basis are individuals assigned to organizational units within the firm? This issue is fundamental and complex. Multinational, multiproduct companies are continually grappling with the issue of whether they should be structured around product divisions, country subsidiaries or functional departments, and periodically they undergo the disruption of changing from one to another. Employees can be grouped on the basis of:

- *common tasks:* cleaners will be assigned to maintenance services and teachers will be assigned to a unit called a 'faculty';
- *products:* shelf fillers and customer services assistants will be assigned to one of the following departments: kitchen goods, tableware, bedding or domestic appliances;
- *location:* the 141 000 associates that work in Starbucks stores are organized by location: each store employs an average of 16 people;
- *process:* in most production plants, employees are organized by process: assembly, quality control, warehousing, shipping. Processes tend to be grouped into functions.

How do we decide whether to use task, product, geography or process to define organizational units? The fundamental issue is 'intensity of coordination needs': those individuals who need to interact most closely should be located within the same organizational unit. In the case of Starbucks, the individual stores are the natural units: the manager, the baristas and the cleaners at a single location need to form a single organizational unit. British Airways needs to be organized by processes and functions: the employees engaged in particular processes – flying, in-flight services, baggage handling, aircraft maintenance and accounts – need to be working in the same organizational units. These process units can then be combined into broader functional groupings: flight operations, engineering, marketing, sales, customer service, human resources, information and finance.

This principle of grouping individuals according to the intensity of their coordination needs was developed by James Thompson in his analysis of interdependence within organizations. He distinguished three levels of interdependence: 'pooled interdependence' (the loosest), where individuals operate independently but depend on one another's performance; 'sequential interdependence', where the output of one individual is the input of the other; and 'reciprocal interdependence' (the most intense), where individuals are mutually dependent. At the first level of organization, priority should be given to creating organizational units for reciprocally interdependent employees (e.g. members of an oilfield drilling team or consultants working on a client assignment).[26]

In general, the priorities for the first level of organization tend to be clear: it is usually fairly obvious whether employees need to be organized by task, process or location. How the lower-level organizational units should be grouped into broader organizational units tends to be less clear. In 1921, it was far from obvious as to whether DuPont would be better off with its functional structure or reorganized into product divisions. In taking over as Procter & Gamble's CEO in 2000, A. G. Lafley needed to decide whether to keep P&G's new-product divisional structure or revert to the previous structure in which the regional organizations were dominant.

In deciding how to organize the upper levels of firm structure, the same principle applies. At Nestlé, it is more important for the managers of the chocolate plants to coordinate with the marketing and sales executives for chocolate than with the plant manager for Evian bottled water: Nestlé is better organized around product divisions than around functions. Hyundai Motor produces a number of different models of car and is present in many countries of the world; however, given its global strategy and the close linkages between its different models, Hyundai is better organized by function rather than by product or geography.

Over time, the relative importance of these different coordination needs changes, causing firms to change their structures. The process of globalization has involved easier trade and communication between countries and growing similarities in consumer preferences. As a result multinational corporations have shifted from geographically based structures to worldwide product divisions.

Alternative structural forms: Functional, multidivisional, matrix

On the basis of these alternative approaches to grouping tasks and activities, we can identify three basic organizational forms for companies: the **functional structure**, the **multidivisional structure** and the **matrix structure**.

THE FUNCTIONAL STRUCTURE Single-business firms tend to be organized along functional lines (Figure 9.3). Grouping together functionally similar tasks is conducive to exploiting scale economies, promoting learning and capability building and deploying standardized control systems. Since cross-functional integration occurs at the top of the organization, functional structures are conducive to a high degree of centralized control by the CEO and top management team.

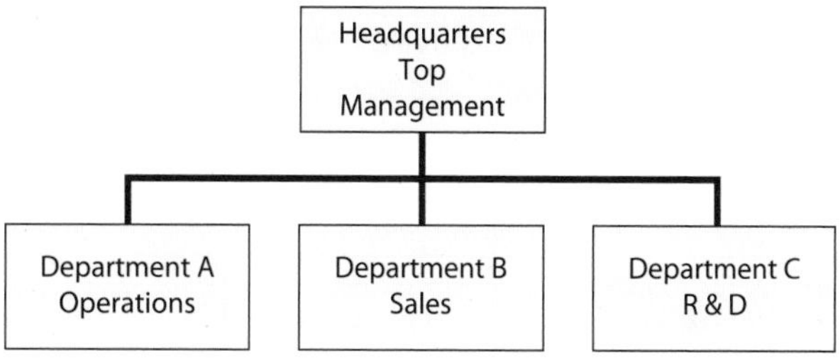

Figure 9.3 A simple functional structure.

However, even for single-product firms, functional structures are subject to the problems of cooperation and coordination. Different functional departments develop their own goals, values, vocabularies and behavioural norms, which makes cross-functional integration difficult. As the size of the firm increases, the pressure on top management to achieve effective integration increases. Because the different functions of the firm tend to be tightly rather than loosely coupled, there is limited scope for decentralization. In particular, it is very difficult to operate individual functions as semi-autonomous profit centres.

The real problems arise when the firm grows its range of products and businesses. Once a functionally organized company expands its product range, coordination within each product area becomes difficult.

However, as companies and their industries mature, the need for efficiency, centralized control and well-developed functional capabilities can cause companies to revert to functional structures. For example:

- When John Scully became CEO of Apple in 1984, the company was organized by product: Apple II, Apple III, Lisa and Macintosh. Cross-functional coordination within each product was strong, but there was little integration across products: each had a different operating system, applications were incompatible and scale economies in purchasing, manufacturing and distributions could not be exploited. Scully's response was to reorganize Apple along functional lines to gain control, reduce costs and achieve a more coherent product strategy.
- General Motors, pioneer of the multidivisional structure, has moved towards a more functional structure. As cost efficiency became its strategic priority, it maintained its brand names (Cadillac, Chevrolet, Buick) but merged these separate divisions into a more functionally based structure to exploit scale economies and faster technical transfer.

THE MULTIDIVISIONAL STRUCTURE We have seen how the product-based, multidivisional structure emerged during the 20th century in response to the coordination problems caused by diversification. The key advantage of divisionalized structures (whether product based or geographically based) is the potential for decentralized decision making. The multidivisional structure is the classic example of a loose-coupled, modular organization where business-level strategies and operating decisions can be made at the divisional level, while the corporate headquarters concentrates on corporate planning, budgeting and providing common services.

Central to the efficiency advantages of the multidivisional corporation is the ability to apply a common set of corporate management tools to a range of different businesses. At

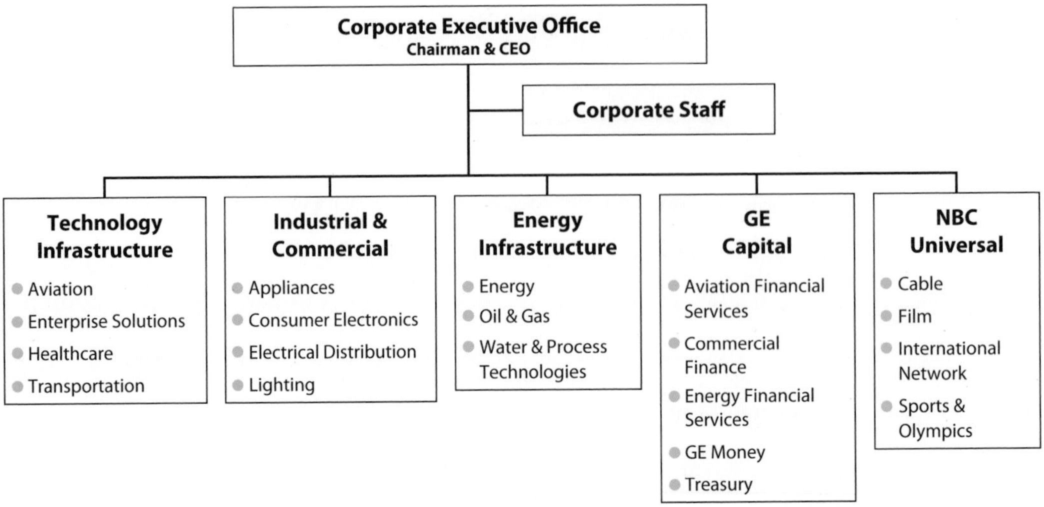

Figure 9.4 General Electric: Organizational structure: 2009.
Source: Based on information in General Electric's Annual Report, 2008.

ITT, Harold Geneen's system of 'managing by the numbers' allowed him to cope with over 50 divisional heads reporting directly to him. At BP, John Browne's system of 'performance contracts' allowed direct reporting by over 20 'strategic performance units'. Divisional autonomy also fosters the development of leadership capability among divisional heads – an important factor in grooming candidates for CEO succession.

The large, divisionalized corporation is typically organized into three levels: the corporate centre, the divisions and the individual business units, each representing a distinct business for which financial accounts can be drawn up and strategies formulated. Figure 9.4 shows General Electric's organizational structure at the corporate and divisional levels.

MATRIX STRUCTURES Whatever the primary basis for grouping, all companies that embrace multiple products, multiple functions and multiple locations must coordinate across all three dimensions. Organizational structures that formalize coordination and control across multiple dimensions are called 'matrix structures'.

Figure 9.5 shows the Shell management matrix (prior to reorganization in 1996). Within this structure, the general manager of Shell's Berre refinery in France reported to his country manager, the managing director of Shell France but also to his business sector head, the coordinator of Shell's refining sector as well as having a functional relationship with Shell's head of manufacturing.

Many diversified, multinational companies, including Philips, Nestlé and Unilever, adopted matrix structures during the 1960s and 1970s, although in all cases one dimension of the matrix tended to be dominant in terms of authority. Thus, in the old Shell matrix the geographical dimension, as represented by country heads and regional coordinators, had primary responsibility for budgetary control, personnel appraisal and strategy formulation.

Since the 1980s, most large corporations have dismantled or reorganized their matrix structures. Shell abandoned its matrix during 1995–1996 in favour of a structure based

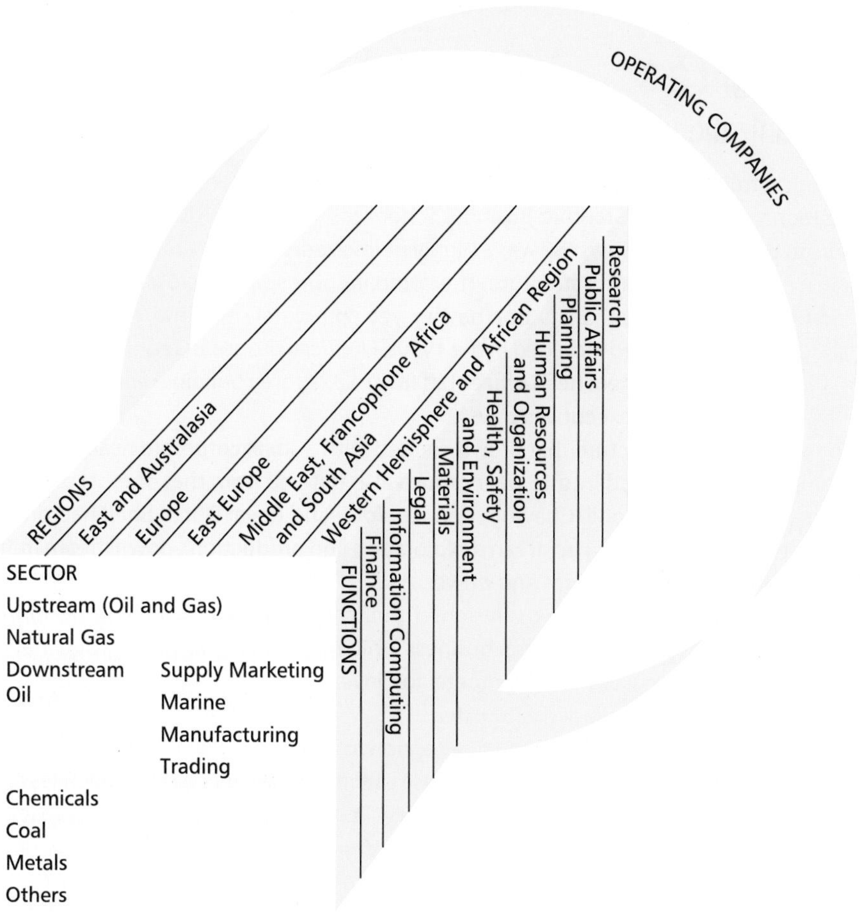

Figure 9.5 Royal Dutch Shell Group: Pre-1996 matrix structure.

on four business sectors: upstream, downstream, chemicals, and gas and power. During 2001–2002, the Swiss/Swedish engineering giant ABB abandoned its much-lauded matrix structure in the face of plunging profitability and mounting debt. In fast-moving business environments, companies have found that the benefits from formally coordinating across multiple dimensions have been outweighed by excessive complexity, larger head-office staffs, slower decision making and diffused authority. Bartlett and Ghoshal observe that matrix structures 'led to conflict and confusion; the proliferation of channels created informational logjams as a proliferation of committees and reports bogged down the organization; and overlapping responsibilities produced turf battles and a loss of accountability'.[27]

Yet, all complex organizations that comprise multiple products, multiple functions and multiple geographical markets need to coordinate within each of these dimensions. The problem of the matrix organization is not attempting to coordinate across multiple dimensions; in complex organizations, such coordination is essential. The problem is when this multidimensional coordination is over-formalized, resulting in a top-heavy corporate HQ and over-complex systems that slow decision making and dull entrepreneurial initiative.

Case Insight 9.3

BP's organizational structure

The 'atomic' structure that Browne introduced was radically different from BP's traditional organizational structure. A Stanford Business School case study describes BP's organizational structure in the 1980s as follows: 'BP was a highly politicized, top-heavy bureaucracy managed through a cumbersome matrix structure. The company was spread across numerous distinct lines of business, the result of its not having yet completely undone the conglomerate diversification in which it had indulged in the 1970s. Financial proposals required 15 signatures before they could be accepted; head office staff filled a 32-storey building; and meetings of 86 committees absorbed top executives' days.'[28]

The decentralized structure that Brown created with a small corporate headquarters and 150 business units organized into 15 peer groups also differed from that of most of the other petroleum majors. ExxonMobil, Chevron, Conoco, Total and Royal Dutch Shell had divisional structures, typically comprising upstream (exploration and production), downstream (refining and marketing), chemicals, and gas and power.

BP's decentralized structure was designed to instil entrepreneurial spirit, performance focus, flexibility and initiative among business unit managers. The peer group networks encouraged the business units to compete for investment funds while collaborating in knowledge sharing and best-practice transfer.

BP's structure was effective in directing attention towards financial performance, especially cost reduction. However, as the introductory case outlines, it appears to have been less suited to maintaining high standards of operational safety. It could be argued that other features of the business environment of the petroleum industry – notably the long-term nature of major projects, the need to develop advanced technologies and the role of geopolitics – also favoured organizational structures that were more conducive to high levels of coordination and control.

Trends in organizational design

Consultants and management scholars have proclaimed the death of hierarchical structures and the emergence of new organizational forms. Two decades ago, two of America's most prominent scholars of organization identified a 'new organizational revolution' featuring 'flatter hierarchies, decentralized decision making, greater tolerance for ambiguity, permeable internal and external boundaries, empowerment of employees, capacity for renewal, self-organizing units, [and] self-integrating coordination mechanisms'.[29]

In practice, there has been more organizational evolution than organizational revolution. Certainly, major changes have occurred in the structural features and management systems of industrial enterprises, yet there is little that could be described as radical organizational innovation or discontinuities with the past. Hierarchy remains the basic structural form of almost all companies, and the familiar structural configurations – functional, divisional and matrix – are still evident. Nevertheless, within these familiar structural features, change has occurred:

- *Delayering:* Companies have made their organizational hierarchies flatter. The motive has been to reduce costs and to increase organizational responsiveness. Wider spans of control have also changed the relationships between managers and their subordinates, resulting in less supervision and greater decentralization of initiative. At Tata Steel, the management hierarchy was reduced from 13 layers to five. In briefing the McKinsey lead consultant, the CEO, Dr Irani, observed: 'We are over-staffed, no doubt, but more damaging is the lack of responsiveness to fleeting opportunities ... Our decision making is not as fast as it should be with everyone looking over their shoulder for approval ... The objective is to redesign job content more meaningfully. The purpose is to rejuvenate the organization by defining richer jobs with fewer hierarchical layers of reporting.'[30]

- *Adhocracy and team-based organization:* **Adhocracies**, according to Henry Mintzberg, are organizations that feature shared values, high levels of participation, flexible communication and spontaneous coordination. Hierarchy, authority and control mechanisms are largely absent.[31] Adhocracies tend to exist where problem solving and other non-routine activities predominate and where expertise is prized. Individual teams involved in research, consulting, engineering, entertainment and crisis response tend to be adhocracies. At a larger organizational scale, companies such as Google, W. L. Gore & Associates and some advertising agencies have adopted team-based structures with many of the features of adhocracies.
- *Project-based organizations:* Closely related to team-based organizations are project-based organizations. A key feature of the project-based organization is recognition that work assignments are for a finite duration, hence the organizational structure needs to be dynamically flexible. Project-based organizations are common in sectors such as construction, consulting, oil exploration and engineering. Because every project is different and involves a sequence of phases, each project needs to be undertaken by a closely interacting team that is able to draw upon the know-how of previous and parallel project teams. As cycle times become compressed across more and more activities, companies are introducing project-based organization into their conventional divisional and functional structures, for example new product development, change management, knowledge management and research are increasingly organized into projects.
- *Network structures:* A common feature of the many descriptions of new approaches to company organization is use of the term 'network'. Bartlett and Ghoshal present the 'transnational organization' as a multinational corporation organized as an integrated global network;[32] Goold and Campbell propose an organizational design that they call the 'structured network'.[33] Viewing organizational structures in terms of networks derives from social network analysis where organizations (and other social institutions) are conceptualized in terms of the social relationships between the individuals and organizational units within them. This emphasis on patterns of communication and interaction rather than the formal relationships puts emphasis on the informal mechanisms through which coordination occurs and work is done within organizations. Advances in information and communications technology have greatly increased the scope for coordination to occur outside of the formal structure, leading many observers to advocate the dismantling of much of the formal structures that firms have inherited.
- *Permeable organizational boundaries:* The benefits of specialization accrue to organizations as well as to individuals; at the same time, the complexity of most products has been increasing. As a result, firms have sought to narrow their corporate scope through outsourcing and refocusing upon core business activities, while relying on close

relationships with partner firms to access a wider range of expertise. Localized networks of closely interdependent firms have been a feature of manufacturing for centuries. Such networks are a traditional feature of the industrial structure of much of northern Italy.[34] Hollywood and Silicon Valley also feature specialized firms that coordinate to design and produce complex products.[35]

These emerging organizational phenomena share several common characteristics:

- *A focus on coordination rather than on control:* In contrast to the command-and-control hierarchy, these structures focus almost wholly on achieving coordination. Financial incentives, culture and social controls take the place of hierarchical control.
- *Reliance on informal coordination where mutual adjustment replaces rules and directives:* Central to all non-hierarchical structures is their dependence on voluntary coordination through bilateral and multilateral adjustment. The capacity for coordination through mutual adjustment has been greatly enhanced by information technology.
- *Individuals in multiple organizational roles:* Reconciling complex patterns of coordination with high levels of flexibility and responsiveness is difficult if job designs and organizational structures are rigidly defined. Increasingly, individual employees are required to occupy multiple roles simultaneously. For example, in addition to a primary role as a brand manager for a particular product category, a person could be a member of a committee that monitored community engagement activities, part of a task force to undertake a benchmarking study and a member of a community of practice in Web-based marketing.

Organizational culture

Edgar Schein defines organizational culture as: 'A pattern of shared basic assumptions that was learned by a group as it solved its problems of external adaptation and internal integration, that has worked well enough to be considered valid and, therefore, to be taught to new members as the correct way you perceive, think and feel in relation to those problems'.[36] Deal and Kennedy put it more simply as 'the way things get done around here'.[37] It is common to distinguish between corporate culture and organizational culture. The term **corporate culture** is typically used to refer to the values and ways of thinking that senior managers wish to encourage within their organization, whereas 'organizational culture' refers to the diverse cultural patterns that exist in the informal organization. In addition, commentators refer to strong and weak cultures. A strong culture is one in which key values and attitudes are widely shared and intensely held. For example, companies such as Starbucks, Shell, Nintendo and Google endeavour to create a strong sense of identity among their employees. A weak culture, in contrast, is one where people tend to hold different views, have different values and may interpret and respond to signals in very different ways. Most organizations contain subcultures within the whole – in an advertising company, for example, the 'suits' are likely to have a different subculture from the 'creatives'; in a university, administrative staff may have a different subculture from academics.

Describing and classifying cultures

Numerous ways of describing cultures have been developed, together with many different classifications of organizational types. Johnson, for example, identifies a number of elements that can be used to describe organizational cultures, which he labels a 'cultural web'.[38] These include the organization's paradigm (its mission and values), its control systems, organizational structures, power structures, rituals and routines and stories and myths. By identifying these elements, managers may be able to influence them.

Schein suggests that culture can be understood at three different levels:[39]

- The first level comprises the organizational attributes that an outsider visiting the company for the first time could see, hear or feel. Schein refers to these features as 'artefacts'. Artefacts include corporate logos, the way people dress, the premises in which the firm's activities are located, the stories people tell about the organization, even the look and feel of the washrooms! We can see something of these differences between companies if we compare the images of Google's and Microsoft's logos. Google deliberately attempts to portray itself as a playful and informal organization, whereas Microsoft comes across as more traditional.
- The second level refers to the values and attitudes that organizational members express. Managers often try to articulate the values they desire organizational members to share in mission statements or codes of conduct.
- The third and deepest level is that of 'unspoken rules' and tacit beliefs. Some attitudes and beliefs become so deeply ingrained in the organization that they are taken for granted and moved beyond expression and challenge. It is this third facet of culture that is considered by Schein and others the most influential but also the most difficult to change.

Featured Example 9.1

Was Nokia's culture partly to blame for its failure?

Some commentators argue that Nokia's engineer-driven culture was, in part, to blame for the firm's inability to make headway in smart phones and its subsequent failure in the mobile devices market. Nokia, once the global market leader in mobile phone handsets, sold its entire handset business to Microsoft in April 2014 and laid off large numbers of workers. Some claim that an engineering perspective was so embedded in Nokia's psyche that the company focused too much on technical improvements to existing products (many of which were not valued by customers) and failed to notice the emergence of stiff competition in both the upper and lower ends of the market.[40]

A full discussion of many different typologies of culture and framework for assessing organizational cultures is beyond the scope of the chapter but the key questions for strategists are: 'Can organizational cultures be changed in ways that better align them with a firm's strategy and is it ethical to try to do so?' and 'Is there any evidence that a strong corporate culture has a significant impact on a firm's performance?' In the following sections, we will examine these questions.

Case Insight 9.4
Exploring BP's organizational culture

As a starting point for exploring BP's culture, we could look at some of the symbols the company uses and value statements it selects to publicize on its website. The company's current logo was introduced in 2000 and designed as a representation of the Greek sun god Helios. The Helios design was chosen to replace the old shield because it was suggestive of light, heat and nature, reinforcing the company's portrayal of itself as progressive and environmentally concerned. However, even though these symbols (what Schein would call 'artefacts'[41]) tell us something about the company, unless the values expressed in the company's documentation are evident in the day-to-day behaviour of its senior team and are embedded in its structure, processes and practices, they are more likely to be seen as part of the organization's public relations efforts rather than indications of its corporate culture. Large organizations are typically made up of many different cultures and subcultures. In BP, for example, interviews that took place with operatives following the *Deepwater Horizon* incident revealed that engineers and managers viewed risk and safety in very different ways. The *Deepwater Horizon* Study Group suggested that the engineers tried to quantify risks by calculating probabilities and evaluating possible consequences, whereas managers saw risk in terms of 'risk and reward', that is to say the bigger the reward, the bigger the risk that was worth taking.[42] Some of those commenting on the disaster suggested that the managerial interpretation of risk had come to dominate the organization and that over time BP's strategy had become one of 'elephant-hunting', that is to say the company focused its efforts and resources on the biggest, most lucrative (and, by inference, the riskiest) prospects while ignoring more conventional projects. This, it was argued, gradually resulted in the emergence of a culture in which it was legitimate to cut corners in order to reduce costs. In the words of one report, 'BP forgot to be afraid.'[43] This claim was strongly denied by BP, who pointed out that there was no evidence whatsoever that any individual had put cost saving and profit above safety. From BP's point of view, the accident was unprecedented and unforeseeable. While few would argue that BP made a conscious decision to put cost cutting above safety, the debate centres on whether the 'unconscious mind' or deeply engrained culture of the company contributed in any way to the accident.

Can organizational cultures be changed?

We have seen that the development of a strong culture can act as an efficient and effective coordinating device because if employees share the same values there is less need for direct supervision and employees can act on their own initiative. Strong corporate cultures play to employees' hearts rather than their heads and encourage loyalty and commitment. They are built by recruiting the 'right' people, holding induction events, establishing corporate rites and ceremonies that reinforce the approved ways to behave (for example, annual dinners or 'employee of the month' awards), holding team briefings, organizing social activities and paying attention to symbols (for example, the architecture of buildings or the design of the corporate logo). Critics argue that the current emphasis placed on building strong corporate cultures is misplaced, because it represents an attempt to 'engineer' employees' 'souls' and is profoundly unethical.[44] Others point out that management attempts to engineer a corporate culture are unlikely to succeed because the company can never completely shut out other cultural influences on employees. People are not machines, easily subject to managerial manipulation. Any attempts to change values that are not seen as authentic tend to be met with cynicism and resistance. For example, corporate statements that declare 'people are our most valuable assets' or 'excellence in all we do' that do not ring true with organizational members' experiences tend to be treated as meaningless slogans. From the manager's point of view, it is impossible to know whether an employee has truly internalized the desired norms and values or merely pays lip service to them.

Does a strong corporate culture have an impact?

There is limited empirical evidence on the links between corporate culture and organizational performance, in part because of the difficulties of measuring these broad concepts. Those studies that have been attempted suggest that organizations with strong corporate cultures do have better long-term financial performance than those that do not, but the methods that have been used to test this assertion have attracted significant criticism.[45] Regardless of whether a link between corporate culture and firm performance has been established statistically, a large number of business practitioners believe that corporate culture and performance are linked. For example, in a survey that Heskett undertook, asking questions about the relative importance of strategy, execution and culture in an organization's success, culture came out on top by a wide margin.[46] We shouldn't forget, however, as Barney points out, that for an organization's culture to confer a competitive advantage it needs to be valuable, rare and inimitable.[47] If it were easy to engineer then it would cease to be rare and inimitable and all companies could create a 'strong' culture. On the other hand, if culture is difficult to manipulate then, while having a 'superior' culture can confer an advantage on the firm, the basis of its advantage would be luck because culture would be outside managerial control.

Summary

Strategy formulation and strategy implementation are highly interdependent. The formulation of strategy needs to take account of an organization's capacity for implementation; at the same time, the implementation process inevitably involves creating strategy. If an organization's strategic management process is to be effective and strategy is to be realized in practice then its strategic planning system must be linked to actions, commitments, monitoring and the allocation of resources. Hence, operational plans and capital expenditure budgets are critical components of a firm's strategic management system.

Realizing strategy involves the entire design of the organization. By understanding the need to reconcile specialization with cooperation and coordination, we are able to appreciate the fundamental principles of organizational design.

Applying these principles, we can determine how best to allocate individuals to organizational units and how to combine these organizational units into broader groupings, in particular the choice between basic organizational forms such as functional, divisional or matrix organizations.

We have also seen how companies' organizational structures have been changing in recent years, influenced both by the demands of their external environments and the opportunities made available by advances in information and communication technologies. We have also seen that informal aspects of an organization's social structure – its organizational culture – have an important role to play in strategy implementation.

In the final chapter, we have more to say on the organizational structures and management systems appropriate to different strategies and different business contexts, when we explore some of the new trends and new ideas that are reshaping our thinking about organizational design.

Summary table

Learning objectives	Summary
Understand how strategic planning links to operational planning, performance management and resource allocation in implementing strategy	Whereas small companies may be able to operate successfully without an explicit strategy in larger organizations, procedures need to be established so that individuals and groups commit to the strategies that have been agreed. Typically, these procedures involve an annual planning cycle in which strategic plans are linked with operating plans and capital budgeting. Figure 9.1 summarizes some of the main links.
Appreciate the basic principles that determine the structural characteristics of complex human organizations	Allowing individuals to specialize greatly enhances the efficiency with which tasks are completed but at the same time creates the challenge of ensuring cooperation and coordination. Several mechanisms are available to managers to manage this challenge. Control mechanisms include hierarchical supervision, shared values and performance incentives. Coordination mechanisms include rules and directives, routines and mutual adjustment
Select the organizational structure best suited to a particular business context	The basic design for complex organizations is hierarchy, but companies still need to grapple with the bases on which divisions or business units are established and what the relationships between these different divisions of entities should be. Three main organizational forms have been identified – functional, multidivisional and matrix – each with different advantages and disadvantages and with a different degree of fit with different business contexts
Recognize how companies have been changing their organizational structures in recent years and the forces that have been driving these changes	We have outlined a number of the changes that have occurred in the structural features and management systems of industrial enterprises in recent decades. These include: delayering, adhocracy, project-based organizations, networks and permeable organizational boundaries. In practice, these changes are more evolution than revolution
Appreciate the role an organization's culture plays in realizing strategy	We have explored what is meant by organizational culture and the different levels at which it operates. We have seen how in recent years culture has been seen as an important way of controlling and coordinating work activity but we have also recognized that there are significant limits to managers' ability to influence culture

Further reading

The following article by Harold Leavitt is a good place to start to understand the role that hierarchies play in organizing business activity:

Leavitt, H. J. (2003). Why hierarchies thrive. *Harvard Business Review*, 81(3), 96–102.

Henry Mintzberg has also written extensively on organizational design:

Mintzberg, H. (1980). Structure in fives: A synthesis of the research on organisation design. *Management Science*, 26(3), 322–41.

Mintzberg has also made a significant contribution to the debate on strategic planning systems:

Mintzberg, H. (1994). The rise and fall of strategic planning. *Harvard Business Review*, January–February, 107–14.

In terms of more recent organizational forms, Bartlett and Ghoshal's work on matrix organizations remains a classic:

Bartlett, C. and Ghoshal, S. (1990). Matrix management: Not a structure, a frame of mind. *Harvard Business Review*, July–August, 138–47.

DeFilippi and Arthur extend the discussion to project-based organizations:

DeFilippi, R. and Arthur, M. (1998). Paradox in project-based enterprise: The case of film making. *California Management Review*, 40(2), 125–40.

For those wishing to understand the debates around cultural control, the article by Grugulis *et al.* provides an illuminating insight into employment practices within a consultancy company:

Grugulis, I., Dundon, T. and Wilkinson, A. (2000). Cultural control and the culture manager: Employment practice in a consultancy. *Work, Employment and Society*, 14(1), 97–116.

Self-study questions

1 You are employed as a manager by a fashion retail chain and have been asked to put forward suggestions about ways in which the organization could encourage sales staff to offer better customer service. Suggest some of the alternative control mechanisms the firm might put in place and outline the advantages and disadvantages of each.

2 Can a firm's organizational structure contribute to the acceleration of innovation? If so, how?

3 Draw an organizational chart for an organization with which you are familiar. How would you characterize this structure (e.g. functional, multidivisional, matrix)? What suggestions would you make to reorganize the structure to make the organization more efficient and effective?

4 Whereas in the past many universities were organized as self-organizing collectives of scholars, today most have well-formulated strategic plans. What are the benefits to a university of having formalized planning and budgetary systems? What are the limitations?

5 Google regularly features in the higher end of the Fortune 500 list of the top 100 companies to work for. Use the Internet to research the key features of Google's corporate culture and explain why this culture is attractive to new recruits. What could be the downsides of working in this type of culture?

Closing Case

Designing and redesigning Cisco

Cisco Systems Incorporated is a multinational company, headquartered in the US, that designs, manufactures and sells Internet-protocol-based products relating to the information and communication technology industry and provides services associated with these products and their use. Cisco is best known for its routing and switching technologies but its products and services have evolved in ways that reflect the changing demands of users and the rapid pace of technological innovation. For a short while in early 2000, Cisco was the most valuable company in the world by market capitalization, but its time in the top spot was short lived as the bursting of the dot.com bubble saw its share price drop dramatically. Since that time, Cisco has faced mixed fortunes. Like many other companies, it has been adversely affected by the turbulence in the world economy following the banking crises of 2008 and by increased competition and, as a result, its financial performance has been somewhat lacklustre in recent years. Despite its change in fortune since the heady days of the early 2000s, in 2013 Cisco still employed more than 70 000 employees, had an annual sales revenue of around $49 billion and a net income of approximately $10 billion.[48]

Cisco built its reputation and sustained its early growth by designing and selling equipment that guided data through the Internet. As this market matured and margins were squeezed, Cisco branched out into new product areas such as wireless equipment, Internet telephony and optical networks. While the decision by a company located in maturing markets to diversify is unremarkable, Cisco is interesting because it explored many new markets, pursuing 30 or more opportunities in what the company labelled 'market adjacencies', simultaneously.

In the early years, following its start-up in 1984, Cisco organized its business on the basis of its product lines, but as the business grew it moved towards a more customer-focused structure. In 1997, it re-organized its business into three main divisions based on its three main customer segments: telecom operators, large businesses and small businesses. The aim was to provide customers with complete end-to-end solutions, including integrated software, hardware and network management. Over time, however, this structure proved problematic. As markets matured and greater emphasis was placed on cost reduction, this structure was increasingly seen as inefficient. The product requirements of different customer segments were becoming increasingly blurred and the structure was resulting in unnecessary duplication as different lines of business developed similar equipment independently of each other.

The dip in Cisco's financial performance following the dot.com crash resulted in the company finding itself under pressure to further reduce its costs. To achieve this aim, it undertook more restructuring, this time moving to a more traditional functional structure. The functional groupings included marketing, engineering, R & D, operations and customer service. The rationale behind this structure was that it would: facilitate the design of equipment that used a standard architecture, allow economies of scale to be realized and enhance knowledge sharing across Cisco's product groups. While the functional structure delivered some efficiency gains, it also had some drawbacks. The emphasis on cost cutting and standardization meant that the company was less in touch with the needs of its consumers and as functions developed their own subcultures cooperation between functions became more problematic.

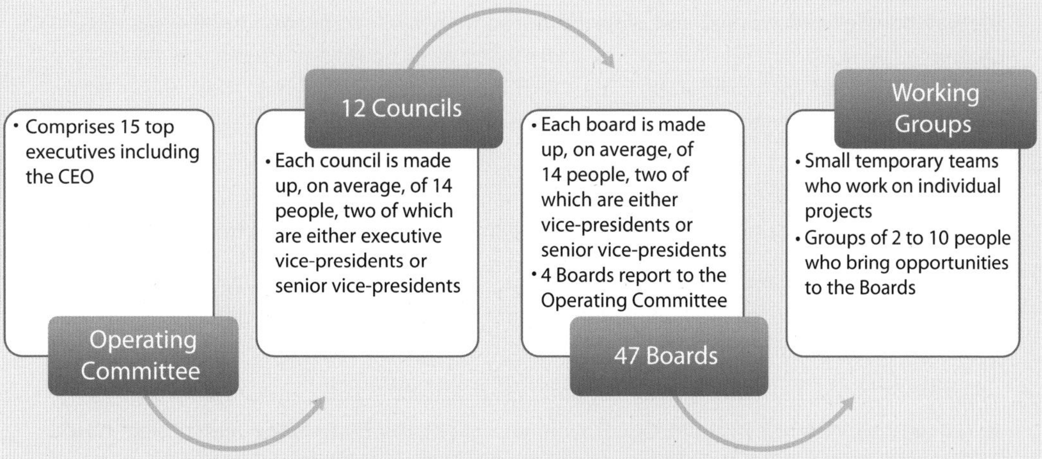

Figure 9.6 Illustrative organization chart for Cisco 2007.

Instead of going back to one of its earlier structural forms, based on customers or products, in 2007 the chief executive officer, John Chambers, announced a new 'technology organization' designed to make the most of the opportunities and to counter the challenges, created by the next phase of Internet growth. The new structure comprised an elaborate system of committees made up of 'councils', 'boards' and 'working groups' with their membership drawn from managers operating in different business functions (see Figure 9.6). There were initially around 12 councils that looked after new markets that might have reached sales of $10 billion. There were more than 40 boards focused on prospective markets of around $1 billion and both boards and councils were supported by working groups, which were temporary project teams. Many managers had roles on both councils and boards, and how well managers performed in these teams contributed to their annual bonuses.[49]

The opinions of the company's managers and industry observers were very mixed about whether this new structure would work. On the one hand, the hierarchy of cross-functional teams made it easier for the organization to react quickly to new opportunities and to innovate. On the other hand, there was a real danger that the whole structure was too complex and would slow down decision making and lead to burn out for senior managers. As a consequence of the restructuring, a number of senior managers left the company, citing frustration with the councils as part of their reason for going.[50]

In May 2011, following uninspiring financial results, Cisco announced it was to restructure yet again. Chambers announced that the councils and boards were to be reduced in number and the company would instead focus on five key areas it was targeting for growth, but despite these changes Chambers remained committed to the devolved organizational structure he had introduced.[51] In a keynote address in 2014, he pointed out that when he joined Cisco (19 years previously) about a thousand devices connected to the Internet and by 2014 that number had grown to 10 billion and forecast that by the end of the decade the figure would rise to 50 billion. Referring to this step change in connectivity as the 'Internet of Everything', he argued that the convergence of mobile and cloud technologies would transform not only the way people lived, worked and played but also the way firms needed to be organized. In Chambers' view, command and control approaches were no longer sustainable and future success depended on collaboration, partnerships and team-work but, most importantly, collaborative working needed to be supported by replicable processes.

Case questions

- Why has Cisco chosen to change its organizational structure on such a frequent basis?
- What are the advantages and disadvantages of the different organizational structures Cisco has adopted over time? (Hint: consider the extent to which different structures facilitate innovation and learning, incur coordination and control costs, address market requirements and facilitate the exploitation of scale economies.)
- In your opinion, how could Cisco avoid the problems that matrix and project-based organizations typically face?

Notes

1 L. Bossidy and R. Charan, *Execution: The discipline of getting things done* (New York: Random House, 2002): 71.

2 *The Transformation of BP* (London Business School Case Study. 302-033-1 March 2002).

3 http://www.ogj.com/articles/print/volume-96/issue-16/in-this-issue/general-interest/common-financial-strategies-found-among-top-10-oil-and-gas-firms.html, accessed 29th September 2014.

4 N. O'Regan and A. Ghobadian, 'Revitalizing an oil giant: An interview with Dr Tony Hayward, chief executive of BP', *Journal of Strategy and Management*, 3 (2009): 174–83.

5 The National Commission on the BP Deep Water Horizon Oil Spill and Offshore Drilling, 'The BP Deep Water Horizon oil disaster and the future of offshore drilling: Report to the president' (January 2011).

6 H. Mintzberg, 'Patterns of Strategy Formulation', *Management Science* 24 (1978): 934–48; 'Of Strategies: Deliberate and emergent', *Strategic Management Journal*, 6 (1985): 257–72.

7 *MCI Communications: Planning for the 1990s* (Harvard Business School Case No. 9-190-136, 1990): 1.

8 R. M. Grant, 'Strategic planning in a turbulent environment: Evidence from the oil majors', *Strategic Management Journal*, 24 (2003): 491–518.

9 P. F. Drucker, *The Practice of Management* (New York: Harper, 1954).

10 Bossidy and Charan (2002) op. cit.: 227.

11 H. Mintzberg, *Structure in Fives: Designing effective organizations* (Englewood Cliffs, NJ: Prentice Hall, 1993): 2.

12 A. Smith, *The Wealth of Nations* (London: Dent, 1910): 5.

13 S. Ross, 'The Economic Theory of Agency', *American Economic Review*, 63 (1973): 134–9; K. Eisenhardt, 'Agency Theory: An assessment and reviews', *Academy of Management Review*, 14 (1989): 57–74.

14 T. Kay and S. Van Ritten, *Myths and Realities of Executive Pay* (Cambridge: Cambridge University Press, 2007): Chapter 6.

15 W. G. Ouchi, *Theory Z* (Reading, MA: Addison-Wesley, 1981).

16 'Interim report on causes of the Deepwater Horizon oil rig blowout and ways to prevent such events', National Academy of Engineering and National Research Council (16th November 2010).

17 M. Weber, *Economy and Society: An outline of interpretive sociology* (Berkeley, CA: University of California Press, 1968).

18 T. Burns and G. M. Stalker, *The Management of Innovation* (London: Tavistock Institute, 1961).

19 H. Mintzberg (1993), op. cit.: Chapter 9.

20 H. A. Simon, 'The architecture of complexity', *Proceedings of the American Philosophical Society*, 106 (1962): 467–82.

21 J. D. Orton and K. E. Weick, 'Loosely Coupled Systems: A reconceptualization', *Academy of Management Review*, 15 (1990): 203–23.

22 On organizational modularity, see R. Sanchez and J. T. Mahoney, 'Modularity, flexibility, and knowledge management in product and organizational design', *Strategic Management Journal*, 17 (Winter 1996): 63–76; M. A. Schilling, 'Toward a general modular systems theory and its application to interfirm product modularity', *Academy of Management Review*, 25 (2000): 312–34; C. Baldwin and K. Clark, 'Managing in an Age of Modularity', *Harvard Business Review* (September/October 1997): 84–93.

23 Burns and Stalker (1961), op. cit.

24 'The Contingency Theory of Organizational Design: Challenges and opportunities', in R. M. Burton, B. Eriksen, D. D. Hakenssen and C. C. Snow (eds), *Organization Design: The evolving state of the art* (New York: Springer-Verlag, 2006): 19–42.

25 J. Nickerson and T. Zenger refer to this as 'structural modulation': 'Being efficiently fickle: A dynamic theory of organizational choice', *Organization Science*, 13 (2002): 547–67.

26 J. D. Thompson, *Organizations in Action* (New York: McGraw-Hill, 1967). The nature of interdependence in organizational processes is revisited in T. W. Malone, K. Crowston, J. Lee and B. Pentland, 'Tools for inventing organizations: Toward a handbook of organizational processes', *Management Science*, 45 (March 1999): 489–504.

27 C. A. Bartlett and S. Ghoshal, 'Matrix management: Not a structure, a frame of mind', *Harvard Business Review* (July/August 1990): 138–45.

28 J. Podolny and J. Roberts, *British Petroleum (A2): Organizing for Perfomance at BPX*, Case Study S-IB-16A2 (Graduate School of Business Stanford University, revised 2nd April 1999): 7.

29 R. Daft and A. Lewin, 'Where are the theories for the new organizational forms?' *Organization Science*, 3 (1993): 1–6.

30 R. Kumar, 'De-Layering at Tata Steel', *Journal of Organizational Behavior Education*, 1 (2006): 37–56.

31 H. Mintzberg (1993), op. cit.: Chapter 12.

32 C. Bartlett and S. Ghoshal, *Managing across Borders: The transnational solution*, 2nd edn (Boston, Harvard Business School, 1998).

33 M. Goold and A. Campbell, *Designing Effective Organizations* (San Francisco: Jossey-Bass, 2002).

34 M. H. Lazerson and G. Lorenzoni, 'The firms that feed industrial districts: A return to the Italian source', *Industrial and Corporate Change*, 8 (1999): 235–66; A. Grandori, *Interfirm Networks* (London: Routledge, 1999).

35 R. J. DeFilippi and M. B. Arthur, 'Paradox in project-based enterprise: The case of film making', *California Management Review*, 40 (1998): 186–91.

36 E. Schein, *Organizational Culture and Leadership* (San Francisco: Jossey Bass, 2004): 17.

37 T. Deal and A. Kennedy, *Corporate Cultures: The rites and rituals of corporate life* (Harmondsworth: Penguin Books, 1982).

38 G. Johnson, 'Strategy through a cultural lens', *Management Learning*, 31 (2000): 403–27.

39 Schein (2004), op. cit.

40 N. Bilton, 'The engineer-driven culture at Nokia', *New York Times* (1st June 2011).

41 Schein (2004), op. cit.

42 W. E. Gale, 'Perspectives on changing safety culture and managing risk', http://ccrm.berkeley.edu/pdfs_papers/DHSGWorkingPapersFeb16-2011/Perspective-on-ChangingSafetyCulture-and-Managing-Risk-WEG_DHSG-Jan2011.pdf, accessed 29th September 2014.

43 Final Report of the Investigation of the Macondo Well Blowout. *Deepwater Horizon* Study Group (1st March 2011): 76.

44 See, for example, J. Lozano, 'Ethics and corporate culture: A critical relationship', *Ethical Perspectives*, 5 (1998): 53–70.

45 See, for example, T. Peters and R. Waterman, *In Search of Excellence* (New York: Profile Books, 1982) or D. Denison, 'Bringing corporate culture to the bottom line', *Organizational Dynamics*, 13 (1984): 5–22.

46 J. Heskett, *The Culture Cycle: How to shape the unseen forces that transform performance* (London: FT Press, 2011).

47 J. Barney, 'Organizational culture: Can IT be a source of sustained competitive advantage?' *Academy of Management Review*, 11 (1986): 656–65.

48 Cisco Systems Inc. 2013 Annual Report.

49 'Reshaping Cisco: The world according to Chambers', *The Economist* (27th August 2009).

50 P. Burrows and J. Galante, 'Cisco reins in management system that spurred exodus at the top', *Bloomberg Business Week* (5th May 2011), http://www.bloomberg.com/news/2011-05-05/cisco-departures-reflect-frustration-over-management-structure.html, accessed 29th September 2014.

51 J. Duffy, 'Cisco restructures and streamlines operations', *Network World* (5th May 2011), http:// www.networkworld.com/news/2011/050511-cisco-reorginization.html, accessed 29th September 2014.

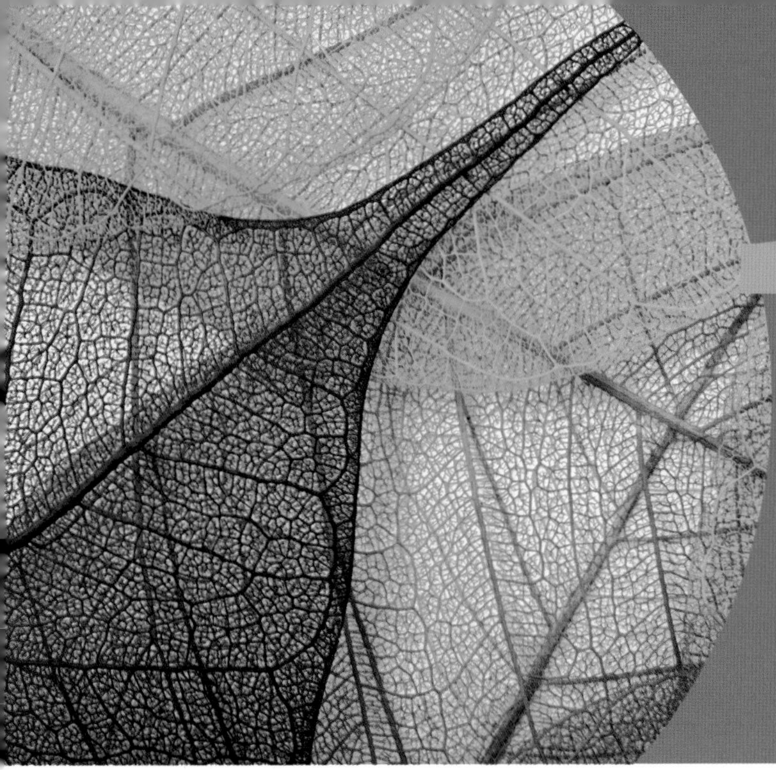

10

Current trends in strategic management

www.foundationsofstrategy.com

Introduction and objectives

In this final chapter, we assess some of the key changes that have taken place in the business environment in recent years and discuss their implications for strategic management. Unlike other chapters of the book we will not be introducing tried-and-tested strategy tools and techniques, instead our approach is more speculative. We identify some of the forces that are reshaping the business environment and introduce a number of concepts and approaches that are influencing current thinking in strategy. We look to draw lessons from leading-edge companies about strategies, organizational forms and management styles that could prove effective during a period of rapid, unpredictable change and introduce you to some new ideas that are emerging in the field of strategic management.

By the time you have completed this chapter, you will:

- be familiar with some of the key changes that have occurred in the business environment in recent years;
- understand the reasons for recent calls for change in a number of areas of management practice;
- be aware of some of the new directions in strategic thinking;
- be alert to the ways in which organizations are being redesigned and be able to reflect on how the role of managers is changing.

The new environment of business

Firms are having to contend with a business environment of increasing complexity and increasing volatility. The 21st century began with the bursting of the dot.com stock market bubble. March 2000 marked the beginning of the NASDAQ's decade-long bear market in technology stocks. The following year saw the terrorist attacks of September 11th, which triggered a train of events including the invasions of Afghanistan and Iraq. In November 2001, Enron, one of America's most successful and admired energy companies, declared bankruptcy – the first of a series of financial scandals that engulfed companies on both sides of the Atlantic. Bigger shocks were to follow. In September 2008, the failure of Lehman Brothers, a US investment bank, and the collapse of the Icelandic banking system heralded the start of a global financial crisis.[1] National governments were soon drawn in: in March 2012, the Greek government defaulted on its debt, casting doubt upon the survival of the euro. Meanwhile, political turbulence reached new peaks with the overthrow of the Tunisian, Egyptian and Libyan governments in the Arab Spring of 2011, civil war in Syria and Iraq and rising tension between Russia and the West following Russia's annexation of Crimea in 2014. Instability also affected the natural world with an increased incidence of hurricanes, earthquakes and extreme weather conditions causing droughts, forest fires, floods and snowstorms.

The transition from the optimism and prosperity of the last decade of the 20th century into the gloom and apprehension of the 21st century has caused a major reorientation of firms' strategies. To understand how companies are adjusting to the new conditions and the strategic options available to them, let us look more carefully at the major characteristics of today's business environment.

Turbulence

In reviewing the events of the 21st century, our focus has been on the turbulence and unpredictability that has characterized the business environment. Almost all the events we listed – from the September 11th attacks of 2001 to the crisis in Ukraine in 2014 – were highly improbable and unpredicted, what have been called 'black swan events' (see Featured Example 10.1).

A key issue is whether the black swan events we have witnessed between 2000 and 2014 simply reflect an unusual preponderance of extreme events or whether we are witnessing systematic changes that have made the business environment more crisis-prone. The latter seems likely. A feature of the global economy, and human society in general, is increasing interconnectedness through trade, financial flows, markets and communication. Systems theory predicts that increasing levels of interconnectedness within a complex, nonlinear system increase the tendency for small initial movements to be amplified in unpredictable ways.

Shifts in the global balance of economic power will continue to undermine the ability of the leading industrial nations to control these disruptive forces. The rise of the BRIC countries (Brazil, Russia, India, China) with MINT countries (Mexico, Indonesia, Nigeria and Turkey) following in their wake is creating a multi-polar world where the Old Order – the US, the EU, Japan and the institutions they created (the World Bank, the IMF and the OECD) are less able to offer global leadership. Looking ahead to 2025, the US National Intelligence Council predicts:

> The international system – as constructed following the Second World War – will be almost unrecognizable ... owing to the rise of emerging powers, a globalizing economy, an historic transfer of relative wealth and economic power from west to east, and the growing influence of non-state actors.[2]

Featured Example 10.1
Black swan events

The term 'black swan', a metaphor popularized by Nassim Taleb, refers to events that are extremely rare, have a major impact and are unpredicted, despite the fact that they are rationalized retrospectively (i.e. they *could* have been predicted). The term derives from the widespread belief that all swans were white until black swans were discovered in western Australia at the end of the 17th century. Taleb argues that almost all significant events in human history are black swans: despite their rareness, the sources of black swan events are many, and their impact is amplified by the fact that they are not predicted.[3]

Our vulnerability to black swan events is exacerbated by conventional approaches to risk management. These typically assume, first, that past events provide a basis for predicting future events and, second, that the probabilities of these events tend to be normally distributed. Extrapolating the past into the future makes strong assumptions about the stability of the underlying processes that generate uncertain events, while the very rareness of unusual events makes it very difficult to understand their causes. Growing awareness of 'long tail' or 'power law' distributions has called into question conventional assumptions about the normal distribution of uncertain events.

Thus, Taleb's conclusion is that managing black swans is essentially about building robustness to reduce vulnerability to negative events and responsiveness to exploit positive ones.

Competition

Among the wide array of uncertainties that firms face when looking at the immediate future, there is one near certainty: economic growth, especially in the advanced economies, will remain sluggish throughout the medium term. The aftermath of the consumer-led, debt-fuelled growth and the financial crisis has been the need for massive deleveraging by households, companies and governments. The corporate sector is the least of the problems: debt/equity ratios are generally modest (indeed, a bigger problem is channelling firms' cash balances into productive investment). However, for the household and government sectors the problems are both serious and long term. For the governments of the US, Europe and Japan, expansive fiscal and monetary policies are making the problem increasingly intractable. With the economies of China, India and Brazil also decelerating, the prospects for robust global growth seem far off.

In most sectors of the global economy, with a few notable exceptions, such as agriculture, excess capacity is the norm. Such conditions will fuel strong price competition and squeeze profit margins.

An additional source of competitive pressure is internationalization by companies from emerging-market countries. Firms that were once contract manufacturers are now competing with products sold under their own brand names. By 2014, more than 30 Chinese and Indian firms were supplying Android smartphones under their own brands. Haier, a Chinese company, is now the global market leader in domestic appliances, while Beko, a Turkish-owned, white-goods company, is the UK market leader. The entrance of emerging-market firms onto the world stage has also involved increasing numbers of cross-border acquisitions from companies from emerging economies. See Table 10.1.

Technology

The potential for digital technologies to undermine established positions of competitive advantage and redraw industry barriers appears as great now as it was 20 years ago. Indeed, the pace of creative destruction is accelerating. Just as Netflix sealed the fate of Blockbuster,

Table 10.1 Emerging-market corporations acquiring Western companies: Some illustrative examples.

Year	Acquirer	Country	Target	Country	Value ($billion)
2014	Lenovo	China	IBM servers division	US	2.3
2014	Lenovo	China	Motorola Mobility	US	2.9
2012	PETRONAS	Malaysia	Progress Energy Resources	Canada	4.7
2011	HTC	Taiwan	S3 Graphics	US	0.3
2011	Geely	China	Volvo	Sweden	1.8
2009	Grupo Bimbo	Mexico	Sarah Lee	US	1.0
2008	Tata Motor	India	Jaguar Land Rover	UK	2.3
2007	CEMEX	Mexico	Rinker Group	US	14.2
2007	United Spirits Ltd	India	Whyte & Mackay Ltd	UK	1.2
2006	Mittal Steel	India	Arcelor	Lux/Fr.	32.8
2006	Tata Steel	India	Corus	UK/Neth.	7.8

so Netflix struggles with the displacement of DVDs by video streaming. Such uncertainties are part of a broader picture of disruption within what was once known as the 'television industry', which is now part of a much broader arena where the producers of a wide array of digital content distribute through various channels for viewing on a multitude of mobile and home-based digital devices. A pervasive feature of digitization is industries converging then reconfiguring. Only a few years ago Nokia cell phones, Apple iPods, Nintendo Gameboys, Palm PDAs, Blackberry smartphones and Nikon cameras occupied different markets. Increasingly, mobile hand-held devices share functions and compete in a shared market space.

New information and communications technologies are also revolutionizing industrial and business processes. The *Economist* magazine predicts that 3D printing, new materials, advanced robotics and intelligent, automated administrative and logistical systems will result in a third industrial revolution in which economies of scale are undermined and manufacturing relocated from low-wage to technology-rich countries.[4]

Social pressures and the crisis of capitalism

For organizations to survive and prosper they must adapt to the values and expectations of society – what organizational sociologists refer to as 'legitimacy'.[5] One fallout from the 2008/9 financial crisis was the loss of legitimacy that many businesses suffered, and financial service firms in particular. This negatively affected their reputations among consumers, the morale of their employees, the willingness of investors and financiers to provide funding and the government policies towards them. The loss of social legitimacy that affected many commercial and investment banks was a greater threat to their survival than their weak balance sheets. Similar legitimacy challenges face Rupert Murdoch's News Corp. media empire following the 'phone hacking' scandal at its British newspapers.[6]

The notion that business enterprise is a social institution that must identify with the goals and aspirations of society has been endorsed by most leading management thinkers, including Peter Drucker, Charles Handy and Sumantra Ghoshal.[7] The implication is that when the values and attitudes of society are changing so must the strategies and behaviours of companies. While anti-business sentiment has for the most part been restricted to the fringes of the political spectrum – neo-Marxists, environmentalists and anti-globalization activists – the events of 2001 to 2014, including corporate scandals such as Enron and WorldCom and the financial crisis of 2008–2009, have moved disdain for business corporations and their leaders into the mainstream of public opinion.

A feature of growing disenchantment with market capitalism has been the undermining of the Washington Consensus: the widely held view that the competitive market economy based on private enterprise, deregulation, flexible labour markets and liberal economic policies offers the best basis for stability and prosperity and, according to the World Bank and the IMF, the primary foundation for economic development.

Central to the fraying legitimacy of market capitalism has been widespread dismay over changes in the distribution of income and wealth. Figure 10.1 shows evidence of the growing income disparities that have been characteristic of increasing inequality in almost all countries of the world. In the US, attention has focused on 'the 1%': the top percentile of the population that owns 42% of America's personal wealth. This propensity of the capitalist system to generate increasing inequality is the core thesis of French economist Thomas Piketty.[8]

The economic decline of the US, Europe and Japan relative to China and other emerging-market countries has reinforced this waning confidence in free market capitalism. Between 2000 and 2013, the number of Global Fortune 500 companies from the BRIC countries grew

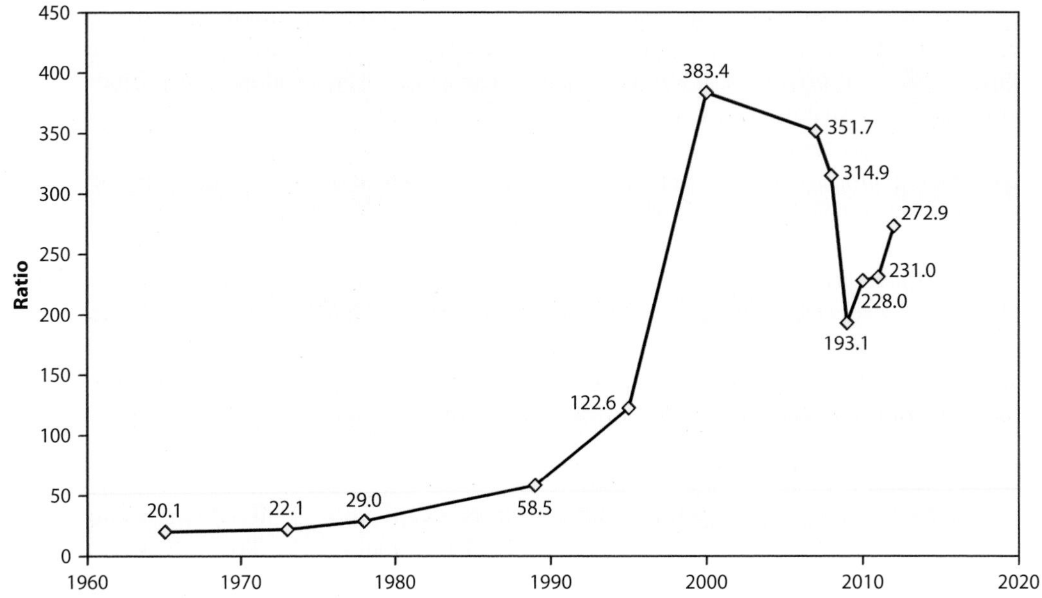

Figure 10.1 CEO-to-worker compensation ratios 1965–2012.
Source: Economic Policy Institute based on options realised data at US dollars 2011.

from 16 to 83. In 2010, China overtook Japan as the world's second-biggest economy. The growing prominence of Chinese state-owned multinationals in global markets has triggered debate over the merits of **state capitalism**. As the *Economist* reported: 'the Chinese no longer see state-directed firms as a way-station on the road to liberal capitalism; rather, they see it as a sustainable model. They think they have redesigned capitalism to make it work better, and a growing number of emerging-world leaders agree.'[9]

Recognition of the merits of state capitalism in combining the entrepreneurial drive of capitalism with the long-term orientation and coordinated resource deployment of government planning is one aspect of a growing interest in alternative forms of business enterprise. The United Nations' designation of 2012 as the 'International Year of Cooperatives' did much to raise the profile of businesses that are mutually owned by consumers (e.g. credit unions), employees (e.g. the British retailing giant John Lewis Partnership) or independent producers (e.g. agricultural marketing cooperatives). Cooperatives account for 21% of total production in Finland, 17.5% in New Zealand and 16.4% in Switzerland. In Uganda and other African countries, cooperatives are the dominant organizational form in agriculture.[10]

Adapting to society's growing demands for fairness, ethics and sustainability presents challenges for business leaders that extend beyond the problems of reconciling societal demands with shareholder interests. Should a company determine unilaterally the values that will govern its behaviour or does it seek to reflect those of the society in which it operates? Companies that embrace the values espoused by their founders are secure in their own sense of mission and can ensure a long-term consistency in their strategy and corporate identity (e.g. the Walt Disney Company and Wal-Mart Stores, Inc. with respect to founders Walt Disney and Sam Walton). However, there is a risk that these values become out of step with those of society as a whole or with the requirements for business effectiveness. Thus, at British retailer Marks & Spencer and chocolate maker Cadbury, social responsibility and paternalism towards employees became a source of rigidity rather than a competitive advantage. Other companies have experienced the reverse: by taking account of the interests and needs of different stakeholders and of society at large, some companies report a greater responsiveness to their external environment, greater commitment from employees and enhanced creativity.

New directions in strategic thinking

The external pressures affecting firms is evident in the worldwide rise in company failures over the past decade. Major US bankruptcies of 2011–2014 have included AMR (the parent of American Airlines), Eastman Kodak, MF Global, Dynegy Holdings, Borders Group, Blockbuster LLC and Cengage Learning. Across the globe, companies are facing a more demanding business environment that is forcing them to rethink their strategies.

Reorientating corporate objectives

Distaste over the excessive compensation and short-term thinking of many corporate leaders has fuelled increasing criticism of the notion that companies exist to enrich their shareholders. Yet adapting corporate goals to accommodate wider social and environmental responsibilities can hamper companies' ability to cope with increasingly intense competition. Recent efforts to reconcile a broader societal role with the need for profit maximization have emphasized either the need for companies to maintain social legitimacy or the potential for such a broadening of goals to open up new avenues for value creation – the central theme of Porter and Kramer's 'shared value' concept.[11] The appeal of this broader concept of the role of the firm is that it maintains the fundamental orientation of the firm towards earning profit or, equivalently, value creation.

The key reorientation of the doctrine of shareholder value creation is away from its 1990s preoccupation with stock market valuation towards a refocusing of top management priorities on the fundamental drivers of enterprise value. This reflects a recognition that management cannot create stock market value: only the stock market can do that. What management can do is to generate the stream of profits that the stock market capitalizes into its valuation of the firm. Indeed, as we argued in Chapter 1, the critical focus of top management should not even be profits; it should be the strategic factors that drive profits: operational efficiency, customer satisfaction, innovation and new product development.

The implication is not that business leaders abandon shareholder value maximization in favour of some woolly notion of pursuing stakeholder interests or to seek some new model of capitalism but that they focus more determinedly on identifying and managing the basic drivers of value creation.[12] Common to most of the corporate disasters of the 21st century from Enron and Parmalat to Royal Bank of Scotland and MF Global have been poor corporate strategies. Hence, to improve corporate performance, it is unlikely that a massive extension of government regulation, a new model of capitalism or a re-engineering of human nature offers the best solution. The most useful antidote to the threats of corporate empire building, CEO hubris and blind faith in new business models is likely to be a stronger emphasis on the basic principles of strategy analysis. As Richard Rumelt has pointed out: 'Bad strategy abounds!'[13]

Seeking more complex sources of competitive advantage

Focusing on strategy fundamentals does not necessarily lead to simple strategies. As we observed in Chapter 4, in today's dynamic business environment competitive advantages are difficult to sustain. As the rate of technology diffusion increases and new competitors with unassailable cost advantages emerge from newly industrializing countries, established firms are under increasing pressure to access new sources of competitive advantage. A key feature of companies that have maintained both profitability and market share over many years – for example Toyota, Walmart, 3M, Canon, Swatch and Samsung – is their development of multiple layers of competitive advantage, including cost efficiency, differentiation, innovation, responsiveness and global learning. As we shall see, reconciling the different requirements of different performance dimensions imposes highly complex organizational challenges that are pushing companies to fundamentally rethink their structures and management systems.

Thus, the ability of some companies to combine multiple capabilities recalls Isaiah Berlin's classification of intellectuals into foxes and hedgehogs: 'The fox knows many things; the hedgehog knows one big thing.'[14] Despite Jim Collins' praise for companies that have a single penetrating insight into the complexities of their business environments, it appears that companies which have built their strategy on such insight often have difficulty in adapting to subsequent changes in their markets: Toys 'R' Us with big-box retailing, Dell with its direct sales model, General Motors with its multi-brand market segmentation strategy, AOL with dial-up Internet access.[15]

Looking more closely at processes and practices

The pursuit of more complex sources of competitive advantage as well as the need to respond more frequently to external shocks and black swan events has focused attention on organizations' abilities to implement strategic change. Because the issues firms face are entangled and messy rather than simple and easily resolved, making sense of situations, generating ideas and proceeding on a trial-and-error basis can often offer a better way forward than sticking to a grand plan. Recognition of the important role that sense-making, experimentation and 'learning-through-doing' plays in strategy has rekindled interest in the everyday practices, processes and activities through which strategy 'happens'. As we noted in Chapter 1 the work of Henry Mintzberg, Richard Pascale and others shows strategic decision making to be based more on ad hoc and emergent processes than rational accounts suggest.[16] Some critical theorists go further and suggest that strategy is 'a vessel that managers fill with politically important issues'.[17] They argue that strategy is best understood as a discourse, that is to say a particular way of talking about and understanding the world which does not, as we may first suppose, merely reflect the world but actively shapes the way organizational members make sense of events and act upon them. From this perspective the process of creating and enacting strategy is inextricably entwined in the structures, cultural contexts and networks of social and power relationships that form the backdrop of everyday organizational activities. The discourse of strategy shapes how problems are framed, whose voices are heard and which strategy statements gain acceptance. In this sense, strategy can never be politically neutral even though issues of power are rarely acknowledged explicitly – a shortcoming that critical theorists seek to address.

The recognition that strategy is not something a firm *has* but something that people *do* has also spawned approaches which focus on the micro-foundations of strategy and the 'practice' of strategy. Researchers adopting these approaches draw on a wide range of social science disciplines – such as anthropology, psychology, sociology and linguistics – to explore how strategy is actually defined and enacted on a day-to-day basis. As March pointed out many decades ago: 'The composition of the firm is not given; it is negotiated. The goals of the firm are not given; they are bargained.'[18] While there is, as yet, no clear consensus on what constitutes 'micro-foundations', scholarly attention is focused on the ways in which individual level factors build to form the collective. Barney and Felin, for example, suggest that there is significant value in posing very finely grained questions such as: 'Who – with what skills, abilities, capabilities and knowledge – selects into (or leaves) organizations and with what aggregate effects?', 'How is [organizational] capability built?' and 'Where do firm level expectations and information come from?'[19]

Similarly, the strategy-as-practice approach highlights the social context in which strategy is enacted and, in part, connects with earlier analysis by Mintzberg and others who explored what top and middle managers did in their day-to-day activities. Strategy-as-practice scholars have extended this earlier work by focusing attention on 'the routines, interactions and conversations that lead to the definition and enactment of strategy, as well as the linkages between these practices and their organizational and institutional contexts'.[20] Studying managerial practices in this detailed way not only helps us to understand what constitutes professional practice in the strategy arena but also provides us with a better view of the skills and abilities that managers at different levels draw on when engaged in strategy work. However, to suggest that the strategy-as- practice approach is limited to the study of the actions and linguistic practices of individuals would oversimplify a complex body of research. Many strategy-as-practice researchers draw on seminal theorists, such as Bourdieu and Foucault, to provide a critical understanding of the role that strategy plays in society. While the work of these theorists lies outside the scope of a foundational strategy text, suffice it to say that this kind of research directs attention to the ways in which strategy is interpreted and understood in a societal context, causes us to reflect on our assumptions about the who, how and why of strategy and gives us a better understanding of its hidden and contextual dimensions.

Managing options

During turbulent times, it is important that firms keep their options open. Managing 'real options' as opposed to 'financial options' requires firms to actively consider how they can retain the potential – but not necessarily the obligation – to undertake new business initiatives and grasp new opportunities when they arise. Luehrman explains real options using the metaphor of a tomato grower.[21] He suggests that a gardener looking at his tomatoes during the summer months will find some that are ripe and ready to pick and others that are rotten that need to be discarded. In between, however, there will be a range of tomatoes with differing prospects. Some tomatoes could be picked now and would be edible but they would benefit from further ripening on the vine. By leaving them to mature, however, the gardener runs the risk that they are attacked by pests or ruined by bad weather. Others aren't ripe enough to be picked yet but given enough water, sun and plant food could do well. The active gardener inspects his tomatoes regularly and cultivates them to get the best possible crop. The message is, of course, that the gardener managing his tomato crop is analogous to the business manager managing real options. Firms need to be alert not only to the costs and benefits of particular courses of action but also to the ways in which their decisions can open options up or close them down.

Taking real options into account has typically required firms to adjust their investment appraisal methodologies so that option values are incorporated into capital budgeting decisions. For example, a firm may choose to invest in research and development so that it can keep abreast of new technologies that could prove promising in the future even though these technologies offer little immediate prospect of commercial development. Similarly, a firm may choose to acquire land to retain the option to grow even though it has no immediate expansion plans. However, the implications of options thinking extend further than this and affect fundamental aspects of strategy. To take just one example of how a failure to take account of option value can lead to a misguided strategy, consider conventional approaches to corporate finance. The attraction of leveraged buyout has been to create shareholder value through substituting low-cost debt (the interest payments on which are tax deductible) for high-cost equity. Yet, such reductions in the cost of capital also destroy option value: highly leveraged firms have fewer opportunities to take advantage of unexpected investment opportunities (including acquisition) and have less flexibility in adjusting to an unexpected downturn.

Viewing strategy as the management of a portfolio of options shifts the emphasis of strategy formulation from making resource commitments to the creation of opportunities. Strategic alliances offer a particularly potent tool for creating growth options: they allow a firm to make limited investments in new technological and market opportunities that can be 'exercised' through larger investments (possibly in the form of a joint venture or an outright acquisition) as more information emerges.

The adoption of options thinking also has far-reaching implications for our tools and frameworks of strategy analysis. For example:

- Industry analysis views the attractiveness of an industry in terms of its profit potential. However, once industry structure becomes too unstable to forecast profitability, attractive industries are increasingly ones that are rich in options. For example, an industry that produces many different products, comprises multiple segments, has many strategic groups, utilizes a diversity of alternative technologies and raw materials and where internal mobility barriers tend to be low offers wider options than a commodity industry, where member firms converge around a single dominant strategy. Thus, fashion clothing, semiconductors, packaging and investment banking tend to offer more option potential than electricity generation, steel or car rental.
- An options approach also has major implications for the analysis of resources and capabilities. In terms of option value, an attractive resource is one that can be deployed in different businesses and can support alternative strategies. A technological breakthrough in nanotechnology is likely to offer greater option value than a new process that increases the energy efficiency of blast furnaces will. A relationship with a rising politician is a resource that has more option value than a coalmine. Similarly, with capabilities: a highly specialized capability, such as expertise in the design of petrochemical plants, offers fewer options than expertise in the marketing of fast-moving consumer goods. Dynamic capabilities are important because they generate new options: 'Dynamic capabilities are the organizational and strategic routines by which firms achieve new resource combinations as markets emerge, collide, split, evolve and die.'[22]

Understanding strategic fit

Central to just about everything in this book is the notion of strategic fit. In Chapter 1, we looked at how strategy must fit with the business environment and with the firm's resources and capabilities; in Chapter 5, we saw how complementarities between strategy, structure and management systems can act as barriers to change. In Chapter 9, we looked at contingency approaches to organizational design: the idea that the structure and management systems of the firm must fit with the firm's business environment. In recent years, our understanding of fit (or contingency) has progressed substantially as a result of two major concepts: complementarity and complexity. These concepts offer new insights into linkages within organizations.

COMPLEMENTARITY RESEARCH Complementarity research addresses the linkages among a firm's management practices. A key focus has been the transition from mass manufacturing to lean manufacturing, where it has been observed that reorganizing production processes tends to be counterproductive without the simultaneous adaptation of a range of human resource practices.[23] Similarly, a six-sigma quality programme needs to be accompanied by changes in incentives, recruitment policies, product strategy and capital budgeting practices.[24]

At one extreme, recognition of complementarities in management practices makes it difficult to make generalizations about strategic management: every firm is unique and must create a unique configuration of strategic variables and management practices. In practice, strategic choices tend to converge on a limited number of configurations. Thus, successful adaptation among large European companies was associated with a small number of configurations of organizational structure, processes and boundaries.[25]

COMPLEXITY THEORY Organizations – like the weather, ant colonies, flocks of birds, human crowds and seismic activity – are complex systems whose behaviour results from the interactions of a large number of independent agents. This behaviour of complex systems has interesting features that have important implications for the management of organizations:

- *Unpredictability:* The behaviour of complex adaptive systems cannot be predicted in any precise sense. There is no convergence on stable equilibria; cascades of change are constantly interacting to reshape competitive landscapes. The outcomes tend to follow power law distributions: small changes typically have minor consequences but may also trigger major movements.[26]
- *Self-organization:* Complex biological and social systems have a capacity for self-organization. A bee colony or shoal of fish shows coordinated responses to external threats and opportunities without anyone giving orders. Groups of human beings also display coordinated behaviour patterns, e.g. when walking along crowded pavements. Quite sophisticated synchronized behaviour can be achieved through adopting just a few simple rules. There are three main requirements for self-organization: identity that permits organizational members to develop shared interpretations of organizational life and make sense of events in similar ways, information that provides the possibility of synchronized behaviour and relationships that are the pathways through which information is transformed into intelligent, coordinated action.[27] We will discuss self-organization in the next section.
- *Inertia, chaos and evolutionary adaptation:* Complex systems can stagnate into inertia (stasis) or become disorderly (chaos). In between is a region where the most rapid evolutionary adaptation occurs. Positioning at this edge of chaos results in both small, localized adaptations and occasional evolutionary leaps that allow the system to attain a higher fitness peak.[28]

THE CONTEXTUALITY OF LINKAGES WITHIN THE FIRM Common to both the complementarity and complexity approaches to analysing linkages among a firm's activities is the concept of 'contextuality': the extent to which the benefits from any particular activity depend upon which other activities are taking place. Porter and Siggelkow identify two dimensions of this contextuality:[29]

- *Contextuality of activities:* Some management activities are generic: their performance effects are independent of other activities, e.g. using computers for managing accounting systems is optimal for virtually all firms independently of what business the firm is in or how other activities are organized. The benefits from other activities are dependent upon what other activities are taking place, e.g. payments linked to individual employee output only boost productivity if employees work independently.

- *Contextuality of interactions:* Do activities interact in similar ways across firms? Generic interactions are the same for all firms. For example, the benefits from flexibility in manufacturing will always increase with increased product differentiation. Other interactions are context-specific, e.g. in the case of Ryanair's activity system, the complementarity between a point-to-point route structure and 25-minute aircraft turnarounds in achieving high aircraft utilization is dependent upon the airline's policy of no through-ticketing and no baggage transfers.[30]

Acknowledging the different ways in which a firm's activities interact offers insight into some of the complexities of strategic management. In particular, it helps us to understand why a strategy that has worked well for one company is a dismal failure when adopted by a competitor; it points to the risks in attempting to transfer 'best practices' either from another firm or even from another part of the same firm; it allows us to see why piecemeal adaptations to external change often make the situation worse rather than better.

Redesigning organizations

A more complex, more competitive business environment requires companies to perform at higher levels with broader repertoires of capabilities. Building multiple capabilities and achieving excellence across multiple performance dimensions requires managing dilemmas. A company must produce at low cost while also innovating; it must deploy the massed resources of a large corporation while showing the entrepreneurial flair of a small start-up; it must achieve reliability and consistency while also making local adaptations to meet individual circumstances. We addressed one of these dilemmas, the challenge of ambidexterity (optimizing efficiency and effectiveness for today while adapting to the needs of tomorrow) in Chapter 5. In reality, the problem reconciling incompatible strategic goals is much broader: the challenge of today is reconciling multiple dilemmas – this requires multi-dexterity.

Implementing complex strategies with conflicting performance objectives takes us to the frontiers of management knowledge. We know how to devise structures and systems that drive cost efficiency; we know the organizational conditions conducive to innovation; we know a good deal about the characteristics of high-reliability organizations; we have insights into the sources of entrepreneurship. But how on earth do we achieve all of these simultaneously?

Multidimensional structures

Organizational capabilities, we have learnt (Chapter 3), need to be embodied in processes and housed within organizational units that provide the basis for coordination between the individuals involved. The traditional matrix organization allows capabilities to be developed in relation to products, geographical markets and functions. And the more capabilities an organization develops, the more complex its organizational structure becomes.

- The total quality movement of the 1980s resulted in companies creating organizational structures to implement quality management processes.
- The adoption of social and environmental responsibility by companies has resulted in the creation of structures devoted to these activities.

- The dissemination of knowledge management during the 1990s resulted in many companies setting up knowledge management structures and systems.
- The need to develop and exercise capabilities to meet the needs of large global customers has resulted in multinational corporations establishing organizational units for managing key accounts.[31]
- The quest for innovation and organizational change has resulted in the establishment of organizational units that conduct 'exploration activities' (see the discussion on ambidexterity in Chapter 5). These include project teams for developing new products and incubators for developing new businesses. They also include organizational change initiatives such as General Electric's 'Work-Out' programme and innovation structures such as IBM's online 'Innovation Jam', a temporary organization that administers a biannual, 72-hour online session involving tens of thousands of contributors from inside and outside the company, then harvesting the results.[32] Such organizational structures that are outside companies' formal operating structures for the purposes of fostering dynamic capabilities have been described as parallel learning structures.[33]

Coping with complexity: Making organizations informal, self-organizing and permeable

If firms expand their range of capabilities, the implications for organizational complexity are frightening. In Chapter 9, we observed that traditional matrix structures that combined product, geographical and functional organizations proved unwieldy for many corporations. We are now introducing additional dimensions to the matrix!

INFORMAL ORGANIZATION The solution to increased complexity is to rely upon informal rather than formal structures and systems. The organizational requirements for coordination are different from those required for compliance and control. Traditional hierarchies with bureaucratic systems are based on the need for control. Coordination requires structures that support modularity, but within each module, team-based structures are often most effective in supporting organizational processes and coordination between modules does not necessarily need to be managed in a directive sense. Coordination can be achieved by means of standardized interfaces, mutual adjustment and horizontal collaboration (see discussion of 'The Coordination Problem' and 'Hierarchy in Organizational Design' in Chapter 9).

The scope for team-based structures to reconcile complex patterns of coordination with flexibility and responsiveness is enhanced by the move toward project-based organizations. More companies are organizing their activities less around functions and continuous operations and more around time-designated projects where a team is assigned to a specific project with a clearly defined outcome and a specified completion date. While construction companies and consulting firms have always been structured around projects, a wide range of companies are finding that project-based structures featuring temporary cross-functional teams charged with clear objectives are more able to achieve innovation, adaptability and rapid learning than more traditional structures are. A key advantage of such temporary organizational forms is that they can avoid the ossification of structures and concentrations of power that more permanent structures encourage. W. L. Gore, the supplier of Gore-Tex and other hi-tech fabric products, is an example of a team-based, project-focused structure that integrates a broad range of highly sophisticated capabilities despite an organizational structure that is almost wholly informal: there are no formal job titles and leaders are selected by peers. Employees ('associates') may apply to join particular teams, and it is up to the team members to choose new members. The teams are self-managed and team goals are not assigned from above but agreed through team commitments. Associates are encouraged to work with multiple teams.[34]

Reducing complexity at the formal level can foster greater variety and sophisticated coordination at the informal level. In general, the greater the potential for reordering existing resources and capabilities in complex new combinations, the greater the advantages of consensus-based hierarchies, which emphasize horizontal communication, over authority-based hierarchies, which emphasize vertical communication.[35]

SELF-ORGANIZATION When discussing complexity theory, we identified three factors that are conducive to self-organization in complex systems: identity, information and relationships. There is ample evidence of the role that these can play in substituting for traditional management practices.

- *Identity:* For coordination to be effective in the absence of top-down directives, it requires shared understanding of what the organization is and an emotional attachment to what it represents. These form the organizational identity: a collective understanding of what is presumed core, distinctive and enduring about the character of an organization.[36] Having a clear and coherent identity is an enormous organizing advantage. In a chaotic world, organizational identity can offer a foundation for stability. Structures and programmes come and go, but an organization with a coherent centre is able to sustain itself through turbulence because of its clarity about who it is and confidence in where it is going.[37] Consensus around organizational identity provides a powerful basis for coordinated action that permits flexibility and responsiveness to be reconciled with continuity and stability. Of course, organizational identity can be an impediment to, rather than a facilitator of, change. The key challenge for organizational leaders is to reinterpret organizational identity in a way that can support and legitimate change. Michael Eisner at Disney, Lou Gerstner at IBM and Franck Riboud at Danone all initiated major strategic changes, but within the constancy of their companies' identities. Organizational identity creates an important linkage between a firm's internal self-image and its market positioning. With the increase of symbolic influences on consumer choices, the linkages between product design, brand image and organizational identity become increasingly important. For companies such as Apple, Alessi and Bang & Olufsen, product design is an important vehicle for establishing and interpreting organizational identity.[38]
- *Information:* The information and communication revolution of the past two decades has transformed society's capacity for self-organization. Mobile telephony and social networks played a critical role in coordinating the London riots of 2011, anti-Putin protests in Moscow in 2011–2012 and insurrections across the Arab world. Within companies, information and communication networks support spontaneous patterns of complex coordination with little or no hierarchical direction. Indeed, real-time coordination is increasingly characterized by automated process where human intervention is absent (see Featured Example 10.1).
- *Relationships:* According to Wheatley and Kellner-Rogers, 'Relationships are the pathways to the intelligence of the system. Through relationships, information is created and transformed, the organization's identity expands to include more stakeholders, and the enterprise becomes wiser. The more access people have to one another, the more

possibilities there are. Without connections, nothing happens ... In self-organizing systems, people need access to everyone; they need to be free to reach anywhere in the organization to accomplish work.'[39] There is increasing evidence that a major part of the work of organizations is achieved through informal social networks.[40]

BREAKING DOWN CORPORATE BOUNDARIES Even with informal coordination mechanisms, modular structures and sophisticated knowledge management systems, there are limits to the range of capabilities that any company can develop internally. Hence, in order to expand the range of capabilities that they can deploy, firms collaborate in order to access the capabilities of other firms. This implies less distinction between what happens within the firm and what happens outside it. Strategic alliances, as we have already seen, permit stable yet flexible patterns for integrating the capabilities of different firms while also sharing risks. While localized networks of firms – such as those that characterize Italy's clothing, furniture and industrial machinery industries – offer potential for building trust and inter-firm routines, Web-based technologies permit much wider networks of collaboration. The open innovation efforts described in this book – Procter & Gamble's 'Connect & Develop' approach to new product development and IBM's 'Innovation Jam' – both point to the power of ICT technologies to enable firms to draw upon ideas and expertise across the globe. The collaborative potential of the Internet is most strongly revealed in open-source communities that build highly complex products, such as Linux and Wikipedia, through global networks of individual collaborators.[41]

Featured Example 10.2

The automated economy

Management has always been closely identified with the management of people. This reflects the primary role of labor as a factor of production. Yet a growing feature of the modern economy is the replacement of people and human decision making by information technology. The economist Brian Arthur points to the emergence of a 'second economy' where economic activity is coordinated entirely by machines. One example is the issuing of boarding cards by self-service machines at airports. On inserting a frequent-flyer card or credit card, the machine issues a boarding pass, receipt and luggage tag within the space of four or five seconds. Within these seconds, observes Arthur, a complex conversation takes place entirely among machines. With your identity established, your flight status is checked with the airline along with your past travel history. Your name is checked with the database of the Transportation Security Administration, and possibly with the National Security Agency. Your seat choice is confirmed, your frequent-flyer status checked and mileage credited. Your seat allocation takes account of the aircraft's loading system, which ensures an even weight distribution of the fuselage. The disintermediation of human decision makers by intelligent systems that process information, optimize decisions and coordinate subsequent activities is an increasingly common feature of distribution systems, financial services and even petroleum reservoir management. When you use a self-service checkout at a supermarket, an integrated information system links your purchases to shelf-filling activity within the store, deliveries from warehouse to store, and production planning and supply logistics by manufacturers.

Source: S. Hoover, 'Digitized Decision Making and the Hidden Second Economy', Techonomy Conference, October 9, 2011; W. B. Arthur, "'The Second Economy', *McKinsey Quarterly* (October 2011).

The changing role of managers

Changing external conditions, new strategic priorities and different types of organization call for new approaches to management and leadership. The era of restructuring and shareholder focus was associated with 'change masters' – highly visible, individualistic and often hard-driving management styles of CEOs such as Lee Iacocca at Chrysler, John Browne at BP, Michael Eisner at Disney and Rupert Murdoch at News International.[42] These leaders were, first and foremost, strategic decision makers, charting the direction and redirection of their companies, and making key decisions over acquisitions, divestments, new products and cost cutting.

In the emerging 21st-century organization, this 'buck stops here' peak decision-making role may no longer be feasible, let alone desirable. As organizations and their environments become increasingly complex, the CEO is no longer able to access or synthesize the information necessary to be effective as a peak decision maker. Recent contributions to the literature on leadership have placed less emphasis on the role of executives as decision makers and more on their role in guiding organizational evolution. Gary Hamel is emphatic about the need to redefine the work of leadership:

> The notion of the leader as a heroic decision maker is untenable. Leaders must be recast as social-systems architects who enable innovation ... In Management 2.0, leaders will no longer be seen as grand visionaries, all-wise decision makers, and ironfisted disciplinarians. Instead, they will need to become social architects, constitution writers, and entrepreneurs of meaning. In this new model, the leader's job is to create an environment where every employee has the chance to collaborate, innovate, and excel.[43]

Jim Collins and Jerry Porras also emphasize that leadership is less about decision making and more about cultivating identity and purpose:

> If strategy is founded in organizational identity and common purpose, and if organizational culture is the bedrock of capability, then a key role of top management is to clarify, nurture and communicate the company's purpose, *heritage*, personality, values, and norms. To unify and inspire the efforts of organizational members, leadership requires providing meaning to people's own aspirations. Ultimately this requires attention to the emotional climate of the organization.[44]

This changing role also implies that senior managers require different knowledge and skills. Research into the psychological and demographic characteristics of successful leaders has identified few consistent or robust relationships – successful leaders come in all shapes, sizes and personality types. However, research using 'competency modelling' methodology points to the key role of personality attributes that have been referred to by Daniel Goleman as 'emotional intelligence'.[45] These attributes comprise: 'self-awareness', the ability to understand oneself and one's emotions; 'self-management', control, integrity, conscientiousness and initiative; 'social awareness', particularly the capacity to sense others' emotions (empathy); and 'social skills', communication, collaboration and relationship building. Personal qualities are also the focus of Jim Collins' concept of 'Level 5 Leadership', which combines personal humility with an intense resolve.[46]

A similar transformation is likely to be required throughout the hierarchy. Informal structures and self-organization have also transformed the role of middle managers from being administrators and controllers to being entrepreneurs, coaches and team leaders.

The insights provided by complexity theory also offer more specific guidance to managers, in particular:

- *Rapid evolution requires a combination of both incremental and radical change:* While stretch targets and other performance management tools can produce pressure for incremental improvement, more decisive intervention may be needed to stimulate radical change. At IBM, Sam Palmisano's leadership between 2002 and 2012 refocused IBM on research and innovation, expanded IBM's presence in emerging markets, and inaugurated a new era of social and environmental responsibility.[47]
- *Establishing simple rules:* If the coordinated behaviors of complex systems can be simulated with a few simple rules, it seems feasible that companies can be managed by a few simple rules with limited managerial direction. For instance, rather than plan strategy in any formal sense, rules of thumb in screening opportunities (boundary rules) can locate the company where the opportunities are richest. Thus, Cisco's acquisition strategy is guided by the rule that it will acquire companies with fewer than 75 employees of which 75% are engineers. Rules can also designate a common approach to how the company will exploit opportunities (how-to rules). Thus, Yahoo! has a few rules regarding the look and functionality of new Web pages, but then gives freedom to developers to design new additions.[48]
- *Managing adaptive tension:* If too little tension produces inertia and too much creates chaos, the challenge for top management is to create a level of adaptive tension that optimizes the pace of organizational change and innovation. This is typically achieved through imposing demanding performance targets that are also appropriate and achievable.

Summary

Our review of the changes that have taken place in the business environment since 2000 reveals the new challenges that face firms and their leaders, in particular the need to compete at a higher level along a broader front. A common feature of these challenges is that almost all of them present dilemmas: between competing for the present and adapting to the future, between efficiency and innovation, between centralized resource deployment and decentralized responsiveness, and so on.

In responding to these challenges, business leaders are supported by two developments. The first comprises emerging concepts and theories that offer both insight and the basis for new management tools. Key developments include complexity theory, the principles of self-organization, real option analysis, organizational identity, practice-based approaches and new concepts of innovation, knowledge management and leadership.

A second area is the innovation and learning that results from adaptation and experimentation by companies. Long-established companies such as IBM and P&G have embraced open innovation; technology-based companies such as Google, W. L. Gore, Microsoft and Facebook have introduced radically new approaches to project management and human resource management, including allowing individuals to choose which projects to work on and giving them autonomy in innovation initiatives. In emerging-market countries, we observe novel approaches to government involvement in business (China), new initiatives in managing integration in multi-business corporations (Samsung), new approaches to managing ambidexterity (Infosys) and novel approaches to encouraging employee engagement (Haier).

At the same time, it is important not to overemphasize the obsolescence of either existing principles or methods of management. Many of the features of today's business environment are extensions of well-established trends rather than fundamental discontinuities. Indeed, it has typically been radically new management concepts and ideas that have been found wanting: the dawning of the 'new economy', the new era of 'virtual corporations', the revolutionary potential of 'knowledge management' and the coordination benefits of the 'networked organization' have all failed to convince. Certainly, our strategy analysis will need to be adapted and augmented in order to take account of new circumstances; however, the basic tools of analysis – industry analysis, resource and capability analysis, the applications of economies of scope to corporate strategy decisions – remain relevant and robust. One of the most important lessons to draw from the major corporate failures that have scarred the 21st century – Enron, WorldCom, Lehman Brothers and Royal Bank of Scotland – has been the realization that the rigorous application of the tools of strategy analysis outlined in this book could have helped these firms to avoid their misdirected odysseys.

Summary table

Learning objectives	Summary
Be familiar with some of the key changes that have occurred in the business environment in recent years	We have examined a range of economic, social, political and technological changes that together have changed the nature of the business environment. We have focused, in particular, on increased environmental turbulence, increased competitive pressure, technological change and the 'crisis in capitalism'
Understand the reasons for recent calls for change in a number of areas of management practice	We have explored how recent events have increased societal pressure for greater fairness, ethical behaviour and environmental sustainability and have resulted in calls for an end to the hard-driving management styles and practices that were lauded in the first decade of the 21st century
Be aware of some of the new directions in strategic thinking	Some of the new directions in strategic thinking include the re-orientation of corporate objectives towards the drivers of enterprise value, the quest for more complex sources of competitive advantage, a focus on the processes and practices through which strategy is defined and enacted, the management of options and a concentration on strategic fit
Be alert to the ways in which organizations are being redesigned and be able to reflect on how the role of managers is changing	We have discussed how a more complex and competitive business environment requires companies to perform at a higher level with a broader repertoire of capabilities. Reconciling multiple dilemmas requires multi-dexterity and has resulted in organizations becoming more informal, self-organizing and permeable. The new strategic priorities have also required senior managers to acquire new knowledge and skills and adopt different styles of leadership

Further reading

Paula Jarzakowski and Paul Spee provide a review of the strategy-as-practice literature in:

Jarzakowski, P. and Spee, P. (2009). Strategy-as-practice: A review and future directions for the field. *International Journal of Management Reviews*, 11(1), 69–95.

Rita McGrath has written extensively on strategy and real options, see:

McGrath, R. and Boisot, M. (2005). Option complexes: Going beyond real options reasoning. *Emergence: Complexity and organization*, 7(2), 2–13.

Heifetz *et al.* explore the challenges of business leadership in the aftermath of the financial crisis in:

Heifetz, R., Grashow, A. and Linsky, M. (2009). Leadership in a (permanent) crisis. *Harvard Business Review*, 87(7/8), 62–9.

Raisch and Birkinshaw look at the issues of organizational flexibility and adaptation in:

Raisch, S. and Birkinshaw, J. (2008). Organizational ambidexterity: Antecedents, outcomes and moderators. *Journal of Management*, 34(3), 375–409.

Self-study questions

1 Outline the advantages and disadvantages of adopting formalized strategic planning processes.

2 Global firms such as Starbucks, Google and Amazon have recently come under fire for avoiding tax on their sales in some countries. Should companies voluntarily pay more tax than they are legally obliged to?

3 To what extent does complexity theory provide practical assistance to managers facing increasingly complex business environments?

4 Research suggests that chief executives consistently overestimate their influence on a company. Does the leadership style of a company's CEO matter? If so, why? If not, why not?

Notes

1 The Financial Crisis Inquiry Commission. *The Final Report of the National Commission on the Causes of the Financial and Economic Crisis in the United States* (January 2011), http://www.gpo.gov/fdsys/pkg/GPO-FCIC/pdf/GPO-FCIC.pdf, accessed 29th September 2014.

2 US National Intelligence Council, *Global Trends 2025: A transformed world* (Washington, DC, November, 2008), http://www.aicpa.org/research/cpahorizons2025/globalforces/downloadabledocuments/globaltrends.pdf, accessed 29th September 2014.

3 N. N. Taleb, *The Black Swan: The impact of the highly improbable* (New York, Random House, 2007).

4 'The third industrial revolution', *The Economist*, 21st April 2012.

5 D. Barron, 'Evolutionary theory', in D. O. Faulkner and A. Campbell, *Oxford Handbook of Strategy* (Oxford, OUP, 2003): 96–7.

6 'CSR's importance is underlined by the NoW hacking scandal', http://www.theguardian.com/sustainable-business/blog/csr-now-hacking-scandal, accessed 29th September 2014; H. Mance, 'Murdoch empire has already regained its swagger', *Financial Times* (25th June 2014).

7 P. F. Drucker, *Managing in the Next Society* (New York: St Martin's Press, 2003); S. Ghoshal, C. A. Bartlett and P. Moran, 'A new manifesto for management', *Sloan Management Review* (Spring 1999): 9–20; C. Handy, *The Age of Paradox* (Boston: Harvard University Press, 1995).

8 T. Piketty, *Capital in the Twenty-First Century* (Boston, Harvard University Press, 2014).

9 'The rise of state capitalism', *The Economist* (21st January 2012); D. Barton, 'Capitalism for the long term', *Harvard Business Review*, 89 (2011): 85.

10 http://www.worldwatch.org/membership-co-operative-businesses-reaches-1-billion, accessed 29th September 2014.

11 M. E. Porter and M. R. Kramer, 'Creating shared value', *Harvard Business Review* (January, 2011): 62–77.

12 See, for example, P. Barnes, *Capitalism 3.0* (San Francisco: Berrett-Koehler, 2006); and D. Rodrik, *The Globalization Paradox: Democracy and the future of the world economy* (New York: W. W. Norton, 2011).

13 R. P. Rumelt, 'The perils of bad strategy', *McKinsey Quarterly* (June, 2011).

14 I. Berlin, *The Hedgehog and the Fox* (New York: Simon & Schuster, 1953).

15 J. Collins, *Good to Great* (New York: HarperCollins, 2001).

16 See H. Mintzberg, 'Patterns of strategy formulation', *Management Science*, 24 (1978): 934–48; R. T. Pascale, 'Perspective on strategy: The real story behind Honda's success', *California Management Review*, 26 (Spring, 1984): 47–72.

17 S. Clegg, C. Carter, M. Kornberger and J. Schweitzer, *Strategy: Theory and practice* (London: Sage, 2011).

18 J. G. March 'The business firm as political coalition', *Journal of Politics*, 24 (1962): 67.

19 J. Barney and T. Felin 'What are microfoundations?' *Academy of Management Perspectives,* 27 (2013): 138–55.

20 L. Rouleau 'Strategy-as-practice research at a crossroads', *M@N@GEMENT*, 16 (2013): 574–92.

21 T. Luehrman, 'Strategy as a portfolio of real options', *Harvard Business Review*, 76 (1998): 89–99.

22 K. M. Eisenhardt and J. A. Martin, 'Dynamic capabilities: What are they?' *Strategic Management Journal*, 21 (2000): 1105–21.

23 K. Laursen and N. J. Foss, 'New human resource management practices, complementarities and the impact on innovation performance', *Cambridge Journal of Economics*, 27 (2003): 243–63.

24 Six sigma is a quality management methodology first developed by Motorola in 1986 that aims to reduce defects among products and processes to fewer than 3.4 per million. See C. Gygi, N. DeCarlo and B. Williams, *Six Sigma for Dummies* (Hoboken, NJ: John Wiley & Sons, Inc., 2005).

25 R. Whittington, A. Pettigrew, S. Peck, E. Fenton and M. Conyon, 'Change and complementarities in the new competitive landscape', *Organization Science*, 10 (1999): 583–600.

26 P. Bak, *How Nature Works: The science of self-organized criticality* (New York: Copernicus, 1996).

27 M. J. Wheatley and M. Kellner Rogers, *A Simpler Way* (San Francisco: Berrett-Koehler, 1996).

28 P. Anderson, 'Complexity theory and organizational science', *Organization Science*, 10 (1999): 216–32.

29 M. E. Porter and N. Siggelkow, 'Contextuality within activity systems and sustainable competitive advantage', *Academy of Management Perspectives*, 22 (May 2008): 34–56.

30 Porter and Siggelkow (ibid.) discuss these issues in greater depth.

31 G. S. Yip and A. J. M. Bink, *Managing Global Customers: An integrated approach* (Oxford: OUP, 2007).

32 O. M. Bjelland and R. C. Wood, 'An inside view of IBM's 'Innovation Jam',' *MIT Sloan Management Review* (Fall 2008): 32–40.

33 G. Bushe and A. B. Shani, *Parallel Learning Structures* (Reading, MA: Addison-Wesley, 1991): Chapter 5.

34 Ibid.

35 J. A. Nickerson and T. R. Zenger, 'The knowledge-based theory of the firm: A problem-solving perspective', *Organization Science*, 15 (2004): 617–32.

36 D. A. Gioia, M. Schultz and K. G. Corley, 'Organizational identity, image and adaptive instability', *Academy of Management Review*, 25 (2000): 63–81.

37 M. J. Wheatley and M. Kellner-Rogers, 'The irresistible future of organizing', (July/August 1996), http://margaretwheatley.com/articles/irresistiblefuture.html, accessed 29th September 2014.

38 D. Ravasi and G. Lojacono, 'Managing design and designers for strategic renewal', *Long Range Planning*, 38 (February 2005): 51–77.

39 Wheatley and Kellner-Rogers (1996), op. cit.

40 L. L. Bryan, E. Matson and L. M. Weiss, 'Harnessing the power of informal employee networks', *McKinsey Quarterly* (November 2007).

41 A. Wright, 'The next paradigm shift: Open source everything', http://www.brighthand.com/default.asp?newsID=14348, accessed 29th September 2014.

42 R. M. Kanter, *The Change Masters* (New York: Simon & Schuster, 1983).

43 G. Hamel, 'Moon shots for management?' *Harvard Business Review* (February 2009): 91–8.

44 J. C. Collins and J. I. Porras, *Built to Last* (New York: Harper Business, 1996).

45 D. Goleman, 'What makes a leader?' *Harvard Business Review* (November/December 1998): 93–102. See also J. C. Hayton and G. M. McEvoy, 'Developing and assessing professional and managerial competence', *Human Resource Management*, 45 (2006): 291–4.

46 J. Collins, 'Level 5 Leadership: The triumph of humility and fierce resolve', *Harvard Business Review* (January 2001): 67–76.

47 'IBM's Sam Palmisano: A super second act', *Fortune* (4th March 2011).

48 For discussion of the role of rules in strategy making, see K. M. Eisenhardt and D. Sull, 'Strategy as simple rules', *Harvard Business Review* (January/February 2001): 107–16.

Glossary

Absolute cost advantages – a firm has an absolute cost advantage over a rival producing a similar product or providing a similar service when its average costs of production are lower than its rivals at all levels of output

Adhocracies – a type of organization characterized by the absence of bureaucracy and hierarchy. Decision-making authority is diffused and located within organizational members' areas of specialization. Coordination is achieved informally through mutual adjustment

Adverse selection – refers to the propensity for a market to be dominated by low-quality or risky offerings as a result of information asymmetry. This is also known as 'the lemons problem'

Agency relationship – the arrangement that exists when one person (known as the agent) acts on behalf of another (known as the principal). For example, the arrangements by which the managers of a firm (the agents) act on behalf of its owners (the principals)

Ambidextrous organization – an organization that can handle both gradual and revolutionary change

Architectural advantage – a term coined by Michel Jacobides to describe the benefits associated with particular ways of configuring a firm's boundaries

Architectural capabilities – the ability of a firm to innovate at a product or systems level, i.e. to change the way in which component parts fit together

Barriers to entry – the obstacles a firm faces in trying to enter a particular market

Barriers to exit – the obstacles a firm faces in trying to leave a particular market

Benchmarking – the process by which one organization gathers information on other organizations in order to evaluate and improve its own performance

Bilateral monopolies – a single seller (a monopoly) and a single buyer (a monopsony) in the same market

Born global companies – a company that operates internationally on start-up

Bounded rationality – The principle that the rationality of human beings is constrained ('bounded') by the limits of their cognition and capacity to process information

Brand extension – the use of an established brand name in a new product category

Business environment – all the external influences that affect a firm's decision making and performance

Business strategy – strategic decisions concerning *how* a firm competes within a particular industry or market. Also referred to as competitive strategy

Capabilities – what organizations are able to 'do'

Capital expenditure budget – that part of a company's overall financial plan that deals with expenditure on assets such as equipment and facilities

Causal ambiguity – the situation where it is difficult or impossible to map the connections between actions and results. When causal ambiguity exists the source of a successful firm's competitive advantage is unknown

Clusters – groups of firms that form part of a close network, usually because of their geographic proximity to each other

Codifiable knowledge – knowledge that can be written down

Comparative advantage – a situation in which a country or a region can produce a particular good or service at a lower opportunity cost than rivals

Competencies modelling – involves identifying the set of skills, content knowledge, attitudes and values associated with superior performers within a particular job category and then assessing each employee against that profile

Competency trap – a barrier to change which results from an organization developing high levels of capability in particular activities

Competitive advantage – the ability of one firm to earn (or have the potential to earn) a persistently higher rate of profit than rivals who operate in the same market

Competitive strategy – see 'business strategy'

Complementary resources – mutually dependent assets that enhance the value of an industry's products, for example petrol stations are a complementary resource to cars

Component capabilities – the ability of the firm to innovate at the level of component parts or sub-systems

Concentration ratio – the combined market share of the leading firms

Core competencies – a unique set of abilities that a firm possesses that adds value for customers and is hard for others to imitate

Corporate culture – the values and ways of thinking that are promoted by the senior management team within an organization

Corporate governance – refers to the set of processes, institutions, regulations and policies that affect the way companies are directed, administered and controlled

Corporate incubators – are facilities established to fund and nurture new businesses, based upon technologies that have been developed internally, but have limited applications within a company's established businesses

Corporate planning – a systematic approach to resource allocation and strategic decisions within a company over the medium to long term (typically 4 to 10 years)

Corporate social responsibility – a business organization's accountability for the social and environmental as well as the economic consequences of its activities and its commitment to having a positive impact on society

Corporate strategy – A firm's decisions and intentions with regard to the scope of its activities in terms of the markets and industries in which it competes

Cost advantage – when a firm is able to supply an identical product or service to its rivals at a lower cost

Cost drivers – the determinants of a firm's unit costs (cost per unit of output) relative to its competitors

Creative abrasion – frictions or differences that generate new ideas

Cross-subsidization – using profits or surpluses generated by one part of a business to support other parts of the business that perform less well

De alio entrants – entrants that are established firms from another industry

De novo entrants – entrants that are new start-ups

Differentiation advantage – a competitive advantage that is built on providing something unique that is valuable to buyers beyond simply offering a low price

Disruptive technologies – technologies that displace established technologies and overturn existing business practices and value networks

Distinctive competence – those things that an organization does particularly well relative to its competitors

Diversification – the expansion of an existing firm into another product line or field of operation

Dominant design – a product architecture that defines the look, functionality and production method for the product and becomes accepted by the industry as a whole

Dynamic capabilities – a firm's ability to integrate, build or reconfigure its internal and external capabilities in response to rapidly changing environments

Economies of scale – reductions in unit costs that result from increases in the output of a particular product in a given period of time

Economies of scope – reductions in unit costs that result from increases in the output of multiple products, i.e. using a resource across multiple activities

Emergent strategy – decisions that are derived from the complex process in which individual managers interpret the intended strategy and adapt to changing external circumstances

Emotional intelligence – the ability to perceive and understand one's own and others' emotions and to manage emotions in a way that facilitate communication, collaboration and relationship

Entrepreneurship – the process through which individuals identify opportunities, allocate resources, create value and assume risk for new ventures

Evolutionary strategy – a strategy that involves incremental rather than radical change. In the context of high-tech industries, an evolution strategy is often used to describe the decision by a firm to retain backward compatibility with earlier products

Firm as property – a viewpoint that sees management's responsibility as acting in the interests of shareholders

Firm as social entity – a viewpoint that sees management's responsibility as acting in the interests of a broad set of stakeholders and making a positive contribution to society at large

First-mover advantage – refers to the advantages that an initial occupant of a strategic position or niche gains by pre-empting the best resources or by using early entry to build superior resources and capabilities

Fixed costs – costs that do not change when a firm's output changes

Franchise – a contractual agreement between the owner of a business system and trademark (the franchiser) and a licensee (franchisee) that permits the franchisee to produce and market the franchiser's product or service in a specified area

Functional analysis – identifying organizational capabilities in relation to each of the principal functional areas of the firm, e.g. operations, sales and distribution etc.

Functional structure – organization around specialized business functions such as accounting, finance, marketing and operations

Global industries – industries which internationalize through both trade and direct investment

Hierarchy – an ordered grouping of people with an established pecking order

Human resources – the people who staff and run an organization

Hypercompetition – a situation characterized by intense and rapid competitive moves, where firms constantly strive to build new advantages and erode the advantages of their rivals

Industry lifecycle – the notion that industries, like products, go through distinct phases which comprise introduction, growth, maturity and decline

Innovation – is the initial commercialization of invention by producing and marketing a new good or service or by using a new method of production

Institutional isomorphism – the tendency for organizations that are subject to common social norms and pressures for legitimacy to develop similar organizational characteristics

Intangible resources – non-financial assets without physical substance, e.g. reputation, organizational culture, specialist knowledge

Intellectual property – creative products of the mind that have commercial value, for example literary or artistic works or ideas for new products or processes

Intended strategy – the strategy as conceived by the top management team

Internal capital market – the mechanism by which the headquarters allocates funds to various divisions of the business

Internal environment – all the factors within an organization that affect its strategic decision-making and performance for example, its organizational structure, management systems and human resources

Internal labour market – the system by which a company looks inside its own organization to find a suitable person for a job

Invention – the creation of new products and processes through the development of new knowledge or from new combinations of existing knowledge

Isolating mechanisms – the barriers that protect a firm's profits from being driven down by the competitive process

Key success factors – those factors within the firm's market environment that determine the firm's ability to survive and prosper

Lead time – the time it will take followers to catch up

Long-term contract – a contract involving a commitment to undertake agreed activity over several time periods

Matrix structure – hierarchies that comprise multiple dimensions; these typically include product (or business) units, geographical units and functions

Multidivisional structure – a company structure comprising separate business units, each with significant operational independence, coordinated by a corporate head office that exerts strategic and financial control

Multidomestic industries – industries that internationalize through direct investment in overseas markets

Network effects – the effect that one user of a good or service has on the value of that good or service to other people

Network externalities – linkages between the users (or producers) of a product or technology that result in the value of that product or technology being positively (or sometimes negatively) related to the number of users

Not-for-profit organizations – organizations that do not distribute the surplus funds that may result from their operations to those in control

Open innovation – an approach to innovation where a firm seeks solutions from organizations and individuals outside the firm and shares its technologies with other organizations

Operating budget – A detailed projection of all estimated income and expenses based on forecasted sales revenue during a given period

Organizational capability – the firm's capacity to deploy resources for a desired end result

Organizational culture – the values, traditions and social norms that exist informally within organizations

Organizational identity – is that which organizational members collectively perceive to be central, distinctive and enduring about their organization

Organizational processes – those sequences of actions through which a specific task is performed

Organizational routines – patterns of coordinated activity through which organizations are able to perform tasks on a regular and predictable basis

Path dependent – the recognition that history matters and that an organization's strategy, structure and management's options for the future are determined by past decisions

PEST analysis – an environmental scanning framework that classifies external influences by source, i.e. political, economic, social and technological

Planned emergence – a strategy-making process that combines design with emergence, i.e. there is a planned strategy but this strategy is continually enacted through decisions that are made by every member of the organization and evolves and changes over time

Positive feedback – a response that results in a self-reinforcing cycle of amplification or growth

Product lifecycle – the notion that products go through distinct stages from their introduction to eventual withdrawal from the market

Realized strategy – the strategy that is pursued in practice

Regime of appropriability – describes the conditions that influence the distribution of returns from an innovation

Relational contracts – agreements based on informal social relationships between transacting partners rather than on formal legal documents

Resource-based view – a theoretical perspective that highlights the role of resources and capabilities as the principal basis for firm strategy

Resources – assets that the organization 'has' and that it can use to pursue its objectives

Resource leverage taking advantage of resources to improve competitiveness

Revolutionary strategy – a strategy that involves radical rather than incremental change. In the context of high-tech industries, a 'revolutionary strategy' is often used to describe the decision by a firm to produce products that are not compatible with its earlier offerings

Routinization – the process by which the regular activities performed by an organization become a set of customary, standardized procedures

Satisficing – a decision-making strategy that aims for a satisfactory or adequate result rather than the optimal solution

Scale economies – see 'economies of scale'

Scenario analysis – a systematic way of thinking about how the future might unfold that builds on what is known about current trends and signals

Segmentation – the processes of partitioning a market on the basis of characteristics that are likely to influence consumers' purchasing behaviour

Shared service organizations – organizations with central departments that supply common administrative and technical services to the operating businesses

Sheltered industries – industries that are protected from international competition

Social legitimacy – popular acceptance of business organizations' rights to behave in particular ways

Spot contracts – a contract for the immediate sale and delivery of a commodity

Stakeholder analysis – the process of identifying, understanding and prioritizing the needs of key stakeholders so that the questions of how stakeholders can participate in strategy formulation and how relationships with stakeholders are best managed can be addressed

Stakeholder approach – viewing the business organizations as a coalition of interest groups where top management's role is to balance these different – often conflicting – interests

Standard – see 'technical standards'

State capitalism – a market-based economy where a large proportion of leading enterprises are owned by the government

Strategic alliances – refers to collaborative arrangements between firms

Strategic fit – strategic fit refers to the consistency of a firm's strategy with its external environment (especially its industry and the market it serves) and its internal environment (especially its goals and values, resources and capabilities and structure and systems)

Strategic innovation – creating value for customers by creating new value propositions, services or production processes

Strategic management – the label given to an approach that places less emphasis on corporate planning and focuses more on competition as the central characteristic of the business environment and competitive advantage as the primary goal of strategy

Strategy – the means by which individuals or organizations achieve their objectives

Strategy process – the way in which strategy is conceived and put into practice

Substitutability – the extent to which goods or services can be interchanged or act as replacements for one another

Sunk costs – costs that have already been incurred that cannot be recovered regardless of future events

Tangible resources – assets that can be touched or seen

Technical economies – refer to the reductions in unit costs that businesses are able to reap when they employ production techniques associated with large-scale manufacture

Technical standards – agreed, consistent rules or established norms with regard to technical systems. These often take the form of formal documents that establish uniform engineering or technical criteria, methods, processes and practices

Time-based competition – rivalry based on speed to market

Tipping – movement towards a market situation where the winner takes all (i.e. a single firm dominates)

Trading industries – industries in which internationalization occurs primarily through imports and exports

Transaction costs – the costs associated with participating in a market, e.g. the costs of searching for a particular product or negotiating a price

Uncertain imitability – the situation where there is ambiguity associated with the causes of a competitor's success

Value chain analysis – separates the activities of the firm into a sequential chain and explores the linkages between activities in order to gain insight into a firm's competitive position

Variable costs – costs that change when a firm's output changes

Vertical integration – where a firm extends its activities into the preceding or succeeding stages of the value-creation process

Virtual corporation – a firm whose primary function is to coordinate the activities of a network of suppliers and downstream partners. Coordination typically takes place through the use of information and communication technologies

Index

Note: Page numbers in italics refer to illustrations